MW00844764

HOSPITAL OPERATIONS

HOSPITAL OPERATIONS

PRINCIPLES OF HIGH EFFICIENCY HEALTH CARE

Wallace J. Hopp

William S. Lovejoy

Vice President, Publisher: Tim Moore
Associate Publisher and Director of Marketing: Amy Neidlinger
Executive Editor: Jeanne Glasser Levine
Consulting Editor: Barry Render
Editorial Assistant: Pamela Bolad
Development Editor: Russ Hall
Operations Specialist: Jodi Kemper
Marketing Manager: Megan Graue
Cover Designer: Chuti Prasertsith
Managing Editor: Kristy Hart
Project Editor: Andy Beaster
Copy Editor: Gill Editorial Services
Proofreader: Debbie Williams
Indexer: Erika Millen
Senior Compositor: Gloria Schurick
Manufacturing Buyer: Dan Uhrig

© 2013 by Wallace J. Hopp and William S. Lovejoy

Published by Pearson Education, Inc.
Upper Saddle River, New Jersey 07458

For information about buying this title in bulk quantities, or for special sales opportunities (which may include electronic versions; custom cover designs; and content particular to your business, training goals, marketing focus, or branding interests), please contact our corporate sales department at corpsales@pearsoned.com or (800) 382-3419.

For government sales inquiries, please contact governmentsales@pearsoned.com.

For questions about sales outside the U.S., please contact international@pearsoned.com.

Company and product names mentioned herein are the trademarks or registered trademarks of their respective owners.

All rights reserved. No part of this book may be reproduced, in any form or by any means, without permission in writing from the publisher.

Printed in the United States of America

Second Printing: February 2014

ISBN-10: 0132908662
ISBN-13: 9780132908665

Pearson Education LTD.
Pearson Education Australia PTY, Limited.
Pearson Education Singapore, Pte. Ltd.
Pearson Education Asia, Ltd.
Pearson Education Canada, Ltd.
Pearson Educación de Mexico, S.A. de C.V.
Pearson Education—Japan
Pearson Education Malaysia, Pte. Ltd.

Library of Congress Cataloging-in-Publication Data

Hopp, Wallace J.
  Hospital operations : principles of high efficiency health care / Wallace J. Hopp, William S. Lovejoy.
    pages cm
  ISBN 978-0-13-290866-5 (hardcover : alk. paper)
  1. Hospitals—United States—Administration. 2. Health facilities—United States—Administration. I. Lovejoy, William S. II. Title.
  RA971.H575 2013
  362.11068—dc23
                        2012029261

To Melanie, Elliott, and Clara
—Wallace Hopp

To Lois and Julia
—William Lovejoy

CONTENTS

1

INTRODUCTION TO HOSPITAL OPERATIONS   1

2

EMERGENCY DEPARTMENT   21

3

NURSING UNITS   127

4

OPERATING ROOMS   243

5

DIAGNOSTIC SERVICES   339

ACKNOWLEDGMENTS

We are forever grateful to our incredible co-authors, Dr. Jeffrey Desmond, MD; Christopher Friese, BSN, PhD; Dr. Stephen Kronick, MD, MS; Dr. Michael Mulholland, MD, PhD; and Dr. Jeffrey Myers, MD whose ability to turn around manuscripts in the midst of saving lives and running a major hospital left us in constant awe. We are also indebted to many other colleagues at the University of Michigan whose wide-ranging expertise in health care and generosity in sharing it has shaped our thinking in more ways than we can describe. In particular, we thank Dr. Carolyn Blane, MD; Mark Daskin, PhD; Deborah Harkins RN, MBA; Dr. Jack Iwashyna, MD, PhD; Dr. Christopher Kim, MD, MBA; Dr. Timothy Rutter, MD; Soroush Saghafian, PhD; Joan Scheske, MBA; Dr. Paul Taheri, MD, MBA; Mark Van Oyen, PhD; and Dr. Jeffrey Warren, MD, PhD for their wise counsel and stimulating conversation.

No one learns in isolation, and we have benefited greatly from years of guiding student project work in hospitals and clinics. There is no faster way to be exposed to a wealth of institutional detail than mentoring teams of bright, energetic students. These include the following University of Michigan doctoral students who used the health care setting to ground their work, and in the process helped us to higher levels of understanding: Thunyarat Amornpetchkul, Ana Ruth Beer, Hakjin Chung, Yao Cui, Ying Li, Liang Ding, Jihyun Paik, Anyan Qi, Santhosh Suresh and Yan Yin. The undergraduate, Master's level, and executive students who participated in several iterations of project coursework in hospitals and clinics are too numerous to list. However, some teams generated insights that we incorporated directly into examples and cases in this book and therefore warrant special mention. These include Matt Blahunka, Penn Chou, Lauren Elkus, Meredith Eng, Kelvin Fong, Joungwook Lee, Neha Mehta, Patricia Mencia, Jaime Ontiveros, Chris O'Rourke, Sukutu Patel, Michael Paulsen, and Jeffrey Robbins. This does not come close to exhausting the list of students to which we are indebted for embedding themselves in health care systems and feeding back to us, as their instructors, a wealth of insights. We also owe a deep debt of gratitude to the many hospital personnel (at the University of Michigan, Henry Ford, Northwestern Memorial, Trinity, and Spectrum Health Systems) who took time from their overly busy days to welcome our students and/or ourselves. These, also, are too numerous to list individually, but their wisdom and insights permeate this book. These rich encounters would not have been possible without the support and encouragement of key principals and administrators in these various health systems, including Melanie Barnett, MBA; Dr. Christopher Beach, MD; Rick Breon, MHA; Robert Casalou, MBA, MHA; Anthony Denton, JD, MHA; Mary Duck; Dr. David Dull, MD; Dr. Bradley Hubbard, MD; Crystal January Craft, MLIR; Martin Lutz, MPH; Dan Oglesby, MPA; Alice Peoples; Dr. Jonathan Schwartz, MD, MBA; and Douglas Strong, MBA.

There are many others that contributed to our enculturation into the world of health care. We know that some names will appear to us in a flash shortly after publication. To those we extend apologies and gratitude. Your voices and insights are not lost, they live on every page.

Wallace Hopp

William Lovejoy

ABOUT THE AUTHORS

Wallace J. Hopp is the Herrick Professor of Manufacturing and Associate Dean for Faculty and Research in the Ross School of Business, and a Professor of Industrial and Operations Engineering, at the University of Michigan. His research focuses on the design, control, and management of operations systems, with emphasis on manufacturing and supply chain systems, innovation processes, and health care systems. His prior publications include the books *Factory Physics* and *Supply Chain Science*, in addition to numerous research papers and book chapters. He has served as editor-in-chief of *Management Science*, president of the Production and Operations Management Society, and consultant to a wide range of companies. Hopp's research and teaching have been recognized with a number of awards, including the IIE Joint Publishers Book-of-the-Year Award, the IIE Technical Innovation Award, the SME Education Award, and Fellow Awards from IIE, INFORMS, MSOM, POMS, and SME.

William S. Lovejoy is the Raymond T. Perring Family Professor of Business Administration and Professor in the Operations and Technology department of the Ross School of Business, University of Michigan, with a joint appointment in the School of Art and Design. Professor Lovejoy held positions in both the private and the public sectors before joining academia. He works with companies on new product development, the management of innovation, and process assessment and improvement; he works with hospitals and clinics on health care operations. His courses have enjoyed coverage by CNN, *The Wall Street Journal*, *The New York Times*, and *Businessweek*. His past editorial activities include department editor for the Operations and Supply Chains department of *Management Science*, and senior editor for *Manufacturing and Services Operations Management*. He is a fellow in the Production and Operations Management Society.

Jeffrey S. Desmond is an Associate Chief of Staff at the University of Michigan Health System and Associate Chair for Clinical Operations in the Department of Emergency Medicine. He is a Clinical Associate Professor at the University of Michigan Medical School. He received his MD from the University of Texas Health Science Center at Houston and did his residency in Emergency Medicine at the University of Massachusetts. He is the co-founder of the Graduate Medical Education Health Care Administration Track and has a strong interest in the development of physician leaders. His research focuses on the operational aspects of emergency care, and in addition to publishing in peer-reviewed journals he has guided or mentored numerous applied operations design and improvement projects.

Christopher R. Friese received his BSN and PhD from the University of Pennsylvania and is an Assistant Professor at the University of Michigan School of Nursing. He remains clinically active as an inpatient staff nurse at the University of Michigan Health System and holds advanced oncology certification. His research focuses on patient, provider, and system-related factors that influence care outcomes. His findings have been cited by the Institute of Medicine's Future of Nursing report, the American Association of Colleges of Nursing, and two state Boards of Nursing to reform nursing educational policy. His work has helped guide oncology nurses in daily patient care, and through his leadership positions with the American Society of Clinical Oncology and the National Quality Forum he broadened quality measurement initiatives to include nursing-sensitive outcomes. In October 2012, he will be inducted as a Fellow in the American Academy of Nursing in recognition of his nursing leadership.

Steven L. Kronick is the Service Chief of Adult Emergency Medicine and an Associate Professor in the Department of Emergency Medicine at the University of Michigan. He received his MD from the University of Texas and his MS in Clinical Research Design and Statistical Analysis from the University of Michigan School of Public Health. He completed residencies in Internal Medicine at the University of Michigan and Emergency Medicine at Henry Ford Hospital. He is the director of Advanced Cardiac Life Support programs at UMHS and chairs the institutional CPR Committee. He is an item writer for the American Board of Emergency Medicine and has served on the American Heart Association's ACLS Committee and on the International Liaison Committee on Resuscitation's Task Force on the Consensus on Science. His research interests focus on emergency medicine operations and cardiac arrest in the hospital setting.

Michael W. Mulholland is the Frederick A. Coller Distinguished Professor and Chair, Department of Surgery at the University of Michigan Medical School. He also serves as Surgeon-in-Chief of University Hospital. His clinical interests are in gastrointestinal surgery with expertise in the treatment of pancreatic and biliary cancer, neoplastic diseases of the gastrointestinal tract and biliary reconstruction. His research interests include neurocrine control of pancreatic exocrine secretion and enteric neurobiology. He is the principal director of a research laboratory that has been continuously funded by the NIH since 1986. In 2004, he received the MERIT Award from the NIH for his work. In 2004 he was elected a member of the Institutes of Medicine of the National Academies. Dr. Mulholland is the senior editor of the textbook *Surgery: Scientific Principles and Practice* which has become the leading text in the field.

Jeffrey L. Myers is the A. James French Professor of Diagnostic Pathology, Director of the Divisions of Anatomic Pathology and MLabs, and Associate Director of the Medical Innovation Center at the University of Michigan. He received his MD from Washington University where he completed his residency in Anatomic Pathology at Barnes and Affiliated Hospitals followed by fellowship training at the University of Alabama at Birmingham. His research interests include pulmonary and general surgical pathology, patient safety, and practice innovation. He has published widely in the peer reviewed literature, co-authored multiple book chapters, and is co-editor of a textbook. Prior to Michigan he was a member of the Mayo Clinic staff where he was selected as a Distinguished Clinician in 2004. In 2010 he received the Outstanding Clinician Award and is a member of the League of Clinical Excellence at the University of Michigan Medical School.

1

INTRODUCTION TO HOSPITAL OPERATIONS

1.1 Stakeholders' Perspectives

Thursday March 25, 2010, 8:46 p.m.

"#@%&*)^%#@!" Dr. Nate Greene swore as he clanged an easy layup clumsily off the rim.

Greene was an emergency physician from University Hospital who joined several of his medical colleagues to play basketball on Thursday evenings at a local elementary school gym. Because swearing was almost as rare as defense at these games, one of Greene's teammates, orthopedic surgeon Dr. Ben Arnold, took notice. When the game ended and the players began leaving the gym, Arnold hung back with Greene.

"You okay?" he asked. "You seem a bit off tonight."

"Aw," Greene groaned. "My layups were just bricks tonight."

"I don't mean your shooting. That's always terrible." Arnold smiled. "But you seem kind of distracted tonight."

Greene dropped the basketball banter and grew serious. "A woman I treated in the Emergency Department died in the hospital this morning. Bowel obstruction."

"Mmmm." Arnold commiserated. "That's tough."

"I knew her a little." Greene continued. "She was taking care of both her elderly parents and a handicapped son. The family is completely devastated."

"That is sad," agreed Arnold. "But when it's your time…"

"But that's just it." Greene's voice rose. "I'm not sure it *was* her time to go."

"Oh, oh. Did somebody screw up?" Arnold winced. "The surgeon?"

"No, not exactly." Greene rubbed the basketball in his hands abstractedly. "I've been thinking about the case all day and I can't put my finger on an outright error anywhere in the process. But we were slow at every step. The Emergency Department was crammed on Monday as usual, so she waited a long time. It took a while to get the CT scan and even longer to get the report. By the time we realized it wasn't a virus, we'd already lost a day. Then the operating room was full, so it was another day before we got her on the schedule and a half day of delays after that. By the time they opened her up, there was no hope." Greene dropped the ball and his voice. "I can't help thinking that if we had been faster, she'd still be here."

"Then it was the system that failed!" Arnold picked up the ball and began thumping it on the floor. "Every one of the people on the case did his or her job. So blame the hospital, not the people in it."

"What are you talking about?" Greene grabbed the ball back and heaved up a shot that missed the rim by more than a foot. "The hospital *is* the people in it. We control what goes on there. So if it failed; we failed."

"Are you kidding?" Arnold jeered, and not just about the wild shot. "Nobody controls the hospital. It's too big, too complicated, and too set in its ways. That's why I'm leaving."

"What!" Greene had taken a step to retrieve the ball but stopped and turned to face Arnold. "Where are you going?"

"I've signed on with Andry Ortho," Arnold replied. Nicolas Andry Orthopedic Surgery Center was a small physician-owned specialty hospital founded several years ago by a group of physicians from University Hospital. Greene was aware that the facility had undergone an expansion at the beginning of the year, right before the health care bill put a ban on further growth of physician-owned hospitals. But he didn't know that Arnold had been considering joining them.

"Are you an owner?" Greene asked incredulously.

"Well, I have a piece," Arnold admitted. "But it's not the money that sold me. It's the fact that the docs run the place. The hospital is small, simple, and new. We run on schedule. The IT system actually works. We can practice medicine instead of fighting the bureaucracy. The kind of system failure you had today won't happen to us."

"That does sound pretty good." Greene recovered the basketball and flipped it to Arnold.

"You should join us." Arnold launched a perfect jump shot that swished neatly through the center of the net. "We've been staffing the emergency facility with specialists, but demand has grown to the point where we could use a real Emergency Department doc. Specialty hospitals are the way of the future."

"Hmmm…" Greene mused softly. "I'll think about it."

Flows Imp — material, patient, workflow etc.

1.2 A Metaphor for Hospital Operations

Recently, an estimated 20,000 people from the community turned out for the grand opening of an architecturally and aesthetically stunning new children's hospital. As they streamed through the sparkling entrance, the enchanted visitors were struck by the success of the design in captivating the young. Wide-eyed children stared at dynamic sculptures and mixtures of professional and elementary school art. Upbeat colors and vaulting spaces gave reassurance that this was a place to get well. Operating rooms (ORs) were large and flexible, inpatient rooms state of the art. Panoramic views of the surrounding trees and rivers inspired parents and children alike. The site even contained an onsite hotel to enable parents to stay close to their sick child, and the Neonatal Intensive Care Unit (NICU) had convertible furniture to provide sleeping accommodations for parents who could not emotionally tolerate even a few floors of separation.

Unfortunately, however, many visitors never saw the full wonder of the new hospital. Stairwells had been closed off during the open house for safety reasons, and only the central elevators were operational. Insufficient elevator capacity led to long lines on every floor. Worse, although eager guides were positioned throughout the hospital to answer questions, neither they nor the signage steered people along the planned route from top to bottom. The resulting random traffic patterns served to further aggravate the congestion. Frustrated with their inability to move from floor to floor, many people gave up and went home.

This (true) story is an apt metaphor for modern hospital operations. Infrastructure and equipment are exquisite, but flows are ill-designed and confused. Visible capital assets are awe inspiring, but invisible processes are frustratingly inefficient. Technology is state-of-the-art, but management is not. People are dedicated and knowledgeable in their fields, but they are largely unaware of operations. The net result is a system that performs far below the sum of its parts.

But it need not be like this. Just as there is a science of medicine that guides the treatment of patients, there is a science of operations that can and should guide the design and management of hospitals. For example, the physics of flows implies that it is impossible to respond quickly to highly variable demand without surplus capacity. In an acute care hospital, patient arrivals are highly variable, both over time and in levels of severity. Capacity, in the form of nurses, physicians, and high-tech equipment, is costly and therefore not installed in abundance. So the delays that are prevalent in hospitals are completely predictable.

Fortunately, the physics of flows also tells us that when resources are busy, with long queues of patients and other tasks waiting for attention, even small capacity enhancements or demand reductions will yield disproportionately large returns. That is, a little bit goes a long way. Modest increases in staffing, improvements in resources, and efforts to eliminate waste, if applied in the right places, can achieve major improvements in responsiveness. These insights can be used to speed the flow of visitors through a new hospital or the flow of patients through an existing one.

In this book, we define, explain, and apply management principles related to physical flows, decision making, quality, and human behavior. These principles encapsulate essential insights about management that can be used throughout the hospitals of today to significantly improve responsiveness, throughput, quality, patient satisfaction, and financial viability. But, because principles are by their nature timeless, they also provide the conceptual building blocks for ultra-high performance hospitals of the future.

1.3 Health Care in Crisis

Few things affect our quality of life more than health, so few issues are more important than health care. But, while we often speak of it as such, health care is not a single, monolithic topic. It ranges from delivery of basic public health in the poorest regions of the globe to stimulation of scientific breakthroughs in the advanced research laboratories of the world's wealthiest nations. As such, health care is too vast a subject for any single book. In this one, we focus specifically on a key part of the health care system: hospitals in developed countries. In addition to constituting a significant percentage of total health care expenditures, these hospitals are central to the delivery process, which makes them candidates as catalysts for improvements in the quality and efficiency of the overall health care system.

Compared to other developed countries, the United States spends significantly more on health care. Exhibit 1.1 shows that health care consumes 17.6% of the gross domestic product (GDP), which is 47% more than the next highest country (The Netherlands, at 12%) in the OECD (Organization for Economic Cooperation and Development, consisting of 34 largely developed countries). Exhibit 1.2 shows that the per capita expenditure in the United States is $8,233, which is more than double the OECD average of $3,268 and significantly higher than the next most profligate country (Norway at $5,388).

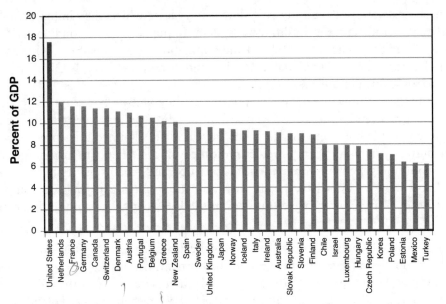

Exhibit 1.1   Health expenditures as a percent of GDP, 2010 or nearest year.

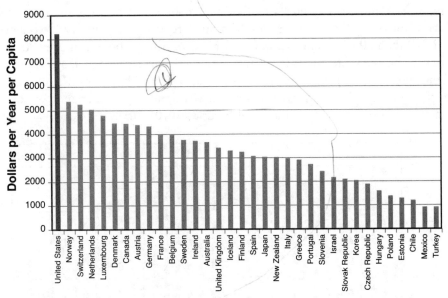

Exhibit 1.2   Health expenditure per capita, US$ PPP[1], 2010 or nearest year.

As high as these costs are now, projections are for U.S. health care costs to escalate significantly in the future. The U.S. Department of Health and Human Services predicts that health care will consume 19.8% of GDP by 2020 (CMS 2011). The high cost of health care, and particularly the gap with the rest of the world, threatens the competitiveness of the U.S. economy.[2]

Financial costs are not the only cost dimension along which the United States fares poorly; America's current health care system imposes costs beyond expenditures. Almost 50 million Americans (16% of the population) are uninsured, and even more are underinsured. The United States, Mexico, and Turkey are the only OECD countries without some form of universal health coverage (OECD 2008). What is the "cost" of the anxiety of nonwealthy Americans wondering if they will be bankrupted by a single major medical event? What is the social cost of the labor frictions injected into the economy when people hold onto jobs they don't like and are ill-suited for, simply because it is the only way they can get affordable medical coverage? When vibrancy in the economy is commonly tied to entrepreneurial start-ups and small businesses, what is the social cost of tying affordable health insurance to employment by large companies? These issues place an even bigger burden on the U.S. economy than that indicated by direct costs alone.

While the United States spends much more on health care than any other country in the world, we do not get a good return on our investment. Exhibit 1.3 shows life expectancy in the 34 OECD countries (2010 data). The United States is below the OECD average and lower than all the OECD countries except the Czech Republic, Poland, Estonia, Mexico, the Slovak Republic, Hungary and Turkey. It is also well below the leaders (Japan, Switzerland, Spain, and Italy). Exhibit 1.4 shows infant mortality in the OECD countries, and again the United States does not fare well, with rates above the average and higher than all but Chile, Turkey, and Mexico. Also, although insured Americans experience shorter wait times for elective surgeries than citizens of many other countries, the percentage of people able to see a doctor within 48 hours is lower in the United States than in Australia, France, Germany, New Zealand, the Netherlands, Switzerland, and the UK according to a Commonwealth Fund (2010) survey.

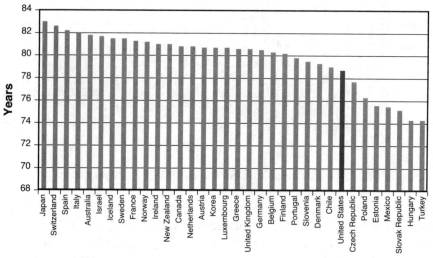

Exhibit 1.3   Total life expectancy in OECD countries, 2010 or nearest year.

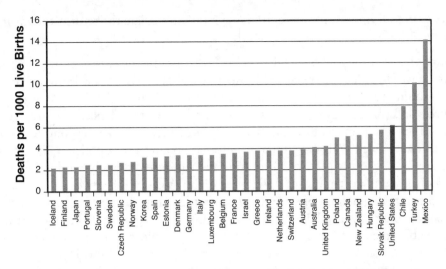

Exhibit 1.4 Infant mortality (deaths per 1,000 live births) in OECD countries,
2010 or nearest year.

The U.S. health care system does some things very well, as evidenced by the fact that some people travel great distances to come here for treatment. However, such "medical tourism" travel is typically for advanced procedures at the highest end of the health care spectrum, in which the United States excels. It is not exotic procedures for the rich that drive our embarrassing macro-statistics; it is in the inefficient (or absent) delivery of basic care (both prevention and cure) for the general population. The benefits of superior health care are not distributed evenly in the U.S. population, where death rates tend to correlate with income, race, and education (see Anderson et al. 2007, Barr 2008). To address this imbalance, we do not need more exotic procedures. We need a rationalization of basic care delivery. In this book, we focus on that rationalization within hospitals.

1.4 A Focus on Practice

Hospitals are part of a larger health care system in the United States, which has been shaped by a complex and often contradictory public policy structure. Fundamentally, health care policy debates revolve around this basic question: What is the appropriate political and economic structure for the promotion of health and health care in the country? Whether this is a centralized system with single-payer prices set by committee, a decentralized system with prices determined by a market, or anything in between, the debate tends to abstract away from actual hands-on medical practice. This abstraction is a dangerous oversimplification. All the value in any conceivable system is only realized in the actual delivery, when hands touch patients. Everything else is prelude. The closer we get to this all-important transaction, the more immediate the returns on our investment will be.

Pundits gloss over the health care delivery process because they assume that if incentives (prices, rewards, costs) are set correctly, the rest will follow as people rationally respond by consuming more of this, less of that, and so on, reaching the desired allocation of resources and consumption. This faith is unfounded. "Correct" incentives are necessary but insufficient for efficient operations. Different firms routinely respond to the same market environment with very different internal organizations, policies, and practices. For example, the Toyota Motor Corporation revolutionized the way production is managed globally, with no significant differences in the prices or incentives it was facing relative to competing automobile companies. Granted, Toyota served a Japanese market (smaller in volume, but still demanding high variety) and was located in more rural settings where cynical models of management and labor did not hold sway. These differences may have facilitated, but cannot fully explain, the rise of the Toyota Production System, now known as "lean" or "just-in-time" production. Rather, a combination of individual genius (and near fanaticism) by one individual, Taiichi Ohno, a supportive management structure, and two decades of trial and error led to innovations that greatly enhanced the efficiency and competitiveness of Toyota. The company simply found a better way to do things. This sort of process innovation makes it possible to do more with existing resources or to achieve the same level of output using fewer resources.

In general, external incentives influence, but do not determine, outcomes. What takes place within the hospital, and how well internal processes are managed, governs how efficiently and well patients are served. Simply put, there are many ways to manage internal processes, and some ways are better than others. It is this observation that motivates this book. We seek to provide a framework for identifying the causes of inefficiencies and the path to improvement for hospital operations.

The potential social gain is significant. Hospital expenditures (including inpatient and outpatient hospitals, Emergency Departments [EDs], and ambulatory surgical centers) account for 36.3% of total health care expenditures in the United States (Exhibit 1.5). Improving these operations can have a major impact on the total social cost and benefits of our health care system. It is commonly assumed in consulting circles that if a system grows up in an ad hoc fashion, bringing some rationalization to its design can easily reduce costs by 10% or more. Applying this logic to the $2.1 trillion in health care expenditures in 2009 (of which 36.3% are spent on hospitals), we estimate that rationalizing hospital operations has the potential to achieve annual savings of at least 10% of 36.3% of 2.1 trillion, or $76 billion. We expect that the actual upside potential is significantly higher, because in the authors' experience internal processes in a typical hospital are less mature than those in most other industries.

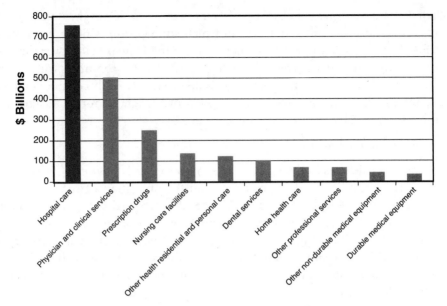

Exhibit 1.5   How to spend $2.1 trillion.

1.5 The Time Is Now; The Tools Are Known

People have voiced the need for health care reform in the United States for years, but no significant changes have been able to get past the political and organizational hurdles to implementation. However, there is evidence that we are finally in a critical transition phase where inaction is not an option. The economic surpluses that historically masked our inefficiencies are disappearing, and the various binders that hold the entire system together are straining to the point of failure.

1.5.1 The Unraveling

The surpluses masking our inefficiency are no longer affordable.

One advantage of surplus resources that accrue in a rich economy is that they can mask inefficiencies. Excess resources can, in general, cover for inefficient management and organization. For example, a firm with a substantial excess capacity can continue to serve customers well even if it uses that capacity inefficiently. In a rich economy, patients can happily enjoy continuity of care even with inefficient health care processes. However, when surpluses dwindle, those excesses are no longer affordable and must be removed, exposing the inefficiencies in the underlying process.

The United States has emerged from a post-war era in which it was the dominant economy on earth, and it has entered an era in which competition is fierce from multiple continents. The natural surpluses that characterized the United States over the past 50 years are no longer automatic. The retirement of post-war baby boomers will soon place an increasing load on the nation's health care system, which already consumes too much of the country's GDP. In short, we can no longer afford to ignore our inefficiencies. Our economic future, and indeed our very lives, are at stake.

Our reliance on values is at risk.

Health care policy debates in the United States tend to oscillate around the proper role of personal responsibility for one's own fate and the obligation of society to care for those who cannot care for themselves. Sometimes this debate devolves into a "markets" versus "socialism" caricature, which remains unresolved because neither works in pure form. Markets will visit the highest costs on the sickest people, who will therefore die if they are poor. This is socially unacceptable. Yet, universal coverage without individual incentives leads to overuse of expensive resources and produces high levels of avoidable waste. This is unaffordable.

These natural and unresolved tensions have resulted in a complex potpourri of reimbursement structures for hospitals and physicians. To serve patients in this bewildering environment, the industry has relied more than most people realize on its people being guided by principles that transcend the sometimes perverse incentives they face. This is, after all, a profession that deals with life and death, and therefore ethics. Before the government assumed responsibility for health care, charities provided care, or doctors charged based on ability to pay. That is, society expressed its values in organic rather than formally legal ways. This continues today through free clinics, volunteerism, and hospitals incurring (on average in the United States) 6% of their total expenditures providing care for people who cannot pay for it.

Further, the professional code of doctors is one that puts the patient first, and patients put some faith in this code when seeking medical care. Indeed, overt pursuit of profits in the medical arena arouses suspicion and antagonism on the part of patients when choosing physicians, or referring physicians when choosing hospitals. As Arrow (1963) observed, "The social obligation for best practice is part of the commodity the physician sells, even if it is a part that is not subject to thorough inspection by the buyer."

Not surprisingly, trust plays a more critical role in health care interactions than in other business transactions. We expect our doctors to act in our best interests, more than we expect the sellers of other services to do so. Insurance companies can ask patients to get physical exams to reduce the information asymmetry between themselves and patients, trusting an honest report from the physician. Given the convoluted and often opaque reimbursement jumble that hospitals face from multiple insurers and Medicare/Medicaid, hospital administrators could slavishly maximize profits by exploiting accounting confusions at the expense of patients and society at large. Yet we trust them not to. This system does not work perfectly, but trust and professional conduct that transcend the profit motive are central features of current health care markets. To date, values-based behaviors in medicine have been sufficient to keep the wheels from falling off this wagon.

This values-based glue is now coming under increased stress as economic surpluses disappear. Uninsured patients who cannot pay for their care are still cared for in hospital emergency rooms, but the cost of their care has to come out of a buffer of resources somewhere in the hospital-insurance-customer system. As buffers become unaffordable, the mere presence (or not) of an emergency room can become a matter of fiscal survival for hospitals. A 2011 report by the American Medical Association (Hsia et al. 2011) noted that urban and suburban areas have lost more than a quarter of their ED capacity over the past 20 years. EDs are more likely to close if they provide a lot of uncompensated care, are in for-profit hospitals, or are in competitive markets where margins are thin.

"Safety net" hospitals, which provide care for people who cannot access it anywhere else, are increasingly at risk. The travails of one such hospital, Grady Memorial Hospital in Atlanta, are not unique. Grady almost closed its doors in 2007, and since that time it has continually struggled to balance its social mission with financial realities. Grady remains dependent on outside funding (for example, federal funding for indigent care) that is increasingly at risk (Williams and Schneider 2011).

It is a unique feature of the health care industry that hospitals often do not want a competitor to close. If a hospital providing a significant amount of uncompensated care closes, nonpaying patients will either get no care (and die) or show up in the EDs of other hospitals. Hospitals like Grady have been kept afloat by financial transfusions from the outside because everybody realizes the consequences if they close. But this is more reactive crisis management than proactive rational policy. The reliance in the United States on values and charity will come under increasing stress as financial realities become more pressing.

Further, as doctors' salaries stagnate, the temptation to shade decisions, consciously or not, toward profit maximization becomes stronger. Nallamothu et al. (2007) studied the rates of various coronary procedures in specialty hospitals relative to general hospitals. Specialty hospitals provide care limited to specific medical conditions or procedures, and two-thirds of Medicare payments to specialty hospitals are related to heart conditions. There are arguments based on both physics and economics that can justify the spinning off of specialty hospitals from general hospitals, based on economies of scale and concepts of a "focused factory" (see Skinner 1974 and Chapter 6 of this book). However, critics claim that specialty hospitals focus primarily on low-risk patients and provide less uncompensated care than general hospitals.

Nallamothu et al. found that the frequency of three key coronary procedures was higher in regions after the opening of a specialty hospital when compared with the opening of new cardiac programs in general hospitals. The authors did not comment on the appropriateness of the procedures, but their findings raise the concern that procedure utilization in specialty hospitals was higher than one might expect based on medical need alone. The authors state in their conclusions that, "Among the potential mechanisms underlying our findings, the most concerning is physician ownership." Physician ownership allows physicians to collect not just their professional fees, but a share of the facility fee as well, creating a potential conflict of interest between the physician's financial incentives and a patient's clinical needs. Estimates of physician ownership of cardiac specialty hospitals range from 21% to 49%, and hospitals are currently exempted from anti-kickback laws that prevent referral of patients to facilities in which physicians have a significant financial stake. Although we cannot say for certain that economics is trumping values in these instances, we can conclude that values will be increasingly stressed as the economic climate becomes more challenging.

A similar concern applies to the rise of ambulatory surgical centers (ASCs) in the United States. An ASC performs surgical procedures that do not require hospitalization (for example cataracts, some knee and ear surgeries, and colonoscopies). Between 2000 and 2007, the number of such facilities increased by nearly 50%. This growth was largely financed by physician-owners, who had a financial stake in 83% of them and complete ownership of 43%. Hollingsworth et al. (2010) found that physician-owners, on average, had higher caseloads and operated on healthier (fewer accompanying health conditions) and better insured (more private and Medicare, less Medicaid) patients. Further, physicians who started as nonowners and became owners during the study period increased their caseloads after ownership. As always in such complex territory, there could be reasons for these results unrelated to financial incentives. But results like these raise concerns that physician-owners may increase caseloads beyond what is clinically necessary and route the lowest risk and most well-insured patients to their own facility, leaving the rest to be treated in a general hospital. This, of course, will increase the financial stress on the general hospital, decreasing its ability to manage their higher risk, lesser insured patients.

It is difficult to overstate the consequences if profit-maximization comes to dominate historical values in medical practice. The rush away from the poor, sick, and uninsured will accelerate, like a game of hot potato in which each party tries desperately to pass the ball. The cracks in the system are already beginning to show and will only get worse as baby boomers age.

As policy makers argue, there is a crisis to be met. Fortunately, with or without coherent leadership at the federal and state levels, we can do more with our current resources within hospitals. As the economic surpluses that have masked high levels of inefficiency disappear, hospitals must begin an evolutionary process that we have seen in other industries. These prior experiences have revealed general principles that can serve as tools with which we can manage this process.

1.5.2 The Tools Are Known

There is a famous scene in the film *Apollo 13* in which an engineer dumps a pile of spacecraft parts and materials onto a desk and demands that the team make a CO_2 filter out of them. The situation they faced was new, and conditions under which the filter would have to operate were uncertain, but the basic building blocks they had to use were known. Hospitals face an analogous situation, in which the policy structure that society will adopt is uncertain, but there are known tools, the principles of management, available with which to craft a response. These principles and their application to management challenges are what this book is all about. We articulate and apply concepts that will stand the test of time so that hospitals can excel regardless of the policy regime to which they are subjected. We will say more about which tools apply in which environments in Chapter 6, after we lay the building blocks in the context of existing hospitals. Appendix A provides a standalone summary of the management principles that we employ. This can be read as a basic management primer or consulted as a reference for the problem-oriented chapters.

1.6 Principles-Driven Management: Marrying Theory and Practice

The skill and judgment of experienced clinical practitioners is critical to quality outcomes. Yet it would be a mistake to rely on clinical experience alone, unsupported by theory, to advance the field. We could watch a surgeon all day without understanding why she is doing what she's doing. To understand the "why" behind the "what," we would need courses in chemistry and anatomy, physiology and neurology. Modern medical practice relies heavily on science.

This was not always the case. For example, doctors used leeches in ancient times for all manner of maladies (even headaches) without any scientific basis. As long as some patients got better, doctors continued to use leeches. But with only experience as a guide, outcomes were unreliable and usage of leeches steadily declined. However, more recently, science demonstrated the anesthetic and anticoagulant features of leech saliva, and modern circulatory theory helped explain when using leeches (or genetically engineered equivalents) might be beneficial and when it would be foolhardy. As a result, leech usage has made something of a comeback. Theory tells us why things work as they do, and by so doing both explains practice and provides us with the tools to improve it.

A *theory*, according to *The American Heritage Dictionary* (1985 edition), is "systematically organized knowledge applicable in a wide variety of circumstances, especially a system of assumptions, accepted principles, and rules of procedure devised to analyze, predict or otherwise explain the nature of behavior of a specialized set of phenomena." Practice without theory is just trial and error, with no guiding principles beyond what "seems to work." At the same time, theory without practice is ultimately sterile. In academic disciplines, it is a constant temptation to develop theories on theories, moving ever further into the sterile realm of abstraction and away from the real world of actual practice. Yet, it is practice that directly adds value to people's lives. The best theories are focused on informing real problems that real decision makers face.

Theory development involves separating out phenomena that are idiosyncratic to a certain narrow context from those that are more universal in application. The latter can be expected to stand the test of time, more so than any particular practice. Some theories are more predictably accurate (most laws of physics can be counted on to hold and to predict outcomes) than others (theories of human behavior are less reliable given the open-ended and evolving nature of human understanding and culture). But, in all cases, researchers seek guiding principles that provide fundamental understanding, inform practice, and give us the tools to improve outcomes. As new diseases, risks, and contexts evolve over time, practice can become obsolete. Theory, however, is semipermanent and should apply in circumstances old and new. Theory can therefore provide guidance in new territory, which is why we need it now.

In this book, we strive to marry the worlds of theory and practice by taking a principles-driven approach to hospital management. We identify key hospital management challenges, and for each we base potential responses on general principles that can be relied on to be applicable in a variety of circumstances and help predict or otherwise explain behaviors. Because the same principles apply to a range of specific hospital management challenges, we avoid excessive repetition by accumulating them in Appendix A. Readers who are not yet familiar with one or more of them can consult Appendix A for descriptions, explanations, and examples.

The result is a book that uses general principles of management, derived from many years of research in a variety of business subfields, to inform and improve practical hospital operations. In this way, we allow medically oriented readers to acquire general management knowledge by focusing on specific hospital issues that are familiar to them but that, once mastered, provide an approach that is applicable to new problems in the evolving future.

1.7 The Structure of This Book

Our focus is within the walls of the hospital, but occasionally it extends to extra-hospital initiatives. For example, if inpatient capacity is strained, one possibility would be to reduce demand by promoting healthy lifestyle choices or home therapies, possibly through a website. If the ED receives a pulse of older patients on Monday morning because no registered nurse (RN) was on duty in local nursing homes over the weekend, one response could be to put a hospital staff RN into the homes. In this way, we recognize the close interdependence between the hospital and the community it serves, but we consider it through the lens of hospital management rather than the broader perspective of public policy.

Until the final chapter, we assume a hospital configuration that is consistent with current practice. Specifically, we view the hospital as divided into four identifiable areas: ED, nursing units, ORs, and diagnostic facilities. We devote a chapter to each of these, and within each chapter we follow the common content format shown in Exhibit 1.6.

```
Stakeholders' Perspectives
Introduction
        History
        Physical Assets
        Human Assets
        Flows
Management
        Performance Metrics
        Management Decisions
Key Management Issues
        Issue 1
                Problem
                Principles
                Practices
                Case(s)
        Additional Issues Repeat This Format
Conclusions
Stakeholders' Perspectives
References
```

Exhibit 1.6   Hospital Operations general chapter outline.

We begin each chapter with a "stakeholders' perspective" narrative (that continues through all of the chapters) before turning to unit-specific material, beginning with an introduction, brief history, and the unit's assets and flows. We then list common metrics by which the unit's performance is judged and some management decisions that the unit must make in practice. This is followed by two or more key management challenges, and for each we provide an introduction, affected metrics, relevant management principles, and a translation of principles into practices followed by illustrative case examples. Each chapter then ends with a continuation of the narrative.

1.7.1 Principles-Driven Brainstorming

To solve problems for complex organizations, it is helpful to begin with a broad landscape of options from which to choose. It is universal in books on brainstorming and innovation that one should not narrow the focus too early to only a few options. Rather, one should start with a long, open-ended, and uncensored list of possibilities to be sure that all options are considered. Then, using judgment, this list should be winnowed down to the most promising few, which are subjected to more detailed and rigorous analysis. The most difficult part of this exercise for many people is not the analysis part, for which tools exist, but the brainstorming part that involves coming up with a wide array of options. This is called the *concept generation* stage of an innovative process and entails a long list of concepts being generated prior to the *concept selection* phase of choosing one or a few for closer scrutiny and eventual implementation.

Principles-driven management provides a helpful tool for concept generation. Principles relate precursors to consequences, so if we want to improve the consequences, we should work on the precursors. For example, suppose the management challenge is to reduce delays getting onto the surgical schedule. What can we do to shorten delays? By turning to the principles, we can list the causes of delays and look at each of these individually as an opportunity. Delays, for example, can result from excessive workload, insufficient capacity, poor synchronization of demand and capacity, high variability, or poor sequencing of the jobs in queue. Improvements can be achieved by working on any one of these subtopics. So, in a brainstorming exercise, we can think of all the ways the hospital can work on each subtopic. For example, the hospital can reduce workload by reducing the patients served per day or reducing the time per patient in surgery. Likewise, increasing capacity, improving synchronization, reducing variability, and improving sequencing can be broken down into more detailed components. By continuing in this fashion—breaking down higher-order concepts into more detailed concepts—we will eventually reach a level of implementable specificity. By this process of cascading refinement, a few general principles beget a wide array of specific potential solutions.

Because each higher-level concept generates many lower-level offspring, after two or three levels we will have constructed a long list of possible action items. This is good and signals a robust concept generation phase. Many of the options may be infeasible, undesirable, or difficult to implement for various practical reasons, but all of them should still be listed. The worst enemy of a productive concept generation activity is premature censoring. Sometimes an option that appears impractical can, with a small twist, become a novel and winning solution.

This principles-driven brainstorming approach is used for the key management challenges covered in each chapter. The reader may want to flip through a few chapters and inspect the tables. Their size will be striking. The illustrative cases then describe how to analyze or implement one or a few of the options in practice. Once a reader is familiar and comfortable with this approach, he or she can use it for other challenges not covered in this book. The principles and our approach are generic.

While examining the management challenges of the different units of the hospital, it quickly became apparent that three issues—responsiveness, patient safety, and organizational learning—are ubiquitous. Responsiveness is a common problem because delays negatively affect both patient satisfaction and clinical consequences. Whether the challenge is to reduce delays in the ED, the ORs, on nursing units, or in the lab, the underlying principles driving delays are the same. Similarly, ensuring and protecting patient safety and promoting organizational learning are issues that arise in many contexts and are amenable to some general principles regardless of context. So, for each of these generic management challenges, we have constructed the first three levels of the brainstorming process and have summarized them in three generic tables in Appendix A. When addressing one of these three generic challenges, a reader can start with a prepopulated generic table and then continue to break down the third-level list of options into specific action items.

1.7.2 Policies Progress but Principles Persist

The management principles presented in this book will continue to apply regardless of how the health care policy regime eventually evolves or what internal hospital structures dominate in the future. Although our division into the four subunits (ED, OR, nursing units, and diagnostics) is common in modern hospitals, one criticism of this structure is that it accepts as given the one thing that most impedes seamless patient care: a lack of cohesive integration between these subunits. Patients (and their information) often must pass through all of them during their acute-care experience (see Exhibit 1.7), and lack of coordination among them leads to poorer clinical, patient satisfaction, operational, and financial outcomes. While we focus on individual sections of the hospital, because each has its own culture of practice, the need for coordination between sections cannot be ignored.

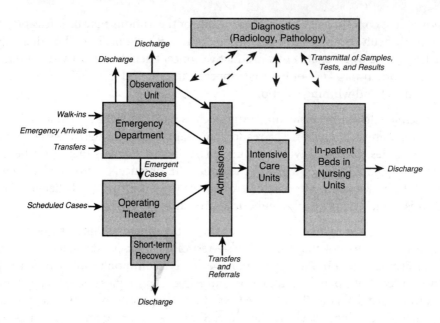

Exhibit 1.7   Hospital flows.

We pay attention to this need in some of our managerial challenges. For example, sizing inpatient units must take into account the need for post-surgery beds for patients coming out of the ORs (see Section 3.4.1). In other cases, the unit-specific managerial challenge that we cover can extend to interunit issues. For example, managing shift-to-shift patient handoffs on a nursing unit has the same character as managing ED to bed floor admissions handoffs (see Section 3.4.3).

However, we delay until Chapter 6 a more thorough discussion of alternatives to current practice in the internal organization of hospitals. There, we contrast the evolution of hospitals as service organizations to known evolutionary trajectories in other industries. We note that hospitals have been sheltered from the natural economic and competitive pressures that force firms in most industries to transit from "job shops" with poorly connected islands of expertise to "flow shops" of seamless processes as time and technology advances. The life-saving mission of hospitals does not exempt them from these pressures, but it does make addressing them significantly more complicated. In the end, however, the same erosion of economic surpluses that is threatening values-based conduct will challenge the current organization of health care services.

However, there is nothing in the future of health care that changes the basic principles of management. By focusing on these principles in the context of current practice, we equip readers to think strategically about their future and leverage fundamental management insights to get there. In the midst of an acknowledged health care crisis featuring high expenditures, mediocre outcomes, and confusion at the policy level, there are things we can and should do at the level of the most important transaction of all—that between patient and caregiver. It is to these we turn in the remainder of the book.

1.8 References

Abernathy, W., and J. Utterback. "Patterns of Industrial Innovation." *Technology Review*, July 1978, 41–47.

Anderson, R., T. Rice, and G. Kominsky. *Changing the US Health Care System*. John Wiley & Sons, SF, 2007.

Arrow, K. "Uncertainty and the Welfare Economics of Medical Care." *American Economic Review*, 53(5), 1963, 941–973.

Barr, D. *Health Disparities in the United States*. Johns Hopkins Press, Baltimore, 2008.

CMS 2010. "National Health Expenditure Projections 2010–2020." Centers for Medicare and Medicaid Services, U.S. Department of Health and Human Services: https://www.cms/gov/NationalHealthExpendData/downloads/proj2020.pdf [accessed November 7, 2011].

Commonwealth Fund 2010. "2010 Commonweatlh Fund International Health Policy Survey in Eleven Countries": http://www.commonwealthfund.org/Charts/In-The-Literature/How-Health-Insurance-Design-Affects-Access/Access-to-Doctor-or-Nurse.aspx

Hammer, P., D. Haas-Wilson, M. Peterson, and W. Sage. *Uncertain Times: Kenneth Arrow and the Changing Economics of Health Care*. Duke University Press, Durham NC, 2003.

Hardin, G. "The Tragedy of the Commons." *Science*, 162, Dec 1968, 1243–1248.

HCS report: "America's Uninsured Crisis: Consequences for Health and Health Care." Board on Health Care Services, Institute of Medicine. National Academies Press, 2009.

Hollingsworth, J,. Z. Ye, S. Strope, S. Krein, A. Hollenbeck, and B. Hollenbeck. "Physician-Ownership of Ambulatory Surgery Centers Linked to Higher Volume of Surgeries." *Health Affairs* 29(4), April 2010, 683–689.

Hsia, R., A. Kellermann, and Y. Shen. "Factors Associated with Closures of Emergency Departments in the United States." *JAMA* 306(9), 2011, 1978–1985.

Legorreta, A., J. Silber, G. Costantino, R. Kobylinski, and S. Zatz. "Increased Cholecystectomy Rate After the Introduction of Laparoscopic Cholecystectomy." *JAMA* 270(12), Sept 22–29, 1993, 1429–1432.

Mendes, E. "Percentage of Uninsured Adults in U.S. Remains Elevated." Gallup website. http://www.gallup.com/poll/126791/percentage-uninsured-adults-remains-elevated.aspx. March 17, 2010.

Nallamothu, B., M. Rogers, M. Chernew, H. Krumholz, K. Eagle, and J. Birkmeyer. "Opening of Specialty Cardiac Hospital and Use of Coronary Revascularization in Medicare Beneficiaries." *JAMA* 297(9), March 7, 2007, 962–968.

Noah, T. "A Short History of Health Care." A slate blog posting (March 13, 2007) summarizing J. Cohn's book *Sick: The Untold Story of America's Health Care Crisis—and the People Who Paid the Price.*

OECD: Organization for Economic Cooperation and Development, see www.oecd.org.

OECD report Economic Survey of the United States, 2008. http://www.oecd.org/document/51/0,3746,en_2649_34587_41809843_1_1_1_1,00.html.

Schwartz, W., and D. Mendelson. Eliminating waste and inefficiency can do little to contain costs. *Health Affairs* 13(1), 1994, 224–232.

Skinner, W. "The Focused Factory." *Harvard Business Review* 52 (1974): 113–121.

Williams, M., and C. Schneider. "Grady Memorial CEO to Resign." *Atlanta Journal-Constitution*, Wednesday March 30, 2011.

---

1   PPP = Purshasing Power Parity, meaning exchange rates are adjusted to reflect the cost of a fixed basket of goods among countries being compared, equating the purchasing power of currencies in those countries.
2   For example, when General Motors went bankrupt in 2009, hourly wages for production workers were only slightly higher than those at Toyota, but health care costs were seven times greater, resulting in a $1,500 per vehicle penalty for GM.

2

EMERGENCY DEPARTMENT

Coauthored with Jeffrey S. Desmond, MD and Steven L. Kronick, MD

2.1 Stakeholders' Perspectives

Monday March 22, 2010, 12:05 p.m.

"Hi Lucy, it's me." Sally pinched the cell phone to her ear with her shoulder as she rummaged through her purse for her keys. "Can you pick up Charlie after school? I need to go to the hospital."

"Um, sure, of course," Lucy replied haltingly. "Are you okay? What's wrong?"

"I think it's just the flu." Sally finally located her keys. "But I've been pretty sick all night and my doctor suggested going to the emergency room to get checked out. So if you'll drop Charlie with Mom and Dad, he'll be okay until I get home tonight."

"Okay." Lucy wasn't assured by Sally's matter of fact tone, but she knew better than to press her fiercely private sister-in-law for details. "Call me from the hospital when you know more."

"Okay, bye."

Sally Barbar Oldham was a 55-year-old widow with a 22-year-old disabled son Charlie. Although born normal, Charlie had begun having seizures at the age of three and had slowly declined physically and mentally thereafter. Passionately protective of her only son, Sally had never considered institutionalizing him. So when her husband was killed in a traffic accident ten years ago, she had moved in with her parents for help in caring for Charlie. But now that her parents were in their 80s, Sally was increasingly caring for them as well as her son. Lucy, wife of Sally's younger brother Mark, marveled that Sally did all this without complaint while managing to work nearly full time as a paralegal.

Yesterday morning, while driving her mother home from church, Sally had experienced a sudden abdominal pain. This persisted throughout the day, accompanied by occasional vomiting. Since Sally knew several people at work who had missed days due to the flu, she assumed she had picked up a bug from someone there. From what she had heard, the worst of the symptoms would be over within 24 hours, so she had applied her considerable resolve to getting through the night.

In the morning, Sally was still feeling very ill. She managed to drive Charlie to his program for developmentally disabled adults (which she persisted in calling "school"), but vomited again in the parking lot. She returned home, called in sick to work, and dialed her primary care physician. The nurse apologized but said it was high flu season and the doctor did not have any openings to see her, but she should go to the emergency room just to be safe. Sally hesitated because the only medical plan she could afford had a very high deductible. She lay down to see if anything improved, but by noon the pain was even more acute, and she reluctantly decided to go to the Emergency Department (ED). She told her parents she was going to see the doctor, without mentioning the emergency room, called her sister-in-law to make sure Charlie would have a ride home, and headed for the hospital.

Sally followed the red signs to the emergency room, passed up the short-term parking spaces (thinking *those are for real emergencies*), and parked in the adjacent ramp. She walked slowly to the entrance holding her stomach and entered through the sliding glass doors. Passing a full waiting room to her left, she approached the registration desk. A young woman in white with a clipboard stood beside it.

"Hello," the young woman greeted. "What brings you to the emergency room today?"

"Nausea," replied Sally. "I think I have a bad case of the flu."

The woman instructed Sally to check in at one of the two kiosks opposite the desk. One of these was already in use by a fiftyish man who had a teenage girl with a bulky bandage wrapped around her right calf. Sally slid into the chair of the other station and filled out the electronic form, which dealt with identification and medical insurance information but also asked for the reason for her visit and some other questions about symptoms. She checked the box for "abdominal pain" and filled out the rest as best she could. When she was finished, the woman in white directed her into the waiting room.

Only a few chairs were unoccupied. Sally selected a seat on the end of a row where she could watch the registration desk and scanned the room. A few people were noticeably sick or injured, but the majority just looked bored—sleeping, slouching, or staring listlessly at a television blaring the cacophony of a daytime game show.

One person who was not bored or listless was the man who had been at the other registration kiosk. He was angry.

"I can't believe this emergency room makes you check in by computer!" he fumed. "What if you're dying? Do they want you to enter the time of your death into the computer?"

"Shhhh, Dad!" the girl hissed, her face contorted in mortified embarrassment. "You're too loud!"

The girl was 17-year-old Chelsea Saline, who had gashed her leg on a metal bed frame and needed stitches. Her father stopped his tirade but scowled for the next 15 minutes, keeping a careful eye on the double doors next to the registration desk. When a uniformed man finally came through those doors, the father jumped up and hustled over to him.

"Excuse me," he said, "my daughter and I have been here for 20 minutes, and we haven't even talked to anyone yet. Can you please tell me what's going on?"

"I'm sorry sir," the man replied. "I'm just a security guard. Someone on the medical staff will be out soon."

"How soon?" asked the father.

"I don't know." The security guard slowly sidled backward. "Soon." And he disappeared back through the double doors.

"For crying out loud!" The father wasn't moderating his voice any more. "Come on Chelz. Let's go to General Hospital. They can't be any worse than this."

They left, with the father muttering something about hoping their computer registration would at least "screw up their records." At General, they would be checked in by a human being. But they would still wait nearly three hours to reach an examination room and would spend a total of four and a half hours in the emergency room for Chelsea to receive four stitches. On the evaluation card at General Hospital, Chelsea's father would note sarcastically that their visit took more than an hour per stitch.

In addition to Chelsea, Sally noticed a young man in his twenties, who was sitting alone in a chair close to hers. He clutched a fully thawed ice pack in his left hand. He announced his exasperation with an occasional deep sigh.

Sally did not know that 26-year-old Darrell Johnson had injured his hand the previous evening while out with some of his buddies. He slipped (or was pushed if Darrell's alcohol-impeded memory could be trusted) and fell on his hand, bending his index and middle fingers backward. Darrell swore he heard a crack, but his friends told him to "cut the drama" because "it's just a sprain." But the pain got progressively worse overnight, and his fingers swelled up to half again their normal size. By morning, he had had enough and took a bus to the hospital.

When Sally arrived in the ED at 12:20 p.m., Darrell had already been waiting for more than two hours. The only words Sally heard him speak during the time they shared in the waiting room were "Damn straight!" in response to a comment from another patient about their long wait, "They wouldn't treat us like this if we had insurance." Darrell would eventually (after a six-hour wait) receive an x-ray, a splint, and a $1,500 bill, which he never paid despite hounding from a collection agency.

Shortly after Chelsea and her father left, a woman dressed in purple scrubs emerged from the double doors and began clicking on the computer at the registration desk. Sally immediately seized the opportunity to find out what was going on.

"Excuse me," she said softly, as she walked gingerly toward the desk. "I'm Sally Oldham, and I've been here for almost half an hour and haven't talked to anyone yet."

"I'm sorry ma'am," the nurse replied. "We're really busy here today. Did you check in at the desk?"

"Yes," replied Sally, "but…"

"Good," the nurse interrupted, glancing down at her monitor and standing up. "I'll be with you in just a sec. There's just one person ahead of you." She stepped out from behind the desk and called "Ms. Saline! Chelsea Saline!"

When Chelsea didn't answer, the nurse looked again at her computer screen and then up at Sally. "Sally Oldham?" Sally nodded and the nurse led her to an examination area.

"How can we help you?" the nurse asked while peering at a computer screen and clicking a mouse.

"I think I have the flu," Sally replied. "But it's pretty bad and my doctor recommended coming here to get checked."

"Nausea? Vomiting?" The nurse's gaze alternated between the computer and Sally as she went through a list of questions very much like those asked in the computer check-in process. Then she took Sally's temperature and blood pressure. After making some final entries into the computer, the nurse told Sally that she could go back to the waiting room.

"A doctor will see you as soon as possible," she said. "But because we're so busy, it will probably be a little while."

Sally returned to the same seat in the waiting room. What she did not know was that both the computer check-in system and the nurse had classified her as an ESI-3 (Emergency Severity Index level 3), which meant she was not in any immediate danger. But she realized soon enough that she was not a high priority as she continued to wait for two more hours.

Just after 3:30 p.m., Sally, who was hunched over with her head in her hands, was startled by a light touch on her shoulder.

"Sal?" Lucy asked softly. "How are you doing?"

"Lucy!" Sally sat up. "What are you doing here? Where are the kids?"

"They're with your mom." Lucy continued to stand because the seat next to Sally was occupied. "I picked up Charlie on the way to get Sandra and Conner."

"Why?"

"Because I'm concerned about you!" Lucy's voice adopted a slightly scolding tone. "And you didn't call or pick up your phone."

"Oh." She often forgot to take her phone off silent. "Sorry." Sally put her head back down.

"It's okay," Lucy rubbed Sally's shoulder, all accusation gone from her tone. "But how are you? What's happening here?"

"Nothing's happening," Sally sighed. "I'm not that sick by the standards of this place. So I'm not a top priority."

"But how are you feeling? You look kind of pale." Lucy reached over and felt Sally's forehead. "And you feel a little warm."

"I've been really nauseous since yesterday morning." Sally smiled wanly. "But I think everyone who's had this flu has been pretty sick for a day or so. I just hope the kids don't get it."

"I'm sure they'll be fine," Lucy reassured her. *If she were on death's door, she'd still be thinking about others.* "Let's worry about you for now. I'll go see what's up."

Lucy went up to the registration desk and talked briefly with the clerk and then the nurse. Both were polite and sympathetic, but neither could give Lucy an estimate of how much longer it would be before Sally would be seen. But only ten minutes later another nurse, whose badge identified her as Betty, came out and asked Sally to follow her. Lucy picked up Sally's coat and purse and held her arm as they walked.

"I'm sorry we've kept you waiting so long," she said as she pushed open one of the double doors. "As you can see, we have a lot of people here today."

Betty guided them to a space in the hallway that had been outfitted with a mobile bed, a heart monitor, and other equipment to serve as an auxiliary, if unprivate, examination room. "The doctor will come to see you here." She waved Sally to the bed and vanished.

"Not too private," whispered Lucy, self-conscious about being overheard. "I wonder how this complies with HIPAA."

Sally glanced around. From her recumbent vantage point, she could see several other patients in the hall, none of whom were being attended to. Three nurses (again in purple scrubs, evidently the standard uniform) were conversing at a circular desk at the intersection of two halls. A door on the other side of the nurse's station opened, and a young-looking doctor hurried out, conferred briefly with one of the nurses, and strode down the hall and out of sight.

Sally and Lucy waited uneasily, watching doctors, nurses, and people of unknown occupations pass through the corridor, occasionally attending to patients waiting in hallway beds. Finally, a little after 4 p.m., a dark-haired man with glasses emerged from a doorway on the other side of the nurse station and walked briskly over to Sally's bed. He was wearing a white coat over green scrubs that agreed reassuringly with Sally's expectations of a physician.

"Hello Ms. Oldham. I'm Dr. Greene." He shook hands with Sally and turned to Lucy.

"Nate!" Lucy was surprised to recognize a fellow parent from her children's school. While she had known that Nate was a doctor, she had never known where he worked or that he was an emergency physician.

"Lucy! How nice to see you." Dr. Greene looked from Lucy to Sally. "How are the two of you connected?"

"Sally is Mark's sister." Lucy turned to Sally. "Dr. Greene and I are on the PTA together."

"It's a pleasure to meet you." Dr. Greene smiled at Lucy. "Your sister-in-law speaks very highly of you. But let's talk about how you're feeling today. I know you've already told the nurse, but I'd like to go over your symptoms."

Sally described her stomach pain and vomiting. She then answered questions about her medical history—diabetes, hypertension, and high cholesterol—and surgeries—hysterectomy for fibroids five years ago and tonsillectomy when very young. Dr. Greene also physically examined her, noting that her abdomen was very tender, and listened to her stomach with his stethoscope.

"Does it look like the flu?" Lucy asked as Dr. Greene completed his examination.

"It could be," said Dr. Greene. "There's been a lot of that going around. But I want to do some tests just to make sure. The first thing I'll need is a blood test. Someone will come in just a bit to get a sample. I'll be back as soon as I get the results." He patted Sally's arm and left with a nod to Lucy.

At 4:20 p.m., a technician named Sanjay arrived. He collected four vials of blood and, after a failed attempt that required a tight bandage on her wrist, inserted an IV into Sally's forearm. Lucy wondered about the IV but did not want to alarm Sally and so said nothing. While they waited, Lucy told Sally that Nate had two children in the same grades as her own and that he was a stand-up guy.

"You're in good hands," she assured her sister-in-law.

At 5:45, Dr. Greene received the lab reports, which showed a white blood count (WBC) of 14,500, compared to a normal range of 4,000–10,000, blood urea nitrogen (BUN) of 32 compared to a normal range of less than 20, and a creatinine (Cr) level of 1.4, compared to a normal reading of 1.0. He indicated a working diagnosis of viral gastroenteritis (stomach flu) in the record and placed an order for intravenous hydration of 1 liter and intravenous pain medication. He then returned to Sally.

"Hello Sally. Lucy." Dr. Greene noted that Sally was holding her abdomen and had an expression of pain on her face. "Are you feeling worse?"

She shook her head vaguely, so he went on.

"No? Okay. I got your test results, and there's nothing too out of the ordinary. But we're going to try to make you more comfortable by giving you some fluids and medication. Before we do that, however, we're going to get you into an actual room."

Sally was moved from her hallway space to an enclosed examination room and hooked up to an IV drip. Her abdominal pain subsided somewhat, but she remained nauseous. Shortly before 6 p.m., when Lucy had stepped out in search of a better cell phone signal with which to call home, Dr. Greene returned. He examined Sally and found that her abdomen was still distended and tender. Despite the fluids, she had not urinated since coming to the hospital. Although gastroenteritis remained the most likely explanation, Greene wanted to rule out other more dangerous conditions.

"I'm glad you're feeling a little better," said Dr. Greene. "But I'd like to do another test."

"What test?" asked Sally. "What do you think is wrong?"

"Well, it's likely that you do have the flu," replied Dr. Greene cautiously. "But your symptoms could also be consistent with some kind of intestinal blockage. To make sure, I want to get a CT scan."

"Is a blockage dangerous?"

"Yes. It can require surgery." Dr. Greene came around the side of Sally's bed. "I don't mean to scare you Sally, and the odds are this is just the flu. But we shouldn't take any chances."

"Okay. What is a CT scan, and how long will it take?"

"A CT scan is an advanced form of an x-ray that can produce a detailed image of almost any organ." Dr. Greene explained. "But it will take a while. It's really busy in here tonight, so there's going to be a wait for the scanner. Also, you'll need to drink a contrast agent an hour before the exam. Depending on how things go, we may want to keep you here overnight."

"Overnight?" Lucy had reentered the room as Dr. Greene was speaking. "Are you going to be here overnight, Nate?"

"No, I'm afraid not," Dr. Greene apologized. "I've been here since seven this morning, so I'm going to be leaving soon. But before I go, I'll brief my colleague, Dr. Jennifer Gray, on your case. You'll be in very good hands."

As Dr. Greene predicted, the CT scanner was busy. It was past 9 p.m. before Sally received her scan. Prior to that, she was given contrast agent, but she vomited after drinking it. Without sufficient material in the gastrointestinal tract, the image was not as informative as it might otherwise have been. Moreover, the only radiologist available to read the scan was a resident who issued a preliminary report; the final report would not be issued until morning. In the report, the radiologist noted distended small bowel loops and a distended, fluid-filled stomach. No definitive obstruction was observed, but, due to the quality of the image, the radiologist could not rule this out. However, the report also noted that the observed inflammation could be consistent with gastroenteritis.

Dr. Gray examined Sally and concluded that she was too sick to send home and recommended she be admitted. Because the hospital was very busy, it took some time to get Sally transferred up to a floor. The most probable diagnosis being gastroenteritis, Dr. Gray recommended that Sally be admitted to Internal Medicine (IM) unit 6A. However, the bed management team told her IM could not accept any more patients, but there was a bed available on 5B, the General Surgery unit. It was almost midnight before two transfer techs arrived to take Sally up to 5B.

Thursday March 25, 2010 1:45 a.m.

The mechanical buzz of the cell phone on his nightstand was working its way gradually into Dr. Greene's consciousness when a nudge from his already awakened wife jarred him alert. He reached over and grabbed the phone.

"Oh, hello Lucy, what's going on?"

There was a long pause.

"I am very, very sorry."

After a few more pauses, punctuated by sympathetic "Hmms" and apologies, he hung up. He turned to his wife, "A patient…a friend is dying in the hospital."

Thursday March 25, 2010 11:00 a.m.

Dr. Greene was tired during his ED shift, having spent a sleepless night after Lucy's call. He looked up Sally's medical record, which confirmed the worst. Sally had expired at 10:15 a.m. On his first break, he went to the Intensive Care unit (ICU) to see if Lucy and her family were still there.

He saw them from the doorway but hesitated. Not knowing what to do or say, he waited silently outside for a few full minutes before going in.

"I know this will be of no use to you," he said, "but I am really sorry." Lucy and her husband Mark thanked him in subdued mumbles. Greene almost added, "We did our best," but in truth he did not believe that. They clearly did not do their best, and Sally was the face of that failure.

The rest of his shift followed a familiar pattern, with delays, adjustments, and occasional chaos. Although this was typical, Dr. Greene was less tolerant than usual of the barely-under-control chaos. He was acutely aware, in a way he had not acknowledged previously, that these increasingly commonplace features of life in the ED were life threatening to patients. Each delay, each perceived inefficiency, each miscommunication added fuel to his inner fire. By the end of the day he was angry and discouraged, not because of the usual grind but because he could not see it getting better. He desperately needed to run off some steam at his weekly basketball game.

When his shift ended, he hurriedly pulled on his sweats, grabbed his duffel, and jogged to his car. He pulled out of the parking ramp and drove the two miles to the elementary school site of the weekly game. On the way, he reviewed everything he knew about Sally's case and realized he did not know much. There were too many open questions, but one thing stood out in his mind: *She was not supposed to die!*

He got out of the car and stood holding the door. *I got into this business to help people, not to have friends die unnecessarily on my watch!*

"#@%&*)^%#@!" He slammed the door and ran into the school.

2.2 Introduction to the ED

2.2.1 History

Treatment of medical emergencies is as old as medicine itself. Transportation of wounded soldiers to care facilities dates back at least to the ancient Greeks (Sternberg 1999). But systematic prehospital treatment of injuries was not practiced until the French Revolution in 1794, when Baron Dominique Jean Larrey trained medics to treat wounded soldiers in the field prior to transport to a field hospital (Pozner et al. 2003).

Larrey is also credited with introducing the practice of triage (from the French *trier*, which means "to sort") as a means of separating wounded soldiers into those who needed immediate attention in the field, those who could wait for treatment until after being transported to a field hospital, and those who could not be saved and therefore should receive only pain relief (that is, alcohol) but not medical care. The concept of triage found its way into hospital EDs, although the details of how patients are classified and how the classification information is used to allocate treatment differ from hospital to hospital.

From the time of Larrey's initial innovations, military emergency medical services progressed steadily through a progression of wars. However, civilian emergency medical services lagged behind. Although the Commercial Hospital of Cincinnati (now Cincinnati General) and Bellevue Hospital in New York introduced the first civilian ambulance services in the 1860s, most municipal "ambulances" were actually hearses from local funeral homes until the latter half of the twentieth century (Blackwell 1993). Inside hospitals, emergency rooms were manned on a rotating basis by staff physicians (surgeons, internists, psychiatrists, dermatologists, and so on) or even foreign medical school graduates, with no training in emergency medicine (Rosen 1995) and offered little more than first aid (Institute of Medicine 1993). Emergency physician John Wiegenstein recalled the emergency rooms of the 1950s as "dismal places, staffed by doctors who couldn't keep a job: alcoholics and drifters" (University of Michigan 2003).

Emergency medicine began to emerge as a discipline when researchers showed the value of mouth-to-mouth ventilation in 1958 and the effectiveness of cardiopulmonary resuscitation in 1960 (Institute of Medicine 2007a). These clinical advances demonstrated that rapid response to cardiac emergencies could significantly improve patient survival and health. Emergency medicine received a huge boost when the landmark report *Accidental Death and Disability: The Neglected Disease of Modern Society,* by the National Academy of Sciences and the National Research Council (1966), reported that, in 1965, 52 million accidental injuries killed 107,000 Americans, temporarily disabled more than 10 million, and permanently impaired 400,000 more at a cost of approximately $18 billion. The report concluded that accidental injury is "the neglected epidemic of modern society" and "the nation's most important environmental health problem."

A wave of public and private funding of initiatives to improve the emergency medical system led to development of portable external defibrillators, nationwide adoption of the 9-1-1 system, and construction of regional emergency medical service (EMS) systems. To elevate the professional status of emergency medicine, the American Medical Association (AMA) formed a committee on emergency medicine in 1967, and the above-mentioned John Wiegenstein and seven colleagues founded the American College of Emergency Physicians (ACEP) in 1968. In 1970, the University Association for Emergency Medical Services (UAEMS) was formed for scientific and educational purposes by medical school faculty practicing emergency medicine (American Academy of Emergency Physicians 2008). The first residency in emergency medicine was established in 1970 at the University of Cincinnati. By 1975, there were 32 residency programs for training physicians in the practice of emergency medicine (NAEMT 2008). The first nationally recognized training course for emergency medical technicians (EMTs) was held in Wausau, Wisconsin, in 1969. Today, EMT training, with some variations by state, is offered through hundreds of community colleges, technical schools, hospitals, and universities, as well as EMS, fire, and police academies.

In the 1980s, categorical federal funding for EMS was replaced by general health service block grants to states. Because most states used these discretionary funds for other areas of need, EMS experienced a sharp decrease in funding (Institute of Medicine 2007a). In addition to slowing the overall advance of emergency medicine, this shift led to a fragmentation of state policies. For example, although Maryland took a strong central role and established statewide emergency air and ground transportation systems and a sophisticated trauma system, California delegated responsibility for EMS to the county and regional level, resulting in high diversity among and limited coordination between local systems. The National Research Council (1985) cited limited progress in EMS during the 1980s and called for a federal agency to focus on injuries as a public health problem. This led to an injury program being established at the Centers for Disease Control and Prevention (CDC), which later became the National Center for Injury Prevention and Control (NCIPC) within the CDC (Institute of Medicine 2007a).

Another important development in the 1980s, which had a large impact on the modern ED, was passage in 1986 of the Emergency Medical Treatment and Active Labor Act (EMTALA). This act states that any patient who "comes to the Emergency Department" requesting "examination or treatment for a medical condition" must be provided with "an appropriate medical screening examination" to determine if he/she is suffering from an "emergency medical condition." If he/she is, then the hospital is obligated to either provide him/her with treatment until he/she is stable or transfer him/her to another hospital in conformance with the statute's directives. Passed to prevent hospitals from "dumping" uninsured or Medicaid patients on public hospitals, the law had the effect of increasing the amount of uncompensated care provided by EDs. Indeed, according to a May 2003 AMA study, emergency physicians provide an average of $138,300 of uncompensated care per year, and one-third of emergency physicians provide more than 30 hours of EMTALA-related care each week (American College of Emergency Physicians 2008). The resulting financial strain is one reason that many hospitals have closed their EDs; the number of hospitals with EDs has declined from 5,318 in 1982 to 4,061 in 2008, a decrease of 24%.

By the 1990s, hospital "emergency rooms" were increasingly being designated "Emergency Departments" to reflect their association with the new academic discipline of emergency medicine. Innovations in scanning and surgical technology continued to increase the efficacy of care for injured and critically ill patients. But, as noted by the National Highway Transportation Safety Administration (1996), integration of EMS, hospital health care and public safety systems was still inadequate. The lack of interoperability and communication between these systems was exposed during the response to the terrorist attacks of September 11, 2001 (National Commission on Terrorist Attacks upon the United States 2004). This led to calls for improved surge capacity and system integration to improve preparedness (Center for Catastrophe Preparedness and Response NYU 2005).

Although disaster preparedness remains a critical concern, congestion is the primary challenge cited in editorials by ED professionals (for example, Derlet 2002, Hollander and Pines 2007). The underlying cause of this congestion is the fact that the decrease in hospital-based ED capacity was accompanied by an increase in demand (see Exhibit 2.1). The number of ED visits has steadily risen over the past 15 years due to several factors. One is an increase in the number of uninsured patients for whom the ED is the only guaranteed access to health care. Another is rising wait times to see primary care physicians, which has made the ED a more convenient choice for many patients seeking prompt care. A third factor is the increased sophistication of care in the ED, which has broadened the set of patients who can be served effectively in the ED. The net result has been severe overcrowding conditions in many EDs.

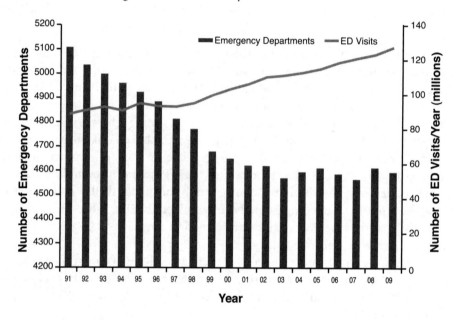

Exhibit 2.1   ED visits and EDs in community hospitals, 1991–2009
(data source American Hospital Association 2011).

Long waits, boarding of patients waiting for hospital beds, ambulance diversions, patients leaving without being seen, and increased adverse events are examples of the negative consequences of congestion in the ED. Given this, it is not surprising that a key finding of the recent Institute of Medicine report *Hospital-Based Emergency Care at the Breaking Point* (2007b) is that there is a great need to improve operational efficiency by adopting industrial engineering and operations management techniques proven to be effective in other sectors of the economy.

Another issue looming on the horizon for EDs is cost. More sophisticated equipment, shortages of key labor categories, and the need to respond to higher volumes have steadily driven up costs. At the same time, reimbursement rates have been under serious downward pressure. Hence, the efficiency methods needed to address operations issues are needed to address financial issues as well. By encapsulating the essential insights that underlie these techniques in the form of management principles, we seek in this book to provide health care professionals with a framework for improving ED performance in operational and financial, as well as clinical, terms.

2.2.2 Physical Assets

The physical configuration of EDs varies greatly between hospitals. Size is one reason; an ED in a small community hospital may have a simple layout with a waiting room and registration desk feeding a single examination and treatment area, whereas a major academic medical center or large private hospital may have an ED with several units, dozens of examination rooms, a helipad, and imaging/laboratory facilities. ED layout also differs across hospitals due to legacy considerations. EDs must fit within the physical constraints of the hospital. Because the workload and complexity of EDs has increased substantially over the past few decades, most hospitals have had to find ways to expand their ED capabilities within these constraints. As a result, no two EDs are exactly the same in either structure or function.

Nevertheless, most EDs have many features in common. Exhibit 2.2 shows a schematic of a sample layout of an ED. Typical components of an ED, which are represented in this sample layout, are described in the list that follows.

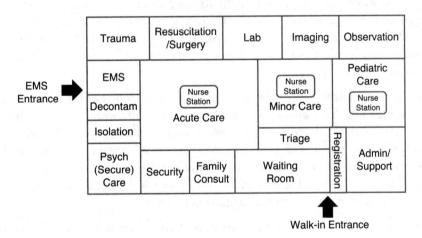

Exhibit 2.2 A sample layout of an ED.

Note that, although we present these as physical areas, they are really functions. Although all hospital EDs perform the functions associated with these areas, they use different physical spaces to support them. Indeed, within a given ED, a function may be carried out in a flexible manner, sometimes using a designated space and sometimes not. With this caveat, we summarize the main areas/functions of the ED as follows:

- **EMS entrance**—The EMS (emergency medical services) or ambulance entrance is usually physically separate from the walk-in entrance. In small hospitals, these two entrances may be adjacent to one another. But in larger hospitals, they are often separated by a substantial distance to prevent congestion.

- **Triage area**—The purpose of the triage process is to classify patients according to their treatment needs. Typically, this is done in a triage area adjacent to the reception/waiting room area to facilitate efficient assessment of walk-in patients. However, some EDs handle triage flexibly, with the triage nurse assessing patients' needs in the waiting room, at the registration desk, or in regular examination rooms. In EDs that have a formal triage location, it is typically an examination room equipped with standard precaution equipment (hand-washing facilities, gloves, and so on), communication devices (such as phone and intercom), and information technology (terminal for entering patient information, paper forms, and so on).

- **Waiting room**—The waiting room is where patients wait to begin treatment. The waiting room can range from a cold, forbidding space with a few chairs and little else to a comfortable, inviting entry to the ED that facilitates exchange of information and family support. Because time spent in the waiting room generally has a negative impact on performance metrics, some EDs try to avoid using it at all when possible. That is, patients are brought directly into examination rooms. But because some waiting is inevitable in busy EDs, hospitals have introduced equipment aimed at increasing efficiency (such as self-registration stations) and comfort (such as TVs and computers, and in pediatric waiting rooms, toys).

- **Registration area**—Registration is where patient information is collected. Traditionally, this consisted of a desk, where patients would check in. But in modern EDs, the registration process is often flexible, taking place where and when convenient. For instance, a patient may not be registered until he/she has been moved to an examination room and has begun treatment. In such settings, registration is defined less as an area and more as a process, which is supported by an information system and work procedures.

- **Nurse stations**—Nurse stations are almost always centrally located. Because these are the information hubs of the ED, it is vital that they be in close contact with the examination rooms. So most EDs are designed with the examination rooms encircling the nurse station(s). Notice that in the ED shown in Exhibit 2.2, the trauma (resuscitation) areas are not directly adjacent to the nurse station in the sample diagram. This is because patients in trauma/resuscitation rooms often require continual staff presence, whereas patients in the regular examination rooms are only visited periodically. So visibility of examination rooms within units (such as Acute Care, Minor Care, and Pediatric Care) from a nurse station is more important than is visibility of the rooms used for more intensive care.

Nurse stations are equipped with whatever information systems are in use. Computers are a given. Electronic white boards that display patient and room status are common. But despite the progress of electronic information systems, paperwork is still ubiquitous. Patient files on clipboards, compliance forms, ED status records, and a host of other documentation and transaction data are recorded and transferred via paper. The effort involved in paperwork, whether carried out electronically or with actual paper, is substantial; the American Hospital Association (2001) reported that every hour of patient care in the ED involves an hour of paperwork. Given this, the mundane furniture and equipment that facilitate information recording, storage, display, and transfer are important parts of a well-designed ED.

- **Diagnostic units**—These units contain imaging and other test equipment dedicated to the ED. The diagnostic unit is almost always equipped with x-ray units, which may be fixed or portable. Many larger EDs have full radiology facilities, including CT scanners and ultrasound equipment. Some EDs also have their own labs to ensure rapid turnaround of blood counts, blood typing, toxicology screens, and so on. Other hospitals handle ED laboratory services on a priority basis in the central lab.

  Diagnostic units are frequently located on the periphery of the ED. Because ED patients share X-ray, CT scan, and other imaging equipment (in contrast to a vital signs monitor, which is dedicated to a single patient during his/her stay), patients are typically moved to these devices as needed. As such, they do not justify prime real estate near the nurse station and hence are relegated to more distant spaces. When EDs have their own lab, it is similarly positioned on the perimeter of the unit.

- **Resuscitation unit**—Larger EDs may contain a separate unit designed to treat unstable (for example, critically ill or injured) patients who need life-sustaining intervention. This typically consists of one or more resuscitation bays, each equipped with a defibrillator, airway equipment, oxygen, suction, intravenous lines and fluids, emergency drugs, and a telephone. Surgical instruments, organized in trays for specific emergency procedures (such as tracheostomy, cricothyroidotomy, thoracotomy, peritoneal lavage, and others), are typically accessible to the bays. Resuscitation areas also have electrocardiogram (ECG) machines and may contain X-ray facilities, noninvasive ventilation (NIV), and portable ultrasound devices.

- **Observation unit**—Many EDs maintain rooms for observing patients whose symptoms require time to evaluate. In the case shown in Exhibit 2.2, specific rooms are reserved for psychiatric observation (for example, suicide watch). But many EDs also maintain observation rooms in a Critical Decision unit (CDU) for cardiac and other patients for whom lengthy (24 hours) observation periods are needed to assess their condition. Because observation rooms are less expensive to construct and are generally not subject to the "certificate of need" restrictions imposed on other hospital resources, they are often deemed an economical means of preventing slow-moving patients from tying up critical examination rooms and delaying treatment of other patients.

- **Acute Care (Major) unit**—The main unit of the ED, where stable patients with serious or complex medical problems are diagnosed and treated, is often called the "Acute Care" or "Major Unit," or sometimes just the "main ED." This unit almost always consists of multiple examination rooms that are equipped with beds (which are typically mobile gurneys or trolleys, rather than fixed beds), vital sign monitors, IV equipment, surgical kits, and other standard equipment.

- **Fast-Track (Minor) unit**—In recent years, many EDs have established separate units to diagnose and treat patients with minor injuries/illnesses who do not require extensive ED resources and are likely to be released after treatment. Examination rooms are similar to those in Acute Care, although they may be more lightly equipped. If the Fast Track is implemented via logical, rather than physical, flow, the examination rooms may be shared with Acute Care.

- **Pediatric unit**—This unit is for treatment of children under the age of 17. Equipment in the examination units is similar to that in the Acute Care unit, although the décor is usually different (including bright colors, animal characters, and TV screens). More recently, some EDs have introduced analogous geriatric units designed to serve the needs of older patients.

- **Psychiatric unit**—Some hospitals contain units for assessing and treating psychiatric patients in crisis. The unit for providing psychiatric emergency services may be housed in the ED or elsewhere in the hospital (such as in a Psychiatric Services Department). Although patient rooms are usually minimally equipped from a medical standpoint, they are often secured with locks and closed-circuit camera monitors.

2.2.3 Human Assets

Like physical assets, the human assets of EDs vary from hospital to hospital. Again, size and focus are key determinants of the personnel makeup of an ED. But tradition and local practices are also influential. The main staff categories found in most EDs are:

- **Medical director**—The director of the ED is a practicing physician with responsibility for hiring, firing, physician review, and scheduling. In larger EDs, the director may be assisted by other physicians with administrative responsibilities (service, quality, and so on).

- **Emergency physician**—As we noted earlier, EDs were once staffed by various hospital physicians without specific training in emergency medicine. But since 1970, residencies specifically in emergency medicine have been available. Consequently, more and more physicians in EDs are specialists in emergency medicine. To become board certified in emergency medicine, physicians must complete an approved residency program or graduate training program and be accredited by the American Board of Emergency Medicine (ABEM). As of 2001, there were approximately 32,000 emergency physicians practicing in the United States, of which 17,000 were certified by ABEM.

In teaching hospitals, senior members of the medical staff who have completed their training are generally referred to as attending physicians ("attendings" for short). They have ultimate responsibility for care of patients, as well as supervision of medical students and residents when present. Attending physician duties include diagnosis, decision making, and direct care for patients.

- **Trauma surgeon**—Because patients with *trauma* (a bodily injury severe enough to pose a threat to life and limb) typically enter the medical system through the ED, trauma surgeons play an important role in the ED. Trauma surgeons complete a five-year residency in general surgery, followed by one or two years of fellowship training in trauma surgery and surgical care. There are roughly 3,000 trauma surgeons practicing in the United States (Institute of Medicine 2007b). Because this is substantially fewer than the number of hospital EDs, many EDs must rely on on-call general surgeons for trauma surgery. High levels of uncompensated care, malpractice risk, and disruption of family life have discouraged surgeons from pursuing trauma surgery fellowships, many of which have not been filled in recent years. Consequently, a national shortage of these specialists is looming.

- **Physicians in training (residents, interns)**—Teaching hospitals have training programs for physicians and are usually affiliated with a medical school. Interns are in their first year of training after graduating from medical school. After the first year, the physician in training is called a resident. These physicians participate in the diagnosis and care of patients, but an attending physician supervises them. The level of independence granted to physicians in training depends on their experience level and demonstrated skill.

- **Mid-level practitioners**—Many EDs utilize physician assistants (PAs) and nurse practitioners (NPs), who are collectively called mid-level practitioners (MLPs). MLPs work under the supervision of an emergency physician to examine, diagnose, and treat patients. In most states, they can prescribe medications. Although they play a role similar to that of residents, PAs do not go to medical school. Both types of MLPs have graduate training, prior to which NPs generally have a bachelors in nursing degree and are certified as RNs, whereas PAs often have a bachelor's degree in a science field, in addition to experience in health care (usually four years). MLPs must also pass a licensing exam. The NP and PA professions were founded in the 1960s and have grown steadily since then. Currently, there are approximately 160,000 nurse practitioners (Health Resources and Services Administration 2010). There are roughly 83,000 licensed PAs in the United States, of which 10% work in emergency medicine (American Academy of Physician Assistants 2010). Because their training tends to be more pragmatic and experience-oriented than that offered in medical school, MLPs are generally well equipped to deal with the realities of the ED.

- **Emergency nurse**—Nurses play a wide range of essential roles in the ED, including administration, triage, diagnosis, stabilization/resuscitation, prioritization, treatment (for example, suturing), and evaluation. After completing a two- or four-year academic nursing program (or a three-year diploma program through a hospital), graduates take an exam to become a registered nurse (RN). Although they are not required to work in an ED, many emergency nurses take an additional exam to become a certified emergency nurse (CEN). Some EDs still use licensed practical nurses (LPNs), who have one year of vocational training, to provide direct care for patients. There are roughly 90,000 nurses of all types working in EDs (Nurses for a Healthier Tomorrow 2008).

  Beyond their titles and training, emergency nurses are distinguished by the roles they play. The nurse manager is responsible for recruiting, training, staffing, scheduling, and educating the nursing team in the ED. Depending on the size of the unit, the nurse manager may delegate day-to-day supervision to a nurse supervisor. The triage nurse is responsible for classifying patients according to their treatment needs. The charge nurse is responsible for overall operations, including assignment of patients to rooms and staffing of nursing resources. A primary nurse provides and coordinates care for patients in the ED. Larger EDs may also employ clinical nurse specialists, who work to integrate care, improve nursing practices, and facilitate education of the nursing staff.

- **ED technician**—In response to recent shortages of nurses, many EDs have introduced emergency technicians to perform a variety of tasks depending on the institution and state laws. These may include taking vital signs, drawing blood, starting an IV, performing EKGs, and transporting patients to and from various tests. Training varies widely, but these technicians are often former ambulance personnel (paramedics and EMTs).

- **Pharmacist**—Although not yet common practice, some EDs include pharmacists on their staff to oversee patient medical needs and to improve medication billing and inventory control. Some EDs also have satellite pharmacies that provide medication support specifically for ED patients.

- **Unit secretary/clerks**—In addition to medical staff, the ED needs administration to run. The unit secretary generally serves as the receptionist, coordinates test orders, and handles the communication needs of the ED. For instance, the unit secretary may help a physician contact a patient's family, assist families calling about their loved ones, or talk to patients calling for medical advice. In larger EDs with more administration, additional clerks may carry out similar tasks.

- **Social workers**—Many EDs have social workers on staff to deal with suicidal or homicidal patients, alcoholics, addicts, abused children, and patients with mental illness. They also work with patients and family members dealing with crisis situations and help ensure that patients are discharged into safe environments.

- **On-call specialists**—Because the ED must serve patients with almost any problem, they cannot possibly rely on internal staff for all the expertise they need. So EDs use on-call specialists for consultation and support. Traditionally, hospitals required physicians to cover some on-call hours in return for admitting privileges. This enabled hospital EDs to provide specialist support and gave young specialists a way to build up their practices by gaining new patients. But in recent years, specialist shortages in many markets have enabled physicians to fill their practices without ED patients. For instance, there are many fewer neurosurgeons than there are EDs in the United States (Institute of Medicine 2007b). This, combined with the facts that reimbursement rates are lower and malpractice rates are higher for work in the ED relative to an office, has made it increasingly difficult for EDs to find sufficient on-call specialist coverage.

2.2.4 Flows

Exhibit 2.3 provides a schematic of the flow of patients through a typical ED. Because it provides a broad array of services to a wide range of patients, there is no single path through the ED. Patients can arrive by car, ambulance, or helicopter, or they can just walk in. Once in the ED, patients are triaged to determine their priority of care, usually by assigning a triage score or category. In most cases, patient triage is done in a designated area by a triage nurse. However, in some hospitals, triage can be done flexibly in different locations, and in some EDs at least some triage is done by an MLP or physician. Triage is usually a quick process, often requiring only two minutes and almost never more than five.

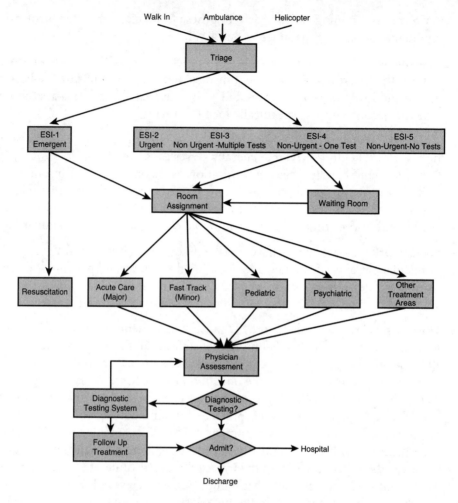

Exhibit 2.3   Typical patient flow through an ED.

Traditionally, triage focused exclusively on urgency. A typical three-level triage system would classify patients into "emergent" (needs treatment right away), "urgent" (would benefit from prompt treatment), and "nonurgent" (can wait for treatment). However, in more recent years, many American EDs have adopted the five-level Emergency Severity Index (ESI) system, in which ESI-1 indicates a life-threatening situation, ESI-2 indicates an emergency situation, and ESI-3, 4, and 5 indicate nonurgent patients with different resource (for example, diagnostic testing equipment) needs. By taking into account resource needs as well as urgency, triage information can be used to prioritize patients for purposes of efficiency and exigency.

Based on the information gathered at triage, patients may be tracked into different units (Resuscitation, Acute Care, Fast Track, Pediatric, or Psychiatric). The number of tracks an ED has depends on the size of the ED and the range of services it offers. Based on criteria set by the American College of Surgeons (ACS), EDs are classified from Level I trauma centers, which offer the most advanced surgical care and a full range of specialists and equipment, to Level V trauma centers, which provide basic evaluation, stabilization, and diagnostic capabilities.

Regardless of the level of the ED, the basic patient flow is similar. Once they have entered a unit within the ED, patients undergo various tests and treatments, which may result in their being moved within or beyond the ED or having resources and people moved to them. Ultimately, patients are discharged, admitted to the hospital, or transferred to another care facility.

A large ED receives as many as 100,000 patients per year, which is more than 250 per day. The patients are treated in several tracks competing for a range of resources, including people, equipment, and facilities. Making sure that these resources get to patients in a timely and accurate fashion is the fundamental management challenge of the ED. If this is not done successfully, patients will wait, causing them frustration and possibly adverse medical outcomes. The resulting congestion may cause staff to feel pressure to hurry, possibly leading to oversights or errors.

So much of the performance of the ED hinges on the manner in which flows are managed. This is why there has been increased interest for many decades in operations management methods to manage material flows in production systems. Indeed, the Institute of Medicine (2007b) explicitly recommended that "hospital chief executive officers adopt enterprise-wide operations management and related strategies to improve the quality and efficiency of emergency care." Included in these strategies are programs based on Lean, the Toyota Production System, and Six Sigma, which are fundamentally about improving system flows.

But porting methods from manufacturing to hospitals is not straightforward. Flows are complex because decisions made during the process determine them. These decisions require sophisticated judgment on the part of ED personnel. Errors can be matters of life and death. Employee contracts are complicated and varied (for example, some surgeons are hospital employees, whereas others belong to independent practices but have hospital privileges). These and other differences present unique challenges for flow management in hospital EDs, which are distinct from those in manufacturing systems.

Nevertheless, the underlying principles used to design and control efficient manufacturing systems can be helpful in improving ED performance. To do this, we cannot simply copy practices from manufacturing. Instead, we must first state the performance metrics and management decisions we seek to improve. Then, in the context of specific problems in the ED, we can highlight basic management principles and use them to systematically explore improvement alternatives.

2.3 Managing the ED

2.3.1 Performance Metrics

Performance of the ED is measured in clinical, operational, and financial terms. Clinical metrics attempt to measure the quality of patient care. Operational metrics seek to characterize the process efficiency of the unit. Financial metrics track monetary flows in an effort to monitor the ED solvency.

Clinical metrics can be divided into three subcategories: process, outcome, and patient satisfaction. *Process metrics* measure the extent to which the treatment process conforms to specifications established by regulatory agencies, professional societies, or the hospital itself. An example of such a metric is the percent of myocardial infarction patients with door-to-balloon time within 90 minutes, as recommended by the American College of Cardiology (ACC) and the American Heart Association (AHA). In addition to individual procedures, process metrics can seek to measure overall process effectiveness. For example, the Agency for Healthcare Research and Quality (AHRQ) provides a standardized survey of the culture of safety in a hospital setting. *Outcome metrics* measure the result of treatment. An example is the number of patients who return to the ED and are admitted to the hospital within 72 hours of their initial visit to the ED. *Patient satisfaction metrics* measure the subjective approval by patients of their experience. These are generally collected via surveys, which typically ask patients to rate their caregivers and other aspects of the system (such as the waiting room) on a scale from "very dissatisfied" to "very satisfied."[1] Table 2.1 gives more examples of clinical performance metrics for the ED.

Table 2.1   Sample Performance Metrics for the ED

Clinical Metrics	Operational Metrics	Financial Metrics	Organizational Metrics
Process	Time	Costs	Learning
Percent EMTALA forms completed	Average door-to-triage time (by patient type)	Staffing	Attendance in training sessions
Percent pneumonia patients who receive blood cultures prior to antibiotics	Average triage-to-room time (by patient type)	Overtime per week/month	Number of items submitted through suggestion boxes
Percent compliance with sepsis resuscitation bundle	Average room-to-provider time (by patient type)	Premium labor (for example, agency nurses)	Number of suggestion box items acted upon
Percent sepsis patients transferred to ICU within 6 hrs	Average provider-to-disposition time (by patient type)	Consumables (drugs, supplies, and so on) per visit	Average number of "links" beyond an individual's home unit
Percent pediatric patients whose weight documented at triage	Average disposition-to-bed time (by patient type)		Improvement in targeted metrics (for example, change in AMI door-to-balloon time)
Percent pediatric patients whose vital signs documented per protocol	Length of stay (LOS) (by patient type)		
Percent pneumonia patients who receive appropriate antibiotics selection	Percent ESI- 2 patients seen within various threshold times		
Percent AMI (acute myocardial infarction) or chest pain patients who receive EKG within 10 min	Percent ESI-3 patients seen within various threshold times		
Percent AMI patients who receive thrombolytic agent within 30 min	Percent of ESI-4,5 patients discharged within various threshold times		
Percent AMI patients door-to-balloon time within 90 min	Average time from disposition to out		

Table 2.1 Sample Performance Metrics for the ED

Clinical Metrics	Operational Metrics	Financial Metrics	Organizational Metrics
Percent eligible stroke patients who receive t-PA within 3 hours	Percent patients transferred to higher level care within 24 hours of initial disposition		
Percent cases with consent documented	Average order to completion time (and percent completed within various threshold times) for lab tests		
	Average order to completion time (and percent completed within various threshold times) for general x-rays		
	Average order to completion time (and percent completed within various threshold times) for CT scans		
	Percent time waiting room is closed		
Outcome	**Volume**	**Revenues**	
Total deaths within 24 hours of ED visit	Average number of ED visits per day (could be broken down by ESI level)	Total ED charges per month	
Unscheduled returns to the ED within 72 hours (with and without admission to hospital)	Percent bed utilization	Relative value units (RVUs) per hour for the ED and for individual physicians	
Total cases reviewed at M&M (mortality and morbidity) conference	Percent bed hours utilized in ED and OU	Percent of expenses billed	
		Percent of billings reimbursed	

Clinical Metrics	Operational Metrics	Financial Metrics	Organizational Metrics
Percent patients left without being seen (before and after triage)	Average age of patients	Facility and professional billings	
	Percent time ED is on diversion		
	Resource (CT scanner, operating room [OR], and so on) utilization		
Patient Satisfaction			**Staff Satisfaction**
Average overall patient satisfaction score from survey			Average overall staff satisfaction score from survey
Average patient rating of attending physician			Average response to specific survey questions (for example, rating of physisian/nurse working relationship)
Average patient rating of nurse			Staff turnover rate
Likelihood to recommend ED to others			

Operational metrics can be divided into two categories: time and volume. *Time metrics* track the speed at which patients flow through the unit. The most basic time measure is LOS (Length of Stay), which is usually measured separately for patients who are admitted to the hospital, patients who are kept for observation, and patients who are released. But because patients wait at many points in the process, it makes sense to track metrics that measure specific wait times, as illustrated in the table. *Volume metrics* measure the workload the unit receives. The most direct metric is the average number of patients per day who visit the ED. But because patients are clearly not equal in terms of the degree of care required, other metrics, which are sensitive to the complexity of patient treatment needs, are typically used. Some examples are shown in the table. Finally, we can track behaviors that influence operational performance. For example, the percent of time the waiting room is closed (so that patients bypass it and go directly into an examination room) can serve as a proxy for short arrival-to-room times. Other examples are composite metrics that combine time and volume measures into single number metrics of overcrowding.[2]

Financial metrics can be broken down into costs and revenues. *Cost metrics* characterize ED expenses, which include staff salaries, equipment expenses, and consumable purchases. These are relatively straightforward to measure, although it requires some accounting sophistication to associate expenses with individual patients. In contrast, *revenue metrics* can be subtle because payments to the ED are affected by not only the procedures performed, but also whether they are billed for, whether the patient has insurance coverage, and whether they are approved by the insurance company. To break down revenue generation by provider and to document charges for insurance purposes, many hospitals use relative value units (RVUs), which standardize costs (including physician time, overhead, and liability insurance) of providing specific procedures. A physician's RVUs per hour is a measure of his/her financial productivity. Multiplying the RVU by a conversion factor determines the reimbursement rate to the hospital from an insurance company or government agency. For expenses not covered by insurance, revenue depends on the collection percentage from patients.

Finally, organizational metrics can be divided into two categories: staff satisfaction and organizational learning. *Staff satisfaction metrics* measure how content staff members are with working conditions and how engaged they feel in the mission of the hospital. This is most directly measured by means of a survey asking general questions, such as "How satisfied are you?" as well as more focused questions, such as "Do the physicians and nurses have a good working relationship?" But indirect measures, such as employee turnover rate, can also offer insight into staff satisfaction levels. *Organizational learning metrics* seek to measure the extent to which the ED acquires, shares, and uses knowledge. Because it is not easy to measure organizational knowledge directly (for example, by giving the organization an exam), learning metrics focus either on process (for example, number of training sessions attended, number of ideas expressed in suggestion boxes, number of new initiatives adopted) or outcome (for example, fraction of error-free medication orders, door-to-EKG time for MI patients). Note that clinical compliance metrics can serve as organization learning metrics if they are used to follow up on knowledge acquisition/sharing/use initiatives.

2.3.2 Management Decisions

Like any organization, management of an ED involves decisions at the long, intermediate, and short term. Roughly speaking, long-term decisions revolve around capacity, intermediate-term decisions center on scheduling, and short-term decisions focus on flow.

Long-term capacity decisions include facility decisions (for example, expanding the number of examination rooms, obtaining a dedicated CT or MRI scanner for the ED, and locating a lab within the ED) as well as personnel decisions (for example, adding emergency physicians or nurses to the regular staff and setting the number of physician assistants and residents assigned to the ED). In addition to capacity for handling patients, long-term decisions must deal with capacity for handling information. Equipment and procedures for storing, displaying, and transferring information about patients and ED status are becoming increasingly essential to performance.

Intermediate-term scheduling decisions determine how the resources established by the long-term decisions are used. A big part of this is staffing, which determines who is scheduled to work when. ED management set work schedules for regular conditions and exceptional (for example, mass casualty) situations. Hospital management must set a schedule for on-call personnel for specialized consulting needs. These schedules in turn affect nonstaff resources, such as makeup and layout of mobile carts within the ED.

Finally, once staff and equipment are in place, *short-term flow decisions* must be made to promote speed and quality in patient care. These cover a wide range of issues, including the order in which to treat patients, assignment of staff and resources to patients, test and treatment decisions, admission/discharge decisions, and a host of others. In addition to decisions, the flow of patients involves many routine processing activities, including collection, entry and transfer of information, transport of patients, collection of materials and supplies, and of course, actual treatment (for example, resuscitation, surgical procedures, wound sterilization, suturing, and administration of medication). The efficiency with which routine activities are carried out can have a major impact on performance. That is why they are an important focus of ED management.

2.4 Key Management Issues in the ED

One way to approach the problem of improving management of the ED is to select a performance metric from Table 2.1 and then seek policies with which to improve it.

However, almost any policy will affect more than one performance metric. For instance, suppose we decided to focus on the percent of time the ED is on diversion as a performance metric and considered the long-term option of adding staff as a potential improvement strategy. This would obviously affect the cost metrics by increasing the staff budget. It might also increase equipment expenses and physical overhead charges if additional facilities are needed to effectively use the extra staff. Moreover, the extra staff would affect waiting times, volumes, process metrics, and possibly even outcome metrics. So, to fairly evaluate the wisdom of adding staff, we would need to consider all these ramifications.

Because of this, and because identifying policies for addressing all the performance metrics in Table 2.1 would wear out the patience of even the most tolerant reader, we adopt a more intuitive, issue-oriented approach. That is, we identify two major management challenges facing most EDs today—alleviating overcrowding and enhancing patient safety—and analyze each in a systematic fashion. We will do this by first identifying the set of performance metrics to measure progress for the specified management challenge. Then we invoke selected management principles from Appendix A to identify policy levers for improving those performance metrics. Finally, we translate these levers into practical policies for addressing the management challenge.

The goal is to be as comprehensive as possible by using the management principles to identify all possible levers. This leads to a broad enumeration of high-level improvement policies, each of which could be pursued to identify concrete action items. However, because detailed implementation policies depends on the environmental specifics of the ED being considered, it is not possible to be comprehensive at the detailed level. That is why we offer concrete policies as illustrations of how this approach can be used to explore ways to resolve a given issue. By doing this for a handful of important issues in the ED, we hope to offer both useful suggestions and a framework for exploring additional solutions to these and other challenges in managing an ED.

2.4.1 ED Overcrowding

2.4.1.1 PROBLEM

We begin with a widespread problem in U.S. EDs: overcrowding. As illustrated in Exhibit 2.1, the number of visits to EDs has increased in recent years, but the number of hospital-based EDs has declined. There are a number of interrelated reasons for this. The U.S. population has aged, and older people tend to experience more health care emergencies. The fraction of the population with medical insurance has declined, and by law (EMTALA) the ED is the one part of the hospital required to give patients at least some care regardless of ability to pay.[3] Finally, lower reimbursements by Medicare,

Medicaid, and private insurance companies have put financial pressure on hospitals, which has been partially responsible for a decline in the number of hospital-based EDs.

These trends have led to fewer EDs handling more patients than ever before. So it is no surprise that the number one problem cited by ED professionals is overcrowding. Indeed, in a national survey, 91% of EDs cited overcrowding as a problem, with 40% reporting that the problem occurred on a daily basis (Derlet et al. 2001). As shown in Exhibit 2.4, a high percentage of hospitals, particularly teaching and urban hospitals, put their EDs on diversion during periods of high congestion, forcing ambulances to divert patients to other hospitals until the congestion clears.

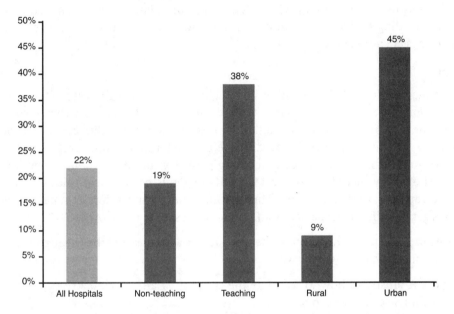

Exhibit 2.4   Percentage of hospitals reporting time on ambulance diversion in 2010
(data source American Hospital Association 2011).

Overcrowding is a serious problem because it degrades performance in clinical, operational, and financial terms. In clinical terms, overcrowding can lead to delays in treatment and rushing by the ED staff, which in turn can cause departures from compliance with standard procedures, adverse health outcomes, and dissatisfied patients. In operational terms, overcrowding inflates length of stay (LOS) and, because it increases the amount of time the ED is on diversion and the number of patients who leave without being seen, reduces the volume of patients who are treated. In financial terms, the loss of patients means a loss of revenue, particularly if those who leave without being seen tend to be insured patients with a higher likelihood of reimbursement. Consequently, finding ways to alleviate the overcrowding problem is an essential management challenge to the ED and to the hospital as a whole.

To analyze the overcrowding problem in a way that will help us identify promising management responses, we start by identifying the management principles applicable to improving responsiveness. These fall into four categories. First, we consider *capacity* and the role of capacity overloads in causing patient backlogs. Second, we examine *variability* and how it can cause congestion even when the ED has enough capacity on average to meet patient arrivals. Third, we discuss *sequencing* and its effect on patient waiting times. Finally, we introduce *psychology* and explore how perceptions of waiting can influence patient satisfaction with their care.

Here we only list the relevant principles with brief comments on their connection to the ED overcrowding problem. For additional motivation and discussion of the principles, the reader is encouraged to consult Appendix A.

CAPACITY

The simplest cause of ED congestion is capacity overload, which occurs when the ED receives work (patients) at a rate faster than it can handle. That is, the arriving workload exceeds the *capacity* of the ED. But, although it is easy to refer to the capacity of the ED informally, what exactly does this mean? The ED isn't a monolithic entity. It is a composite of many different resources, including people, equipment, rooms, supplies, and so on. The ability of the ED to treat patients depends on all these things. Hence, to define a capacity overload, we must first define what we mean by ED capacity. We do this by first defining the capacity of an individual resource as follows.

Definition (Resource Capacity)—The capacity of a resource is the throughput it can achieve if it is never starved for work.

Appendix A illustrates how to compute the capacity of an individual resource, such as the triage nurse or a CT scanner.

To get from the capacity of a single resource to the capacity of the ED as a whole, we invoke the concept of *utilization*, which is defined as follows:

Definition (Utilization)—Utilization of a resource is the long-term fraction of time it is busy, which is given by the average arrival rate of work (for example, patients per hour) at the station divided by the resource capacity over the long term.

This is important because the resource in a system with the highest utilization has the least capability to catch up from a capacity overload. Hence, we define the following:

Definition (Bottleneck)—The bottleneck of a system is the resource with the highest utilization.

For instance, the emergency physicians might be the most highly utilized resources in the ED. If so, they constitute the bottleneck. Because the bottleneck constrains the maximum rate of the system and hence defines its capacity, we have the following principle:

Principle (System Capacity)—The capacity of a system is defined by its bottleneck, which is the resource in the system with the highest utilization.

So, if the emergency physicians are the bottleneck of the ED, then throughput (patients per hour) cannot exceed the capacity of these physicians to treat patients. This also means that to increase the capacity of the ED we must increase bottleneck (physician) capacity.

The following principle describes how capacity impacts congestion:

Principle (Utilization)—Utilization magnifies queueing in a highly nonlinear fashion.

In the ED, this principle implies that busier resources (people, equipment, rooms, and so on) will result in longer patient waits. Furthermore, as utilization approaches 100% (for example, physicians are continuously occupied with patient care), waiting times will increase dramatically. This is important, because it implies that capacity and utilization are key levers with which to address ED overcrowding.

VARIABILITY

Overloaded resources are not the only reason for ED congestion. Congestion can occur even when capacity exceeds demand. The reason is the other major driver of patient waiting, which is variability, as stated in the following key principle:

Principle (Variability)—Unsynchronized variability causes queueing.

In the ED, variability comes in two major forms: arrival variability (fluctuations in patient arrival rate) and treatment variability (fluctuations in the rate at which patients are processed). Note that if these two types of variability were synchronized (that is, the processing rate increases and decreases in precise proportion to workload), then congestion would not occur. But when arrival and treatment variability are unsynchronized, periodic bursts in arrivals or delays in treatment will cause backups that will take time to clear. Hence, (unsynchronized) variability combined with high resource utilization leads to patient queueing, which results in ED overcrowding, even when ED capacity meets or exceeds demand.

The consequences of variability can take on multiple forms, as described by the following:

Principle (Variability Buffering)—All unsynchronized variability will be buffered by some combination of inventory, capacity, time, quality, and system degradation.

The most obvious impact of variability in the ED is increased patient waiting (a time buffer). But variability can also lead to poor use of resources (a capacity buffer), such as idle clinicians who are on duty to be ready for periods of peak demand. It can also lead to hurrying and mistakes (a quality buffer) or a long-term decline in performance (a system degradation buffer). Although in many systems (for example, a pharmacy or a supply cabinet) variability can lead to inflated inventories, an ED is a service system, so the following reduced version of the Variability Buffering principle applies.

Corollary (Variability Buffering in Service Systems)—In a pure service system, inventory is not available as a buffer, so holding quality and system degradation costs constant, there is a trade-off among variability, excess capacity, and waiting time.

The implication in the ED is that if we want to reduce overall patient waiting times, we must either add capacity or reduce variability. Moreover, the following principle implies that the average waiting time of patients waiting in the ED is proportional to the average number of patients waiting:

Principle (Little's Law)—Over the long term, the rate (R), in-process inventory (I), and waiting time (T) of a system are related in the following manner:

$$I = R \times T$$

Hence, whatever we do to reduce waiting times (via capacity additions or variability reductions) will also reduce the number of people waiting , and hence ED overcrowding.

Although adding capacity is a transparent way to reduce waiting and overcrowding in the ED, reducing variability is more subtle. The following principles describe generic ways of reducing variability:

Principle (Buffer Flexibility)—Flexibility in variability buffers reduces the buffering required for a given amount of variability.

Principle (Pooling)—Combining sources of variability so that they can share a common buffer reduces the total buffering required to achieve a given level of performance.

Principle (Task Simplification)—Reducing task complexity reduces the mean and variance of the task times and the likelihood of errors.

Principle (Task Standardization)—Using clearly specified best-practice procedures for repetitive tasks reduces the mean and variance of task times and the likelihood of errors.

We will exploit these later to identify specific policies for reducing ED overcrowding by reducing variability.

SEQUENCING

Variability and utilization affect congestion and waiting regardless of the order in which patients are treated. But patient sequencing is an important activity in the ED. Indeed, the reason for triage is to sequence patients so that those with urgent needs are seen first. But sequencing also has operations implications, which leads to the third level of our analysis of the causes and cures of ED overcrowding.

Typical five-level triage systems divide patients into five Emergency Severity Index (ESI) classes. Note that classification of a patient into the most serious levels of ESI-1 or ESI-2 is based entirely on medical needs. These patients are treated as quickly as possible, regardless of the time required, which is vital to the clinical performance of the unit. But classification as ESI-3, ESI-4, or ESI-5 is done with consideration of how many resources are required, which provides some indication of how much treatment time a patient needs. The fact that patients differ according to their treatment needs means that sequencing can also be used to influence operational performance.

Key principles related to sequencing are the following:

Principle (Critical Ratio Sequencing)—In a multiclass system with dynamic arrivals, prioritizing entities according to the ratio c/t, where c is the delay cost per unit time and t is the expected process time, minimizes total cumulative delay cost over the long term.

Corollary (SPT Sequencing)—Processing entities in order of shortest processing time (SPT) minimizes average wait time.

The Critical Ratio Sequencing principle justifies treating ESI-1 and 2 patients first; because the cost of waiting for these patients is so high, they have high critical ratios. But for ESI-3, 4, and 5 patients, waiting costs are similar (because none are at elevated risk of mortality or morbidity). So the critical ratio depends primarily on patients' expected treatment time. The SPT Sequencing corollary implies that patients with similar treatment times should be treated in order of quickest patients first (that is, ESI-5 before ESI-4 before ESI-3). In addition to simple sequencing, there are other ways to organize the ED to take advantage of this concept, as we will enumerate in section 2.4.1.3.

PSYCHOLOGY

All the preceding principles deal with factors that affect actual waiting times. As such, they are important to many of the metrics given in Table 2.1. But the satisfaction metrics in the clinical category are also affected by *perceived* waiting times. That is, actions that influence how people feel about their waits also influence their satisfaction levels. Indeed, researchers have found that people who feel more informed about wait times are less likely to leave the ED without being seen (Arendt et al. 2003).

The key principle (from Maister 1985) dealing with how patients perceive waits is:

Principle (Waiting Time Psychology):

a. Occupied time feels shorter than unoccupied time.

b. People want to get started.

c. Anxiety makes waits seem longer.

d. Uncertain waits feel longer than known, finite waits.

e. Unexplained waits feel longer than explained waits.

f. Unfair waits feel longer than equitable waits.

g. The more valuable the service, the longer the customer will wait.

h. Solo waits feel longer than group waits.

These are intuitive, yet they are violated all the time in service industries like health care. For example, in the story that opened this chapter, Chelsea and her father gave the ED a poor score on their exit survey, largely due to their frustration with the wait. This frustration stemmed from a combination of the actual waiting time and the nature of the wait. They also sat for a long time doing nothing (items a and b). Certainly, Chelsea was anxious about her injury (item c). Because they did not get information on why the wait was so long and when they could expect to be seen, the wait seemed even longer than it was (items d and e). Finally, without information, they may well have felt that it was unfair that patients who arrived after they did were treated sooner (item f). The only thing that would have made Chelsea's wait even more frustrating would have been to do it without her father (item h). The implication is that, even without reducing Chelsea's actual waiting time, the hospital might have been able to make her more satisfied by giving her more activities and information during her wait.

2.4.1.3 PRACTICES

ED overcrowding is a specific instance of the responsiveness problem, which is ubiquitous throughout the hospital (tests wait for processing in the lab, images wait for reading in Radiology, surgical teams wait for ORs, patients wait for beds in the inpatient units, and so on). Because responsiveness problems are so common, we have invoked the preceding principles to generate Table A.1 of Appendix A to provide a comprehensive set of generic options for improving responsiveness.

Applying the generic options of Table A.1 to the particular environment of the ED results in Table 2.2. This more extensive table logically traces the alternatives for improving responsiveness to a broad set of policies for reducing ED overcrowding. In terms of the performance metrics of Table 2.1, these policies are intended to increase the volume of patients that can be handled by the ED, reduce the length of stay (LOS) experienced by patients, and improve patient satisfaction with their ED experience. Improvements in these key performance metrics will in turn generate improvements in other metrics, such as increasing revenue generated by the ED, reducing the fraction of patients who leave without being seen, and enhancing the clinical outcomes of patients.

Table 2.2   Generic Operations Improvement Policies: ED Overcrowding

Level 1 Objectives	Level 2 Objectives	Level 3 Objectives	Example Policies
Reduce workload	Reduce patient arrival rate	Reduce need for patient care	Install public blood pressure machines
		Encourage patients not to seek ED care	Post average and real-time congestion statistics on website
		Divert patients seeking care to alternate facilities	Establish in-hospital clinic
	Reduce work per patient	Improve preventive care	Distribute stoke symptom pamphlets
		Push work upstream	Authorize EMTs to administer infusion therapy, intubation, and ventilation
		Push work downstream	Board admitted patients in inpatient units instead of ED
Increase capacity	Add physical resources	Add capital equipment	Implement mobile X-ray units in ED
		Add supplies	Implement mobile Rapid Medical Evaluation (RME) cart with common supplies and medications
	Add human resources	Add medical personnel	Hire a physician assistant to perform routine examination, screening, and treatment procedures in place of physicians
		Add support staff	Use volunteers to track down supplies, medications, and information in place of nurses
	Eliminate steps	Automate tasks	Use radio frequency identification (RFID) bracelets to track patient location and room occupancy without manual data entry

Table 2.2   Generic Operations Improvement Policies: ED Overcrowding

Level 1 Objectives	Level 2 Objectives	Level 3 Objectives	Example Policies
	Eliminate steps	Eliminate redundancy	Standardize patient data so questions are repeated less often
		Streamline procedures	Build supply kits for specific procedures (to eliminate search task)
	Reduce process times	Use technology	Implement an e-triage system to speed triage process
		Standardize procedures	Implement an e-triage system to standardize triage process
		Simplify tasks	Use 5S to organize examination rooms
	Balance workloads	Long-term balancing through task reassignment	Train physician assistant to conduct preliminary exams to reduce load on attending physicians
		Real-time balancing through work sharing	Reassign a nurse to help triage nurse when number of patients exceeds a specified level
	Increase task parallelism	Perform diagnostic tasks in parallel with other tasks	Order all lab tests likely to be needed for diagnosis simultaneously, rather than sequentially
		Perform treatment tasks in parallel with other tasks	Prepare patients for surgery while setting up instruments
		Perform administrative tasks in parallel with other tasks	Use bedside registration
	Reduce blocking/starving	Reduce unnecessary starvation of ED resources	Use pull signals to draw patients into CT scanner

Level 1 Objectives	Level 2 Objectives	Level 3 Objectives	Example Policies
	Reduce blocking/starving	Reduce blocking of ED resources	Create observation unit; create discharge lounge to clear patients out of exam rooms sooner; relax nurse-to-patient ratios in inpatient units
Improve synchronization	Adjust demand	Adjust total rate of patients seeking care	Post real-time waiting statistics so nonurgent patients can avoid peak times
		Adjust fraction of patients who come to ED	Divert patients to another hospital when ED is overloaded
	Adjust capacity	Adjust staffing	Call in staff during overcrowded periods
		Adjust facilities/equipment	Borrow beds from inpatient units during periods of overcrowding
		Adjust protocols	Use physician at triage during busy periods to streamline discharge of minor patients and initiate care of more serious patients; Lower admission standard during busy periods so that patients who obviously need admission are admitted quickly rather than waiting for more tests
Reduce variability	Reduce arrival variability	Smooth arrival of urgent patients	Provide real-time workload data to paramedics; trace causes of predictable demand spikes
		Smooth arrival of nonurgent patients	Allow nonurgent patients to make "appointments"

Table 2.2   Generic Operations Improvement Policies: ED Overcrowding

Level 1 Objectives	Level 2 Objectives	Level 3 Objectives	Example Policies
Reduce variability	Reduce treatment variability	Reduce diagnosis time variability	Establish and follow standard protocols
		Reduce direct patient care time variability	Establish and follow standard protocols. Institute Fast Track to handle quick patients
		Reduce setup time variability	Use flexible examination room furniture to facilitate rapid preparation
		Reduce variability in ancillary service times	Establish ED lab or use priority system for ED orders in shared lab. Use teleradiology
		Reduce rework/delay due to errors	Use colored arm bands to identify patient risk factors (for example, Yellow = allergies)
Improve sequencing	Improve information needed to sequence patients	Improve patient sequencing	Visual display of patient status and services required
		Improve ancillary services sequencing	Label tests with patient priorities that give first priority to medical urgency and second priority to shortest processing time
	Improve sequencing decisions	Improve patient sequencing	Use SPT to sequence nonurgent patients, subject to a maximum waiting time constraint
		Improve ancillary services sequencing	Sequence lab/imaging orders for ED according to priorities, subject to constraint on wait time for non-ED orders

Level 1 Objectives	Level 2 Objectives	Level 3 Objectives	Example Policies
Enhance patient perceptions	Keep patients occupied	Involve patients in treatment process	Self-registration; fill out health information for triage
		Involve patients in nontreatment activities	Wireless Internet connection
	Get patients started	Start actual treatment process more quickly	Order tests at triage
		Make patients feel like treatment process has started more quickly	Convert waiting room into observation room, staffed by nurse who actively monitors patients
	Reduce patient anxiety	Provide information	Provide pamphlets that explain ED processes and what patients can expect
		Provide human contact	Have staff person regularly check on waiting patients
		Improve ambiance	Soft lighting, soothing music (instead of blaring TV), comfortable furniture, fish tanks, and so on in waiting room
	Provide explanations of waiting times	Written explanations	Display screen with priorities and estimated wait times by patient ID number
		Oral explanations	Have staff person regularly visit waiting room to explain status to patients
	Make waits more equitable	Minimize "cuts"	Use first-in-first-out except when medical urgency or operational efficiency overrides it
		Avoid extreme waits	Move patients to highest nonurgent priority once they have waited more than a specified amount

Table 2.2 Generic Operations Improvement Policies: ED Overcrowding

Level 1 Objectives	Level 2 Objectives	Level 3 Objectives	Example Policies
Enhance patient perceptions	Make waits proportional to value	Reduce waits of patients with minor illnesses/injuries	Use Fast Track Department or other separate value streams
	Facilitate group waiting	Facilitate waiting with friends/family	Allow family members to accompany patient into examination room and testing facilities
		Facilitate waiting with others	Encourage dialogue among waiting patients by giving them shared information (for example, about status of ED)

Although Table A.1 is fairly compact, Table 2.2 is dauntingly large. This is because there are many specific ways to implement each of the generic improvement avenues identified in Table A.1. So, even though we restrict the breakdown to three levels of objectives and only one (at most two) policies are suggested for each Level Three Objective, this still results in a lot of candidate policies. Obviously, more improvement options could be generated by further breaking down some of the more complex objectives and by being more exhaustive in identifying practical policies for implementing them. But this table gives a good overview of the process and of the range of options that exist for mitigating congestion in the ED.

The bad news is that studying Table 2.2 takes some time. The good news is that the sheer breadth of improvement options contained in it implies that there are many ways to improve patient flow through the ED. Even if some of the options are impractical in a given setting, for whatever reason (political constraints, physical restrictions, resource limitations, and so on), many more are available. Furthermore, as we will see, some policy options address more than one objective. For example, using an electronic triage system may help increase capacity *and* reduce variability of the triage process. Options like this that improve the system in more than one way may be particularly attractive.

We now survey the basic structure of Table 2.2 and discuss some specific improvement policies.

REDUCE WORKLOAD

ED workload can be reduced by either lowering the arrival rate of patients or decreasing the amount of work per patient who arrives.

There are three basic ways to reduce the arrival rate of patients: (a) reduce the need for treatment in the first place, (b) reduce the number of patients with a need who seek ED treatment, or (c) reduce the number of patients who seek ED treatment that choose our ED.

Examples of policies that might limit the need for treatment include better preventive care through changes in Medicare policies, improved nursing home care, public health awareness programs (for example, blood pressure machines in public places), and improved public safety (for example, alcohol restriction policies at sporting events or gun control legislation). Although most of these are beyond the scope of an individual hospital, there is no question that prevention should be an important focus from a public health perspective. The high cost of ED treatment of preventable emergencies can and should be used to argue for intelligent public spending on better preventive health care.

But an individual hospital is limited in its ability to influence the need for care. So an overcrowded ED might have more luck with policies that divert patients to more efficient sources of care. For example, a hospital might consider setting up its own internal clinic for seeing nonurgent patients. This would be analogous to a "factory within a factory" strategy, which has become common in manufacturing systems. There the basic idea is to avoid producing highly customized, low-volume products on the same production lines as high-volume, standardized products. The two product categories require very different operational capabilities. Low-volume, high-variety products (such as circuit boards for use as repair parts in old model computers) require a line that can switch rapidly from one type of product to another after producing a small batch. This type of performance is best achieved by a highly flexible *job shop* structure (that is, general-purpose machines and routings that can be rapidly adapted to produce a variety of products). High-volume, low-variety products (such as circuit boards for assembly into current model computers) require low cost and high reliability. This type of performance is best achieved by a highly efficient *flow shop* structure (that is, special-purpose machines and highly focused product routings that can produce a narrow range of products).

We can think of the ED in a level-one trauma center as a high-flexibility job shop and a specialty clinic as a high-efficiency flow shop. Having a patient with a minor rash receive treatment in a level-one trauma center makes no more sense than producing brake pads for a production model car on a sophisticated prototyping line. It is a waste of expensive equipment and personnel. So, hospitals that can figure out how to divert low-acuity patients requiring few resources to a simple treatment system (such as an internal clinic) will alleviate ED overcrowding, and reduce the overall cost of treatment, thereby (with the right business model) gaining a competitive advantage.

In addition to diverting patients to non-ED care facilities, an ED can seek to divert them to other (less crowded) EDs. At the municipal level, this can be done by enhancing the EMS system so that EMS personnel have access to real-time ED congestion data, allowing them to direct patients to the ED best able to treat them. However, because systems that provide such detailed data are not yet widely available, individual EDs often provide a coarser version of congestion information by going "on diversion" (that is, turning away patients) during busy intervals. Because of the potentially detrimental health consequences of diverting a patient to a more distant or less suitable ED, hospitals do not use this option cavalierly. Nevertheless, nearly half of urban hospitals spent some time on diversion in 2004 (see Exhibit 2.4).

A potentially less dangerous policy for diverting patients from the ED would be to publish congestion and waiting time statistics so that physicians (who advise patients to seek care in an ED) and individuals can make informed decisions. For example, Detroit Medical Center posts expected waiting times at their EDs, online, and via mobile phone apps. If a patient with a non-urgent malady knows that the expected wait in Hospital A is 5 hours, but the average wait in nearby Hospital B is only 3 hours, he/she may choose Hospital B, thereby helping to balance the workload among EDs in the region.

Note that reducing the number of patients who come into the ED is only one way to reduce workload. The other is to decrease the average work per patient. If patients require less time to treat, then congestion will be less, even if the number of patients does not decline. There are three basic ways to reduce the time required to treat a patient: (a) reduce the total amount of treatment required, (b) push some of the treatment upstream (before the ED), or (c) push some of the treatment downstream (after the ED).[4]

An example of a policy to reduce patient treatment time would be an educational campaign to educate the public about symptoms of stroke or myocardial infarction, which would encourage earlier calls to 911 and less seriously ill, and hence less time-consuming, patients.[5] An example of pushing workload upstream would be a policy encouraging EMTs to administer endotracheal intubation for patients in need of cardiopulmonary resuscitation.[6] Finally, an example of pushing workload downstream would be a policy to admit patients to the hospital more quickly. An obstacle to such a policy, however, is the fact that, in many hospitals, it takes longer to get tests on inpatients than on ED patients. Consequently, patients are sometimes held in the ED longer than necessary in order to get their tests more quickly. If the hospital were to adopt a system to speed testing for such patients after admission, there would be less incentive to hold them in the ED where they contribute to the overcrowding problem.

INCREASE CAPACITY

From Table A.1, we note that options for increasing ED capacity are adding physical/human resources, eliminating steps, redesigning workflow, reducing process times, balancing workloads, increasing task parallelism, and reducing blocking/starving.[7]

Adding physical or human resources is an obvious (and generally expensive) way to increase capacity. If a physical resource (such as an X-ray machine) or a staff member (perhaps a triage nurse) is overloaded (and hence a bottleneck), the most straightforward way to reduce utilization is to add more units of the resource. Although there is nothing complicated about hiring people or buying equipment, there is still room for creativity in how these resources are added. For instance, a creative way to add supplies might be to introduce Rapid Medical Evaluation (RME) carts so that common supplies and medications can be quickly transported to wherever they are needed in the ED. Such carts could be specialized by patient type (for example, an orthopedic cart would contain supplies specific to bone and joint injuries). A creative way to add human capacity might be to have a physician assistant (PA) perform some of the simpler duties currently handled by physicians.

A more subtle way to increase effective capacity is by eliminating steps. Any activity that does not contribute directly to patient welfare is "nonvalue added" and therefore a candidate for elimination. Generic ways to eliminate tasks include (a) automation, (b) redundancy elimination, (c) and procedure streamlining. For example, equipping patients with RFID bracelets could automate patient tracking and, with the right software, automate calculation of wait time and queue lengths. Patient background information (such as, "Are you currently taking any medications?") could be requested less frequently (subject to safety considerations, of course). Supply kits could be constructed in advance and stored in examination rooms to eliminate the need to search for supplies.

Reducing process times is closely related to task elimination, but instead of making tasks go away, the focus is on making the tasks that remain go faster. The default way to do this is to simply work harder. However, although most ED professionals agree that they do work faster during heavy demand periods, this is not a sustainable strategy. Consistently working beyond a healthy, vigorous pace leads to frustration and errors. The negative consequences of handling too many patients are apparent in statistics showing that medical outcomes degrade when the ED is overloaded (see, for example, Cowan and Trzeciak 2005).

Three standard ways of speeding tasks without working harder are (a) using technology, (b) standardizing procedures, and (c) simplifying tasks. For example, using an e-triage system, which structures the sequence of questions and examinations needed to classify patients according to their treatment needs, is an option for speeding the triage task. Because it imposes a set procedure, an e-triage system is also a means of standardizing the process. An example of a task simplification policy might be using a 5S system to organize the examination rooms, to position materials and equipment in a manner that supports rapid deployment as needed.[8]

All of the above options serve to increase overall effective capacity. But, even if we cannot add capacity in the aggregate (for example, by adding staff), we can add capacity at bottlenecks by borrowing it from nonbottlenecks. This practice, which we term *workload balancing*, shifts work from high-utilization resources to low-utilization resources. This can be done in both the long term through reassignment of tasks and the short term through dynamic sharing of tasks. An example of a long-term task reassignment would be training an MLP to do a task, such as suturing minor lacerations, normally done by a physician. An example of short-term work sharing would be having another nurse help perform triage when the triage nurse has more than a specified number of patients waiting for triage.

Workload balancing works by removing constraints on work assignments. Another way to increase effective capacity by removing implicit constraints is "task parallelism." Increasing task parallelism does not speed up or eliminate tasks, but instead reduces the total time required to treat a patient by performing some tasks in parallel (by eliminating precedence constraints). A common example of task parallelism in the ED is bedside registration. By using a Mobile Registration unit to collect patient information at any point in the treatment process (for example, while in the examination room), the ED can avoid delaying patients for registration at the outset of the process. Similarly, drawing blood from patients before sending them to X-ray would enable lab tests to proceed in parallel with imaging. Such parallelism could extend beyond the hospital, for instance, by having an EMS tech get a patient EKG in the field and transmit either the reading or the results to the hospital so that preparation can start before the patient arrives. Finally, a more aggressive example of task parallelism is ordering all lab tests likely to be needed for a patient right at the outset, rather than ordering some tests initially and ordering others later if needed. For example, an ED physician might order a CT scan of the spine when a patient is receiving a brain scan. Such just-in-case testing would ensure that patient would not have to wait for subsequent tests if needed. However, this could increase costs. So such a policy would have to be used judiciously.

One final way to increase the effective capacity of the ED is to reduce blocking or starving of ED resources. Although some starving of resources is inevitable (for example, an X-ray machine that is only 30% utilized will frequently be starved for patients without consequences for patient waiting), unnecessary starving can cause delays later on. For instance, a heavily utilized CT scanner that is not currently being used because a patient who needs it has not been transferred to the test room will have to process this patient later, possibly when other patients are waiting. So, using pull signals (for example, in the form of an electronic display that indicates when the CT is available, thereby encouraging ED personnel to expedite transfer of the next patient requiring a CT scan) could avoid some unnecessary waiting.

Blocking of ED resources can prevent them from serving other patients, resulting in longer patient waits. For example, if an examination room is occupied by a patient who needs a long time to diagnose (for example, a patient with chest pains who may or may not be experiencing a cardiac event), then other patients may be blocked from treatment due to lack of a room. Hence, implementing an Observation unit, where such patients can be watched overnight, would free up the examination room more quickly and make its capacity available to other patients. Similarly, if an examination room is occupied by a patient waiting for a ride home to be discharged, establishing a discharge lounge (in which discharged patients would wait for nonmedical issues, such as transportation, to be resolved) would free up (unblock) the examination room and enable it to handle another patient. An even simpler way to prevent blocking of ED resources is to speed up discharge procedures through better administrative efficiency and coordination. For example, a patient with a minor injury who has completed treatment but is sitting in an exam room waiting for an approval signature from the attending physician is occupying a resource that may be needed by other patients. Systems such as whiteboards, pagers, and wireless devices that help ED personnel know when their input is needed to discharge a patient could reduce delays like this. Similarly, systems such as simplified forms and electronic forms for streamlining the process of discharging or transferring patients can help speed patients out of the ED when they are ready.

Although speeding up internal discharge/transfer procedures can certainly help, a more serious source of output delay is blocking by external resources. In particular, patients who have been admitted to the hospital are often held (boarded) in the ED due to lack of a bed. A 2003 survey of hospitals found that 73% of EDs were boarding two or more patients on a typical Monday evening (Institute of Medicine 2007b). There are many reasons for the lack of available beds, ranging from hospital discharge policies to OR scheduling policies to nurse-to-patient ratio restrictions. A specific problem is that, in many hospitals, admissions of early morning surgical patients and ED arrivals take place before most discharges occur, which leads to a "mid-day crunch" between 1 and 3 p.m., during which beds are often in short supply. Measures that push discharge times earlier in the day would help ameliorate this. The bottom line is that blocking of patient output from the ED into the hospital is a major problem that compromises both operational and clinical performance. Dealing with it requires a collaborative effort that extends across the hospital.

Another way to prevent blocking is to provide alternate space to hold patients while they await transfer. As we noted previously, admitted patients are frequently boarded in examination rooms or hallways. An alternative used by some hospitals is a "share the pain" strategy, in which other units in the hospital are required to board patients awaiting a room (Viccellio 2008). That is, patients are shifted from the ED hallway to an inpatient ward hallway to spread out the congestion and make the rest of the hospital aware of the problem. But admitted patients are not the only ones who experience delays in discharge/transfer. Patients who have been approved for discharge may wait in the ED because they do not have transportation or because they are too intoxicated to be released safely. For these patients, establishing discharge lounges or "wet shelters" (for intoxicated patients) could free up precious examination rooms and hallway space more quickly.

Finally, we note that many of these policies for increasing effective ED capacity could be invoked in dynamic fashion. For example, the ED could use streamlined discharge policies only when congestion is severe. The hospital could implement accelerated discharge policies for the bed floors specifically when the ED is approaching an overcrowded state. The ED could open up discharge lounges or implement "share the pain" strategies for boarding patients only when conditions necessitate them.

IMPROVE SYNCHRONIZATION

Reducing workload or increasing capacity reduces utilization of the ED, which enables it to better respond to spikes in demand. But we do not necessarily need to reduce workload or increase capacity all the time to achieve this. Synchronizing capacity and demand over time can also reduce the likelihood of a delay-causing overload. We can achieve such synchronization by either adjusting the demand rate or adjusting the capacity.

We can adjust the demand rate by (a) regulating the total rate of patients seeking health care (for example, by posting expected waiting times on the web so that nonurgent patients can check the status of the ED before deciding to come in) or (b) adjusting the fraction of patients seeking care who come to our ED (for example, by increasing primary care/clinic access or diverting ambulances to other EDs when our ED is full).

We can adjust capacity during peak demand times by (a) adjusting staffing, (b) adjusting facilities or equipment, or (c) adjusting protocols. We can do this in either the intermediate term (by scheduling) or the short term (by dynamically responding to changes in system status). To match scheduled capacity to anticipated demand, ED managers first need to collect time-of-day arrival data like that shown in Exhibit 2.5. They could also collect similar data for days of the week or different seasons. Going beyond simple averages, they might try correlating arrivals with external factors (temperature, precipitation, first day of hunting season, and so on). Finally, they could set up a real-time dashboard for monitoring workloads. Note that such a system should not just keep track of the number of patients in the ED or in the waiting room, but ideally should estimate the total number of hours of work waiting for key resources (for example, physician, nurse, technician, test equipment, and so on). With these profiles, the ED can schedule or dynamically allocate resources accordingly.

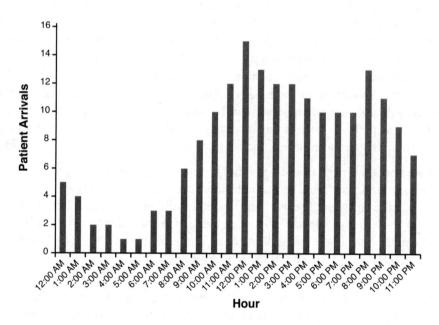

Exhibit 2.5   A representative profile of patient arrivals to the ED over the course of a day.

The ED can schedule people, facilities and equipment, and procedures to provide more capacity when it is expected to be needed. Ideally, these resources would be scheduled to match demand (for example, the profile shown in Exhibit 2.5). But people considerations place constraints on the extent to which staff resources can be adjusted over the course of the day. In general, people must work tolerable shifts. Although some companies like FedEx use split shifts, with drivers working one shift in the morning for delivery and a second one in the afternoon for pickup, most organizations insist on contiguous shifts. What this means is that if there is an anticipated spike in demand between noon and 1 p.m., we cannot bring people in to cover it. However, if staff take their lunch breaks during this hour, then effective capacity will go down right when demand is going up, which will lead to a pile up of patients and longer waiting times. So one scheduling response to this demand profile might be to spread out lunch breaks by having some people go to lunch before 12 and others go to lunch after 1.

Physical resources of facilities and equipment do not have preferences for work times. But they can be more difficult to flex. However, a policy of "borrowing" resources such as beds from another unit could allow the ED to increase physical capacity to meet peak periods. There may be some resources, such as a room that could be used as a Surge unit or an after-hours Radiology recovery room, whose utilization profile is out of phase with the needs of the ED and so present options for borrowing.

Finally, the option that probably offers the most room for creativity is adjusting protocols. Any policy that speeds up treatment during busy times could reduce ED congestion. These could be internal ED practices, such as deferring documentation work until the ED is less busy, reducing non-essential conversation (small talk) with patients, or allowing patients to be seen in hallway beds. Or they could be practices that involve other units of the hospital, such as lowering the standard for admitting patients to the hospital during busy periods, so that patients who are obviously in need of admission can be moved more quickly into the hospital, shortening their LOS in the ED and freeing up personnel to treat other patients. Collectively, such practices can be termed *full capacity protocols*, since they become active only during busy periods.[9]

REDUCE VARIABILITY

We can reduce the need to increase capacity or to synchronize capacity with demand by eliminating some of the variability that periodically causes demand to exceed capacity. This can be done by reducing either arrival variability, treatment variability, or both.

Arrival variability can be reduced by (a) smoothing the arrival of urgent patients or (b) smoothing the arrival of nonurgent patients. Because many urgent patients arrive by ambulance, one way to level arrivals of urgent patients is to provide workload information to ambulance drivers in real time. With this information, they can collectively spread out patient deliveries, to the extent possible given patient safety constraints. Many EDs already do this by going on diversion. But diversion is a coarse and extreme form of information, because it simply closes the ED to all ambulance deliveries. As we noted earlier, more refined workload information, which would let paramedics know that an ED is approaching diversion status even though it is not yet there, would enable ambulance drivers to divert patients whose condition allow it. Patients whose condition requires them to be taken to the nearest ED, or an ED with particular capabilities, would not be diverted. Implementing such a system would require developing a methodology for tracking ED workload and devising a means for communicating the information to paramedics in the field.

Another way of reducing fluctuation in the number of patients seeking urgent emergency care is to look for predictable peaks and trace their causes. For instance, if nursing homes tend to send a higher than average number of patients to the ED on Mondays because their nursing staff levels are low on the weekends, it might be productive (both for patient health and for ED efficiency) to find long-term options to improve weekend monitoring of residents of these nursing homes.

In contrast to urgent patients, nonurgent patients are usually transported to the ED by private means. So smoothing their arrival would require coordination with the patients themselves. One option would be to allow patients to make appointments, which would give them priority over other nonurgent patients who arrive in a specified time window. Such a system would be analogous to the FastPass system used at Disney theme parks. Under FastPass, patrons can reserve a future time for a ride or exhibit. When they arrive, they enter through a separate line from that for patrons without a FastPass reservation. Because the FastPass line receives priority, and because Disney only issues a limited number of reservations for any given time window, patrons are guaranteed a short wait. Because many patients who come to the ED only need attention within a short time (for example, a day or two) rather than right away, issuing reservations would be a way to smooth out arrival of such patients and thereby bring down waiting times.

Although far from common in EDs, the FastPass idea is being tried. InQuickER is a private firm that facilitates reserved appointments with emergency physicians at participating hospitals (Poole 2009). Patients pay a fee to book an appointment time online and then wait at home until their scheduled time. If they are not seen within 15 minutes of this time, their visit is free. Although this may sound like something a Disney Imagineer would come up with, reservations of some kind may well be in the future of EDs.

To limit variability on the treatment side, there are many options. We can generate a reasonably comprehensive list by addressing the different components of patient waiting time by (a) reducing variability in the time to diagnose a patient, (b) reducing variability in direct patient care time, (c) reducing setup (preparation) time variability, (d) reducing variability in ancillary service times, and (e) reducing variability due to rework or errors. Although there are far too many ways to achieve these improvements for us to be comprehensive, we offer some illustrative examples here.

For example, we could reduce variability in the time it takes to diagnose or treat a patient by establishing and following standard protocols for questioning, testing, and treating patients with specific symptoms. The goal is to prevent the physician from omitting a possibility or going down a "blind alley" and thereby winding up spending too much time identifying and executing the proper treatment. Establishing this type of *standard work procedure* is an essential tool of the Toyota Production System. Although it is harder to standardize a complex task like diagnosing a patient than a simple task like installing a spare tire, the goal is the same. Some best diagnostic and treatment practices can be discovered by experience (for example, if Nurse X is particularly efficient at inserting IVs on the first try, she could be asked to demonstrate her methods to other nurses with IV responsibilities). Others require formal analysis. (For example, see Gomez et al. (1996) for a streamlined procedure for ruling out myocardial ischemia.) A technological option for standardizing diagnosis and treatment is computer decision support, which has been touted as coming for many years (see Graber and VanScoy (2003) for a discussion of performance in ED settings) but has yet to see widespread use. An approach that could involve experience, research, and technology would be developing standard pathways for work-up of certain complaints. Regardless of how it is accomplished, variability reduction through task standardization is an on-going challenge that should be a visible part of the ED culture.

Even if we cannot directly reduce variability in treatment times via standardization, we can still reduce variability by streaming patients into similar cohorts. The most common approach to this is use of a Fast Track unit. By sending patients with short treatment times into the Fast Track and patients with long treatment times into the Acute Care unit, this policy reduces process time variability, and hence variability-related queueing, in both units. Another way to group similar patients is by separating patients expected to be discharged from those expected to be admitted to the hospital. (See Saghafian 2012 for a discussion.) A third way, which is becoming increasingly popular, is to create separate geriatric units. Finally, because all these patient streaming criteria are proxies for patient complexity, a sensible, but not yet common, approach would be to separate patients at the time of triage into simple and complex cases. (See Vance and Spirvulis (2005) for a study of how this can be done.)

Reducing setup (preparation) variability can also be addressed through standardization (such as developing a checklist for setting up an examination room for a particular procedure). For example, the steps for applying various types of ortho splints are discrete and well specified. Reducing these to clear checklists would reduce delays in starting the splinting process and avoid errors. But there are many other ways to reduce and stabilize setup times. Kitting (gathering materials needed for a particular procedure into a ready-to-use kit), externalizing tasks (performing the preparation steps while other activities, such as patient education, are taking place), and technology (reconfigurable furniture to facilitate rapid transformation of an examination room for a given procedure) can all help eliminate variable delays in getting procedures started. Indeed, the

---

well-known "crash cart" (sometimes called a "crisis cart") has been used in EDs for decades to transport preassembled kits of drugs, equipment, and supplies to cardiac arrest patients. But carts for other conditions (for example, burns, respiratory failure, and orthopedic injuries) and functions (for example, anesthesia and infection control) can also be used to reduce setups and increase efficiency.

Reducing variability in ancillary service (such as lab testing and radiology imaging) times can be achieved by eliminating excessive waits. Simply adding capacity (perhaps by establishing a lab in the ED or using teleradiology to access image reading capacity beyond boundaries of the hospital, or even the country) will reduce the likelihood of having to wait for a test. Prioritization schemes (such as by giving priority to ED tests that have taken longer than a specified time) can also avoid letting some tests languish for lack of attention.

A huge potential source of variability in patient length of stay is rework (that is, having to repeat patient treatment or correct problems due to errors). Of course, all hospitals focus on avoiding errors for medical reasons. But research suggests that diagnosis and treatment errors also lead to unscheduled returns to the ED (Nuñez 2006), which further aggravate congestion. The operational benefits of "doing it right the first time" are well known in almost all industries. In the ED, a key way to accomplish this is by improving availability and communication of information. For example, using colored arm bands to identify patient risk factors (such as allergies to medication) can help prevent health tragedies but can also smooth and speed the flow of patients through the ED.

Because variability reduction is a rich and varied activity, it is important to make it part of the culture of continual improvement. For example, we know of a highly successful manager in the auto industry who led significant turnarounds of plants in multiple companies. He did so by first educating his workforce about the importance of variability reduction and then by supporting and recognizing their efforts. His essential insight was that a thousand brains throughout the organization are vastly more effective than a few at the top. By harnessing the energy and creativity of the line workers to drive out variability in hundreds of tiny ways (for example, reorganizing tool layout, altering job procedures, improving cleaning practices, and so on), he was able to achieve overall performance improvements that could not have been attained by a few large-scale initiatives.

IMPROVE SEQUENCING

Reducing utilization and synchronizing/reducing variability are the most effective ways to lower congestion. But even without making changes in these fundamental parameters, we can still reduce the average LOS of a patient by making changes in the order in which patients are treated. From Table A.1, two ways to improve sequencing of patients are (a) generating information that can be used to make better sequencing decisions, and (b) improving the sequencing decisions themselves.

The SPT Sequencing Corollary can be invoked to improve sequencing of patients. The basic idea is to treat quick patients before slow ones wherever clinical conditions permit. To sequence patients by speed of treatment, however, we must estimate treatment times at the beginning of the process. Triage is the natural place to do this. Indeed, most five-level triage systems include some form of assessment of treatment complexity. For instance, the ESI system considers the number of resources (for example, test equipment) that each patient requires. An ESI-3 patient requiring multiple resources almost certainly needs more treatment time than an ESI-5 patient requiring no resources. So a simple SPT rule would be to process ESI-3, 4, and 5 patients in reverse order of their severity index, unless their wait time exceeds the designated limit. But if the triage nurse can make a more refined estimate of treatment time (for example, by classifying patients according to the level of physician care required), SPT logic can be applied more effectively to reduce average LOS. Once we have an estimate of treatment time, we can include it, along with the current time in the system, as part of the central display used by ED personnel to track patients and make sequencing decisions.

Note that the SPT rule cannot be invoked blindly. In addition to taking medical severity into account, we should consider fairness. For instance, a patient with a broken arm that will require some time to set, who is forced to wait for hours behind several patients who arrived later with less time-consuming, nonlife-threatening conditions, may understandably feel unfairly treated. So, although shortest processing time logic can be applied to nonurgent patients (that is, patients with ESI levels of 3, 4, and 5), it makes sense to establish a limit on waiting time. For instance, once a nonurgent patient has been waiting for more than 90 minutes, he/she gets priority over other nonurgent patients regardless of his/her expected treatment time.

In addition to improving sequencing of patients directly, we can seek to improve sequencing of ancillary services. In the lab or Radiology, where process times do not differ greatly between tests, priorities can be set to match the patient sequence in the ED (that is, if patient A has a higher priority than patient B, either because of medical severity or because A has a shorter process time than B, then A should also have a higher priority for lab or image results). But to make such a system work, there must be a mechanism for communicating priorities from the ED to the lab. Within the lab, prioritization would have to extend to tests from other sources besides the ED (for example, OR, inpatient units, outpatient units). Of course, if laboratory turnaround times are short enough, sequencing ceases to be an issue. We discuss responsiveness in the lab in Chapter 5.

Finally, a policy that is part sequencing/part variability reduction is *value stream division*, which refers to separating patients into streams based on their treatment needs. For example, a Fast Track unit provides a way for patients with short treatment times to jump ahead of patients with longer treatment times, which is an implementation of the SPT rule. But, by separating low acuity patients requiring routine procedures from more serious patients requiring complex procedures, separate tracks also serve to reduce variability of treatment times within tracks. In factories, such policies are called *cellular* or *modular* manufacturing. By establishing lines or cells dedicated to producing narrow ranges of products or parts, these policies increase efficiency by reducing variability. Because EDs handle such a wide range of patients, policies such as value stream division, which improves focus, are attractive options.

ENHANCE PATIENT PERCEPTIONS

Even if actual waiting times cannot be reduced, patients can be made more content about their waits if (a) they are kept occupied, (b) they are started promptly, (c) their anxiety is reduced, (d) they're given explanations about their waiting times, (e) waits seem equitable, (f) waits are proportional to the value of services received, and (g) group waiting is facilitated.

Patients can be kept occupied by either involving them in the treatment process (for example, through self-registration at a kiosk in the waiting room) or involving them in nontreatment activities (for example, a wireless Internet connection to provide individual distractions to those for whom the network programming on the single television in the waiting room is not pleasurable).

Patients can get started by either beginning treatment or having attention focused on them. The former might be accomplished by ordering obvious tests at triage rather than waiting for the physician examination. The latter might be accomplished by converting the waiting room into an observation room, staffed by a nurse who actively monitors (and reassures) patients.

Reducing patient anxiety can be achieved by providing them with information that removes uncertainty about their condition (for example, by providing pamphlets that explain ED processes for various categories of ailments), providing human contact (for example, having a volunteer regularly check on patients and their families), and improving the ambiance of the waiting environment (for example, with lighting, music, and furniture chosen to soothe rather than jar the senses).

Providing explanations of waiting time can be done through written explanations (for example, a display that shows ED workload and estimated waiting times by patient number) and oral explanations (for example, having the volunteer who visits patients in the waiting room update them on their expected wait based on ED status). Some hospitals, such as Detroit Medical Center, have chosen to post expected waiting times in the hospital, online, and via mobile phone apps. Some have even taken a cue from Disney and have deliberately biased their wait time quotes to be a little bit high to pleasantly surprise patients with a shorter-than-expected wait (Goldstein 2008).

Waiting times can be made more equitable by minimizing "cuts" (for example, handling patients in first-in-first-out order except when differences in medical severity or treatment time dictate an alternate sequence) and avoiding extreme waits, which will be perceived as particularly unfair (for example, by moving patients to highest nonurgent priority once they have waited longer than a specified amount).

Making waiting times proportional to the value of services received implies that patients with minor complaints should not wait as long as patients with serious problems. However, medical urgency often requires that serious patients receive treatment first. In small EDs with only a single track, this can mean that nonurgent patients may wait a long time. For these, some form of the registration policy mentioned earlier might be a viable way to minimize such waits. But in larger EDs with enough staff to process many patients in parallel, it makes sense to use multiple tracks, including a Fast Track, to customize patients' treatment to their needs. Although many EDs have implemented Fast Track Departments, they are not uniformly effective.[10] A Fast Track Department must use the other congestion-reducing measures discussed in this section if it is to live up to its name.

Finally, the ED can make waits more tolerable by facilitating group waiting. The most obvious form of group waiting is that by the patient with his/her family. So, policies that allow family members to accompany the patient along the treatment path (for example, to Radiology or the laboratory) will help ameliorate anxiety and stress. More subtly, the ED can help socialize the waiting process by enhancing opportunities for patients and their families to talk with other patients and their families. For instance, giving oral updates about the status of the ED can serve as conversation starters ("It sounds like there was a major auto accident, with a bunch of people hurt." "No wonder we're waiting." "I hope everybody's okay." Et cetera.)

Although the preceding may seem obvious, waiting time perceptions are routinely mismanaged, in health care and in other industrics. For example, the earlier story about Chelsea and her father, who left the ED after a wait during which they saw no one other than a security guard, actually happened to one of the authors and his daughter. Certainly no ED professional would choose to leave patients waiting in the ED for long periods of time without human contact, but such incidents happen all the time. This anecdote suggests that there is considerable opportunity for EDs to make patient waits more informative and less stressful. Moreover, in most cases, achieving this will not require technological advances or sophisticated management programs. Clear communication and helpful attention, practices that even the smallest retailer knows intimately, are all that is required. Even if the policy is no more than having a staff person periodically come out into the waiting room and talk to patients about what is going on in the ED, the improvement over the unattended waits common today in EDs could be vast.

2.4.1.4 CASE: IMPROVING ED RESPONSIVENESS AT OAKWOOD HOSPITAL

Oakwood Hospital was founded in Dearborn, Michigan, in 1953. After 30 years of growth as an independent hospital, Oakwood began to expand through acquisition in the 1980s. In 2010, the Oakwood Healthcare System consisted of four Acute Care hospitals and 52 primary/specialty care sites spread across Southeastern Michigan, with 1,267 licensed beds, 1,308 physicians, 9,375 employees, and $2.9 billion in annual gross revenue. In 2011, the system handled more than 180,000 emergency visits.

However, back in 1999, neither the hospital nor the ED was a model of effectiveness. The LOS was almost 7 hours for ED patients who were ultimately discharged and from 8–14 hours for patients admitted to the hospital (Full Circle Group 2004). Ambulance diversions were common, patients left without being seen, and physicians were disinclined to refer their patients to Oakwood's ED. Consequently, the hospital was losing significant revenue, both directly from the ED and from lost hospital admissions through the ED.

Recognizing that the ED served as a "front door" to the hospital, which accounted for roughly 50% of admissions, senior management embarked on an ambitious plan to enhance the hospital by radically improving the ED. Based on an analysis indicating that hospital revenue could be increased by $20 million per year or more with modest capital investment, Oakwood set a target to increase ED visits by 20%. But to achieve this, Oakwood would need to distinguish itself from a number of strong hospitals in the region. Consequently, management set a goal of reducing ED waiting time to half of the region's average.

To start the improvement process, Oakwood established a cross-functional Integration Team with physicians, nurses, and staff members from the ED, as well as from other units closely associated with the ED (for example, Radiology, labs, ICUs, Admitting). This team mapped the patient experience from arrival to discharge/admission and highlighted points with excessive waiting. Smaller Pathfinder Teams were appointed to analyze specific problems and propose solutions. Taken together, these teams not only provided analysis horsepower, they helped achieve buy-in from the many people needed to support the change initiatives. Consistent with the insights of the Key Stakeholders and Veto Power Principles, these broadly constituted teams ensured that people with power to block change were instead tasked with making change happen.

The Integration Team found that nursing coverage in the ED was adequate but that physicians and some technical specialists were serious bottlenecks. So a first step toward bringing down LOS was to add staff in these categories. Other bottlenecks outside the ED were also identified and addressed. Specifically, an inpatient bed availability problem was addressed via an initiative to speed the room cleaning process. Similarly, turnaround times were reduced in Radiology and the laboratories. All of these exploited the Utilization principle, which implies that adding capacity to highly utilized resources can have a dramatic effect on waiting.

These capacity increases were not limited to simple additions of resources. The logic of the Task Simplification principle was used to simplify the registration process by reducing the number of questions asked of patients to five: name, address, age, SS number, and reason for visit. The team made use of task parallelism to increase capacity by performing registration at the patient bedside in parallel with other activities.

In addition to making use of the responsiveness principles we have laid out here, the Integration Team also devoted considerable effort to improving teamwork, invoking the concepts of the Information principles (specifically, Handoffs and Knowledge Sharing) and Behavioral principles (namely Inertia), which are discussed in Appendix A. The culture change that accompanied the operations changes was so significant that roughly a quarter of the staff left the ED during the redesign.

After a year of implementation, Oakwood rolled out a marketing campaign to capitalize on its new capabilities. Under the slogan "We're an emergency room, not a waiting room," they made a pledge that patients would see a physician within 30 minutes of arrival. If they failed to do this, patients would receive a written apology and two tickets to a local movie theater. Among the first 50,000 patients treated under the new policy, only 55 movie passes were given out.

In less than two years from the initiation of the program, the average time from arrival to being seen by a physician had been reduced to 22 minutes. The LOS for patients who were discharged was reduced from more than 7 hours to less than 2 hours. For patients who were admitted to the hospital, LOS was reduced from 8–14 hours to less than 3.5 hours. Customer satisfaction increased from 79% to 91%, and 95% of patients indicated on comment cards that they were "likely" or "almost certain" to recommend Oakwood to others.

Predictably, the improved responsiveness in the Oakwood ED attracted more patients. Interestingly, the increase occurred in both low- and high-acuity patients. As a result, two years after the initiation of the project, admissions to the hospital from the ED had increased by 300 per month, generating millions of dollars of revenue annually.

The Oakwood ED transformation illustrates the power of focusing on a clear performance metric (LOS) and applying the insights from the Flow Principles, Information Principles, and Behavioral Principles in an integrated fashion. This case also highlights the evolution of an improvement campaign over time. Quick but critical steps, such as adding physician capacity, were instituted immediately, whereas more complicated changes, such as reducing turnaround times of diagnostic services, were rolled out over time. Finally, the Oakwood case shows how operational change can be coupled with promotional marketing to advance a hospital's ability to meet its core mission.

2.4.2 Patient Safety

2.4.2.1 PROBLEM

The primary objective of all health care is to improve the health of patients. Hence, *patient safety*, which can be defined as freedom from accidental injury due to medical care, or medical errors, is of paramount importance. Indeed, the familiar dictum "First, do no harm" places patient safety at the top of a physician's priorities.[11]

In spite of this, hospitals are dangerous places. The Institute of Medicine (1999) estimated that between 44,000 and 98,000 Americans die each year because of preventable medical errors. Brennen et al. (1991) estimated that preventable injuries from care affect 3–4% of hospital patients. More recently, the Hearst Media Corporation reported that deaths in the United States due to preventable errors and infections number about two million over the decade prior to 2009, or about 200,000 per year (Hearst Newspapers 2009).[12]

The ED is particularly challenging from a patient safety standpoint for a number of reasons, including these:

- Providers usually do not have a prior relationship with patients, so they have limited background information.
- Patients present a wide range of illnesses and acuity levels.
- Multiple individuals are typically involved in the care of an individual patient.
- High utilization and narrow time windows place considerable stress on providers.
- Interruptions, distractions, and multitasking make focusing on a single patient difficult.
- Fatigue and shift work may cloud acuity.

As a result, EDs tend to experience relatively high rates of medical errors compared to other parts of the health care system. For instance, in a study of hospitalized patients, Leape et al. (1991) found that although only 3% of adverse events in a hospital occurred in the ED, 70% of these were attributed to negligence, so the ED was responsible for 11% of adverse events due to negligence.[13]

This risk of adverse events carries with it a liability challenge. For example, a 2004 survey found that 42% of private neurosurgeons had been sued by a patient seen through the ED (Seaver 2004). Another survey showed that orthopedists who regularly take on-call duty at an ED pay 75% more for malpractice insurance than orthopedists who do not take call (Taheri and Butz 2004). This, combined with difficulty in obtaining payment for on-call services,[14] has created problems for many EDs in providing adequate specialist coverage.

Therefore, although patient safety is an overriding concern in all health care systems, it is particularly critical in the ED. As a result, considerable research attention has been devoted to ED patient safety. For example, the book by Croskerry et al. (2009) contains 56 papers, each of which cites 20–100 other papers, dealing with various facets of patient safety in emergency medicine. This large and growing literature is motivated by the fact that ED patient safety is both important and complex.

Because a host of factors contribute to adverse clinical outcomes, no single perspective can hope to capture them all. Indeed, there have been so many attempts to place structure on adverse events that Cosby (2009) constructed a "taxonomy of taxonomies" to classify 24 different studies that proposed classification schemes. Some of these focus on the people in the system (for example, decision-making breakdowns). Others focus on the point in the process where the error occurred (for example, prearrival, referral, triage, ED care, post-treatment care). Still others focus on the function that led to the error, such as diagnosis, treatment, or prevention. Finally, most studies mention contributing factors including workload, fatigue, communication, support systems, and so on, that play a role in errors. Clearly, patient safety can be viewed through many lenses.

A fundamental dichotomy in the literature on medical errors is that between an emphasis on the *individual* and an emphasis on the *system*. (See Reason 2000 for a discussion.) Individual caregivers are obviously essential in all health care; their innate ability, training, and behavior have an enormous impact on patient safety. So research on cognitive functions and other individual diagnosis and treatment activities (see, for example, Croskerry 2002, 2003, Weingart and Wyer 2006) can play an important role in preventing medical errors. But EDs often go beyond this by focusing on individuals to the point of blame. In a survey by Magid et al. (2009), 61% of ED clinicians reported that individuals are sometimes or often blamed when safety problems occur. Obviously, if adverse events are viewed as the result of mistakes by individuals, or even cause for disciplinary action, these individuals will have incentive to underreport problems. This is particularly the case for "near misses," which do not result in observable adverse events. Without an event, a problem that *almost* led to an incident will go uninvestigated unless the people involved bring it to light. Hence, emphasizing individual responsibility for errors can impede long-term efforts to improve patient safety.

In contrast, an emphasis on the system takes individual capabilities (including human fallibility) as given and seeks ways to reduce adverse outcomes by improving the physical and logical infrastructure that supports the individuals. For example, if people make errors due to fatigue, a systems approach might address the problem by modifying schedules to reduce fatigue. If errors are the result of information lapses, then a systems approach might address them by improving the quality and accessibility of information. Focusing on system improvements can help individuals improve the quality of their work. Furthermore, by making patient safety a matter of shared organizational responsibility, rather than one of individual blame, a systems approach can motivate people to share information essential to the improvement process.

Once we adopt a systems perspective on patient safety, operations become a critical consideration. This is well known in manufacturing, where the interactions between quality and operations performance have been studied for decades (see, for example, Hopp and Spearman 2008, Chapter 12). For instance, long queues of work imply delays between the time a defect is created and the time it is detected, which translates to larger amounts of scrap or rework when a process goes "out of control." (That is, poor operations hinder quality performance.) At the same time, correcting errors via rework or replacement introduces variability into the system, which creates congestion and impedes flow. (In other words, poor quality degrades operations performance.) Because of their manifest interdependencies, quality and operations are often combined in industry practice programs. For instance, total quality management (TQM) was an integral part of the original Toyota production system (Schonberger 1982); in more recent times, Lean (operations) and Six Sigma (quality) initiatives have been combined into Lean Six Sigma (George 2002).

As in manufacturing, operations are central to quality (patient safety) in the ED. The most direct connection results from the effect of waiting on outcome. Several studies have shown that the rate of adverse outcomes increases in patient LOS (see, for example, Diercks et al. 2007, Richardson 2006, Sprivulis et al. 2006). The underlying reason, of course, is that sometimes speed of treatment matters. Hence, operational improvements that speed patient flow can also help ensure that patients get timely, and hence more effective, treatment.

Operations also affect patient safety in more subtle ways. For instance, research has shown that decision making often degrades when individuals are stressed by a chaotic environment (Williamson and Runciman 2009) and when they are interrupted (Collins et al. 2006, 2007). So, smooth, continuous flow also supports better decisions.

To increase patient safety in the ED by improving operations, it is useful to invoke basic management principles. These can identify areas of leverage and organize improvement policies into a logical taxonomy. But changes require more than principles. Implementation practices, which have been honed in industry lean and quality programs, are also essential. The fact that most of these techniques will simultaneously address the (operations) problem of ED overcrowding and the (quality) problem of patient safety is a happy coincidence that should increase their appeal to ED managers.

We summarize the relevant principles next and then appeal to these to suggest appropriate practices.

2.4.2.2 PRINCIPLES

Causes of preventable adverse outcomes can be classified into the following:

- **Delay**—Patient is not treated or is not treated quickly enough.
- **Mistreatment**—Patient is given incorrect or unhelpful treatment when an effective treatment could have been identified and applied.
- **Injury**—Actions within the system actively harm the patient.

Although there may be some overlap between these causes, they generally suggest three distinct prevention strategies:

- **Speed of Treatment**—Avoiding adverse events due to delay requires speeding patient flow to reduce waits.

- **Accuracy of Treatment**—Avoiding adverse events due to mistreatment requires better information, decision making, and execution in the treatment process to decrease the likelihood of errors.

- **Patient Protection**—Avoiding direct injury of patients requires a safe environment to systematically protect patients.

We will explore the management principles relevant to each of these categories next. Following each of these to their logical implications leads us to the policies for improving safety summarized in Table 2.3.

SPEED OF TREATMENT

The first line of defense against adverse events that lead to patient injuries is a system ensuring that patients who need care quickly get it. The ED is specifically tasked with handling patients for whom speed is critical. Indeed, the triage system is designed to identify such patients; the emergency severity index levels ESI-1 (delay could cause death) and ESI-2 (delay could cause injury) classify delay-sensitive patients.

But delays happen. A tragic and highly publicized case involved a woman with acute myocardial infarction who died after waiting for two hours in an ED in Waukegan, Illinois (SoRelle 2006). Although such cases are unusual, this particular case was made even more unusual when a coroner's jury ruled the woman's death a homicide, citing the delay in the waiting room as "a gross deviation from the standard of care, which a reasonable person would exercise in the situation." Such sensationalism was probably counterproductive, but it served to put an exclamation point on the importance of timely care in the ED.

Magid et al. (2009) surveyed 3,562 clinical workers at 65 EDs and found evidence of serious problems with the speed of treatment. Respondents reported that the number of patients exceeded ED capacity to provide safe care most (32%) or some (50%) of the time. Only 41% of clinicians indicated that specialty consultation for critically ill patients usually arrived within 30 minutes of being contacted. Finally, half of the surveyed clinicians reported that ED patients requiring admission to the ICU were rarely transferred from the ED to the ICU within one hour.

From our previous discussion of ED overcrowding, we already know that there are structural reasons that patients wait, sometimes for a long time. The key principles that describe the drivers of waiting in the ED are the Variability and Utilization Principles:

Principle (Variability)—Variability causes congestion.

Principle (Utilization)—Utilization magnifies congestion in a highly nonlinear fashion.

High variability (due to unpredictable arrivals and uneven treatment requirements for patients) and high utilization (due to the increasing demand and decreasing capacity for emergency medical services) combine to produce a powerful tendency toward overcrowding and delay. By probing the causes of variability and utilization, we can identify some policies for reducing delay (many of which we have already discussed in the previous section on ED overcrowding).

Two of the most effective ways to reduce variability and utilization are task simplification and task standardization, whose effects are summarized in the following principles:

Principle (Task Simplification)—Reducing task complexity reduces the mean and the variance of the task times and the likelihood of errors.

In the ED, many procedures are complex, multitask procedures, which may be amenable to simplification. For example, Schuur et al. (2007) studied the ED of an urban teaching hospital and found that the hospital admission process from "decision to admit" to "left ED" involved 37 steps, only 8 of which added value from the patient's perspective. So, by simplifying the process through elimination of 11 of the 37 steps, the ED was able to reduce process time for this task by 54%.

Principle (Task Standardization)—Using clearly specified best practice procedures for repetitive tasks reduces the mean and variance of task times and the likelihood of errors.

In the ED, many repetitive tasks are candidates for standardization. For example, registering patients, taking blood pressure, and cleaning a wound are routine in nature and should therefore be conducted using a single best-practice approach. Leaving these to individual preferences only introduces variability into the system, which causes delay that can prevent patients from obtaining timely treatment.

Invoking the preceding principles to reduce overall delays is a primary means of assuring timely treatment to avoid patient errors. But it is not the only way. Patients do not need the same speed of care. A stroke victim may require immediate intervention to survive, whereas a trauma victim may suffer only discomfort if forced to wait. So it is vital to direct care first to those who need it most. This is what the triage process is designed to do. The relevant management principle at play is this:

Principle (Critical Ratio Sequencing)—In a multiclass system with dynamic arrivals, prioritizing entities according to the ratio c/t, where c is the delay cost per unit time and t is the expected process time, minimizes total cumulative delay over the long term.

For patients with serious conditions (that is, those classified as ESI-1 and ESI-2), the delay cost, c, is enormous, because delay can result in death or serious injury. So their critical ratio, c/t, will be large, even if treatment (process) time, t, is long. Hence, the Critical Ratio rule calls for these patients to be treated first, no matter what.

But for many ED patients, the cost of delay, c, is much smaller than that for patients facing a life-or-death situation and is roughly similar across patients. For example, for patients classified as ESI-3, 4, 5, the cost of waiting is largely due to discomfort and inconvenience. So it is reasonable to assign these patients the same delay cost rate, which will be much smaller than that of ESI-1 and ESI-2 patients. When this is the case, a patient with a short process time (for example, an ESI-5 patient) will have a higher critical ratio, c/t, than a patient with a longer process time (for example, an ESI-3 patient) and should be treated first. This special case of the Critical Ratio rule is known as the SPT rule.

Corollary (Shortest Process Time Sequencing)—Processing entities in order of SPT minimizes average waiting time.

Note that the Critical Ratio Sequencing principle addresses ED patient safety in two ways. First, giving top priority to patients known to be most at risk avoids delays where they are most costly. Second, reducing the average time spent waiting by "nonurgent" patients (via the SPT Corollary) reduces the risk of an adverse outcome due to mis-triage. That is, if a patient's condition is more serious than originally thought (for example, the previously mentioned example of the Waukegan woman who died in the waiting room), a sequence that reduces average waiting time may help him/her be treated in time.

ACCURACY OF TREATMENT

Treating patients in a timely fashion is necessary, but not sufficient, for patient safety. For treatment to be effective, it must be properly administered. This requires *information*, on which treatment must be based; *planning*, in which a course of treatment is determined; and *execution*, in which the treatment is carried out. Conceptually, these phases are sequential, with information feeding planning, which governs execution. But in practice they may be iterative. For instance, execution (administration of a medication) may yield information (a patient reaction reveals a drug allergy) that alters planning (leads to a revised diagnosis). Nevertheless, because they involve different types of activities, thinking about treatment in terms of information, planning, and execution phases can help us identify how and where errors can occur.

We can also use other taxonomies for classifying errors to help structure the problem of increasing treatment accuracy in the ED. For instance, some authors separate the *blunt end* of the treatment process, which refers to the organizational systems that support caregivers, and the *sharp end* of the treatment process, which refers to the activities directly involved with providing care to patients (Byers and White 2004). The information and planning phases generally deal with the blunt end, whereas the execution phase deals with the sharp end. Other authors divide errors into *latent* errors, which occur due to lapses in system support (blunt end activities), and *active* errors, which occur due to direct care actions (sharp end activities) (Reason 2000).

In keeping with the systems approach to understanding and improving patient safety, we must be careful about making too much of a distinction between blunt end (latent) and sharp end (active) errors, because they are all part of the web of events that lead to a patient injury. Although it is tempting to focus on the direct commission of the error at the sharp end (for example, administration of an improper dosage of a medication), a host of blunt-end actions (communication of the prescription, color coding of different dosages, establishing "high alert" procedures for potentially dangerous drugs, educating patients to monitor their own medications, and so on) could have a large impact on the likelihood of the error being committed. Because a positive action at the blunt end could offset a negative action at the sharp end, or vice versa, it is impossible to precisely assign blame for an error. Hence, it is vital to maintain a broad focus on the overall system, in order to exploit safety improvement opportunities of all types.

Carrying out an even-handed assessment of a system is challenging because latent and active errors differ with respect to their ease of detection. Before the fact, active errors can be difficult to anticipate. Predicting that a nurse will misinterpret a specific patient's prescription and administer the wrong medication is nearly impossible. However, after the fact, active errors are manifestly evident if they lead to a negative outcome. For instance, an improperly medicated patient who has an adverse reaction will serve as a highly visible indicator of a medication error. In contrast, latent errors may not be at all evident after the fact. Finding out that a medication error was made more likely by the fact that two similar-looking drugs were placed in close proximity on a cart may be difficult to determine, because the cart will have been emptied before any follow-up investigation takes place. However, before the fact, it may be possible to anticipate the risks posed by latent errors. Studying the layout of the medication room, procedures for loading carts, appearance of different medications, handwriting on prescriptions, warning signs (or lack of them) in key locations, and so on, could reveal opportunities for errors before they are committed.

With this perspective in mind, we return to our three-phase model of treatment accuracy: information, planning, and execution. We examine each phase and note the management principles that can be invoked to identify improvement opportunities.

Information Phase

Information in the ED (and the hospital as a whole) is varied and pervasive. Accurate treatment requires information about individual patients (symptoms, allergies), staff members (including who is responsible for what and who is on duty), equipment (operating instructions, current location), medications (administration procedures, side effects), and many other parts of the system. Although the specific information needed for a given factor or in a given situation is highly context dependent, we can make the following general observation about all information:

> *Information becomes actionable knowledge only through communication.*

For example, a nurse can only use information from a textbook on a particular procedure once that information has been communicated to him/her, through reading, lecture, conversation, or some other means. A physician can use information about a patient's symptoms only after it has been communicated to him/her, through direct observation, oral conversation with the patient, indirectly from another staff member, or another means.

This has enormous implications for patient safety because, according to the Joint Commission of Accreditation of Healthcare Organizations (JCAHO), communication failures account for more than 60% of root causes of sentinel events (Lingard 2004).[15] While this is not surprising, given the complex, multistage, multiperson processes involved in patient treatment, it highlights the central role of communication in improving patient safety.

Because communication is essential to all management, established principles pertaining to it are vital. The most straightforward, which is a direct consequence of the Task Simplification principle we discussed earlier, is the Intuitive Information principle.

Principle (Intuitive Information)—Providing essential information visually or orally in tight association with a task reduces the mean and variance of task times, as well as the likelihood of errors.

Intuitive information improves task speed and accuracy in two ways. First, by making the appropriate information easily available, it reduces the time spent sifting through inappropriate information and the likelihood of using the wrong information. Second, by displaying this information in a simple (visual) form, it reduces the likelihood of a transcription or interpretation error.

Hospital EDs have adopted various types of visual and oral displays of information. Specific examples of visual/oral information designed to promote patient safety are colored wristbands that indicate patient allergies, color-coded medications to prevent switching errors, whiteboards to display patient status to prevent delay problems, and red lights and audio alarms on monitors to indicate dangerous readings.

A second management principle that deals with person-to-person communication is the Handoff Principle.

Principle (Handoff): Unless new knowledge is contributed by the individuals, information is degraded as it is passed from one individual to another.

In the ED, several people contribute to the treatment of an individual patient. The reason, of course, is to take advantage of the efficiencies of labor specialization. Dividing the tasks involved in treating a patient (for example, triage, registration, examination, x-ray, medication administration, discharge, and so on) among individuals with specific skills makes better use of ED capacity and can provide better quality of care. But, because such division of labor also means that the patient is handed from one person to another, it also presents opportunities for information errors. Hence, managing handoffs in the ED is an essential component of patient safety.

Planning Phase

With information in hand, we progress to the planning phase, in which individuals make decisions about a course of action. These decisions may deal directly with the sharp end of the treatment process, for instance, by planning the specific treatment of an individual patient. They can also deal with the blunt end of the process, for example, by establishing procedures, policies, and infrastructure that support patient care. In either case, decision makers must consider the information available to them and formulate a plan. Such a plan could involve ordering tests, administering medications, staffing, setting standards for information display, or any of a host of short- and long-term decisions regarding the management of the ED.

The fast-paced and sometimes chaotic character of the ED makes it a difficult environment in which to craft a plan that may involve life and death decisions. Consequently, there are many opportunities for errors (that is, decisions that are inferior to those that should be made by qualified professionals equipped with the available information). A host of factors can make such errors more likely, including workload pressure, interruptions, and fatigue. Therefore, the following principles are relevant to ED patient safety.

Principle (Workload)—Work efficiency and accuracy exhibit an inverted-U shaped relationship with workload.

As we noted in the previous section on ED overcrowding, EDs are subject to spikes in workload, which can lead to haste and errors.

Principle (Interruptions)—Interruptions degrade decision making in complex tasks.

In a study of five hospitals and 22 primary care physician offices, Chisholm et al. (2001) found that emergency physicians were interrupted an average of 9.7 times per hour, compared to 3.9 times per hour for primary care physicians. Particularly when the ED is busy, a caregiver who is trying to diagnose or treat one patient is frequently pulled away to tend to another patient or is interrupted by another staff member with questions.

Principle (Fatigue)—Fatigue impairs decision making.

Stretching out shifts to cope with patient backlogs can lead to tired staff and more errors. In the ED, where backups are most extreme in the late afternoon, "catch-up" periods can extend late into the evening, further contributing to fatigue.

Execution Phase

With information and a plan, execution of treatment can proceed. Two principles that are central to reducing errors by reducing opportunities for them are the Task Simplification and Task Standardization principles that were mentioned earlier as means for reducing delays.

Principle (Task Simplification)—Reducing task complexity reduces the mean and variance of the task times and the likelihood of errors.

For example, Jolly et al. (1995) found that simplifying written discharge instructions in the ED at the George Washington University Medical Center improved patient understanding and presumably their post-discharge care. Inside the ED, placing calculators in preparation areas to simplify calculations involved in making up intravenous narcotics could reduce dosage errors.

Principle (Task Standardization)—Using clearly specified, common procedures for repetitive tasks reduces the mean and variance of task times and the likelihood of errors.

Unfortunately, although standardization is a way of life at Toyota, it is not nearly widespread enough in EDs. For example, Sinha et al. (2007) conducted a survey of emergency medicine program directors and found that 89.5% of EDs have no uniform written policy regarding patient sign-out. A majority (71.6%) of the surveyed directors felt that standards to encourage specific practices regarding transfer of care in the ED would improve patient care. A majority (72.3%) also agreed that a standardized sign-out system would improve communication and reduce medical error.

PATIENT PROTECTION

Exhibit 2.6 illustrates the Swiss cheese model of system failure (Reason 2000), which posits that errors are often the result of breakdowns of multiple defense systems. This insight is consistent with the systems perspective of medical errors and is essential to creation of a high-reliability organization.

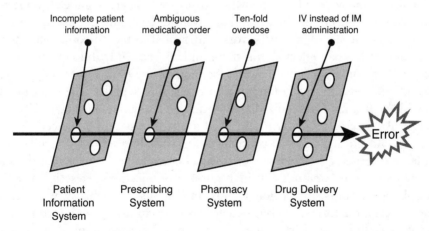

Exhibit 2.6   Swiss cheese model of multiple defense systems (Reason 2000).

To illustrate the implications of the Swiss cheese model for ED patient protection, we consider the 1996 death of a day-old infant in a Denver hospital (Smetzer and Cohen

1998). In this case, the mother had a prior history of syphilis and, because the infant's parents could not speak English, hospital staff could not confirm current status or past treatment of the disease. After consulting with specialists and the Health Department, they decided to treat the infant for congenital syphilis. The attending physician placed an order for a dose of "Benzathine penicillin G 150,000U IM."

Unfamiliar with this drug, the pharmacist misread the "U" in the dosage as a zero and prepared a 10-fold overdose. Without a procedure for dosage checking, this error was not detected, and 2.5 ml of medication was dispensed to the nurses with instructions to administer intramuscularly. However, because of the infant's size, standard procedure was to inject no more than 0.5 ml at a time, which would require 5 injections. Seeking to minimize pain to the infant, the nurse practitioner checked a medication reference book to see if the medication could be administered intravenously. But the book did not specifically mention penicillin G benzathine. Because the physician had written "Benzathine" with a capital letter on a separate line above "penicillin G," the nurse practitioner interpreted it as a brand name. So she assumed the instructions for "aqueous crystalline penicillin G," which said that administration by IV slow push was allowed, were applicable. None of the nurses saw the "IM use only" warning, which was placed inconspicuously on the back of the syringe. They went ahead and administered the penicillin via slow IV push.

Tragically, benzathine penicillin G is insoluble, so IV administration resulted in obstructed blood flow in the lungs and death to the infant. Even more tragically, the autopsy revealed that the baby did not have congenital syphilis and had not required treatment at all.

Not surprisingly, many people blamed the nurses for this error. Indeed, three nurses were indicted for negligent homicide, and one went to trial. But, as posited in the Swiss cheese model, a host of system-level errors contributed to the outcome. The attending physician did not have an effective translator and consequently did not obtain patient information that would have revealed that the mother had been successfully treated for syphilis and had two other children without congenital syphilis. The drug order was unclear, with "Benzathine" capitalized and written on a separate line and a "U" for units that looked like a zero. The pharmacy lacked a warning system to detect the 10-fold overdose and did not have special procedures for a rarely used (nonformulary) drug, such as the one in this case. There was no formal system to flag a suspicious drug order, such as one that implied an unusually high number of injections. Prescriptive authority of a nonphysician (nurse practitioner) was ambiguous, particularly with regard to changing prescription orders. Reference materials were confusing, with inconsistent references to "penicillin G" and "penicillin G benzathine," and incomplete, with no mention of penicillin G benzathine in the paragraph on penicillin G. Warnings against IV administration, in the order and documentation, as well as on the syringe, were either missing or obscure. If any one of these, or a host of other, failures had not occurred, the tragedy would probably not have happened. The accused nurse was acquitted by arguing precisely this point.

This case highlights several principles that are fundamental to high-reliability organizations. First, the insight that underlies the Swiss cheese model is the Redundancy Principle.

Principle (Redundancy)—Independent layers of protection increase the reliability of a system.

In the preceding case, there were several points in the process where redundancy could have prevented the failure. Special procedures for nonformulary drugs, which require the pharmacist to consult with a colleague or physician when dispensing a rarely used drug, could have clarified the meaning of the "U" in the dose. A computerized dose range-checking system could have flagged the overdose before the medication was dispensed. A policy requiring nonphysicians to consult with the attending physician before altering prescription orders could have prevented the nurse practitioner from changing from IM to IV administration (and might have caught the overdose).

Note that these second opinions will only be helpful if they are independent. If everyone consults the same source of information (for example, the inadequate reference materials available to the nurse practitioner), they might not provide independent inputs. This should be considered when designing safety checks; for example, having a pharmacist check a nonformulary drug order with a supervisor or physician may be more effective than having him/her check it with a colleague.

Redundancy is not the only way to increase safety. Also, because it implies doing things more than once, redundancy can be expensive. So, high-reliability organizations combine redundancy with other error reduction steps. A common and effective technique is foolproofing.

Principle (Foolproofing)—Using constraints to force correct actions reduces the likelihood of errors.

Foolproofing is an attractive way to prevent equipment-related errors. For instance, Fairbanks et al. (2007) reported that defibrillators are easy to misuse, resulting in unsynchronized defibrillation when the intent is to perform a synchronized cardioversion on a patient with supraventricular tachycardia. The reason is that many defibrillators are designed to passively reset out of synchronized mode after a synchronized shock is delivered. Hence, users were required to check and reset the unit to "synchronized" in order to deliver a correct second shock. A design that forces the user to actively choose the mode with each use (and makes the setting easy to set and visible) could prevent these potentially serious errors.

In the preceding case, issuing IM drugs in single dose syringes that do not fit into an IV tube would have prevented the decision by the nurse practitioner to administer the medication intravenously. Having to prepare five syringes also might have alerted the pharmacist to the overdose.

A less forceful, but still effective, method for error prevention is to present key information in an intuitive format.

Principle (Intuitive Information)—Providing essential information visually or orally in tight association with a task reduces the mean and variance of task times, as well as the likelihood of errors.

In the case of suspected congenital syphilis, color-coded containers for IM-only drugs would have provided a clear signal to the nurses not to use IV administration. The non-visual information provided by the reference books did not make this key message clear, thereby contributing to the tragedy.

2.4.2.3 PRACTICES

Table A.2 of Appendix A invokes the previous principles to generate options for improving patient safety via improved treatment timeliness, treatment accuracy, and patient protection. Here, we start with that table and flesh out these generic options into specific actions relevant to patient safety in the ED. The result is Table 2.3.

Table 2.3 Generic Operations Improvement Policies: ED Patient Safety

Level 1 Objectives	Level 2 Objectives	Level 3 Objectives	Example Policies
Improve responsiveness	Reduce workload	Reduce arrivals	Divert low-acuity patients to clinics
		Reduce work per arrival	Reduce number of tests/patient
	Increase capacity	Add physical resources	Dedicate CT scanner to ED; install Observation unit
		Add human resources	Use physician assistants/nurse practitioners to treat simple, low-risk patients
		Eliminate steps	Streamline layout to reduce walking; eliminate steps needed to issue medications
		Reduce process times	Electronic patient data entry; standard room layouts
		Balance workloads	Float nurses between main ED and Fast Track based on workloads
		Increase task parallelism	Use bedside registration
		Reduce blocking/starving	Board admitted patients in hospital hallways (rather than in ED)

Level 1 Objectives	Level 2 Objectives	Level 3 Objectives	Example Policies
	Improve synchronization	Adjust demand to match capacity	Coordinate with EMS system to divert arrivals during peak periods; Offer "reservations" to non-acute patients to divert them to off–peak periods
		Adjust capacity to match demand	Improve shift scheduling to better match staffing to arrival patterns; call in staff to cope with workload spikes
	Reduce variability	Smooth arrivals	Appointments for noncritical patients; level loads between ED tracks
		Simplify tasks	Order tests all at once, rather than sequentially; streamlined forms in place of full assessment paperwork
		Standardize tasks	Distributed supply locations
	Improve sequencing	Increase triage accuracy	E-triage system; physician triage during peak periods
		Improve sequencing decisions	SPT within ESI classes; stream patients by disposition
Improve decisions	Improve information	Improve information availability	Facilitate communication with pharmacists; Measures to encourage people to bring their medications to the ED
		Make information visual and connected to tasks	Whiteboard displays of patient status; CPOE system that highlights risk factors, such as possible drug interactions
		Improve information transfer	Standard protocol for EMS to ED transfer of patient data; read-back protocols for handovers within the ED

Table 2.3 Generic Operations Improvement Policies: ED Patient Safety

Level 1 Objectives	Level 2 Objectives	Level 3 Objectives	Example Policies
	Improve assignment	Internal	Clarify staff authority for decision making
		External	Formal referral protocols
	Improve training	Cognitive process training	Exercises that illustrate decision biases
		Technical domain training	Medical refresher courses; professional conferences
		Decision support systems	Diagnostic decision trees
	Improve incentives	Financial	Bonus to ED from hospital for reducing unnecessary tests, as measured by periodic audits
		Non-financial	Recognition of individual physicians for low 48-hour patient revisit rate
	Simplify/standardize decision process	Simplify	Bedside ultrasound diagnosis of deep vein thrombosis; reduce number of medication/dosage choices available in CPOE system
		Standardize	Algorithms for emergency diagnosis and response scenarios
	Improve focus	Optimize workloads	Match physician staffing to arrival patterns; call in physicians to cope with spikes in demand
		Avoid fatigue	Shift length restrictions; casino scheduling
		Minimize interruptions	Use whiteboards and other visual displays and written protocols to reduce interruptive queries

Level 1 Objectives	Level 2 Objectives	Level 3 Objectives	Example Policies
	Increase redundancy	Active checks	Encourage pharmacist review of medication orders
		Passive checks	CPOE system that intercepts dangerous drug combinations or dosages before orders are placed
Improve execution	Improve information	Improve information availability	Posters documenting key procedures
		Make information visual and connected to tasks	Color coded bottles/syringes; standardized drug bar codes
		Improve information transfer	Read-back protocols; written sign-out templates
	Improve assignment	Within function	Assign most experienced nurses to most at-risk patients
		Across function	Defer blood draw responsibility for difficult patients from nurse to phlebotomist
	Improve training	Technical training	Safety short courses
		Organizational training	Simulation-based teamwork training
	Improve incentives	Financial	Bonus pay for meeting safety improvement targets
		Non-financial	Public recognition of nurses for procedural innovations
	Simplify/standardize execution process	Simplify tasks	Kit supplies for procedures
		Standardize tasks	E-triage and other DSS systems; written discharge forms and other checklists

Table 2.3   Generic Operations Improvement Policies: ED Patient Safety

Level 1 Objectives	Level 2 Objectives	Level 3 Objectives	Example Policies
	Improve focus	Optimize workloads	Match nurse staffing to arrival patterns; use worksharing to shift tasks from one nurse to another to level imbalances
		Avoid fatigue	Shift length restrictions; casino scheduling
		Minimize interruptions	Improve written communication (for example, whiteboards) to eliminate unnecessary verbal queries
	Increase redundancy	Active checks	Procedures requiring checks of equipment settings before use
		Passive checks	Separate IV/IM syringes; spread out patients with similar names to avoid mix-ups
Improve protection and mitigation	Improve information	Remove reporting disincentives	Independent observers monitor medication administration during specified intervals; Confidential/anonymous incident reporting; Flexible, easy-to-use reporting system; Protect "whistle blowers"
		Track contextual data	Accurate time stamps of events; report forms with fields for environmental conditions; systematically investigate "near misses"
		Identify contributing factors to errors and near misses	Root cause analysis of failures; event tree analysis of potential events
	Increase redundancy	Active checks	Safety rounds; read-back protocols
		Passive checks	Dual patient identifiers; firsthand interpretation of images

Level 1 Objectives	Level 2 Objectives	Level 3 Objectives	Example Policies
	Mitigate harm	Increase response speed	Clear monitoring policy to detect symptoms of medication errors; Ready availability of antidotes and reversal agents
		Increase response accuracy	Written rescue protocols for classes of errors; Open disclosure policy that allows full response to error

Next we survey the basic structure of Table 2.3 and discuss some specific improvement policies.

IMPROVE RESPONSIVENESS

The first set of improvement options in Table 2.3 deal with reducing treatment delays to decrease the patient injuries these may cause. Note that the options listed here are almost the same as those listed in Table 2.2. That is because increasing responsiveness of treatment serves both to reduce ED overcrowding and to enhance patient safety. The options listed in Table 2.2 that do not carry over to Table 2.3 are those related to patient perceptions. Although making people feel better about their waits can make patients happier, it does not make them safer. We must physically reduce wait times to reduce the risk of delay-induced patient injuries.

However, not all wait times are equal when it comes to improving patient safety. Keeping an emergent patient (for example, one classified as ESI-1) waiting is likely to result in an adverse outcome, whereas keeping a nonurgent (for example, ESI-5) patient waiting may produce complaints but is unlikely to cause a clinical failure. Hence, one might be tempted to conclude that measures that reduce congestion caused by nonurgent patients will have little or no effect on patient safety. For instance, diverting low-acuity patients by offering them reservations (for example, Disney-like "fast passes" like those offered through the InQuickEr service) would reduce ED wait time for them but presumably would not affect the high-acuity patients who would be given priority in any case.

But this reasoning is not completely accurate because (a) having all examination rooms filled with patients, including some low-acuity patients, may delay treatment of high-acuity patients because of the extra time required to make space for them, and (b) triage classifications are not perfect, so some patients classified as low acuity may actually be high acuity; hence, a reduction in their waiting time may avoid adverse outcomes. For example, the previously cited case of the woman who died in a Waukegan ED waiting room was waiting precisely because she had been incorrectly triaged as a low-risk patient (SoRelle 2006). If the ED had implemented responsiveness improvement measures like those suggested in the top portion of Table 2.3, including those aimed at reducing waiting times of nonurgent patients, she might have been seen quickly enough to have been saved. The bottom line is that all investments in responsiveness are potentially investments in patient safety, because we can never be certain who is in need of timely treatment.

IMPROVE DECISIONS

The second set of improvement options in Table 2.3 deal with decision making, which is the most important role of the physicians in the ED. What tests to order, what specialists to consult, what interventions to apply, and in what order—these and many other decisions critically affect the care patients receive in the ED. Nurses also make many important decisions, such as how to administer a medication, what steps to take to ease a patient's pain, when to consult a colleague about an uncertain situation, and so on. Decision errors can become treatment errors that impact patient safety.

For example, Santell et al. (2004) reviewed data of 11,000 medication errors observed over a five-year period in 484 EDs and concluded that drug administration (predominantly an execution function) was the most prevalent source of errors, comprising 48% of the total. However, prescribing (primarily a decision-making function) was second, constituting 29% of the total. Patanwala et al. (2010) reported analysis of errors over 28 shifts in a single ED and observed that some type of medication error occurred in 59.4% of patients, and 37% of patients had an error that reached them. Of these, 53.9% were classified as prescribing errors, whereas 34.8% were deemed administration errors.

IMPROVE INFORMATION

Improving decisions in the prescribing process, as well as elsewhere in the ED, requires accurate information (on which to base the decision), appropriate assignment (the right person to make the decision), suitable training (of the person who makes the decision), alignment of incentives (of the decision maker with the desired outcome), a suitable (simple or standard) decision process, proper focus (of the decision maker), and some measure of redundancy (as protection against incorrect decisions).

For example, a prescription error could result from the physician not knowing what medicines a patient is currently taking. Because patients can be an unreliable source of the needed information, measures that encourage patients to bring their medications to the ED could help avoid potentially dangerous drug interactions. Posting a notice on the ED website, reminding patients who contact the ED by phone in advance of a visit, training paramedics to request patient medications, encouraging family physicians to talk to their patients, and participating in a public ad campaign, are various ways to improve the likelihood of getting accurate medication information about patients. Of course, in the long term, having a central database that contains reliable patient data would be a superior solution to the information availability problem.

Beyond making information available, it is important to make it useable. For instance, patient information that is buried in a record the physician doesn't see, or drug interaction data that is contained in a publication the physician doesn't read, won't help avoid a decision error. So steps to make the information visible (for example, highlighting key patient information on a whiteboard, computer screen, cell phone app, or whatever is most convenient) or tied to the task (for example, calling out possible drug interactions directly in response to a prescription entry by the physician in a computerized physician order entry [CPOE] system) would make the information more likely to be effective.

Finally, making information available and useful often involves transfer of the information from one person to another. Hence, making information transfers efficient and accurate can help prevent decision errors. Examples of actions for doing this include standard protocols that indicate what information is to be communicated and in what form for specific situations (for example, transfer of patient from an EMS technician to the ED) and read-back protocols for oral information (to make sure the information has been heard correctly).

IMPROVE ASSIGNMENT

Even with accurate and appropriate information, humans can make decision errors for many reasons. For instance, Peth (2003) noted that, in the ED, the "two most common factors associated with prescribing errors are lack of knowledge pertaining to the drug prescribed and lack of knowledge regarding the patient for whom the drug is prescribed." Knowledge about patients is an information problem, as discussed earlier. Knowledge about drugs is a function of innate ability and training.

We can take advantage of innate ability to improve patient safety by ensuring that decisions are made by those competent to make them. For instance, in the previously mentioned case involving misadministration of benzathine penicillin G, the nurses made a decision on administration method that (in hindsight) should have been made by someone else (such as a pharmacist or physician). Tragically, in spite of the ambiguity of information in the medical reference books, the nurses did not seek confirmation of their decision to use IV push to administer the medication. A policy that withheld authority for medication administration decisions for drugs not explicitly listed in the reference materials might have prevented this error. In addition, a protocol that required a second opinion (and specified who that opinion should come from) on medication decisions involving a change in administration method might well have prevented the error.

IMPROVE TRAINING

Of course, people's ability to make specific types of decisions can be influenced by training. For example, the constant evolution of medical knowledge makes it essential for medical staff to update their domain knowledge by attending courses and conferences.

But another type of training, which is not generally offered in medical or nursing school, is instruction in basic cognitive processes. Learning about decision biases and heuristics can make medical caregivers aware of pitfalls in their thinking processes, and hopefully help them avoid mistakes. For example, Weingart and Wyer (2006) note that when a patient does not completely match a known illness script, physicians tend to rely on cognitive shortcuts for resolving uncertainty. Some of the more common ones are

- **Rule out worst scenario**—If the ED physician does not know the correct diagnosis for a patient, he/she may seek to rule out the incorrect diagnoses. If all serious diagnoses can be eliminated, then the physician can conclude that it is safe to defer diagnosis to someone else (for example, a hospitalist). Although this may protect some patients by ruling out the most serious causes of their symptoms, it can also result in unnecessary, and possibly intrusive, testing and workup for many others.

- **Sick/not sick dichotomy**—If a patient cannot be fully diagnosed, the ED physician may simplify the decision to one of determining whether the patient is sick (and should be admitted to the hospital) or not sick (and should be discharged). This heuristic can fail disastrously when a serious disease presents with benign symptoms (for example, a pulmonary embolism may cause only shortness of breath or mild pleuritic chest pain, but could cause sudden death; acetaminophen overdose may initially cause only nausea/sweating but later could cause liver damage, kidney failure, or death).

- **Shotgunning**—When a patient's presentation is vague, the ED physician may order an array of tests and images.[16] This strategy delays the need to make a decision and sometimes leads to a good outcome. But often it results in unnecessary tests and delays.

Diagnosis can also be impaired by common biases in human decision processes. Two common ones are

- **Anchoring**—A predisposition to stick with an initial diagnosis despite contradictory evidence can lead to early termination of the evaluation process and erroneous conclusions.

- **Satisficing**—A tendency to stop looking for alternate diagnoses when we find one that fits can also lead to errors and oversights (for example, finding one fracture on an X-ray but failing to see the second fracture in the same extremity).

Many other heuristics and biases are common in the decision processes used by clinicians facing uncertainty. (See Croskerry 2002 for an excellent overview.) Training ED staff members to recognize these is a first step toward reducing cognitive errors.

Beyond training, an ED can take more proactive measures to improve diagnostic decision making by adopting various types of decision support. These can take the form of sophisticated algorithms embedded in clinical information systems (for example, an annoying cartoon tongue depressor that pops up to ask if you've considered carbon monoxide poisoning). Or they can be simple checklists that embody best practice. For example, Williamson and Runciman (2009) summarize several algorithms for use in emergency medicine, such as the ABCD (airway, breathing, circulation, drugs) mnemonic, which can help ED physicians avoid diagnostic oversights.

SIMPLIFY/STANDARDIZE DECISION PROCESS

Procedures, such as the ABCD protocol, can help avoid errors of omission by standardizing the decision process. Closely related to standardization is simplification, in which errors of commission are avoided by reducing the complexity of the decision task. This could be achieved by reducing the number of options, for example, by restricting prescriptions to a limited number of medications available in a CPOE system. It could also be achieved through a technological advance, such as bedside ultrasonography for diagnosing deep vein thrombosis, which provides a clear and simple process for making a diagnosis.

IMPROVE FOCUS

No matter how much we improve the decision process, errors are still possible if the decision maker lacks focus. We know from the Workload, Interruption, and Fatigue Principles that a host of environmental factors can degrade the quality of decision making. Hence, environmental improvements can help avoid errors.

As we noted earlier, ED congestion leading to work overloads is associated with an increase in errors and adverse outcomes. So all the practices we have mentioned earlier for reducing ED congestion and delay will have the additional benefit of improving decision making and treatment accuracy. These include scheduling staff to better match patient arrival patterns, work-sharing policies (for example, shifting residents from the "Fast Track" to the "Acute Care" track if workloads become imbalanced), and many other practices for better matching ED capacity to patient demand.

Another environmental factor associated with medical errors is fatigue. Of course, one cause of fatigue is work overloads. Another is excessive shift lengths. A third is shift timing that clashes with circadian rhythms. So, implementing restrictions on shift lengths, even if it results in longer delays in clearing out an evening backlog of patients, may be necessary to avoid long-term staff fatigue that compromises safety. Yet another way to reduce fatigue is by avoiding scheduling people to consistently work through the "anchor period" from 1 a.m. to 5 a.m., during which sleep is particularly important (Croskerry 2009). This can be accomplished by using "casino schedules" (named for their use by casino managers to schedule employees during nighttime hours), as shown in Exhibit 2.7. By covering the night with shifts that switch near the center of the anchor period (say 3 a.m.) rather than by a single midnight-to-8 a.m. shift, EDs can reduce the disruption to the circadian rhythms of their staff members. Over the long term, this will lessen fatigue and decision errors.

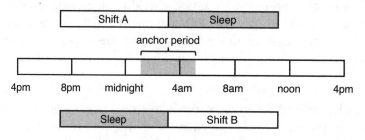

Exhibit 2.7 Casino scheduling.

One final environmental factor that disrupts decision making is interruptions, which are particularly common in the ED. France et al. (2005) reported a case study suggesting that interruption rates are lower in an ED in which an electronic whiteboard is present. Presumably, the reason is that people are able to get needed information from the whiteboard (for example, in the form of notes, instructions, and key forms attached to the whiteboard with magnets), rather than by interrupting other staff with questions. This suggests that other types of visual display (color-coded medications, computer displays, graphical instructions accompanying tasks, and so on) could similarly eliminate the need for some questions (interruptions). Many of the other information transfer practices (for example, read-back protocols, standard sign-out forms) could also reduce the need for questions, and thus would improve both productivity and accuracy of decision making in the ED.

INCREASE REDUNDANCY

If all else fails, we can seek to prevent a decision error through some form of redundancy. An example of an active intervention would occur if a physician consulted a pharmacist about a medication and the pharmacist recognized and prevented a potential drug combination error. An example of a passive intervention would be an automated warning from the CPOE system about a potential dosage error.

IMPROVE EXECUTION

Once a decision has been made, it must be executed. Prescribed medications must be administered. Ordered tests must be carried out. Requested patient transfers must be made.

At a generic level, the options for improving execution are the same as those for improving decision making: improve information (relevant to the execution task), improve assignment (by ensuring that the right person does the task), improve training, improve incentives, simplify/standardize the tasks involved, improve focus, and improve redundancy. Of course, the details of how to translate these into specific policies will differ on the specific type of execution being addressed. We offer some illustrative examples next.

IMPROVE INFORMATION

To be useful in the execution of a task, information must be *available* and *visible*. For example, in the case of the infant who died from improper administration of penicillin G benzathine, the medication reference book did not contain information specifically for penicillin G benzathine. Key information was not available. An up-to-date medication reference that contained instructions for penicillin G benzathine might have prevented the error.

At the same time, the "IM use only" warning on the back of the syringe was so inconspicuous that none of the nurses saw it. Key information was not visible. A bolder warning, color-coded syringe, or other form of visual reminder of the administration instructions might also have prevented the error.

Finally, to be available, information must often be *transferred* effectively between people. In the case of the infant death, the prescription information was not communicated accurately from the physician to the pharmacist. A "U" that looked like a "0" led the pharmacist to dispense the overdose. A CPOE system that eliminated the need for handwriting interpretation might have avoided the sequence of events that led to the tragedy.

There are many ways to promote more effective information transfer between members of ED teams (see Coiera 2009):

- **Read-back protocols**—Requiring individuals to repeat information (for example, medication instructions), to make sure they have received and understood it, can reduce errors due to information degradation of the type described by the Handoff Principle.

- **Written sign-out templates**—Forms with mandatory fields for specific types of patient data (for example, resuscitation status, pending test results, special instructions, and so on) in a standard format can help ensure that key information is transferred between ED team members.

- **Computer and communication technology**—Various technologies can facilitate communication between ED team members. For instance, in trauma cases, some members of the team are the EMTs in the field. A survey of trauma centers by Xiao et al. (2001) found that the majority of communication between hospital ED personnel and field personnel took place via shortwave radio. However, mobile phones and land line phones were also used. For the future, mobile phones on broadband networks offer the prospect to bring visual information to remote communication (for example, forms and images), which should improve accuracy and decision making.

IMPROVE ASSIGNMENT

As with decision making, execution can be improved by making sure the person performing the task is qualified to do so. This can be done in the short term by assignment (choosing the right person) and in the long term by training (creating the right person). In the case of the infant death, the initial error might have been prevented had the pharmacist who was unfamiliar with penicillin G benzathine deferred the dispensing task to another pharmacist who was. Similarly, had the nurses been able to defer the administration task to a more experienced nurse, the final error might have been avoided.

IMPROVE TRAINING

Of course, it is not always possible to defer tasks to someone more expert. So training to increase ED staff skill is an obvious means for improving execution and patient safety. Of course, all ED personnel have had classroom training in their respective areas of expertise, which is vital. But, because the ED must function as a team, training beyond individual instruction is also important. Studies (for example, Shapiro 2004) indicate that simulation-based teamwork training is an effective mechanism for reducing errors and improving overall performance. Simulation-based training has been used for many years in aviation, military, and other industries. In recent years, simulations using mannequin-, procedural-, and screen-based simulators have become increasingly common in emergency medicine residency programs. Team-based simulations, involving actual hospital ED teams and possibly conducted onsite, are not yet common. But this appears to be a promising path for improving system-wide quality in the ED.

Regardless of how much individual or team training the ED staff members receive, execution accuracy and patient safety can always be increased by improving the processes they use to deliver treatment. This is the essence of the "systems view" of quality.

IMPROVE INCENTIVES

As in all types of work, monetary and nonmonetary incentives can be used to signal desired types of behavior. For example, an ED could give nurses a bonus (in the form of extra pay or a present, such as a restaurant gift certificate) for identifying near misses (good catches) or suggesting safety-improving changes. Or they could be recognized without money with a patient safety award (complete with a plaque and parking space). Although few would argue that nurses need rewards to care about patient safety, these types of recognition serve to highlight and encourage the activities needed to achieve it. It is possible that such an incentive system might have provided just enough encouragement for a staff member to identify and correct one of the system flaws (for example, an incomplete drug reference) before it led to the tragedy in the penicillin G benzathine case.

Simplify/Standardize Execution Process

Task simplification and standardization have already been cited multiple times as improvement options because they are core to virtually all workplace efficiency and quality enhancement efforts. Simplification options in the ED that could improve the accuracy of treatment include reducing the number of medications or dosage levels available (to make it easier to make the right choice and know the right administration procedure); kitting supplies to be used for specific treatments (to make oversights or mistakes less likely); and reducing the number of steps involved in medication delivery (to reduce likelihood of errors). Standardization options that could improve ED treatment accuracy include standardizing supply locations and presentation (to prevent mix-up errors); using e-triage and other decision support systems that standardize routine decision processes (to prevent oversights and faulty logic); and using checklists (for example, discharge forms) that enumerate required steps in a task (to ensure that best practices are followed by everyone). Many, many opportunities exist for simplification and standardization of specific procedures in the ED.

In the penicillin G benzathine case, a CPOE system that simplified the prescribing process by eliminating the step of writing out the prescription also would have eliminated the information transfer error that started the chain of events leading to the infant death. A standardized checklist, with which nurses indicate that they have followed the recommended process, including checking the syringe for an "IM use only" warning, also might have prevented the tragedy.

Improve Focus

Almost all tasks are degraded by lack of focus. So steps that enhance focus can improve execution. In the case of the infant death, the physician might have been hurrying to keep up with a heavy workload, leading to a rushed and less legible prescription. The pharmacist might have been fatigued from working an extra shift, leading to a misread prescription. And the nurses administering the medication might have been interrupted by someone asking a question, leading them to forget to check the syringe for a warning. Hence, steps to balance workloads (for example, accounting for complexity when assigning patients to physicians, to level workload, not just patient load), prevent fatigue (for example, limit extra shifts and double shifts), or reduce interruptions (for example, post patient information on white boards or in computer data bases so that some oral questions become unnecessary) would improve focus and hence execution accuracy.

Increase Redundancy

Execution redundancy refers to layers of security within the execution process and can take the form of active and passive checks. An example of an active check, which requires action on the part of someone, was the "IM use only" warning on the syringe in the infant death case. Unfortunately, the check was not executed, as is the risk of active checks. An example of a passive check (also called foolproofing), which requires no extra action on the part of the person executing the task, would be IM and IV syringes designed so that they cannot be interchanged.

Other foolproofing strategies include using different sized hoses for blood and food transfusion so they cannot be used improperly for each other, using premixed medications to prevent dilution error, using medical devices that require settings to be input anew for each use (for example, a defibrillator that must be set to synchronized or unsynchronized mode) to prevent erroneous assumptions about prior settings leading to errors, and using pin indexing on gas delivery systems to ensure that pressurized gases are not connected to the wrong yoke. Because foolproofing is specific to the process to which it is applied, there are many, many opportunities to use it in ED systems. Toyota claims to have an average of 12 foolproofing (poka-yoke) measures per station in its assembly plants. Sadly, in health care, where errors are much more costly than in automobile manufacturing, there are not nearly this many protections.

IMPROVE PROTECTION AND MITIGATION

The first three avenues for increasing patient safety focus on specific treatment steps: getting information, making decisions, and executing treatment tasks. But safety can also be improved by enhancing the system within which these steps take place. This can be done by improving system information, increasing system redundancy, and mitigating harm from errors that occur.

Improve Information

Collecting information to evaluate and improve safety requires (a) tapping into the knowledge and observations of a broad range of people, and (b) recording information about the diverse factors that influence the risks of injuries.

Hence, the first requirement of a system for reporting incidents and issues is that it involves many different people (doctors, nurses, technicians, administrators, patients, and so on). To accomplish this, a system must be perceived as *safe* and *convenient*. A safe system is one that provides protection from reprisals to those who make reports, by allowing these to be confidential or even anonymous. This involves more than simply designing paper or electronic report forms without name fields. To be credible, this confidentiality or anonymity must be maintained throughout any follow-up procedures. An important mechanism for doing this is producing standardized reports so that ED staff and patients can see that data is used in a systems approach to quality improvement, rather than blaming individuals. Indeed, individuals who report errors should be (publicly or privately) praised or rewarded.[17]

A convenient system is one that is easy to use. For instance, allowing individuals to choose paper, electronic, or voice format; select between check boxes or free text; and make reports either immediately at the time of an incident or later, are design features that make reporting systems convenient. These present a design challenge, because we want to make the system flexible on the front end (to encourage people to use it) but standardized on the back end (to produce standard reports for display and analysis purposes). However, this challenge has been faced for decades in other fields (such as aviation) and affects the design of the various types of systems used in EDs. (See Stella et al. 1996, Vinen 2000, Khare et al. 2005, Haller et al. 2007 for discussions of ED incident reporting systems.)

In addition to being safe and convenient to encourage submissions, a reporting system needs to capture the right kind of data for use in safety evaluation and improvement efforts. This should include contextual data, such as the time of an incident, and environmental factors (such as congestion status of the ED and workloads of individuals involved in an incident). Although having open text fields on report forms provides an opportunity for individuals to report whatever information they wish, these do not prompt individuals for information beyond a description of the incident or issue. So it may be helpful to include check boxes or questions to encourage reporters to provide broader information. Note that this suggests that reporting forms may need to be revised periodically. For example, if a careful evaluation of time stamp data reveals that a particular type of error is more likely when the ED is boarding a large number of admitted patients, it might make sense to add a question about the patient boarding situation to the standard form.

Of course, raw reports are data, not information. To convert these into information that can be used to assess and improve patient protection processes, reports must be analyzed. Although there are many techniques from the field of reliability analysis (fault tree analysis, event tree analysis, failure modes and effects analysis (FMEA), hazard analysis and critical control points (HACCP), hazard and operability study (HAZOP), and others), these basically break down into two modes of analysis:

- **Retrospective analysis**, which works backward in time to identify contributing causes of an incident that has already occurred. Root cause analysis (sometimes called "fishboning" or Ishikawa diagramming) and its variants fall into this category.

- **Anticipatory analysis**, which works forward in time from an event (for example, equipment failure, labeling mistake) to anticipate consequences. Event tree analysis, fault tree analysis, and FMEA are examples of methods that seek to anticipate failure modes before an incident occurs.

The information developed from these collection and analysis processes will highlight risks and areas of potential improvement. Then the problem becomes one of acting on these to create a highly safe environment. There are two basic ways to do this: (1) *redundancy*, which refers to layers of protection designed to prevent errors from impacting patients and (2) *mitigation*, which involves reducing the harm done to patients by errors that do reach them.

Increase Redundancy

Redundant layers of protection come in two forms: active and passive. Active checks explicitly force a redundant step, whereas passive checks imply redundancy without explicitly adding a step to check quality. An example of an active check is use of "safety rounds," in which a high-level team of medical and administrative staff makes a periodic (perhaps biweekly) review of the ED. In this nonpunitive process, the reviewers observe practices, identify opportunities for improvement, educate employees about safety procedures, and highlight the need for full involvement in patient protection. Mandatory read-back procedures are another example of an active safety check. Examples of passive safety checks include dual patient identifiers (to provide a check against misidentification of a patient) and firsthand reading of images by ED physicians (to provide a check against an oversight or error by the radiologist).

Mitigate Harm

Because all systems, no matter how safe and well managed, will experience errors, a final line of defense against patient harm can be established through mitigation policies, which minimize the impact of errors on patients. As in most ED activities, speed and accuracy matter. Examples of policies that speed the response to an error include appropriate monitoring of patient symptoms to detect an error if one occurs and stocking antidotes and reversal agents in accessible locations to facilitate quick administration if needed. A simple example of a policy that facilitates an accurate response to an error is having a clear protocol for what to do in case of an overdose. A more subtle example is a policy of open disclosure that reveals the error to all key parties (including patient and family) so that they can participate in the decision of how best to respond. Although policies like these won't prevent errors from happening, they can help ameliorate the consequences to the patient.

2.4.2.4 CASE: ELIMINATING ICU INFECTIONS AT JOHNS HOPKINS HOSPITAL

The Johns Hopkins Hospital (JHH) is a 1,039 bed tertiary care hospital with seven ICUs and a reputation so sterling it was named the top hospital in the United States by *U.S. News & World Report* 21 consecutive times. But even the very best hospitals face serious patient safety challenges. So, in 1998, Peter Pronovost, an intensive care physician at JHH, and several of his colleagues set out to address a specific safety concern: catheter-related bloodstream infections (CR-BSIs). In the United States, an estimated 80,000 CR-BSIs per year result in $45,000 in care costs per patient, for a total of $2.3 million annually, and are responsible for 28,000 deaths per year (Berenholtz et al. 2004).

Although CR-BSIs are common and dangerous, they are preventable. Several medical societies have developed guidelines for controlling infections, which include simple measures such as these:

- Physician hand washing.

- Cleaning the patient's skin with chlorhexidine

- Using sterile drapes over the entire patient during central venous catheter insertion

- Wearing a sterile mask, hat, gown, and gloves

- Putting a sterile dressing over the catheter site to maintain a sterile field during insertion

But, even though the effectiveness of these measures had been documented by multiple research studies, a gap persisted between best and actual practices. So, instead of seeking to develop new infection control methods, Pronovost and his team sought to ensure use of existing methods. They did this in the JHH surgical ICU (SICU) via five interventions (implementation dates in parentheses):

- **Developing a mandatory training module (February 1999)**—The Department of Hospital Epidemiology and Infection Control (HEIC) unit at Johns Hopkins Medical School created a web-based training module on evidence-based infection control practices. In 2002, the hospital required proof of completion of this module for physicians to receive credentials.

- **Creating a catheter insertion cart (June 1999)**—Recognizing that an obstacle to compliance with evidence-based practices was the dispersion of equipment, which required SICU staff to collect tools and supplies from eight different locations, the team constructed a cart that included everything needed to support the catheter insertion process. They also established a policy of restocking the cart every four hours to ensure that everything was consistently available.

- **Asking providers daily whether catheters can be removed (June 2001)**— Because a central venous catheter cannot cause an infection if it is not there, the team added a question to the daily rounding form, which asked whether any catheters or tubes could be removed.

- **Implementing a checklist to be completed by bedside nurses (November 2001)**—The team encapsulated the evidence-based procedures (hand washing, cleaning patient's skin, and so on) in a standardized checklist. During central venous catheter insertion, nurses would fill out this checklist to indicate which procedures had (and had not) been followed. Initially, physicians did not know they were being observed, and nurses merely recorded compliance. In a study of 26 procedures (8 new catheter insertions and 18 catheter exchanges), the rates of compliance were as shown in Table 2.4, which makes it clear that some procedures, particularly hand washing, were not being followed religiously.

- **Empowering nurses to stop procedures if guidelines were not followed (December 2001)**—After the initial study, the team empowered the SICU nurses to stop a procedure (except in an emergency) if any step on the checklist was not followed. In the event that a resident failed to correct a violation, nurses were instructed to page the attending physician. During the first month after the nurse empowerment intervention, nurses completed the checklist for 38 procedures (8 new insertions and 30 replacements). In 12 (32%) of these, the nurse intervened to stop the procedure.

Table 2.4 Compliance with Evidence-Based Infection Control Guidelines in a Study of 26 Insertion/Exchange Procedures in a SICU (Berenholtz et al. 2004)

Guideline	Percent Compliance
Cleaned hands	62
Sterilized procedure site	100
Draped patient in sterile fashion	85
Used hat, mask, and sterile gown	92
Used sterile gloves	100
Applied sterile dressing	100
Compliance with all guidelines	62

In the first quarter of 1998, before these interventions had begun, the SICU experienced a CR-BSI rate of 11.3 infections per 1,000 catheter days. In the fourth quarter of 2002, after all the interventions had been implemented, the rate was an astounding 0 (that's right, zero) infections per 1,000 catheter days. Between January 2003 and April 2004, the SICU experienced two CR-BSIs, which translated into a rate of 0.54 per 1,000 catheter days. In their 2004 article, the unit reported that it had not had a single CR-BSI in nine months.

In 2003, Pronovost and his team extended their analysis to a Michigan study called the Keystone ICU project, which involved 108 ICUs. The participating hospitals made the same interventions as those in the Johns Hopkins study. Prior to these interventions, the mean rate of infections was 7.7 per 1,000 catheter days; in 18 months following the interventions, the mean rate had fallen to 1.4 infections per 1,000 catheter days (Pronovost et al. 2006). Based on these numbers, the team estimated that 1,500 lives and $100 million had been saved during the first 18 months. Moreover, the reduced infection rates were still being reported almost four years later (Gawande 2007).

In addition to representing a simple and effective approach to reducing infection rates, this case illustrates the application of several principles discussed earlier and improvement paths presented in the execution section of Table 2.3. These include

- The web-based training module is a direct implementation of the Table 2.3 recommendation to improve execution through training.

- The policy of removing catheters where appropriate is an application of the Simplification Principle, because it eliminates the possibility of errors by eliminating their presence altogether.

- The catheter insertion cart is another application of the Simplification Principle because it eliminates the search and collection activities within the catheter insertion task.

- Putting a checklist on top of the catheter insertion cart to guide the restocking process is an example of the Intuitive Information Principle, because it provides information on what should be in the cart in a simple format in direct association with the restocking task.

- The procedures checklist is a classic example of the Standardization Principle. Because of the existence of evidence-based practices, this was an instance in which the dictum "rationalize the repeatable" most definitely applies. Moreover, not only did JHH require everyone to adopt known best practices, it established an enforcement mechanism to discourage deviations from these practices.

- Nurse oversight of the checklist constituted an application of the Redundancy Principle, because it added a layer of protection against physician oversights.

- Finally, the implementation of the checklist and attendant policies showed sensitivity to the Key Stakeholders Principle. Nurses, who easily could have resisted a blunt policy that asked them to oversee physician practices, were co-opted by (a) initially asking them to fill out the checklist without intervening in the procedure so that they could see the level of noncompliance for themselves, and (b) empowering them to page the attending physician if a resident did not correct an omission upon notification. Taken together, nurses were both motivated to support the initiative and protected from potential fallout from it.

In addition to illustrating the preceding concepts, this case shows how powerful simple interventions can be. If a straightforward checklist can have such a dramatic effect on SICU infections, other equally modest mechanisms for propagating best practices can certainly play a major role in improving safety in the ED and elsewhere in the hospital.

2.4.3 ED Observation Unit Design

2.4.3.1 PROBLEM

One of the causes of ED congestion is the presence of patients whose conditions require a long time to diagnose. For example, patients with chest pain who are deemed to have a low probability of acute myocardial infarction (AMI) are often held for an extended period, usually overnight, to rule out AMI. If these patients are held in ED examination rooms, they contribute to ED overcrowding, which inflates waiting times and jeopardizes patient safety. If they are moved into hospital beds, they contribute to high occupancy levels, which can also contribute to ED overcrowding by causing "bed block" that prevents admission of other ED patients into the hospital. Bed block can also result in cancellation of elective surgeries in the OR.

A hospital could reduce the overcrowding and bed block problems caused by patients under observation by expanding the number of ED examination rooms or hospital beds. But, in addition to being expensive, these resources are frequently subject to "Certificate of Need" (CON) requirements.[18] So a key challenge is to find a less expensive way to monitor patients in need of extended observation.

The Institute of Medicine (2007b) suggested that Clinical Decision units (CDUs), also known as Observation units, are a particularly promising alternative. Because CDUs cost less to build and staff, and are usually not subject to certificate of need requirements, they offer an economical way to divert patients undergoing long-term observation from the ED without filling up hospital beds.

However, although beds in CDUs are less costly than regular ED or hospital beds, they are not free. So a hospital still must justify the expense. Furthermore, they must determine an appropriate size (number of beds) for an Observation unit.

2.4.3.2 PRINCIPLES

The key tool for evaluating the economic attractiveness of an Observation unit, and for making sizing decisions, is Little's Law.

Principle (Little's Law): Over the long term, the rate (R), in-process inventory (I), and waiting time (T) of a system are related according to

$$I = R \times T$$

This principle is important because an Observation unit is designed to hold patients who are being evaluated for conditions like AMI. The set of patients being observed constitutes an inventory (I). If we know the average arrival rate of such patients (R) and the average duration of their observation (T), then we can compute the average number of patients (I) requiring space in the Observation unit. This gives us a means for determining the needed size of the Observation unit. By considering the economic value of the ED and/or hospital beds freed up by shifting patients from them, we can make a business case for an Observation unit.

2.4.3.3 PRACTICES

CDUs were originally introduced for patients with chest pain. In 2007, the Centers for Medicare and Medicaid Services allowed reimbursement for stays in the CDU for three conditions: chest pain, asthma, and congestive heart failure (Institute of Medicine, 2007b). Because of their effectiveness at reducing ED congestion, their use has been expanded to other conditions, such as fainting, drug reactions, kidney stones, acute hypertension, and others.

To determine whether a CDU is a good alternative for a given hospital, we must (a) determine the appropriate size of the CDU and (b) evaluate the economics of adding an appropriately sized CDU. Because these are specific questions, we will not use the approach employed for the broader management challenges of addressing ED over-crowding and patient safety, in which we invoked several principles and a generic improvement table from Appendix A to generate an array of candidate improvements. Instead, we will rely on a single principle (Little's Law) and address the questions in the context of a case study.

2.4.3.4 CASE: DESIGNING AN OBSERVATION UNIT FOR LINCOLN HOSPITAL

Lincoln Hospital (LH) is a congested tertiary care hospital. (Only the name is fictional.) At the time of this case, occupancy rates were averaging over 90% with substantial fluctuation from day to day and week to week, leading to frequent events in which the hospital became full. When this occurred, patients in the ED were boarded for lack of a bed, and transfers from other hospitals were refused. In the prior year, more than 20% of patients admitted from the ED were delayed, and over 15% of transfer requests were refused for lack of space. Delaying admissions compromises patient safety, and refusing transfers negatively impacts both patient safety and hospital revenues. Consequently, the administration was considering adding a CDU (Observation unit) to hold patients who require extended observation.

Todd and Mary, two Lincoln analysts who had taken a short course on hospital operations, were assigned to "run the numbers" necessary to answer the sizing and economics questions. They decided to use Little's Law because it is simple, can be rapidly executed with available data, and is readily accessible to physicians and administrators. Their analysis, summarized next, follows that presented in Lovejoy and Desmond (2011).

After reviewing data from the past year, Todd found that an average of 11.1 patients/day were put into inpatient beds on observation status, and they stayed on average 1.14 days before being either discharged or admitted. Hence, by Little's Law there were, on average,

$$I = R \times T = 11.1 \text{ patients/day} \times 1.14 \text{ days} = 12.65 \text{ patients}$$

in observation status occupying inpatient beds on any given day.

If Lincoln were to build an Observation unit to accommodate these patients, designed for 90% utilization, they would need $12.65 \div 0.9 = 14$ beds. This provided an answer to the sizing problem.

To address the economics question, Mary and Todd needed to estimate the costs of installing an Observation unit and the benefits that would result from it. On the cost side, Todd made a detailed analysis of construction and operating costs and concluded that it would cost about $5.9 million to construct and equip a 14-bed unit, and that staffing it (with RNs, LPNs, techs, clerks, and supervisors) would cost about $2 million per year with benefits. Hence, the costs of an observation unit would include a one-time fixed investment of $5.9 million and annual operational costs of about $2 million.

On the benefits side, Mary noted that there are two components: (1) cost savings from moving observation patients currently occupying inpatient beds to lower cost observation beds, and (2) added revenues from new patients who could be accommodated in the inpatient beds that are freed up because of the Observation unit. Of course, Mary recognized that the added revenues would only be realized if the empty inpatient beds could be backfilled with additional patients. But, given the large number of transfer patients that were currently being turned away, she was confident that these beds would be filled.

To compute the benefits from lower cost monitoring observation patients, Mary estimated the average net contribution of an observation patient held in an inpatient bed to be $4,642 and the average net contribution of an observation patient held in an Observation unit bed to be $4,733. The $91 difference was attributable to the lower cost of staffing an Observation unit bed. Because the hospital received 11.1 observation patients per day, the net benefits from the reduced cost beds in the Observation unit would be

$$11.1 \text{ patients/day} \times \$91/\text{patient} = \$1,010/\text{day} = \$368,865/\text{yr} = \$0.37 \text{ million/yr}$$

To estimate the increased revenues from backfilling the inpatient beds vacated by the 12.65 patients (on average) who move to the Observation unit, Mary computed the increase in volume of patients by again applying Little's Law. First, she noted that

$$I = R \times T$$

so

$$R = I/T$$

Because she knew that $I = 12.65$ patients, she only needed to estimate the average time (length of stay) of an inpatient. Using data for the past year, she found that $T = 5.34$ days. Hence, the additional space for inpatients provided by redirecting observation patients to a CDU would support a backfill patient flow of

$$R = 12.65 \text{ patients} \div 5.34 \text{ days} = 2.37 \text{ patients/day.}$$

The additional revenue from these patients would be

$$2.37 \text{ patients/day} \times \$4,642/\text{patient} = \$10,996/\text{day} = \$4 \text{ million/year}$$

Thus, a CDU would require an initial outlay of $5.9 million but would generate annual positive cash flows of

$$\$0.37 \text{ million} + \$4 \text{ million} - \$2 \text{ million} = \$2.37 \text{ million}$$

This cash flow represented a payback period of 2.5 years, a 5-year net present value (NPV) of $2.8 million (at a 10% interest rate), and a 5-year internal rate of return (IRR) of 29%. With these encouraging numbers, Todd and Mary were able to make a plausible case for the Observation unit.

However, they cautioned in their final report that there could be significant qualitative effects not captured in these calculations. For example, patient satisfaction might suffer for observation patients because beds in the Observation unit would be in a ward, rather than in private or semi-private rooms as is the case in the inpatient units. But, with an average stay of about 1 day for observation purposes, the administrators did not believe this will be significant. There might also be some additional financial exposure to staffing the Observation unit if the reimbursed professional fees for attending physicians did not fully cover the physicians' costs. However, with the preceding numbers, this exposure could be as high as $813,000 each year before the 5-year net present value of the investment dropped to zero. So Todd and Mary recommended the Observation unit as a safe and profitable investment. The administration agreed, and Lincoln Hospital proceeded with the construction of a 14-bed Observation unit.

2.5 Conclusions

The ED is the hospital unit where operations problems are most visible. As we noted, a number of trends have conspired to produce significant increases in the number of ED visits simultaneously with a decline in the number of hospital EDs. The resulting high utilization of most EDs, combined with the high variability that is a consequence of unscheduled arrivals and widely different patient treatment needs, has resulted in a perfect storm for ED congestion. Long waits, crowded hallways, and harried staff are highly visible symptoms of this congestion and unmistakable signals of the operational stress faced by EDs.

Given this, it is not surprising that the Institute of Medicine (2007b) cited the need to adopt modern operations management practices from other industries, such as manufacturing, at the top of its list of recommendations for addressing the crisis in emergency health care. But saying this and actually making it happen are two different things. The ordered environment at Toyota, where a limited number of vehicle models are produced to preset schedules, is a far different place from an ED that receives patients with an unlimited range of symptoms in an unscheduled fashion. So we cannot simply borrow practices from Toyota. For instance, Toyota's famous kanban and single minute exchange of die (SMED) systems are not likely to be of much use in the ED.

What hospital managers can borrow from Toyota and other leading practitioners of lean production methods are the principles that underlie their practices. Many of Toyota's methods are essentially variability reduction tools. Production smoothing, setup reduction, total preventive maintenance, work standardization, and many other key components of the Toyota Production System are designed to systematically eliminate variability in their system. But the specific tools have been evolved over decades to meet the specific needs of Toyota. What hospital EDs need is a similar evolution of detailed methods that apply the insights of basic management principles to the specific needs of the ED.

In this chapter, we have highlighted several management principles that are relevant to key issues facing the ED. By tracing the implications of these in a systematic manner, we were able to identify a comprehensive set of generic policies for addressing these issues. For illustration, we translated these generic policies into options for specific action items. But we could not be comprehensive in tracing all the ways the generic policies could be operationalized because these depend on the environmental specifics of the particular ED.

Therefore, as is the case at Toyota, where everyone in the organization is tasked with continually improving the system by finding new and better ways of applying fundamental principles to everyday practice, professionals in hospital EDs must take responsibility for generating the next generation of management practices in their system. The framework laid out in this chapter provides a conceptual basis for identifying levers for improving performance. For specific issues, we have generated checklists of generic improvement options that can help ED managers be comprehensive in their consideration of alternatives. Developing and implementing actual improvement policies will require thorough analysis, substantial creativity, and active leadership on the part of ED managers. But, because the need is so great, the rewards to these efforts in the ED can also be great.

2.6 Stakeholders' Perspectives

Thursday June 24, 2010

"I've been thinking exactly the same thing," said Tony Tenore, the COO, to Dr. Greene. "In fact, I'm delighted you're here. Let's talk."

Three months ago, after the tragic death of Sally Oldham, Greene had begun talking to various physicians across the hospital about why it happened and what they could do to avoid similar tragedies in the future. He found that many others shared his concern that the hospital was just on the edge of being out of control with major congestion and delay problems. Ironically, despite the concerns of the staff, University Hospital was widely considered a leader in implementing lean management techniques, with projects, champions, teams, workout events, charts, and celebration dinners. Greene himself had participated in some of those efforts in the ED.

Why didn't all those kaizen events help Sally? Green wondered. The more he discovered about her experience, the more obvious the answer became. Sally's trajectory spanned the entire hospital, from the ED to diagnostics to the nursing units and the OR, but the kaizens addressed only narrow slices of the system. Although these were individually worthwhile, there was no overarching strategy for selecting and coordinating individual improvement efforts. As a result, system-wide performance remained largely static. *Without a better way to make improvements*, he thought, *I might as well give up and join Ben in his less complicated life.*

It was with these thoughts that Greene had gone to see Tony.

"You're right Nate," Tony said. "We have been doing projects for a long time without really connecting them. We have also been applying the same methodology to all projects, to the point where our process has become highly bureaucratic and not very innovative. I think it's time for us to take a clear-eyed, open-minded look at our operations and how they can be improved. If that means continuing to use a Lean/kaizen lens, fine. If it means using something else, fine too. We just want results!"

"Well, that makes sense." Greene hesitated, pondering how much he wanted to reveal his growing concerns about the future of full service hospitals. *What the heck!* He decided to plunge ahead. "But to tell you the truth, I'm seriously considering making a change. I'm worried that integrated hospitals have become too big and too complex to deliver quality health care."

"You're thinking of Mrs. Oldham, right?"

"Yes," Greene acknowledged. "But I can name any number of cases like Mrs. Oldham's. They don't all die, but they're delayed or treated improperly or injured or hassled or all of the above!"

"You're absolutely right. That's why I'm happy that at least you, one of our most respected physicians, understand the need to change!"

"Yes, but what if that change really should be to a specialty hospital where confusion and bureaucracy wouldn't be such obstacles?" Greene asked bluntly.

"If all of our most talented docs defect to specialty hospitals," Tenore countered, "where will that leave patients like Mrs. Oldham?"

"What do you mean?"

"Do you think that a case like Mrs. Oldham's would wind up in a specialty hospital?" Tenore asked.

"No, I guess not." Greene admitted.

"Then what you're proposing would leave people like her in EDs that are congested, confused, *and* staffed by second-rate physicians." Tenore went for the jugular. "And that will result in more people like Mrs. Oldham's family whose lives have been devastated unnecessarily." Greene listened pensively as Tenore continued. "We have no choice. We have to fix our hospitals. But if smart docs like you don't do it, who will? Let's work together on this! I'm not just offering you a chance to become a better doctor; I'm offering you a chance to make every physician in this institution a better doctor. Come on! Take the chance."

Greene was impressed by Tenore's passion. In his heart of hearts, Greene wanted to believe in the big teaching hospital as a place of healing and support, rather than one of frustration and inefficiency. Tony was offering a way to work toward that vision, rather than abandoning it. In honor of Mrs. Oldham and all those like her, he had to try.

"Okay." Greene smiled. "Where do we start?"

Tenore explained that he knew they were fighting an uphill battle against indifference generated by so many marginally productive lean projects in the past, so the first step was to find a champion to work on one part of the hospital. With some success there, they could develop a hospital-wide strategy and expand outward. "Fortunately," he said, "I think I've just found a champion."

Tenore suggested that Greene become the lead flow advocate within the ED, with an eye toward taking a role as a hospital-wide champion.

"But the ED is so different from the OR," Greene protested. "Why would a good idea in the ED work in the OR or vice versa? Isn't this just the same piecemeal approach we just finished trashing?"

"Ah!" Tenore smiled and pointed his index finger in the air. He reached behind him and pulled a book from a cluttered shelf. "The practices are very different between units, but if you think in terms of flows, the principles are the same! I've been reading this book that I think might provide the perspective we need."

As he took the book from Tenore, Greene noted the title—*Hospital Operations*.

Surgery? Greene gave Tenore a skeptical look.

"You'll see what I mean." Tenore continued waving away Green's protests before they were made. "And I'll buy some release time for you to really work on this. If you can make it work, it will be worth it a hundred times over."

Greene devoured the book over the next three days. It turned out to have nothing to do with surgical operations and everything to do with flows—flows of patients moving through treatment stages, flows of information moving between individuals, and even cash flows moving (or not) through the administrative system. It was a revelation. He'd always thought of patients as "cases." The book taught him to view the sequences of hospital processes encountered by patients as "flows," in which any variation or stoppage degrades patient service. Further, it offered a coherent explanation of why such degradations occur. With this new perspective, Greene began seeing all kinds of inefficiencies he had never noted before. Delays were no longer an inevitable fact of life, but something that could be actively managed.

"Why is that patient waiting?" "Why do those two nurses use different methods for the same task?" "Why is that PA backed up with work, while that other one has nothing to do?" "Why don't we inform patients about their wait times?" "Why did that lab result take so long to come back?" Greene began asking "Why?" constantly.

His newfound perspective also deepened his understanding of Sally Oldham's experience. He began viewing her trajectory as two interacting flows, of Sally herself and of the information associated with her case. He became more and more interested in using the principles of the book to find ways to improve flows like Sally's that cut across the entire hospital. But Green knew well how difficult it was to work across unit boundaries and how weary the staff was with improvement initiatives. So he committed himself to demonstrating concrete progress in the ED before taking on any hospital-wide initiatives.

In his first two months, Greene made relatively straightforward improvements along the physical and information flow paths. He encouraged earlier ordering of tests, including at triage for some patients, so that results would be available more quickly. He standardized kits for some procedures to reduce the time spent by nurses accumulating materials and equipment. And he gave the reception and triage team the responsibility to sweep through the waiting room every 20 minutes to see how people were doing and give them brief updates on how long their wait was likely to be. He had enough seniority and credibility in the ED that people listened to him and gave his changes a chance.

As he probed more deeply into the ED processes and discussed his findings with his staff, Greene began to realize that, although standardization was a powerful way to speed flow and improve efficiency, it was far more applicable to some procedures than others. Some simple procedures were amenable to a formal checklist and a standard material kit, whereas others, being more uncertain and complex, required creativity and flexibility on the part of the physician. Trying to standardize the latter was actually counterproductive.

This led to a minor epiphany for Green: There was a place for Lean, but its use had to be strategic. With this in mind, he reached out to the hospital expert on the Toyota Production System (TPS), Dexter Jackson.

"I think the reason we didn't get very far with Lean in the past," explained Greene, "was that we tried to apply it to the full range of patients. But I'm working on a system that will track simple patients separately from complex ones. I think TPS tools will work great in the simple track. We could make it flow just like a production line."

"Hmmm…" Jackson responded. "Maybe we can…"

Over the next six weeks, Greene worked with his staff to separate the ED into pods—one to handle simple cases, and the other to handle complex ones. On the simple side, the goal was to keep patients moving production-line style, like the fast lane in a supermarket. On the complex side, the plan was to work in the more familiar team problem-solving mode. To track patients into the proper pod, Greene worked with the triage nurses to design a system rating a patient's complexity and medical urgency. When in doubt, nurses were to direct patients into the complex pod to ensure that the patients in the simple pod were amenable to high-efficiency flow methods.

Knowing that mistakes in assignment were inevitable, Greene worked with the ED to develop procedures for moving patients from the simple to the complex queue, and vice versa, as information unfolded during examination.

The next month, as implementation of the new system was approaching, Greene took time out for his weekly basketball game. When he arrived, Dr. Arnold was already there, practicing free throws so intently that he did not hear Greene slip through the door.

"Hey Ben!" Greene called. "How's the life of the medical entrepreneur?"

"Hey Nate." Arnold swished a shot. "Actually, things are pretty terrific. Business is really picking up since the expansion. How about you? What's the haps at the hosp?"

"We're doing okay." Greene dropped his duffel in the corner and knelt to tighten his shoelaces. "I think we're finally starting to get some traction on improving flows in the ED. We've been simplifying a bunch of our procedures, and I think it's going to make a real difference."

"Congratulations," offered Arnold. "Of course, as I've said before, my hospital is already simple. There is no way you'll ever match the efficiency we already have. If you'd join us, you could do things you can only dream of at University."

"But I dream of treating the full range of patients—young and old, rich and poor, easy and complex." Greene stood up. "As I've said before, you gave up doing that."

"That's true." Arnold had heard this before. "But we don't need to treat everyone in our hospital. If other specialty hospitals can do as good a job with other kinds of patients as we're doing with ours, we'll have a network that serves patients better than any integrated hospital can ever do. The large, integrated hospital is just too unwieldy to be successful and is going the way of the dinosaur."

"Not going to happen," Greene countered. "Nobody is going to start a specialty hospital to serve unprofitable patients. But if you and your mates continue picking off all the profitable patients, you might be able to put us out of business. Then what will happen to all the patients you don't serve?"

"I think you are underestimating the power of the market," said Arnold earnestly. "But come on, let's play."

2.7 References

American Academy of Emergency Medicine. 2008. "AAEM History." [Online]. Available: http://www.aaem.org/about-aaem/aaem-history [accessed July 27, 2012].

American Academy of Physician Assistants. 2010. "2010 AAPA Physician Assistant Census Report." [Online]. Available http://www.aapa.org/uploadedFiles/content/Common/Files/2010_Census_Report_Final.pdf [accessed July 27, 2012].

American College of Emergency Physicians. 2008. "EMTALA." [Online]. Available: http://www.acep.org/patients.aspx?LinkIdentifier=id&id=25936&fid=1754&Mo=No&acepTitle=EMTALA [accessed July 6, 2008].

American Hospital Association. 2001. "Patients or Paperwork: The Regulatory Burden Facing America's Hospitals." [Online]. Available: http://www.aha.org/aha/content/2001/pdf/FinalPaperworkReport.pdf [accessed July 6, 2008].

American Hospital Association. 2011. "TrendWatch Chartbook 2011." [Online]. Available: http://www.aha.org/research/reports/tw/chartbook/2011chartbook.shtml [accessed July 27, 2012].

Arendt, K.W., A.T. Sadosty, A.L. Weaver, C.R. Brent, and E.T. Boie. 2003. "The Left-Without-Being-Seen Patients: What Would Keep Them from Leaving? *Annals of Emergency Medicine* 42(3), 317–323.

Aspden, P., J.A. Wolcott, J.L. Bootman, L.R. Cronenwett (editors). 2007. *Preventing Medication Errors.* Institute of Medicine of the National Academies, National Academies Press, Washington, D.C.

Berenholtz, S.M., P.J. Pronovost, P.A. Lipsett, et al., 2004. "Eliminating Catheter-Related Bloodstream Infections in the Intensive Care Unit." *Critical Care Medicine* 32(10), 2014–2020.

Blackwell, T.H. 1993. "Pre-Hospital Care." *Emergency Medical Clinics of North America* 11, 1–14.

Brennan, T.A., L.L. Leape, N.M. Laird, L. Hebert, A.R. Localio A.G Lawthers, J.P. Newhouse, P.C. Weiler, and H.H. Hiatt. 1991. "Incidence of Adverse Events and Negligence in Hospitalized Patients." *New England Journal of Medicine* 324(6), 370–376.

Byers, J.F., and S.V. White. 2004. *Patient Safety: Principles and Practice.* New York: Springer.

Center for Catastrophe Preparedness and Response NYU. 2005. *Emergency Medical Services: The Forgotten First Responder—A Report on the Critical Gaps in Organization and Deficits in Resources for America's Medical First Responders.* New York: Center for Catastrophe Preparedness and Response, New York University.

Chisholm, C.D., A.M. Dornfeld, D.R. Nelson, and W.H. Cordell. 2001. "Work Interrupted: A Comparison of Workplace Interruptions in Emergency Departments and Primary Care Offices." *Annals of Emergency Medicine* 38(2), 146–151.

Coiera, E. 2009. "Communication in Emergency Medical Teams." in P. Croskerry, K.S. Cosby, S.M. Schenkel, and R.L. Wears (eds). *Patient Safety in Emergency Medicine.* Philadelphia: Lippincott Williams & Wilkins.

Collins, S., L. Currie, S. Bakken, J.J. Cimino. 2006. "Interruptions During the Use of a CPOE System for MICU Rounds." *AMIA 2006 Symposium Proceedings,* 895.

Collins, S., L. Currie, V. Patel, S. Bakken, and J.J. Cimino. 2007. "Multitasking by Clinicians in the Context of CPOE and CIS Use." in K.A. Kuhn, J.R. Warren, and T.-Y. Leong (eds). *MEDINFO 2007 Proceedings of the 12th World Congress on Health (Medical) Informatics Volume 129 Studies in Health Technology and Informatics.* Amsterdam: IOS Press, 2007.

Cowan, R.M., and S. Trzeciak. 2005. "Clinical Review: Emergency Department Overcrowding and the Potential Impact on the Critically Ill." *Critical Care* 9, 291–295.

Croskerry, P. 2002. "Achieving Quality in Clinical Decision Making: Cognitive Strategies and Detection of Bias." *Academic Emergency Medicine* 9(11), 1184–1204.

Croskerry, P. 2003. "The Importance of Cognitive Errors in Diagnosis and Strategies to Minimize Them." *Academic Medicine* 78(8), 775–780.

Croskerry, P., K.S. Cosby, S.M. Schenkel, and R.L. Wears. 2009. *Patient Safety in Emergency Medicine.* Philadelphia: Lippincott Williams & Wilkins.

Derlet, R.W., J. Richards, and R. Kravitz. 2001. "Frequent Overcrowding in U.S. Emergency Departments." *Academic Emergency Medicine* 8(2), 151–155.

Derlet, R.W. 2002. "Overcrowding in Emergency Departments: Increased Demand and Decreased Capacity." *Annals of Emergency Medicine* 39(4), 430–432.

Diercks, D.B., M.T. Roe, A.Y. Chen, W.F. Peacock, J.D. Kirk, C.V. Pollack, Jr., W.B. Gibler, S.C. Smith, Jr., M. Ohman, and E.D. Peterson. 2007. "Prolonged Emergency Department Stays of Non–ST-Segment-Elevation Myocardial Infarction Patients Are Associated with Worse Adherence to the American College of Cardiology/American Heart Association Guidelines for Management and Increased Adverse Events." *Annals of Emergency Medicine* 50(5), 489–496.

Fairbanks, R.J., S.H. Caplan, P.A. Bishop, A.M. Marks, and M.N. Shah. 2007. "Usability Study of Two Common Defibrillators Reveals Hazards." *Annals of Emergency Medicine* 50(4), 424–432.

France, D., S. Levin, R. Hemphill, et al., 2005. "Emergency Physicians' Behaviors and Workload in the Presence of an Electronic Whiteboard." *International Journal of Medical Informatics* 74, 827–837.

Full Circle Group. 2004. "Oakwood Hospital and Medical Center Healing an Ailing Emergency Department, Case Study." [Online.] Available: http://www.fcg-global.com/case-studies/Oakwood [accessed May 18, 2011].

Gawande, A. 2007. "The Checklist: If Something So Simple Can Transform Intensive Care, What Else Can It Do?" *The New Yorker* December 10, 2007. [Online] Available: http://www.newyorker.com/reporting/2007/12/10/071210fa_fact_gawande [accessed May 23, 2011].

George, M. 2002. *Lean Six Sigma.* New York: McGraw-Hill.

Goldstein. J. 2008. "Inflated Wait Time Estimates Make ER Patients Happier." *Wall Street Journal Health Blog*, October 30, 2008, http://blogs.wsj.com/health/2008/10/30/inflated-wait-time-estimates-make-er-patients-happier/ [accessed 12/14/2010].

Gomez, M.A., J.L. Anderson, L.A. Karagounis, J.B. Muhlestein, and F.B. Mooders. 1996. "An Emergency Department-Based Protocol for Rapidly Ruling Out Myocardial Ischemia Reduces Hospital Time and Expense: Results of a Randomized Study (ROMIO)." *Journal of the American College of Cardiology* 28(1), 25–33.

Graber, M.A., and D. VanScoy. 2003. "How Well Does Decision Support Software Perform in the Emergency Department?" *Emergency Medicine Journal* 20, 426–428.

Haller J.S. 1990. "The Beginning of Urban Ambulance Service in the United States and England." *Journal of Emergency* Medicine 8, 743–755.

Haller, G., P.S. Myles, J. Stoelwinder, et al., 2007. "Integrating Incident Reporting into an Electronic Record System." *Journal of the American Medical Informatics Association* 14(2), 175–181.

Harrison Y., and J. Horne. 2000. "The Impact of Sleep Deprivation on Decision Making: A Review." *Journal of Experimental Psychology: Applied.* 6, 236–249.

Health Resources and Services Administration. 2010. "The Registered Nurse Population." U.S. Department of Health and Human Services. [Online]. Available: http://www.acnpweb.org/files/public/HRSA_2008_Initial_RN_National_Survey.pdf [accessed May 5, 2011].

Hearst Newspapers. 2009. *Dead by Mistake.* Available: http://www.timesunion.com/local/article/Dead-by-mistake-547875.php [accessed July 27, 2012].

Hollander, J.E., and J.M. Pines. 2007. "The Emergency Department Crowding Paradox: The Longer You Stay, The Less Care You Get." *Annals of Emergency Medicine* 50(5), 497–499.

Hopp, W.J., and M.L. Spearman. 2008. *Factory Physics: Foundations of Manufacturing Management,* Third Edition. New York: McGraw-Hill.

Institute of Medicine. 1993. *Emergency Medical Services for Children*. Washington, DC: National Academy of Sciences.

Institute of Medicine. 1999. *To Err Is Human: Building a Safer Health System*. Washington, DC: National Academy of Sciences.

Institute of Medicine. 2007a. *Emergency Medical Services at the Crossroads*. Washington, DC: National Academy of Sciences.

Institute of Medicine. 2007b. *Hospital-Based Emergency Care at the Breaking Point*. Washington, DC: National Academy of Sciences.

Jolly, B.T., J.L. Scott, and S.M. Sanford. 1995. "Simplification of Emergency Department Discharge Instructions Improves Patient Comprehension." *Annals of Emergency Medicine* 26(4), 443–446.

Jones S.S., T.L. Allen, T.J. Flottemesch, and S.J. Welch. 2006. "An Independent Evaluation of Four Quantitative Emergency Department Crowding Scales." *Academic Emergency Medicine* 13(11), 1204–1211.

Khare, R.K., B. Uren, and R.L. Wears. 2005. "Capturing More Emergency Department Errors via an Anonymous Web-Based Reporting System." *Quality Management in Health Care*. 14(2), 91–94.

Landrigan C.P., J.M. Rothschild, J.W. Cronin, R. Kaushal, E. Burdick, J.T. Katz, C.M. Lilly, P.H. Stone, S.W. Lockley, D.W. Bates, and C.A. Czeisler. 2004. "Effect of Reducing Interns' Work Hours on Serious Medical Errors in Intensive Care Units. *New England Journal of Medicine*. 351, 1838–1848.

Lingard, L., S. Espin, S. Whyte, G. Regehr, G.R. Baker, R. Reznick, J. Bohnen, B. Orser, D. Doran, and E. Grober. 2004. "Communication Failures in the Operating Room: An Observational Classification of Recurrent Types and Effects." *Quality and Safety in Health Care* 13, 330–334.

Lovejoy, W., and J. Desmond. 2011. "Little's Law Flow Analysis of Observation Unit Impact and Sizing." *Academic Emergency Medicine* 18, 183–189.

Magid, D.J., A.F. Sullivan, P.D. Cleary, S.R. Rao, J.A. Gordon, R. Kaushal, E. Gaudagnoli, C.A. Camargo, and D. Blumenthal. 2009. "The Safety of Emergency Care Systems: Results of a Survey of Clinicians in 65 US Emergency Departments." *Annals of Emergency Medicine* 53(6), 715–723.

Maister, D.H. 1985. "The Psychology of Waiting Lines." [Online.] Available: http://davidmaister.com/articles/5/52/ [accessed July 22, 2008].

McGlynn, E.A., S.M. Asch, J. Adams, J. Keesey, J. Hicks, A. DeCristofaro, and E.A. Kerr. 2003. "The Quality of Health Care Delivered to Adults in the United States." *New England Journal of Medicine* 348(26), 2635–2645.

NAEMT. 2008. "EMS: Where We've Been and Where We're Going." [Online.] Available: http://www.naemt.org/Libraries/NAEMT%20Documents/History%20of%20EMS.sflb [accessed July 27, 2012].

National Academy of Sciences, National Research Council. 1966. *Accidental Death and Disability: The Neglected Disease of Modern Society.* Washington, DC: National Academy of Sciences.

National Commission on Terrorist Attacks upon the United States. 2004. *The 9/11 Commission Report.* Washington, DC: National Commission on Terrorist Attacks Upon the United States.

National Highway Transportation Safety Administration. 1996. *Emergency Medical Services Agenda for the Future.* Washington, DC: Department of Transportation.

National Research Council. 1985. *Injury in America: A Continuing Health Problem.* Washington, DC: National Academy of Sciences.

Nuñez, S. A. Hexdall, and A. Aguirre-Jaime. 2006. "Unscheduled Returns to the Emergency Department: An Outcome of Medical Errors?" *Quality and Safety in Health Care* 15, 102–108.

Nurses for a Healthier Tomorrow. 2008. "Emergency Nurse." [Online.] Available: http://www.nursesource.org/emergency.html [accessed August 22, 2008].

Patanwala, A.E., T.L. Warholak, A.B. Sanders, et al., 2010. "A Prospective Observational Study of Medication Errors in a Tertiary Care Emergency Department." *Annals of Emergency Medicine* 55(6), 522–526.

Parshuram, C.S., T. To, W. Seto, A. Trope, G. Koren, and A. Laupacis. 2008. "Systematic Evaluation of Errors Occurring During the Preparation of Intravenous Medication." *Canadian Medical Association Journal* 178(1), 42–48.

Peth, H.A. 2003. "Medication Errors in the Emergency Department: A Systems Approach to Minimizing Risk." *Emergency Medicine Clinics of North America* 21, 141–158.

Poole, S. 2009. "Online Service Holds Your Spot at Hospital." *The Atlanta Constitution-Journal,* May 31, 2009. Available: http://www.ajc.com/business/content/business/stories/2009/05/31/InQuickER_ER_hospital.html [accessed December 15, 2010].

Pozner, C.N., R. Zane, S.J. Nelson, and M. Levine. 2003. "International EMS Systems: The United States: Past, Present, and Future." *Resuscitation* 60, 239–244.

Pronovost, P., D. Needham, S. Berenholtz, et al., 2006. "An Intervention to Decrease Catheter-Related Bloodstream Infections in the ICU." *New England Journal of Medicine.* 355(26), 2725–2732.

Reason, J. 2000. "Human Error: Models and Management." *British Medical Journal* 320, 768–770.

Richardson, D.B. 2006. "Increase in Patient Mortality at 10 Days Associated with Emergency Department Overcrowding." *Medical Journal of Australia* 184, 213–216.

Rosen, P. 1995. *History of Emergency Medicine*. New York: Josiah Macy, Jr. Foundation. 59–79.

Rudkin, S.E., J. Oman, M.I. Langdorf, M. Hill, J. Bauche, P. Kivela, and L. Johnson. 2004. "The State of ED On Call Coverage in California." *American Journal of Emergency Medicine* 22(7), 575–581.

Russ, S., I. Jones, D. Aronsky, R.S. Dittus, and C.M. Slovis. 2010. "Placing Physician Orders at Triage: The Effect on Length of Stay." *Annals of Emergency Medicine* 56(1), 27–33.

Saghafian, S., W. Hopp, M. Van Oyen, J. Desmond, and S. Kronick. 2010. "Patient Streaming as a Mechanism for Improving Responsiveness in Emergency Departments." *Operations Research*, in press.

Santell J.P., R. Hicks, and D. Cousins. 2004. "Medication Errors in Emergency Department Settings." ASHP Summer Meeting, Las Vegas (NV).

Shonberger, R.J. 1982. *Japanese Manufacturing Techniques: Nine Hidden Lessons in Simplicity*. New York: The Free Press.

Seaver, M. 2004. "Baseline ER Survey Explores System's Cracks." *AANS Bulletin* 13(4), 19–24.

Sefrin, P. 1998. "'Scoop and Run'" Or "'Stay and Play.'" *The Internet Journal of Rescue and Disaster Medicine* 1(1). Available: http://www.ispub.com/journal/the-internet-journal-of-rescue-and-disaster-medicine/volume-1-number-1/scoop-and-run-or-stay-and-play.html [accessed July 27, 2012].

Shapiro, M. J. Morey, S. Small et al., 2004. "Simulation Based Teamwork Training for Emergency Department Staff: Does It Improve Clinical Team Performance When Added to an Existing Didactic Teamwork Curriculum?" *Quality and Safety in Health Care* 13, 417–421.

Sinha, M., J. Shriki, R. Salness, and P.A. Blackburn. 2007. "Need for Standardized Sign-Out in the Emergency Department: A Survey of Emergency Medicine Residency and Pediatric Emergency Medicine Fellowship Program Directors." *Academic Emergency Medicine* 14, 192–196.

SoRelle, R. 2006. "Homicide Charges Against Illinois ED Stun EM." *Emergency Medicine News* XXVIII(12), 1.

Smetzer, J. L., and M.R. Cohen. 1998. "Lessons from the Denver Medication Error/Criminal Negligence Case: Look Beyond Blaming Individuals." *Hospital Pharmacy* 33(6), 640–657.

Speier, C., J.S. Valacich, and I. Vessey. 1999. "The Influence of Task Interruption on Individual Decision Making: An Information Overload Perspective." *Decision Sciences* 30(2), 337–360.

Sprivulis, P.C., J.A. Da Silva, I.G. Jacobs, A.R.L. Frazer, and G.A. Jelinek. 2006. "The Association Between Hospital Overcrowding and Mortality Among Patients Admitted via Western Australian Emergency Departments." *Medical Journal of Australia* 184, 208–212.

Stella, D., J. Hendrie, J. Smythe, and I. Graham. 1996. "Experience with Critical Incident Monitoring in the Emergency Department." *Emergency Medicine* 8, 215–219.

Sternberg, Rachel H. 1999. "The Transport of Sick and Wounded Soldiers in Classical Greece." *Phoenix* 53(3/4), 191–205.

Schuur, J.D., D. Collins, A. Smith, R. Lisitano, R. Kulkarni, and G. D'Onofrio. 2007. "Use of Lean Techniques to Simplify Admission Procedures and Decrease ED Process Time." *Annals of Emergency Medicine*, 50(3), S90.

Streitenberger, K., K. Breen-Reid, and C. Harris. 2006. "Handoffs in Care—Can We Make Them Safer?" *Pediatric Clinics of North America* 53, 1185–1195.

Taheri, P.A., and D.A. Butz. 2004. "Specialist On-Call Coverage of Palm Beach County Emergency Departments." Palm Beach County, FL: Palm Beach County Medical Society Services.

University of Michigan. 2003. "The Emergence of Emergency Medicine." *Medicine at Michigan* 5(3), Summer 2003 [Online]. Available: http://www.medicineatmichigan.org/magazine/2003/summer/classnotes/wiegenstein.asp [accessed July 4, 2008].

Vance, J., and P. Spirvulis. 2005. "Triage Nurses Validly and Reliably Estimate Emergency Department Patient Complexity." *Emergency Medicine Australasia* 17 382–386.

Viccellio, P. 2008. "Reducing Emergency Department Crowding Through the Full Capacity Protocol." Robert Wood Johnson Foundation. Available: http://www.rwjf.org/qualityequality/product.jsp?id=28816 [accessed April 10, 2011].

Vinen, J. 2000. "Incident Monitoring in Emergency Departments: An Australian Model." *Academic Emergency Medicine* 7(11), 1290–1297.

Weber, E.J., et. al. 2008. "Are the Uninsured Responsible for the Increase in Emergency Department Visits in the United States?" *Annals of Emergency Medicine* 52(2), 108–115.

Weick, K.E., and K.M. Sutcliffe. 2007. *Managing the Unexpected: Resilient Performance in an Age of Uncertainty, Second Edition.* San Francisco: Wiley.

Weingart, S., P. Wyer. 2006. *Emergency Medicine Decision Making: Critical Choices in Chaotic Environments*. New York: McGraw-Hill.

Williamson, J.A.H., and W. Runciman. 2009. "Thinking in a Crisis: Use of Algorithms." in P. Croskerry, K.S. Cosby, S.M. Schenkel, and R.L. Wears (eds). *Patient Safety in Emergency Medicine*. Philadelphia: Lippincott Williams & Wilkins.

Wood, D.L., M.D. Brennan, R. Chaudhry, A.A. Chihak, W.L. Feyereisn, N.L. Woychick, P.T. Hagen, J.W. Curtright, J.M. Naessens, B.R. Spurrier, and N.F. LaRusso. 2008. "Standardized Care Processes to Improve Quality and Safety of Patient Care in a Large Academic Practice: The Plummer Project of the Department of Medicine, Mayo Clinic." *Health Services Management Research* 21(4), 276–280.

Xiao, Y., Y. Kim, S. Gardner, et al., 2006. "Communication Technology in Trauma Centres: A National Survey." *Journal of Emergency Medicine* 30(1), 21–28.

Yerkes, R.M., and J.D. Dodson. 1908. "The Relation of Strength of Stimulus to Rapidity of Habit-Formation." *Journal of Comparative Neurology and Psychology* 18, 459–482.

Zimmermann, P.G. 2006. "Cutting-Edge Discussions of Management, Policy, and Program Issues in Emergency Care." *Journal of Emergency Nursing* 32, 435–441.

---

[1]   Many hospitals employ a third party, such as Press Ganey, to compile survey statistics and compare them to benchmarks computed by averaging responses from many hospitals.

[2]   Four composite overcrowding metrics that have been proposed are National Emergency Department Overcrowding Score (NEDOCS), Emergency Department Work Index (EDWIN), Real-time Emergency of Demand Indicators (READI), and Emergency Department Crowding Scale (EDCS) (Jones et al. 2006).

[3]   Although the EMTALA provisions have led some to speculate that hospital EDs are being inundated by the indigent, Weber et al. (2008) found that the increase in ED visits between 1996 and 2003 was predominantly due to an increase in visits by nonpoor people (not uninsured patients) whose usual source of care is a physician's office. They speculate that factors underlying this trend are an aging population, more patients requiring time-sensitive interventions that need a state-of-the-art hospital, and difficulty in obtaining timely appointments from one's usual source of care.

[4]   We can also reduce the time required to treat patients by adding capacity or by using existing capacity more efficiently. We consider these in the "Increase Capacity" discussion coming up next.

[5]   Swifter treatment is not always less time consuming. For instance, delays in seeking treatment for heart attacks may result in dead patients, who do not require treatment at all. But, in keeping with our assumption that no hospital would sacrifice patient safety in the pursuit of operational efficiency, we will not consider exploiting such scenarios.

[6]   The debate in the emergency medical service field over "scoop and run" (that is, giving patients minimal treatment in the field in order to get them to the ED as quickly as possible) versus "stay and play" (that is, administering treatment beyond basic first aid in the field) has focused on cost and patient safety (Sefrin 1998). But a reasonable question to ask is whether "stay and play" policies can have a beneficial impact on ED overcrowding by reducing patient treatment time within the ED.

7   A seventh generic option is to improve batching, which is useful when entities can be processed in batches (for example, blood samples can be collected in batches). But, since patients in the ED are almost always treated individually, we do not consider batching as an improvement lever.

8   5S stands for "Sort, Straighten, Sweep, Standardize, Sustain" and refers to a workplace organization methodology that achieves "a place for everything and everything in its place" on an ongoing basis. As a standard lean tool, 5S is described in almost all books on lean production. Viewed through the lens of the Utilization and Variability Principles, 5S is a tool for reducing both utilization and variability by eliminating long and variable search times to find tools, equipment, materials, paperwork, or other inputs to tasks.

9   In many hospitals, *full-capacity protocol* refers only to the specific practice of moving admitted patients to inpatient units whether or not a bed is available, to free up ED space. But it is certainly possible to define other practices that "kick in" only when the ED is facing an overload.

10   For example, the wife of one of the authors once spent three hours in an ED sitting under a sign that read "God Bless Our New Fast Track Department" while she waited for a simple X-ray of her finger. Evidently, the Radiology lab was unaware of her presence, despite her periodic visits to the reception desk to inquire about her status. Finally, after the X-ray was completed, she was told she had a fracture and would have to come in the next day for an examination and possible cast. But when she did this, the new physician informed her that the X-ray did not indicate a fracture and that she should just "take it easy" and let the strain heal on its own.

11   It is a widely held misconception that this phrase is part of the Hippocratic Oath. Although this is not the case, many scholars believe that Hippocrates did originate the phrase. Furthermore, most versions of the Oath do contain a phrase like "abstain from whatever is deleterious and mischievous" that proscribe harmful behavior.

12   Although the Hearst estimate is at least double the Institute of Medicine estimate, it does not necessarily imply that fatal medical errors doubled in the decade from 1999 to 2009. Many states do not have a standard system for reporting medical errors, so all estimates are based on multiple data sources and a host of modeling assumptions. But the Hearst study provides support for the Institute of Medicine conclusion that medical errors are a serious and widespread problem.

13   The OR was the source of the highest fraction of adverse events (40%), but only 14% of these were due to negligence, so the OR accounted for 31% of adverse events due to negligence. The highest fraction of adverse events due to negligence (45%) occurred in patient rooms, which was responsible for 26% of total adverse events, with 41% of these due to negligence.

14   For example, Rudin et al. (2004) reported that 79% of members of the California Medical Association reported significant difficulty obtaining payment for on-call services, and 54% reported that they had provided services for which they received no payment.

15   JCAHO defines a sentinel event as "an unexpected occurrence involving death or serious physical or psychological injury, or the risk thereof."

16   This is sometimes referred to as the "Casablanca strategy," in reference to the closing scene of the movie, in which the chief of police gives the order to "round up the usual suspects."

17   For example, such rewards could encourage a person who has made an error (for example, mixed up patient medications) that did not harm a patient (for example, because that person caught his/her own error) to report it. This would allow follow-up analysis of the factors (for example, confusing labels, undifferentiated containers, similar patient names) that contributed to the "near miss," which could guide development of safer systems without the need for a patient injury as stimulus.

18   CON programs are the result of state laws that attempt to limit the cost of health care by avoiding overcapacity situations. Under them, hospitals cannot acquire, replace, or add specified types of equipment and facilities without government approval. The net result is that it may be infeasible or slow to add capacity governed by CON requirements. These requirements typically apply to operating rooms and hospital beds but not to Observation units.

3

NURSING UNITS

Coauthored with Christopher Friese, RN, PhD

3.1 Stakeholders' Perspectives

February 15, 2010, 3:45 p.m.

Ed Escobedo did not remember hitting the car in front of him. As he slid from behind the deployed air bag, noting that neither he nor the occupants of the other car appeared to be hurt, he thought *Any accident you can walk away from is a good one.*

But he knew that, as an 80-year-old, his ability to drive would be called into question. One of his friends had been forced to retake a driving exam after her recent accident. Although Ed was confident he could pass he was nevertheless unnerved.

Did I have a momentary lapse in concentration? Or were the other car's brake lights not working? He just didn't know.

The cars were towed, reports were filed, and Ed went home. His license was temporarily suspended, pending a new driving exam scheduled for three weeks hence.

Over those weeks, Ed's life was fairly normal, except he had to rely on mass transit and taxis to get around. He was surprised how easy this was. He did not go out much at night, and during the day the bus system was efficient and gave senior citizen discounts. His only complaint was a worsening cough, which Ed attributed to a cold he must have picked up waiting at bus stops or being with all those people on the bus.

Slowly, Ed's cold got worse, and he felt weaker. Even modest exertion like climbing bus steps left him short of breath. His daughter Muriel, who visited Ed regularly from her home in a neighboring county, noticed Ed's lack of energy.

"Stay in bed for a couple of days," she advised. "I'll do your shopping until you're back on your feet."

Always self-sufficient, Ed did not like that idea, although he did enjoy her visits.

One cold day in March, Muriel was delayed by traffic getting to Ed's house. She arrived to find him in bed, looking weak and gray. She asked him if he had a temperature, and Ed said he did not know. Muriel found a thermometer and confirmed a reading of 103 degrees. This certainly looked like more than a cold, and she berated herself for not suspecting something sooner. She immediately bundled Ed up and drove him to the emergency room of University Hospital.

In the Emergency Department (ED), Ed was taken into one of the examination rooms, and after about 20 minutes he was interviewed and examined by Dr. Greene, who ordered a bedside X-ray using one of their mobile units. The X-ray image showed a white haze in the lower part of his right chest cavity. This could have been due to pneumonia or a pleural effusion (liquid either inside the lung or outside the lung in the chest cavity), which in turn could be indicative of a wide range of serious diseases including pneumonia, cancer, pulmonary embolism, infection, and tuberculosis. The combination of high fever and pleural fluid suggested empyema (infection with accumulated pus in the pleural space). The latter possibility suggested a surgical, rather than internal medicine, consult. Dr. Greene contacted an on-call thoracic surgeon.

The surgeon heard no *rales* (rasping sounds) as Ed breathed, so he strongly suspected an accumulation of fluid and possible infection in the pleural space, confirming Dr. Greene's suspicions. She recommended that Ed be admitted to the hospital while she had some further tests done. Often, however, a diagnosis in cases such as this can only be made with a *thoracentesis* (putting an aspirating tube into the pleural space and withdrawing fluid) and analysis of the withdrawn fluid. That would require a surgical procedure.

Dr. Greene recommended to the bed management team that Ed be admitted to the hospital on the Thoracic Surgery unit. However, that unit was short staffed and could not receive another patient, so the bed management team called up to 5B, the General Surgery unit.

Thursday March 18, 2010, 8:00 a.m.

Allan Ruell, the day shift charge nurse on 5B, took stock of his unit as he always did at the beginning of the day. How many beds were filled, and with what manner of patients? Were any patients awaiting transfer onto the floor? How many were likely to be discharged today? With this information, he determined how many nurses and techs he would need and compared that to the number scheduled to work. He had not been "overstaffed" in a long while. Rather, in recent months it had been all too common for Allan to have to ask an unscheduled nurse to come in or to request a "floater" from the nursing float pool. Once he had secured enough nurses, he tried to balance their workload by assigning a mix of "sick" and "better" patients to each nurse.

It was high flu season, and recently 5B had been full or almost full, often with sick patients. Staff had been working very hard, with some taking on unsustainable overtime. This made it even harder for Allan to ask for extra help, because many staff were just too exhausted to want more overtime.

"I can't wait until flu season is over," he muttered to himself as he set up the day's nursing assignments.

At 1:00 p.m., Allan received a call from the bed management team.

"Can you take a thoracic surgery patient? 7A has no beds, and you just discharged some patients, so we're hoping you have room."

"Well, it's not ideal; we're still tight up here. But we can do it if you really need us to."

"We do. Thanks."

An elderly gentleman, Ed Escobedo, arrived on 5B on a gurney pushed by a transfer tech. Allan assigned a nurse to him, who joined the admitting physician in taking Ed's "story" from Dr. Greene, the Emergency physician. Ed was tucked into one of the few empty beds on the unit and put on an antibiotic regimen. This left Allan with only a single bed, which was soon filled with another patient from the ED.

Later that afternoon, Ed's nurse reported a deteriorating condition and alerted the attending physician, who was a thoracic surgeon and therefore did not normally spend time in the General Surgery unit. It took him a while to walk over, but once he saw Ed, he quickly recognized the possibility of a deteriorating infection and ordered a semi-emergent thoracentesis. Ed's surgery was scheduled for the following day at 2:00 p.m.

On Friday, Muriel, Ed's daughter, visited her father on 5B. Shortly before his scheduled surgery, a pair of transport techs arrived and moved Ed to a gurney for his trip to pre-op prep. Muriel walked alongside the gurney, her hand on her father's shoulder. Allan watched as they rolled off the unit. This freed up a bed, at least temporarily, and Allan notified the techs to clean up Ed's room for a new patient. He knew that Ed might eventually require a bed back on the unit, after he recovered in the Post Anesthesia Care unit (PACU), but the way things had been going he also knew that he might well be full by then.

As luck would have it, the comings and goings of patients did result in a bed being freed up. Allan was not on duty, because he did not work weekends, but Ed wound up returning to 5B on Saturday, when he was stepped down from the PACU.

Ed's daughter Muriel came to visit him daily, before and after work. At first Ed was listless and pale. But by Sunday his energy was up and his color was good. However, that afternoon bubbles showed up in the fluid being drained from Ed's intercostal tube, indicating air in his pleural space (a *pneumothorax*) between his lungs and chest cavity. An X-ray showed that Ed's right lung had not reinflated as it should. It was possible that Ed's lung had been damaged during the operation. To try to reinflate Ed's lung, talc was injected into the pleural space through Ed's drain tube. This procedure, called *pleurodesis*, was intended to irritate the two pleural linings (one around the lungs, the other lining the chest cavity) so that they would stick together, helping to "pull" the lung open to fill the entire space. After Ed's pleurodesis, the bubbles appeared to stop, giving everyone hope of success (and discharge).

Monday March 22, 2010, 11:00 a.m.

Ed Escobedo's stay on 5B lasted days longer than expected. Bubbles had reappeared in his drained fluids, and another pleurodesis was administered. Situations like these complicated Allan's attempts to forecast his patient census and accommodate requests for beds on his unit. He would not have been surprised if on any morning Ed was cleared for discharge, but then again he would not have been surprised if he had to stay in his bed for another day. As it was, Ed was occupying a bed he had hoped to have open by now, and he had just one empty bed on the unit, 5B-09.

What Allan did not know was that Ed would be on the floor three more days, requiring three pleurodeses in all, which was rare but not unheard of. By ignoring his cough and condition for weeks, Ed had put himself in a life-threatening situation. By requiring three pleurodeses, Ed had occupied a bed that the unit, and the hospital, sorely needed, far longer than expected given his diagnosis.

At 7:00 p.m., Allan went off shift and handed the 5B charge nurse duties to Safiya Rana. Safiya inherited the one open bed and all the full beds, including flu patients who were likely to need attention during the night. As usual, it was not shaping up to be a relaxing evening shift.

Monday March 22, 2010, 11:38 p.m.

Safiya took a call from the ED asking her to accept a patient, Mrs. Sally Oldham, with a probable diagnosis of flu. She had been recommended to the Internal Medicine unit, but they were full.

"This is my last bed, you know, but what the hey, she can join the club," Safiya told the ED nurse. "We've got other flu patients tonight, and they're all pretty sick. This is a bad strain. But I don't know where Dr. Park is, and he has the only admissions pager. When he answers, I'll let you know."

Twenty minutes later, Dr. Park answered his page and arranged to take Sally's story from the ED team. Around midnight, Sally was transported to room 5B-09; her sister-in-law Lucy was still with her. Sally, despite her nausea and pain, insisted that Lucy go home and get some sleep.

"I just need to get through this bad stretch," Sally assured her. "The kids need you more than I do. I'll see you tomorrow."

Lucy reluctantly agreed, and she departed tired and anxious, but confident that Sally was now in good hands.

Safiya assigned nurse Kristina Chung to take care of Sally.

"Another stomach flu." Michelle told Kristina, "Let's put her on a 4-hour monitoring cycle because I know you've got some other sick patients."

Kristina entered 5B-09, a private room, introduced herself to Sally, and wrote her name on the whiteboard opposite Sally's bed. She explained the call button and bed controls and put on a pair of compression stockings to help prevent blood clots. "Is there anything else you need now?" Sally shook her head no. She was tired and just wanted to sleep.

Around 2 a.m., Sally felt nauseous, but she was unsure of how to unhook her compression stockings or move her IV. She grabbed her bed pan and caught most of the vomit but not all, and with great embarrassment pushed the call button to call Kristina to clean up.

"I'm terribly sorry, Kristina," Sally said. "I didn't know how to get out of bed with all these tubes and socks."

Kristina showed Sally how the stockings came off easily with Velcro straps and asked Sally to move temporarily to the only chair in the room, trailing her IV tubes. Kristina then changed Sally's bedding.

"This is normal for a flu," Kristina explained. "Don't worry about it. And, don't hesitate to call me if you feel sick again. I'm also going to leave you a larger receptacle. I will come as soon as I can, but if I'm delayed it's only because I have several other sick patients to care for tonight."

Sally got back to sleep about 2:45 a.m. but was not peaceful for long. She felt nauseated again about 4 a.m. and vomited twice more before dawn. It was a miserable night.

Tuesday March 23, 2010, 7:00 a.m.

Dr. Henry Bennett, an internal medicine resident, was conducting morning rounds. Neither Kristina, the outgoing nurse assigned to Sally on 5B, nor Claire Woods, the incoming nurse, were present for rounds. Physicians conducted rounds at various times, so it was hit or miss whether the patient's nurse was free to attend. Dr. Bennett usually rounded on Internal Medicine unit 6A, but because Sally was being boarded on 5B, he had to walk over. He had two other patients in various parts of the hospital, in addition to some on 5B. Not only did this impose a lot of nonproductive walking, it also made predicting his rounding times difficult to specify in advance. More often than not, the floor nurse was busy with something else when he showed up to round.

Dr. Bennett noted that Sally's vital signs included a 101.6-degree fever. In response to his questions, Sally told him she had thrown up three times during the night but did not have diarrhea or any form of bowel movement. Dr. Bennett became concerned that she might have more than a flu; it could be a blockage in the small intestine. He examined Sally's abdomen by first palpating and then listening for bowel sounds. Her abdomen was distended and tender, but he did not hear anything. Often, an intestinal obstruction is associated with a high-pitched bowel sound, but the absence of this sound was not conclusive.

Dr. Bennett ordered a nasogastric (NG) tube, which was inserted through Sally's nose and into her stomach to allow gastric secretions to drain. He also ordered a catheter to be inserted, to measure Sally's urine output, which would be another data point in the diagnosis. Finally, Dr. Bennett consulted Sally's electronic medical record, which only contained the ambiguous CT reading. He called Radiology to see if there were any updates, now that more senior staff were on duty. The Radiology tech promised Dr. Bennett that somebody would get back to him shortly.

Twenty minutes later, Dr. Bennett received a page to call Dr. Claudia Perez in Radiology.

"This is a really bad image," Claudia explained. "I think it is moderately likely that she has a small bowel obstruction with associated volvulus, although the image is not conclusive and clinical correlation is definitely warranted."

Dr. Bennett asked the daytime charge nurse, Allan Ruell, to request a general surgery consult, explaining that there was an outside chance Sally had an obstruction.

Shortly before 10:30 a.m., the General Surgery resident Leon Pearson arrived and interviewed Sally. In a private consultation afterward, he agreed with Dr. Bennett that an obstruction was a definite possibility. But the flu diagnosis remained persistent in people's minds, and Dr. Pearson believed that flu was still the most likely diagnosis. In any case, he had checked, and the day's surgery schedule was full. The earliest any surgery could happen without a major schedule disruption would be much later in the day. In addition, the entire surgery team was changing that evening. Because Leon would not be on service after today, he would pass the information about Sally to the new team in the 7 p.m. handoff. He felt it prudent to leave Sally to the new team, which could offer continuous care and make the call for surgery if necessary.

During the day, the nursing team on 5B recorded that Sally had a continued low fever of 101.4 degrees and an increase in pulse from 88 to 118 BPM. Drainage output from the NG tube was 400 cc for an 8-hour shift, and urine output was 15–20 cc per hour. Sally seemed less nauseous, which suggested the NG tube was making a difference. Satisfied that she was making progress, the nursing team focused on other patients.

Shortly after 7 p.m., the surgical shift change took place. Leon Pearson handed off Sally to the incoming resident, Joanne Chandler.

"I'm following a patient in 5B-09, a Mrs. Oldham, with possible gastroenteritis or small bowel obstruction. She was stable the last time I saw her, and the floor team is apprised of the situation, so I am sure they will call if anything unusual happens tonight. We'll get her into the OR tomorrow and have a look."

Joanne, who had a busy night ahead of her, interpreted this to mean that no visit to Sally was required unless she heard from the floor that there was a problem.

Wednesday March 24, 2010, 6:07 a.m.

After another uncomfortable night, Sally was awakened by a phlebotomist who had come for a blood sample. At 8:15 a.m., Dr. Bennett visited her on his morning rounds. The lab readings of WBC 22,000, BUN 41, and Cr 1.8 were worse than yesterday. Sally had become *oliguric* (low urine output), which he knew could be a sign of dehydration, renal or multiple organ failure, obstructions, or infections—a worrisome sign. Finally, his examination showed Sally's abdomen to be more distended and tender; she reported a pain level of 8 on a 10-point scale. Concerned even more than before that Sally's condition might be the result of a blockage, he called General Surgery again.

A little after 10:30 a.m., Joanne Chandler visited Sally in 5B-09, reviewed her charts, and consulted with Dr. Bennett. She agreed that an obstruction was now likely enough to warrant surgery and said she would put Sally on the schedule as soon as she could. She felt, but did not say, that Dr. Pearson should have lobbied to get Sally into the operating room (OR) the previous day, but she understood the administrative difficulties that implied and understood the uncertain nature of the diagnosis at that point.

Joanne called the main OR scheduling desk but was told that all ORs were currently in use and a full elective schedule had already been listed. Joanne protested, but the schedulers were always making judgment calls about when to disrupt schedule, and the ambiguity around Sally's condition tipped the decision toward scheduling her after the last elective surgery was scheduled to close at 5:00 p.m. Joanne called Dr. Bennett with the news, who informed Sally of the planned surgery. Sally, in turn, called her sister-in-law.

"Lucy, I'm going into surgery this afternoon at 5. I had a bad night, and I guess they are worried enough to want to look at something." Lucy immediately began planning how to arrange her life so she could be there.

Joanne also called her attending surgeon, Dr. Ranier, who was on call and would be performing Sally's surgery with Joanne as first assist. Dr. Ranier had plans for the evening and was not pleased that he would be delayed. This had been a frequent occurrence lately, and he was extremely frustrated.

I did not go into this profession to give up my family and personal life, he thought as he hung up the phone. He went to look for his wife to tell her the news, holding out some hope that they could still enjoy the evening. "This is exploratory," he told her. "It might be nothing, and anyway a 5:00 surgery could easily be complete by 7:00, so let's not cancel our plans yet."

The after-hours surgery process was started with calls to an on-call anesthesiologist and a team of surgical nurses, all of whom were informed that they would need to come in for Sally's late procedure. Nobody was pleased about this.

Wednesday March 24, 2010 10:00 a.m.

A patient, Paul Roscoe, was transferred to 5B from the Intensive Care unit (ICU). As a result, Allan Ruell again had a full unit. However, he expected five to seven patients to be discharged later that day.

"Maybe there is light at the end of this tunnel," he confided to Claire Woods, one of his best nurses.

Allan was getting tired of fighting with the ED and bed management people. The ED managers, in particular, accused the nurses on 5B of "hiding" beds that were really available, causing patients to back up in the ED hallways and wait room because nobody could move upstairs. Allan knew there were times when the bed management database was not updated immediately upon a discharge, but that was not deliberate. He was managing patients as well as his charge nurse duties and could not do ten things at once. The ED team was not sympathetic and occasionally threatened to just send patients up on gurneys. "I'll bet you will find beds faster if these patients were in your hallways and not ours," was one common remark. They had not made good on this threat, however, knowing that patients are not well served by being used as political footballs.

Lab reports were delivered to the unit by 9:00 a.m., providing valuable information on each patient's status. By 11:00 a.m. Wednesday, rounds were complete, and Allan was delighted to learn that four patients were cleared for discharge. He would soon start the paperwork in concert with the discharge planners. Family members would be coming to receive home-care instructions and then take the patients home. Allan hoped that these beds would be empty and the rooms cleaned by early afternoon.

These hopes were only partially realized. By 1:00 p.m., there were still three patients cleared for discharge, with paperwork complete, who remained in their beds.

"What's the holdup with 5 and 12, Mr. O'Connell and Ms. LeFarge?" he asked the discharge coordinator.

"They have no place to go," she explained. "Mr. O'Connell is homeless, and Ms. LeFarge does not have family members who can deal with her needs. Social Work has been notified, and we are waiting for a resolution."

"Has the ride for room 5B-16 arrived yet?"

"No. His wife cannot get off work to pick him up until after 5:00."

"Great!" Allan thought to himself, "He was supposed to be one of my easy discharges. Now I won't have that bed until 6:00 or later!"

At 3:47 p.m., Allan heard a nurse on the phone talking about Paul Roscoe, the patient he had accepted earlier that day. Paul had been operated on for pancreatic cancer.

"We see blood in his intra-abdominal drains, and he has become hypotensive."

After hanging up, she explained that Mr. Roscoe's initial postoperative recovery was smooth. However, today, his second postoperative day, they saw blood in his drains, and she just paged Dr. Emma Payne, the surgical resident who performed his procedure with Dr. LeMaster. Dr. Payne was on the way up.

When Dr. Payne arrived, she determined that Paul was hemorrhaging internally and that he needed to be returned to the OR emergently. Allan knew that Mr. Roscoe would go to the PACU or ICU post-operatively. So, although this is not the way he wanted it, he could see getting another bed before the end of the afternoon. He also knew, however, that eventually he was likely to get another bed request for Mr. Roscoe, as he was stepped down from intensive to regular care.

Meanwhile, Sally was getting psychologically prepared for her surgery. Her sister-in-law Lucy and brother (Lucy's husband) Mark arrived around 4 p.m. to be with Sally before she left for the OR. They had, somewhat nervously, left their own children and Sally's son Charlie with Mark and Sally's parents. Sally was gracious in thanking them for being there, but it was apparent that she was in considerable pain. Lucy and Mark tried to distract her by talking about pleasant family matters, but as time passed Lucy grew restless. At 4:45 p.m. Lucy went down the hall to the nurse's station to inquire about what was going on.

"My sister was scheduled for a 5 p.m. surgery," she said. "But no one has come for her or done anything to prepare her."

Allan said he would get an update and let them know. A half hour later, Sally's internal medicine resident Dr. Bennett came to the room.

"I'm sorry Sally," he said. "Some of the operations before you ran long. And now there are some emergencies ahead of you. So it might be a couple more hours before they get you in. They are moving as rapidly as they can."

What neither Dr. Bennett nor Sally and her family knew was that another reason for Sally's surgery delay, in addition to Paul Roscoe's emergency, was the lack of a place for her to go afterward. Hospital policy was not to begin a procedure until there was a PACU or an ICU bed available. So Sally, Lucy, and Mark waited.

By the time his shift ended, Allan had turned only three beds, and the ED and bed managers were, as usual, complaining. During the shift change, nurses on the outgoing shift pass patient-relevant information to the incoming shift in a process called *shift report*. This usually exacerbated the blockage of flows onto the floor because, during this time, nurses were too busy to learn the stories of admitted patients and begin their care. They had tried parallel processing admissions with shift reports, but that was too fractured and distracting, resulting in important information being missed in shift reports, and some serious incidents had resulted. Reports were now done in a less distracted context, but admissions had to wait.

"Maybe tomorrow will be better," thought Allan, as he handed the reins over to Safiya Rana for the night shift.

Wednesday March 24, 2010, 7:30 p.m.

After the shift change, things went smoothly, for once. Some of the patients originally targeted for 5B were boarded elsewhere, and some of the delayed discharges were eventually cleared from their rooms. Safiya actually had one available bed! But this did not last long. At 7:37 p.m., she received a call from bed management.

"Can you board an intensive surgery patient? The PACU and ICU are full, and this is an emergent case."

"You know we staff down at night!" Safiya replied, "And we don't have all the equipment we need."

"I know, but you've got the best team for this patient. We're full up in the ICU and PACU. In addition to the emergent cases already in surgery, we had some readmits. We had a case that we thought was downgraded to a regular bed, but the patient got violent and sick and is now back with us in restraints. He can't go back to a floor unit. We need beds here, badly, and are delaying some surgeries until we find them. We've been looking for somebody who maybe can be transferred out. We identified this patient as being the safest. But, this is like air traffic control, you know."

Safiya knew; she was a 20-year veteran of the hospital. She reluctantly agreed to take the patient onto her unit and put him in the one empty bed she had. Materiel Services brought in some mobile equipment, and Safiya asked for another ICU-trained nurse so she could offer ICU-level attention. Everything worked well, except the oxygen sensor on the patient's finger kept tripping its alarm for no good reason. This was common in all the rooms and something that the nurses had lived with for a long time.

Meanwhile, Sally Oldham was waiting and in pain. It was 8:30 p.m. before the transport techs came to take Sally to pre-op. Safiya watched the techs roll Sally down the hall to the elevators with Lucy and Mark walking along side her.

Lucy and Mark, by now extremely frustrated with the delays, stayed with her right up to the double doors leading to the preparation area. There, they said their goodbyes.

"See you soon," said Lucy, "I know you will be feeling a lot better!" Sally did her best to smile as Lucy squeezed her hand in encouragement and Mark, in a rare show of affection for his big sister, kissed her on the forehead.

Wednesday March 24, 2010 10:57 p.m.

Safiya received another call from bed management. "We're sending over that ICU patient," she explained. "That bed we needed to free up here? It will be filled by a very sick, potentially dying patient…not a good day." Safiya understood and took steps to get ready for her new boarder.

3.2 Introduction to Nursing Units

3.2.1 History of Nursing

Nursing means to care for or tend, as when trying to cure or treat an ailing person. However, this definition applies to the activities of physicians as well as nurses. In practice, nursing in U.S. hospitals is differentiated from physicians' practices along several dimensions. Nursing refers to the continuous care of patients on the floor, in contrast with the more episodic diagnose-and-prescribe nature of a physician's activities. Nurses have professional degrees but do not hold medical doctorates (MDs) or Doctorates of Osteopathy (DOs) and thus do not have the same level of authority to prescribe and treat that physicians have. The boundaries of a nurse's responsibility and authority are a continual topic of debate that is centrally relevant to modern cost-effective health care but one that also bears the imprint of history. The development of the nursing profession has been greatly affected by larger social events, such as wars and the women's and labor movements. Reviewing this history informs many current issues faced by nurses and nursing units in modern hospitals.

The earliest practices of medicine were a mixture of mysticism, empirical observation, and rational thought. The ebb and flow of rationalism and mysticism throughout history went in both directions. It started with early priest-healers in Egypt (2000 B.C.), progressed to the Greek rational school of Hippocrates (460–370 B.C.), and regressed due to the loss of classical knowledge and intellectual stagnation in Western Europe in the Middle Ages. A reintroduction of this knowledge to Western Europe was made possible after the Crusades by the preservation of Greek texts and medical knowledge in Arabic and Byzantine capitals. The history of nursing inherits this rich religio-scientific drama and intertwines evolving cultural issues like the role of women in society and perceived class differentials after the Industrial Revolution. The following brief history of nursing draws heavily from Kalisch and Kalisch (1995) and Chitty (2001).

The hospital as a central location for patient care is a relatively modern phenomenon. During most of history, the continuous care of patients was largely in the hands of family and friends in an informal system of caring and healing. However, religious orders also established and staffed hospitals for the poor, sick, or displaced. Between 1000 and 1300 A.D., monks and Crusaders set up and operated hospitals for pilgrims to the Holy Land who had fallen ill. One of the most famous, named after St. John, was also the catalyst for a nursing-soldiering order, the Knights Hospitalers of St. John of Jerusalem. The Knights Hospitalers and another order, the Knights Templars, became the finest fighting forces in the Crusades, but the Hospitalers retained as part of their mission caring for their wounded brethren. Women formed a related female order, the Hospitaler Dames of the Order of St. John of Jerusalem, and established many additional hospitals to care for the sick and wounded. This represented a common theme in the history of women in nursing—the desire to support their cause in warfare but being culturally prevented from fighting on the front lines. As a result, women frequently contributed in a healing capacity. The importance of these early hospitals was to give order and structure to the ancient tradition, found in many religions, of helping the needy (Gordon 2005). A by-product of these organized health centers was the evolution of hospital practice.

During the ensuing centuries, hospitals were built across Europe, with patient care handled by men and women of various religious orders. In the twelfth century, women midwives trained at a famous medical school in Salerno, beginning a more formal, institutional context for the practice of nursing. Between the sixteenth and nineteenth centuries, various women's religious orders were formed under both Catholic and Protestant banners dedicated to patient care; the famous Sisters of Charity was founded in Paris in 1633. The first step toward the professionalization of nursing was the establishment of training programs to address the highly variable quality of hospital staff. The Kaiserwerth School in Germany (founded in 1836) featured standard courses of instruction that disseminated current best practices with the goal of reducing arbitrariness in patient care.

The modern nursing profession took a leap forward through the efforts of Florence Nightingale of Britain, born in 1820. Nightingale resisted her family's pressure to marry into society and consistently pursued an interest in nursing, spending time with the Sisters of Charity during a family vacation, and attending the nursing school at Kaiserwerth. She was involved in a variety of nursing activities in England when the Crimean War (1853–1856) broke out pitting Britain, France, and Turkey against Russia for control of the Black Sea. London newspaper accounts of atrocious conditions in hospitals for casualties of the war prompted England's Secretary of War to ask Nightingale to go direct women nurses in the Crimea. She accepted the charge and took a cadre of 39 women to the Barrack Hospital in Scutari. Designed to accommodate 1,700 patients, the Barrack Hospital housed 3000–4000 patients in squalor when Nightingale arrived. Through shear tenacity, and against the resistance of the army bureaucracy and surgeon antipathy, Nightingale redesigned diet and sanitary standards and brought a learned but comforting tone to patient care. Numerous accounts from patients attest to their admiration for her tireless efforts, and by the time the war ended and Nightingale returned to England, mortality had declined from 60% to just over 1% in the hospital.

In England, Nightingale established a school for nurses, again against physician opposition, and wrote several treatises on nursing and hospital administration that are still read today. Her innovation in compiling statistical data on the outcomes of patients was revolutionary; she was the first female invited to join the Royal College of Statistics. Her techniques to measure *iatrogenic mortality* (deaths inadvertently caused by treatments or diagnostics) remain the gold standard to this day.

Some common historical themes are represented in Nightingale's efforts. Nurses wished to professionalize their activities but were resisted by doctors and hospitals in the medical establishment. Nurses wanted the greater consistency and higher-quality patient outcomes that one would expect with professional training, but they also wanted the higher wages and better working conditions that they felt would accompany that training. Doctors were concerned that increased nursing education could blur the professional boundaries between nursing and medical work and lead to nurses making decisions beyond their training. Also, more educated and empowered nurses could threaten the status of physicians. Hospital administrators wanted highly trained professionals for good patient outcomes, but they also wanted lower wages for their largest workforce, so they would resist any training that they felt was beyond the level necessary. Much of the work of continuous patient care is routine, and the administrators did not want to over pay for it.

Another theme in the Nightingale story that parallels the evolution of nursing in general is the role of wars as major punctuation points socially and professionally. Wars took many men out of the workforce. They were replaced by women who, by performing admirably, eroded cultural resistance to women in professional jobs. In hospitals, perhaps because in wartime men were fighting and women were healing, nursing in America became a predominantly female profession. The carnage of war forces attention to healing by whatever means possible, eroding resistance to an expanded role for nurses that is based on non-health-related motives. However, the patriotic zeal of war nurses was not always matched by training and expertise, leading to a variable quality of care.

In the United States during the Civil War (1861–1865), close to 10,000 women, including the Sisters of Charity and nuns of various orders, served as nurses to the sick and wounded. Louisa May Alcott wrote a short book, *Hospital Sketches*, based on her experiences as a Union army volunteer nurse in a military hospital. Many Civil War nurses were poorly trained and assigned to do menial work for male nurses and physicians. However, several alumni of this experience worked after the war to establish nursing schools to increase the quality of nurse training and practice. The Civil War resulted in both greater public acceptance of female nursing and the beginnings of professional nurse training in the United States.

Many of the early pioneers of American professional nurse training visited, at one time or another, Florence Nightingale and her colleagues in Europe, who continued to work to establish a nursing profession both at home and abroad. An early nursing school in New York was modeled after Nightingale's famous St. Thomas' Hospital in London. The model included an intense apprenticeship program, whereby student nurses staffed the units under the supervision of a senior nurse. The first American school for nursing was founded in New England in 1872 and graduated its first professionally trained nurse in 1873. More professional schools followed, despite continued opposition from the medical profession. A rise in demand for nurses paralleled the rise in building of community hospitals in the latter part of the nineteenth century. A large hospital at that time could not be successful without an affiliated training school for nurses, because the trainees did most of the work and were not paid very well. Trained nurses typically left the hospital to be home nurses in the employ of wealthy families, to be replaced by new (poorly paid) trainees. These forces, and the limited alternatives for professional women, contributed to the explosive growth of nursing schools.

In the nineteenth and twentieth centuries, these warfare-punctuated dynamics were joined by the social winds of the Industrial Revolution in America. In broad strokes, the Industrial Revolution expanded the number of wage earners dependent on a company rather than a farm for subsistence and accelerated the urbanization of America as workers moved to live closer to factories. However, the working conditions for large numbers of unskilled men, women, and children in the urban manufacturing centers of the late nineteenth century were appalling by modern standards. Because their work was routine, they could be replaced at a moment's notice provided there was surplus labor available. Steady waves of immigration and continued migration to cities assured that supply. Factory laborers worked long hours at physically demanding jobs for wages that were driven down, by competition for the job, to subsistence levels. Muckraking exposés in the 1920s of the working and living conditions of this "other half" of society catalyzed a trend of legislative protection for the health and safety of children and other workers. By that time, however, workers had already begun to organize to attain in aggregate what they could not attain alone—some power in their relationship to the factory owners. The growth of labor unions was slow and difficult, opposed at first by the U.S. government. However, unions gained legitimacy as the worst management excesses came under public scrutiny.

These social dynamics intersect nursing history in several places. First, hospitals depended on nurses for patient care, but the limited economic options for women meant they could be hired at low cost. At the end of the nineteenth century, nurses still had rigid boundaries on what they could do and were at all times to obey physician authority without question. Aspiring nurses working as "probationers" in hospitals were asked to do the most menial tasks over long hours, seven days a week. With the mixed motives already mentioned, the drive for professionalism and stature in nursing was opposed at first by the American Medical Association (AMA, founded in 1847) and the American Hospital Association (founded in 1899). At the risk of oversimplifying some complex historical dynamics, the major parties had conflicting objectives: Hospitals wanted low-cost labor, doctors wanted to limit competition, and nurses wanted higher wages and job security. Intuitively, one can associate nurses with labor, and hospitals and doctors with management, in the early twentieth century.

Eventually, cultural changes in the twentieth century, including increased opportunities for women and a rise in the divorce rate without social stigma, gave women more options for economic independence. This, in turn, meant more women in the workplace, leading to more care in hospitals than at home and an increased demand for nurses. Hospitals had to compete for women employees with other female-friendly professions, such as education, endowing nurses with some bargaining power.

Whenever wages were not sufficient to compensate nurses for their hard-working conditions, a nursing shortage followed. In 1946, the average starting salary for a staff nurse was $35.75 for a 48-hour week. Bookkeepers and seamstresses were paid more per hour, and typists made a little less. Finally, although registered nurses had achieved the status of a "professional," they were often not treated as such by doctors or administrators in hospitals. Hospital nurses perceived themselves as working under more rigid discipline than women in other occupations. Women returning from war nurse duties often did not stay in the profession, citing job conditions and salary. Having had real responsibility as a military nurse, they did not want to go back to a subservient role.

These events placed many nurses philosophically closer to workers than to managers in economic and philosophical terms. This, together with their intimate familiarity with the working poor, made them more receptive to socially egalitarian movements such as labor unions early in the century, New Deal legislation in 1935, and Medicare in 1965. For example, the AMA was against any use of Social Security to finance the health needs of the aged, but the American Nursing Association (ANA) was in favor of it. In 1959, an *American Journal of Nursing* editorial titled "Taking a Stand" hypothesized that these differences of opinion were because nurses were closer to families on a day-to-day basis and knew that many had no way of paying for high medical bills. Nurses, having low salaries themselves, shared the sense of personal vulnerability prevalent in the general population.

These status differentials between physicians and nurses led to different tactics in forwarding their profession. In 1955, the average gross monthly starting salary for a general duty nurse was $253, below that of a teacher, librarian, or other alternative professions then available to women. In 1966, approximately 2,000 nurses in 33 San Francisco Bay area hospitals resigned during a salary dispute, which began a series of battles over the right of nurses to organize and strike. In 1973, the ANA, fearing that if they did not act swiftly other labor organizations would organize nurses in their place, started a drive to organize the nation's 800,000 registered nurses. All the familiar arguments for and against unions were raised, and nurses themselves were divided over the benefits of organizing. Currently, less than a third of the nation's nurses are organized (in a variety of different organizations). In February 2009, the United American Nurses, the California Nurses Association/National Nurses Organizing Committee, and the Massachusetts Nurses Association merged into a national organization, the 150,000 member United American Nurses-National Nurses Organizing Committee, UAN-NNOC (AFL-CIO), hoping to gain more negotiating power.

Estimates about the nursing fraction of total hospital costs vary widely, from as low as 10% to as high as 40%, due to the variety of hospital types and accounting methods. By any measure, however, nursing costs are a significant portion of a hospital's inpatient costs. The current macroeconomic health care climate of budgetary pressures and increases in the ranks of the uninsured drive some important workplace issues for nurses. Current cost pressures drive demands for higher nurse case loads. In parallel, uninsured patients often delay their care and then arrive at the hospital with more acute conditions. This, and a trend toward more outpatient therapy when appropriate, means that nurses today are required to treat more, sicker patients. Several nurse surveys indicate that short-staffing leading to work overload is a major source of nurse dissatisfaction (c.f. Aiken et al. 2001; Davidson et al. 1997, Shader et al. 2001, Shaver and Lacey 2003). Nurses consistently report that higher workloads decrease the quality of the technical and psychosocial care they are able to provide to patients and families. Finally, hospitals cannot go idle on nights and weekends, and unstable work schedules (such as mandatory late shifts or weekends) can negatively impact satisfaction (Shader et al. 2001). It is well known that job satisfaction and turnover are correlated, so an increase in nurse dissatisfaction will increase nurse turnover and career changes. Although nursing wages have risen to competitive levels in many places, a significant number of trained nurses (over 500,000 by one estimate) do not work in nursing, suggesting the ongoing barriers nurses perceive in clinical practice.

In the 1980s, motivated by a desire to stem nursing vacancy and promote continuity of care, Dr. Joyce Clifford, nurse-in-chief of the Beth Israel Hospital in Boston, implemented a series of reforms that established a standard for professional hospital nursing practice. With the support of her chief executive officer, Clifford only hired nurses with a bachelor's degree, assigned primary nurses who held 24-hour accountability for patient care, and revolutionized admission flows so patients were placed on units where their primary nurses were located. Numerous studies have documented positive nurse and patient outcomes from this model of care (Clifford, 1990; Aiken, et al. 2001, 2002, 2003; Rosenstein 2002, Gordon 2005).

In the 1990s, however, hospitals essentially abandoned these reforms to cut costs (Weinberg 2003). Many of these changes were championed by consultants but lacked an evidence base, and some hospitals lost—rather than earned—money as a result (Walston, Burns, and Kimberly, 2000). It was also during this time that the staffing, educational preparation, and working conditions of nurses were linked empirically to patient outcomes (Aiken, et al. 2002; Aiken, et al. 2003; Friese, et al. 2008; Needleman, et al. 2002). This period in hospital administration amplified historical tension between administrators (cost) and nurses (wages) with patient care in the balance.

Today's nurses perform the hard, essential work of continuous patient care in hospitals, with shifting boundaries of authority and a range of working relationships relative to medical doctors. Nursing care still has to be provided overnight and on weekends, sick patients are still physically and emotionally taxing, and nurses in general have limited authority relative to doctors. Cost containment efforts have put increased stress on everybody working in the health care industry. Management perceives unionized nurses as inflexible, not without some cause, but nurses know well how hospitals treated them when they had little power. The challenge today is to manage the patient units with nurses as the primary caregivers in a way that responds to the need to contain costs

and provide quality patient care, with working conditions that are sufficiently rewarding to keep nurses on the job.

The future is uncertain. Hospital care increased relative to home care after the Industrial
Revolution for the reasons stated earlier. However, given the costly nature of hospital
infrastructure and a trend toward outpatient therapy, the increasing patient concentration
in hospitals may not be permanent. Despite her dedication to the improvement of patient
care in hospitals, Florence Nightingale had a different vision for the future of nursing:

> My view, you know, is that the ultimate destination of all nursing is the nursing
> of the sick in their homes...I look to the abolition of all hospitals...But no use
> to talk about the year 2000.
>
> —Florence Nightingale 1867

3.2.2 Assets

The nursing unit is one of the places in the hospital where hands actually touch patients.
All the decision-making and clinical paths, all the planning and budgeting activities in
these complex organizations, are ultimately support activities for these all-important
personal transactions where the social value of a hospital is delivered. The assets used in
this delivery include the physical unit itself and the nurses, doctors, specialists, and technicians who interact with the patient. The dominant organization of these assets is for
the patient to occupy a bed in a nursing unit, with continual care by nurses and cyclical
visits by physicians, specialists, and technicians (Exhibit 3.1).

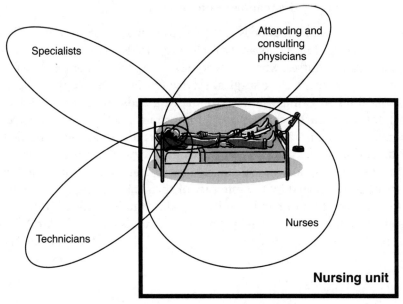

Exhibit 3.1   Visit cycles on a nursing unit.

3.2.2.1 PHYSICAL ASSETS: THE NURSING UNIT

A nursing unit in a modern hospital (in a developed country) looks more like a special-purpose hotel than the large open wards of Florence Nightingale's time. Although Ms. Nightingale's reforms were patient-centric in their day, they would hardly be viewed as such today. In her time, wealthy patients were cared for at home, so only the poor or soldiers at war went to hospitals. Economically and logistically, large numbers of patients had to be placed in close proximity to scarce caregivers. Today, concerns for privacy, the spread of infection, and attention to the patient experience have shifted hospital nursing units toward designs based on private or semiprivate rooms that are designed to reduce stress for patients and staff. Modern patient-centrism finds a strong voice in the design philosophy of the Planetree Alliance (started by Angelica Thieriot in 1978, c.f. the Planetree website), which stresses "human touch" relationships among caregivers, patient, and family; access to complete information; architectural designs that are functional but also welcoming and comfortable; and expanded attention to the arts, spiritual nourishment, and options for alternative therapies. Windows are an important feature for day/night orientation and emotional well-being. Color accents or artwork are chosen to promote rest and calm.

The appropriate architecture for the future of health care delivery is evolving along with advances in technology (telemedicine), economics (reducing costs), and changing demographics (an aging population and the associated care challenges). In the United States, these trends are evolving in a context of partial competition, fostered by some amount of patient choice. In this competitive landscape, different market segmentation strategies suggest different room designs from those that focus on low cost to those meant to support a luxury destination health program.

Despite these changes, inpatient beds are still predominantly organized using the nursing unit as its basic module. Units are typically organized so that patients will pose similar care challenges to nurses, who can then develop special expertise. Most often, this means organizing by medical or surgical service (such as Oncology or Neurosurgical units). A typical nursing unit will have rooms with beds and bathrooms for patients; nurses' stations where nurses can perform administrative duties, communicate with off-unit personnel and monitor the patient rooms; a storage area for often-needed supplies and pharmaceuticals and a private space for conferencing. Each bed will have monitoring equipment and call/alarm capabilities appropriate for its intended occupant. Patients are often segregated by the intensity of their monitoring requirements, which increase from observation to regular units, step-down units, and ICUs. Table 3.1 summarizes some common design objectives for nursing units (adapted from Miller, R. and E. Swensson. *Hospital and Healthcare Facility Design*. WW Norton and Co., NY, 2002).

Table 3.1

Patient needs	Nurses and floor staff needs	Physicians needs

Cleanliness
Security
Privacy, peace and quiet
Dignity
Access to bathroom and shower
Sense of being observed in case help is needed
Isolation from other patients, when required
Company of other patients, when appropriate
Interesting area for ambulation, diversion and entertainment
Easy access to nurse's call signal, phone, lighting, bed and television controls
Accessible place for personal belongings
Accommodation for visitors
Aesthetic, pleasing environment with good glare-free lighting, outside view
	Line of vision from nurses' station
	    Easy access to patients
	    Ability to see patients
	    Minimize walking distances
	Access to patient information, "knowing what is going on"
	Ability to communicate with patients, caregivers and other departments
	Ability to move beds, equipment, supplies in and out of rooms as appropriate
	Ability to accommodate different approaches to staffing (e.g. team vs primary)
	Ability to work with changes in acuity levels
	Ability to work effectively day or night
	Access to high usage medications, supplies and other needs
	Easy disposal of supplies as appropriate
	Ability to confer privately
	Access to lounge, and conference space
	Security
		Patients and information easy to find
		Spaces to confer privately, or for private dictation
		Proper equipment
		Access to clerical support
		Sufficient space to support team care, if appropriate

Visitors and family members needs	General therapeutic needs	General logistical needs
Easy access and wayfinding Access to information Privacy for conversations with staff and patients Designated restrooms	The nursing unit should be a healing environment that reduces anxiety and confusion. The unit should provide for infection control, e.g. accommodate the isolation of soiled material, and frequent hand-washing.	The nursing unit must be designed to support transportation of patients to and from the floor, and the cyclical activities of doctors, phlebotomists and other technicians to and from the bedside.

This chapter focuses on the most important physical and human assets on the unit: the beds and nurses. Beds fall into four main categories:

- **ICU**—An ICU (Intensive Care unit) is designed for the most fragile patients, requiring the highest levels of continuous monitoring and care. Nurses staffing the ICU are specialists in critical care. Separate ICUs are often used for different types of patients (medical, surgical, pediatric, neonatal, coronary, or burn) because differential knowledge is required and patients can be in proximity to the appropriate service upon leaving the ICU. Similar to an ICU is a PACU (Post Anesthesia Care unit), where patients may need to go after a surgical procedure for pain management, stabilization of vital signs, and recovery from the effects of anesthesia. Like the ICU, the PACU is staffed by specialists in critical care and features high levels of monitoring. The nurse/patient ratio is usually highest in ICUs.

- **Step-down**—A step-down bed is a transition place between the ICU and the standard level of care in a regular hospital bed, and contains an intermediate level of staffing and monitoring. For example, patients with stable but irregular heart rhythms or patients who require long-term mechanical ventilation may be placed here. The nurse/patient ratio in a step-down unit is between that for the ICU and general care bed.

- **General care bed**—This is the familiar hospital bed, typically situated in a nursing unit occupying a floor or part of a floor in the hospital. Beds can be private with a single patient in the room, or semiprivate with two or four patients per room and retractable curtains around beds for privacy. A daytime patient-to-nurse ratio of 4 to 1 is typical in larger hospitals, but ratios will vary with hospital, clinical complexity, and time of day.

- **Observation bed**—Sometimes it is not clear whether a patient should be admitted to the hospital or sent home for home care, and a waiting period or tests are required before a decision is made. These patients, not yet officially admitted to the hospital, can stay in observation status beds, which feature lower levels of monitoring and care. The average stay will be about one day only, before the patient is either admitted or discharged. Observation units are often wards (with multiple beds in one room) and feature higher patient/nurse ratios than elsewhere in the hospital.

The total bed inventory in a hospital may also include various types of specialty beds (such as telemetry beds with heart monitors, stroke beds, and psychiatric beds). There may be some negative pressure rooms (isolation rooms) with ventilators that draw air out to prevent cross-contamination of other rooms by airborne contagions.

Allocating admitted patients to units, rooms, and beds is a crucial activity in any hospital, because it matches patient needs with floor expertise and it can be a patient flow bottleneck. This activity is complicated by the mix of private and semiprivate rooms covered by insurance or appropriate for care, possible uncertainty in the appropriate service for the clinical needs of patients, cross-infection issues, and the desire not to mix genders or dramatic age differences in the same room.

3.2.2.2 Human Assets

The people who "live" on the nursing units are primarily the nurses and the patients, with some administrators. Other important stakeholders (physicians, specialty consultants and surgeons, technicians) cycle through the floors to see the patients, and transportation techs handle the transport of patients to and from the floors.

Nurses

As hospitals have evolved, so has nurse training. The first nursing programs in the United States, set up in the latter half of the nineteenth century, were affiliated with hospitals and lasted one year in length. The primary reason for their existence was to staff the hospitals that supported them. By 1900, there were 432 hospital-owned nursing schools in the United States, with courses of study differing in length from 6 months to 2 years, and each school set its own standards (Chitty 2001). These diploma programs, which peaked from 1920–1930, followed an apprenticeship model where trainees worked in the hospital first and took classes after work. Nurse trainees essentially ran the day-to-day aspects of the hospital. But, in part because the primary reason for their existence (in some hospitals) was for labor rather than education, the training programs were of highly variable quality.

In 1903, North Carolina was the first state in the union to register nurses who had completed a training course. Beginning in 1905, nurses also had to pass a licensing examination to register (Johnson 2004). Although each state's board of nursing sets the explicit criteria by which a nurse can be registered in that state, common themes include completion of an accredited nursing program and passage of the National Council Licensing Examination for Registered Nurses (NCLEX-RN) or for Practical Nurses (NCLEX-PN). The National Council of State Boards of Nursing develops and supervises these examinations. However, licensure is still state specific, so if nurses relocate they must follow state-specific procedures to transfer their licenses.

One of the first major national studies of nursing education, the Goldmark report of 1923, noted the diversity of quality and mixed incentives in hospital-based diploma programs and recommended that schools of nursing affiliate with universities. The first Baccalaureate degree in nursing in the United States was established in 1909 at the University of Minnesota, and the Yale School of Nursing (opened in 1924) was the first with its own budget and dean. After the Goldmark report, hospital-based diploma programs lost ground to university-based training. In the 1930s, there were about 2,000 diploma programs in the United States, declining to about 800 by 1960, 300 by 1980, and less than 100 today.

University-based training had its critics. Many doctors and administrators felt that university-based training was too academic, when much of the work was hands-on and had to be learned by actual practice. This was partially addressed by including more clinical practice in nurse training programs. Another problem with a four-year degree program is that it is expensive in time and money for the students, and it injects long lag times into workforce dynamics. In times of severe nursing shortages, the ability of the workforce to rapidly adjust to changing needs was slowed by these frictions in time and money.

Associate degrees in nursing started in 1952, fueled in part by the 2-year community college movement in the 1950s. At first, these were intended to prepare nurse technicians to work under the supervision of a professional nurse, doing much of the bedside or long-care work. However, over time, the associate degree has increased its nursing content and can be used as a stepping stone to the BS degree. Currently, the associate degree is the most common form of training for registered nurses (RNs). In 1998, there were 1,526 basic programs preparing registered nurses in the United States, of which 58.6% were associate degree programs, 34.9% baccalaureate programs, and 6.5% diploma programs. In addition, there were 1,107 practical nursing programs (Chitty 2001).

Administrators and Technicians

A typical nursing hierarchy in a hospital is shown in Exhibit 3.2. Nurses on a unit will be part of a larger nursing organization headed by the director of nursing. Just under the director will be nurse supervisors who are responsible for several units. At the unit level, the nurse manager or head nurse interfaces between the unit and these higher-level administrators.

Nurse Executive or Director of Nursing: Part of the executive team of the hospital, and responsible for all nursing services. The director of nursing participates in strategic and long-range planning and in the design of nursing services. S/he is more actively engaged in planning and organizing than in day-to-day operations.

Nurse Supervisor: Coordinates care over multiple nursing units. The nurse supervisor is responsible for staffing on a day-to-day basis.

Nurse Manager or Head Nurse: Responsible for the day-to-day operations of one or more nursing units. The head nurse is primarily responsible for the delivery and evaluation of patient care, and also acts as a communication link between the units' nurses and upper levels of management.

Charge Nurse: Duties vary but usually include handling the administrative end of admits and discharges, as well as generally helping out where needed. Is usually an RN, often rounds with physicians, and sometimes assigns nurses to patients at the start of each shift. Sometimes the charge nurse also has patients, but in other cases is 100% administration and support.

Staff Nurse: Directly gives care to patients and maintains patients' records, often rotating through day, evening, and night shifts. There are several types of staff nurse:
> APN-Advanced Practice Nurses are registered nurses (RNs) who have one or two years of advanced training. Specialties include clinical nurse specialists, nurse practitioners and certified practical nurses.
> RN = registered nurse, the basic nursing degree
> LVN = licensed vocational nurse

UAP = Unlicensed Assistive Personnel, also known as nurse's aids, orderlies, patient care technicians, nurse extenders, certified nursing assistants (CNAs), and other titles. UAPs carry out routine activities under the supervision of a registered nurse. The use of UAPs for routine tasks lowers the labor cost structure in the hospital, and can free up RN time for higher level patient care.

Exhibit 3.2   Typical nurse hierarchy (c.f. Rowland and Rowland 1997).

In addition to these connections within the nursing community, physicians will rotate through the floors inspecting, diagnosing, and prescribing for patients. Prescribed tests or diagnostic procedures may be performed by nurses or by representatives of specialty services (such as Pathology and Radiology) who rotate through the floors and answer to their own hospital-wide decision hierarchy.

Doctors

Physicians are highly trained professionals who have weathered a long regimen of study starting with pre-med courses in their undergraduate colleges. Exhibit 3.3 shows the steps required to become a doctor in the United States. A doctor may simultaneously care for a number of patients ranging from healthy and at home to acutely ill in hospitals. Consequently, he/she can spend only a small amount of time with each. In a nursing unit, this results in a doctor *doing rounds* where he/she will see all of his/her patients in that location before leaving for other locations (office or another floor, or hospital). During rounds, a doctor will review any relevant information from the nurse(s) and charts and records, visit the patient for a hands-on update, and leave instructions to be followed. So, activities on a nursing unit include cyclical accommodation of rounds and the resulting instructions, in addition to continual patient care.

1. Focus on pre-medical content in undergraduate education: The menu of pre-med coursework usually includes specific courses (e.g. biology or organic chemistry) in which a high grade is recognized as being a key determinant of admission into post-graduate medical schools.

2. Attend an accredited medical school: In the U.S. medical schools are accredited, meaning certifiably maintaining standards, by an accrediting organization. For example, the Liaison Committee on Medical Education (LCME) and American Osteopathic Association (AOA) monitor schools granting Doctor of Medicine (M.D.) and Doctor of Osteopathic Medicine (D.O.) degrees, respectively. Getting into medical school is a very competitive process, because capacity is limited. In medical school, which takes 3 to 4 years, the first two years include basic courses in anatomy, physiology, and biology before moving to a survey-type exposure to a range of medical specialties (e.g. internal medicine, surgery, pediatrics) and types of care (emergency, acute, chronic, and rehabilitative, as well as preventive).

3. Spend 3 to 7 years in residency: After graduating from medical school the student spends three to seven years (depending on their intended specialty) of residency gaining experience by caring for patients in a hospital under the supervision of an "attending" physician (a licensed and experienced doctor who is responsible for a group of residents and their patients). While terms are used loosely and are constantly evolving, doctors-in-training beyond medical school are often known as "house officers" (originating most likely from the fact that they practically live "in house" at the hospital), and among house officers a first-year resident is sometimes called an "intern," while beyond the first year they become "junior residents" until, in their final year of residency they will be "senior" or "chief" residents.

4. Take the licensing examination: The United States Medical Licensing Examination (USMLE) tests aspiring doctors in their understanding of the basic science and practice of medicine. Upon passing all parts of this test, the M.D. is a licensed physician.

5. Become board certified: A "board" is an organization that sets standards for membership, and the best medical boards will require a combination of education, experience and an examination to join. Three well-known boards in the U.S. are the American Board of Medical Specialties (ABMS), American Osteopathic Association (AOA), and American Board of Physician Specialties (ABPS). There are others. Within a board there will be specialties and subspecialties, each with their own requirements. For example, the ABMS currently has 36 specialties (e.g. anesthesiology, dermatology, pediatrics) and 145 subspecialties (e.g. critical care, hospice and palliative care, pain management; dermatopathology, pediatric dermatology; pediatric cardiology, pediatric endocrinology). Maintaining board certification requires some continuing education courses and practical guidelines. Board certification is a signal to the market that the physician has passed further tests beyond licensing, and is remaining current in his/her specialty. The proliferation of boards can weaken this signal, so some customer due diligence is recommended.

Exhibit 3.3   Becoming a doctor.

Thes preceding description of the rounding physician is typical in community hospitals. In teaching hospitals, where medical school graduates (now **residents**, c.f. Exhibit 3.3) are training to become doctors, residents conduct the rounds under the guidance of an attending (licensed and experienced) physician. In some hospitals, doctors are employees rather than in private practice, but periodic rounds are still the norm as they alternate between caring for patients in the hospital and other activities, such as seeing patients "in clinic" for consultations. In research hospitals (many of these are also teaching hospitals), doctors may alternate between rounding, clinic, and research. Doctors certified for surgery have yet another claim on their time.

Several different doctors may be involved in a patient's care. For admitted patients in a hospital bed, there is always an **attending physician** who has primary responsibility for the patient, is available in person or by pager, and to whom nurses appeal for decisions beyond the authority of an RN. The patient may have been admitted to the bed floor on the recommendation of an "admitting" doctor who was responsible for the patient's initial diagnosis. For example, an admitted patient may have her family doctor as the admitting doctor, and a hospitalist physician as the attending doctor. In other cases, the admitting and attending physicians can be the same person. Finally, consulting physicians can be called in to advise on the patient's care or to take over portions of her care. For example, a thoracic surgeon may be called in for suspected lung infections, or a cardiologist for heart arrhythmias, and these individuals will leave their own sets of instructions or schedule procedures for the patient.

Key issues at the intersection of the nursing unit with the (more sporadically present) technicians and doctors include the transfer of information among these groups, the degree to which nurses can act autonomously without doctor approval, and the timing and coordination of rounds with other activities. Any transfer of information from one individual to another usually loses some fidelity en route, so information completeness and accuracy during handoffs is a critical issue on bed floors. This is not restricted to doctor-nurse handoffs during rounding, but also nurse-nurse handoffs or doctor-doctor handoffs during shifts changes or between specialties. There are fewer attending physicians than nurses for each patient, so sometimes critical decisions are delayed because the attending is not available. Deciding which decisions nurses can make without physician approval is a challenge affecting responsiveness, appropriateness, and legal exposure.

Finally, the efficiency of patient care is affected by the timing of physicians' visits. Decisions that update instructions, or clear a patient for discharge, are typically made during rounds, so it is important that the information available at rounding time be as up to date as possible. For example, consider a phlebotomist who draws a patient's blood at 7 a.m. and takes the sample to a lab that processes it and posts a report by 9 a.m. If rounds are at 8 a.m., the rounding physician will not have the most current information, and in fact a report that becomes available at 9 a.m. may remain unread for another 23 hours! Moving the blood draw to 6 a.m. may save an entire day in the decision-making process and potentially the discharge process. In congested hospitals where empty beds in nursing units are at a premium, coordinating the rounding and information flows among the various groups that intersect at bedside can make more efficient use of the nursing unit's (and the hospital's) scarce capacity.

3.2.3 Flows

Exhibit 3.4 shows a patient's flow through the hospital. A patient who arrives to the ED is "undifferentiated" and, once stabilized, requires some analysis to diagnose symptoms, determine whether or not he should be admitted, and if so to which nursing unit. A patient who arrives by transfer or for scheduled surgery has more available data for consideration and his appropriate unit is easier to identify. In congested hospitals, however, there may not be enough beds in the desired unit and a patient assigned to service A (for example, Cardiology) may be placed in a bed in service B (for example, General Medicine). This means that the nurses in B may not be intimately familiar with that patient's issues, and the rounding team from service A must travel to service B to see their patient. In a recent study, hospitalist physicians in a highly utilized hospital spent more than 7% of their time traveling to see patients (Kim et al. 2010).

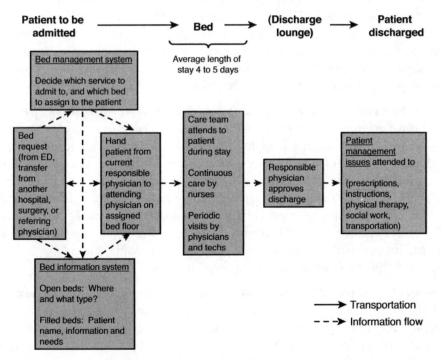

Exhibit 3.4   Patient and information flows.

As noted in the previous section, physicians from the appropriate service and any required diagnostic personnel (phlebotomists to draw blood, radiologists to take X-rays, physical therapists to exercise patients) will rotate through the patient's room as required. Sometimes the patient will be transported to another location for a service (such as MRI, CT-scan, or physical therapy) and then return to bed. Patients may also change locations if they change acuity levels (for example, from ICU to step-down, or to a standard bed), if they were originally admitted to the "wrong" service, or if changes in their diagnosis or condition suggest a service change.

With DRG (diagnostic-related groups, introduced by Medicare in 1983, c.f. Carey 2002) payment schemes, in which the hospital is paid a flat fee for serving a patient with a given diagnosis, there is a strong incentive to treat patients in the lowest-cost setting possible. In particular, there is no incentive to extend a patient's stay unnecessarily, and lengths of stays (LOS) have been declining nationwide. Yet, medically unnecessary delays in discharges do occur, for example due to incomplete paperwork, communication delays, lack of attention or diversion of attention to sicker patients, or social service issues (in some cases a patient has nowhere to go and nobody to take him).

Some delays are the result of rational human reactions to a difficult environment. For example, a patient cleared for discharge is likely to require only low levels of care and attention (he is nearly well, which is why he is ready for discharge), but once that patient is gone, the bed is likely to be filled by a new, sicker patient. It takes a lot of time and energy to understand a new patient's "story" and personality and settle down to a regimen of care. A harried nurse who is already overworked has little incentive to exchange an easy patient for a difficult one and might rationally delay the discharge or delay recording the bed as "empty" and available for a new admission. This is known as *hiding* a bed.

A patient who is ready for discharge but is not released creates three problems. First, the hospital is paying more for the patient than is necessary, which a net loss with DRG payments. Second, if the hospital is highly utilized, bottlenecks in the discharge process limit all patient flows. A failure to release beds in a timely manner can be a primary reason for overcrowding in the ED, delays in getting patients into and out of surgery, and being unable to honor requests for transfers. These in turn can have financial and clinical consequences and decrease patient and staff satisfaction. Finally, hospitals are dangerous places because they are filled with sick people. Keeping a well patient, ready for discharge, longer than necessary increases his chances of contracting a hospital-acquired infection (also known as a *nosocomial* infection).

It is natural for the physical presence of patients to demand attention in a hospital setting, but the "invisible" admissions and discharge process can also significantly affect clinical and financial outcomes. Analyzing any system requires attention to its physical flows, information flows, and human resources. Managing a nursing unit requires the right levels and types of capacity in physical and human assets; appropriate information flows among the nurses, doctors and staff to coordinate those assets; and sufficient incentives for each member of this team to work in the best interests of the system as a whole.

3.3 Managing a Nursing Unit

3.3.1 Performance Metrics

Key metrics on a nursing unit that correspond to the core healing mission of the hospital are clinical compliance and outcome measures. Compliance means conformance to best practices, and outcomes include not just discharge versus death, but safety events (such as falls and medication errors), complications, and emergency visits or readmissions within some specified time period. Some sample clinical metrics are shown in Table 3.2.

Table 3.2   Sample Performance Metrics for a Nursing Unit

Clinical Metrics	Operational Metrics	Financial Metrics	Organizational Metrics
Compliance and Best Practice	*Time*	*Costs*	*Staff Satisfaction*
Adherence to evidence-based care guidelines	Average patient LOS, adjusted for DRG or acuity	Labor cost per patient or patient-day	Nurse satisfaction
Physical plant maintenance records	Time between being ready for discharge and leaving the room	Labor costs adjusted for patient acuity/complexity	Technician and other staff satisfaction
Process consistency (for example, timely updating of records in proper format)	Time between formal admission to floor and actual transport to floor	Labor cost per dollar of revenue	Physician satisfaction
Information availability (for example, lab reports in time for rounding)	Time to turn over a room (clean and prepare) between patients	Labor cost per dollar of profit	Employee retention/turnover
Continuity of care (how many different nurses during a stay?)	Patient throughput (patients discharged per unit time)	Fixed and overhead costs for the unit	Measures of safety culture
	Nursing hours per patient day (HPPD) or hours per patient (HPP)	Consumables and inventory costs	
	Fraction of surgeries experiencing bed holds	Use of overtime, contingent/agency staff	

Table 3.2 Sample Performance Metrics for a Nursing Unit

Clinical Metrics	Operational Metrics	Financial Metrics	Organizational Metrics
Outcome	*Volume*	*Revenues*	*Organizational Learning*
Clinically specific outcome measures	Admissions, discharges, transfers (both in/out)	$ charged (or collected) per month/year due to patient throughput on the unit	Nurse training and continuing education
Patient safety events (falls with injury, pressure ulcers, hospital-acquired infections)	Patient census	Average revenue per patient (charged, and received) based on patient mix	Trends in clinical, operational or satisfaction metrics
Staff safety events (back injuries, absenteeism, needlestick injuries)	Utilization of beds and other physical assets	Payer mix (% from Medicare, Medicaid, private insurance)	Suggestion program entries, and fraction implemented
Complication rates	Fraction of attractive transfers rejected due to lack of a bed	Uncompensated care ($ and %)	Committees or other organizational structures for data gathering, analysis, and improvement recommendations
Emergency visits within 30 days	Equipment availability		
Readmissions within 30 days			
Rates of reported adverse events (both "near-miss" and events that reach the patient)			
Patient Satisfaction	*Other*		
Patient satisfaction	Skills mix ratios (% of care provided by RNs, LVNs, UAPs, others)		
Patient's family satisfaction			

In addition to compliance and outcome metrics, nursing units must consider nonclinical metrics (financial, operational, and organizational), which are driven in large part by how well the two most important assets on a nursing unit—beds and nurses—are managed. Two characteristics are essential to measuring the nonclinical performance of a nursing unit. The first is the difference between fixed- versus variable-cost assets (beds being the former, nurses the latter). The second is the whole-system consequences of a bottleneck resource, which can impact metrics far from the nursing unit and introduce distortions into the local (that is nursing-unit specific) measures of performance.

3.3.1.1 FIXED VERSUS VARIABLE COST ASSETS

Beds are part of a physical infrastructure that is largely a fixed cost. Once they are in place, the bonds (loans) that put them there must be paid off whether or not patients are occupying them. In contrast, nursing (and other staff) schedules can dynamically respond to changes in the patient census on a unit, so these are (semi-) variable costs that will change with changing patient volumes and lengths of stay. This difference affects the key management challenges in nursing units.

For decisions made infrequently and impacting long-term fixed costs, such as building a new bed tower, a key challenge is the initial capacity decision. How many beds should the hospital have? This decision has long-term consequences for whole-hospital performance, due to its fixed nature and the capacity constraints it imposes on all future operations.

It is common to manage expensive, fixed-cost assets by measuring their utilization. No industry wants to invest in an expensive asset just to see it lying idle. Bed utilization is typically calculated based on a midnight census of patients, divided by the total number of beds in the hospital. If there are 450 patients in a 500-bed hospital, the bed utilization is $450/500 = 90\%$. Note, however, that if LOS is high, the patient census can be high even if throughput (and therefore revenue production) is low. So, in addition to utilization, hospitals track LOS and throughput (discharge rate, in patients/week for example). In the long run, these must be related via Census = Throughput rate × LOS by Little's Law (see Appendix A).

Although the number of beds is fixed, the number of patients is not. That is, the patient load placed upon the fixed-bed capacity is variable, and we know from the physics of queues (Variability and Utilization Principles) that we cannot operate in a context of high variability and high utilization without dramatically compromising customer service (in the form of intolerable delays). So, by being overly attentive to the financial management of high-cost fixed assets (that is, by managing their utilization up toward 100%), we invite deterioration in both operational and clinical performance.

Unlike fixed-cost assets, a variable-cost resource is not paid for until it is used. The use (and cost) of variable-cost resources fluctuates with patient demand. This is important because costs will rise and fall with revenues (patients), in contrast with fixed-cost resources whose costs are fixed regardless of revenues. For purely variable-cost resources, which can be purchased and released as required, the original "capacity" decision is moot because capacity can be marshaled as needed. Few resources are purely variable in nature, however, so some judgment is used when accountants put certain resources in the fixed-cost category and others in the variable-cost category. Labor costs are typically considered variable in accounting systems, despite the fact that most labor costs (and professional labor costs in particular) are partially fixed. Nurse labor costs, in particular, have both fixed and variable attributes. In the face of nursing shortages and long training times, hospitals will want to retain their nursing resources. That is, nurses will not be laid off during short-term depressions in demand, because laid-off nurses may find employment elsewhere, and the hospital will not want to lose them in case demand picks up again. If employees are not laid off, they become essentially fixed-cost resources, and the initial capacity (hiring) decision rises in importance. On the other hand, the use of nursing resources does vary with patient load via a nurse scheduling system that assigns nurses to shifts in an attempt to match supply and demand. Further, if too many or too few nurses (relative to patient needs) show up on a given day, there are typically contractual options available to remedy the imbalance. So the use (and cost) of nurses varies with patient demand, albeit imperfectly. Due to this hybrid fixed-/variable-cost nature, key nurse management challenges include both longer-term hiring strategies and shorter-term adjustment (scheduling) strategies.

Variable-cost resources tend to be measured on a resources-per-unit-flow basis. That is, a nursing unit will pay attention to things like hours per patient day (HPPD), hours per patient (HPP), or analogous metrics in dollars (for example, cost per patient day, or CPPD).

3.3.1.2 METRICS FOR BOTTLENECK RESOURCES

The second important characteristic to understand when measuring the performance of a nursing unit is the whole-system consequences of a bottleneck resource. (See Appendix A for a definition and discussion of a bottleneck.) In conformance with our practice in other chapters, Table 3.2 lists metrics that measure things over which the nursing unit has significant control or responsibility. It is demotivating to measure anybody's performance based on things over which they have no control. However, when either beds or nurses are potential bottlenecks (to patient flows through the hospital), there will be whole-hospital consequences that may not be apparent on the unit itself. In fact, the performance metrics on the nursing units themselves may improve when they are a bottleneck resource, even as overall the hospital's performance deteriorates. This is because many of the consequences of congestion at a bottleneck are felt elsewhere in the system, as upstream assets are blocked and cannot proceed with their work and downstream assets are starved, with the same consequence. The real effects of a bottleneck in the nursing units (due to overutilization of either beds or nurses) will be felt by the ED, the operating rooms and surgical services, referring physicians, and transferring hospitals.

Consider, for example, a unit that strives for 100% utilization of its beds and nurses. Financially, the dollars and resources invested per patient on the unit might be very commendable, but we know that such high utilizations will cause disruptions elsewhere because patients cannot get out of the OR or the ED. In this case, the most salient operational metrics, in addition to the important clinical compliance and outcomes measures, will be those at the interface of the nursing unit and the rest of the hospital. These include the fraction of surgeries experiencing a bed hold, the time between being cleared for admission from the ED and actual transportation to an in-patient bed, the time between being ready for discharge and actual discharge, and the fraction of attractive transfers that must be rejected for lack of a bed.

3.3.1.3 METRICS OVERVIEW

From earlier, there are likely two types of hospitals relevant to the discussion of nursing unit performance metrics: those for which the beds, nurses, or both are bottleneck resources, and those for which they are not. From current national statistics, we can expect the former to be larger hospitals (urban and academic medical centers) and the latter to be smaller (more rural) ones; see Section 3.4.1. Clinical metrics are always central to the core mission of any hospital. Operational metrics include unit-specific time and flow measurements, and if units are highly utilized, important bottleneck metrics can include the delays imposed elsewhere in the hospital.

There are some natural interactions among these metrics. If the nursing units are not bottlenecks (are lightly utilized), there should be no operational problems with rapid patient throughput and quality care. That is, these facilities should enjoy enviable operational performance (for example, short delays getting into a bed, or between being cleared for discharge and actual discharge), high patient satisfaction, and low overtime rates. If this is not the case, the hospital has a management problem. Low utilizations mean that there is ample capacity, so poor performance means the installed capacity is not being used efficiently. In contrast, high bed or nurse utilizations on the unit will be associated with bottleneck status and compromised performance in delays getting out of the ED, bed holds in the OR, or refused transfers.

3.3.2 Management Decisions

Achieving excellent clinical outcomes for patients, while optimizing financial performance and not compromising patient or staff satisfaction, poses a multidimensional challenge to the design and operation of a nursing unit. As usual, these management decisions can be nested according to time horizon. Long-range strategic plans (with multiyear time horizons) determine the aggregate resources that will be put in place and their positioning in the competitive landscape. Intermediate-range planning (six months to a year) provides a general method for the allocation of resources to physical locations and activities. At the lowest level of the decision hierarchy, real-time day-to-day accommodations are made as required to respond to dynamically unfolding events.

3.3.2.1 LONG-RANGE STRATEGIC PLANNING

Key long-range decisions include the mission and the strategy of the hospital, which drive its intentions for patient care, and the procurement or construction of sufficient capacity to fulfill that mission. The strategic goals suggest a basic hospital design and first-cut allocation of resources. Specifically, nursing units are designed and located in the hospital along with their bed count and staffing needs. Taking a hospital-wide perspective, key strategic decisions include

- **What demands will be served?** Will the hospital focus on particular patient types? What is the demand for these types likely to be? What are the health care needs of the community? Does the hospital have "destination health" (sufficiently distinctive services that can attract patients from outside its natural catchment area) aspirations?

- **What physical and human assets will be required to meet the demand?** How many nursing units? Of what types? How many beds in each? Of what types? How many nurses? What types? How many ORs? How many exam rooms in the ED?

- **What is the competitive reaction?** How will installing new physical and human capacity influence the competitive landscape? Will it discourage investment by competitors and increase the hospital's market share, or will competitive reactions reduce margins for everybody?

- **What revenues should derive from the demand?** What volume and payer mix is anticipated, at what reimbursement rates?

- **What is the planned financial performance?** After considering construction and staffing costs, demand for services and competitive reactions, and reimbursement trends, how will the hospital perform financially?

Once these decisions are made, if the plan makes business sense, the hospital can be designed in more detail. Analogous comments hold for strategic additions to existing hospitals, or reorganizations of resources. From the perspective of a nursing unit, once this long-range planning process is complete, the nursing unit will be designed with an anticipated mission, expertise, room mix, bed count, and staff.

3.3.2.2 INTERMEDIATE-RANGE SCHEDULING: ALLOCATING CAPACITY TO DEMAND

In the intermediate range (six months to a year), general planning and scheduling protocols are designed to facilitate a dynamic matching of available staff capacity to forecasted patient demand. Support systems will be designed, including the admissions system, workload planning and scheduling systems, bed management system, and discharge systems.

Assets may also be reallocated in the intermediate range. For example, if one nursing unit is underutilized and another overutilized, the hospital administration might take resources from one and reassign them to the other.

Once the intermediate range planning, scheduling, and control systems are operational, the hospital is prepared to process patients.

3.3.2.3 SHORT-TERM SCHEDULING

Nurse labor schedules are typically set weeks in advance so that nurses can schedule their nonwork lives. However, over the intervening weeks, the inherent variability in patient requirements, staff illnesses and absences, emergencies, and other unanticipated events can result in patient needs in excess of, or short of, scheduled nurse capacity.

If too many nurses are scheduled for the immediate patient load, options include staffing them anyway, having a "float pool" so that overstaffed nurses in one unit can work in an understaffed unit elsewhere in the hospital (contingent on their training), sending the extra nurses home on call, sending them home with or without some pay, or using their time for educational or other programmatic activities. If too few nurses are scheduled for the immediate patient load, extra nurses can be added from a float pool (if it exists) or "off duty" nurses can be called in, usually for premium pay. Trained temps from nursing agencies may also be used to address an urgent shortage of personnel. The nurse manager or a shift's charge nurse makes these decisions daily, trying to match staff to patient needs.

In addition to adjusting overall nurse staffing levels on a given day, the charge nurse or nurse manager matches specific nurses to patients on a given shift. A typical patient-to-nurse ratio in a large hospital is four patients per nurse, although this can vary widely. Some hospitals report assigning seven or even eight patients to each nurse, whereas the ratio for critical care beds is often lower than four. In addition, ratios may be different for evening, night, weekend, or holiday shifts. For example, a single nurse can manage more patients during the night shift because most patients are sleeping and require less hands-on attention.

When matching patients to nurses for a shift, the charge nurse typically considers the following factors:

- **Training and experience**—More experienced nurses can handle harder cases. Patients with special care needs (for example, chemotherapy, specific types of infusions, special monitoring) will only be assigned to nurses who have completed the requisite training.

- **Balancing work load**—One nurse should not get four very complicated patients while another nurse gets four patients with minimal complexity.

- **Continuity of care**—Most nurses and patients prefer to stay with one another, developing a relationship that yields the psychological benefits of comfort and familiarity, the medical benefits of a consistent set of eyes tracking patient progress, and the efficiency benefits of a nurse who thoroughly understands a patient's needs. Also, upon discharge, patient education (regarding home care, for example) is facilitated when nurses know the patient.

- **Training needs**—More experienced nurses can work with less experienced nurses on difficult cases to increase the latter's skill set.

- **Geography**—Many units choose to assign nurses to patients who are located contiguously to increase their presence with the patients and reduce the amount of time spent walking between rooms. This also makes locating the responsible nurse easier when necessary.

3.4 Key Management Issues in a Nursing Unit

Each of the metrics listed in Table 3.2 could be the object of a detailed process improvement effort. An encyclopedic catalog of these opportunities is unrealistic. Instead, we present a selection of key management issues that nursing units in most hospitals will face.

The two key assets on a nursing unit are nurses and beds. As described in Section 3.3.1, beds are integrated into an infrastructure (a building and floor plan) that represents fixed and sunk costs. The key management challenge, then, is deciding how many beds to have in the first place. Nursing costs are semi-variable. So, in addition to the long-range capacity decision of how many nurses to hire, there is an intermediate range problem of designing a nurse scheduling system to match the potential supply of nursing hours to patient demands for attention and care. The first two management challenges we review below are long-range capacity planning for both beds and nurses (Section 3.4.1) and intermediate- and short-range nurse scheduling (Section 3.4.2).

We then turn to a management challenge that is driven by information flows rather than decision flows. Most people are familiar with the old "telephone game," in which a series of people pass along a message, one to the other, by whispering in their ear. What emerges after many "handoffs" of the information is something so distorted that the original message is all but lost. Information is handed off in just that fashion (one person talking to another) from one nursing shift to the next. Any distortions injected into the information can have serious clinical and financial consequences. Handoffs are widely recognized as a place where mistakes originate. The final challenge we address in this chapter is the management of handoffs between nursing shifts (Section 3.4.3).

3.4.1 Long-Range Bed and Nurse Capacity Planning

3.4.1.1 PROBLEM

Patients admitted to hospitals require beds, so an insufficient number of beds will disrupt the flow of patients through the hospital and cause congestion and delays upstream. Patients in the ED awaiting hospital beds to be admitted occupy ED beds and therefore can cause long delays for other patients to be examined. Some may tire of waiting and leave before they are seen by a doctor (LWBS = Left Without Being Seen, or LBE = Left Before Examined). A 2006 study of 4.3 million patient visits to Canadian hospitals revealed an emergency room LWBS rate of 3% (129,000 patients leaving). The situation was worse in higher-volume hospitals with a high number of admissions through the ED, and for younger patients with less acute triage scores (Baibergenova et al. 2006). It is conventional wisdom that patients who can leave are those who have an alternative primary or urgent care clinic to go to, and are likely to be insured. Consequently, a high LWBS rate can significantly deteriorate the hospital's financial performance if paying customers leave and nonpaying customers stay.

Many patients leaving the operating rooms also require beds both pre- and post-operatively. An insufficient number of beds can cause elective surgeries to be delayed or cancelled. In one large hospital, 6% of all surgical procedures experienced a *bed hold*, which means that a patient who was ready to leave the OR could not do so because there was no ICU or PACU bed to receive them. Upon further investigation, it was found that the ICU and PACU had patients who were ready to move to a step-down or regular care unit but could not because no beds were available. Of course, when patients do not move out of the OR, no new cases can move in, which delays procedures. In the worst case, elective surgeries are cancelled because the day has extended too long, or because no post-operative bed can be guaranteed.

Finally, transfers from other hospitals or referrals from private practice physicians must be refused if there are no beds available. The same goes for emergency arrivals, when a hospital lacking beds must go "on diversion" and instruct ambulances to go elsewhere. Diversions and refused transfers can represent a significant loss of revenue and margin.

There are both upside and downside risks when deciding on the number of beds to design into a hospital. An insufficient number of beds will restrict the patient flows as described, causing backups and delays that will translate into compromised clinical outcomes, financial performance, and patient and staff satisfaction. Yet, having too many beds is inefficient. As noted, beds do not exist in isolation. They are embedded into an expensive physical infrastructure (including rooms, bathrooms, and monitoring equipment). Building this infrastructure and then not using it is wasteful. Indeed, many of the rural health facilities built after the Second World War were seriously underutilized (see Appendix B), resulting in a socially suboptimal allocation of resources.

Regulators also worry about the incentives to use something just because it exists. In 1961, Milton Roemer published a paper (Roemer 1961) that found a positive correlation between the number of hospital beds available and the number filled, leading to a conclusion that supply may induce demand (rather than vice versa), especially when a third party pays for it. This "if we build it, they will come" hypothesis became known as Roemer's Law and prompted regulators to take an active stand to prevent overbuilding by passing Certificate of Need legislation in many states (Appendix B). The perceived market failures (that justify government intervention to limit bed capacity) include limited consumer information and understanding, consumption decisions made primarily by providers rather than consumers or payers, the fundamental nature of disease (different psychological processes are at play when we bargain with death, versus buying a car, for example), and the ethical requirement to treat even unprofitable cases.

The result is an intense social and local interest in the total number of beds available in a region. Both overbuilding and underbuilding have clinical, financial, operational and organizational, and ultimately social consequences.

Current Practice: Bed Inventories

The average hospital bed utilization in the United States is only 67%, so there are many underutilized hospitals. Table 3.3 shows that the average small hospital is significantly overcapacitated. This means it has built and is paying for expensive beds and infrastructure but is not recouping revenues to match its expenditures. It is doubtful that the need to buffer variability alone can account for utilizations less than 70%. This dramatic overbuilding is costly and raises the cost of health care without improving the care itself.

Table 3.3 Hospital Bed Utilization (source: American Hospital Association, 2004)

Category (Bed Size)	Average Number of Beds	Admissions/Year (000)	LOS (Days)	Bed Utilization
25–49	34	1,104	5	45.0%
100–199	143	5,840	5.6	62.8%
300–399	343	16,424	5.3	69.5%
500+	706	32,348	6.0	75.3%

However, there are also large urban hospitals and academic medical centers that are highly utilized and in which beds are a clear bottleneck. These highly congested hospitals consistently operate on the cusp of cancelled surgeries, LWBSs, lost revenues, dissatisfied patients and staff, and compromised clinical outcomes. As noted, in these hospitals underinvesting in beds may make unit-specific metrics look good (highly utilized resources, for example). But, by restricting flows through the hospital, the unit restricts total profitability and limits care. These hospitals would have been better off incurring higher fixed costs (build more beds) to facilitate greater throughput and margin generation.

Clearly, when designing a hospital, the question, "How many beds should we build?" is an important one that requires thoughtful analysis.

Current Practice: Staffing Levels

An abundance of beds does not mean that a nursing unit will not be a bottleneck. Remember that the capacity of a work system is determined by its most highly utilized resource, which could be nurses and not beds. Indeed, beds without nurses are of little use. Further, although medical equipment manufacturers will gladly supply more beds upon demand, the labor markets have not been so accommodating with nurses. The value proposition for nurses has not been sufficiently attractive to prevent recurring nursing shortages in the United States. Although the criticality of shortages varies with economic conditions and economic alternatives for nurses, the United States is expected to be short more than 260,000 registered nurses by 2025 (Buerhaus et al. 2009, also see Bureau of Health Professionals 2004). Nursing can be rewarding, but it is stressful. When patients require care, it must be provided without delay. Nurse managers need flexibility from their staff resources to adjust to patient needs, which translates into mandatory overtime and other spontaneous intrusions into the nonwork aspects of a nurse's life. Added to this is the psychological stress of dealing with sick patients, and it is little wonder that many nurses leave the profession prior to their natural retirement age.

Table 3.3 shows lower bed utilizations in smaller hospitals, but nursing units could still constrain whole-hospital performance if their nurses are overutilized. Table 3.4 shows that smaller hospitals (which have low bed utilization on average) do tend to have fewer nurses per bed and make more use of LPNs relative to RNs.

Table 3.4 Nurses per Bed (source: American Hospital Association, 2004)

Size category (beds)	RN/Bed Full Time	Part Time	Total	LPN/Bed Full Time	Part Time	Total	Grand Total
25–49	0.79	0.47	1.26	0.25	0.11	0.36	1.62
100–199	0.74	0.46	1.2	0.12	0.06	0.18	1.38
300–399	1.08	0.58	1.66	0.12	0.05	0.17	1.83
500+	1.28	0.57	1.85	0.09	0.03	0.12	1.97

However, one would naturally expect fewer nurses if the beds are not full, because nurses are semiflexible resources who respond to patient load. If the patient load is low, some beds will be unoccupied and unstaffed. Hence, a better way to investigate the potential for a nurse bottleneck is to look at nurses per patient, as shown in Table 3.5. This shows that smaller hospitals use relatively more nurses per patient, making it unlikely that nurses are bottleneck resources in these facilities.

Table 3.5 Nurses per Patient (source: American Hospital Association, 2004)

Size category (beds)	RN/Patient Full Time	Part Time	Total	LPN/Patient Full Time	Part Time	Total	Grand Total
25–49	1.75	1.05	2.8	0.55	0.23	0.78	3.58
100–199	1.35	0.84	2.19	0.22	0.1	0.32	2.51
300–399	1.56	0.84	2.4	0.17	0.07	0.24	2.64
500+	1.7	0.76	2.46	0.12	0.04	0.16	2.62

We conclude that there is a dichotomy in hospital types. In many smaller hospitals, neither beds nor nurses are bottleneck resources. Indeed, these hospitals appear to have overinvested, at least in their physical assets. Better matching of long-range capacity decisions to demand would significantly improve the cost structure of these hospitals. It is not clear from the data whether nurses are underutilized in these hospitals or not, but in any case a better matching of supply to demand will improve their cost structure without an ancillary deterioration in other metrics.

There are, also, a smaller number of larger urban or academic research hospitals in which either beds or nurses (or both) are bottleneck resources that restrict whole-hospital flows. For these hospitals, it is even more critical to bring nursing and bed capacity in line with demand, because it will improve both financial and clinical performance. It is clear that improvements can be made in capacity planning at both ends of this utilization spectrum.

3.4.1.2 PRINCIPLES

Nursing units should be sized, staffed and located to respond to an anticipated patient volume and mix. These long-range decisions typically suppress operational details so as not to lose the forest for the trees. So, the management principles that apply to the capacity planning problem are those that relate, at a high level, key clinical, operational, financial, and organizational performance metrics. Our overview of these management principles is brief so we do not exhaust readers already familiar with them. The principles we invoke are described more completely in Appendix A, which readers needing more elaboration can consult for details and examples.

The first key relationship is one that must hold in any processing system and is known as *Little's Law*.

Principle (Little's Law)—Over the long term, the rate (R), in-process inventory (I), and waiting time (T) of a system are related according to:

$$I = R \times T$$

Little's Law is general and can be used to analyze delays to get into a bed from the ED, lengths of stay on nursing units, delays in the discharge process, and many other flow scenarios. To apply Little's Law to a nursing unit, we can associate T with the LOS in days, I with the average patient census (number of patients), and R with the throughput rate (patients/day), which in the long run will also equal the admission rate and discharge rate (assuming deaths are also "discharged"). That is, in the long run we must have, on average, Census = Throughput Rate × LOS on any nursing unit. We use the latter to design the capacity of nursing units. If we know the planned throughput rate for the unit and the LOS, we can compute the average patient census and translate this into the number of beds and staff we will need. The expression Census = Throughput rate × LOS also has some intuitive consequences. If beds are full on a nursing unit (census is constant at its maximal level), the only way to increase throughput (admission or discharge rate) is to decrease the LOS. Also, for any fixed throughput rate in a hospital, if LOS is decreased, patient census will also decrease.

In general, "performance" is measured by the collection of metrics in Table 3.2, but we will simplify things by focusing on cash flow and patient satisfaction as two key performance metrics. A primary driver of cash flow in a hospital is throughput rate (each patient represents some margin), and a primary driver of patient satisfaction is LOS (because delays in being seen, operated on, or discharged degrade the patient experience).

We first focus on the throughput rate of the hospital, which will be determined by the capacity of its bottleneck resource (terms we will now define). The *capacity* of a resource is the maximum processing rate for that resource.

Definition (Resource Capacity)—The capacity of a resource is the throughput it can achieve provided that it is never starved for work.

For example, if the LOS for a patient in a single-occupancy room is 3 days, the average capacity of the room is 1/3 patients/day. The capacity of a complex system such as a hospital can be determined from the capacities of its constituent resources. For example, nurse and room capacities determine the capacity of a nursing unit, and nursing unit capacities contribute to the capacity of the hospital. Clearly, the nurse's (and hence the hospital's) capacity depends on the character of the patients who arrive (are they simple or complex? Does the hospital do simple hernias or triple transplants?), the capabilities of its internal human and physical assets, and how those assets are organized.

If we know the capacities of a nursing unit's constituent resources, how can we determine the capacity of the nursing unit itself? We need to know the *utilization* of each resource, from which we can identify the *bottleneck* resource.

Definition (Utilization)—Utilization of a resource is the long-term fraction of time it is busy, which is given by the average arrival rate of work (for example, patients per hour) at the station divided by the resource capacity over the long term.

A resource's utilization can equivalently be computed by dividing its long-run average workload by its capacity. For example, if a nurse who can manage 4 patients on every 10-hour shift (that is, supply 40 patient-hours per shift, or 160 patient-hours per 40-hour week) is asked to manage an average of 3 patients per shift (120 patient-hours per week), his utilization will be 120/160 = 75%. The bottleneck resource(s) will be those with the highest utilization(s), and these will constrain the throughput of the entire system.

Definition (Bottleneck)—The bottleneck of a system is the resource with the highest utilization.

Principle (System Capacity)—The capacity of a system is defined by its bottleneck, which is the resource in the system with the highest utilization. If the capacity of a system is less than the demand placed on it, the demand will not be met.

So, if beds in a nursing unit are 76% utilized and nurses are 89% utilized, nurses are the bottleneck resource, and nurse capacity will constrain the throughput of the nursing unit. We will not be able to increase the capacity of this unit by adding beds. We need to increase the capacity of the nurses.

In a world without variability, we would exactly balance the utilizations of all our resources at 100%. Clearly, if two resources are required to process patients and one is 100% utilized and the other is 75% utilized, we have overinvested in the latter. But, in a variable world, we do not want a resource utilized at 100%, and we may not choose to balance utilizations. This is because utilization and variability combine to generate delays (such as LOS, an important metric for nursing unit performance).

Throughput rate and time are related to patient census through Little's Law. But Little's Law does not fully characterize LOS, because, for a given average throughput rate, the LOS can be long or short (with the patient census being correspondingly large or small to satisfy Little's Law). What determines LOS is the interplay between utilization and the level of "variability" or "burstiness" in the arrival or treatment times of patients. Variability on a nursing unit increases if patients arrive randomly (arrival rate variability) or are highly heterogeneous in their nursing requirements (service time variability). These combine to cause queuing of patients and other important "jobs" on, or trying to enter, the unit.

Principle (Variability)—Unsynchronized variability causes queueing.

The Variability principle points out that variability per se is not the real problem; rather, it is *unsynchronized* variability. Variability is unsynchronized when increases in demand may coincide with decreases in capacity, or vice versa. There will be less congestion and delay if variability is synchronized, so that every time demand increases capacity does also. So, less overall capacity is required if that capacity is flexible to adjust to demand levels, or if demand can be adjusted dynamically to current capacity levels. For example, cross-trained nurses who can float between units can allow capacity to flow to where the demand is, thereby synchronizing demand and capacity and improving performance.

The relationship between variability, utilization, and nursing unit performance is captured in the following.

Principle (Utilization)—Utilization magnifies queueing in a highly nonlinear fashion.

The previous two principles, taken together, say that unsynchronized variability will cause a queue of patients (or other "jobs") to build, and this queue gets larger in an explosive and nonlinear fashion as utilization increases. Nursing units and many other health care contexts can be highly variable, meaning that the utilization of their resources cannot be driven up to 100% without incurring dramatic and unacceptable delays. In industry in general, it is conventional wisdom that a target utilization of 85% is practical, and in the absence of any more detailed information on the level and character of variability in the system, this is a decent rule of thumb. We can do better with a better understanding of the levels of variability in our processes. Highly variable resources may have utilization targets less than 80%, whereas standard processes (for example, some administrative tasks, room turnover tasks, or automated lab tests) may have design targets of up to 95% utilization.

But, in general, and on nursing units in particular, utilizations below 100% will be required for acceptable levels of patient care. Utilizations below 100% mean that, on average, resources have some "slack" underutilized capacity. A key to efficiency, then, is to manage variability. The problems imposed by variability can be managed by either reducing it directly, synchronizing it, or "buffering" it. If there are natural daily, weekly, or seasonal variations in patient demand for nursing services, and if nurse capacity can be adjusted to meet these predictable variations, then the problems of queuing, congestion, and delay can be greatly reduced. Remaining unsynchronized variability will require buffering.

Principle (Variability Buffering)—All unsynchronized variability will be buffered by some combination of inventory, capacity, time, quality, and system degradation.

Nursing units serving patients with random arrival patterns and random nursing needs have to design extra capacity into the system, live with delays getting onto the unit, or risk poor-quality care. However, the amount (and hence cost) of buffering required can be reduced by exploiting pooling or flexibility.

Principle (Pooling)—Combining sources of variability so that they can share a common buffer reduces the total amount of buffering required to achieve a given level of performance.

For example, rather than having two separate nursing units, each staffed independently, it is better (from a physics perspective) to pool them into one unit. When they're separate, there can be congestion on one unit but idleness on the other, whereas this will never happen when the units are combined so that variability in their patient census is pooled. Of course, issues of required training/expertise on nursing units and the administrative overhead of managing larger staff populations may limit the extent to which pooling is desirable.

It has already been mentioned that flexible resources (beds, rooms, and nurses) can provide benefits without physical combination by enabling resources to flow where they are needed.

Principle (Buffer Flexibility)—Flexibility in variability buffers reduces the buffering required for a given amount of variability.

For example, flexible nurses trained in two different units can move to where the greatest demand is, flowing capacity to demand and reducing the corrupting effects of unsynchronized variability between nurse capacity and patient demand.

Because long-term capacity decisions place constraints on future activities, they have a significant impact on all relevant metrics. Some of this impact is direct. By definition, capacity is the maximal throughput rate for the nursing unit, which directly affects financial performance because each patient produces some margin; therefore, higher throughput means higher margins. Some effects are indirect. For example, lower-capacity investments relative to demand implies higher utilizations, which in a variable environment will cause longer patient delays and higher stress on nurses, all with clinical, organizational, operational, and financial consequences. At the same time, capacity (human or physical) costs money, so overinvesting also has financial consequences. The Newsvendor principle provides a quantitative tool for striking a balance between too much and too little capacity.

Principle (Newsvendor)—In a single demand period with uncertain demand, the capacity level that optimally balances the cost of too much capacity with too little capacity is given by Q^* where

$$F(Q^*) = c_u / (c_o + c_u).$$

and

$F(\bullet)$ = cumulative distribution function of demand (that is, $F(x)$ = probability that demand is less than or equal to x)

c_o = "cost of overage" = cost per unit overstocked relative to demand

c_u = "cost of underage" = cost per unit understocked relative to demand

Note that for symmetric demand distributions (Normal, for example) the common practice of staffing to the mean, or expected demand is only optimal if the underage and overage costs are equal. This is seldom the case in nurse staffing, so the optimal staffing level will not be equal to the average demand level. See Appendix A section A.2.1.1 for details.

Finally, we note that, at the capacity planning level, a great deal of detailed information about daily operations (including mechanics, logistics, job descriptions, and IT systems) is suppressed. However, there is a natural interaction between these levels of detail. (Better operations at the detailed level mean less capacity required to meet demand at the design level.) But considering all operational details at the capacity planning stage is impractical. Instead, assumptions are made based on current evidence and practice regarding things like the capacity of human resources, and the right number of patients per nurse or per physician to achieve desirable clinical outcomes. These are combined with strategic decisions about target patient loads and consideration of the need for buffers to choose design levels of physical and human assets.

3.4.1.3 PRACTICES

A hospital's mission is to heal the sick in the most socially efficient way, but an ancillary supporting mission is to make enough money to survive. A hospital's strategy balances these objectives. There are health care needs in a community, as well as market opportunities. The first step in capacity planning is determining what services will be offered and forecasting demand for those services. Then sufficient capacity is installed to meet those forecasted needs, taking into account demand rates, average LOS, and variability. In common with most service industries, delays can be costly. However, avoiding delays (in the presence of variability) requires extraordinary (and extraordinarily costly) capacity investments. So, capacity decisions involve a fundamental trade-off between the cost of capacity and the cost of delay.

As noted earlier, the capacity of a system is the capacity of its bottleneck resource. In a hospital, this can be any one of the complex mixture of assets, including the number and type of beds, the capacity of the nursing or medical staff, the capacity of the clinical support services (including diagnostic services like pathology or radiology, and the pharmacy), or floor support services (supply, laundry, housekeeping, food service, and security).

All this is supported by HVAC systems, power and emergency power systems, sewage systems, toxic and nontoxic waste flows, and an information infrastructure. Any one of these interdependent pieces can be a bottleneck resource determining overall system capacity. A good hospital plan has neither too much nor too little capacity in each of these areas.

Planning requirements for the ED, ORs, nursing units, diagnostic facilities and labs, pharmacy, stores, and so on will differ in specifics but are united by the need to handle their part of the anticipated volume and types of patients the hospital wishes to accommodate. If any one of these departments is out of balance with the whole, it can become a system bottleneck.

In capacity planning for nursing units, one begins with the business case for the hospital, the anticipated patient volumes, the division of the bed floors into nursing units, and the number of beds and staff required per unit. These nursing unit design decisions are merged with similar ones for the ORs, Emergency, and other departments as inputs to the more detailed architectural and operational planning processes for the hospital as a whole. The steps follow:

1. Adopt a strategy that seeks to serve or attract certain types of patients.

2. Forecast demand for the desired services and the level of natural or seasonal variability in that demand.

3. Install the right capacity to meet forecasted demand for each type of targeted service, adjusted for variability and subject to regulatory controls.

Step 1 considers the competitive landscape and the potential for a hospital to differentiate itself in the market. Step 2 recognizes that the appropriate bed and staffing levels will depend on more than the average supply and demand for bed-days in the hospital. It will also depend on the levels of variability in those rates, because high variability must be buffered with extra (or more flexible) capacity. Most hospital employees are familiar with oscillations between frantic congestion and relative calm as patient demand waxes and wanes about its average. These oscillations are the result of periodic mismatches between the supply of labor-hours and the demands of the current patient load, and any such mismatch is typically costly.

Hence, the "right" capacity (step 3) depends on the average rate and variability in patient demands that the hospital aspires to serve. Some variability is purely random, such as variations in the mean number of cardiac admissions. Other types of variability might be predictable, such as births peaking in September, trauma in the summer, and respiratory ailments in the fall. Still other sources of variability may be internally generated, such as demand for ORs peaking midweek as surgeons seek to avoid post-operative weekend rounds. Any of these sources of variability, if not addressed, will reduce the achievable occupancy rate of the hospital. Managing variability-related costs includes improving forecasting to better predict (and schedule nurses to match) upcoming patient demand and putting in place buffers to absorb any remaining random variation. In a "typical" hospital, an occupancy target of 85% is a common recommendation (Green and Nguyen 2007), meaning there is a 15% capacity buffer to absorb variability. If variability can be reduced or eliminated, so can the buffer capacity and cost.

In modern hospitals, beds are typically grouped into nursing units associated with particular specialties (cardiology, thoracic surgery, gastroenterology, neurology) to take advantage of and develop caregivers with specialty skills and experience. Within a unit, there may be private and semiprivate rooms. Private rooms are more expensive (each room has a bathroom, while bathrooms are shared in semiprivate rooms) but more flexible in terms of usable capacity. For example, admissions policies try to avoid mixing genders or extreme age differences in the same room. So, if a semiprivate room already has a male occupant, the remaining bed(s) in that room cannot be assigned to a female patient. Also, patients with contagious pathogens (for example, *Clostridium dificile*, or MRSA, Methillician-Resistant Staphylococcus Aureus) generally require private rooms and special disposable equipment (and sometimes "isolation rooms" with negative air pressure to prevent cross-contamination via air flow). Clearly, in hospital capacity planning, the devil can be in the details. However, bringing too much detail into capacity calculations makes computations opaque and risks losing the forest for the trees.

A good capacity planning exercise mixes methods, approaching the question from multiple independent directions and checking for consistency. For planning the appropriate bed count in a hospital, the following approaches are available, ordered roughly from the simplest to the most complicated.

Standard bed-to-population ratios—There exist historical ratios for the demand for hospital beds per 1,000 people in a patient population (see Appendix B). The average should be adjusted for demography (for example, higher for an older population), technological trends (for example, outpatient services replacing hospital stays), and seasonality (for example, vacation destinations experience higher seasonality and require more beds during the busy season). This gives a rough estimate for the total number of beds the population can support, which is then adjusted for the market share the hospital aspires to. After the Second World War, a national effort to upgrade hospitals resulted in ratios of 4–5 beds per thousand people in the population. However, since then shorter lengths of stay and economic pressures have reduced this to an average of 2.7 beds per thousand nationwide (but with high variation across regions of the country).

Average hospitalization rates—On average how many people, per thousand in the catchment area, require a hospital bed each year? This average changes with technology and demographics, but often some data is available. Multiplying the average hospitalization rate by the population size gives the number of admissions per year, which divided by 365 gives the admissions per day. Multiplying this by the hospital's target market share gives the forecasted admissions per day to the hospital. By Little's Law (see Appendix A), multiplying this admissions/day by the LOS, in days, gives the average patient census. Finally, dividing this by the intended occupancy rate (percent full, 85% say) gives the number of beds required.

For example, if a hospital enjoys a 60% market share in a population of 250,000 with an average hospitalization rate of 9%, it will expect to see $(.09)(250,000)(.6) = 13,500$ admissions per year, or 37 admissions per day. If the LOS is 5 days, then the average number of patients in the hospital will be (by Little's Law) $(37)(5) = 185$. If the hospital is being designed for 85% bed utilization, then the average census must equal 85% of the number of beds (call this N), so 185 = .85N or N = 185/.85 = 218 beds. Note that we accounted for variability by assuming 85% occupancy (15% buffer capacity). If variability is expected to be low in the patient population (for example, a specialty hospital doing only uncomplicated hernia procedures), the hospital can plan for utilizations higher than 85%, which will reduce the required capacity and costs. If variability is extreme (vacation destinations, or trauma and transplant centers), more buffer (and lower utilizations on average) may be required. In the absence of additional information, 85% is not a bad rule of thumb.

Service-line forecasting—This is a bottom-up process where total demand is built up one service line at a time. We can again use Little's Law, but now at the level of individual services. By doing this, the hospital can access and benefit from the richer understanding each service is likely to have of its own market. That is, each service line can be asked to forecast how many patients per year it expects to handle. As a consistency check, administrators can analyze the historical demand for the various services over the past few years to estimate trends and seasonality. Then this statistical model can be used to predict future demand. Inconsistencies between the service-line forecasts and the statistical model calibrated with historical data are discussed and resolved.

Just because statistical models are objective (unlike service-generated forecasts, which tend to be optimistic) does not mean they are correct. Any statistical method that is calibrated using past data needs to be adjusted if the future is expected to differ from the past in significant ways, for example due to demographic, clinical, technological, or reimbursement changes. Information about these issues is most richly resident in the professional services themselves, which is why they should be consulted.

The combination of statistical models and service-line forecasts results in an anticipated number of patients per year the hospital should be designed to handle. Repeating the previous Little's Law calculation, but at the service-line level, gives the number of beds required for each service. Aggregating across services provides the required overall bed inventory for the hospital.

Queueing theory—The previous techniques used Little's Law to go from forecasted demand per day and LOS to the average patient census, and then divided by the target bed utilization rate to give an estimate for the number of beds required. In the absence of a more refined analysis, we used 85% as our target utilization. More sophisticated methods based on queueing theory (see, for example, Green 2002) can go from primary data on patient demand rates and its variability to predicting the probability distribution of the number of patients in the hospital. Then that distribution can be combined with the costs of over- and undercapacity to choose bed inventories rationally. This requires more thought (and data) than the simple 85% rule and requires more specialized skills to apply accurately, but it is also more attentive to hospital-specific conditions. The analysis may suggest when 85% is too generous, or insufficient.

Monte Carlo Simulation—Simulation is a computer-based method in which virtual patients are conjured up by software and tracked as they move virtually through the system, much like popular video games. General purpose simulation software allows an analyst to define the arrival rates, trajectories, service times, and so on, for patients according to user-specified probability distributions (see, for example, Law and Kelton 1982). When thousands of virtual patients have been simulated, summary performance statistics for the virtual hospital can be generated. Simulation methods can predict the performance of general patient flow models, but they can be time consuming to write and debug and typically require the expertise of a specialist to do well. Also, the many assumptions that must be made when building these models are often hidden in the software, which compromises model transparency.

Nurse staffing levels are addressed in an analogous fashion to bed inventories. Historical (or in some states legally mandated) ratios of patients per nurse can relate the forecasted average patient census to staffing needs. Then the right amount of buffer nurse capacity is determined using either rules of thumb (85% utilization of nurse resources) or more sophisticated (queueing theory or simulation) techniques.

As with all long-term planning exercises, it is best to take more than one approach to the problem and look for consistency. Lack of consistency means one or more sets of underlying assumptions are wrong and provides an opportunity to learn and upgrade one's assumptions and intuition. Achievement of consistency from two or more different methods generates confidence in the results.

3.4.1.4 CASE: CAPACITY PLANNING AT SEABERG HOSPITAL

The Northampton Health System (NHS) is considering building a community hospital in suburban Seaberg that can serve the local population of about 200,000 people. Although there is already a competing 250-bed general hospital in the greater Seaberg area, NHS believes the area is still underserved. It believes that a new Seaberg Hospital could be profitable by itself but could also serve as a portal to the larger urban NHS main hospital, to which Seaberg could transfer specialty cases. In addition, NHS hopes to capitalize on two other strategic opportunities in the Seaberg area.

Birthing center—It is conventional wisdom that women who give birth in a hospital and develop a positive relationship with the institution will bring their children to the same health system and their spouses will follow, producing downstream revenues. People also do not want to travel too far from home to give birth. So, there is an opportunity to gain a loyal local following, as well as to use Seaberg Hospital as an entrée for families to the larger NHS health system. This is important to management because people who live in Seaberg tend to be well insured, whereas the core hospital is in an area with rising rates of uninsured (contributing to a rise in NHS's levels of uncompensated care). To be a top-quality birthing center, Seaberg needs resident expertise in obstetrics, gynecology, and pediatrics.

Physical Medicine—Many people in the Seaberg area work in warehouse and manufacturing jobs that, in an aging population, can easily result in back pain and other ailments that are typically covered by insurance (such as workman's compensation) that pays relatively well for quality care. People also prefer not to travel too far from home for regular physical therapy (PT) sessions, so a new Seaberg Hospital would occupy a natural catchment area for these patients. PT is most often handled on an outpatient basis, but to be a preferred destination NHS wants to plan for sufficient inpatient capacity at Seaberg to serve the subset of patients that do require a hospital bed. This requires expertise in occupational health, neurology, orthopedics, radiology, physical medicine and rehabilitation (PM&R), occupational therapy, and PT.

Normal mix of patients for a community hospital—NHS is also targeting a share of the naturally occurring demand for hospital beds from the local population.

Executing the Seaberg strategy requires attention to the capacity and staffing needs of many off-floor services, including anesthesia, ORs, emergency room, medical and surgical ICUs, pharmacy, ultrasounds, infusions, outpatient services, radiology and other diagnostic services, and more. Here we focus on a capacity analysis for the nursing units to demonstrate the general approach. We can apply the same approach to sizing other departments.

Patients will arrive to the units from the emergency room, the ORs (via the ICUs or PACUs), or transfers from other hospitals. The admissions process will determine which nursing unit is right for the patient. Bed capacity and staffing decisions must be made at both the aggregate level (how many total beds in the hospital) and unit level (how many for each unit). For example, birthing and gynecology, obstetrics, and pediatric services are typically kept physically separate from the other units, meaning that the number of beds must be computed independently for each.

Many activities scale with the number of beds in a hospital, so "beds" is a common measure of hospital size. The NHS administration looks at sizing the proposed Seaberg facility from three different angles:

- **Standard bed-to-population ratios**—There are 200,000 people in the natural catchment area for Seaberg Hospital, and there is a 250-bed competing hospital close by. Statewide, the ratio of beds to population is about 3 beds per thousand people. Accordingly, the Seaberg area can support 600 beds and, given the existing 250-bed competitor, a rough cut estimate is that Seaberg can support an additional 350 beds. The dangers of using this number are many. First, most of the state is more rural than Seaberg, and the state-wide occupancy rate is only 66%. This means that 350 beds translates into an average patient census of only 231 patients. Seaberg plans for 85% utilization, so 231 patients would be 272 beds. The planners realize that the Seaberg population density and demographics are sufficiently different from the state-wide averages to make the 272 bed estimate very rough. They have more faith in methods using more locally relevant data.

- **Average hospitalization rates**—Each year about 13% of the population in the Seaberg area requires hospitalization, for a total demand rate of 26,000 admissions per year (71.2 admissions per day). If they target 60% market share relative to the local competitor, Seaberg Hospital would have to handle 42.7 admissions per day. With an average stay of about 5 days, by Little's Law 214 beds are expected to be occupied on any given day. At a target utilization of 85%, this implies a bed inventory of 251 beds.

- **Service-line forecasting**—The Seaberg strategy is to provide an entrée into the main NHS hospital, but also to distinguish itself locally in maternity services and pain management. The birthing-related beds will be kept on a different floor. Assuming an average birth rate of 14 births per thousand people, the Seaberg catchment area will support about 2,800 births per year (7.7 births per day). Targeting 60% of that market, they hope to accommodate 4.6 births per day. Childbirth lengths of stay vary by delivery type (1.5 days for spontaneous or induced, 3.5 days for cesarean sections) but average 1.9 days. This implies (by Little's Law) an average census of $(4.6)(1.9) = 8.74$ maternity patients, which at 85% utilization requires 10.3 beds. When seasonal variation is considered, and the strategy of making this a high-service facility, they estimate the right number of maternity beds at about 14.

Repeating this service-line approach for various adult nonmaternity patient types yields the bed numbers shown in Table 3.6.

Table 3.6   Beds for Seaberg Hospital Based on Service-Line Forecasting

		Arrivals per day	LOS (days)	Average census	Total	Beds @ 85% util
Cardiology	Emergency	0.859	3.3	2.84		
	Other	7.027	2.5	17.57	20.402	24.00
Thoracic	Emergency	0.210	5.2	1.09		
	Other	0.675	1.9	1.28	2.377	2.80
Oncology	Emergency	0.145	5.1	0.74		
	Other	3.134	4.9	15.36	16.096	18.94
Hospitalist	Emergency	6.040	5.5	33.22		
	Other	18.900	3.2	60.48	93.700	110.24
Neurology	Emergency	0.145	9.7	1.40		
	Other	0.298	4.8	1.43	2.834	3.33
PM&R	Emergency	0.324	58	18.81		
	Other	0.684	56	38.29	57.109	67.19
	TOTAL	38.441			192.5	226.5

Based on these numbers, they decide to divide adult nonmaternity patients into four main nursing units: Cardiothoracic, Oncology, Hospitalist, and Neurology-PM&R (NPM&R). After adjusting for seasonal variations (higher in the maternity, hospitalist, and NPM&R units) and considering their desire to distinguish Seaberg in maternity and physical therapy services, they arrive at the following estimated unit sizes:

Maternity	14 beds
Cardiothoracic	27 beds
Oncology	20 beds
Hospitalist	5 units of 25 beds each
NPM&R	3 units of 25 beds each
	Total = 261 beds

The Pain Management units (NPM&R) will have some beds for acute orthopedic and neurology patients, and others for longer-stay physical medicine and rehabilitation patients. It is hoped that there will be close interaction between these two subunits; in fact, a patient may flow from the Acute Care area to the PM&R area. Not included here is the substantial investment they will make in outpatient PT.

The Hospitalist unit is for generalists who can handle an array of patient types (urology, gastro-intestinal, vascular surgery, otolaryngology, burn) that could be in their own units in larger hospitals. The unit includes some extra "surge capacity" that can be used for periodic overflows from the other services.

Although some oncology patients will be referred to the central hospital, the administration decides to have a standalone Oncology unit at Seaberg, and a set of chemotherapy infusion chairs. Travel is a major inconvenience to people undergoing chemotherapy on an outpatient basis.

These three relatively independent approaches recommend that Seaberg have 251, 261, and 272 beds. This is a gratifying level of consistency for such rough calculations. Triangulating these three estimates, the planners decide to look at the business case for a 260-bed facility. This is also the size recommended by the most detailed service-line estimates.

Initial costs will be for construction (including architectural fees, land purchase and site development, and sanitary, electrical, HVAC, water, sewage, and safety systems) and equipment as appropriate for the various departments and services. Given the relatively high real estate prices in the Seaberg area, construction and equipment costs are expected to be about $1 million per bed. Ongoing operational costs will include staffing, supplies, and maintenance.

Staffing levels are a little less "permanent" than hospital construction decisions, and hence a little less critical to specify exactly this far in advance. But, NHS still wants to know what level of staff to target in their hiring process, which has to begin before construction is complete, and estimates are also required for their financial analysis. Nationwide, average nurse-to-bed staffing levels are shown in Table 3.4.

There are economies of scale up to about 175 beds, and then some diseconomies. Based on 260 staffed beds, the planners propose a staff of 230 full-time RNs, 130 part-time RNs, 36 full-time LPNs, and 13 part-time LPNs, in addition to techs, clerks, and some administration personnel. At average area salaries with benefits, these employees will cost about $25 million per year.

Similar bottom-up workforce estimates are carried out for other employees, including physical therapists, techs and transportation workers, office and administration, computer system specialists, social services, maintenance and housekeeping, and lab and other support service personnel. Adding anticipated maintenance, supply, and debt service costs increases the total labor cost by an estimated $30 million. The expected reimbursements for the forecasted patient load will be $110 million per year.

So, the business case for Seaberg Hospital is made based on $110 million per year revenues minus $55 million per year in expenses, and a one-time construction cost of $260 million. This data is sufficient to compute standard financial metrics. (See any basic business finance or accounting text for information on these.) The payback period for this investment is 5 years, and at a 10% cost of capital, it will be net present value (NPV) positive in 7 years. The 10-year internal rate of return is 16.6%. This appears to be a good investment. In fact, the administration considers expanding their objectives and building an even larger facility, reaching for even more market share.

Numbers never tell the whole story, and the administration also considers some hard-to-quantify dimensions to this investment. Their revenue calculations are for reimbursements to the Seaberg facility only and do not include the benefits to NHS for having a feeder hospital (into the main campus). Nor do their calculations consider the strategic benefits of building capacity in a contested area, which may stave off another entrant into that market. Also, construction costs are currently low, due to low levels of economic activity in general, but that is not expected to last. So, building some speculative capacity now could save the system millions in expansion costs downstream. All of these amplify the attractiveness of the investment and argue for being aggressive in their expansion strategy.

However, it is apparent that these numbers are very rough because no one really knows what will happen to costs or reimbursement rates over the next 10 years. Also, it is not clear whether the longer-term trend will be for hospitalization or encouraging more home or outpatient care. Many cardiac units were left with excess capacity when stenting and other catheter-based treatments supplanted surgery for heart patients. There is considerable uncertainty in the health care business, and the NHS administration decides to remain conservative, foregoing speculative capacity and beginning the process of more detailed planning for a 260-bed Seaberg hospital.

The approach used in this example was to start with a competitive strategy that translates into the choice of services rendered and a forecast of the admission rates (hospital wide and by individual service) and lengths of stay. We then computed the average daily census from Little's Law and adjusted this for planned utilization levels to estimate the quantity of resources required. As suggested previously, more sophisticated approaches to hospital sizing use queueing theory or simulation. These approaches can relate capacity, demand, and variability to probabilities of delay and average delays, which are good service-oriented performance metrics that can also estimate pooling economies (for example, by combining two services into one nursing unit, Green and Nguyen 2001). Their major disadvantages are (a) they require more data—specifically data on the levels of variability in demand and service times, which is typically less available, and (b) the analysis is more complex and requires some special training.

3.4.2 Nurse Scheduling

In Section 3.4.1 we considered long-range capacity planning, one part of which is determining the total head count of nurses that the hospital can draw on. Given that total, the nurse scheduling system determines the actual number of nurses assigned to show up for work on any given day. This number can be adjusted, within reason, to respond to changes in patient load. The scheduling system must balance the goals of supporting quality care to patients, remaining cost effective, and promoting staff satisfaction and retention.

3.4.2.1 PROBLEM

A nursing unit's performance metrics (see Table 3.2) are divided into clinical, operational, financial, and organizational categories.

Clinical—A number of empirical studies conducted across many hospitals have confirmed a relationship between nurse staffing and patient outcomes that is significant both statistically and clinically. Researchers have identified higher mortality rates for patients who receive care in hospitals with lower hours of nursing care provided per day of admission (Aiken et al. 2002, Needleman et al. 2002, Kane et al. 2007). In another multisite study of 621 patients, satisfaction with care was higher when nurses reported adequate nurse staffing (Vahey et al. 2004). However, patient heterogeneity and differences among measures of nurse staffing preclude definitive answers from the empirical health services research literature as to the "right" number of nurses in all circumstances (Kalisch, et al. 2011).

Operational—The speed of patient flows from admission through discharge is greatly affected by work practices on the nursing units. With DRG-driven reimbursements, faster throughput means less cost per patient and higher margins for the hospital, so operational improvements on nursing units can be direct precursors to improved financial performance. Likewise, standardized best practices can be direct precursors to improved clinical performance. Even if throughput remains the same, rationalizing tasks can reduce the required nursing HPPD (hours per patient day).

Financial—The hospital seeks to minimize total nurse staffing costs, subject to the constraint that clinical outcomes are not compromised. Total staffing costs include both day-to-day labor costs and the longer term costs of turnover (which is driven in part by nurse satisfaction). Also, nurses' schedules are set weeks or a month in advance, which allows them to plan other aspects of their lives. However, given the random nature of patient arrivals, it is often the case that the number of scheduled and available nurses on a particular day either falls short of, or exceeds, the number needed to attend to the patients on a unit. In the field of Operations Management, these situations are called *overage* (too much nurse capacity) and *underage* (too little nurse capacity), both being inevitable when you must choose a single level of capacity (number of nurses scheduled on the unit) to treat random demand. Hospitals have coping mechanisms for overage and underage, but all of them are costly. If there are too few nurses, more have to be called in, at a premium if necessary. If there are too many nurses, some can be sent home "on call" but, depending on the nurses' contract, the hospital may have to pay them for this. Even if there is no direct financial consequence for overage, nurses who are scheduled and show up ready to work at full salary but are then told to go home are often upset, as anybody would be. Schedule volatility of this sort leads to job dissatisfaction, a contributor to turnover.

The "right" number of nurses for a given patient census can be established in several ways.

Some hospitals strive for a specified maximum patient-to-nurse ratio. More sophisticated systems estimate the required nursing capacity using an acuity-adjusted patient classification system (PCS) designed specifically to estimate the nursing workload demanded by a given patient mix by considering criteria that translate directly into the complexity of nursing care required. We will say more about this later. Once the "right" staffing level is established, then for any given patient census, the cost for the number and types of nurses required is preordained and unavoidable. In contrast, overage and underage costs are the costs of a mismatch between the actual number of nurses scheduled and the "right" number of nurses required that day. The hospital can reduce these with no violation of clinical imperatives and no impact on patient care. These mismatch costs are a direct result of unmanaged variability in the patient load and available nurse capacity. Without variability, there would be no problem scheduling just the right number of nurses (even a month in advance), and mismatch costs would be zero. Consequently, understanding how to manage variability is central to managing nursing labor costs.

Organizational—As described earlier, nurse staffing policies have a direct impact on nurse satisfaction and turnover. Nurse continuing education and training are another claim on a nurse's time, but they can be flexibly scheduled into fallow periods in patient demand if these can be anticipated.

As with all complex operations, these metrics can be in tension. Patient needs must be met 24 hours a day, 7 days a week and can change on short notice, yet most nurses want predictability in their schedules and prefer day to night shifts and weekdays to weekends. Attempts by the hospital to cut costs by reducing nursing hours can result in overworked nurses, affecting compliance to best practices and clinical outcomes. However, a system that is too generous with resources or too flexible in response to nurses' desires may put the financial metrics at risk. Freezing schedules far enough ahead for nurses to plan their lives means using less accurate, longer range forecasts, resulting in more overage and underage costs or more need for day-to-day flexibility to respond to mismatches between supply and demand for nurses. Nurses trained on multiple units can float as needed, reducing overage and underage. However, floating nurses from an overstaffed unit to an understaffed unit can send nurses into unfamiliar surroundings, leading to dissatisfaction and potentially poor clinical outcomes, and a drain on local nurses who must provide orientation instructions to the newcomer.

Nurse scheduling is an important, multidimensional challenge with significant clinical, operational, financial, and organizational consequences. This challenge is made even more difficult by the market for nurses. Nurses follow a career trajectory of education and training, employment, maturing in experience and skills, and then retiring and being replaced by new nurses. If nurses retire too soon, the hospital incurs the costs of too many inexperienced nurses, and the remaining experienced nurses are burdened with greater training and mentoring costs. Yet, as mentioned already, many nurses do leave the profession before their natural retirement age. Their work is hard, with mandatory overtime and inflexible schedules that impose on all aspects of a nurse's nonwork life.

Further, the current economic context of costs outpacing reimbursements is forcing hospitals into financial difficulties and potential downsizing. Nurses in aggregate comprise about 25% of the average hospital's costs, and often more than 50% of its labor costs, so nurse employment levels and compensation are closely monitored. Yet, underinvesting in nurses can be false economy, as low staffing levels can significantly impact clinical outcomes and at the same time encourage more nurses to leave as their workload increases.

The relationship between the number of nurses scheduled to work and labor costs is direct. The relationship between the schedule and longer-term turnover costs is less direct, and therefore more easily overlooked. Turnover costs include the cost of search and acquisition of new hires and efficiency losses while new nurses learn how to integrate with the hospital's culture and systems. Turnover is linked to job satisfaction.

Managing nurse turnover requires that administrators understand what nurses find satisfying and unsatisfying in their jobs. Several surveys of large numbers of nurses indicate that short-staffing leading to work overload is a strong detractor from nurse satisfaction (Davidson et al. 1997, Shader et al. 2001, Shaver et al. 2003). It is not just that overloads make the job harder, although they do, but that nurses report satisfaction from continuity of care (seeing, and potentially developing a relationship with, a patient from admission to discharge). Increased workloads do not allow them appropriate time with each patient. Also, in at least one survey (Shader et al. 2001), unstable work schedules (such as mandatory overtime on weekends) negatively impacted nurse job satisfaction. This can be partially mitigated if nurses have some control over their work requirements (substantial input to schedules, for example, to accommodate other aspects of their lives).

A good nurse scheduling system strives for (Rowland and Rowland 1997):

- **Quality coverage**—Adequate numbers of appropriately trained nurses are available to provide quality care for patients.

- **Efficiency**—Low cost in terms of resources consumed.

- **Flexibility**—Ability to adjust rapidly and efficiently to unanticipated circumstances.

- **Staff satisfaction**—Nurses should perceive the scheduling system as fair and satisfying.

Based on the preceding evidence, a satisfying system should offer enough schedule stability for nurses to plan the nonwork portion of their lives, enough input from nurses for them to have a sense of control, and enough continuity of patient care to develop relationships and see the fruits of their labors.

The general scheduling process, repeated each planning period (as noted, schedules are set in advance), is as follows:

1. Develop a forecast of patient mix and volume in the nursing unit.

2. Translate the patient forecasts into required nursing hours per shift.

3. Consider nurses' availability, corrected for vacations, training, and other absences.

4. Assign specific nurses to work specific shifts (two weeks to a month hence).

5. Have in place contingency plans for managing overstaffing and understaffing due to unforeseen changes in nurse availability or patient census and needs.

Steps 1 through 4 are repeated for each planning period. Step 5 prepares for an activity that is performed on a daily, or even shift-to-shift, basis. At the start of each workday, two administrative activities take place: Nurses showing up for work are assigned to individual patients, and the contingency plan for overstaffing or understaffing is implemented if necessary. These steps are described in more detail next.

Some hospitals have centralized scheduling systems, in which a single entity schedules all the nursing units, but most hospitals decentralize the scheduling function to the unit managers. These two models have the familiar advantages and disadvantages of centralized versus decentralized decision making. Centralized schedulers have a more global perspective on the hospital and can avoid the pitfalls of local politics driving feelings of favoritism or unfairness at the unit level. However, centralized entities lack the rich unit-specific information that unit managers have about their patients and nurses, and these are primary inputs to appropriate staffing. The best model might be a hybrid, with a few similar nursing units being scheduled jointly (and nurses being able to float from one to the other), but not the entire hospital.

In terms of controlling costs, everything starts with the forecasts. If steps 1 and 2 are done poorly, understaffing and overstaffing costs increase. Many hospitals do not do a good job of data mining to reveal trends and seasonality. There may be predictable daily, weekly, or annual variations in patient load and acuity, which if understood can be planned for. Absent this, fluctuations in demand for nurses appear as "random" shocks to the forecasts and require last-minute remedies.

As we have noted, nurses require advance notice of their schedule so step 4 is typically frozen two weeks to a month in advance. Other common strategies for increasing the predictability of a nurse's schedule include

- **Block scheduling**—In a block schedule, a nurse works the same days each week. This offers predictability but not much flexibility. Also, fixed schedules can seldom distribute evening and weekend hours uniformly among the staff, which can cause resentment.

- **Cyclical scheduling**—A scheduling cycle is a series of weeks after which the schedule repeats itself. So, for example, in a four-week cycle, a nurse will know exactly when he is scheduled to work for each week in the four. He may work different days from one week to the next over the next four weeks, but then the schedule resets and repeats itself. So, in theory, a nurse can tell exactly what days he will be working far into the future. Although cycles repeat, weekly schedules within the cycle can be different, so undesirable days can be distributed more evenly than with block scheduling. This has the advantage of predictability but is still not a very flexible system.

In addition to schedule stability, step 4 assignments strive for

- **Equity**—Each nurse gets a fair share of unappealing shifts, and the scheduler attempts to honor requests for specific time off.

- **Appropriateness**—Assigning the right mix of training and capabilities for the patients' needs.

- **Unit preference and experience**—Nurses who have experience on a unit may be more comfortable and capable on that unit, so constant floating of nurses to other units is avoided if possible.

- **Cost**—Serve patients at the lowest appropriate cost.

- **Seniority and other external factors**—In some hospitals, nurses with more years of experience on a unit receive their preferred shifts. Alternatively, if nurses are represented by a collective bargaining unit or union, the bargaining agreement may constrain nurse schedules and patient assignments.

- **Ownership**—Nurses have input to and some ownership of the scheduling process.

There are a range of ownership options. In one, nurses on a unit fill out requests for shifts for the next scheduling period, and the nurse manager combines all the requests into a schedule that tries, within fairness and institutional constraints, to accommodate those requests. Another option is a nurse shift auction (NSA, described more completely in section 3.4.2.6), in which nurses bid on shifts and there are fixed rules for allocating work based on the bids received. In smaller units, nurses may gather in a room and work cooperatively to fill out a blank schedule, which is a form of "self-scheduling." An extreme form of ownership is where staff on a unit form a responsibility center that internally and autonomously organizes to guarantee proper coverage. That is, if a nurse is absent, the others must pick up the slack, without resort to external float or agency nurses unless needs are extreme. On the other hand, if workload is low on the unit, nurses do not expect to be floated off or sent home. So, the nurses rather than the hospital inherit the upside and downside risks of varying workloads.

All this planning comes to fruition at the start of each day, when the nurse manager or charge nurse observes the patient census and the nurses who have shown up for work and matches the two. As noted in Section 3.4.2, the charge nurse considers balance, training, logistics, and continuity of care when assigning individual patients to nurses. He or she also implements step 5, the contingency plans for overstaffing or understaffing relative to patient needs. These overage and underage situations are often defined using simple ratios like the "right" number of patients per nurse. However, as noted earlier, one patient may require more attention than another, and simple patient/nurse ratios do not take these patient differences into account when estimating workload. A better method is to weight patients by acuity, with sicker patients requiring more nursing hours than well patients. Acuity scores can be as simple as where the patient is located (ICU, step-down, or floor) or more detailed "sickness" scores like Apache scores (a weighted average of standard measures like age, temperature, blood pressure, and heart rate, c.f. Sinclair 1991). Most standard acuity scores like Apache, however, are designed to predict mortality for use in risk-adjusted clinical outcome measures and may be only indirectly related to how many nursing hours a patient requires.

A better approach is a PCS designed specifically to estimate the nursing workload demanded by a given patient by considering criteria that translate directly to the complexity of nursing care required. For example, Marquis and Huston (2003) suggest the following drivers of workload, each of which is rated from 1 to 4:

- Feeds self

- Bathing and grooming, self-sufficient to completely dependent

- Toilet needs

- Comfort and pain management

- General health, emotional state

- Treatments required (simple to complex)

- Medications (simple to those requiring close monitoring)

- Teaching requirements (for example, new diabetics, tubes, any major lifestyle changes)

By summing scores over all patients in the unit, the nurse manager can estimate the nursing hours required for patient care (and in more detailed models, time by skill level). By adding in the expected administrative overhead time, lunch, breaks, and education or orientation time, the nurse manager can estimate the total nursing hours required. This is then compared with scheduled nursing resources, and an adjustment strategy is implemented if necessary.

How are such adjustments made? If too many nurses have been scheduled to work relative to the patient load, paying them for a day of work is inefficient. Common options include sending excess nurses home to remain "on call" (in case a burst of patient arrivals makes it necessary to call them back in) for a nominal hourly payment, nurses taking a paid vacation day, nurses taking unpaid vacation, or nurses "floating" to other units. Many hospitals have a "float pool" of nurses who can be assigned to any unit. If there is an extra nurse in one unit, she can join the float pool and potentially be assigned to work in another, understaffed unit. If too few nurses show up relative to the patient load, more have to be called in. Options include calling in nurses who are waiting "on call," calling in nurses who were not on call (in emergencies), requesting an additional nurse from the float pool, or using a temporary nurse employee (from a temporary work agency). Also, roughly 20% of nurses (in 40% of hospitals) in the United States are unionized, which can result in additional constraints on how management addresses nurse/patient imbalances.

The challenge is to use a combination of forecasting, planning, and daily execution to assign nurses to patients in a way that maintains good clinical outcomes, responsible cash flows, and good patient and staff satisfaction.

3.4.2.2 PRINCIPLES

As usual, we briefly list the most relevant principles here, allowing readers already familiar with them to move ahead quickly. All these principles are described more completely in Appendix A for readers who need to refresh their understanding. The primary operational purpose of a nurse scheduling system is to reduce, to the extent possible, the unsynchronized variability between patient needs and nursing capacity (Variability principle). All such variability must be buffered with some combination of excess capacity or time, or risk deteriorated quality and general system degradation (Variability Buffering principle). The general process, as described earlier, is to forecast patient needs, plan accordingly, and have contingency plans in place in case of deviations of needs from forecasts. General strategies for efficiently matching supply to demand include better forecasting and less costly contingency plans. Better forecasting would allow planned staffing to more closely match required staffing, reducing the need for contingency solutions. However, inherent variability in the demand for medical attention and natural variation in nurse availability means that accurate forecasting will be difficult in facilities that treat a heterogeneous mix of patients. The hospital can reduce its need for better forecasting by improving its ability to respond rapidly and efficiently to the inevitable mismatches. Strategies for doing this include leveraging the operational features of cross-training (Buffer Flexibility principle) and resource pooling (Pooling principle).

New to this section are a discussion of deriving optimal staffing levels from the economics of overage and underage costs, captured in the "newsvendor model" discussed in section A.2.1.1. in Appendix A.

Also, implementing any program in a hospital needs to account for the preferences of the key stakeholders who are impacted by it. No proposal will succeed unless key stakeholders approve it, and key stakeholders will map any proposal into what it means for them and things they believe in. These insights are summarized in the following four principles, which are justified in greater detail in Appendix A.

- **Principle (Self-Interest)**—Individuals, not organizations, are self-optimizing.

- **Principle (Key Stakeholders)**—All organizations have key stakeholders with veto power whose approval is necessary to implement changes.

- **Principle (Veto Power)**—For a proposal to be implemented, all key stakeholders must perceive themselves to be better off with the proposal than without it.

- **Principle (Pareto Efficiency)**—If benefits can be transferred from one group to another (for example, via the transfer of money or time or some other medium of exchange) and if there exists a policy that improves the overall performance of a system, there exists an allocation of the total benefits that makes all key stakeholders better off.

A key implication of these principles is that proposals often flounder not on their intrinsic value to the system, but due to a failure to distribute the benefits of the change sufficiently broadly to overcome resistance by key stakeholders. Fortunately, if a proposal offers sufficient improvement over the status quo, and there is way to share the benefits, the Pareto principle implies that the proposal should be implementable. That is, as long as every key stakeholder is willing to give a little to gain even more, any proposal with substantial whole-system benefits can overcome impending vetoes by an appropriate distribution of the gains.

There are other principles that play a less prominent role in the discussion to follow but contribute to the theoretical underpinnings of Table 3.7. See Table A.1 in Appendix A.

3.4.2.3 PRACTICES

The basic goal of nurse scheduling is to match the available capacity of nurses to patient demand for nursing care. As such, it is closest to a "responsiveness" problem, as we define it in Appendix A. Consequently, we will use generic Table A.1 as a point of departure in our brainstorming exercise to generate a landscape of options to consider. The generic table uses principles of management to generate a range of options for improving the responsiveness of a resource. In Table 3.7, we build on the generic table, revising it for the specifics of the scheduling challenge. The Level 1 and Level 2 initiatives are the same as in generic Table A.1, with an additional staff satisfaction section. Level 0 explains the relationship between the scheduling challenge and a general responsiveness challenge.

Table 3.7   Objectives and Practices for Nurse Scheduling

Level 0 Objectives	Level 1 Objectives	Level 2 Objectives	Example Policies
Buffer variability by having excess nurse capacity relative to average demand	Reduce workload	Reduce case rate	Restrict patient throughput
			Use more home treatment
			Change strategy to focus on higher-paying, lower-volume diseases
		Reduce workload per case	Shift to target lower acuity patients
			Use labor-saving technologies
			Reduce the overall acuity in the population with community health programs
	Increase capacity	Add physical or human resources	Hire more nurses
			Hire more nurse extenders (techs, certified nursing assistants [CNAs], UAPs)
			Automate some manual processes
			Increase work hours per nurse per week
		Eliminate steps	Streamline admission, discharge, and other standard, time-consuming processes
		Reduce process times	Lean initiatives focused on reducing redundant tasks, eliminate steps, and so on, in nurse's work

Table 3.7   Objectives and Practices for Nurse Scheduling

Level 0 Objectives	Level 1 Objectives	Level 2 Objectives	Example Policies
		Balance workloads	Have accurate patient classification system to evenly balance work across nurses
		Increase task parallelism	Do admission, discharge, or other process steps in parallel instead of sequentially
		Improve batching	Stagger shifts to smooth the pulses of work at shift changes
		Reduce blocking/ starving	Install an IT system for information dissemination and availability, reducing "waiting for information" times
			Make lab results more available for rounding and discharge decisions
			Install a "discharge lounge" so patients medically cleared for discharge can leave a room
			Adopt new communication technologies to reduce wasted time trying to communicate to a doctor or other nurse
			Reduce time spent waiting for social work, transportation, and so on, before a patient can be discharged

Level 0 Objectives	Level 1 Objectives	Level 2 Objectives	Example Policies
Reduce asynchronicity between demand and capacity	Improve synchronization	Adjust demand rate to match the supply of nurses	Divert patients when hospital-wide nurses' workload is full
			Coordinate elective surgery schedule and nurse staffing schedule
			Coordinate referring physicians' schedules and nurse staffing schedule
			Board patients "off unit" when unit is up to nurse capacity
			Actively solicit patients from neighboring hospitals when a nursing unit is not full
			Email alerts to referring physicians, with a potential incentive or bonus, if they send patients to a unit that is not full
		Adjust capacity to match demand	Hold mandatory training and other required overhead activities during lighter shifts and times
			Use data mining to uncover predictable trends and generate better longer-range forecasts of demand (for example, one month in advance)
			Use a PCS system to better anticipate required capacity

Table 3.7 Objectives and Practices for Nurse Scheduling

Level 0 Objectives	Level 1 Objectives	Level 2 Objectives	Example Policies
			Shorten the lead time over which the hospital can change schedules, so only shorter-range forecasts are required
			Have open contract with temp nurse agency for same-day fill-ins
			Use nursing schedules that include guaranteed hours and "buffer" hours that may or may not be required
		Develop flexible capacity that can flow to demand	Develop and deploy a float pool of flexible and cross-trained nurses that can move capacity from over-staffed units to under-staffed units
			Have a tiered work-force with some nurs-es on fixed schedules, supplemented by another job class of nurses who must live with more uncertainty
			Design nursing teams as self-governing responsibility centers
			Schedule 4-hour shifts instead of 8- to 12-hour shifts to increase scheduling flexibility
			Install a website where nurses can register, at 6 a.m. each morning, their willingness to come in for unsched-uled work that day

Level 0 Objectives	Level 1 Objectives	Level 2 Objectives	Example Policies
Work directly on the variability of demand and capacity	Reduce variability	Reduce arrival variability	Divert patients who would spike variability in the arrival rate
			Close the ED, temporarily or permanently
			Rotate (share) admissions among all the nursing units to distribute and smooth the arrival stream to each unit
			Spread out admissions more evenly across shifts
		Reduce treatment variability	Make a strategic change to target more predictable diseases
			Use standardized best practices clinical pathways whenever appropriate for patients
			Divert patients who would spike variability in workload
			Include community health programs to reduce the overall acuity in the population
			Segment nursing units by acuity level
			Use observation units to advance patient diagnosis and optimize clinical pathways prior to arriving to the nursing unit

Table 3.7   Objectives and Practices for Nurse Scheduling

Level 0 Objectives	Level 1 Objectives	Level 2 Objectives	Example Policies
			Have physician work on the bed management team to help decide where to place patients
			Standardize best practices on nursing units, and have robust orientation efforts to implement them
			Use better handoffs to enhance communication and reduce rework
			Reduce batching (for example, batching admissions at a shift change)
			Limit consecutive hours worked, reducing stress and errors
			Decrease absenteeism to reduce variability in nurse availability
			Decrease turnover, resulting in fewer untrained nurses and more stable capacity on nursing units
Prioritize tasks during the day	Improve sequencing	Prioritize patients	Prioritize patients ready for discharge
			Prioritize new patients to get care plan stabilized
		Prioritize tasks	Study bottleneck tasks in nurse processes and prioritize these

Level 0 Objectives	Level 1 Objectives	Level 2 Objectives	Example Policies
Enhance the perceptions of patients and staff	Enhance patient perceptions	Keep patients occupied so they push their call buttons less frequently	Install engaging bedside entertainment systems
			Have strolling musicians
			Have simultaneous multi-bed video games
		Get patients started	Make admission and discharge processes fast and efficient
		Reduce patient anxiety so they push their call buttons less frequently	Have updated information system on upcoming rounds, meds, exercises, trajectory toward discharge, and so on
			Decorate with soothing paint colors and decor
			Design rooms to be less noisy, or to have piped-in soothing music
		Make waits proportional to value	Process admissions and discharges for easy cases first
		Facilitate group waiting	Use dedicated "admissions rooms" in addition to discharge lounges to gather patients waiting for admissions
Enhance staff perceptions	Increase staff perception of fairness in work allocation	Fair as equal work	Distribute extra work evenly among nurses on the unit
			Use a PCS to more evenly allocate workload to nurses

Table 3.7 Objectives and Practices for Nurse Scheduling

Level 0 Objectives	Level 1 Objectives	Level 2 Objectives	Example Policies
		Fair as earned priorities	Use a seniority system for allocating work
			Use a mutually accepted metric of performance as a means for allocating work
	Increase schedule stability	Longer notice	Freeze schedules further in advance
		More rigid commitments	Have some "guaranteed days" where nurse cannot be sent home; rotate these among the nurses
	Increase understanding of the scheduling challenge	Administrative training	Use tutorials on arrival rates and costs to illustrate the logic behind difficult scheduling decisions
	Increase ownership	Increase nurses' ownership of schedules and work assignments	Give nursing teams ownership of how work gets allocated among them, who goes home, who gets called in, and so on
			Use a nurse suggestion program with robust follow-up
			Use nurse shift auctions where nurses get to bid on their willingness to work different shifts
	Increase continuity of care	Increase continuity of nurse-patient experience	Allow nurses to stay with a patient until discharge
			Form patient-centric "nurse teams"
			Increase nurse responsibility for totality of care for patients on their unit

Central to the nurse scheduling challenge is the day-to-day matching of asynchronously varying demand (patients) and capacity (nurses). This task is made much easier if there is a lot of capacity to use (this may be expensive, but it will certainly mean we can meet demand), which can result from increasing raw capacity or decreasing demand. These options, however, are likely to either increase costs or decrease revenues. Most scheduling improvement options focus on reducing the variability (in both demand and capacity) itself, or on synchronizing it. That is, they focus on reducing overage and underage costs.

For example, if the hospital could smooth out the arrival rate of patients to nursing units, it would facilitate more accurate forecasting of patient loads and more accurate assignments of capacity. One way to smooth out the arrival rate of patients on the floor is to manipulate the manageable aspects of patient admissions, in particular the elective surgery schedule and transfers from other hospitals. Alternatively, the hospital could consciously divide admitted patients evenly among all its nursing units, so each unit gets roughly the same number of patients. This would eliminate inequalities among the various units and smooth out the volatility in any one unit (but may also result in suboptimal assignment of patients to units according to their specialized care needs). The hospital may also accept the patient stream as is and improve its ability to marshal the right amount of capacity. More day-to-day flexibility to change nurse staffing levels would allow nurse managers to adjust daily capacity to match the current patient load. For example, a judicious amount of cross-training to support efficient floating of nurses from one unit to another would allow capacity to flow to demand, reducing the mismatch.

Each of the options in Table 3.7 has its own costs and benefits. The idea at first is not to assess these ideas too critically, but simply to list a broad array of options to consider. Then the most promising ideas can be subjected to more detailed analysis.

The best ideas may well combine several of the initiatives listed in Table 3.7. For example, asking for more nurse flexibility (that is, reducing their guaranteed hours) may decrease nurse satisfaction, but satisfaction is itself a multidimensional issue. If increased flexibility lowers costs by X dollars, say, would the hospital be willing to pay nurses an additional X/2 dollars for agreeing to be more flexible? Would nurses be willing to make this trade-off? It is usually necessary to pull several levers at once to find an implementable win-win solution.

In the following three subsections, we present some detailed examples of nurse scheduling challenges and resolutions. The first describes ways to reduce overstaffing and understaffing costs in a large east coast hospital. The second case describes scheduling in a trauma-burn center. These specific situations and data are composites based on actual hospitals and centers as described in Beer et al. (2011), Harkin (2009), Chou at al. (2009), Klein et al. (2006), and Brasel et al. (2002). The final example describes nurse shift auctions, which at the time of writing are still being vetted in the industry.

St. Mary's Hospital is a large, tertiary care hospital on the east coast. Like many hospitals, St. Mary's was seeing its margins squeezed as a result of decreasing reimbursement schedules; increasing material, technology, and information costs; and an increase in the number of uninsured or underinsured patients it serves. The hospital prided itself on high-quality, patient- and family-friendly care, which it accomplished through its dedicated workforce. St. Mary's did not pay salaries to its doctors, who were not employees. Doctors were either independent contractors or belonged to a separate group practice that charged separately for services to patients. The majority of St. Mary's labor costs were for nurse and staff salaries, which accounted for a high percentage of its operating costs. CEO Bob Driscoll wanted to look carefully at his labor costs to see if there were any potential savings that could be achieved without compromising patient care. He hired a consulting firm that recommended a rotating patient placement schedule, where after a certain target population is reached in the nursing units, newly arriving patients were rotated evenly among all units. This, Bob was told, would reduce costs by decreasing the variability in the patient census across units. Indeed, after implementation of this new patient assignment system, the cost trends were encouraging. However, Bob also got vocal pushback from both doctors and nurses about problems with the new system. He was experienced enough to know that any new way of doing things, being unfamiliar to staff, often incurs blame for everything that goes wrong (whether or not the new system was really at fault). However, he also had faith in the excellence of his staff, and this prompted him to look more closely at the theory, and reality, of the new patient placement and staffing system.

Nurse Staffing Costs

Nurses were trained for and worked on a specific unit in the hospital (Cardiology, Neurology, and so on). They were paid hourly, and their schedules were set a month in advance. However, given the random nature of patient arrivals, it was often the case that the number of scheduled and available nurses either fell short of, or exceeded, the number needed to attend to the patients in each unit, which led to overage and underage costs. If there were too many nurses, some could be sent home "on call" but St. Mary's had to pay them for this (not their full salary, but it could still add up). Also, nurses who were scheduled and showed up ready to work at full salary, but were then told to go home on call, were often upset. Schedule unreliability regularly showed up on nurse staff surveys as a significant dissatisfier.

Overage and underage costs were, for all practical purposes, the only manageable nurse labor costs at St. Mary's. For clinical reasons, the hospital strived for a maximum patient-to-nurse ratio of four, so for any given patient census, the number of nurses required was preordained and unavoidable. In contrast, overage and underage costs were the costs of a mismatch between demand and capacity, and the hospital could reduce these with no impact on patient care. These mismatch costs were a direct result of unpredictable variability in patient load. Without unpredictable variability, there would be no problem scheduling just the right number of nurses. So, these labor costs followed from the variability in demand for nurses generated by variability in the numbers and types of patients admitted to the hospital (demand variability) and the unpredictable patterns of personal issues that prevented a scheduled nurse from coming to work (capacity variability). Here we will focus on the variability imposed by the heterogeneity in patient arrivals.

Patient Placement

In recent months, 52% of patient admits to St. Mary's came from referring physicians, 35% through the ED, and 13% from transfers from other hospitals. In each case, there was a physician (for example in the ED, or the referring physician) who had diagnosed the patient and could suggest which nursing unit was best (in terms of skill set) to manage the patient. Nurses on different units were trained for, and more experienced in, different types of diseases. The common intuition was that patients are best served by nurses most experienced with their particular ailment and, in some cases data (lengths of stay, complications, or adherence to checklists of standard best practices) confirms this.

However, patients did not always end up on St. Mary's recommended unit. When a patient was put in a non-ideal unit, it was known as *boarding* the patient on that unit. There were several reasons for boarding patients. First, each nursing unit had finite capacity, and if a unit was already full, it was not possible to place another patient there until someone was discharged, regardless of that patient's recommended designation. However, there was also suspicion that too much specialization was counterproductive, because it allowed caregivers to miss important disease complications that did not conform to their original narrow diagnosis. Indeed, older patients who often had several simultaneous and interacting comorbidities might be best served by nurses who were broadly rather than narrowly trained. Combined with the finite time that ED and other physicians had to diagnose a patient, this injected some doubt into the "right" unit for a patient. For example, a referring or ED physician may diagnose congestive heart failure, which by itself would recommend admission to a cardiology unit. But, the patient may also have been suffering from a complex of diseases, of which heart failure was just one, and a team of nurses focusing only on the heart may miss some important signals of that broader complex. So, it was not clear that the referring physician's recommendation was always the right one, although it was always important information that entered seriously into the patient's bed assignment.

St. Mary's had a bed management team (BMT) of four people who took requests for beds from referring physicians, the ED, the elective surgery schedule, interhospital transfers, and within hospital transfers (for example, from the ICU or step-down to a regular bed) and matched these demands against the bed availability in each unit. Bed availability was tracked on a *bed board*, which was a visual display of all the beds in each unit and the status of each (occupied, awaiting discharge, empty awaiting cleanout, or available). They then matched patients to available beds, taking into consideration the referring physician's recommendation. In some cases, a particular patient designation was "mandatory" due to the nature of the patient's disease. For example, patients with arrhythmias should go to a Cardiology unit, and patients for chemotherapy should go to a unit equipped with infusion chairs and with a trained staff for that activity. In other cases, one or more units may be preferred but not mandatory. For example, there are preferred places for patients with bronchitis, pneumonia, and pulmonary medical problems. In still other cases, no particular unit was preferred over all others. Of course, if a unit was already full, even "mandatory" patients had to be placed elsewhere. The BMT looked at the list of bed requests, considered the referring physician's recommendation, the resulting mandatory and preferred locations, and the bed availability on each unit before assigning patients to beds.

The physician assigned to oversee the patient's course of therapy was always "appropriate," in the sense that he would be of the type recommended in the original admission decision. For example, a cardiologist may have five patients: three on the Cardiology nursing unit and two others boarded elsewhere in the hospital. For that physician, rounds involve traveling to different nursing units. When a patient is boarded on another unit, the difference in his care is not due to a change of physician, but to the different skill sets of the nurses caring for him.

The New Patient Placement System

The manageable labor costs in the nursing units at St. Mary's were driven by the level of unpredictable variability in the number of patients assigned to that unit. Traditional thinking about managing these costs was aimed at getting better forecasts of patient loads. If St. Mary's could forecast exactly how many patients would be in each unit one month into the future, it could schedule just the right number of nurses. Unfortunately, although some improvements were made, these were limited and the problem persisted.

The consulting firm that Bob hired took a different approach. It sought to decrease variability in patient load on the units by rotating new arrivals through them. The "mandatory" patient designations were still honored, and many "preferred" were also, but other patients were handled differently. Specifically, the patient placement system that the consulting firm recommended would begin a day by assigning patients to their "proper" unit (as determined by the referring physician), but after a certain target census in the unit, newly admitted patients (without a mandatory destination) would be assigned to the other nursing units in a fixed sequence, regardless of the patient's original designation. For example, the next five arriving patients might go to units 1, 2, 3, 4, and 5 in that order regardless of where they were "supposed" to go. The logic behind this was that the responsible physicians would still be from the "proper" unit even if the patients were housed in a different place in the hospital, and by honoring the mandatory assignments, this system would not compromise clinical outcomes. The belief was that nurses were skilled enough to follow the instructions of doctors from any discipline, and the rotated patients were not those for whom a "must" designation applied. By rotating patient assignments, this system spread the patients more evenly throughout the hospital, eliminating major peaks and valleys in one nursing unit versus another. That is, it smoothed out variability at the nursing unit level. Some variability would remain because of variations in the total patient census in the hospital and variability in staff capacity. But patients would be distributed more evenly among the nursing units, reducing the current unevenness among them.

Table 3.8 shows the patient census in a sample of five different nursing units over a 6-month period (before patient rotations) and the results of a simulation experiment conducted by the consulting firm of what would happen to the census if those same patients were rotated through the units in the recommended way. The average number of patients per unit is the same, of course, but by rotating patients the standard deviation of the number of patients in each unit decreases, sometimes dramatically. For example, the standard deviation in unit 3 decreases from 4.4 to 2.6, and in unit 4 from 3.5 to 1.8. Overall, the average standard deviation over the five units declines from 4.1 to 3.0 as a result of cycling admissions among the units. The consulting firm forecasted that this reduction in variability would translate into reductions in overage and underage costs and lower nurse labor costs at St. Mary's with no serious compromises to clinical care. As a result of this analysis, the BMT was instructed to implement the new patient cycling system.

Table 3.8   Patient Census Before and After Cycling Admissions

Unit	Before Patient Rotations		After Patient Rotations	
	Mean	Standard Deviation	Mean	Standard Deviation
1	32.4	3.7	29.8	2.6
2	24.8	4.6	25.8	4.8
3	28.9	4.4	28.4	2.6
4	18.5	3.5	22.1	1.8
5	30.6	4.1	29.5	3.0
Average	27.1	4.1	27.1	3.0

Problems with the Patient Rotation System

After six months with the new system, St. Mary's had not yet realized the forecasted cost savings. Bob was also receiving an increasing number of complaints about it from physicians and nurses. Physicians did not like the increase in the number of boarded patients that resulted from the new system. Not only did doctors have to walk further on rounds, they had to deal with multiple nursing units, each with different staff and practices. The physicians complained to Bob that this was inefficient and possibly even dangerous because medical outcomes might be compromised due to patients being placed with staff unfamiliar with their particular disease.

Surprisingly, the nurses also complained. Bob had anticipated that more reliable staffing, with fewer nurses being called in or sent home, would be well received, and indeed that aspect of the new system was not part of the nurses' concerns. However, the nurses felt that the clinical and administrative parts of their job were suffering. Specifically, they reported that at times they were unsure what a particular patient needed and had trouble identifying and finding the responsible physician, who could be anywhere in the hospital. Also, the overhead activities for taking care of many different types of patients took time—time that came out of direct patient care.

Upon further investigation, it also appeared that the new system was not being followed as prescribed. That is, even after 6 months of data gathering, it was impossible to tell how much the new system could potentially save, because it was never fully implemented. That's because the BMT was not immune to emphatic input from doctors and nurses. Hence, although the BMT tried to implement something close to the desired cycling, in the case of any one patient there could be passionate voices arguing for specific nursing units, so the BMT frequently departed from the prescribed recipe. This resulted in less cycling than was anticipated by the consultants, who assumed all patients not in the "mandatory" category (and about half those in the "preferred" category) would be cycled. The result was less of a variability reduction, and therefore lower cost savings than anticipated.

Bob knew that people resist change in general, but he also knew that both physicians and nurses were key stakeholders in the organization, and he had to address their concerns to make headway.

Bob's Analysis

Bob took note of the fact that all the complaints from doctors and staff had to do with boarding patients, which was always a part of hospital operations but had become more pronounced under the new system. Doctors did not like walking long distances between patients, and nurses did not like the clinical and administrative complications of having boarded patients on their units. Yet, St. Mary's margins were not so robust that he could ignore an opportunity to lower costs, even modestly. Was there an approach that could reduce labor costs without boarding patients?

Bob, who had an MBA, recalled his college Operations classes on managing variability in services and looked back over his notes for ideas. He was reminded that somebody always pays a price for variability: patients (longer delays, longer stays, worse clinical outcomes), nurses and staff (higher workload), or the hospital (higher costs). The key to reducing these costs was to actively manage the variability itself so that it would not have to be buffered by increased capacity (and cost), time (delays), or quality (lowered expectations for outcomes).

Bob's notes listed two generic ways to manage variability: Reduce variability, or synchronize it. The first was the most direct way to reduce variability—just attack it head on. What were the sources of variability, and which of these could hospital policies influence? It was important to consider variability in the demand for nurse capacity (due to the number of patients arriving to a unit and the time demanded by each patient) and in nurse capacity itself (due to unplanned absences or sickness, for example). Most of the variability in workload was absorbed by the nurses themselves. St. Mary's staffed to a 4:1 patient-to-nurse ratio, so the required number of nurses on a unit was a function of the number of patients only and not how sick and time-consuming each patient was. So, variations in time demanded per patient were absorbed by the nurses and staff, not the hospital's bottom line. In contrast, variability in patient census on a unit translated directly into overage and underage costs and the hospital's bottom line. It was this variability that the new cycling admissions program tried to address.

Bob knew he could improve operations by reducing "process" variability. Currently, sources of process variability included nonstandard work practices, some frustrating process steps (for example, getting medications out of the secure cabinet was unnecessarily time consuming), and systemic issues such as batched admissions. (Typically, a glut of admissions occurred just after a shift change, for convoluted reasons having little to do with patient care or efficient operations.) There was also inherent variability in how sick each patient was and how much attention each needed for feeding, bathing, toilet needs, medications, pain management, and general emotional healing. Charge nurses attempted to distribute this load fairly when assigning patients to nurses so that no nurse got stuck with four very sick patients.

Variability in nurse capacity due to unplanned absences, premature departures for family emergencies, or nurse turnover (which resulted in a changing mix of nurses at varying levels of experience and efficiency) were important issues at St. Mary's, and Bob had already formed a task force to look at their hiring, training, and staffing policies.

While studying his notes, Bob also recalled that the most costly form of variability was unsynchronized variability between capacity and demand. That is, if demand went up but capacity rose to meet it, or if demand and capacity decreased together, there would be no unnecessary costs incurred. Problems occur when demand and capacity are "unsynchronized" so that high demand meets low capacity (an underage situation, requiring nurses to be called in) or low demand meets high capacity (an overage situation, requiring nurses to be sent home).

Bob realized that synchronizing demand and capacity could be accomplished in a variety of ways. First, if St. Mary's could better forecast patient loads up to one month in advance, nurse managers could better staff to forecast and reduce overage and underage costs. Bob knew that some demand could indeed be forecast, such as the demand for beds required after elective surgeries, but many of those cases were not scheduled one month in advance, and emergent cases were even less predictable. Historically, St. Mary's had not had much success trying to forecast patient loads. Even when the hospital believed it had a valid statistical model, dynamic changes in the economy, insurance legislation, or other exogenous influences rendered a lot of the historical data (and therefore the model) obsolete.

With imperfect forecasts, "synchronization" would have to be accomplished by more near-term initiatives, which strive to better match demand and capacity on a given day. Adjusting the patient demand on nursing units to match their available capacity was already done to some extent at St. Mary's through boarding patients. Adjusting capacity to meet demand was also done at St. Mary's through its practices of sending nurses home, or calling them back, based on patient census. Although this was a primary source of staff dissatisfaction, Bob wanted to consider all alternatives.

A key concept that Bob read about in his notes, and which he had not considered previously in this context, concerned flexible resources. Operations theory implied that flexible capacity that could be assigned where needed would allow an organization to better match capacity to demand and reduce overage and underage costs. At St. Mary's, nurses who could float to several units could be used to reassign nursing capacity to wherever the demand was that day, reducing mismatches between capacity and demand and its attendant costs. That is, instead of staffing each unit individually, St. Mary's could treat its nurses as one big pooled resource to be allocated to units as needed. This would eliminate situations in which one unit had more nurses than required, and another had fewer than required. This idea seemed promising to Bob, because he knew such mismatch situations were common. But he also knew that St. Mary's already floated nurses from one unit to another! So, why then would one unit be sending nurses home on call while another unit had to call in a higher priced additional nurse? Why didn't the required nurse simply float from the overstaffed unit to the understaffed unit?

Flexible Nursing Capacity

As with all process improvement activities, it was important to keep asking the question, "Why?" until the root cause was uncovered. Why would St. Mary's, which officially had systems to float nurses from one unit to another as required, ever be in a situation with overage on one unit (remedied by sending a nurse home) and underage on another (remedied by calling a nurse in at premium pay)? Bob asked his chief operating officer, Nilima Pandya, to find out why this might happen. Nilima, too, was curious. She explained to Bob that nurses at St. Mary's could be certified to work in a variety of areas, and if they arrived at work to an overstaffed unit, they always had the option to join the "float" pool of nurses who could be assigned to any unit for which they were certified and that needed more nurses that day. They could also refuse this opportunity and go home "on call," being paid a modest sum each hour to remain available. If their unit received a high number of admissions that day, nurses sent home on call would get priority in being called back in. Nilima also knew that arriving ready to work, only to be told to go home on call, was a major source of nurse dissatisfaction. So, like Bob, she assumed that most would join the float pool, and this should give St. Mary's the flexible capacity it needed to match its variable demand. But, upon investigation, this turned out not to be the case.

Nilima and her staff went to find out why. After interviewing nurses and nurse managers, they discovered several reasons for nurses choosing to go home rather than joining the float pool. Some actually preferred the day off. Others, however, preferred to work on their home unit but found the floating experience very dissatisfying. Their "certification" meant they had some familiarity with the disease states they would likely see on a foreign unit, but it did not mean they were familiar with the idiosyncratic local processes and culture on that unit. So, they felt inefficient and even disruptive in that unfamiliar territory. To make matters worse, the only time a nurse would float to a unit was when that unit was understaffed, so the local nurses had no time to orient and train the float nurse. This left the float nurse having to go around asking questions of very busy people, being less efficient than the locals, and even fearing that the quality of patient care might suffer. This was less than ideal from the perspective of both the floating nurse and the receiving unit. The nurse managers would also subtly discourage their own nurses from choosing to go to the float pool. They believed that if their surplus nurses floated out instead of going home on call, they would lose a valuable on-call resource that knew the unit well. If the unit experienced an excess of new admissions later in the day, they would not have well-trained capacity on call and would themselves have to tap the float pool for a less efficient nurse. So, contrary to the theoretical staffing policy, in practice St. Mary's was not using its nursing pool in a flexible manner.

A New System

Bob asked Nilima's team to estimate the potential savings if all nurses could float to other units with no loss of clinical efficacy. He knew this level of complete flexibility was not realistic, but he wanted an upper bound on the savings potential before he decided to invest more in this direction. The advantages of being able to float nurses could only be realized if there was at least one unit with an extra nurse and another with a need. Because St. Mary's was a highly utilized hospital, it was likely that many units would need nurses at the same time, so it was not clear what level of savings Bob could expect. However, the team used some simple queueing models to estimate a potential for 6% savings in nurse staffing costs relative to the status quo. This was significant, because nursing costs constituted more than half of the total labor costs at St. Mary's. Bob authorized the team to investigate the literature on flexibility in human resources and make some recommendations. The team reported the following:

1. Cross-training should be more thorough and include an orientation to and familiarity with the work processes on every unit to which a nurse can be assigned. One of the problems with the current certification program was a lack of exposure to everything a nurse had to know to be effective, and welcomed, onto a unit. The new system would train nurses in more than managing a certain disease type; it would also train nurses in the processes and culture on the nursing units to which they may float.

2. Given that training should be thorough, it was impractical to train nurses on more than a few units. That is, complete cross-training so that all nurses could work on any unit was infeasible. The team recommended that, if possible, each "flexible" nurse master at most two units. However, this meant that the 6% potential savings probably could not be fully realized.

3. Once cross-trained, a nurse should invest a minimum number of hours each year on all units that he or she was considered qualified to staff. Processes on units changed continually, so continual exposure was the only way to remain current. Relationships on units were also important to seamless integration, and these required continual exposure to maintain. These considerations also argued for qualifying an individual nurse on just a few units.

4. Not all nurses were excited about being cross-trained. Some preferred to work on just one unit. Fortunately, because the units did the best job they could to staff to patient needs and only had to float nurses to attend to overage and underage situations, most of the benefits of flexibility could be attained by having just a few nurses on each unit who could float. Not all nurses had to cross-trained.

5. The theory of resource flexibility suggested that the benefits of cross-training are concave in the level of flexibility (see Exhibit 3.5). Practically, this means that "a little bit of flexibility goes a long way," and St. Mary's could realize a good fraction of the ideal 6% benefit with just a modest number of flexible nurses—perhaps just one or two on each unit.

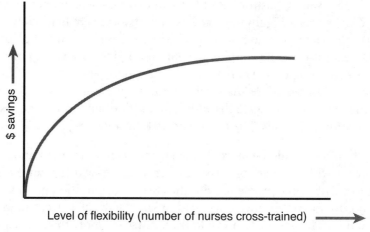

Exhibit 3.5   Benefits are concave in flexibility.

6. The theory of flexibility also provided insight into which cross-training designs might be effective. Exhibit 3.6a shows nurses being assigned to units with no cross-training, where only nurses trained for unit 1 can work on unit 1. The numbers after the nurse labels refer to the units they are qualified to staff. For example, "Nurses 1" refers to a pool of nurses who can only work on unit 1. Exhibit 3.6b shows the complete cross-training scenario, which could reduce staffing costs by 6% if it were feasible. Exhibit 3.6c shows a cross-training pattern that can achieve as much as 95% of the potential benefit (that is, a 5.7% cost reduction). The key idea, first presented by Jordan and Graves (1995), is that a "chain" of abilities will be almost as effective as full cross-training. If, on a given shift, unit 1 has too many patients, nurses can be pulled from unit 4. If this leaves unit 4 understaffed, it can pull nurses from unit 3, which can in turn pull nurses from unit 2 if needed. By chaining the nurses' abilities, any deficiency in any unit can usually be addressed as long as there is an extra nurse somewhere in the hospital. This is why a chained training design can attain most of the benefits of total flexibility, but at a much reduced training cost.

However, Nilima's team believed that cross-training would be easiest and most effective if the units that shared nurses (a) were similar, facing similar clinical challenges, and (b) could share nurses symmetrically to solidify personal relationships. That is, if some nurses from unit 1 could flow to unit 2, some nurses from unit 2 should also flow to unit 1. The nurse managers on units 1 and 2 could jointly decide on staffing levels, and the units could exchange ideas. The team believed that a sense of community would develop between the two units who shared nurses between them, suggesting the term "community cross-training" (Exhibit 3.6d). Although they estimated that in theory this pattern would only achieve 75% of the potential (a 4.5% cost reduction), in practice they believed it would promote many ancillary benefits within the informal and formal culture of paired units, including cross-fertilization of shared ideas for improvements from nurses moving back and forth between them.

Nilima recommended to Bob that St. Mary's select two nursing units with similar clinical challenges but variable and uncorrelated patient loads to pilot a community cross-training and cooperative staffing model. Data would be taken on nurse staffing costs, clinical outcomes, and patient and staff satisfaction. After 6 months, they would review the data and decide whether or not to roll out the system to the entire hospital.

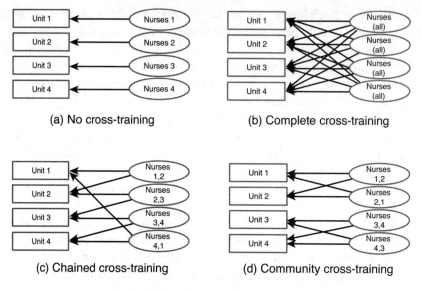

(a) No cross-training   (b) Complete cross-training

(c) Chained cross-training   (d) Community cross-training

Exhibit 3.6   Cross-training patterns.

At the 6-month review, the pilot did indeed lead to a 4% cost reduction, and both nurses and doctors associated with the two pilot units were happier with the community floating system than they were with the old patient rotation system. As a result, Bob asked Nilima to propose a rollout sequence of the community cross-training system to the other nursing units in St. Mary's.

3.4.2.5 CASE: SCHEDULING THE TRAUMA-BURN CENTER AT MERCALON HOSPITAL

The Mercalon Hospital Trauma-Burn Center (TBC) is verified as a Level 1 Pediatric and Adult Trauma and Burn Center by the American College of Surgeons (ACS). Verified centers offer specialized care, services, equipment, and staff who are trained to treat serious burn and trauma injuries. There are only 56 verified burn centers in the United States, or about one for every 5.4 million people, and 132 centers that self-declare burn expertise, or one for every 2.3 million people (Klein et al. 2006). Consequently, burn centers can cover large populations and geographic regions. Patients may receive preliminary care at a local hospital or from an emergency response team, but this is usually for stabilization only, and definitive care ensues only upon transfer to the regional center. Lengths of stay for burn victims are associated with the extent and depth of the burn. At Mercalon, arriving burn patients are 70% male and average about 30 years old with 10% total body surface area (TBSA) burned. The LOS for burn patients is about 9 days. Patients leave for home, a skilled nursing facility, or another acute care facility, and about 4% will die. Trauma patients arrive with a wide range of conditions and severities, dominated by orthopedic and head injuries, and about 25% require an operation of some sort. Trauma patients stay an average of 6 days prior to discharge or death. (Mortality is also about 4% for trauma patients.) The Mercalon TBC treats on average 1,200 patients each year, of which about 1,000 are trauma patients and the rest are burn patients.

Burn care is an extreme form of wound management that requires a high level of training and experience to manage a range of activities including initial intake and resuscitation or stabilization, rehabilitation, and end-of-life care. Although nurses practice in an environment of healing and hope for both patients and their families, burn care is a critical, highly skilled, emotionally draining job. Wound and dressing management, careful bathing, and other activities for these very sick patients are time- and labor-intensive. Trauma patients similarly generate a range of hope and despair in their caregivers. The worst of car accident and burn victims from all age groups end up at Mercalon, and there are more unsatisfying endings than any person would want. In addition to caring for their own patients, staff in the TBC may be called into the ED or other hospital units to advise on wound management issues in which they are expert. The TBC experiences higher than average turnover, in large part due to the emotionally draining nature of the work. In an environment where training periods are long, high turnover puts the TBC's critical reservoir of skill and experience at risk.

Karina Reisman, the nurse manager in the TBU, was responsible to her patients for quality care, to her staff for good and fair schedule management, and to the hospital administration for keeping costs under control. A particular challenge Karina faced was determining the "right" staffing level for the unit. Rules of thumb like "patients per nurse" imported from elsewhere in the hospital were not applicable in an environment where the level of severity of an injury can vary tremendously; one burn is not like another. Yet, acuity-based staffing rules were not in place at Mercalon, so Karina used a simple staffing model that assumed the unit would be at full capacity. Staff schedules were prepared and frozen four weeks in advance. When there were fewer, or less sick, patients in the TBC than assumed in the schedule, excess nurses could be transferred to the float pool for possible work in an understaffed unit, they could be put on call for $4.77/hour, they could take a paid vacation day, or they could take an unpaid vacation day. When the unit was overstaffed, who got reassigned was driven largely by seniority. When admissions or acuity spiked above "capacity," as was inevitable in the TBC's highly variable environment, too few nurses would be on hand. Extra nurses could be procured from the "float pool" (if they are TBC trained) or called in from off-duty TBC nurses for 1.5 to 1.75 times their normal wage. Because Karina scheduled assuming that the unit would be at full patient capacity, overstaffing was a more frequent problem than understaffing.

All the options for addressing over- or understaffing were costly for the hospital and disruptive for the nurses. Staffing uncertainty was a significant part of nurse dissatisfaction, which contributed to nurse turnover. Turnover was a significant problem in the TBC because training times were long due to the specialized and delicate nature of the required care. Yet, the unit had been running over budget, so cost control was a key concern. Karina wanted a better and more cost-effective way to match nursing capacity to the uncertain patient demand.

Karina knew that there were some periods when the unit was not full, so her at-capacity staffing policy could be improved, but she was not sure what changes were necessary. She decided to use historical data to estimate the seasonality of activity in the TBC to help her anticipate staffing requirements. She found that trauma arrivals were significantly higher in the summer than in the winter. Exhibit 3.7 shows the mean and standard deviation of daily trauma patient arrivals, by month.

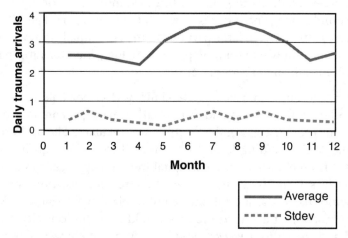

Exhibit 3.7   Trauma average daily arrivals by month.

The burn arrival rate was lower and fairly even for three quarters of the year before dipping lower in the fourth quarter (October–December), as shown in Exhibit 3.8.

Another source of variation in staffing needs was the level of acuity among the patients. The TBC had an ICU unit for very sick patients, a step-down unit for intermediate needs, and a regular floor unit for patients with less care-intensive needs. Patients in the ICU required, on average, one nurse for every one to two patients. The nurse-to-patient ratios for step-down and the floor were 1:2 and 1:3, respectively. Elsewhere in the hospital, lower nurse-to-patient ratios were used; the TBC was highly labor intensive.

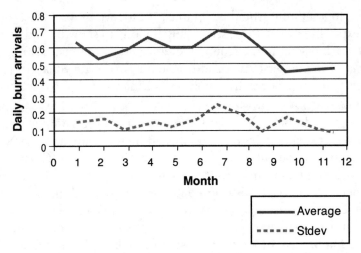

Exhibit 3.8 Burn average daily arrivals by month.

Karina collected historical work records for the TBC and found that she used, on average, 11 nurses per day. The TBC patient census and staffing needs by month are shown in Exhibit 3.9.

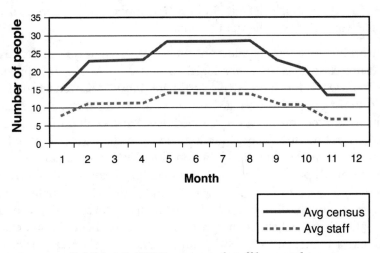

Exhibit 3.9 TBC census and staff by month.

Because Karina planned staff at full capacity, scheduling 15 nurses for each day, she frequently had to resort to one of the overstaffing remedies. She realized that she could use this new seasonality information to do better. Karina's liberal staffing policy was not completely irrational, however. On any given day, the actual patient census was likely to be different from the average, either on the upside or downside, and the costs of accommodating these forecast errors should be taken into account when staffing the unit. For example, if recovering from overstaffing was costless but understaffing was expensive, always staffing to a full unit would be optimal. If the reverse were true, costless understaffing and expensive overstaffing, scheduling nobody to show up and bringing nurses in (costlessly) each day up to the required level would be optimal. Staffing to the mean is only optimal if the understaffing and overstaffing costs are equal. To relate her seasonal forecasts to appropriate staffing policies, Karina wanted to consider these costs.

Managing the Understaffing and Overstaffing Costs

Variability in required TBC staff derived from the seasonal variation in staffing needs as described earlier, as well as daily variation in staffing needs due to variability in patient census and acuity. Overall, 40% of arrivals to the TBC went to ICU beds requiring a high nurse-patient ratio, but many of these patients migrated to step-down or regular beds before being discharged. Historical data for required staffing in the TBC showed that the "coefficient of variability" (standard deviation divided by the mean) for staffing needs each month was roughly constant across the year at .15. For example, on average in January Karina needed 7.65 nurses on staff each day, with a standard deviation of .15(7.65) = 1.15 nurses. The data also supported a normal distribution for staffing needs, implying that 95% of the time, staffing needs were within 2 standard deviations of the mean. So, for example, 95% of the time, a day in January would require between 7.65 − 2(1.15) = 5.35 and 7.65 + 2(1.15) = 9.95 nurses. Likewise, 99.7% of the time, staffing needs would be within 3 standard deviations of the mean, or between 4.2 and 11.1 nurses. Clearly, Karina's default "full staffing" policy was suboptimal in January. But, what, she wondered, was the right number?

This sort of problem—choosing a level of capacity to face uncertain demand—can be addressed using classical *newsvendor* logic. (See section A.2.1.1 in Appendix A.) To invoke this framework, Karina needed to estimate the cost of overstaffing (c_o) and the cost of understaffing (c_u). The average base salary for a TBC nurse was $27.26 per hour, plus benefits. When too few nurses were scheduled, Karina could marshal more capacity in one of several ways. She could get a nurse from the float pool if a TBC-trained nurse was available, or she could call in an off-duty TBC nurse at an average premium of 60% above normal pay. The former was not charged against her, and the latter costs .6(27.26) = $16.36 per hour ($130.84 for an 8-hour shift) above what she would pay if she had the right number of nurses scheduled. She used the base pay, without benefits, in this calculation because benefit charges were largely fixed and did not change significantly with extra hours. Because TBC-trained nurses were scarce, Karina could only find an appropriate nurse in the float pool about 30% of the time. So, 70% of the time she had to rely on calling in an off-duty nurse, and her average "cost of understaffing" c_u = .7(130.84) = $91.59. That is, she would incur a cost of $91.59 per nurse understaffed. But Karina knew this might actually underestimate the true cost of understaffing, because float nurses were less familiar with the TBC procedures and hence would be less efficient.

If Karina scheduled too many nurses to come in, then the excess nurse(s) could be floated out to another unit if the need arose, take a paid or unpaid vacation day, or put on-call for $4.77 per hour ($38.16 per shift). TBC nurses were well trained, and at least half the time they could be floated out to other units, so on average the overage cost per nurse is c_o = .5(38.16) = $19.08. That is, Karina incurred a cost of $19.08 for each nurse overstaffed on a given day. Being sent home was not popular with nurses, so considering their satisfaction, $19.08 might underestimate the true cost of overstaffing.

By explicitly considering the costs of overstaffing and understaffing nurse capacity and the probability distribution of the demand that would be placed on the TBC's capacity, the newsvendor model allowed computation of an economic staffing decision that would minimize expected total staffing costs. The Newsvendor principle (see section A.2.1.1 of Appendix A) states that the optimal staffing level can be computed as follows:

$$F(s) = \frac{c_u}{c_o + c_u}$$

where $F(\ )$ is the cumulative probability function for the demand for nurse staff. That is, $F(s)$ is the probability that demand will be less than or equal to s. This number could be computed in the Mercalon case (see next paragraph) because Karina knew that monthly demand for nurses in the TBC was normally distributed, with known mean and standard deviation.

The newsvendor ratio for the Mercalon TBC is 91.59 / (91.59 + 19.08) = 0.828, so the appropriate staffing level given uncertain patient demand was to staff to a level that will meet or exceed patient demand with probability 0.828. That is, given the random demand for nursing hours each day, Karina concluded from the preceding analysis that she should schedule enough nurses to cover all demand 82.8% of the time. Demand should only exceed capacity 17.2% of the time (see Exhibit 3.10). Note that staffing to the mean would cover demand 50% of the time, so in fact it is optimal to staff to a level higher than the mean. This is a result of the overstaffing costs being lower than the understaffing costs.

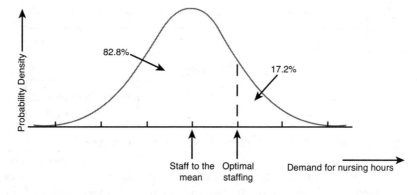

Exhibit 3.10   Staffing in the Mercalon TBC required to meet demand 82.8% of the time.

When daily demand is normally distributed, the staffing level that achieves this target 82.8% probability equals the mean plus 0.945 standard deviations. So, for any given day, Karina should schedule enough nurses to cover the expected patient demand plus 0.945 standard deviations. Putting this together, if μ denotes the mean (expected value) of the staffing needs per day for a specific month, its standard deviation $\sigma = .15\,\mu$. Taking into account the costs of overstaffing and understaffing, Karina should schedule $S^* = \mu + .945\,\sigma$ nurses to come to work. So, $S^* = \mu + .945(.15\,\mu) = 1.14\mu$ nurses. That is, each month Karina should start with the forecasted expected value of her daily staffing needs, based on her seasonal analysis, and then bump it up by 14% when scheduling nurses to come to work.

For example, Karina's seasonal analysis revealed that, in January, her mean required staffing level was 7.65 nurses, so in January Karina should plan to staff each day with $1.14(7.65) = 8.72$ nurses. Karina understood that the financial costs of under- and over-staffing can underestimate the true costs for the reasons stated, so she used her judgment to choose between staffing 8 or 9 nurses. (Both would be reasonable with a staffing target of 8.72.) When all aspects of her scheduling problem were considered, she chose to schedule 9 nurses in January.

During the summer months, adding 14% would actually increase her staffing level beyond 15 nurses, so she truncated her staffing to the full complement of 15. In summary, Karina's target staffing levels for each month were revised to the levels shown in Exhibit 3.11.

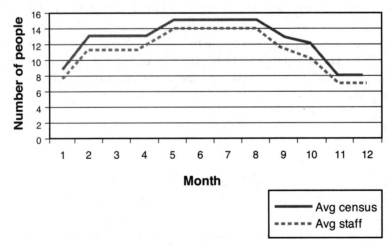

Exhibit 3.11   Average staff and staff target by month.

Implementing this forecast-driven staffing model saved Karina a full 5% in her labor costs over the next year. It also increased her and her unit's understanding of the pacing and seasonality of demand for their services.

A Refined Patient Demand Model

Armed with her success, Karina wondered if she could extract more from the data. Specifically, staffing needs are driven by both census and acuity, and some hospitals had detailed PCSs recognizing that all patients are not alike, and that some will require more care (and nursing time) than others. A more refined staffing model would go beyond simply counting patients and take variations in patient mix and acuity into account when estimating how many nurses were needed on any given day. She did not have the time or resources to explore and implement a complicated PCS, but she did have historical records containing a detailed breakdown of how many patients were in the ICU, step-down, and floor each day. Because these bed designations were correlated with acuity, she decided to see what she could do using bed status as a proxy for a patient's sickness and therefore demand on her nurses.

For example, on average over the year, there were 24 patients in the TBC, broken down into 17 trauma patients (6 ICU, 3 step-down, 8 floor) and 7 burn patients (3 ICU, 2 step-down, 2 floor). 40% of all new arrivals went into ICU beds requiring a high nurse-patient ratio, but these patients would (hopefully) migrate to a step-down bed, regular bed, and then discharge, changing their required level of care as they go. Karina assumed patients could be in one of four possible states: ICU, step-down, floor, or discharged/deceased. On the recommendation of a systems analyst in the hospital, Karina read up on and developed a "Markov chain" model of patient trajectories through the TBC. This is a type of statistical mathematical model assuming that the probability of a patient being in a given state tomorrow is determined by his state today. For example, based on TBC historical data, a burn patient who is in the ICU today has

- An 89% chance of remaining in the ICU tomorrow

- A 10% chance of being in step-down tomorrow

- A 1% chance of dying or being discharged

A burn patient who is in step-down today has

- A 75% chance of remaining in step-down tomorrow

- A 7% chance of reverting to an ICU bed

- A 12% chance of improving to floor status

- A 6% chance of dying or being discharged

A detailed description of Markov chains is beyond the scope of this book, but treatments can be found in any basic Operations Research text. Essentially, given the census of patients in each state (ICU, step-down, regular, discharged) today and the estimated transition probabilities, Karina could estimate the census in each state tomorrow, and by repeating the process she could estimate that census two days hence, three days, and so on.

For example, if Karina has 3 ICU burn patients today, and each will have an 89% chance of remaining in the ICU, a 10% chance of moving to step-down, and a 1% chance of leaving the TBC by tomorrow, the expected number of patients tomorrow (due to these 3 ICU patients today) will be 2.67, .3, 0, and .03 in the four categories, respectively. Repeating calculations like this for each type of patient today gave Karina an estimate of the expected number of patients in each state tomorrow and for any day into the future. These calculations ignored new arrivals, so the actual number of burn patients Karina could expect one day into the future would be these computed numbers plus the average daily arrivals to each bed status. Similar calculations could be performed for trauma patients. In summary, given the current census in each bed type and the known daily arrival rates for the season, Karina could forecast the census in each bed type for any number of days into the future.

Table 3.9 shows the results of these calculations for one day in July. The required staff for trauma and burn care are shown in the table, and Karina would add those two columns to get the total number of nurses required. Karina truncated this at a maximum of 15 nurses. For example, the forecasted total number of nurses required today (day 0) is 6.28 + 2.86 = 9.14, and for tomorrow (day 1) is 7.02 + 3.02 = 10.04. The expected number of nurses required for days 2, 3, 4, and 5 into the future are 10.82, 11.51, 12.12, and 12.66. Because one month ago Karina scheduled 15 nurses to work each day, she would be overstaffed for at least the next five days. However, one week out, her target staffing level would be up to 13.56 nurses, and within two weeks, she would want to staff up to the regular July target of 15 nurses. That is, the unusually low census of 17 patients on this one particular July day has little effect when Karina looks ahead four weeks, which is her planning horizon for nurse scheduling. The LOS for trauma and burn patients is 9.23 and 6.15 days, respectively, so looking 28 days out, most patients currently in the TBC will have left, and the future census is driven primarily by future arrivals, not by the current census. The best data Karina had on future arrivals was just the historical July long-run averages. So, there was little opportunity to leverage current census information to improve forecasts when staffing 4 weeks into the future.

Table 3.9   Mercalon TBU Forecast Starting on a Day in July, and Looking Out Four Weeks

	Trauma patient forecast Census at acuity levels			Expected Staffing	Target Staffing		Burn patient forecast Census at acuity levels			Expected Staffing	Target Staffing
Days ahead	ICU	Step down	Floor	Expected Staffing	Target Staffing	Days ahead	ICU	Step down	Floor	Expected Staffing	Target Staffing
0	2	5	5	5.51	6.28	0	2	1	2	2.51	2.86
1	3.21	3.69	6.49	6.16	7.02	1	2.13	1.12	1.98	2.65	3.02
2	4.09	3.12	7.24	6.71	7.65	2	2.25	1.22	1.98	2.78	3.17
3	4.75	2.91	7.66	7.19	8.19	3	2.37	1.31	1.99	2.91	3.31
4	5.26	2.88	7.94	7.60	8.67	4	2.48	1.39	2.01	3.03	3.45
5	5.65	2.92	8.16	7.96	9.08	5	2.59	1.46	2.03	3.14	3.58
6	5.96	3.00	8.35	8.28	9.43	6	2.68	1.53	2.06	3.25	3.70
7	6.22	3.08	8.53	8.54	9.74	7	2.78	1.58	2.10	3.35	3.82
8	6.42	3.15	8.70	8.77	10.00	8	2.86	1.64	2.13	3.44	3.93
9	6.58	3.22	8.85	8.97	10.23	9	2.94	1.68	2.16	3.53	4.03
10	6.72	3.28	8.99	9.14	10.42	10	3.02	1.73	2.20	3.62	4.12
11	6.83	3.33	9.12	9.28	10.58	11	3.09	1.77	2.23	3.70	4.21
12	6.92	3.38	9.23	9.39	10.71	12	3.15	1.81	2.26	3.77	4.30
13	6.99	3.41	9.32	9.49	10.82	13	3.21	1.84	2.30	3.84	4.37
14	7.05	3.44	9.41	9.58	10.92	14	3.27	1.88	2.33	3.90	4.45
15	7.10	3.47	9.48	9.65	11.00	15	3.32	1.91	2.36	3.96	4.52
16	7.14	3.49	9.54	9.70	11.06	16	3.37	1.94	2.39	4.02	4.58
17	7.17	3.51	9.59	9.75	11.12	17	3.41	1.96	2.41	4.07	4.64
18	7.20	3.52	9.63	9.79	11.16	18	3.45	1.99	2.44	4.12	4.70
19	7.23	3.53	9.67	9.83	11.20	19	3.49	2.01	2.46	4.17	4.75
20	7.24	3.54	9.70	9.85	11.23	20	3.53	2.03	2.48	4.21	4.80
21	7.26	3.55	9.72	9.88	11.26	21	3.56	2.05	2.51	4.25	4.84
22	7.27	3.56	9.74	9.90	11.28	22	3.60	2.07	2.53	4.28	4.88
23	7.28	3.56	9.76	9.91	11.30	23	3.62	2.09	2.54	4.32	4.92
24	7.29	3.57	9.77	9.92	11.31	24	3.65	2.10	2.56	4.35	4.96
25	7.30	3.57	9.79	9.93	11.33	25	3.68	2.12	2.58	4.38	5.00
26	7.31	3.57	9.80	9.94	11.34	26	3.70	2.13	2.60	4.41	5.03
27	7.31	3.58	9.81	9.95	11.34	27	3.72	2.15	2.61	4.44	5.06
28	7.32	3.58	9.81	9.96	11.35	28	3.74	2.16	2.62	4.46	5.09

Karina realized that unless nurses would accept schedule changes with only one to two weeks' notice, the immediate daily census was not directly relevant to her nurse scheduling problem. Acutely aware of how valuable her nurses were, and unwilling to inject more uncertainty into their lives, Karina did not wish to change her four-week planning horizon at this time.

However, the refined system did make some efficiencies possible. By being able to forecast scheduled overstaffing and understaffing up to a week in advance, Karina was able to make adjustments with several days' lead time and avoid the disruptive nature of same-day staffing changes. For example, all nurses were required to take periodic continuing education courses to keep their knowledge current, and Karina could schedule those for times when she knew she would be overstaffed. If not enough nurses were scheduled to show up, Karina could proactively ask nurses days in advance if they wanted to work. These changes, while not immediately financially impactful, were well received by her staff.

Karina was discussing her staffing project with a family friend, an economist at a local university. The economist was a strong advocate for market-based solutions to allocation problems, meaning some form of marketplace that brings buyers and sellers together—in this case, Karina in need of nurses and nurses in need of work-hours and pay.

"Why not design an electronic marketplace to match buyers (a hospital willing to pay) to sellers (nurses willing to work)?" the economist asked. "One example I know of is a 'nurse shift auction' (NSA), in which hospitals post the shifts that they need to cover and nurses bid their price for working the shift! Auctions are now fairly common, and well understood, market mechanisms in other industries. Under the right conditions, markets can distribute goods to those who most value them, so market-based mechanisms are potentially beneficial to both hospitals and nurses."

Karina realized that a shift covered at a wage lower than her premium costs would be financially beneficial to the hospital. If nurses were not forced to work, so they only work at wages they themselves specify, shifts might go to those who most value them with no strong dissatisfying consequences. This seemed so intuitively attractive that she invested some time to research shift auctions.

Karina's Research

By simply conducting a web search on the key words "nurse auctions," Karina was able to uncover a wealth of information. She found that the basic outline for an NSA is as follows. First, the hospital schedules itself the best it can. If shifts are unfilled, they are placed up for auction. A qualified pool of bidders can bid on the shifts, with the lowest bidder getting the work. Within this basic framework, however, there are many different design considerations. Each of these has been explored in industrial auctions (more prevalent than health care applications), so there was some inherited wisdom about how to manage them. Exhibit 3.12 shows the auction design decisions that Karina was able to list.

Hospital-run shift auctions are not the only electronic marketplace models that Karina found. Nurse agencies can auction off nurse time to hospitals, basically reversing the tables and running the auction from the supply side. Also, "double auctions" are possible, in which hospitals put in needs and their maximum willingness to pay, nurses put in their availability and minimum acceptable wages, and the buyers and sellers are electronically matched. All of these were being experimented with in various forms, and as she visited websites, Karina saw advertisements by a number of consulting companies standing ready to provide auction services to hospitals and nurses.

1. Open or sealed bids? In an open bid auction each nurse knows what the current best bid is. In a sealed bid auction nurses do not know what their competitors are bidding. Both have strengths and weaknesses. Sealed bids are believed to reduce the chance of collusion among bidders, and are simple in that nurses submit one bid and don't have to worry about tracking other bids and potentially updating their own as competing bids come in. However, hospitals experimenting with shift auctions have not found collusion among nurses to be a big problem, and open bidding has appeal as a more transparent and information-rich process. Both designs are in use.

2. What constraints should be put on legitimate bids? That is, what is the maximal acceptable bid to the hospital and the minimum a nurse can bid? It seems reasonable that the maximal bid should be somewhere around the agency cost, since this is what the hospital would have to pay in the absence of bidding. The minimal bid is more debatable. If a nurse really needs money and is willing to work at depressed wages rather than not work at all, why not allow this? The problem is that many auction frameworks give natural power to the "auctioneer" who defines the rules, and so can be used to put nurses in competition with each other to drive down wages. In the short run this may save some money for the hospital, but in the longer run may breed resentment and further defections from the profession. It seems reasonable to disallow bids lower than a mutually agreed upon fair wage.

3. Opening and closing time for bids. When is the auction held? How long is bidding open? The further in advance the auction is held the more stable the planning process can be for all stakeholders (nurses and the hospital know their time commitments well in advance), but the less the auction can respond to shorter-term fluctuations in patients and nurse availability. Some hospitals open the auction weeks before the work is required, and some open one at the beginning of each scheduling cycle. Likewise, some close the auction weeks in advance, and others let it go until days before the shift must be worked. One common feature in open auctions with fixed termination times is "sniping," where bidders wait until the last minute and then jump in and just undercut the current best bid, hoping that the competing bidder does not have time to respond. This is less of an issue with sealed bid auctions, because nobody knows what to undercut.

4. Who can bid? How are they qualified? Some hospitals allow only staff RN's to bid, others any staff, and still others extend the bidding to nurses outside the hospital. In all cases, issues of who is qualified must be carefully managed. Hospitals need to engage a form of "vendor qualification" (common in industrial practice) to be sure that only qualified nurses bid on a shift. For example surgery, ED, or ICU shifts may require specialty training. Also, there are likely to be cultural issues on any specific unit that make temporary nurses, unfamiliar with the way things are done, less efficient. Qualification can include some mandatory experience on the unit. Once the qualifications required for specific shifts are determined, only qualified bidders can bid for those shifts.

5. What is the wage paid to the winner? This is more of a theoretical question than a practical one. It is natural and intuitive for the wage paid to be the wage bid. But, there is some

Exhibit 3.12 The results of Karina's research on the design decisions for nurse shift auctions.

theoretical justification for paying the second lowest bid (which will be higher than the lowest bid). While this may seem counterintuitive, bidders use different bidding strategies under a "second-lowest" design, and the hospital may not end up paying any more (see the "revenue equivalence principle" in Krisha 2002). Also, sometimes the wage bid will be very close to the second best anyway. Consider an open bidding contest, in which bidders compete with each other, each alternately undercutting the other. The winner will cease aggressive bidding when her last remaining competitor drops out, so will win the shift at a wage that reflects the second best nurse's value. Only if there is a significant difference in how much the most competitive nurses value the shift will there be a significant difference in the winning wage. So, paying the first best or second best bid may not end up being that different, in the end. However, second-best pricing lacks the virtue of intuitive transparency, and no hospital interviewed by Li (2005) used a second-best wage design in their auctions.

6. Include an "instant win" option? This is where a hospital will award the shift to the first nurse bidding a specified wage. Instant-win options can co-exist with regular bidding. Bidding occurs as usual, but if at any time some nurse wants to guarantee he gets the shift he can bid the instant-win price (if he is the first to do so). This sort of option is used in some commercial auctions. There may be benefits from an earlier closing of the bidding and maybe an enhanced sense of control by nurses.

7. Can more than one shift be auctioned off simultaneously? There may be windows of time in which a nurse prefers extra work only if she gets a lot of added work, not just one shift. In these cases the nurse would benefit from bidding on a block of shifts, not just one at a time. This gets complicated quickly as one contemplates the many different ways to mix and match shifts (these are called "combinatorial auctions" in industrial practice, because of the many ways the pieces can combine, and are notoriously difficult to manage). It may be advantageous for a hospital to auction off blocks of time that are longer than a shift, but full blown combinatorial auctions where nurses can bid on different combination packages of shifts is beyond current practice.

Exhibit 3.12   The results of Karina's research on the design decisions for nurse shift auctions.

Some health systems reported millions of dollars in cost savings by auctioning off shifts to staff nurses instead of hiring agency nurses (Li 2005), but the more she read into these systems, the more complicated assessing their true potential benefits became.

Win-Win or Win-Lose?

Karina was intrigued by the testimony of a nurse at the Spartanburg Regional Medical Center in South Carolina who, every two weeks, entered her preferences for shifts into a website (Koeppel 2004). She usually worked three 12-hour shifts each week and was paid $20.11 an hour, but she could bid for extra hours to help pay her expenses, which included raising two children and taking master's level classes. She could bid in a way that least interfered with these other obligations, and when she won, her pay was often in the $39/hour range. Agency nurses cost the hospital about $50 per hour, and the hospital set a reservation price (maximum bid) of $40.50 per hour. So, filling the shift at $39/hour was a win-win for the nurse and the hospital. As the nurse explained, "Shift bidding helps out my family and presents a great opportunity for nurses to take advantage of." According to Spartanburg's chief nursing officer, the center auctioned 350 to

500 shifts every two weeks, and about one-third of the center's 1,200 nurses had used the system. The average winning bid was $36/hour, and the hospital had saved $1.2 million since implementing the system in 2002 (Koeppel 2004).

There was evidence that shift bidding can be appreciated by nurses to the extent that it enhances their control over their schedules, which is important for family life and their interface with the outside world. In a survey of 153 nurses in Israel, Sagie and Krausz (2003) looked at the influence of objective job characteristics (demographics, regular shiftwork versus rotating schedules, night versus day, ICU Department versus non-ICU) and subjective perceptions (demands of the job and degree of control over one's own schedule) on the dependent variables of job satisfaction, commitment to the organization, burnout, and intention to leave the hospital. They found that the subjective variables were the most significant drivers of the dependent variables, and that the deleterious effects of highly demanding jobs could be partially compensated for by some degree of schedule control. This suggested that some control over schedule is appreciated by nurses and can reduce their intention to leave the workplace, a desirable outcome because turnover in the TBC is particularly costly given the special skills required in the unit.

Detractors of shift bidding, including some nurses' union leaders, pointed out that the dynamic of low pay leading to longer hours, just to make ends meet, was a common historical theme in labor history and had an abusive end-point. They maintained that higher wages and improved working conditions were better long-term solutions to any nursing shortage (Koeppel 2004). They also saw a dangerous precedent in nurses competing with one another for shifts, which might undermine the solidarity needed to make demands of management. Koeppel (2004) noted that almost none of the hospitals employing NSAs were unionized.

It is also true that, in any auction design, the entity that gets to design the auction has a natural advantage. Bidders can only play by the rules declared by the auctioneer, so those rules can be written for unilateral advantage. For example, a reservation price can be set so low that only the most desperate apply, and even these may perceive only marginal personal value in the extra work due to the depressed wage. Being acutely aware of how valuable her trained staff was at the TBC, Karina knew that if she used any sort of NSA, she would have to be careful to share the potential gains with the nurses (ensure a win-win), rather than extracting as much as possible in an adversarial manner. Of particular interest to Karina were any clinical consequences of NSAs, but there was no data to shed light on this. Depending on how it is implemented, she speculated that shift bidding may affect the skills mix on a floor or unit and continuity of patient care. Based on what she could find in the literature, the full financial, operational, organizational, and clinical consequences of shift auction systems were not yet fully understood.

Because the full costs and benefits for NSAs were still being worked out in hospitals across the country, Karina adopted a cautious approach. She decided that she would continue to use her upgraded scheduling method using statistical forecasts and her Markov chain model for near-term forecasts. However, if her near-term needs exceeded her scheduled capacity, Karina allowed nurses to bid on the extra slots, but she placed a relatively high minimum bid level to maintain a decent wage close to the status quo. If more than one person bid at the minimum, she broke ties based on seniority. The same general system was used in reverse when she forecast that she would be overstaffed. Nurses were able to bid for their wage consequences of being asked to stay home, where again she bounded the allowed levels to be close to the status quo and broke ties by seniority. This cautious approach generated only modest savings but helped her and her team learn about the pros and cons of NSAs, a knowledge base they intended to build on over time and with experience.

3.4.3 Managing Handoffs

Health care delivery in hospitals is performed 24 hours a day, 7 days a week. Caregivers cannot be on duty continuously, so there are inevitable transfers of care responsibilities between them. Also, patients often require multiple services or procedures during a hospitalization, which are delivered by multiple providers. Consequently, communication between health care personnel is an essential component of safe, effective care. Handoffs, or transfers of information, occur frequently between health care providers. We focus here on one particular type of handoff: the shift-to-shift nursing report. This report is important because patient needs change as they get better, or worse, in the hospital. Monitoring, medications, and plans of care change dynamically over time. So, when one nursing shift leaves the hospital to be replaced by another, patient information must be transferred from the departing shift to the arriving one. This shift-to-shift handoff is known as a *report* (commonly a *nursing report, nursing shift report,* or *shift-to-shift report*). Although practices vary widely across nursing units and hospitals, nursing reports commonly entail the exchange of both verbal and written information.

3.4.3.1 PROBLEM

In her ethnographic study, Wolf (1988) identified the shift-to-shift nursing report as an "occupational ritual" whereby nurses formally release and accept responsibility for patient care. Wolf's observations revealed the concept of "suspended time" that enabled on- and off-duty nurses to focus on the data surrounding their patients. In a recent literature review, Hilligoss and Cohen (2010) concluded that the goal of any handoff between health care providers is:

to establish a shared understanding of the patient and his or her trajectory sufficient for the receiving party to anticipate likely and possible emergent needs and to move care forward in a smooth, appropriate and effective manner.

Several studies have identified important correlations between faulty handoffs and safety events. In a classic paper by Donchin et al. (1995), four months of detailed observation in ICUs showed that errors by nurses had peaks just after physician rounds, and again at each shift change. The authors conclude that communication errors between physicians and nurses (during or after rounds) and between nurses and nurses (at shift changes) contributed significantly to the error rate.

In 2005, the Joint Commission reviewed its registry of sentinel events from acute care hospitals (for example, chemotherapy errors, wrong-site surgery, patient elopement, and patient suicides) and identified communication problems in two-thirds of these events (Croteau 2005). In an Australian study, 17% of 14,000 admissions experienced an adverse event, and in 11% of those events, communication problems were identified as a contributing factor (Wilson et al. 1995). In a 2009 "safety culture" survey of 196,462 staff members in 622 hospitals (Sorra et al. 2009), information loss during handoffs and transitions received the lowest (only 44% positive) score among all the contributors to safety culture. Information loss during transitions is a recurring theme in safety studies in hospitals, with quality losses in physician-to-physician communication (during handoffs from the ED to the nursing unit, or transferring a patient between units, for example), in physician-to-nurse communication (for example, during rounds), and nurse-to-nurse communication (for example, during shift changes). Here we focus on nurse-to-nurse communications, but the insights extend to other contexts.

As a result of their root-cause analyses of operational failures in patient care, the Joint Commission on Accreditation of Healthcare Organizations (JCAHO) established improved "effectiveness of communication among caregivers" as a National Patient Safety Goal in 2006. To achieve this goal, nurses must have sufficient time, space, and resources to administer shift-to-shift reports. Barriers identified to effective nursing handoffs include interruptions, lack of standardized reporting processes, and underdeveloped information and communication technologies.

In terms of hospital performance metrics, handoffs directly affect clinical outcomes, patient and staff satisfaction, and time and cost. Handoffs take time, and ineffective communication can result in longer shift-to-shift report times or nurses staying late to complete requisite documentation or complete care, resulting in overtime and increased labor costs. Faulty handoffs impair the ability of providers to advance the plan of care, follow up on diagnostic tests and therapeutic treatments, and facilitate safe discharges. These increase the risk of complications and can result in costly adverse outcomes and increased LOS. Naturally, the delivery of poor care will reduce patient satisfaction and increase the moral distress of providers, which can result in poor unit and team morale.

3.4.3.2 PRINCIPLES

As before, we briefly list the management principles relevant to this section, allowing readers who are not already familiar with them to refer to Appendix A, where each principle is explained in greater detail.

Principle (Handoffs)—Unless the individuals contribute new knowledge, information is degraded as it is passed from one individual to another.

This is the root of the problem, and the remaining principles are used to increase the quality (and thereby reduce the negative impact) of handoffs. These principles include the following.

Principle (Value of Information)—The value of information is determined by the expected improvement in outcome with the information over that without it. This implies that information that will not change a decision has no value.

Choosing what to report between nurses is important because it can affect both time (reporting too much takes too much time to communicate irrelevant information) and outcomes (reporting too little can contribute to adverse events). The Value of Information principle tells us that only information that can change a decision has value, so nurses should report just the information required to forward the course of therapy.

Once one knows what to report, execution of the handoff requires enough time (capacity) to do it correctly. If too much time is required relative to the time available, one of two things will happen. Either nurses will go overtime, costing money or delaying care, or they will truncate their reports, risking incompleteness and patient harm. The **System Capacity**, **Utilization**, and **Variability principles** (all reviewed previously) tell us that high-utilization and high-variability resources (nurses) experience these problems most acutely.

A nurse can accomplish more or less in a given amount of time, depending on the nature of the task. If the content of the exchange is not compromised, nurses are better off with less complex reports.

Principle (Task Simplification)—Reducing task complexity reduces the mean and variance of the task times and the likelihood of errors.

Principle (Task Standardization)—Using clearly specified best-practice procedures for repetitive tasks reduces the mean and variance of task times and the likelihood of errors.

Given finite time, nurses may benefit from different sequencing of patients in their reports. SPT (**Shortest Processing Time**) sequencing will get the most reports done in a finite amount of time, and **Critical Ratio Sequencing** argues for completing reports for the most valuable (or vulnerable) patients first. For a complete discussion of these, the reader is referred to Appendix A.

In information transfer, "quality" is the extent to which the right information is accurately communicated. Several principles influence the quality of a transfer.

Principle (Foolproofing)—Using constraints to force correct actions reduces the likelihood of errors.

Principle (Redundancy)—Independent layers of protection increase the reliability of a system.

Principle (Intuitive Information)—Providing essential information visually or orally in tight association with a task reduces the mean and variance of task times, as well as the likelihood of errors.

Checklists of things that must be covered in a nurse report would be a "foolproofing" initiative. The Redundancy principle states that repetition or replication can uncover oversights, such as one nurse repeating the message from another to be sure the communication is clear and complete. The Intuitive Information principle says that information presented in a clear visual format is more easily assimilated than information in a cluttered written format. For example, clear icons with commonly understood meanings can be more effective than written instructions when describing a patient's care needs.

Information is more easily and accurately transferred if both the sender and the receiver are free of interruptions and distractions and are alert.

Principle (Interruptions)—Interruptions of complex tasks degrade the quality of decision making and the efficiency of execution.

Principle (Fatigue)—Fatigue impairs decision making and task execution.

The Interruption principle has clear implications for nurse shift reporting, implying that this critical handoff should occur in a space and at a time that is free of interruptions. The Fatigue principle implies that overworking nurses will have a deleterious effect on critical activities, shift reporting included.

The capacity and ability to do a task must be accompanied by a willingness to engage the task. Individuals, not organizations, are self-optimizing (**Self-Interest principle**), so handoffs can improve as nurses perceive a better connection between a quality report and their own personal satisfaction. Some of this satisfaction is intrinsic to the job, the pride that is associated with a job well done. This can be augmented with extrinsic rewards that are attached to quality handoffs. For example, metrics (compliance, or incidence rates of complications traced to miscommunication) can be in place to measure quality handoffs, and some meaningful recognition can be attached to superior performance.

3.4.3.3 PRACTICES

Because handoff activities are important drivers of patient safety, we begin with our generic "patient safety" matrix (Table A.2) from Appendix A and adapt it to the specific context of handoffs. We retain the "improve responsiveness" objective with its close attention to nurse capacity for properly managing handoffs. We combine "decisions" (about what to do) and "execution" (doing it) into one level 1 objective, to avoid excessive redundancy in the table. In their review of the literature on nursing handoffs, Riesenberg et al. (2010) identified the following as generic strategies for effective handoffs: communication skills, standardization of practices, technological aids, environmental issues, training and education, staff involvement, and leadership. Table 3.10 includes these and other suggestions for improving handoffs.

Table 3.10 Objectives and Practices for Nurse Shift Handoffs

Level 1 Objective	Level 2 Objective	Level 3 Objective	Example Policies
Improve responsiveness to the reporting task	Reduce workload	Decrease patient load	Decrease the nurse-to-patient ratio in nurse staffing
			Admit fewer patients to the unit
		Decrease load per patient	Offload some nursing activities to others
			Initiate process improvement activities to streamline patient care
			Critically review current clinical documentation to reduce redundancy and streamline clinical charting
			Reduce travel time by streamlining all clinical documentation to one location so all disciplines are charting in the same place
		Offload tasks to nurse extenders	Hire more unlicensed assistive personnel (UAPs) such as certified nursing assistants (CNAs) to take some load off nurses

Level 1 Objective	Level 2 Objective	Level 3 Objective	Example Policies
	Increase capacity	Increase capacity of each nurse per day	Extend paid shift by 30 minutes after next shift has arrived to allow for reporting during overlap
			Initiate process improvement activities to streamline nursing duties
		Increase the number of nurses	Hire more nurses
			Have special "handoff" personnel who specialize in information transfer
	Improve synchronization	Synchronize time demanded and time available	Avoid having nurse reports coinciding with physician rounds, or other peak demands on nursing time
		Synchronize nursing pairs	Use teleconferencing technologies to conduct reports without the need for colocation
		Synchronize patients and nursing pairs	Have nurses in two adjacent shifts manage the same patients to reduce the number of different people who must communicate during handoffs
		Synchronize information availability and transfer	Delay transfers if the patient is unstable or if significant uncertainties need to be resolved
	Reduce variability in nursing time demands	Spread reporting times more evenly across the day	Have nurse shift times spread more evenly across the day, so not all nurses go off and on at the same time
		Reduce competing workload during reporting	Reassign regular duties to others when a nurse is engaged in reporting

Table 3.10 Objectives and Practices for Nurse Shift Handoffs

Level 1 Objective	Level 2 Objective	Level 3 Objective	Example Policies
	Improve sequencing	Sequencing motivated by "shortest processing times"	Report from the least to the most complicated cases, to avoid running out of time on multiple case reports
		Sequencing motivated by urgency	Report urgent needs first, to be sure all critical questions are answered
		Sequencing ordered by time to discharge	Report ready to discharge patients first so discharge process can begin
Improve handoff content and execution	Improve information about what to communicate during handoffs	Learn what information begets high quality	Track adverse events and identify important areas that currently lack reliable information transfers
			Conduct a survey of current literature on nurse reports
		Improve recall of what information to cover	See "Simplify, standardize process" entry later in the table
	Improve assignment	Give nurses some ownership over the process of shift reporting	Convene a team of nurses from varying shifts and levels of clinical expertise to establish the principles and practices of shift-to-shift report
		Assign nurses to patients to reduce reporting errors	Assign the most highly trained nurses to the most complicated patients
	Improve training	Train nurses in handoff best practices; what manner of information and conduct is most effective?	Incorporate handoffs in nurse training
			Have videos of both excellent and poor reporting practices for review

Level 1 Objective	Level 2 Objective	Level 3 Objective	Example Policies
			Perform informal and formal audit and feedback activities
		Train nurses in communication skills	Train nurses in clear listening and communication skills when getting information from physicians
			Train nurses in clear listening and communication skills with peers
			Discuss human factor issues (stress, fatigue) in communications
	Improve incentives	Improve incentives at the unit level	Nursing leadership focuses attention on communication and reporting practices
			Establish nursing unit quality metrics and reward nurses for superior performance
			Measure and reward compliance with best practices in handoffs
		Improve incentives at the nurse level	Create peer-to-peer award for outstanding communication
			Find early adopters for improved practices whose testimony is trusted by nurses
	Simplify, standardize process	Standardize content	Generate a standard list of topics and questions to follow during handoffs
			Adopt models of formal release, as used in aviation and nuclear power safety

Table 3.10 Objectives and Practices for Nurse Shift Handoffs

Level 1 Objective	Level 2 Objective	Level 3 Objective	Example Policies
	Use technology to enhance the completeness and accuracy of the report	Simplify the process	Redesign report forms to be visually clean and clear about what information goes where
			Generate from nursing staff a standard web-based platform to enter data
		Prepopulate fields	Investigate how current health information systems could prepopulate report sheets with data
		Create backups	Record verbal reports and store for easy searching if required
		Foolproofing	Foolproof report by disallowing report entry until all required fields are complete
	Improve focus	Reduce interruptions during reporting	Assign nursing assistants to cover call lights during report times, except for emergencies
		Reduce visual and audio distractions during reporting	Avoid coscheduling many different communication and conferencing activities in the same space and time
			Redesign work space for multiple private areas with reduced ambient noise where conferencing can occur
	Increase redundancy	Use redundant personnel	Report to at least two nurses, who compare notes
		Use redundant information	Require the arriving nurse to repeat (echo) the information he just received back to the departing nurse

3.4.3.4 CASE: IMPROVING THE SHIFT-TO-SHIFT NURSING REPORT PRACTICES ON A MEDICAL-SURGICAL UNIT AT MERCY ACADEMIC MEDICAL CENTER[1]

Mercy Academic Medical Center (MAMC) is a large teaching hospital with 556 licensed Acute Care beds. It is part of a larger hospital network that includes MAMC and four community hospitals. MAMC is considered the "flagship" due to its focus on tertiary and specialty services. Occupancy is high, averaging 89% on a daily basis. MAMC is adjacent to prominent schools of medicine and nursing, and accordingly is a major training site for these programs. Thompson 6 (The Thompson building is MAMC's main bed tower) is a 28-bed nursing unit comprised mostly of two-bed rooms. The patient population is heterogeneous; patients are admitted from multiple medical and surgical services. Predominant patient populations include congestive heart failure exacerbations, patients recovering from recent major abdominal operations, and nursing home residents with pneumonia or urinary tract infections. At the time of this case, Jessica had worked at MAMC for 15 years, the last 4 as nurse manager of Thompson 6.

Jessica reviewed several adverse event reports from nurses in which patient complications ensued because of communication breakdowns between nursing shifts. For example:

- One patient's discharge was delayed by one day because a nurse on evening shift did not obtain a needed specimen to determine whether the patient's anticoagulant medication was dosed appropriately.

- A nursing assistant did not report a patient's fever to the incoming nurse, which resulted in a delayed response to start antibiotics. The patient required an ICU stay for sepsis management.

- A patient's allergy to intravenous contrast dye was not reported across nurses (and subsequently to the ordering physician), and the patient required the assistance of a rapid response team to manage the drug reaction in the Radiology suite.

Jessica raised these issues in a monthly staff meeting and received immediate feedback from nurses that shift-to-shift nursing reports take too long, there were too many interruptions, and patient care was suffering. In parallel, hospital management had encouraged each unit manager to consider reforms to achieve the JCAHO national patient safety goals. Jessica organized a leadership team, which included herself, the clinical nurse specialist, and the unit's assistant nurse manager, in conjunction with a small working group of staff nurses, to examine their current state and propose improvements in shift-to-shift nursing report to improve nurse satisfaction and patient safety.

Change Planning

Jessica and her team reviewed articles on improving the quality of handoffs in health care (Arora and Johnson 2006, 2009), which suggested the following template for change:

1. **Implement standard process improvement techniques**—Principles of lean manufacturing are not limited to the manufacturing environment and have been used successfully in hospitals. A cross-functional team of employees should establish the current state of affairs by mapping the process, estimating the time taken at each step, listing current problems, and identifying possible root causes. The team should then conduct surveys or experiments as necessary to identify the real drivers of performance, forecast a desired future state, and craft a strategy for getting there. They should establish a set of metrics by which the success of the exercise can be judged. The identified root causes can then be addressed and performance tracked over time to confirm the improvements.

2. **Design the intervention for the organizational context**—Effective professional communication has some universal principles. For example, closed loop communication (in which pertinent data is repeated between the two agents engaged in communication), reduction in distractions during handoffs, avoidance of jargon, and helpful technological innovations have all been identified as effective aspects of handoffs (Riesenberg, et al. 2010). However, each clinical or functional area operates differently and has different challenges. A proposed solution should be sensitive to these organizational differences, and in so doing, increase the likelihood of successful implementation. For example, in one hospital the space used by nurses for nurse-to-nurse handoff was shared with the resident physicians. During nursing shift reports, both nurses and physicians used the room, increasing noise and distractions. Relocating shift-to-shift report was one intervention to minimize this issue.

3. **Design an evaluation plan**—It is important to design an evaluation plan prior to the design and implementation of the new handoff process. Evaluation plans should assess all phases of the process change, including adherence to the process, time expended, adverse events, patient and nurse perceptions of the change, and cost implications.

4. **Identify and manage variation**—Once a new handoff process has been endorsed and established, management should seek ways to identify and reduce variation in its application.

5. **Clinical leadership should invoke a sense of professional responsibility**—Clinical leaders in the institution should champion and emulate the proposed process as an example of professional clinical practice. For example, this approach has been used successfully in campaigns to improve hand hygiene in health care facilities.

Jessica identified the need for protected time for her team to strategize, implement, and monitor proposed changes. She sought and received approval from the nursing director to fund a work day. She, along with a clinical nurse specialist, an assistant nurse manager, and six nurses held a 9-hour working session to review shift changes, identify barriers to effective communication, and plan improvements. Over the following year, Jessica allocated 4 hours per 13-week pay period for 4 staff nurses to evaluate satisfaction data and adherence to the change principles and prepare feedback reports to the clinical staff. In addition, the chief nursing officer provided Jessica with 8 hours of assistance from a performance improvement consultant.

A nursing student collected baseline data on actual time spent during shift report, quality of the report, and satisfaction with the reporting process as perceived by nurses. The student observed eight nurses at various shift transitions (days, evenings, and night shifts). The student recorded the time for outgoing nurses to prepare report, time for incoming nurses to review the data, time for nurses to confer, and time until nurses began to deliver patient care. The average time for shift report was 45 minutes (Exhibit 3.13), and because shifts only overlapped by 30 minutes, overtime was almost always necessary.

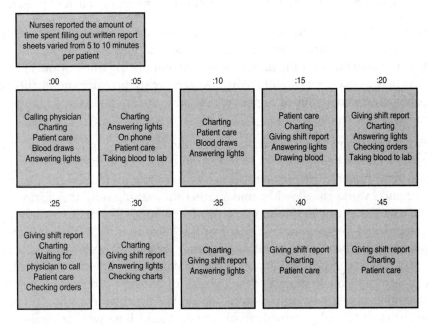

Exhibit 3.13   Current state of nurse-to-nurse shift report, activities of the off going RN.

Physicians also were surveyed to gauge their satisfaction with nursing care. Monthly patient satisfaction ratings were obtained from standard surveys (filled out as part of the discharge process). The planning committee then drafted an idealized flow for the nurse-to-nurse shift report (Exhibit 3.14).

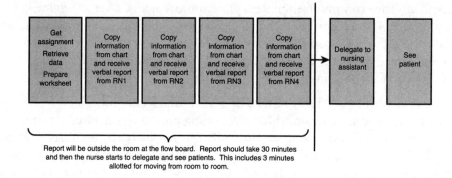

Report will be outside the room at the flow board. Report should take 30 minutes and then the nurse starts to delegate and see patients. This includes 3 minutes allotted for moving from room to room.

Exhibit 3.14   Desired future state of nurse-to-nurse shift report.

Recommendations

The planning committee recommended the following changes to current practice:

- **Standardized report forms**—A standard report form (Exhibit 3.15) was developed by a small working committee of nurses and unit leadership. Recommendations for the future include prepopulating some of the fields using data in the electronic patient records. Adherence to form use and quality of completion were included in peer review performance audits and reported on a monthly basis to staff.

- **Patient assignment guidelines**—Charge nurses were requested to view the current 24-hour schedule, as well as forthcoming days, to identify nursing pairs whenever possible. *Nursing pairs* occur when nurses perform sequential shifts. If one nurse works the day shift, and another the evening shift, they form a nursing pair. For example, if John works 07:00 a.m. to 07:30 p.m. on Monday, Tuesday, and Wednesday, and Nancy works 7:00 p.m. to 7:30 a.m. on Sunday, Monday, and Tuesday, then John and Nancy are a nursing pair for Monday and Tuesday. The charge nurse should strive to align their patient assignments as closely as possible to minimize the number of different people they must talk to at shift change. Charge nurses would be audited for their identification of nursing pairs and asked to provide feedback when guidelines were not followed.

Patient Introduction
- Preferred name, age, diagnosis, and code status if known.

Pain Management/Vital signs
- Patient pain rating, pain management interventions, physiological effects of interventions.

Fluid Intake/Output
- Fluid restrictions, intravenous infusion solutions and rates, surgical drains.

Skin and Wound Assessment and Care
- Current status of patient skin, risk for acquisition of pressure ulcers, interventions to prevent pressure ulcers, wound assessment and location, prescribed treatments and schedule.

Glucose Monitoring and Management
- Serum glucose levels, frequency of monitoring, management and evaluation of interventions.

Cognitive/Perceptual
- Mental status, pain description, and therapies (if not mentioned previously)

Activity/Exercise
- Assessment of circulation status, muscle strength, tolerance of activities, staff assistance required to ambulate

Elimination
- Bowel sounds, nausea/vomiting, stool color/ consistency, urine color/consistency.

Nutrition
- Diet status, plan for advancing diets.

Fall Risk
- Patient risk for falls, related interventions

Other
- Discharge plan, scheduled tests and procedures, documentation needs, education needs, and equipment needs.

Exhibit 3.15   Example of standardized report form.

- **Role changes**—Jessica and the unit leadership team revised the standard procedures and work scope for nursing assistants to reduce interruptions during nurse report. During the shift change times 07:00 a.m. to 07:30 a.m., 03:00 p.m. to 03:30 p.m., 07:00 p.m. to 07:30 p.m., and 11:00 p.m. to 11:30 p.m., nursing assistants were to assume primary responsibility for call lights. Nonurgent requests for nurses would be held until after the report time, which would be communicated to patients and families in their unit orientation. Clerks would also take messages for nurses during these times and only interrupt for urgent matters. If the nursing assistant was not sure of the urgency of a message, he would relay the message to the charge nurse for triage.

- **Changes to rounding schedules by physicians**—With the support of the chief nursing officer, Jessica met with the respective section chiefs in the Departments of Medicine and Surgery to outline a proposed rounding schedule for physician teams. To decrease unit congestion, surgical services would round between 06:00 a.m. and 07:00 a.m., and medical services would round between 08:00 a.m. and 09:00 a.m. To increase team communication, the department chairs and Jessica agreed that rounds would begin when the registered nurse assigned to the patient was present at the bedside. Thompson 6's clerks were to notify nurses on their pager when the physician teams were present. This proposal was brought to the respective department and clinical section meetings and endorsed by the physicians. The chairmen of medicine and of surgery provided further support by implementing the schedule on the month when both of them would be on inpatient service.

Evaluation

After one year of following the change implementation, the average shift report time decreased from 45 minutes to 29 minutes. Overtime was almost completely eliminated. Nurse satisfaction with the reporting process improved from 37% to 78% over the observation period, reflecting significant improvement but opportunities for further intervention. Physician and patient satisfaction rates remained stable across the study period at 83% and 84%, respectively. Clinical outcome data was too confounded by other complicating influences to trace any changes directly to the new handoff system.

A financial analysis of the impact of the intervention contained the following components:

- The initial 9-hour work planning day included 9 people at an average salary with benefits of $50/hour for a total cost of $4,500.

- The annual cost for data collection and evaluation included four nurses for four hours, four times a year, at an average salary with benefits of $44/hour, for a total of $2,816.

- The changes saved an average of 16 minutes of report time per shift change, which at four changes per day and 365 days/year totals 389 nursing hours per year, or $17,131. So, financially the system benefits were estimated at 17,131 − 4,500 − 2,816 = $9,815 for the first year. Each year thereafter would save more because the one-time cost of $4,500 need not be repeated.

- To evaluate the impact on patients for this reduction in nonproductive time, Jessica calculated the amount of time saved in a 24-hour period on the unit, 16 minutes by 20 nurses, which is 320 minutes. If she distributed this time evenly across 28 patients (all beds full), this would translate into an average increase of 11.4 minutes (0.2 hours) per patient. Using the reported statewide median of 4.13 hours of RN care per patient day on medical-surgical units as a base case, the improvement to direct care hours to 4.32 hours of RN care per patient day is 4.8%.

- Staff satisfaction surveys indicated that nurse satisfaction with reports improved, and patient and doctor satisfaction scores remained stable.

- Adverse event reports that could be attributable to nurse-to-nurse communication decreased over the one-year period.

Jessica's efforts were very well received by the administration. Her superiors appreciated that she had faced the challenges of adverse event reports related to the shift report process, nurse dissatisfaction with the process, and the need to improve professional communication across the institution.

3.5 Conclusions

All the planning, budgeting, designing, data-crunching and systems-building in complex hospitals are ultimately support activities for the all-important personal transactions between patients and care-givers. It is at this personal level that all of the social value of a hospital is realized. The dominant design for these transactions is for inpatients to occupy a bed in a nursing unit, with continual care by nurses and cyclical visits by physicians, specialists, and technicians.

The need for 24/7 nursing care demands a mix of nursing responsibilities that range from the unexacting to the complex and poses key managerial challenges to hospitals. Nurses are both a crucial resource for patient care and the source of 50% or more of a typical hospital's labor cost, so the management of this essential resource is central to a hospital's success or failure.

Management issues range from strategic long-term decisions (sizing and configuration of nursing units and their physical and human resources in a hospital's design), through intermediate-range decisions (designing nurse scheduling systems and shift handoff protocols) to day-to-day decisions (adjusting in real time the number of nurses on the unit to respond to unexpected changes in patient census and acuity). Each of these challenges is informed by principles of management. In this chapter we used known relationships between causes and effects to trace desired outcomes back to causal initiatives for consideration. In the process we illustrated a principles-based brainstorming technique that is applicable well beyond the specific challenges we addressed here and thus provides a framework for addressing a wide range of nursing unit management challenges now and in the future.

The intersection of social, political and economic forces that shaped the current nursing profession are still operative, and the precise trajectory nursing practice and management will take is uncertain. But, by standing the test of time and being applicable in a broad range of circumstances, theory-based principles can and will inform and help shape that future.

3.6 Stakeholders' Perspectives

August 2010

Since joining with Tony and accepting the hospital flow improvement challenge, Dr. Greene had internalized the principles in *Hospital Operations* but sometimes wished he hadn't. Armed with a new way of seeing things, possible applications and improvements seemed to be everywhere he looked. The sheer volume of opportunities was intimidating.

However, he was constantly reminded of the power of a key insight in the book that helped make the situation a lot more manageable. It did no good for the system as a whole to work on nonbottleneck processes. This made the complicated world easier to grasp and gave him hope that some mistakes of the past could be corrected. As he and Tony had discussed months ago, the hospital had tried for years to implement lean thinking, and many projects had been pursued. However, the projects were not coordinated, so many of them focused on nonbottleneck activities and therefore had little net impact on the overall system.

Greene had proven to himself that things could be different, at least in the ED. Now it was time to think about expanding his scope. He knew that many problems were systemic, crossing departmental boundaries, and to be successful on a larger scale he would have to reach out into less familiar territory.

But Greene also knew that it would be challenging to apply his ideas beyond the department in which he had natural credibility and implicit authority. Years of relatively unproductive projects had generated a natural resistance among the staff to embrace this sort of effort. All those projects took valuable staff time. Nurses, doctors, techs, physician assistants, and others were interviewed, questioned, shadowed, and charged with implementing many of the changes. Often the core team directly involved in a process improvement activity would become true believers, but it was increasingly difficult to extend their enthusiasm to those outside the team. Because nothing much seemed to change, a justified cynicism gradually developed among the staff. One of the consequences of working on nonbottleneck activities was staff burnout, making it more difficult to sell the importance of the next project.

He started with the nurses on 5B.

"The reason nothing seems to happen," he told them, "is that we have been wasting too much time working on things that are not bottlenecks or parts of critical paths. To make sure we focus on those things that really affect patient care, we're tracing the patient and information flows wherever they go, even when they cross departmental boundaries. Because nursing units are clearly part of our critical paths, I'm very interested to hear about your frustrations and your ideas about what would make your lives and the lives of your patients better."

The nurses regaled Greene with stories of musical beds, irate messages from the ED and the bed managers, and delayed discharges. They mentioned near misses due to handoff information errors and how they sometimes questioned the appropriateness of a care plan, but seldom questioned the doctors about it. This was cultural. Several of them noted that they were frequently unable to locate the appropriate doctor because patients were boarded all over the hospital.

The nurses got increasingly excited, talking about things they cared very much about. Greene knew that one of the biggest prerequisites for change was the psychological attitude that change is possible. As he listened, he became increasingly convinced that things could change on 5B.

He explained this to Arnold at their weekly game.

"Remember when you left, how frustrating it all seemed? How the scope and complexity of the problems made improvements seem just impossible? How no one really believed that the improvement programs would change anything?"

"Yep," replied Arnold, as they took turns missing shots. Eventually Greene abandoned shooting altogether and just rebounded and passed the ball back to Arnold, who was moving around the key.

"Well, I think that your attitude is shared by most of the people at the hospital." Greene zipped a pass to Arnold. "And it's the biggest obstacle we face. Making change happen is as much a psychological challenge as a physical or organizational one."

"Ok, maybe, but so what?" Arnold seemed more interested in his shooting than in this conversation. "The pessimism at UH is well grounded in reality. When things start slipping back to normal, you'll get skeptical, too. And when you do, we'll be happy to have you come over to our side."

"I don't think so," Greene said as he retrieved another of Arnold's missed shots. "I'm beginning to feel like we really can change, because we have a framework that makes sense, and I'm getting so I can describe it convincingly to others. We've already successfully applied it in the ED, and that is just the beginning."

Greene knew he was overstating his confidence. But, maybe not by much.

September 2010

Greene invited Allan Ruell and Safiya Rana, charge nurses on 5B, to work with him on a pilot project to improve patient flow in their unit. He sought and received approval to buy out enough of their time so this work was not just piled on top of their daily tasks. A few residents joined the team, at the recommendation of some attending physicians with whom Greene had good relations.

The *Hospital Operations* text Tony gave to Greene mentioned several of the specific issues he and his team were uncovering and cast them as specific manifestations of more general principles for physical flows, information flows, and human resource practices. His team began to feel more optimistic. They realized that many of their main challenges were generic problems faced by other hospital units and even nonhospital organizations. The idea that knowledge and experience from other sources might be able to help them was encouraging.

The 5B team reviewed Sally's case and concluded that there were both physical flow and information flow issues that contributed to her experience. The team felt the most important physical flow issues were that Sally was delayed being admitted and delayed getting into the OR. The OR issue would be worked on with an OR team. The 5B team focused on their own admission and discharge processes. If patients moved through faster, there would be more free beds and less of the confusion that Sally experienced getting onto a nursing unit.

After some false starts characterized by premature self-censoring of potential solutions, the team succeeded in adapting the generic table of options for improving responsiveness from the *Hospital Operations* book to produce a large list of candidate policies. Team members then began to prune away the less feasible options. Key to this exercise was understanding the reservations of the physicians and staff, because nothing would happen unless all key stakeholders felt themselves better off.

The 5B team felt that the most important information flow issue in Sally's experience was not the original diagnosis, which although incorrect in retrospect, was reasonable given the information available at the time. Rather, it was a delay in realizing this diagnosis was incorrect and reacting urgently to that realization. Because Sally's case passed through a number of people before a final decision was made, the team focused on information handoffs from the ED to 5B, from internist to surgeon, between doctors and nurses, and across surgical and nursing shifts, as well as the translation of information into decisions. Again, they used the generic tables in the *Hospital Operations* book as a basis for brainstorming and analysis.

December 2010

As his year of dramatic professional change came to an end, Greene reflected on his team's accomplishments. He and the 5B team had traced Sally's experience out of the ED up onto the bed floor, and already new procedures for admission handoffs and discharges, and for nurse-to-nurse shift reports, were in place and operating. More than one physician carried an admissions pager to speed the flow onto the unit. Other efforts were ongoing, and with enough converts that the improvement process was beginning to feel self-sustaining.

The staff of 5B worked with several other units to designate a "discharge lounge" for patients medically ready to go home but lacking only transportation or awaiting a family member. This allowed them to clear rooms earlier and increase patient flows onto and off of the nursing unit.

They were easing toward the floor nurses joining the rounding teams to enrich the information flows about each patient's care plan. Under the new process, a doctor would page the charge nurse when he was on the way to the unit, and the charge nurse would notify the floor nurse to be ready. A flag was placed visibly outside the room when the rounding team was inside, so in case the floor nurse was busy when the team arrived, he could see where they were. The practice of having nurses join doctors and residents on rounds was already fostering discussions that promised to break down the cultural barrier of nurses not questioning physicians. Nurses were gradually getting used to asking pointed questions of doctors when their experience or intuition suggested that some more thought might be beneficial.

Longer range plans included staggering shifts so the entire hospital did not pulse with spikes of activity in admissions, transfers, and lab requests at every shift change. Also, the way patients were assigned to beds was under review in an attempt to reduce boarding patients "off unit."

The 5B staff was enthusiastic about the changes, which they had themselves generated and implemented. Greene began hearing stories of them evangelizing to people in other units. Armed with a framework of management principles that made sense and a growing team of converts, Greene not only believed change was possible, he knew it.

That week at basketball, Greene played with more energy and aggression than normal. During a break, Arnold asked him how things were going.

"Really good!" Greene replied vigorously. "We know what to work on, and we're using proven principles of management to figure out what to change. The docs and staff know we need to change. And they're getting it! The psychology is changing—I can feel it!"

"Wow!" exclaimed Arnold. "You sound pumped!"

"I am," replied Greene. "We're not going to say, 'This is the best we can do' until it really is, and we are just beginning to find out how good we can be. Come on, let's play!" To punctuate his remark, Greene squared his shoulders and launched a long 3-point shot. Arnold smiled when it missed by a mile.

"I like your confidence, Nate," he said, "and I don't want to rain on your parade, but you know we've been through this before. I don't doubt that you're making progress. But what is happening now is the result of your personal crusade. When you stop—and you can't go on forever—things will slip back to where they were. It is structural. Your world is just too jumbled and complex. Take it from someone who has seen your system from both the inside and the outside."

3.7 References

Aiken, L., S. Clarke, D. Sloane, J. Sochalski, and J. Silber. "Hospital Nurse Staffing and Patient Mortality, Nurse Burnout, and Job Dissatisfaction." *Journal of American Medical Association* 288(16), 2002, 1987–1993.

Aiken, L.H., S.P. Clarke, R.B. Cheung, D.M. Sloane, and J.H. Silber. "Educational Levels of Hospital Nurses and Surgical Patient Mortality." *Journal of American Medical Association* 290(12), September 24, 2003, 1617–1623.

Aiken, L., S. Clarke, D. Sloane, J. Solchalski, R. Bussse, H. Clarke, P. Giovannetti, J. Hunt, A Rafferty, and J. Shamian. "Nurses' Reports on Hospital Care in Five Countries." *Health Affairs* 20(3), 2001, 43–53.

American Hospital Association Hospital Statistics, 2004, 2006.

The American Journal of Nursing. "Taking a Stand" editorial, v. 59, September 1959, p. 1245.

Arora, V., and J. Johnson. "A Model for Building a Standardized Hand-Off Protocol." *Joint Commission Journal on Quality and Patient Safety,* 32(11), 2006, 646–655.

Arora, V., and J. Johnson. "Implementing and Sustaining Improvement in Health Care." *Joint Commission Journal on Quality and Patient Safety.* Schilling, eds. Joint Commission on Accreditation of Healthcare Organizations, 2009. p. 79–97.

Baibergenova, A., K. Leeb, A. Jokovic, and S. Gushue. "Missed Opportunity: Patients Who Leave Emergency Departments Without Being Seen." *Healthcare Policy* 1(4), 2006, 35–41.

Beer, R., H. Chung, L. Ding, A. Qi, and Y. Yin. "Holistic Patient Placement and Staffing Model." Field report for OMS899 course, "Grounded Operational Research," University of Michigan Ross School of Business, May 2011.

Brasel, K., J. Rasmussen, B. Cauley, and J. Weigelt. "Reasons for Delayed Discharge of Trauma Patients." *Journal of Surgical Research* 107, 2002, 223–226.

Buerhaus, D., D Auerbach, and D. Staiger. "The Recent Surge in Nurse Employment: Causes and Implications." *Health Affairs,* June 2009, 657–668.

Bureau of Health Professionals. "What Is Behind HRSA's Projected Supply, Demand, and Shortage of Registered Nurses?" Report prepared by the Lewin Group for the Bureau of Health Professionals, Health Resources, and Services Administration, Department of Health and Human Service, September 2004. Available at http://dwd.wisconsin.gov/healthcare/pdf/behind_the_shortage.pdf

Carey, K. "Hospital Length of Stay and Cost: A Multilevel Modeling Analysis." *Health Services & Outcomes Research Methodology* 3, 2002, 41–56.

Chitty, K. *Professional Nursing: Concepts and Challenges.* W.B. Saunders Co, Philadelphia, 2001.

Chou, P., K. Fong, N. Mehta, M. Paulsen, and D. Harkins. "Staffing the Burn Unit." University of Michigan Hospital and Ross School of Business student project report, April 2009.

Clifford, J.C. "Professionalizing a Nursing Service: An Integrated Approach for the Management of Patient Care. In: Clifford JC, Horvath KJ, eds. *Advancing Professional Nursing Practice: Innovations at Boston's Beth Israel Hospital.* New York: Springer Publishing, Co, 1990, 30–50.

Croteau R. "JCAHO Comments on Handoff Requirement." *OR Manager* 2005; 21(8):8.

Davidson, H., P. Folcarelli, S. Crawford, L. Duprat, and J. Clifford. "The Effects of Health Care Reform on Job Satisfaction and Voluntary Turnover Among Hospital-Based Nurses." *Medical Care* 35(6), 1997, 634–645.

De Grano, Melanie L., D.J. Medeiros, and D. Eitel. "Accommodating Individual Preferences in Nurse Scheduling Via Auctions and Optimization." *Health Care Management Science* 12, 2009, 228–242.

Donchin, Y., D. Gopher, M. Olin, Y. Badihi, M. Biesky, C Sprung, R. Pizov, and S. Cotev. "A Look into the Nature and Causes of Human Errors in the Intensive Care Unit." *Critical Care Medicine* 1995(2), 294–300.

Friese, C.R., E.T. Lake, L.H. Aiken, J.H. Silber, and J. Sochalski. "Hospital Nurse Practice Environments and Outcomes for Surgical Oncology Patients." *Health Services Research* 43(4), August 2008, 1145–1163.

Gordon, S. *Nursing Against the Odds*, Cornell University Press, Ithaca, NY, 2005.

Green, L., and V. Nguyen. "Strategies for Cutting Hospital Beds: The Impact on Patient Service." *Health Services Research* 36(2), 2001, 421–442.

Green, L. "How Many Hospital Beds?" *Inquiry*—Excellus Health Plan 39(4), Winter 2002–3, 400–412.

Harkin, D. University of Michigan Hospital Trauma Burn Unit. Personal communication, April 2009.

Hilligoss, B., and M. Cohen. *What Is the Goal of Patient Handoff: Implications for the Improvement of Care Transitions.* 2010. Pending publication.

Johnson, P. "Our Future Nursing Workforce: A Regulatory Perspective." *North Carolina Medical Journal* 65(2), 2004, 84–86.

Joint Commission Journal on Quality and Patient Safety. Schilling, eds. Joint Commission on Accreditation of Healthcare Organizations, 2009, 79–97.

Jordan, W., and S. Graves. "Principles on the Benefits of Manufacturing Process Flexibility." *Management Science* 41(4), 1995, 577–594.

Kalisch, B.J., C.R. Friese, S.H. Choi, and M. Rochman. "Hospital Nurse Staffing: Choice of Measure Matters." *Medical Care.* In press, 2011.

Kalisch, P., and B. Kalisch. *The Advance of American Nursing*. J.B. Lippincot Co, Philadelphia, 1995.

Kane, R.L., T.A. Shamliyan, C. Mueller, et al. "The Association of Registered Nurse Staffing Levels and Patient Outcomes: Systematic Review and Meta-Analysis." *Medical Care*. 2007;45(12): 1195–1204.

Kim, C., W. Lovejoy, M. Paulsen, R. Chang, and S. Flanders. "Hospitalist Time Usage and Cyclicality: Opportunities to Improve Efficiency." *Journal of Hospitalist Medicine* 5(6), July/Aug 2010, 329–334.

Klein, M., A. Nathens, D. Heimbach, and N. Gibran. "An Outcome Analysis of Patients Transferred to a Regional Burn Center: Transfer Status Does Not Impact Survival." *Burns* 32, 2006, 940–945.

Koeppel, D. "Nurses Bid with Their Pay in Auctions for Extra Work." *New York Times* June 6, 2004.

Krishna, V. *Auction Theory*. Academic Press, NY, 2002.

Law, A., and D. Kelton. *Simulation Modeling and Analysis*. McGraw-Hill, New York, 1982.

Li, Y. "Hospital Capacity Management: Theory and Practice" (chapter 3). University of Michigan doctoral dissertation, University of Michigan Business School, 2005.

Marquis, B., and C. Huston. *Leadership Roles and Management Functions in Nursing*. Lippincott Williams and Wilkins, Philadelphia, 2003.

Miller, R., and E. Swensson. *Hospital and Healthcare Facility Design*. W.W. Norton & Co, NY, 2002.

Needleman, J, P. Buerhaus, S. Mattke, M. Stewart, and K. Zelevinsky. "Nurse Staffing Levels and the Quality of Care in Hospitals." *New England Journal of Medicine* 346(22), 2002, 1715–1722.

Planetree Alliance website: http://www.planetree.org.

Riesenberg, L.A., J. Leitzsch, and J. Cunningham. "Nursing Handoffs: A Systematic Review of the Literature." *American Journal of Nursing* 110(4), 2010, 24–34.

Roemer, M.I. "Bed Supply and Hospital Utilization: A Natural Experiment." *Hospitals* 35, November 1961, 36–42.

Rosenstein, A. "Nurse-Physician Relationships: Impact on Nursing Satisfaction and Retention." *American Journal of Nursing* 102(6), 2002, 26–34.

Rowland, H., and B. Rowland (eds). *Nursing Administration Handbook*. Aspen Publishers, Gaithersburg, MD, 1997.

Shader, K., M. Broome, C. Broome, M. West, and M. Nash. "Factors Influencing Satisfaction and Anticipated Turnover for Nurses in an Academic Medical Center." *Journal of Nursing Administration* 31(4), April 2001, 210–216.

---

1   The authors acknowledge Julie Grunawalt and Deby Evans for their contributions to this section.

4

OPERATING ROOMS

Coauthored with Michael Mulholland, MD, PhD

4.1 Stakeholders' Perspectives

Wednesday March 10, 2010

Paul Roscoe was a 72-year-old businessman enjoying an active retirement, traveling extensively, and engaging in a number of community projects. Without warning, over a period of a week, Mr. Roscoe's skin became noticeably yellow, his urine turned a dark brown, and he developed a severe itch. Alarmed, he sought the counsel of his internist, Dr. Myron Stein.

"You've got an abdominal mass and skin changes consistent with jaundice," Dr. Stein explained to Paul. "I'm going to order some blood tests, including one for liver function. I'll call you when I get the results."

Paul's blood sample was drawn in the office and sent to a nearby lab. The results came back the next day and were consistent with a biliary tract obstruction. Stein called Paul and ordered an outpatient CT scan to be performed in the Radiology Department of the nearby teaching hospital.

Paul had to call Radiology for an appointment. Luckily, he was able to get in only four days hence. The day after Paul's scan, Dr. Stein received the results indicating a 4 cm mass in the head of the pancreas, consistent with a malignancy, causing bile duct obstruction. The CT showed no evidence of spread of the presumed cancer to other organs and no evidence of invasion of adjacent vascular structures. Dr. Stein called Paul immediately.

"I've got some troubling news," he explained to Paul, "but we're going to manage it. You've got a mass at the head of your pancreas that is blocking the bile duct, and it is possible it is malignant. I'd like you to have an endoscopic biopsy to check. I recommend the hospital's cancer center. We can make the reservation for you."

Paul was stunned, receiving the message nobody wants to hear. He could barely think, so he just agreed. Five days later, the biopsy was performed and confirmed the presumed

■

diagnosis of pancreatic cancer. At the same time, a plastic stent was inserted into Paul's bile duct to relieve the obstruction and to palliate the symptoms of jaundice.

Dr. Stein was sympathetic, but businesslike. "We're going to get on this," he explained. "I will ask my admin to schedule you immediately for a consultation with Dr. LeMaster, a prominent surgeon at the hospital. He's one of the best."

Paul met with Dr. LeMaster the following day. The surgery resident working with Dr. LeMaster, Dr. Emma Payne, interviewed Paul, conducted an examination, and reviewed the imaging and pathology results. She then introduced Dr. LeMaster to the patient. Dr. LeMaster told Paul that he had a serious medical condition.

"Fortunately, the tumor appears to be resectable," he said. "Removing it will require a complicated procedure called a Whipple operation. This procedure is more complicated than most operations and carries substantially greater risk. However, if cure is the goal, there are no other therapeutic options."

Paul was frightened but saw no alternative and agreed to the surgery.

Dr. LeMaster was a busy clinician with many referring physicians. His operating room (OR) block time was completely full for the next three weeks. He told Paul that he would seek additional time within the coming week, but that this might need to be in an afternoon or evening, following the regular schedule of another surgeon. In addition, he recommended reservation of an Intensive Care unit (ICU) bed for postoperative monitoring, given the possibility of a long operation and the potential for finishing late in the day. After negotiating with the main OR scheduling desk, an operative date was set for March 22, five days later.

Friday March 19, 2010

Ed Escobedo's daughter Muriel took off work to be with her father as much as possible. The previous day, Ed's case had been categorized as semi-emergent, meaning next day priority, so today was the day. The surgery was scheduled to start at 2:00 p.m. At 1:30 p.m., Ed was wheeled from unit 5B into the pre-op preparatory area. Muriel said goodbye and watched as Ed's stretcher disappeared behind two large swinging doors.

Ed was scheduled for a thoracentesis with two objectives: to clean up Ed's pleural space, which was likely filled with pus (epyema), and to analyze the withdrawn fluid to help diagnose Ed's disease.

Ed's was the last scheduled case for the day, but after Ed's procedure, the room would be kept open for emergent cases. As was common for afternoon starts, Ed's case did not start on time. The previous case was still ongoing at 2:00 p.m. That case was delayed by its previous case, and then to make matters worse the anesthesiologist had not shown up on time. She was paged urgently when the case was ready to go and eventually showed up scrubbed and ready.

"A scheduled start for 2:00 means the case really starts at 2:30 or 3:00—everybody knows that!" she said. "Nothing in the afternoon starts on time."

Nobody felt like debating the point, because it was generally true, but of course if everybody behaved like this delays would be preordained. Frustrations were mounting all around.

Ed's case finally started at 3:30 p.m. and went well. The appearance and odor of the aspirated fluid strongly suggested epyema, which was confirmed by the path lab analysis. An intercostal drainage tube was inserted between Ed's rib muscles and left in to drain Ed's chest cavity while he recovered. Ed was sent to the ICU for recovery (he occupied the last available bed in either the ICU or Post Anesthesia Care unit [PACU]) and put on an antibiotic regimen.

Monday March 22, 2010 5:00 p.m.

On the day of Paul Roscoe's surgery, the surgeon to whom the regular time block was assigned performed three procedures in sequence. Two were routine, but the third was prolonged by 50% over its expected time by intraoperative complications. Consequently, Paul's six-hour operation began late in the afternoon. Overall, the operation proceeded smoothly. Blood loss was 1400 cc, but transfusion was not thought necessary. Postoperatively, Paul was transferred to the ICU at midnight. The initial postoperative recovery appeared to go well, and by Wednesday morning Paul was ready to be stepped down to a regular nursing unit.

Wednesday March 24, 2010 4:10 p.m.

On the afternoon of the second postoperative day, blood was seen to issue from the set of intra-abdominal drains left in Paul Roscoe at the time of surgery. Paul became hypotensive (low blood pressure), and his blood count fell precipitously. Dr. Emma Payne was called to the bedside. She immediately determined that the patient was hemorrhaging internally and that he must be returned to the OR emergently. Dr. Payne called the main OR scheduling desk. Paul's case was assigned to OR20, where he was operated upon emergently. There were other emergent cases waiting for an OR, but Paul's condition was more critical, so he took priority. In the OR, Paul's arterial bleeder was controlled, and he was returned to the ICU. The remainder of his recovery was uneventful, but this unexpected hemorrhage had prolonged his expected stay by four days and delayed other emergent cases. However, Paul's departure for the OR opened up a bed on 5B, a fact that Allan Ruell, the charge nurse, reported to the bed management team.

Wednesday March 24, 2010, 5:30 p.m.

Dr. Ranier was impatient. He had to stay late for exploratory surgery on Mrs. Sally Oldham, who might have a small bowel obstruction. The elective surgery schedule was complete, but there were two cases going in ahead of Sally. One was a bleeder who had to go emergently into OR20, and the call was made that the case was more critical than

Sally's. There was another late-running procedure in OR17 that would require an ICU bed. There were no ICU or PACU beds available for Sally postoperatively, and it was hospital policy not to begin a procedure until there was somewhere for the patient to go after surgery.

Dr. Ranier called his wife. "Take a friend, or give the tickets away, I'm going to be stuck here for a while." Angrily hanging up, he thought to himself, *We have to change something in the OR schedule and on-call procedures; these ruined evenings have been all too common lately.*

Wednesday March 24, 2010, 8:00 p.m.

The emergent case in OR20 had cleared, and the room was being turned over, but Dr. Ranier and his team still did not have a green light. Dr. Ranier was furious and called OR scheduling to say so.

"This should be an emergent case; you can't just keep us waiting! We've got to get started!"

"I'm sorry, doctor, but we have no place to put your patient postoperatively. The ICU and PACU are full."

"Listen, this is urgent, so find us a bed now!"

The night bed management team did not feel they had the authority to overturn hospital policy, but something had to be done. They called over to the PACU and ICU to see if there were any patients who might step down, because there was a bed available on 5B. They identified a patient who could possibly be cared for on 5B with some mobile equipment and called the night charge nurse on 5B, Safiya Rana, to ask her to accept this patient. Safiya was worried but was convinced of the necessity and agreed.

At 8:30 p.m., Sally was taken to pre-op, where her vital signs were taken again. She was noted to be febrile (T 104 degrees F), with a blood pressure of 85/40 and a pulse of 122. Abdominal distension was marked, and breathing was difficult because of the upward pressure on her diaphragm. The Anesthesiology staff worried aloud about the dangers of anesthetic induction. Dr. Ranier was impatient, "Let's get going. I am sick of waiting around. I've got a full elective schedule tomorrow, you know."

As some of the staff had feared, anesthetic induction resulted in severe hypotension, necessitating aggressive intravenous infusion and vasoconstrictive drugs. Dr. Ranier recognized that his agitation was not helping. He gathered himself and started the procedure. However, when the incision was opened, dark ascetic fluid escaped. *Oh, oh,* Dr. Ranier thought to himself, as all previous emotions quickly turned into concern.

Dr. Ranier proceeded with his exploration, which quickly revealed a volvulus of the small intestine around a point of adhesion from Sally's prior hysterectomy. Worse, Dr. Ranier discovered that all but 60 cm of the bowel was infarcted, dead, and a perforation had resulted in contamination of her peritoneal cavity with bowel contents.

The amount of surviving normal bowel was insufficient for independent survival, and the infarcted tissue and contamination had caused a widespread infection. The surgical team watched Dr. Ranier's eyes and knew the news was bad.

"This is close to hopeless," he announced sadly. "We'll try to stabilize her, but we should all be prepared for the worst. This is a very bad situation."

Dr. Ranier spent the next hour and a half removing the dead intestine and irrigating Sally's cavity. He worked fast, wanting to get her quickly to the ICU so they could try to stabilize her. If this was successful, they could then decide a course of action. As the team closed Sally up, the circulating nurse called the ICU to prepare them for Sally's arrival.

After scrubbing out, Dr. Ranier found Lucy and Mark in the surgical waiting room and asked them to join him in a private conference room.

"I'm sorry," he said, "but I'm afraid I have bad news. Sally's small intestine twisted back on itself, something we call a volvulus, and essentially choked off and killed the rest of her intestines. The problem was likely related to a previous surgery. The dead tissue started an infection that is now close to overwhelming. I'm afraid she is in shock, in very fragile condition, and her chances of survival are not good. You'll be able to see her in the ICU in half an hour or so. I'm really sorry."

Lucy and Mark were too stunned to ask many questions. After a long minute of silence, Dr. Ranier continued.

"Mark is designated as Sally's health care agent in her medical power of attorney document." Dr. Ranier turned to Mark, "You will have to make some decisions about what measures should and should not be taken for Sally."

After an emotional discussion, Lucy and Mark agreed that they should try to control the infection, but if that was not successful and death was inevitable, then only comfort measures should be taken. They both agreed that Sally would want it that way. Neither Mark nor Lucy could believe they were really having this conversation.

Lucy went to the ICU to see Sally while Mark left to get his parents and the children. By the time he returned with them, Sally had opened her eyes. But she was too weak and too groggy to speak. The family gathered by Sally's ICU bed, not knowing what to say. Lucy worried what she would do with her own children, who were with neighbors. The nurse found chairs and blankets for the family.

The ICU nurses stayed in the background except when required to check vital signs and Sally's infusion pump. By 1:00 a.m., Sally was still not responding to broadspectrum antibiotics, and the head nurse came to talk to the family.

"We've done all we can, but she's getting worse. I'm so sorry," she said. "Let me know if there is anybody, a social worker or a chaplain, you would like to speak with. And if there is anything I can do..."

The family thanked her but said they just wanted to be with Sally.

As they sat watching Sally fade, Lucy's anger rose. Feeling a sudden need to vent to someone, she fished Dr. Greene's card out of her pocket and punched in his cell phone number. She did not care that she woke him up in the middle of the night.

"She came to you and you said you would take care of her!" Lucy half sobbed and half shouted. "How could this have happened?"

Dr. Greene did not know the details of Sally's condition, but he inferred that it was bad. "I am very, very sorry," he said, not knowing what else to say.

"Sorry doesn't help," Lucy retorted. "I want a different outcome!"

Thursday March 25, 2010 10:00 a.m.

All of Sally's in-town family members had come to see her. Sally's eyes were open, but she was too weak to speak. Lucy's eyes teared as her own children delivered touchingly sweet goodbyes to their aunt. She choked up as she watched Sally's parents stroke her, murmuring "our sweet girl" over and over. And she nearly broke down completely when Charlie and his mother, neither able to speak, shared a moment of indescribable affection as Charlie reached for his mother's hand and Sally weakly grasped it.

The family took turns being with Sally and resting in the family waiting room. After several hours, Sally's breathing became slow and uneven. Lucy touched her, but Sally was unresponsive. Lucy ran to the nursing station, "Come quickly, I think something is wrong. She is having trouble breathing!" Two nurses converged on Sally's bed. Lucy called Mark, who was sleeping in the waiting room, and told him to alert the others. Sally's breaths became further and further apart. The nurses knew what was happening but said nothing.

They did not have to. The family knew. Finally, after a long pause while they waited for a breath that never came, they looked up at one another.

"She's gone," whispered Lucy.

4.2 Introduction to the OR

4.2.1 History of Surgery

Surgery is unique among the disciplines of medicine in the way it employs invasive procedures that involve incisions in the skin to access deeper tissues of the body. This makes surgery inherently dangerous. The invasive nature of surgical procedures exposes patients to potential hemorrhage, infection, and defects in wound healing. Surgical procedures are among the most complicated and risky activities in the hospital. The high levels of technical expertise required and the resource-intense nature of contemporary practice also make these procedures highly compensated activities for hospitals. It is common for the surgical suite to generate more than 50% of total hospital revenues, not including diagnostic tests, which are also often surgically related (Jackson 2002, Peters and Blasco 2004).

The origins of modern surgical procedures extend to prehistoric times. Stone Age evidence suggests that shaman-doctors may have lanced abscesses with sharp flint instruments and closed wounds with bone needles. Remarkably, a large number of Stone Age skulls have been retrieved in Europe and Russia with holes bored into the cranial bones, an activity called *trepanning*. These procedures, venting the intracranial contents, are speculated to have been performed to cure migraines or epilepsy or to remove bone fragments resulting from head injuries. If correct, this activity implies a recognized connection between human anatomy and pain, and a willingness to intervene by surgical means. About 2500 BC, surgical procedures involved wound management and cultural rites like circumcision.

Cave painting evidence suggests that the earliest doctors were priest-physicians, and the early history of surgery was one of tension between empirical practice and religious mysticism. This tension is understandable given the life and death dimensions of surgical practice. The following historical synopsis comes largely from Walker (1955) and Venzmer (1972). According to Walker, the evolution of surgery had four basic requirements:

1. A knowledge of human anatomy

2. A means to control bleeding

3. Pain control

4. Methods to prevent postoperative infection

4.2.1.1 KNOWLEDGE OF HUMAN ANATOMY

It is difficult to determine what ancient people knew about human anatomy, but if advanced knowledge was present, it did not survive into the early historical period, which begins about 3000 BC. Although accomplished in some aspects of the healing arts, Babylonians, Greeks, and Egyptians were relatively ignorant of human anatomy. Advances in anatomical knowledge were delayed by religious and cultural prohibitions on dissection of the human body. Certainly mysticism, witchcraft, and fear of demons intertwined with medical practice in ancient civilizations, and the interplay of God and man determined what could be investigated.

The first wave of separation of the practical from the mystical occurred in Greece. By 1000 BC, philosopher-doctors articulated fundamental principles guiding life and nature, basing their theories on reason rather than faith. These doctors existed in parallel with temple-healers. A medical school founded on the island of Cos in 600 BC produced one of history's most famous physicians, Hippocrates. Hippocrates represented a wave of empiricism in scientific investigation, but he advanced medicinal thought more than anatomical knowledge due to cultural restrictions on human dissection. Later practitioners extended their knowledge of anatomy by studying animals, making some obvious errors. Other than a brief period of investigation during the Hellenistic period (fourth century BC), the study of animals as models for humans remained the primary source of anatomical knowledge for the next five centuries. The most famous anatomist was Galen (130 AD), a Greek physician in Roman employ. Educated at the medical school in Alexandria, Galen was employed as a surgeon to gladiators, gaining extensive wound management experience. He left that post to practice in Rome. Prohibited from dissecting human bodies, he instead examined apes and pigs and drew some conclusions that, although influential, were incorrect. These misconceptions survived through the Middle Ages in Europe, because after the fall of Rome the church gained ascendance and reduced the role of reason and empiricism in the art of healing.

The knowledge that had been accumulated by the Greeks was preserved and augmented by Arab cultures in great cities like Damascus and Baghdad. This knowledge was reintroduced, but incompletely, to Europe as a result of the Crusades. Amid the constant ebb and flow of the rational and religious, anatomical knowledge remained largely stagnant until the Renaissance. The most famous of the new anatomists working on human bodies (at first illegally) was Andreas Versalius, born in 1515. His painstaking dissections and resulting books disprove many of Galen's claims. His was not an easy victory, as Vesalius was periodically targeted by the Inquisition for heresy because of his repudiation of the venerable Galen. Anatomical engravings after Versalius are significantly more accurate than anything previous.

4.2.1.2 CONTROLLING BLEEDING

Even ancient peoples must have understood the ability of direct pressure to control some types of bleeding. Vedic scripts in India (about 1000 BC) reveal an understanding of cautery, the application of heat to seal a wound. Engravings and other evidence from Europe suggest that cautery was accomplished using hot irons or hot pitch, which was undoubtedly very painful. In 1080 AD, Roger of Palermo, professor of surgery at the famous Medical School of Salerno, advocated ligature (tying off of vessels) to control bleeding. This practice was advanced by the French surgeon Ambroise Pare in the 1500s based on his battlefront experiences. Pare invented special arterial forceps for this purpose. Both cautery and ligature are still used to control bleeding during surgery, but with updated and more efficient equipment.

Closely related to the prevention of blood loss is the replacement of lost blood. Although anatomical knowledge was limited in early civilizations prior to 2000 BC, Middle Kingdom (2697–2597 BC) Chinese understood that blood moves in a constant circle. This knowledge, and the resulting conclusion that lost blood had to be replaced in the closed system, was not widespread in Europe prior to 1500. In the second century, A.D. Galen had proposed a one-way flow of blood from the liver to the heart to the rest of the body, without return.

Miguel Serveto de Reves, a fellow student of Pare, understood circulation but ran afoul of Calvinist doctrine in other areas and was burned at the stake in 1553. The seventeenth century physician William Harvey finally popularized the notion of circulation in Europe. Harvey did this by computing the volume of blood pumped with each heart beat, and then each hour. From the large numbers involved (which equaled many times a person's actual weight), Harvey concluded that circulation could not be a one-way flow. The same blood must return again and again. Harvey waited years to publish his work because he was afraid of the backlash that had greeted other medical pioneers. The public reaction to his theories did hurt his practice, but he survived, and his ideas opened new doors for surgery. The theory of blood circulation implied that one could introduce medicines into the body rapidly by injecting them into the veins, and that blood could be added to the closed system from a donor.

Unfortunately, early transfusions had mixed results, at first because nothing was known of incompatible blood types. Richard Lower of Oxford performed successful transfusions between dogs, after some trial and error. In 1666, Samuel Pepys made diary entries about making up blood loss by borrowing from "a better body." In 1818, the first recorded successful transfusion from human to human was performed by James Blundell and Henry Cline in London. In 1829, a transfusion using syringes was used to save a woman who hemorrhaged in childbirth. In 1901, the existence of agglutinins in the blood was discovered in Vienna and London, and blood types were identified.

Blood typing helped solve the problem of blood incompatibility, leaving one final major difficulty: blockage of the canula (tube used to carry the blood) by clotted blood. In 1914 and 1915, the discovery of potassium citrate as an anticoagulant helped solve this problem.

4.2.1.3 CONTROLLING PAIN

Operations that incise the skin or organs are painful, causing involuntary movements and cries and making unanesthetized surgery difficult or impossible for both surgeon and patient. Lacking the ability to control pain, early surgeons worked as rapidly as possible, which prohibited deep or complex procedures. For patients, pain was an issue not only during the procedure, but sometimes long afterward.

Ancient civilizations in China, India, Egypt, and Greece knew they could control pain with hemp, hashish, opium, or mandrake. These humane methods were largely abandoned during the Middle Ages. Other methods were used, like extreme cold (only in winter), alcoholic intoxication, or induction of unconsciousness by compressing the carotid artery or choking. This crude state of affairs remained until the eighteenth century, when nitrous oxide (laughing gas) was first used in dentistry.

The effects of nitrous oxide are too transitory for longer operations, and in the nine-teenth century ether and chloroform were tried for surgical use. These gasses had longer-lasting effects and created new possibilities for case complexity and duration. Within a year, James Simpson used chloroform as a substitute for ether (Lawrence 1993, Loudon 1997). Interestingly, the tension between religious and secular pursuits persist-ed into the middle 1800s, with the church opposing the use of anesthesia for childbirth, quoting scripture that God told Eve that "in sorrow thou shall bring forth children." Physicians countered by noting that the first operation was carried out under anesthe-sia, when God put Adam to sleep to remove a rib. The debate vanished when Queen Victoria asked for and was administered chloroform during the delivery of her eighth child in 1853 (Loudon 1997).

Not all procedures call for general anesthesia with its attendant dangers, so means were sought to anesthetize local areas of the body. Cocaine, first encountered by Europeans in Peru, was discovered to be of value as a local anesthetic in eye operations in 1884. Later, cocaine solutions were injected into nerve endings. The Incas also developed the drug known as curare, a muscle paralytic that makes surgery feasible by inducing muscular relaxation.

It is difficult to comprehend the pain that must have accompanied early amputations, abdominal surgeries, or tooth extractions prior to the development of anesthetics, or how much patients and physicians alike must have feared an impending procedure. The control of procedural and postprocedural pain is so important to the practice of sur-gery, and so dependent upon precise doses to be effective without being fatal, that the practice of anesthesia is now a specialty in medicine.

4.2.1.4 CONTROLLING INFECTION

Until recently, almost every operation was accompanied by extended fever and pain due to wound infection. The surgical patient was more likely to die of infection than from the procedure, a situation that could not be reversed until the cause of infection was known. Early surgeons suspected the "air" in the hospital was somehow connected to infection, owing to the greater frequency of infection in hospitalized patients, but understanding of infection did not advance greatly until the nineteenth century.

In the 1840s, Ignaz Semmelweiss at Vienna General Hospital was troubled by the high death rate of women in childbirth due to postdelivery infection, a condition termed puerperal fever. The unfortunate death of a colleague who cut his finger during an autopsy suggested a connection between the dead body and the fatal infection. Semmelweiss realized that this connection might provide a key to his puzzle. He had spent many mornings in the mortuary studying deaths during childbirth before going to the operating theater to deliver new children. Could he be the vehicle of transmission of the infection? He decreed that anybody touching the patient must first wash his hands thoroughly in chlorinated water, and deaths in his clinic decreased precipitously.

Despite the compelling logic and evidence of Semmelweiss's work, the medical establishment was loathe to accept that it was the physician who was unclean and the cause of infection. Semmelweiss was dismissed from his post and spent a prematurely shortened career fighting for his ideas, before he succumbed to dementia at the age of 47.

While Semmelweiss was being drummed out of the profession, a successor was already at work. Dr. Joseph Lister, professor of surgery at the University of Glasgow in the 1860s, knew that simple bone fractures almost always healed without infection, but fractures in which the bone pierced the skin almost always became infected. When Lister learned of Louis Pasteur's work on microbes and germ theory, he realized that the real infectious agent was not the air but microbes in the air; hence, killing germs was the key to preventing infection. Lister systematically investigated how the air, the instruments, the surgeon's hands, and everything else in the OR could be cleansed of microbes. Pasteur had already shown that microbes could be killed or excluded by heat, filtration, or antiseptics. Lister found carbolic acid to be an effective antiseptic. So he used it to spray the air in the operating venue and bathe everything that would come in contact with the patient.

Due to suppression of Semmelweiss's work, Lister was unaware of it and found himself facing many of the same criticisms. However, resistance to the notion that surgeons might be a vehicle of infection steadily declined in the face of mounting evidence. By 1875, Lister's work was widely recognized as important, and his techniques, including boiling instruments and the use of antiseptics, found widespread acceptance. Lister first heard of Semmelweiss in 1884 and was quick to credit his Viennese predecessor with the discovery of antisepsis.

The combination of Pasteur's germ theory and the practical experience of physicians resulted in a dramatic increase in understanding of infection and its prevention. Some of these advances can be seen by comparing two famous paintings by Thomas Eakins: *The Gross Clinic* painted in 1875, and the *Agnew Clinic* in 1889. In the latter work, but not the former, the patient is draped, the surgeons are gowned, the light is much brighter and casts fewer shadows (suggesting artificial rather than natural light), and the woman in the picture is a professional nurse rather than a relative cringing in terror. However, the latter painting shows neither masks nor gloves nor, apparently, a rigorously guarded sterile field. These practices were only adopted in the 1890s, little more than a century ago.

A more complete understanding of human anatomy and the control of bleeding, pain, and infection greatly expanded the range of procedures that could be performed. The resulting diversity reduced the ability of any one person to master all procedures, encouraging physicians to specialize in certain areas.

The science surrounding the control of pain and the delicacy with which people must be rendered unconscious or unresponsive, locally or generally, led to specialization in anesthesiology. The need to control infection by preventing the intrusion of microbes into the patient's body led to the development of a sterile OR environment kept separate from the rest of the hospital. Specialty nurses and technicians evolved to manage this new environment. The OR suite is differentiated from the rest of the hospital by these special characteristics and the systems required to support them, which evolved over time to prevent mortality and morbidity during invasive procedures.

From a managerial perspective, advances in diagnostic and surgical technology continually change the equation between the medical conditions likely to be presented by a patient population and the required OR capacity. For example, placing a stent (a rigid tube inserted into a blood vessel to hold it open and prevent blockage) into an artery can be done on an outpatient basis. Angiographic stenting is much less invasive than coronary bypass surgery, in which surgeons remove a vessel from another part of the body and graft it to the blocked vessel to bypass the point of obstruction. A patient with an erratic heart rate may be treated medically or by the implantation of a pacemaker. These examples illustrate the challenges for hospitals that must decide the number and size of rooms in their operating suite, and their configuration, equipment, and staffing.

Recent advances in noninvasive and minimally invasive techniques have also challenged which conditions call for surgery. The need for exploratory surgery (to look at inner tissue for diagnostic purposes) has been greatly reduced by the development of noninvasive imaging techniques like CT scans and MRIs. Minimally invasive (laparoscopic) techniques allow surgeons to perform procedures using fiber optic light systems, miniaturized television cameras, and tools that require only a small incision to enter the body. The surgeon watches a high-definition monitor rather than looking directly at the organ being manipulated. Minimally invasive techniques expose less of the inner tissues to the exterior environment, reducing the risk of infection, blood loss, need for pain medications, healing time and hospital stays, and scarring from surgical incisions. For example, surgical repair of the heart's mitral valve (between the left atrium and ventricle) used to require cutting through the sternum (breast bone) to expose the heart; minimally invasive approaches enter through small incisions between the patient's ribs. Robotic surgery is an extension of minimally invasive techniques in which the surgeon manipulates robotic tools rather than standard laparoscopic tools, with greater precision. Both of these techniques also bring us closer to the day when surgeons will not need to be physically present in the room to perform a procedure, raising interesting questions about the most economical and efficient deployment of surgical expertise in the future.

4.2.2 Assets

4.2.2.1 PHYSICAL ASSETS: THE OPERATING ROOM SUITE

ORs are specially designed and equipped areas for the performance of surgery. The OR complex is designed to accommodate the flow of patients, medical professionals, and equipment to and from the various rooms at the appropriate times to perform scheduled and emergency procedures. Families wait in a room that is open to the public, but they may not enter the OR area. Venturing into the OR requires both authorization and appropriate attire (scrubs).

Because surgery involves crossing the patient's skin barrier, special attention is given to the prevention of infection by either direct contact or through airborne pathogens. To this end, the ORs are separated from the rest of the hospital to prevent infections, and the suite itself is divided into zones of increasing cleanliness. These go by various names, but in general there are public spaces, a "clean zone" transition space, and a "sterile zone" that is kept as aseptic as possible. Strict policies are followed to control the flow of people and materials to ensure that "dirty" people or items do not intrude on the clean and sterile zones. Within each OR, a restrictive sterile field is enforced during a procedure. Nothing unsterilized can cross the boundary into the sterile field, and all individuals working in the field wear scrubs, additional sterile gowns, gloves, and masks.

Exhibit 4.1 shows a sample ambulatory surgery center and its patient, surgeon, and equipment flows. Exhibit 4.2 shows a sample OR suite within a large tertiary care hospital.

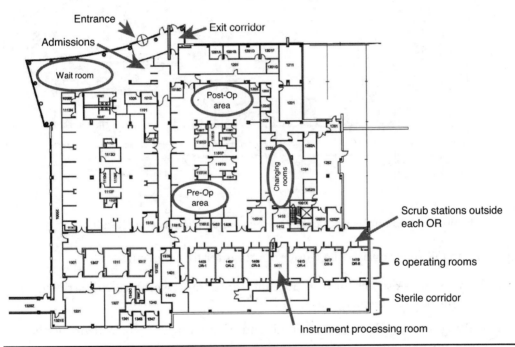

Patient flows: Arrive and check in at front desk, proceed to wait room, called back to pre-op area for preparation, taken to one of the ORs, when procedure is complete patient goes to post-op area for recovery, then out the exit corridor to waiting transportation.

Physician flows: Arrives and goes to changing room, goes to pre-op to meet and talk to patient, takes patient to the OR, scrubs and performs the procedure, takes patient to the post-op area and goes to talk to the patient's family in the wait room, then goes to pre-op to meet the next patient and repeats the cycle.

Instrument flows: After use in the OR "dirty" equipment goes into upper (non-sterile) corridor and into instrument processing room. Sterile equipment leaves instrument processing room and is stored in sterile corridor until needed in one of the ORs.

Exhibit 4.1   An ambulatory surgery center.

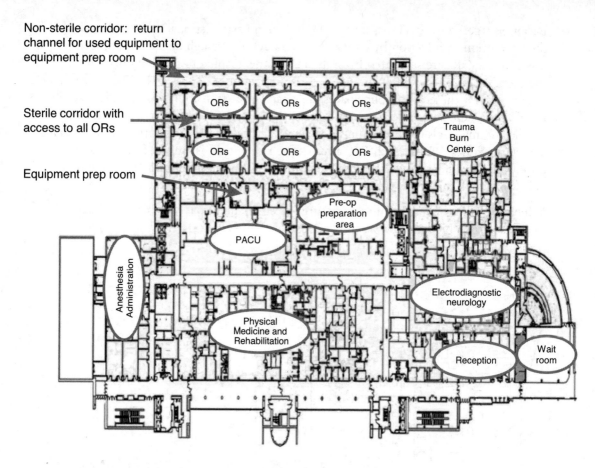

Non-sterile corridor: return channel for used equipment to equipment prep room

Sterile corridor with access to all ORs

Equipment prep room

ORs ORs ORs

ORs ORs ORs

Trauma Burn Center

Pre-op preparation area

PACU

Anesthesia Administration

Electrodiagnostic neurology

Physical Medicine and Rehabilitation

Reception

Wait room

Exhibit 4.2 Example layout of an OR suite within a tertiary care hospital.

Physically, an OR suite consists of a cluster of rooms for the following:

- **Admissions**—Also known as the reception area, this is where patients arriving from the outside are first seen.

- **Waiting room**—Where families and friends wait for news of the patient and the procedure outcome.

- **Preprocedure preparation**—Also known as pre-op, this is for patient preparation that can (or should) be done outside the OR. The patient is gowned, intravenous lines are inserted, telemetry leads and some monitors may be placed, and some paperwork may be completed prior to going into the OR. The surgeon or anesthesiologist also meet the patient here and explain what is to come.

- **Procedure rooms**—Where the operation is performed.

- **Postprocedure recovery**—Where patients first go after a procedure. These spaces, sometimes called the "post-op" area or PACU (for Post Anesthesia Care unit), have more intensive monitoring by nurses and equipment than standard hospital beds. A PACU may be divided into "phase I" (the patient has just emerged from the OR and is waking up) and "phase II" (later stage recovery) areas. Post procedure, patients may also go directly to an ICU.

- **Step-down**—This space is a transition place between Intensive Care in the PACU and the standard level of care in a regular hospital bed. It has an intermediate level of staffing and monitoring.

The preceding spaces trace the physical location of patients as they move through the OR suite. In addition, the surgeons and surgical staff have their own flows:

- **Staff changing rooms**—Where surgeons and surgical staff remove their street clothes, sometimes shower, and get into clean surgical clothes and shoes. There are separate rooms for males and females and sometimes for surgeons and staff.

- **Clean corridor or zone**—There is usually a physical transition area between the hospital and the ORs, through which the surgeons and staff pass en route from the "dirty" outside world into the sterile field. Sometimes this is a physical corridor between the changing rooms and the scrub rooms and ORs.

- **Scrub rooms**—Where the surgeon and surgical staff scrub their hands and arms and put on a sterile gown, gloves, and mask before proceeding to the sterile zone. Scrub rooms are often placed between ORs so surgical staff can go directly from scrubbing into the OR.

In addition to these physical locations along the patient and staff flows, OR suites have a number of support facilities:

- **Sterilizing room(s)**—Sometimes called equipment processing rooms. Used instruments are received on the dirty side of this venue, are cleaned and sterilized, and then moved to the clean side or are stored in a sterile corridor until needed.

- **Clean storage room and equipment storage room**—Used to store clean items and equipment. Sometimes this is a corridor running behind the procedure rooms.

- **Set-up room(s)**—Surgical trays with sterilized equipment are prepared. Each procedure has its own particular inventory of tools, as requested by the physician.

- **Housekeeping room(s)**—To store cleaners and other items required to sterilize a room between procedures.

Each OR is equipped with an operating table and various specialized items of equipment. Special attention is given to keeping the rooms clean, the equipment sterilized, and the air contaminant free, as well as managing the contaminant risk as people and equipment move in and out of the room. Positive air pressure helps prevent cross-contamination from other spaces. Operating room equipment is almost always moveable to aid cleaning and to provide flexibility in room configuration. The operating table pivots so that the patient can be placed in any needed position. The patient's heart rate, blood pressure, and oxygen levels are constantly monitored. Required equipment (such as suction and X-ray) is positioned prior to each procedure. Equipment required for some but not all procedures (such as a heart-lung machine) may not be stored in the OR but should be in an adjacent space outside the general traffic patterns of the hospital.

Practice has evolved to manage the special level of risk that attends many procedures, including the transfer of infection to/from staff and surgical and anesthesia mistakes that can have lasting or fatal consequences. The patient's body is draped to cover all but the area to be operated upon, bright overhead lights illuminate the patient, and the placement of equipment and the design of instruments provide a clear visual field. Careful planning and checks ensure that the right procedure is being done on the right person and that potential complications (for example, interactions with current medications and preexisting health conditions) are recognized and planned for in the procedure and the administration of anesthetic agents (which include gasses and infusions that deaden nerves, induce unconsciousness, reduce pain, relax muscles, prevent infection, and inhibit nausea).

Standard ORs used to be 360–400 square feet, and some procedures (such as urinary tract cystoscopy, requiring only local anesthetic) can still be done in a space of this size. However, as operative procedures have become less and less invasive, the needed equipment and technology has required more and more space. In addition, more room is required for open heart surgery, organ transplants, and other complex procedures that require a heart-lung machine, robotic surgery capability, or other large specialty equipment. A standard OR size today is 600–800 square feet. An increase in the footprint of a single OR reduces the total number of ORs that can fit into a finite space. ORs are also expensive, so it is financially unattractive to overinvest in them. This means that in many hospitals, ORs are scarce resources, and issues of property rights and surgeon scheduling among the various surgical services are important and potentially contentious.

A hospital must anticipate a patient and procedure mix appropriate for its natural demographics and its strategy and translate this into capacity planning for the required physical and human assets.

4.2.2.2 HUMAN ASSETS

A typical procedure involves several, and perhaps many, professionals. The broad categories of people in the OR are as follows:

- **Surgeon**—The surgeon leads the team and personally directs and performs the procedure. In teaching institutions, the attending surgeon may guide a resident through the performance of a procedure.

- **Anesthesiologist**—The anesthesiologist administers anesthetics and other drugs to reduce pain, render the patient unreactive to the trauma of the operation, and reduce the probability of unpleasant or adverse reactions to the procedure. The anesthesiologist and administering equipment is most often positioned at the head of the patient, and the anesthesiologist carefully monitors the patient both visually and via readouts of a variety of physiological monitors.

- **First assistant (surgical technician)**—The first assistant helps the surgeon during the procedure, such as by controlling bleeding as the surgeon makes incisions, clamping or suturing. Recent legal restrictions on the hours per week that surgical residents may work have increased the demand for trained surgical assistants. This development has resulted in new training programs so that registered nurses, nurse practitioners, physician assistants, and some surgical technologists can work in this capacity.

- **Scrub nurse**—The scrub nurse works inside the sterile field (hence, he or she wears scrubs) with the surgeon and assistants. The scrub nurse organizes the equipment on a sterile tray so everything that might be required is readily available and transfers instruments to and from the surgeon and first assistant during the procedure. Depending on the complexity of the procedure, other assistants might handle *retractors* (instruments that hold body tissue aside to provide a clear view of critical areas).

- **Circulating nurse**—The circulating nurse is not scrubbed and may enter or leave the room to get or return equipment during the procedure. He or she is the connection to the world outside the sterile field.

  The scrub nurse and circulating nurse are two examples of *perioperative* nurses, who help the patient and physicians before, during, and after the operation. Perioperative nurses can, with extra training, become first assistants or nurse anesthetists who can administer certain types of anesthesia.

- **Surgical technician**—The definition of a surgical technician varies, ranging from the scrub and circulating nurse to less highly trained assistants who prep and sterilize the room or transport the patient.

The surgical team is supported by a host of others, including receptionists, the crew that prepares and sterilizes the equipment, people who transport patients, and a cleaning and change-over team that cleans the room and gets it ready for the next procedure. Good communication and teamwork among all these people is required for good outcomes. Surgeons can have preferred venues and preferred teams of people familiar with each other and who work well together. This can have efficiency and outcome advantages, but it reduces the ability to use rooms and human resources flexibly.

The personnel in the OR suite tend to be more highly trained, and more costly, than the average health care worker. (See Exhibit 4.3 for some sample requirements.) The OR suite itself is more costly to build and maintain than most other hospital facilities. The high cost of the facilities, the difficulty in replacing these valuable human and physical assets, and their central role in the financial health of the hospital make efficient utilization of the OR suite a managerial imperative.

Surgeon	Undergraduate degree
	4 years of medical school
	5 years of surgical residency in a hospital
	Potentially more for specialties
	Exams and experience requirements for licensing
Anesthesiologist	Undergraduate degree
	4 years of medical school
	1 year general medicine residency
	3 year residency in anesthesia
	Exams and experience requirements for licensing
First assistant	Can be resident or medical practitioner, or a Registered Nurse (RN) or surgical technologist who takes additional courses and has OR experience
Perioperative nurse (includes scrub and circulating nurses)	2 to 4 years of college or a diploma program to be a Registered Nurse (RN)
	Additional clinical experience and continuing education
	Exams for licensing
Surgical technologist	2 year Associates degree
	Additional clinical experience
	Exams for licensing

Exhibit 4.3 Sample training requirements for the surgical team.

4.2.3 Flows

Although different facilities operate differently, in general terms, the people and material flows in an OR suite follow a predictable path.

4.2.3.1 PATIENT FLOWS

A patient is referred to a surgeon on the advice of his primary care doctor. The surgeon meets the patient in a clinic, in an office space where the surgeon holds office hours, to interview the patient, review relevant medical records, and order more tests if necessary. If surgery is indicated, it is discussed with the patient (and the patient's family, as appropriate). Upon consensus, the surgeon places the patient on the surgical schedule. The schedulers check for the availability of a room, a surgical team, the right equipment, and (if required) a bed in the hospital before or after the procedure. When all resources are available, the date and time are set, and the patient is given instructions for when to arrive, how to prepare, and what to bring. The surgical schedule for a given day is closed when all the available resources are used. New requests must then be scheduled on a different day.

The day before a schedule is executed, it is reconfirmed that all required resources are available and scheduled to be at the right place at the right time. If the patient is arriving from the outside, he checks in at admissions, fills out some paperwork, and waits in a public waiting room. If the patient is already in a hospital bed, these administrative tasks can be performed at bedside. The scheduled OR is monitored so that the surgical team knows when the previously scheduled procedure is likely to end. About a half hour prior to the anticipated procedure start time, the patient is called back to a preparatory (pre-op) area to be readied for the operation. The patient is then gowned, intravenous catheters are placed, and telemetry leads and some monitors may be positioned prior to the patient going into the OR.

When the scheduled OR is empty and cleaned, it is prepared for the new procedure with the necessary equipment and instruments. The patient is brought into the OR and positioned correctly on the table. He is draped and scrubbed, the surgical team positions itself around the patient, and the procedure commences.

When the operation is complete, the patient leaves the OR for the post-op area, PACU or ICU, and from there might go home or be admitted to the hospital for postprocedural observation. These general flows are shown graphically in Exhibit 4.4.

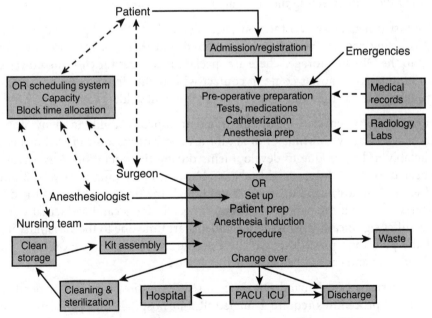

Exhibit 4.4 Daily material and information flows.

4.2.3.2 STAFF FLOWS

Surgeons have access to OR time, and support staff are assigned to surgeons or rooms, via an OR scheduling system to be described later. On the day of a procedure, the surgeon and staff arrive and go to a changing room to get out of their street clothes. The surgeon then goes to the pre-op area to meet and talk to the patient about what to expect. As the patient is transported to the OR, the surgeon goes to the scrub room. There, he scrubs his hands and arms; puts on a sterile gown, gloves, and mask; and proceeds into OR's sterile zone. Nothing dirty is allowed to cross the boundary of the sterile field. After the procedure, staff members discard their gowns and masks, and the surgeon goes out to the wait room to talk to the family of the patient about how the procedure went and what to expect going forward. The surgeon then repeats the cycle with the next patient, until the final case of the day.

4.2.3.3 MATERIAL FLOWS

There is a material flow through the OR that runs concurrently with the patient and staff flows. Prior to each procedure, the surgeon fills out a surgical card requesting specific equipment, which must be pulled from storage and sterilized (if not already sterilized and sealed), prior to being positioned in the OR. After the procedure, there are strict guidelines for cleaning, decontaminating, sterilizing, and storing equipment. The surgical staff discard their gloves and gowns, which leave via their own path that does not intersect the clean zone. Likewise, when the room is cleaned, the waste must leave the room without intersecting the clean area.

Reusable instruments leave via the nonsterile side of the OR and proceed to an instrument processing room. There they are sterilized and then taken to a sterile corridor adjacent to the ORs for storage. There are special procedures for cleaning power equipment or equipment that has come in contact with highly infective or unconventional contaminants, such as the virus that causes Jakob-Creutzfeldt disease.

Challenges to the system derive from the inherent unpredictability in many of its steps. Patients may not arrive on time or at all, for a variety of reasons. Procedures can vary unpredictably in length, due to developments during the operation. A procedure that was expected to take 2 hours might take 1.5 hours if everything is easy, or 3 hours or more due to complications. Consequently, although the first procedure of the day generally starts on time if the patient arrives on time, all others can have actual start times that may differ significantly from the scheduled start time due to the variability in duration of the preceding procedures. In the extreme, cases may be cancelled if they are delayed too long and cannot be performed that day.

Emergency arrivals can demand OR space on short notice, with life or death consequences. Most procedures require a single OR, but hospitals that perform transplants may need to free up two ORs on short notice when an organ becomes available: one room for the donor body, and one room for the recipient. Because emergency cases are given priority, they can greatly disrupt the established schedule unless idle rooms are available.

Delayed and disrupted schedules have many adverse consequences. Patients and their families may have taken vacation days from work and driven long distances to reach the hospital, and families will naturally be anxious about their loved ones. Delays and cancellations inject more stress and turmoil into their lives; asking them to come back at another time imposes a significant practical and psychological burden. Telling a surgical team (that is prepared to operate) to wait or reschedule plays havoc with busy schedules. Procedure disruptions and delays can cause significant reductions in patient and staff satisfaction and can have both clinical and financial consequences.

If the hospital schedules the ORs too tightly, without slack in the schedule, the consequences of unplanned variations are particularly severe. However, insertion of open time into the schedule to accommodate unplanned variations causes the hospital to not fully utilize its expensive physical assets and, by scheduling fewer procedures each day, increases patient delay in having procedures performed. Eventually, patients may go elsewhere for care, with negative revenue implications.

Consequently, the efficient management of flows in the OR requires an understanding of the sources and consequences of variability and how to plan for predictable variability while remaining flexible to respond to unpredictable variability.

4.3 Managing the OR Suite

4.3.1 Performance Metrics

Consciously improving a system requires that one is able to recognize when the system is getting better. A hospital is a complex organization of diverse stakeholders with different and potentially competing agendas, so "getting better" may mean different things to different people, and the adoption of unambiguous measures of "better" can itself be a political process. In our chapters, we present a spectrum of metrics for assessing the various subunits in a typical hospital. The list is diverse, reflecting the multidimensional nature of hospital performance. It reflects a world of trade-offs, where improvement on one metric may require retreat on another. However, one cannot manage what one cannot measure, and any initiative should be evaluated based on its consequences for those metrics salient to any stakeholder with veto power (see the Veto principle in Appendix A). We can divide the OR suite's performance metrics into clinical, operational, financial, and organizational categories. Clinical metrics measure the quality of patient care. Operational metrics characterize the process efficiency of the unit. Financial metrics track monetary flows. Organizational metrics measure staff satisfaction and organizational learning potential.

Clinical metrics are divided into three subcategories. Compliance metrics measure the extent to which the treatment process conforms to specifications. An example of such a metric is the percent of patients who receive the appropriate amount of anticoagulants as determined by current best practice standards. Outcome metrics measure the result of treatment. An example is the number of patients who die within 30 days of a surgical procedure. Satisfaction metrics measure the subjective approval of patients and families, generally collected via surveys.

Operational metrics can also be divided into subcategories. Time metrics track the speed at which patients flow through the unit. Volume metrics measure the workload processed by the surgical suite. For example, the average number of cases performed per day or year is a volume metric, and the length of an average procedure is a time metric.

Financial metrics can be broken down into costs and revenues. Cost metrics characterize expenses, which include staff salaries, equipment expenses, and consumables purchases. Revenue metrics are typically broken down into charges and actual reimbursements, which can differ significantly.

Organizational metrics are in one sense drivers of all the other metrics, because a well-functioning organization performs well clinically, operationally, and financially. However, certain organizational features are important for long-term success yet not captured in the other metrics categories. We divide organizational metrics into current staff satisfaction and related measures (for example, turnover) and organizational learning metrics.

Other metrics may not fall neatly into any of these categories. Also, OR-specific metrics may not tell the whole story. For example, one might be able to reduce the time in the OR at the cost of increasing the time in PACU or in a bed, or for total recovery. The ORs are often bottlenecks in the total flow of patients through the hospital, so activities in the OR can have an important influence on metrics for other units or the entire hospital.

Table 4.1 lists some common metrics for OR suite performance, and Section 4.4 demonstrates the use of these metrics to evaluate proposed initiatives.

Table 4.1 Example Performance Metrics for an OR Suite

Clinical Metrics	Operational Metrics	Financial Metrics	Organizational Metrics
Compliance and Best Practice	*Time*	*Costs*	*Staff Satisfaction*
Patient temperature	Length of time in OR by procedure type	Facilities cost: everything but the physicians, direct and indirect	Staff satisfaction
Standards for serum glucose	Average turnover time between procedures	Professional costs	Staff turnover
Standards for anticoagulation	Time to ambulation	Overtime costs	Ease of recruitment of new staff
Standards for beta blockers	Delay to get on schedule by service and surgeon		
Standards for antibiotic administration			
Outcome	*Volume*	*Revenues*	*Organizational Learning*
Mortality rate by case type	Number of cases performed per day	Charges	Quality improvement projects
Postoperative infection rate	Number of elective cases cancelled	Actual reimbursements	Quality-related meetings/exchanges
Blood loss	Number of elective cases delayed	Uncompensated surgeries	Number of suggestions
Returns to the OR	Frequency of bed delays		Implementation rate of suggestions
Satisfaction	*Other*		
Patient satisfaction	Patient type breakdown		
Patient retention	Fraction of on-time starts		
	Utilization of ORs by service and overall		
	Utilization within assigned block time versus total utilization		

4.3.2 Management Decisions

Managing an OR suite requires a series of planning decisions from long-term strategic planning down to tactical day-to-day execution. The major decision categories differ in their lead time to implementation (the speed with which they can be changed) and the information on which they are based. Long-term decisions take a long time to implement (and so cannot be changed rapidly) and are based on historical data and projections into the future. Short-term decisions are implemented rapidly and are based on real-time data.

Each decision level places significant constraints and consequences on the level below it.

For example, the strategic decision to perform variable, complex procedures relative to routine, predictable procedures has important consequences for rooms and equipment that will, in turn, significantly influence intermediate-range scheduling decisions and shorter range, daily responses to unfolding conditions. In the following subsections, we offer a brief overview of this decision hierarchy, which is shown in Exhibit 4.5.

	Decision type	Lead time to implement	Information requirements	Example
Increasing specificity →	Strategic	5 – 10 years	Historical trends and projections for the next decade	Construction projects, marketing strategy (target case mix, etc.), commitment to grow a discipline
	Intermediate	6 mo -1 year	Forecasts for the next year	Allocation of existing resources to existing services, modest adjustments in human or capital resources
	Short range	Days or weeks	Real time data	Schedule adjustments due to unforeseen circumstances

Each level constrains the next →

Exhibit 4.5   Decision hierarchy.

4.3.2.1 LONG-RANGE STRATEGIC PLANNING

Strategic planning is always a mediation between the external environment and internal capabilities. The long-range planning process, shown graphically in Exhibit 4.6, includes assessing the external environment and regulatory conditions and choosing how to position the hospital in that environment. That decision then has to be supported with an internal configuration. In the end, there must be a balance between the anticipated surgical load and the hospital's surgical capacity, which is determined by its physical and human assets.

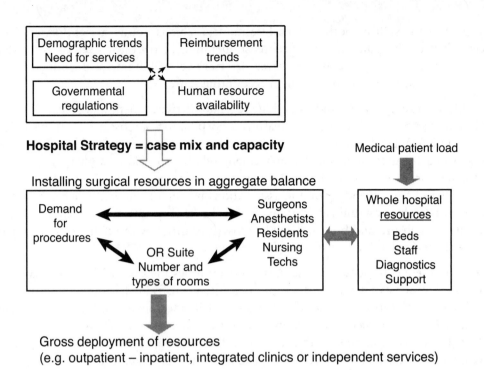

Hospital Strategy = case mix and capacity

Medical patient load

Installing surgical resources in aggregate balance

Gross deployment of resources
(e.g. outpatient – inpatient, integrated clinics or independent services)

Exhibit 4.6   Long-term planning.

Assessing the external environment includes identifying a target patient base. Because most people prefer to go to a hospital close to home, a hospital will have a local "catchment area" that is its natural market. If this market is shared with a local competing hospital, the strategy and investment plans of that competitor should be taken into account in the first hospital's strategy. Will it go head-to-head with the competitor in each service, or should it invest where the competitor has not acted to segment the market? What will each of these options mean for case load, personnel, and financial consequences?

A hospital's target market can extend beyond the natural geographic catchment area. Some hospitals specialize in certain types of procedures and aspire to be "destination health" facilities. This means they are perceived to be sufficiently distinguished to draw patients from around the country or the world. For example, the Mayo Clinic in Rochester, Minnesota, has built a strong brand identity around cancer care and attracts national and international patients. Whether the target market is local, national, or international, the demographics of the patient base suggest their current and evolving medical needs.

Financial forecasts are central to analyzing alternative strategic plans, and the hospital has to understand reimbursement trends and how facilities fees and professional fees interrelate with capacity and staff decisions. Which procedures make money for the hospital or the staff or both? Which lose money? This is not as straightforward as it seems, because hospitals are high fixed-cost operations. How those fixed costs are allocated to various activities can be relatively arbitrary yet will dramatically influence how "profitable" each activity appears in an accounting sense.

Finally, the hospital has to understand the regulatory environment that constrains what it can do. For both ethical and legal reasons, a hospital may choose, or be compelled, to treat some people who cannot pay for their care. This is one of several significant distinguishing features of hospital management relative to standard business practice. Estimates for uncompensated care as a percentage of total costs in U.S. hospitals range from 5% to 13%, depending on the assumptions made, but can be higher in relatively poor areas with many uninsured individuals. The level of uncompensated care that a hospital will absorb and how that will be cross-subsidized by profitable services is part of the strategic plan for its anticipated patient mix.

Based on these considerations, the hospital determines the case load it would want to process if capacity were ample. But capacity is often constrained, meaning that the hospital has to add capacity or decide what parts of its ideal load it will not do. Surgical capacity is driven directly by its physical and human assets, which were listed earlier. The surgical load combines with the medical load to make demands on the hospital's beds, staff, and diagnostic services. The primary output of a long-range strategic plan is an overall strategy for providing health care, a balance between a forecasted case load and the hospital's physical and human assets, and a balance between reimbursements and costs.

The hospital will select an operating suite configuration to support its strategy. Will outpatient and inpatient cases share a common facility, or be separated? The different pacing and needs of outpatient procedures may argue for locating them somewhere other than the high overhead core hospital. However, reimbursement guidelines may argue the opposite. Destination health ambitions may call for integrated clinics, where patients move smoothly from one service to another based on their needs. More traditional organizations have independent services, with the patients having to put together their own integrated schedules. A strategic plan is a decision about who the hospital will serve, with what resources, and how those resources will be deployed in broad terms.

4.3.2.2 INTERMEDIATE-RANGE SCHEDULING: MATCHING PEOPLE AND ROOMS TO TIMES

Once aggregate capacity (rooms, equipment, and staff) is in place, it is allocated to patient needs as demand unfolds through the year. This is done by preparing a schedule, which is a list of the patients, staff, and equipment in each room at each time during the day. Although these detailed allocation decisions are made on short time scales (see next subsection), the process by which this allocation is determined (that is the "scheduling system") is an intermediate-range decision that is only altered or adjusted on time scales of six months to a year or more. This is because any system takes a while to debug and run smoothly, and people plan their private and professional lives around the repeatable aspects of the schedule. So, once it is implemented, it can be difficult to change.

Exhibit 4.7 shows a sample scheduling process. First, the hospital must decide how many ORs are available for prescheduling. This may not be all the rooms, if some are deliberately left open for emergency arrivals. Then the hospital must decide the process by which rooms available for scheduling are allocated to physicians (and patients) as needs arise. Two archetypes for this intermediate-range process are open scheduling and block time. In an open schedule, physicians wishing to perform a procedure look at the existing schedule, anticipate how much time they will need, and sign up for an open slot large enough to accommodate the procedure. In a block time process, surgeons in the various services (for example, cardiothoracic surgery, neurosurgery, orthopedic surgery, surgical oncology, general surgery, and so on) are allocated specific blocks of time in which they are guaranteed a room. Most hospitals use a hybrid system with block time scheduling until close to the day of operation, at which time all unused time is made available to others in an open format.

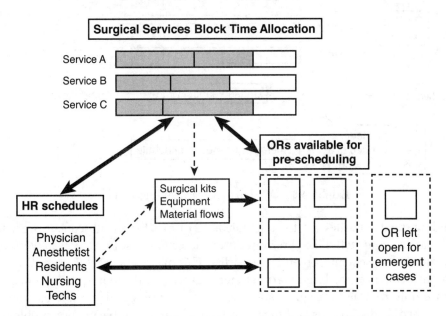

Exhibit 4.7   Medium-term OR scheduling: merging people, resources, and time.

Surgical schedules and block times are related to personnel scheduling systems because all members of a surgical team need to be present for the procedure.

4.3.2.3 SHORT-TERM SCHEDULING

On a daily basis, the planned OR schedule is executed to the extent possible. However, there may be no-shows, unforeseen emergencies, and other disruptions with which the staff must deal. The general situation is depicted in Exhibit 4.8. If an emergency arrives and an OR is open and unscheduled, all is well and the emergency and all scheduled cases can proceed as planned. If no OR is available, the elective surgery schedule must be disrupted to accommodate the emergency arrival. The central OR scheduler must decide whether the day's schedule should be extended (completing the schedule, but later than planned with overtime consequences) or, if not, which scheduled cases to cancel.

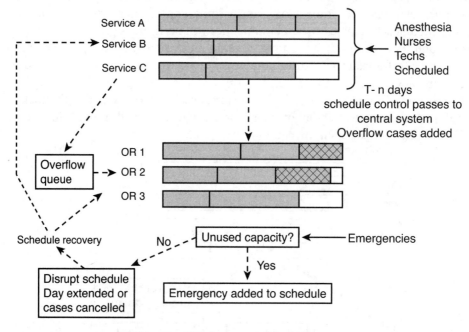

Exhibit 4.8   OR short-term scheduling system.

Extending the day pushes out the scheduled start times for all subsequent procedures, which patients and staff alike perceive poorly. Cancelling cases can be even worse, with the disruptive consequences mentioned earlier. This makes apparent the significant day-to-day consequences for longer-term strategic decisions. If the hospital's strategy is to embrace only routine procedures and refer more complex and variable patients elsewhere, schedule disruptions and their consequences may not be a major problem. If a hospital aspires to be a tertiary care center that accommodates emergency cases, it has to either retain some excess capacity (at a cost) or suffer from frequent schedule disruptions (with reduced patient and staff satisfaction and potentially worse health outcomes). The more routinized the environment, the more the hospital can make use of reliable forecasts of procedure times and standardized work rules for getting things done. The more diverse and complex the mix of procedures the hospital embraces, the more it must rely on flexible resources (human and physical) and systems that adapt rapidly. The hospital's long-range strategy and capacity investments have significant consequences for intermediate-range scheduling, which in turn greatly impacts daily operations.

4.4 Key Management Issues in the OR

Here we introduce some key management problems relevant to managing the OR suite. Each contains a problem statement and the principles that are directly related to that problem. We then illustrate a brainstorming exercise of principles-driven management by populating a generic management table (see Appendix A) appropriate for each challenge and breaking down the higher-level principles into more detailed options for practice. The hospital is not intended to embrace all these options. Rather, we use the objectives and our generic tables as brainstorming stimuli to generate a broad landscape of opportunities for consideration. In any one application, some small subset of this landscape will be adopted, based on the perceived costs and benefits of each option. We illustrate this with specific case examples.

4.4.1 Management Challenge: Delays to Get on the Surgical Schedule

4.4.1.1 PROBLEM

Hospitals with surgical suites tend to depend heavily on them for healthy financial performance. Surgery compensation is high, commensurate with the high levels of human skill and capital investment required. As noted previously, it is common for the surgeries to generate more than 50% of total hospital revenues, not including diagnostic tests which are also often surgically related (Jackson 2002, Peters and Blasco 2004). Clearly, the hospital's financial metrics (revenues and costs) are directly impacted by caseload and case mix in the surgical suite.

Timely access to the ORs is one dimension of the quality of service a hospital offers to patients and physicians. Especially when one or both of these key stakeholders can go elsewhere, timely access can affect caseloads and hence the hospital's bottom line. This is clearly true for hospitals without physician employees, who must attract surgeons to their site by offering something better than competing hospitals. But with impending physician shortages, even physician-employees must be satisfied to prevent their leaving for competing hospitals. Delays in addressing a diagnosed condition can also have health outcome effects.

Delays getting onto the surgical schedule immediately impact patient and staff satisfaction, which in turn can significantly affect the hospital's financial and organizational performance, and potentially health outcomes. This is why many hospitals track delays to get on schedule as a key performance metric, and why it appears as a key operational performance metric in Table 4.1 a few pages back.

Addressing responsiveness issues, such as this, usually involves the possibility of adding resources, which are expensive when we are talking about surgeons, surgical staff, and the physical assets in an OR suite. So, there is a strong cost component to any discussion of surgical delays. If we can speed throughput without adding resources, we also lower the delay to get on schedule, so both the time and volume operational metrics are relevant.

There is also an important subtext to the "staff satisfaction" metric in this context. Surgeons (and some other members of the surgical staff, such as anesthesiologists and potentially surgical nurses) are "key stakeholders" in the organization who have implicit veto power over just about any proposal affecting the ORs. That is, they can refuse to cooperate with any proposed change, thereby effectively vetoing it. So staff satisfaction is not only a metric in its own right, but a means to implementing anything. Consequently key metrics we need to pay close attention to when considering alternative initiatives in this context are health outcomes, revenues and costs, patient and staff satisfaction, and the time and volume operational metrics.

4.4.1.2 PRINCIPLES

We address the management problem of delays to get onto the surgical schedule by starting with a list of relevant management principles and breaking those down into specific policy options. A more complete list and description of the management principles we employ appears in the Appendix A. Here, we briefly review those that are relevant to the current discussion. A delay in getting on schedule is a "responsiveness" problem, so we draw upon the principles underlying our generic responsiveness management table and build those out in the specific context of surgical delays. As we describe in Appendix A, responsiveness issues can be addressed by some combination of managing workload capacity, synchronization, variability, sequencing, and/or perceptions. Finally, we recognize the multistakeholder nature of managing the OR suite by considering the consequences of some individual and group behavioral principles for the implementation of any proposal.

We begin by noting that the following principle:

Principle (Little's Law)—Over the long term, the rate (R), in-process inventory (I), and waiting time (T) of a system are related according to:

$$I = R \times T$$

implies that the long-run average number of patients in the queue to get onto the surgical schedule (I, in patients) equals the product of the throughput rate (R, in patients per day) and the average time a patient waits in queue (T, in days). Hence, we can decrease the waiting time T by either decreasing the queue length (I) for fixed throughput or increasing the throughput rate (R). So, we look for ways to increase capacity or decrease the queue length for any fixed level of capacity.

The simplest cause of delays to get on schedule is a capacity overload, which occurs when the OR suite receives work (patients) at a rate faster than it can handle. That is, the arriving workload exceeds the *capacity* of the ORs. Capacity of a resource, such as an OR, is defined as follows.

Definition (Resource Capacity)—The capacity of a resource is the throughput it can achieve provided that it is never starved for work.

The "throughput" of the OR suite is the long-run average patients per day that it can process. Providing there are ample patients waiting for surgeries, the capacity of the OR suite is the maximum (long-run average) patients/day it can serve. This capacity is determined by many different resources, including people, equipment, rooms, and supplies. Appendix A illustrates how to compute the capacity of an individual resource, such as a room or a surgeon. To get from the capacity of a single resource to the capacity of the OR suite as a whole, we invoke the concept of utilization, which is defined as follows.

Definition (Utilization)—Utilization of a resource is the long-term fraction of time it is busy, which is given by the average arrival rate of work (for example, patients per hour) at the station divided by the resource capacity over the long term.

When computing utilizations, the arrival rate and capacity should be in the same units (for example, patients per day). If demand for OR room-hours is close to the total room-hours available, the rooms will be highly utilized. If the patient and case mix generates a demand for surgeon-hours that is close to the total surgeon-hours available, surgeons will be highly utilized. This concept is important because the resource in a system with the highest utilization has the least capability to catch up from a capacity overload. Hence, we define the following.

Definition (Bottleneck)—The bottleneck of a system is the resource with the highest utilization.

Typically, bottlenecks are expensive resources because one does not tend to overinvest in the most expensive assets, meaning their capacity will be relatively low relative to demand. In the OR suite of a hospital the most likely potential bottleneck resources are the rooms themselves (staffed room time), surgeons or anesthesiologists, or exotic and expensive equipment. Surgical staff (scrub and circulating nurses, assistants) usually are not bottlenecks, not because they are unimportant but because their capacity is typically not as constrained. The bottleneck constrains the maximum rate of the system and hence defines its capacity.

Principle (System Capacity)—The capacity of a system is defined by its bottleneck, which is the resource in the system with the highest utilization.

So, if operating rooms are the bottleneck in the OR suite, throughput (patients per day) cannot exceed the capacity of the rooms. We can improve the performance of the entire system only by improving performance at the bottleneck resource. This principle allows us to focus our scarce managerial attention and resources where they will do the most good. Decreasing the utilization of the bottleneck resource can be accomplished by either increasing its capacity or decreasing the workload imposed upon it (the demand in cases/day or the workload per case). But there is another important driver of queues and delays in service systems, and that is unsynchronized variability in the workload and service times.

Principle (Variability)—Unsynchronized variability causes queueing.

There is an interaction between utilization and variability. In the presence of variability, the effect of utilization is dramatic and nonlinear.

Principle (Utilization)—Utilization magnifies queueing and delays in a highly nonlinear fashion.

So we can decrease queuing and delays by either decreasing utilization (increase capacity or decrease workload at the bottleneck) or decreasing unsynchronized variability (synchronize demand and capacity, or reduce overall variability at the bottleneck). These initiatives form the first three "Level 1" objectives in our management Table 4.2 that follows.

Although capacity, workload, and variability are the main drivers of delays to get onto the surgical schedule, the sequence in which cases are scheduled can also have an impact.

Variability and utilization impact congestion and waiting regardless of the order in which patients are treated. But patient sequencing is an important activity in any service system. Although issues of perceived fairness argue for first-come-first-served sequencing of patients, medical imperatives may require that a cancer or transplant patient be bumped to the front of the queue, even if that means further delay for some patients who have been waiting longer. Sequencing matters for our performance metrics. Two key principles related to sequencing follow:

- **Principle (Critical Ratio Sequencing)**—In a multiclass system with dynamic arrivals, prioritizing entities according to the ratio c/t, where c is the delay cost per unit time and t is the expected process time, minimizes total cumulative delay cost over the long term.

- **Corollary (SPT Sequencing)**—Processing entities in order of shortest processing time (SPT) minimizes average wait time.

The Critical Ratio Sequencing principle justifies treating critical patients first. Among patients with similar criticality scores, critical ratio scheduling reduces to performing the shortest cases first. This is called SPT, or "shortest processing time" sequencing. SPT sequencing on a day's OR schedule has several patient flow benefits.

First, for any fixed time of day, 2:00 p.m. say, more cases will have completed with SPT scheduling than any other format. So, if an emergent case arrives at 2:00 that must pre-empt scheduled surgeries, fewer cases are disrupted with SPT scheduling of elective surgeries. Second, it is common for the variability in case time to increase with expected case length. Longer, more complex procedures are usually more variable than shorter procedures. So, because the variability in the procedure time of one case generates variability in the start time of the subsequent procedure (that is, variability compounds throughout the surgical day), scheduling shorter (less variable) cases first reduces the propagated variability in the day's schedule. There may also be benefits for considering SPT scheduling when constructing longer-range surgical schedules, as we discuss more completely later. There are likely to be medical imperatives, personnel preferences, and issues of politics and fairness that will argue for different ways to sequence cases, but all else equal, it is useful to understand the advantages of SPT sequencing.

Finally, a key metric for any health system is patient and staff satisfaction, so their perception of the system matters. The perception of a wait is not always aligned with the actual chronological duration of the wait. That is, there are ways to make delays "seem" shorter, as enumerated in the following principle.

Principle (Waiting Time Psychology):

    a.   Occupied time feels shorter than unoccupied time.

    b.   People want to get started.

    c.   Anxiety makes waits seem longer.

    d.   Uncertain waits feel longer than known, finite waits.

    e.   Unexplained waits feel longer than explained waits.

    f.   Unfair waits feel longer than equitable waits.

    g.   The more valuable the service, the longer the customer will wait.

    h.   Solo waits feel longer than group waits.

Each of these principles suggests opportunities to improve people's perceptions of the service the hospital provides. Some of these are expanded on in Table 4.2.

We now turn to the "implementability" of prescriptions for decreasing delays to get onto the OR schedule. Changing anything of significance in a hospital requires attention to all key stakeholders who have veto power. As Cyert and March (1963) observe:

> Organizations [can be] considered as coalitions of people who have agreed to join together in return for satisfaction of certain of their objectives. This agreement is arrived at by a process of bargaining and is recorded in the organizational structure, the budgets, and the policies.

A hospital as an organization must strike the necessary compromises to ensure key stakeholder participation. But each stakeholder group may have different priorities and preferences. So, to assess the implementability of proposed policies, we need to consider managing in organizations whose members have diverse preferences. Some principles of individual human behavior, such as **Self-Interest** and **Inertia**, are listed in Appendix A. The connection between these individual behavioral characteristics and organizational improvements is captured in the following.

Principle (Key Stakeholders)—All organizations have key stakeholders with veto power whose approval is necessary to implement changes.

As is clear in Table 4.2, there are many ways to improve timely access to the ORs, but each comes with different costs and benefits to different sets of stakeholders (patients, surgeons, staff, or administration). Depending on the circumstances, some of these stakeholders may have little power to influence decisions and will have to (perhaps grudgingly) accept imposed changes. Other key groups, however, have veto power and can prevent (passively or actively) the implementation of a proposed change. No change will occur unless the preferences of those people are understood and appealed to.

Principle (Veto Power)—For a proposal to be implemented, all key stakeholders must perceive themselves to be better off with the proposal than without it.

Surgeons and anesthesiologists are key stakeholders in hospitals, as is the hospital administration. There may be others, too, such as surgical nurses. An implementable proposal must recognize the interests of each key stakeholder group. An administration focusing on financial performance will prefer more revenues (higher caseloads) with lower costs (fewer expensive resources). However, increasing the workload on fewer resources will, in a variable environment, increase the delays to access those resources. Financial metrics may improve, but patient and staff satisfaction will deteriorate. Surgeons and staff (and patients, at least until the hospital's investment costs show up in their health insurance premiums) will prefer that the administration invest in more human and physical resources so that these are always readily available for use. But, in a variable environment, short delays mean holding excess capacity on average, an expensive proposition that compromises financial performance. The key concept is that *somebody* will bear the cost of variability. The question of who will is a political one negotiated among the key stakeholders.

Focusing on OR scheduling delays, variability in both the demand for surgeries and their time and resource requirements means that the hospital must invest in extra capacity (cost) if it wants to reduce the delay to get on schedule (time) without rushing surgeries (putting quality at risk). Hence, the interests of key stakeholders will not be in perfect alignment, and inventive compromises among them will be required to move forward. Fortunately, there is hope.

Principle (Pareto Efficiency)—If benefits can be transferred from one group to another (for example, via the transfer of money or time or some other medium of exchange), and there exists a policy that improves the overall performance of a system, there exists an allocation of the total benefits that makes all key stakeholders better off.

This principle implies that in situations where one party "wins" at the expense of another, but there is some medium of exchange between them that allows the winners to compensate the losers, anything that benefits the system as a whole can be implemented. "Benefits the system as a whole" means that the total "winnings" are greater than the total "losses," so the winners can fully compensate the losers and still have some left over and remain strictly better off. That is, there is a win-win option.

This is only available when the entire system (sum of winners minus the sum of losers) is better off, creating the surplus that can be distributed. In OR scheduling, if the administration can forecast better financial performance if more procedures are scheduled each day, they should be willing to pay something additional to the staff who are burdened with carrying out an extended schedule. If the offered additional compensation is not enough to overcome the staff's opposition, there is no systemic win-win and the proposal is not implementable. But, if the financial gains to the hospital are greater than the resistance of the staff, a win-win is available by paying the staff enough to entice them voluntarily into an extended day.

Likewise, if surgeons or patients value faster access to resources because it makes their lives much easier, they should be willing to give up something to achieve that end. Hence, there is hope for an implementable compromise solution in which all parties are better off relative to the status quo. The Highland Hospital case in Section 4.4.1.4 illustrates one such situation.

4.4.1.3 PRACTICES

In terms of our generic management challenges (see Appendix A), timely surgical scheduling is a "responsiveness" issue. Our principles-driven brainstorming table begins with the generic ways to improve responsiveness and then breaks these down into specific initiatives applicable to the problem of delays getting onto the surgical schedule. This brainstorming method generates a broad landscape of options to choose from. No hospital wants to embrace all the specific initiatives, and some may be ill advised in certain contexts. The idea is to generate a wide range of options without (at first) being too judgmental as to feasibility or appropriateness. The essence of brainstorming is to avoid being too critical early in the process. Then, one can go back to choose a few promising possibilities for further analysis. If prescreening options happens too early, it is easy to overlook some promising avenues of investigation.

Our principles-driven brainstorming approach begins with the Level 1 initiatives to improve responsiveness: reduce workload, increase capacity, improve synchronization, reduce variability, improve sequencing, and enhance patient perceptions. We then break those down further into more detailed policy options. A more detailed discussion of the table entries follows the table display. Readers who are familiar with our brainstorming approach can skip those details and infer them directly from the table. Although Table 4.2 is extensive and illustrative, it is not exhaustive. Practitioners adopting this technique can, with the advantage of knowing more about their specific hospital context, break out the objectives in Levels 1 and 2 into different potential policies appropriate for their setting.

Table 4.2   Principles-Driven Strategies for Reducing the Delay to Get on Schedule

Level 1 Objectives	Level 2 Objectives	Level 3 Objectives	Example Policies
Reduce workload imposed by current cases	Reduce arrival rate of patients requiring surgical procedures	Use substitute non-surgical technologies	Adopt nonsurgical interventions where appropriate
		Reduce need in the community	Community outreach health and safety programs
			Preventive involvement in retirement homes and extended stay facilities
		Change target patient population	Target a less surgically intensive segment of the population
		Reduce emergent case load	Do not accept emergency transfers requiring surgery
			Outsource emergent surgeries
			Close the Emergency Department (ED)
		Reduce hospital-acquired surgical needs	Have safety programs for fall prevention, sepsis reduction, and so on
	Reduce average length of cases	Select for shorter cases	Transfer or refuse lengthy or complicated cases
			Change strategic case mix pursued by the hospital
		Reduce duration of current cases	Compare case times for the same or similar surgeries to identify "best practices" for surgeons

Level 1 Objectives	Level 2 Objectives	Level 3 Objectives	Example Policies
			Lean activities (process improvements) to reduce average time per case
			Improve preoperative preparation to reduce OR time
			Reduce interprocedure room change-over time
Increase capacity for handling cases	Add physical/human resources	Add resources at the bottleneck	Build new ORs
			Hire more surgeons
		Extend working hours of bottleneck resources	Extend staffed OR times
			Add a shift of surgeons and staff
		Lease or outsource more bottleneck resources	Lease offsite surgical space
			Contract with "surge capacity" surgeons who work as needed
			Outsource elective surgical procedures
	Increase capacity of current resources	Eliminate steps	Eliminate time-consuming steps in prescheduling "paperwork," for example with improved testing and reporting technologies
			Lean activities to reduce OR suite time demanded by surgeries
		Balance workloads to offload tasks from the bottleneck	Offload some tasks from the OR to pre-OR or post-OR rooms, so they can be performed while another case is in the OR

Table 4.2   Principles-Driven Strategies for Reducing the Delay to Get on Schedule

Level 1 Objectives	Level 2 Objectives	Level 3 Objectives	Example Policies
			Increase the work by residents and assistants so surgeon spends less time with each case
		Exploit parallelism	Look for opportunities within the OR to do things in parallel instead of in sequence
			Look for opportunities to perform preoperative testing and so on in parallel instead of in sequence
		Reduce batching	Avoid scheduling procedures in parallel that require the same scarce support resources
		Reduce blocking/ starving	Improve bed allocation system to be sure patients can leave the OR for the PACU, ICU, or a nursing unit
			Improve patient reminder and notification system to reduce no-shows
			Local transportation provided. Driver may perform in-home checklist for preparation compliance
			Phone reminders to improve patient compliance with food intake and other pre-operative restrictions
			Personalized, web-based checklists for compliance with preprocedure preparation

Level 1 Objectives	Level 2 Objectives	Level 3 Objectives	Example Policies
Improve the synchronization of demand and capacity	Level demand to match capacity	Maintain a level schedule for staff hours, and even out demand over the week	Provide incentives for surgeons to operate on Fridays (often avoided because this involves weekend
			Have alternative surgical sites that can handle bursts in demand or can funnel cases to the hospital when demand lags
	"Demand chase" (marshalling flexible capacity to meet variable demand)	Synchronize capacity with forecasted demand	Schedule resources to track predictable peaks and valleys in daily, weekly, or monthly demand for surgeries
		Have flexible human resources that can operate any day, any time	Have on-call teams ready for call-up as needed. Support staff on similar on-call contract to support procedures 24/7
Reduce variability	Reduce variability in the demand for surgeries	Strategic options	Change the strategic posture of the hospital to handle more routine cases
		Make use of external sources of demand and capacity	Refuse or transfer more cases when case load is high
			Advertise, or provide incentives for referring physicians, to invite more cases when case load is low
			Real-time "congestion pricing" for referring physicians based on current load, to move demand from peak to slow times

Table 4.2   Principles-Driven Strategies for Reducing the Delay to Get on Schedule

Level 1 Objectives	Level 2 Objectives	Level 3 Objectives	Example Policies
		Options internal to the hospital	Dynamically adjust the mix of medical to surgical treatments, when both are appropriate, to keep the surgical load level
	Reduce surgery time variability	Reduce variability in start, procedure, and exit steps	Comparison of case times for the same or similar surgeries leads to consistent "best practice" standard procedure for surgeons
			Streamline the kit preparation process, for example using process improvement teams
			Improve the room changeover process
			Provide guidelines or incentives to ensure the entire surgical team is on hand on time, when required
			Have flexible beds that can serve as PACU or ICU beds to avoid bed holds in the OR
Improve sequencing	Generate information	Generate better case length forecasts	Keep track of historical case times for a given surgeon and procedure to better forecast procedure durations
	Give priority to strategic imperatives	Adjust case mix	Give priority scheduling to cases appropriate for the desired strategic case mix; this can reduce delays to get on schedule if the desired case mix contains shorter and less variable cases

Level 1 Objectives	Level 2 Objectives	Level 3 Objectives	Example Policies
	Use critical ratio logic	Putting cases on schedule	Among cases of similar urgency, schedule the shortest cases first to reduce the propagation of variability throughout the day
		Within day scheduling	Use SPT logic, which will minimize the number of cases cancelled due to emergency intrusions
	Use other sequencing logic	Putting cases on schedule	Schedule "like" cases together (that require the same equipment and team) to increase case efficiency
			Sequence cases to smooth out demand for scarce critical equipment (similar to reducing batch demand for those resources)
		Within day scheduling	Schedule "like" cases (that require the same equipment and team) together to increase case efficiency
			Sequence cases to smooth out demand for scarce critical equipment (similar to reducing batch demand for those resources)
			Schedule the lowest variability cases earlier to reduce probability of end-of-day case cancellations

Table 4.2 Principles-Driven Strategies for Reducing the Delay to Get on Schedule

Level 1 Objectives	Level 2 Objectives	Level 3 Objectives	Example Policies
Enhance patient perceptions	Improve patient perceptions of delays to get on schedule	Keep patients occupied	Have "patient learning modules" that explain the disease and surgery and that patients can fill out while waiting
		Get patients started	Stress the dietary, and so on, lead-up to surgery, communicate the procedure as part of a longer process that starts at home
		Provide explanations of wait time	Stress the world-class quality of the service provided, which naturally implies a lot of demand for the best surgeons and facilities
			Provide lists of procedures to be done each day, giving patients visibility into the queue
		Make waits more equitable	Provide delay time statistics so people can see burden is evenly shared
			Compensate families for delays longer than a specified target
		Make waits proportional to value	Give priority scheduling to patients who can easily go elsewhere
			At the margin delay very important, but elective, surgeries more to get less important surgeries in faster
		Facilitate group waiting	Connect families of patients waiting for similar procedures for mutual conversation and support

Table 4.2 translates the generic responsiveness improvement options given in Table A.1 of Appendix A into specific tactics appropriate for managing delays getting onto the surgical schedule. Next we discuss some of these table entries and the logic behind them in more detail. Readers familiar with the underlying concepts and approach can skip this discussion without cost.

We begin with the two most basic ways to reduce queues and delays: either reduce the workload on the bottleneck resources or increase their capacity. Reducing workload can be accomplished by either reducing the arrival rate of jobs or reducing the workload represented by each job. The first can be done by reducing the number of surgeries required, which in turn can happen by substituting medical for surgical treatments, improving community health, changing the hospital's strategy, and so on. Reducing the workload in each case means decreasing the average case duration. This can be accomplished in various ways, such as by changing the case mix to shorter cases or carefully inspecting data on the durations of similar cases to see if there are some generic "best practices" that can decrease the average length without compromising outcomes.

Increasing capacity can be handled by either adding resources or increasing the capacity of current resources. There is an overlap with workload initiatives, because if we decrease the workload per case, we clearly increase the capacity of our resources to process cases. Recall that the bottleneck resource paces the entire system, so we should only add resources at the bottleneck. Adding resources anywhere else does no good. If surgeons are the bottleneck, building new ORs will not help. We need to engage more surgeons by hiring them, subcontracting some part-time, or doing something else. If OR time is the bottleneck, we can build new ORs, lease some off-site facilities, extend hours in existing ORs, and so on.

If we do not add resources, we can look for ways to increase the capacity of current ones. We may be able to eliminate steps in the process of getting on schedule (for example, with better testing and reporting processes to speed up preprocedure preparations). These, however, will not be effective if they do not reduce time on the bottleneck resources. For example, if surgeons or physical room time are the bottlenecks, faster access onto the queue for these resources will not help us.

However, if ORs are the bottleneck and we can offload within-the-OR activities to pre- or post-OR venues, we can improve the entire system. Most hospitals have preparatory areas where catheters and intravenous lines are inserted, telemetry leads and some monitors may be placed, and so on, prior to going into the OR. If surgeons are the bottleneck, can residents and assistants do more of the less complicated aspects of a procedure? Within the OR itself, some tasks may currently be done sequentially that could be done in parallel.

The central role of the bottleneck in whole-system performance means that time saved at the bottleneck helps the entire system. The reverse is also true; time wasted at the bottleneck hurts the entire system. Time is wasted if a bottleneck is blocked (the process is clinically complete, but the patient cannot move downstream to the next stage of his therapy) or starved (the OR is ready to go, but there are no patients to work on, or a complete surgical team has not been assembled so nothing can start). Reducing blocking/starvation is one way to increase the capacity of the bottleneck. We can reduce blockage in the OR by being sure that patients ready to leave the OR have a PACU or ICU bed to go to. We can reduce starvation of ORs and surgeons and staff by ensuring that all patients scheduled for surgery that day are onsite and prepared. One way to do this is to work to reduce "no shows" or people who arrive with improper at-home preparation (for example, violating food intake restrictions). If the ORs but not staff are the bottlenecks, making sure all members of a surgical team are present in a timely fashion can reduce bottleneck starvation (and wasted bottleneck time).

In addition to workload and capacity, the third major contributor to queues and delays is unsynchronized variability, where "unsynchronized" refers to a lack of coherence between the demand for services and the capacity to perform them. In the OR, we will see variability in the case arrival rate, the individual case durations, and the capacity of the surgeons and staff to perform procedures. Queuing and delays would not occur if by some magical process capacity could be instantaneously marshaled to attend to any fluctuations in demand. But, typically demand and capacity are not synchronized, causing alternating cycles of frantic and relaxed days in the OR. Improving synchronization means either adjusting capacity to match demand or vice versa.

In a "demand chase" strategy, the productive resources are organized to flexibly respond to demand, however it unfolds. Human and capital resources have to be "at the ready" to handle bursts in surgical demand. If bursts are predictable by season of the year or day of the month or week, they can be accommodated by scheduling resources appropriately. Fast food restaurants do this every day by staffing up for lunch and dinner, and down again between these times. Can the hospital engage a "safety valve" surgical site that can handle overflow from the main hospital or funnel procedures to the main hospital if demand there lags? Some large health centers use smaller community hospitals in this fashion.

In a "level demand" strategy, the productive resources are organized to work at a level rate, and demand is leveled to match. Although it is true that people injure themselves, develop ulcers or hernias or cancers, and develop coronary or pulmonary problems without regard for a hospital's schedule, it is also true that for elective cases there is some discretion about when the procedure can be done. This flexibility to move procedures a day or two up or back in time can level demand on surgical resources. Block time schedules that are regular each week use this timing flexibility to match demand to block times. However, block times themselves are often uneven across the week. Monday through Wednesday are frequently busy days in the OR, with less activity Thursdays and Fridays. This can be the result of surgeons using their scheduling discretion to operate earlier in the week to avoid weekend rounds. Can physicians be encouraged to work more evenly across the week?

Reducing the absolute variability in demand for surgical resources also reduces unsynchronized variability and its consequences. The hospital can adjust demand-side variability by adjusting its case load toward less variable procedures, filtering the current case load to cut off peaks and fill valleys. This may be done by using external sources of procedures and capacity, or internally to the hospital by adjusting the mix of surgical versus medical approaches, in those cases where both can be appropriate. Procedure-time variability can be reduced by smoothing the time per procedure. For example, the same procedure performed by different surgeons may take dramatically different amounts of time. Why would that be? Is there one "best practice" that all can adopt to smooth out this variability? There may be nonsurgeon-related issues that impose variability on procedure times. For example, the total time required is not just the time required by the patient in the room, but also the time it takes to assemble the right surgical kit, assemble the team, change over equipment, and clean out and sterilize the room between procedures. Reducing the variability in any or all of these can reduce the total variability in the time demanded of the hospital's resources.

Although workload, capacity, and variability are the primary drivers of queues and delays, sequencing can also be important. "Scheduling sequencing" means the order in which cases are put onto the surgical schedule. "Case sequencing" is the order in which scheduled cases are performed in a given OR. Using sequencing rules to improve performance means giving some types of cases priority over others when placing them in queue. If there are quick and simple, but high margin, procedures for which patients have a lot of competitive options, the SPT Sequencing corollary suggests that the hospital give these priority to improve the delay for these patients and avoid patient defections to other hospitals. Likewise, if the hospital has a strategic plan to conduct a certain number of hours of orthopedic, cardiac, and so on, surgeries each quarter, priorities can be used to encourage the desired mix. This sort of strategic initiative can be implemented via the assignment of block time to various services, with the distribution of block time reflecting the desired case mix.

Case sequencing within the day can also affect the delay to get on schedule, if it affects the throughput rate. Sequencing the shortest or least variable cases first within a day can have this effect. Using SPT priority scheduling means that more cases will be complete by any given time during the day, so an emergency intrusion that disrupts the surgical schedule will disrupt fewer cases, causing fewer cancellations and increasing the average number of cases per day performed. Also, as noted, variability in case durations tends to propagate throughout the day. (Procedures tend to be scheduled tightly back-to-back, so if a case is delayed early in the day, it is likely that all later cases in that room will be delayed.) So, putting less variable cases early can decrease the overall volatility of the schedule and the probability of case cancellations (which occurs when there is not enough time to complete the last scheduled case of the day).

Finally, as we noted, from a customer and staff satisfaction perspective, it is the perception of wait more than its chronological duration that matters. The psychological principles of waiting suggest an array of possibilities for improving the perception of the wait. Patients often want to know about the procedure they are about to have. Online learning modules that they can access and, if they wish, become "certified" as an informed patient, may make the delay to get on schedule less onerous. This and other entries in Table 4.2 derive from the psychology-of-waiting principles in Appendix A.

Populating our generic management tables with specific potential action items demonstrates how principles-driven brainstorming can generate a broad landscape of improvement options. In any specific context, some of these options will be more feasible and attractive than others. Some will be more beneficial if implemented, and some will feature lower cost and organizational strain to implement. The best will combine implementability with efficacy, as illustrated in the following case example, which is derived from Lovejoy and Li (2002).

4.4.1.4 CASE: HIGHLAND HOSPITAL

Highland Hospital is a large, 500-bed hospital in the Midwest with 20 ORs. The OR suite is Highland's economic engine; by some estimates, 80% of revenues can be traced to surgical procedures (when one counts tests and pre- and postprocedure stays). At the time of this case, the OR suite was operating Monday through Friday from 8 a.m. to 4 p.m., performing an average of 60 procedures each day (3 procedures per day per room). This, however, was not enough to keep up with demand, and the current wait for a patient to get on schedule averaged 25 days, or 5 weeks. This concerned the administration greatly, because some competitors were able to get patients (for some very profitable procedures) into the OR within 2 weeks.

The most straightforward way to increase capacity would be to add ORs. But this would be expensive, because the cost of adding each new OR is about $3.5 million. Furthermore, it would take several years to bring it online due to regulatory hurdles and construction delays. As a result, new ORs would not meet the hospital's requirement of a 3-year payback period for capital projects.

An alternative to construction would be to increase operating hours of the existing ORs. For a variety of reasons, opening on weekends was not considered feasible. Extending the day during the week was feasible, although physicians and surgical teams opposed it. The main reason for this opposition was that extending the day would mean that some surgeons would get late afternoon starts, which were unreliable (due to the compounded variability of all the preceding cases). Nevertheless, because extending the day would help surgeons clear their queue of waiting patients and would enhance the hospital's bottom line, the administration was determined to consider it.

Under current policy, procedures were scheduled into the OR as follows. Surgeons were assigned "block time," which constituted their allocated time in the OR. For example, Dr. Smith might be guaranteed an OR every Wednesday in which to operate all day. On other days of the week, Dr. Smith would consult with patients in his clinic. If a patient required an operation, Dr. Smith would schedule that patient into the next open Wednesday. He would do this by estimating the length of the procedure and communicating the requirement to a central scheduling system, which would compute and schedule the procedure start times for each day in each room. For example, if Dr. Smith scheduled 3 procedures into a given Wednesday, and estimated durations of 2 hours, 1.75 hours, and 2.25 hours, the scheduling system would add a half hour of clean time after each procedure and schedule start times of 8 a.m., 10:30 a.m., and 12:45 p.m.

With the current case mix at Highland Hospital, the average procedure took 2.4 hours (including cleaning time), and there were on average 3 procedures scheduled into each room each day. Procedures still underway at 4 p.m. would not stop, of course, so the surgical team would stay until everything was complete. Physicians were paid by the procedure via their professional fees, which were billed separately from the "facility fees" for the hospital. The hospital provided all the staff and the rooms and infrastructure, and billed for these at a standard rate. The standard rate did not include overtime expenses for the staff, so the hospital had to absorb these costs when cases ran long. Surgeons were not permitted to schedule so many procedures into a single day that significant overtime would result.

To plan the length of a regular work day, the administration assumed 2.4 hours for each procedure it wanted to perform and rounded up to the nearest hour. Under the current standard of 3 cases per day, this meant a day length of $3 \times 2.4 = 7.2$ hours, which rounded up to an 8-hour day. If, instead, the hospital wanted to schedule an average of 4 cases per day per room, the day would be extended to $4 \times 2.4 = 9.6$ hours, or 10-hour days. To process 5 cases per day per room, they would plan for 12-hour days, and 6 cases per day per room would imply 15-hour days.

The main appeal of extending the OR day was that patient delays to get on the surgical schedule would decline because more procedures could be performed each day. For example, at 4 procedures per day per room, the average delay to get on schedule was estimated to be 21 days. At 5 procedures per day per room, it would be 14 days. At 6 procedures per day per room, it would be only 7 days.

Scheduling more cases into a day would have some significant disadvantages, however. The procedures in each room were run back-to-back, so if the first procedure was estimated to take 2 hours, and the scheduler added a half hour of clean time, the second procedure would be scheduled to begin 2.5 hours later. Because procedures were highly variable, 50% of the time the first patient would be done early and the second patient would go into the OR on time, but 50% of the time the first procedure would run longer than expected and delay the start of the second patient. Such a delay would likely lead to a delay in the completion of the second patient and hence the start of the third patient. The third procedure of the day, for example, could finish up to two hours late, and this would only get worse if more procedures were scheduled into a room on any given day. Because delays tend to stack up, a fourth procedure added to the end of the day would not only have a good chance of being delayed, but that delay could be substantial, sometimes to the point of requiring cancellation. The bottom line was that scheduling more back-to-back procedures would lead to less reliable start times and higher risk of cancellation.

As we've mentioned, in addition to wasting physicians' time, delayed or cancelled cases are emotionally draining for patients and their families, some of whom take vacation days or drive long distances to come to the hospital.

To keep things simple, we highlight the negotiations between the hospital administration and the physicians. The other members of the surgical teams had preferences similar to the surgeons.

Physicians

The block scheduling system was efficient for the physician, who stayed in the OR for continuous blocks of time. However, surgeons believed it was unsafe to work longer than they were currently working on any single day, due to personal fatigue. So, although they would have gladly accepted more block time, they did not want it on the same day as their current block time. This meant that any extension of the day would require that at least two surgeons work in the same room over the course of the day.

This presented a serious problem for surgeons. Each would gladly accept a block of time with an 8:00 a.m. start, but none wanted a block starting in the afternoon. They knew afternoon start times would be unreliable, and cancellation of late-afternoon cases was frequent. Hence, although surgeons would clearly value the increased professional fees they could earn by performing more cases during the added time and would also value reduced wait times to get their patients on schedule, the combination of safety concerns and resistance to unreliable afternoon schedules outweighed these advantages in the surgeons' minds. Consequently, they opposed extending the operating day and instead strongly recommended the more expensive option of building new ORs.

Administration

Using the average cost per hour to keep an OR open and staff on hand and the average costs and revenues per procedure, the administration computed the expected profit per day for any regular time day length and any average number of procedures per day. The result is shown in Table 4.3.

Table 4.3 Financial Consequences for Alternative OR Times and Throughput

Day Length (Hours)	Day Ends	PROFIT ($) per Room per Day — Number of Procedures Scheduled per Room per Day			
		3	4	5	6
8	4:00 p.m.	$ 2,020			
9	5:00 p.m.	$ 1,926			
10	6:00 p.m.	$ 1,801	$ 2,786		
11	7:00 p.m.	$ 1,653	$ 2,711		
12	8:00 p.m.	$ 1,491	$ 2,605	$ 3,549	
13	9:00 p.m.	$ 1,322	$ 2,474	$ 3,490	
14	10:00 p.m.	$ 1,149	$ 2,325	$ 3,401	
15	11:00 p.m.	$ 975	$ 2,164	$ 3,286	$ 4,264

Negotiations

Effective negotiations always begin with each party understanding the perspective of the other. A good rule of thumb is to continue to ask, "Why?" when diagnosing somebody's position. Here, the basic tension was that the hospital wanted to more highly utilize their existing ORs by extending the operating day. Why? Because it would be profitable and would make the hospital more competitive in terms of time to get patients on the operating schedule. Physicians, however, did not want to start in the afternoon or to do more cases in a single day. Why? Because it would compromise safety and because afternoon starts would be unreliable.

Negotiations could easily have stalled at this point of impasse. The key to forward progress was to recognize that it was not the afternoon start, per se, that physicians disliked; it was the unreliable start and finish times that they associated with afternoon starts. If the administration could offer an afternoon block time with a reliable start, would physicians be happy? Probably, because the other consequences for additional block time in the afternoon—shorter delays to get their patients on schedule and more professional fees—were positive.

To manage the unreliable start times that physicians disliked so much, the administration invoked the physics of variability. The data suggested that delays longer than two hours were highly unlikely for the third procedure. This implied that the hospital could operate at 15-hour days broken into two segments separated by two hours to absorb all the variability. That is, the hospital could schedule 3 procedures in the morning segment, have a two-hour fallow period, and then schedule 2 more procedures, all in a 15-hour day. Because 5 procedures, each at 2.4 hours, require 12 hours, adding a 2-hour fallow period results in a total time of 14 hours, which fits well within a 15-hour day.

Under this policy, the hospital would be operating 15-hour days, performing 5 procedures per day, and making $3,286 per room per day (compared to the current level of $2,020 per room per day). This added up to an increase in annual profits of about $317,000 per room per year! Patients would wait on average 2 weeks to get on schedule, as compared to the current 5 weeks. The net result was that the hospital would be both more competitive relative to the competition and more profitable. At the same time, surgeons would be able to do more cases in a timely fashion.

Note that the hospital was giving up something, because the ORs would not be used for two hours in the middle of a day. Table 4.3 suggests that the hospital could make $978 more per day per room, a substantial amount, by scheduling more procedures into the 15-hour day. However, this would compound the variability that is at the core of the surgeon's resistance.

Highland Hospital initiated an afternoon surgical shift with a two-hour break between shifts. At first, not all procedure types were allowed into the afternoon shift because not all the support labs remained open into the later hours. But a sufficient number of labs were activated, and a sufficient number of surgeons voluntarily accepted afternoon starts in addition to their regular block time, to dramatically reduce the average delay to get patients on schedule. An afternoon surgical shift is now standard at the hospital.

4.4.2 Management Challenge: Surgical Patient Safety

Patient health and safety are at the core of a hospital's mission, and nowhere more so than in the ORs. Surgeries are among the most complicated procedures in a hospital. Margins for error are small, and the consequences significant. In this book, we address the challenge of reducing errors and improving safety from two perspectives, which we label "patient safety" and "organizational learning." There is significant overlap between these, but the distinction is useful. Under the heading of "patient safety," we focus on the direct impact of diagnosis and treatment activities on patient outcomes. Acquiring better information, making better decisions, improving the execution of those decisions, and preparing for mistakes if they do happen, are all ways to improve patient safety. In Appendix A, we present a generic "patient safety" managerial brainstorming table focused on these activities. In Table 4.4 to follow, we translate that generic table into specific policies for the OR theater.

Under the heading of "organizational learning," we address the systems that indirectly (but powerfully) influence patient safety by creating a culture of safety. Such systems serve as bookends to direct patient safety improvements. At the front end are systems for clearly articulating organizational goals, disseminating any organizational divergence from those goals, and motivating stakeholders to act on this divergence. At the back end is the dissemination of improved methods throughout the organization in the form of standard operating procedures, which translate local learning into global practice.

4.4.2.1 PROBLEM

According to the Institute of Medicine (IOM) report "To Err is Human" (IOM 2000), somewhere between 500,000 and a million people each year suffer injury due to medical errors, and between 44,000 and 98,000 people die as a result. This exceeds the number of annual deaths from motor vehicle accidents, breast cancer, or AIDS. The three most frequent adverse events are drug complications (19%), wound infections (14%), and technical complications (13%). In the OR, patient safety issues include anesthesia errors, wrong-site surgery and surgical injuries, and infection and other postoperative complications.

One impediment to data collection and analysis is the lack of standardized definitions for patient safety issues. For example, the Joint Commission on Accreditation of Healthcare Organizations (JCAHO) and the Institute of Medicine (IOM) use different taxonomies to describe patient safety. Here we adopt the IOM terminology (see IOM 2000), which defines an *error* as a failure of a planned action to be completed as intended, or the use of the wrong plan to achieve an aim. An *adverse event* is an injury caused by medical management rather than the underlying condition of the patient. An adverse event due to an error is a *preventable adverse event*. An error that does not result in an adverse event is a *near miss*.

For example, the incorrect calibration of a drug infusion pump and the failure of the anesthesiologist to recognize this prior to starting a procedure would be an error. If the patient died or suffered some injury as a result, it would be a preventable adverse event. If the anesthesiologist recognizes the problem and corrects it with no adverse consequences, it would be a near miss (IOM 2000). The reasons for errors include human error, system or process errors, and technological errors.

- **Human error**—It is a human error when individuals make mistakes that should not be made, such as if the technician did not calibrate the infusion pump properly and the anesthesiologist did not double-check it. Reasons for human error include lack of training, overwork and fatigue, time pressures, interruptions, noise and distractions, anxiety, fear, or boredom (IOM 2000). Remedies include relieving these influences with training and more reasonable work cycles, among other things.

- **System or process errors**—Human errors merge into system or process errors when the problem is predominantly communication or coordination. For example, if the anesthesiologist believed it was the tech's job to calibrate the pump, but the tech thought it was the anesthesiologist's job, there was a system (process) breakdown. Remedies include better communication systems and standardized job responsibilities and handoff and/or interface protocols.

- **Technological errors**—The diagnostic, medical, and communication technologies in hospitals are not perfect. If the pump was correctly calibrated but did not hold calibration and drifted off, there was a technological error. Related are human-machine interface problems. For example, if the tech was familiar with another pump and this one had its knobs reversed, causing her to turn up the infusion rate when she thought she was turning it down, the issue is at the tech-machine interface. Remedies include preventive checks and maintenance, fool-proof safety features (a pump that will not allow free flow, or one that will flash an alarm if the flow is outside reasonable limits), and standardized knob configurations or visual icons for common functions (such as off/on and higher/lower).

4.4.2.2 Principles

Increasing and protecting patient safety means making the right decisions and executing those decisions correctly and in a timely fashion. "Timeliness" is a responsiveness issue that can be addressed using our responsiveness principles (workload, capacity, variability, synchronization, and sequencing) and generic Table A.1 from Appendix A. We omit these options here, focusing instead on the process of making better decisions and improving their execution.

Decision-making is a form of information processing. Doctors and staff acquire information and make decisions based on it. Because the ultimate reason for collecting information is to use it to make decisions, the system is working well when the information gathered is appropriate for the decision context and the decision made with that information is appropriate for the patient. In the complex world of many possible diseases, incomplete information, and costly (in time and money) information acquisition via tests, no diagnosis can be 100% certain. Rather, physicians make decisions when their sense of the relative likelihoods for alternative diagnoses are sufficiently clear to begin therapy. This is a judgment call, but one that can be substantially supported by choosing the right information gathering regimen and knowing how to interpret that information appropriately. The following principles cover three stages of action: information gathering, processing that information into a decision, and execution.

We begin with the information gathering stage. Not all information is alike. Some tests are better than others in suggesting diagnoses. The quality of a test is measured by two attributes—sensitivity and specificity—defined as follows:

- **Definition (Test Sensitivity)**—The sensitivity of a test is the true positive rate, which is the probability of yielding a positive result when the condition being tested is present.

- **Definition (Test Specificity)**—The specificity of a test is the true negative rate, which is the probability of yielding a negative result when the condition being tested is not present.

For example, a biopsy is a form of test. One that always gives a positive result for cancer has 100% sensitivity but 0% specificity and is of no use. Likewise, one that always gives a negative result (100% specificity and 0% sensitivity) is of no use. Good tests trade off these two, and it is important to understand these statistical signatures to correctly interpret and act on test results. The right balance depends on the consequences of false positives or negatives; the only thing we can say for sure is the following.

Principle (Test Quality)—All else equal, tests with higher sensitivity and higher specificity are better in supporting rapid and accurate treatment.

We have already suggested that tests should also be chosen with consequences in mind; how will one act on the information? If a course of action has been chosen and would not change no matter what result a test produces, then the test (and its information) has no value. The information contained in a test depends on how significantly that information can change decisions and actions, and therefore outcomes.

Principle (Value of Information)—The value of information is determined by the expected improvement in outcome with the information over that without it. This implies that information that will not change a decision has no value.

If a decision to operate, for example, will not be changed one way or the other by a test result, the test has no value vis-à-vis that decision. Because it states value in terms of the expected improvement in outcomes, this principle implies that two factors determine the value of information: the likelihood that the information will change the outcome, and the magnitude of the change in outcome. The expected improvement is the product of these. So, for example, tests for cancer or a septic joint will be conducted even when their probabilities are low, because the consequences of missing these diseases are significant.

Once the right information has been gathered via patient interviews or tests, the surgeon needs to know how to use that information to support a decision. The first stage of this process is to correctly incorporate new information (from test results, clinical signs, and so on) into updated probabilities that various conditions are present. The second stage of this process is to know when these probabilities are sufficiently mature to make a decision, and which decision is appropriate. It is shown in Appendix A that the statistically correct way to incorporate test information into beliefs regarding different possible diagnoses is to use *Bayes' Rule*, a method for updating "prior" probabilities into "posterior" (post-test) probabilities. See Appendix A for a richer description of this rule and its consequences.

Bayes' Rule is the right way to update probabilities in a rational, unbiased manner. Understanding its application mitigates some of the natural psychological biases common to medical decision making.

Principle (First Impressions)—First impressions are critical inputs to medical decision making because they are psychologically self-reinforcing and because even an objective statistician will not alter strongly held beliefs without significant contrary evidence.

Appendix A describes the phenomena of *anchoring*, *confirmation bias*, and *sunk cost bias* and their contributions to this principle.

Once the information gathering phase of medical decision making has matured to the point that a diagnosis can be made, the surgeon needs to map that diagnosis into a recommended course of action. In addition to improving the training and decision making skills of physicians, this step can be improved by reducing levels of fatigue and distraction that may compromise decisions or by exploiting redundancy.

Principle (Fatigue)—Fatigue impairs decision making and task execution.

Principle (Redundancy)—Independent layers of protection increase the reliability of a system.

For example, if Acute Care surgeons who cover emergency services are scheduled to be on-call too many nights in a row, their performance will likely suffer. When diagnoses and recommended actions are not clear, it is helpful to ask for a second opinion from another surgeon.

Once an action has been decided, optimal patient safety depends on its proper execution.

In hospital settings, the execution of care plans is almost never in just one pair of hands. Primary care physicians hand off patients to surgeons, surgeons rely on nurses to carry out post-operative plans, and nurses change from one shift to the next. A key challenge is maintaining information integrity while information passes through all those hands.

Principle (Handoffs)—Unless the individuals contribute new knowledge, information is degraded as it is passed from one individual to another.

We can again exploit redundancy to improve execution. This principle can be used in handoffs (each person repeats back what was said to confirm consistency) and elsewhere. Multiple independent checks on actions increase one's confidence that they have been conducted properly. It is common for multiple people in pre-op to confirm a surgical patient's name and forthcoming surgery. Although this redundancy can seem silly to patients who must repeat their name and intended procedure several times, these precautions are understandable in view of the serious consequences for errors. Also, it is common for surgical teams to pause (a "time out") before a procedure begins to review, together, the patient's name, why he is there, and what is to be done.

Avoiding mistakes in execution can be accomplished by improved communication about what must be done in which sequence, better execution skills, a reduction in or elimination of the causes of errors, or conformance systems that make errors difficult and catch them if they do get through. Relevant principles include the following.

Principle (Intuitive Information)—Providing essential information visually or orally in tight association with a task reduces the mean and variance of task times as well as the likelihood of errors.

Principle (Foolproofing)—Using constraints to force correct actions reduces the likelihood of errors.

Anesthesiologists will benefit from vital signs in easily understood readout form (intuitive information), and anesthesia pumps may disallow certain flow rates without a deliberate manual override (foolproofing). Large, easily seen marks placed on the correct surgical site help surgeons avoid wrong-site surgeries.

4.4.2.3 PRACTICES

Table A.2 of Appendix A translates the preceding principles into generic options for improving patient safety. We use this table as the basis for our process improvement brainstorming exercise that breaks down its macro-concepts into more detailed objectives and specific management options. As usual, the idea is to generate many possible ideas without being too judgmental at first. After generating a range of options, one should look at them critically to identify appropriate and implementable initiatives for a specific hospital and context.

In Table A.2, the Level 1 objectives are improved responsiveness, improved decisions, improved execution, and improved protection and mitigation. Responsiveness is driven by the same workload, capacity, synchronization, variability, and sequencing interventions that were discussed in detail in the previous section, so we omit them here. In Table 4.4, shown next, we begin with the remaining Level 1 patient safety objectives and break them down into finer detail, leading to specific managerial options.

Table 4.4 Principles-Driven Strategies for Surgical Patient Safety

Level 1 Objective	Level 2 Objective	Level 3 Objective	Example Policies
Improve decisions	Improve information input to decisions	Improve passive information availability	Ensure that personal medical records are always with individuals on small magnetic cards
			Ensure that personal medical records are always available from a secure centralized database
			Install a decision support system with frequency of occurrence of various diseases, given demographic data and symptoms
			Improve vital signs and other data readouts during surgical procedures
			Ensure better access to pharmacology records to verify existing medications
		Improve active information gathering	Implement standard guidelines for optimal patient interview techniques
			Implement improved methods for gathering data from the family of the patient
			Develop less invasive tests
			Develop less labor- or resource-intensive tests
			Develop protocols to query databases, the patient, the family, and so on, to get the most complete current medication list possible
		Improve information content of tests	Have optimal protocols for which test to request as a function of demographics, symptoms, and candidate diseases
			Develop tests with greater sensitivity and specificity (higher true positives and true negatives)

Level 1 Objective	Level 2 Objective	Level 3 Objective	Example Policies
			Purchase higher-quality test equipment
			Develop tests with better information content for specific prior situations (for example, if the prior probability is low, a test with low false positives can be better than one with high true positives)
			Develop tests for diseases you can't afford to miss
			Exploit redundancy by running two independent samples to increase the quality of the test information
			Exploit redundancy by having at least two professionals interpret tests and compare notes before communicating the results to the physician
		Improve administration of tests	Reduce technical errors via preventive maintenance of test equipment
			Reduce human errors via training
			Reduce human errors via foolproofing
			Develop simplified instructions for testing protocols
		Avoidance of psychological impediments to rational information processing	Recognize when the patient uses redundant descriptors for the same symptom, rather than treating these as independent pieces of evidence
			Recognize and adjust for the self-reinforcing nature of first impressions
			Recognize and adjust for the human tendency to see patterns in random data

Table 4.4 Principles-Driven Strategies for Surgical Patient Safety

Level 1 Objective	Level 2 Objective	Level 3 Objective	Example Policies
			Recognize and adjust for the tendency to place too much probability on events that were recently experienced
			Recognize and adjust for the tendency to "find" things that one has recently been exposed to in the medical literature
		Improve information timeliness	See the generic "responsiveness" table for options
		Improve information communication	Reduce information loss during handoffs using standard handoff protocols
			Reduce information loss during handoffs by scheduling time for this activity (for example, time for surgeons to interact with ICU nurses)
			Reduce information loss during handoffs by having a dedicated space that is free of interruptions for this activity
			Make information visual and connected to tasks; for example, color-code preexisting conditions
			Adopt state-of-the-art communication technologies
			Form stable work teams that develop a clear common language
	Improve assignment (who makes decisions)	Improve the decision to operate or not	Have attending physicians rather than residents talk to the patient and family
			Exploit redundancy by having teams of physicians seek consensus in patient care decisions

Level 1 Objective	Level 2 Objective	Level 3 Objective	Example Policies
			Engage a fully informed family by improving the physician's ability to objectively communicate risks and benefits
		Improve decisions during procedures	Have attending physicians present to make decisions during all procedures, in case a complication arises
			Improve real-time consensus building in the OR when complications arise
	Improve training (to use information to make decisions)	Enhance offline individual training	Train residents to better understand the properties of tests (true positives, true negatives, and so on) and the theory of statistical decision making
			Use realistic simulations of medical conditions to develop tacit knowledge
			Have periodic diagnostic quizzes based on complex cases and their resolutions
		Enhance real-time individual training	Improve techniques for extracting lessons from complications faced in the OR
			Improve attending physician—resident training interactions during rounds
	Improve incentives (to make appropriate decisions)	Make clear the multicriteria nature of medical decisions	Identify low-, medium-, and high-cost interventions so physicians can better assess the financial as well as medical consequences for actions

Table 4.4 Principles-Driven Strategies for Surgical Patient Safety

Level 1 Objective	Level 2 Objective	Level 3 Objective	Example Policies
		Publish perform-ance to enhance self-improvement	Make performance on multiple metrics known privately to physicians
			Make performance on multiple metrics public
		Reduce tension between financial and medical imperatives	Reduce cost of existing tests and therapies
			Raise more money
	Simplify/standard-ize the decision process	Change patient population to less complex demo-graphics so deci-sions are simpler	Have a "focused factory" that specializes in specific low-risk procedures, such as hernia repairs or gall bladder operations
			Establish satellite clinics in rich, relatively healthy areas, to feed the main hospital
			Close the ED
		Standardize clinical pathways (treatment guidelines)	Mandate best practices based on scientific clinical evidence
			Install IT systems to provide decision support on recommended courses of action
			Establish a checklist of things to look for, for specific diagnoses or procedures
	Improve focus	Increase the time available to diag-nose patients	Hire more physicians
			Decrease the number of patients each physician sees
			Reduce nonproductive overhead activities

Level 1 Objective	Level 2 Objective	Level 3 Objective	Example Policies
		Reduce fatigue	Schedule clinic, surgery, and other activities with more slack time for reflection
			Have better work-rest cycles
			Offload routine tasks from surgeons so they can focus on that part of the decision process they are uniquely trained to handle
			Optimize staffing to match capacity to patient demand
			Smooth surgical load to eliminate peaks and valleys
		Reduce distractions	Reduce pager and other interruptions
			Have noise abatement policies
			Improve physicians' ability to see relevant data/observations and ignore irrelevant information
	Increase redundancy	Formal requirements	Have at least two knowledgeable people agree on decisions (for example, a pharmacist and anesthesiologist agree on proposed anesthesia, or two physicians agree on a diagnosis and plan)
		Informal techniques	Cultivate a cross-disciplinary social network of people familiar with each other and willing to ask for advice
Improve execution	Improve execution information (how to execute)	Standardize clinical pathways (treatment guidelines)	Create a "best practices" team that suggests best practices based on current scientific evidence
			Install IT systems to remind caregivers of necessary steps
			Establish a checklist of required actions for each diagnosis

Table 4.4   Principles-Driven Strategies for Surgical Patient Safety

Level 1 Objective	Level 2 Objective	Level 3 Objective	Example Policies
		Improve team communication	Have the surgical team review the plan for the procedure before the first incision
			Discuss each case with all significant caregivers: surgeons, ICU nurses, and floor nurses
		Enhance patient understanding of postdischarge instructions	Standardize discharge instructions for specific procedures, based on best practices
			Train nurses for cultural competencies (language and cultural issues) in giving postprocedure discharge instructions
	Improve execution assignment	Require higher levels of skill at key positions	Ensure that attending physicians, not residents, perform surgical procedures
			Upgrade certification requirements to work on a surgical team
	Improve training (skill) to execute	Upgrade skill level of caregivers	Improve resident training programs
			Develop realistic patient training simulators
	Simplify/ standardize the execution process	Standard protocols	Implement checklists and standard guidelines for execution
			Standardized human-machine interfaces (visual controls, icons)
		Foolproofing	Design process so key tests and procedures are impossible to do incorrectly
			Mark on patient to avoid wrong-site surgery
		Signal out-of-compliance	Use equipment that gives visual or audible alarms when use is outside standard parameters
			Standardized human-machine interfaces (visual controls, icons)

Level 1 Objective	Level 2 Objective	Level 3 Objective	Example Policies
	Improve focus	Reduce workload	Hire more surgeons
			Decrease the number of patients each surgeon sees
			Reduce time-consuming overhead activities
		Reduce distractions	Improve within-OR practices to minimize distractions
	Increase redundancy	Within surgical team	Have an attending physician by the resident's side during procedures in teaching hospitals
		Within the greater organization	Have checks at multiple milestones during a patient's course of therapy
			Empower nurses to challenge medications if there is cause for concern
Improve system protection and mitigation	Improve information	Improve data gathering	Improve ability to recognize dangerous postprocedure developments
			Standardize connection between postprocedure warning signs and appropriate response
	Increase redundancy	Preprocedure	Confirm patient's name and surgical procedure multiple times
		During procedure	Have at least two trained eyes review surgical plan
			Have at least two trained surgical staff observe the procedure and comment as necessary
		Post procedure	Have head ICU nurse and pharmacist double-check postprocedure medications
			Have doctor double-check key information with patient or family during rounds
			Have ICU or PACU page a surgeon when patient exhibits unfamiliar symptoms
	Mitigate harm	Standardized responses	Have standard procedures for the "possible but unexpected"

Table 4.4   Principles-Driven Strategies for Surgical Patient Safety

Level 1 Objective	Level 2 Objective	Level 3 Objective	Example Policies
		Patient perception	Train clinicians in how best to handle errors from the patient and family perspective

Table 4.4 is extensive, but it follows a familiar logic. We begin by using the principles for better decision making (information acquisition and processing into decisions, which are then executed), write out general concepts based on those principles, and then break those down into increasingly finer levels of detail, ending with specific action items. In part, Table 4.4 is long because it repeats the same levers (information, assignment, training, incentives, standardization, focus, and redundancy) to improve decisions and to improve execution.

Improving information can be accomplished by improving the ready availability of data or improving active data-gathering activities; improving the quality (specificity and sensitivity) of information that we do gather; improving the execution and administration of tests; removing psychological impediments to processing information; and improving information handoffs. Each of these can suggest several specific actions.

Information only has value if it can influence actions, which are the translations of information into decisions and therapies. The mapping of information into decisions and actions can be improved by placing the decision with more highly trained individuals; exploiting redundancy (engaging more than one trained individual) to validate decisions; improving training; and improving motivation (reducing tensions between multiple goals that might influence decision making).

If there exists a "best practice" that suggests certain types of information should result in certain types of diagnoses and actions, then standardizing around these best practices should improve system outcomes. This can be made available by either reducing the complexity of the cases being treated (for example, close the ED or establish mini-businesses that only handle routine cases) or creating a "best practices" team that makes suggestions based on the most recent clinical evidence.

Decision-makers who are tired or distracted are more likely to make mistakes, so reducing fatigue and interruptions can improve the decision process. This can take a variety of forms, from reducing pager traffic to having better work-rest cycles.

After decisions have been made, the team needs to carry them out. This task, like decision making, responds to initiatives that improve or simplify execution information, upgrade the skills of the primary actors, improve their focus, and exploit redundancy.

Finally, in any complex system, mistakes will happen. Can these be caught and mitigated before they do serious harm? That is, can we catch errors before they become adverse events? In addition to double-checking a patient's name and his understanding of what is recommended for his procedure, other protection and mitigation systems include standard databases of postprocedure symptoms for common surgical errors and recommended remedies, and paging a surgeon from the PACU or ICU if unfamiliar symptoms present themselves. A surgeon familiar with the case may more readily recognize problems than a nonsurgical specialist.

A hospital will follow just a few of the many paths through this extensive table, selected on the basis of value (improvement along an important set of the OR metrics), cost, and implementability. In the following two cases, we illustrate some of these possibilities with examples. The first illustrates how careful testing and updating of information leads to a definitive decision. The second illustrates how an error can be turned into a learning opportunity.

4.4.2.4 CASE: MEDICAL DECISION MAKING: TO OPERATE OR NOT?

Sharon Little is a 50-year-old woman who was referred to otolaryngologist Dr. Carla Valeria with an enlarging neck mass and breathing difficulties. It was visibly clear that Sharon had a goiter (an enlarged thyroid gland), and it was possible that Sharon's breathing difficulties were due to the goiter being so large that it was compressing her trachea. Sharon reported increased enlargement over the past year. What should be done? Dr. Valeria knew that goiters were most often caused by thyroid disease (hypo- or hyperthyroidism, defined in the next paragraph) but could also be caused by thyroid cancer, iodine deficiency, or other nutritional issues. A careful physical examination revealed thyroid nodules, or small tumors, but this is quite common, and most are benign. Overall, only about 5% of people with nodules have cancer. This number is even lower for women but higher for people with a history of radiation treatments around the neck.

The thyroid gland produces hormones (triiodothyronine or T3, and thyroxine or T4) that regulate one's metabolism. Too little hormone production (hypothyroidism) can cause listlessness and weight gain, whereas too much (hyperthyroidism) can cause nervousness and irregular heartbeats. The thyroid itself, however, is regulated by pituitary gland production of "thyroid stimulating hormone" (TSH), so improper T3 or T4 production may result from improper TSH production.

This knowledge influenced the questions Dr. Valeria asked while she completed her patient interview and physical examination. In addition to her thyroid enlargement, Sharon reported fatigue and lethargy, problems with excess body weight, intolerance to cold, hair loss, and dry skin and hair. All of these are signs of hypothyroidism. Also, some members of Sharon's immediate family had had their thyroids removed because of goiters. Sharon appeared to be following a reasonably nutritious and balanced diet, and she had no history of radiation treatments. Iodine deficiency is common in less developed countries but is rare in more highly developed countries where steps have been taken to include iodine in a regular diet.

Based on this examination and interview, Dr. Valeria had high priors (more than 80%) on thyroid disease and much lower (less than 5% each) on cancer, iodine, or diet.

However, cancer was a disease she could not afford to miss because the consequence of being wrong could be catastrophic. In contrast, the consequences of delaying the detection of iodine or dietary deficiencies are not serious, because these situations can be reversed easily. So, Dr. Valeria decided to focus her attention on the most probable (thyroid disease or pituitary disease) diagnosis and the one she could not afford to miss (cancer). She ordered a blood workup focusing on T3, T4, and TSH levels, an X-ray to see if breathing difficulties were due to tracheal displacement by the thyroid, and a fine needle aspiration (FNA) biopsy of the nodules. In this, a thin needle is inserted to withdraw cells or fluid to test for malignancy.

The FNA biopsy was negative, suggesting no malignancy. Because the sensitivity and specificity of FNA is about 85% and 92%, respectively, the negative result reduced Dr. Valeria's estimate of the probability of cancer from 5% to less than 1%. The results of the other tests were not uniform. Sharon's clinical signs pointed convincingly to hypothyroidism, but her labs were in the normal range. (That is, she was "biochemically euthyroid.") However, Dr. Valeria also knew that the "normal range" for T3, T4, and TSH had recently been called into question by new research results, which reduced the information content in these tests. Sharon also had macrophages (white blood cells whose function is to seek out and kill invading micro-organisms) in her thyroid. The X-ray confirmed that Sharon's thyroid was so large that it had significantly displaced her trachea (see Exhibit 4.9), confirming Dr. Valeria's suspicions regarding Sharon's breathing problems.

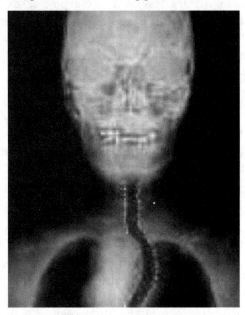

Exhibit 4.9   Displaced trachea due to enlarged thyroid (credit endoconsultants.com).

Despite the lab results, Dr. Valeria knew there was some reason Sharon's thyroid was so large. She also knew that further enlargement of the thyroid could be very dangerous, because it can compress other vital neck structures including the esophagus and blood vessels. Sharon's family history also suggested thyroid disease, and Dr. Valeria knew that people can live quite well without their thyroid glands, provided they take thyroid hormone replacements. She recommended a total thyroidectomy (removal of the thyroid), and Sharon agreed. Alternative treatments (for example, with thyroid-stimulating hormones) would not reduce the size of the goiter and would not address some of the impending medical risks. Sharon was also attracted to the cosmetic improvements of a reduced neck bulge. Postoperatively, Sharon would have to be on thyroid hormone replacement therapy for the rest of her life, but this was a relatively benign consequence relative to the discomfort and dangers of her current condition. For these reasons, the decision to recommend a thyroidectomy would be unlikely to change in the presence of further testing, so such testing had little value. Of course, follow-up visits would pay attention to the now remote, but serious, possibility of cancer.

4.4.2.5 CASE: AN ERROR LEADS TO LEARNING AND IMPROVED PROCESSES IN A SURGICAL TEAM

John Arrieta, a 60-year-old male, underwent surveillance colonoscopy at the direction of his primary care doctor. During the procedure, a malignant-appearing mass was discovered in his right colon. Biopsies confirmed the visual impression of cancer. A preoperative staging CT scan suggested a localized tumor, and John was considered a good candidate for a minimally invasive laparoscopic colon resection.

John's only major chronic medical problem was high blood pressure, which was well controlled with an oral agent, taken daily. He had no prior operative history. John reported a distant history of cigarette smoking, but he had stopped smoking 20 years ago. He stated that he drank maybe "a couple of" beers sometimes in the evening, but not every day.

The operation went smoothly, and John was transferred to a private bed following his recovery from anesthesia. In the evening of the first postoperative day (POD1), John suffered from nausea, vomiting, tachycardia (rapid heart rate), hypertension (high blood pressure), nystagmus (involuntary eye movements), gait ataxia (lack of coordination while walking), and hand tremors. All of these were interpreted to be signs of alcohol withdrawal. John was questioned but strongly contended that he did not drink heavily, and that even during his (past) heavy-drinking periods he had never experienced anything like these symptoms. His physicians transferred John to the ICU. Although the condition of "alcohol withdrawal" is not precisely defined, John's signs were felt by his doctors to be consistent with that diagnosis, and John was kept under close surveillance.

On POD3, John became verbally and physically abusive toward staff, ultimately delirious, and requiring of restraints. In severe cases of withdrawal, coma and death can occur, and airway protection becomes a priority. John was given lorazepam (a sedative with short onset time), haloperidol (an antipsychotic), and clonidine (for high blood pressure). By POD4, John was completely sedated and intubated so that his breathing was secure. His family was consulted and confirmed that, contrary to John's claims, he had been drinking heavily. On POD6, John was weaned off the drugs, extubated, and psychiatry was consulted for an examination. This resulted in no probable alternative explanation for John's behavior, so a diagnosis of alcohol withdrawal was accepted.

After this, there were no further signs of withdrawal, but the team delayed discharge to be sure. John was discharged to home POD9.

There are several obvious aspects of this case that the team did not want to repeat.

In addition to posing a potential safety hazard to himself and staff, John spent an above average time in the hospital relative to other patients having a local colon resection. The team discussed John's case and agreed that they could benefit from additional training in alcohol withdrawal and some structured way to assess future patients for this potential complication.

Their research revealed that 51% of the U.S. population over the age of 12 has consumed some alcohol, and 5% are heavy drinkers (defined as consuming more than 5 drinks per day). Approximately 100,000 people die of alcoholism each year. In medical slang, ingestible alcohol (ethyl alcohol) is referred to as EtOH, because its chemical composition (C_2H_5OH) combines an ethyl group (Et = C_2H_5) with a hydroxyl group (OH). In 1994, the per-capita U.S. consumption of EtOH was 2.21 gallons per year. EtOH withdrawal symptoms are not uncommon, occurring in 16% of surgical cases and a high 31% of trauma cases (attesting to the correlation of EtOH and trauma-inducing behaviors).

Prophylactic treatments can reduce or prevent withdrawal, but anticipating when to use these treatments is complicated by the nonspecific nature of the diagnosis. Several standard checklist-style tests have been validated with scientific data. Upon reviewing these, the team decided to adopt the CIWA-Ar (Clinical Institute Withdrawal Assessment of Alcohol Scale, Revised) (Sullivan et al. 1989) protocol to assess potential withdrawal symptoms. This assessment includes 10 questions and can produce scores between 0 and 67, as shown in Exhibit 4.10. Scores below 10 indicate low risk and no need for additional medications for withdrawal. It became standard policy within the team to use this assessment and, if indicated, prescribe prophylactic treatment. In addition, the team agreed to ask family members about a patient's alcohol consumption, if possible and as appropriate, because patients are not always truthful.

Patient:_____ Date: _____ Time: _____
Pulse or heart rate, taken for one minute:_____ Blood pressure:_____

NAUSEA AND VOMITING -- Ask "Do you feel sick to your stomach? Have you vomited?" Observation:
    0 no nausea and no vomiting
    1 mild nausea with no vomiting
    2
    3
    4 intermittent nausea with dry heaves
    5
    6
    7 constant nausea, frequent dry heaves and vomiting

TREMOR -- Arms extended and fingers spread apart. Observation:
    0 no tremor
    1 not visible, but can be felt fingertip to fingertip
    2
    3
    4 moderate, with patient's arms extended
    5
    6
    7 severe, even with arms not extended

PAROXYSMAL SWEATS Observation:
    0 no sweat visible
    1 barely perceptible sweating, palms moist
    2
    3
    4 beads of sweat obvious on forehead
    5
    6
    7 drenching sweats

AUDITORY DISTURBANCES -- Ask "Are you more aware of sounds around you? Are they harsh? Do they frighten you? Are you hearing anything that is disturbing to you? Are you hearing things you know are not there?" Observation;
    0 not present
    1 very mild harshness or ability to frighten
    2 mild harshness or ability to frighten
    3 moderate harshness or ability to frighten
    4 moderately severe hallucinations
    5 severe hallucinations
    6 extremely severe hallucinations
    7 continuous hallucinations

VISUAL DISTURBANCES -- Ask "Does the light appear to be too bright? Is its color different? Does it hurt your eyes? Are you seeing anything that is disturbing to you? Are you seeing things you know are not there?" Observation;
    0 not present
    1 very mild sensitivity
    2 mild sensitivity
    3 moderate sensitivity
    4 moderately severe hallucinations
    5 severe hallucinations
    6 extremely severe hallucinations
    7 continuous hallucinations

HEADACHE, FULLNESS IN HEAD -- Ask "Does your head feel different? Does it feel like there is a band around your head?" Do not rate for dizziness or lightheadedness. Otherwise, rate severity.
    0 not present
    1 very mild
    2 mild
    3 moderate
    4 moderately severe
    5 severe
    6 very severe
    7 extremely severe

ANXIETY -- Ask "Do you feel nervous?" Observation:
    0 no anxiety, at ease
    1 mild anxious
    2
    3
    4 moderately anxious, or guarded, so anxiety is inferred
    5
    6
    7 equivalent to acute panic states as seen in severe delirium or acute schizophrenic reactions

AGITATION Observation:
    0 normal activity
    1 somewhat more than normal activity
    2
    3
    4 moderately fidgety and restless
    5
    6
    7 paces back and forth during most of the interview, or constantly thrashes about

TACTILE DISTURBANCES -- Ask "Have you any itching, pins and needles sensations, any burning, any numbness, or do you feel bugs crawling on or under your skin?" Observation:
    0 none
    1 very mild itching, pins and needles, burning or numbness
    2 mild itching, pins and needles, burning or numbness
    3 moderate itching, pins and needles, burning or numbness
    4 moderately severe hallucinations
    5 severe hallucinations
    6 extremely severe hallucinations
    7 continuous hallucinations

ORIENTATION AND CLOUDING OF SENSORIUM -- Ask "What day is this? Where are you? Who am I?"
0 oriented and can do serial additions
1 cannot do serial additions or is uncertain about date
2 disoriented for date by no more than 2 calendar days
3 disoriented for date by more than 2 calendar days
4 disoriented for place/or person

Total **CIWA-Ar** Score _____
Rater's Initials _____
Maximum Possible Score 67

This assessment for monitoring withdrawal symptoms requires approximately 5 minutes to administer. The maximum score is 67 (see instrument). Patients scoring less than 10 do not usually need additional medication for withdrawal.

Reference: Sullivan, J.T.; Sykora, K.; Schneiderman, J.; Naranjo, C.A.; and Sellers, E.M. Assessment of alcohol withdrawal: The revised Clinical Institute Withdrawal Assessment for Alcohol scale (**CIWA-Ar**). *British Journal of Addiction* 84:1353-1357, 1989.

Exhibit 4.10   Clinical Institute Withdrawal Assessment of Alcohol Scale, Revised (CIWA-Ar).

When transferring care to the PACU, ICU, or bed floors, the team agreed to communicate any CIWA-Ar score above 15 to the new care providers, despite the fact that these patients had received prophylactic treatment. It was necessary to explain how to interpret scores to the nurses, because this was not part of their general training. The team developed a standard protocol to explain to nurses what symptoms to look for and what to do in case the prophylactics failed and the patients exhibited symptoms of withdrawal. Also, for at-risk patients, the team added standardized discharge instructions asking patients or their families to contact their physician immediately if they experienced withdrawal-related symptoms. The term "withdrawal" was not used in the instructions to avoid the stigma attached to that term and consequent patient reluctance to comply. Rather, the instructions simply listed the constellation of symptoms that would attend withdrawal and instructed the patients and families to be alert for these.

This team's initiatives helped avoid more cases like John's, which put both patient and staff at risk. However, this learning was not efficiently communicated throughout the hospital because there was no systematic way to propose, vet, and implement standard procedures across departments. Learning remained local within this surgical service and those members of the PACU and ICU staff with whom they interacted. This is the way most learning takes place in hospitals: A team experiences a problem that it learns from, but the learning often remains largely within the team. In Section 4.4.3, we consider more systematic organizational structures that encourage the development and dissemination of this sort of learning activity.

4.4.3 Management Challenge: Organizational Learning

The key activities in the Department of Surgery are information gathering, diagnosis, advising a course of action, and execution. In this section, we focus on the systems and culture that promote improvements in those activities.

Individuals learn through education and experience. Surgical teams (for example, an attending physician and her residents) will learn as a team because they work together regularly. Once we move beyond the small work group, however, it is more difficult to propagate lessons across groups. Different surgical services do not interact regularly, relationships are not as close, people are not as interdependent, and there may be competition between groups for recognition or resources. Problems are compounded in the medical profession because discussing medical errors or near misses (both of which can contain learning opportunities) may carry professional or legal risk.

Central to organizational learning systems in hospitals is navigating the turbulent motivational waters of private information. Not many people are motivated to reveal their mistakes, yet it is precisely that sort of revelation that is required to go from the private world of a patient's bad experience to the public world of organizational improvement.

Organizational learning is the process of encoding lessons inferred from past history into routines to guide behavior (Levitt and March 1988). In highly hazardous industries where errors can lead to deaths (such as aviation and health care), errors are rare due to the conservative nature of decision-making processes. But this also means there is little data to work with for organizational learning. Consequently, these industries also gather near miss data, to be analyzed for lessons that can improve safety. Surgical departments are one important example of this. Managing this data collection and analysis process is complicated by the following features:

a. Information on errors and near misses is in many instances local within an individual or team and will not be revealed globally unless the person or team chooses to do so.

b. Revealing medical errors can put surgeons and staff at professional or legal risk.

c. In organizations with complex tasks, legal or bureaucratic requirements to report errors are often ineffective.

We begin by justifying (a) through (c). For (a), it is clear that many of the decisions and actions taken in the care of a surgery patient will be known only to the attending physician and the resident who is managing the patient. Or, if cases are discussed as a group, some things will be known by the attending physician and all her residents. Part (b) is clear without further elaboration. These two together imply a strong disincentive to report errors, but failure to report leaves the greater organization (in this case, the surgical service or department) without data to learn from. How can a surgical department overcome this resistance and learn from errors on a broader scale than just within surgical teams?

One response would be to "require" reporting of all errors or near misses, with strong sanctions for disobeying that requirement. However, when tasks are complex and require a series of judgment calls, it is difficult to define exactly what an "error" is, unless it is blatant. If an exploration of a thoracic cavity results in damaging a lung, has an error been committed? If a patient develops a postoperative infection, has an error been committed? No classification system is perfect, especially for complex tasks, so there will be cases in which an event can be classified in a variety of ways. If some error classifications invite sanction and others do not, there is a strong incentive to choose the more benign classification. Hence, we have (c).

Research has confirmed these dynamics in health care settings (Tamuz 2001, Tamuz and Harrison 2006, Tamuz and Thomas 2006 and references therein), where the mandate to report medical errors and near misses, coupled with an investigative apparatus acting on that information, has deterred reporting. They have also been confirmed in air safety, another hazardous industry with low accident rates. Airline pilots are required to report near midair collisions (NMAC), upon receipt of which the Federal Aviation

Administration (FAA) will check if any regulation had been broken and, if so, will initiate enforcement proceedings. A natural experiment occurred between 1968 to 1971, when the FAA offered immunity from prosecution to any pilot reporting a NMAC, but reinstated the possibility of prosecution in 1972. During the immunity period, the number of reported incidents increased fourfold, but it dropped dramatically again in 1972. That is, the possibility of sanction provided a disincentive to report anything, reducing the total amount of information from which the FAA could learn (Tamuz 2001).

The problem is that using the same reporting system for organizational learning and assigning blame will lead to a disincentive to report, leaving the organization with less information for learning. This is the challenge to learning from surgical errors. As Sagan (1994) puts it, "The social costs of accidents make learning very important; the politics of blame make learning very difficult."

Many states have some form of mandatory adverse event reporting system. A representative system (IOM 2000) would require that all deaths or life-threatening adverse events from unexplained or suspicious causes, medication errors, surgical errors, or transfusion errors be reported to a state agency within 24 hours. These reports would then be used to decide whether further investigation is required. Investigations might result in fines or mandatory plans for improvement. Patient identifiers are always kept confidential, physician identifiers may also be confidential, and in some cases hospital names are confidential. However, these protections are not credible to many doctors or hospitals. In some cases, a Freedom of Information Act (FOIA) request can prompt disclosure, and in others a subpoena would do so. The latter is particularly important, because the basic legal principle in a civil trial is the rule of relevance, meaning that the information can affect the case. Judges have a lot of discretion in deciding relevance, which can potentially apply to much of the data collected by hospitals.

As suggested by (c) above, such systems are unlikely to be effective. By some estimates, less than half (in some studies, significantly less) of the medical mishaps that could plausibly be characterized as an error are officially documented anywhere (Schenkel et al. 2004). In the system described by Rosenthal et al. (2005), the official policy was that every incident be reported to the Risk Management Department, but this actually occurred in less than 10% of the cases.

Some reporting systems are deliberately voluntary, but their record of completeness is no better. For example, U.S. Pharmacopeia (USP, a standards-setting authority for drugs and other health care products, USP 2010a) administered a voluntary Medical Errors Reporting (MER) program between 1991 and 2008 (after which it was transferred to the Institute for Safe Medication Practices or ISMP). According to the Institute of Medicine, only 4,000 reports were received between 1994 and the publication of the IOM report (2000). That same publication estimates about 95,000 adverse drug events each year, implying that less than 1% were reported to the MER.

Most hospitals also have internal reporting systems, often associated with a Risk Management Department, that inherit the same problems of adverse incentives.

In teaching hospitals, these dynamics are further complicated by the hierarchical structure (attending physician—chief resident—junior resident—medical student). As one junior resident noted in Fischer et al. (2006), "I really had this problem which is that the only people who you can talk to about these things really… are the same people who are grading you, and so it creates a very difficult dynamic because if you think that the team made a mistake and your resident doesn't want to talk about it, you really can't talk about it then." About a quarter of the residents interviewed in Rosenthal et al. (2005) said they had reported incidents to their chief resident or attending physician but felt that nothing was reported further, no action taken, or the incident was ignored. So while many hospitals have formal policies and reporting systems for medical errors, these systems are often not effective.

Finally, there is a time and effort cost to documenting events. This time is significant to busy people, many of whom already feel they spend too much time on overhead activities rather than direct patient care. The more onerous the forms to fill out or database interface to negotiate, the less likely it is to be used. To overcome this perceived cost, there must be some strictly positive perceived benefits to the reporting activity, or else one cannot expect widespread use. That is, information is not given freely.

How can the surgical department learn from mistakes in this context of private information (within the attending physician and team) and strong reporting disincentives?

4.4.3.2 PRINCIPLES

The principles we invoke to improve organizational learning focus on the motivation to change and incentives for the embrace of change. These begin with the following.

Principle (Self Interest)—Individuals, not organizations, are self-optimizing.

Principle (Knowledge Sharing)—Knowledge is power, so people need a good reason to share it.

The relevance of these principles to the discussion of errors and near misses (inputs to organizational learning) in a Department of Surgery are self-evident. People will assess the costs and benefits of alternative actions before choosing one, and the potential downside to revealing an error is apparent. Without a commensurate upside, no revelation will take place.

Where does this upside come from? To begin, people must be motivated to improve.

Principle (Motivation for Change)—Motivation for change comes from a perceived or projected divergence between organizational performance and the goals of its key stakeholders.

So, the front end of the change process involves information gathering about current performance relative to the aspirational goals of the surgical staff. However, it is not the motivations of all people that we focus on. In large complex organizations with differing roles and responsibilities, some people matter more than others from the perspective of implementing changes. We already introduced the **Key Stakeholders Principle**, **Veto Power Principle**, and **Pareto Efficiency Principle** in section 4.4.1.2.

In the OR, surgeons and anesthesiologists and other scarce human resources are key stakeholders who have veto power. If they do not feel that a proposal is beneficial relative to the things they want and believe in, they will not cooperate. Real organizational learning, in which changes are made that improve the system overall, will create benefits that were not previously available. Those benefits, if appropriately allocated among all key stakeholders, can make everybody better off. That is, all the personal calculations among key stakeholders can come up positive! The Highland Hospital case in section 4.4.1.4 is an example of the Pareto principle, where both the surgeons and administration compromised to achieve a better outcome for all.

The distribution of benefits to key stakeholders must be sufficient to overcome initial resistances. In Departments of Surgery, the resistances will be the motivational ones already mentioned, and the natural inertia to change.

Principle (Inertia)—People resist change because they know the system they are familiar with, but do not know firsthand the strengths and weaknesses of alternative proposals. Unless there are compelling reasons to believe that significant advantages will accrue, the certain status quo will be preferred to an uncertain future.

In summary, key stakeholders will be motivated to change by a disquieting divergence between current performance and salient goals. So, the organizational learning process begins with information about current performance along dimensions of interest to key stakeholders, and a convincing argument that these are divergent from organizational objectives. Then proposals for change need to be generated, promising candidates selected, validated, and implemented. The implementation phase includes the distribution of benefits so that all key stakeholders support the proposal. The principles introduced here, and previously, are the building blocks for generic Table A.3 in Appendix A, which focuses on improving the organizational learning process. That generic table is the starting point for Table 4.5.

Table 4.5 Principles-Driven Strategies for Organizational Learning in the OR

Level 1 Objective	Level 2 Objective	Level 3 Objective	Example Policies
Improve information about the surgical department's performance	Establish appropriate metrics	Improve understanding of customer expectations	Have surgical patient satisfaction surveys
			Make data public comparing surgery departments or specialties
		Improve understanding of internal stakeholder expectations	Have surgical staff satisfaction surveys
			Interview key stakeholders about what they value in the profession and for the hospital
		Improve understanding of regulatory requirements	Collect regulatory requirements
		Add additional metrics	Publish hospital performance relative to peer hospitals in surgical outcomes
		Improve fidelity of metrics to expectations	Collect data relevant to Department of Surgery strategic initiatives
	Improve passive data collection (does not require extra human effort beyond the routine)	Improved use of current record systems	Track development of comorbidities (already tracked for reimbursement and regulatory purposes)
		Establish new passive systems for focus areas	Automatically generate clinical, financial, operational, and organizational metrics for the Department of Surgery
	Improve active data collection (requires motivation and effort by doctors, nurses, and others)	Reduce incentives to hoard private data	Protect reporting system from legal discovery
			Balance risks of revelation with benefits from improvements

Table 4.5 Principles-Driven Strategies for Organizational Learning in the OR

Level 1 Objective	Level 2 Objective	Level 3 Objective	Example Policies
			Adopt anonymous reporting of unfavorable outcomes
		Reduce the cost of reporting in time and effort	Use easily filled out forms or web interface
			Hire "scribes" to record, in the proper format for reporting, the spoken testimony of doctors and nurses
		Increase incentives to report data	Disburse monetary or symbolic rewards for sharing important information
		Increase revelation of favorable outcomes	Incorporate Grand Rounds, where success stories are shared
			Designate a team that seeks out and disseminates success stories
		Establish a subgroup responsible for data collection and analysis	Establish a department or hospital-level individual responsible for tracking quality metrics
			Adopt a more aggressive pursuit of JCAHO quality system guidelines
	Improved access to external data	Passive approaches	Use published data on surgical outcomes or comparisons of hospitals
			Subscribe to services that provide comparative industry data
		Active approaches	Do one's own benchmarking with site visits
			Form multihospital coalition with focus on data collection and learning

Level 1 Objective	Level 2 Objective	Level 3 Objective	Example Policies
	Improve the interpretation of data into information	Know statistically what data to collect and how to reduce it to conclusions	See entries in Table A.2 of Appendix A for using information to support decisions
		Use better statistical models	Improved statistical techniques
		Improve qualitative understanding of data and events	Enforce "sense-making" meetings, in which multiple perspectives on the interpretation of data are discussed
			Develop improved means for simulating and analyzing several alternative histories from a single sequence of events (for example, a near miss)
			Include individual testimony on events and interpretation
			Have multidisciplinary team focused on understanding data and events
		Improve the financial accounting system	Improve quality of data on surgical department financial performance
Increase motivation	Improve communication of departmental performance	Improve dissemination of information within subgroups	Incorporate weekly Department of Surgery "Death and Complication" conferences
			Activate Grand Rounds
		Improve dissemination of information across functional boundaries or across hospitals	Integrate IT systems that automatically track and display key statistics across surgical services or departments
			Implement quality chat rooms, anonymous or otherwise

Table 4.5   Principles-Driven Strategies for Organizational Learning in the OR

Level 1 Objective	Level 2 Objective	Level 3 Objective	Example Policies
			Improve informal social networking opportunities across surgical services or departments
		Improve accessibility of information	Provide current performance on key metrics using simple visuals or icons
	Justify and communicate aspirational goals for surgical services	Build on current stakeholder expectations	See entries on Level 3 objectives to improve understanding of external and internal stakeholder expectations
		Top-down aspirational goals	Communicate the strategic plan for the hospital and the intended role of the Department of Surgery
Improve execution of the learning process	Increase time and resources allocated to learning	From internal resources	Allow 10% budgeted time for surgeons and staff to work on learning and improving
			Allocate time in key strategic departments or services for process improvement discussions
			Provide internal funding for learning projects
		From external sources	Apply for grants for quality improvements in surgery
			Negotiate pay for performance with payors and an objective metric of performance
			Hire learning coaches
	Improve the concept generation effort	Improve brainstorming skills	Train in effective brainstorming techniques, such as random stimuli and problem decomposition
			Use principles-driven tables such as this one

Level 1 Objective	Level 2 Objective	Level 3 Objective	Example Policies
			Publicize novel approaches to learning in other organizations to make surgeons and staff aware of what is possible
		Reduce search costs for novel concepts	Improve social networking opportunities for idea exchange across services, departments, or hospitals
			Implement automatic news web feeds in certain services to stay abreast of current events
			Encourage membership in a professional society that exchanges information on key surgical issues
		Expand the set of options considered	Form "best ideas of the year" hospital consortia
			Have formal "Idea Contests" with rewards for the winner
			Hire consulting firms to bring in ideas from other industries
			Hire new surgeons with diverse backgrounds to bring in new ideas
			Promote web chat rooms that discuss surgical practices around the world
	Improve the concept selection process	Adopt current industrial innovation and new product development practices	Have each member of a cross-functional team of attending surgeons rate each proposal on a range of key dimensions, and average the scores to rank proposals

Table 4.5 Principles-Driven Strategies for Organizational Learning in the OR

Level 1 Objective	Level 2 Objective	Level 3 Objective	Example Policies
			Have cross-functional team of attending surgeons meet to position each project on a 2-dimensional "risk-return" plot, where each proposal is positioned on the dimensions of risk and return
		Establish a "fair" selection process	Have a democratic vote within the Department of Surgery
			Designate "experts" who can break ties within the process improvement team
		Improve team dynamics	Encourage continuing medical education courses on positive team dynamics
			Assess the interpersonal dynamics on process improvement teams through use of periodic team dynamics questionnaires
		Improve the concept validation effort	Have procedures and resources for "trial runs" in the hospital, measuring results of interest to key stakeholders
			Allocate resources to an intensive data search for corroboration or refutation of claims in refereed medical journals
			Improve web and professional organization searches for validating experiences and data on specific proposals

Level 1 Objective	Level 2 Objective	Level 3 Objective	Example Policies
	Standardize the learning process	Highly respected attending surgeons meet and craft a process of information acquisition, analysis, and recommendations	Have a team of attending physicians with internal formal or informal power design a learning process
			Have a highly respected surgeon work with external coaches to design a learning process
Improve implementation	Improve communication of the need for change	Communicate divergence between current performance and desired performance	Communicate financial realities that require change to improve
			Use public data on current hospital performance relative to national benchmarks and key competitors
			Hire benchmarking service
			Publicize downward trends in key performance metrics
		Communicate change in hospital strategy and required role of the Department of Surgery	Recognize that changing demographics demand better attention to problems of the aged; for example, emphasize orthopedics
			Adopt a "destination health" strategy to attract wealthy patients, which requires better performance on key surgical services
			Communicate the emergence of new competitors in a surgical service that will require a response

Table 4.5 Principles-Driven Strategies for Organizational Learning in the OR

Level 1 Objective	Level 2 Objective	Level 3 Objective	Example Policies
		Identify and disseminate motivational divergences between performance and goals	Form a group of hospitals that agree to share data among themselves
			Benchmark against peer institutions
		Enhance buy-in	Balance costs with benefits to each key stakeholder in terms they value
			Schedule informal quality chats for people to exchange views
			Engage all key stakeholders in the change process, listen to concerns, and seek acceptable compromises
	Reduce resistance among key stakeholders	Communicate benefits of change	Distribute the benefits to appease key stakeholders, and then communicate that
		Present evidence of feasibility	Present evidence from validation tests
			Present evidence of current buy-in from respected others in the organization
			Present testimony of respected people who have been successful in similar endeavors, perhaps in other surgery departments
			Have champions speak to group meetings
		Improve sequence of efforts embraced	Go for "small wins" first to build organizational confidence

Level 1 Objective	Level 2 Objective	Level 3 Objective	Example Policies
		Change the goals of internal stakeholders to be more aspirational	Proselytize among the surgeons and staff
			Hire new internal stakeholders with higher aspirational goals
			Include website material highlighting the proposed changes and rationale
	Make implementation more efficient	Increase capacity, and other responsiveness initiatives (see generic Table A.1)	Allocate enough time and resources to properly implement change, and/or other responsiveness initiatives
		Standardize the implementation process	Employ classic project management (such as PERT/CPM) techniques
			Employ lean techniques
		Have contingency plans	Anticipate problems and have a clear default plan "just in case"

4.4.3.3 PRACTICES

As noted, Table 4.5 is based on the generic organizational learning Table A.3 in Appendix A. We maintain our practice of not repeating large blocks of detailed entries from other tables. For example, "improve the interpretation of data into information" involves making sense of numbers and will benefit from the statistically based recommendations in generic patient safety Table A.2 from Appendix A. In Table 4.5, we simply cite that other table and do not reproduce all its entries. Likewise, managing the process of implementing improvements will benefit from the capacity and workload considerations appearing in generic responsiveness Table A.1. Again, in Table 4.5, these links are alluded to but not repeated in detail.

Table 4.5 is extensive but follows familiar logic. The Level 1 objectives are improving information about current performance, taking note of a motivating divergence between current performance and broadly accepted goals, improving the execution of the learning process, and improving the implementation of recommended improvements. Each of these is broken down further into contributing actions, which are again refined until we get to specific potential action plans. Different contexts may call for different specific breakdowns of the generic table into lower levels.

By following the entries in Table 4.5, readers can generate many different paths to change. Because any change effort must include information, motivation, execution, and implementation, specific applications will simultaneously combine several cells from the rightmost column. As discussed, one aspect of the learning and change process that is significant in Departments of Surgery is the combination of private information among surgeons and residents combined with the disincentives for revelation and the ineffectuality of rules and regulations. The following case illustrates one way to institutionalize organizational learning even in the presence of these adverse motivational issues. The case is based on actual practice, but also benefits greatly from the work of Bosk (1979).

4.4.3.4 CASE: WESTERN HOSPITAL DEPARTMENT OF GENERAL SURGERY

Dr. Jason Allen, chief of surgery at Western Hospital, was granting a visitor permission to observe the Department of Surgery's weekly Death and Complications conference. "This is the holiest hour in our profession," he explains. "What you will see represents surgery as responsibility: responsibility to our patients, to our profession, and to ourselves. Our profession requires that we be knowledgeable, thoughtful, and respectful. We must continually learn and get better."

In Death and Complication (D&C, sometimes called Mortality and Morbidity, or M&M) conferences, surgeons in a department gather to discuss unexpected events, their possible cause, and resulting recommendations for improving the system. The origins of D&C conferences can be traced to an iconoclastic nineteenth century surgeon, Dr. Ernest Codman. Dr. Codman graduated from Harvard Medical School in 1895 and joined the medical staff of Massachusetts General Hospital and the Harvard faculty. While at Massachusetts General, Dr. Codman started the first D&C conferences, in which surgeons met to discuss errors in patient care, their potential causes, and how risks might be mitigated in the future. In *A Study in Hospital Efficiency*, which Dr. Codman self-published in 1917, he says:

> *Every hospital should follow every patient it treats long enough to determine whether or not the treatment was successful, and to inquire "if not, why not," with a view to preventing similar failures in the future.*

Although this sounds eminently reasonable, Dr. Codman made his case with a confrontational approach that, along with the novelty of his ideas, resulted in his resignation from the staff at Massachusetts General and being dropped from the faculty of the Harvard Medical School. He did, however, along with some like-minded colleagues, help found the American College of Surgeons (ACS) and, in particular, its Hospital Standardization Program, which for the next 30 years promoted the embedding of institutional learning from past data into standard operating procedures.

Surgical complications or errors are, in many cases, private information within the surgical team. For these events to be brought forward for public study, with a potential learning outcome, the holders of this private information must be motivated to reveal it. This will happen if, and only if, revealing the information is more beneficial than harmful to their personal motivational concerns. Although people are invariably multi-dimensional, in broad terms the primary motivators of the key players are:

- **Residents**—They want to become surgeons. If revealing a complication or error hurts more than helps their chances of becoming a surgeon, they will not reveal the error.

- **Attending physicians**—They want to maintain and enhance their personal accomplishments and reputation. If revealing a complication or error hurts more than helps this objective, they will not reveal the error.

The motivational landscape for error reporting systems has some clear and powerful elements, and others that are more subtle and intricate. It is clear that a malpractice lawsuit does no good for, and may significantly harm, any of the preceding motivators. There will be a strong disinclination to reveal anything discoverable in a lawsuit. However, a professional desire to treat patients well also calls for a level of honesty that may be in tension with one's exposure to legal risk.

Revelation outside the department to the hospital level has few benefits because learning potential is perceived to be diminished the further one gets from discussion among skilled surgeons. What can the hospital administration add that one's colleagues cannot? An exception would be a discussion among similar surgical departments across several hospitals, which would have greater learning potential.

Revelation within the department and from resident to attending physician has some interesting motivational dynamics. Because residents are just beginning to build their surgical resumes, any error can significantly impact their reputation within the department and their chances of being favorably reviewed. Their preference would be to learn from errors privately, without public disclosure. Even that goal is compromised if the attending physician does not know of the error, because he can offer advice, based on experience, for avoiding mistakes in the future. So, a resident's willingness to reveal private information, even to his attending physician, will depend on what will happen with that information.

Attending physicians' motivations are mixed about the revelation of complications and errors within the team, within the department, within the hospital, or across several hospitals. Within the team house officers (residents), may fear being asked to leave the residency program, but attending physicians may support that outcome for those who are not destined to be good surgeons. Graduating poor surgeons would diminish and not enhance the senior surgeon's professional reputation. To properly assess residents' potential, attending physicians want to know everything that happens on their team. So, while residents may fear revealing mistakes to their attending physician, attending physicians have every motivation to demand that they do exactly that. Attending physicians will cease to trust or favorably evaluate residents who hide things from them. This generally has the desired outcome of residents perceiving more harm than benefit from hiding mistakes from their senior leader.

For attending physicians, the discussion of errors within the greater department of surgery generates mixed emotions. Professionally, the occasional human error does little to impact an attending surgeon's total body of work, so public disclosure of a modest number of adverse outcomes is less inhibited. Also, public admission of errors reinforces the culture of truthful revelation that they want to encourage within their team. However, too many errors on a team can suggest that the attending physician is not a skilled surgeon, not a good teacher, or does not have control of the team. Department-level discussions also have a feedback effect to residents' behavior. A revelation of a mistake that stays within the team is less feared by the resident than one that results in public departmental sanction. The attending physician must walk a fine line between setting an example of truthful transparency, yet avoiding consequences that will cast the team in a poor light or result in public humiliation of a resident, which will in turn discourage residents from honest disclosure.

One of the senior surgeons at Western Hospital is Dr. John Lemaster. Dr. Lemaster considers himself a surgeon and a mentor. He uses a relatively hands-off teaching style. For example, he allows his house staff, and especially his chief resident Emma, considerable latitude in making decisions and in performing procedures, but he retains final responsibility for the outcome. Dr. Lemaster rounds with his house staff twice weekly, and he is in the OR at the beginning of most procedures. He demands that all issues of potential interest be fully disclosed by his house staff. He is, after all, responsible for the results. He can tolerate technical mistakes, which can also be teaching moments. He cannot tolerate dishonesty or hiding relevant information. He wants no surprises. For the most part, his staff complies because he has power over their careers. Dr. Lemaster is a key voice in deciding whether his residents can complete their surgical training at Western or must move on to a less prestigious hospital.

Revelation is not easy, especially when mistakes by the house staff reflect poorly on their judgment or capabilities or place a patient at risk. Dr. Lemaster realizes that as long as the resident has the potential to grow into a good surgeon, public criticism and humiliation serve no useful purpose. Residents know that revealing mistakes to Dr. Lemaster risks short-term criticism, but it will not compromise their professional aspirations or standing in the greater community as long as they are conscientious in trying to improve. By discussing mistakes within the team, the whole team learns.

The science of surgery is advanced by looking closely at cases that do not conform to expectations, because there is learning potential in such events. Abstracting away from the human drama that is an integral part of every case, there is little learning potential in a procedure that is expected to go well and does. Likewise, a heroic intervention to save an extraordinarily sick individual, which in the end fails to do so, is not an unexpected result and may offer little learning potential. However, when a patient is expected to die and survives, or vice versa, then expectations based on current knowledge are violated and reflection is called for. Extraordinarily happy outcomes are discussed by attending physicians and house staff in a meeting called Grand Rounds, an educational forum where interesting, usually successful, cases are presented. Deaths, expected or not, and unexpected complications are discussed in the weekly D&C Conference.

In Western Hospital's Department of Surgery, every death or complication is to be reported to Dr. Allen. A complication is anything outside ordinary expectations or something that disrupts the normal course of events. These include issues in the OR, but also issues such as postoperative infection or delays going home. Near misses can also be learning opportunities, even if there was no adverse outcome for the patient. Dr. Allen chooses from the weekly submissions those cases that will be presented to the entire department. His staff contacts the relevant attending physician or chief resident and confirms they will be in attendance to make the presentation. The resident present during the procedure in question is usually asked to prepare the presentation and present the case, and he is then given a week to put the presentation together. In this fashion, the agenda for each week's D&C conference is decided.

Dr. Allen chooses a case for presentation based on its learning content, and he strives to cover (over the course of a year, say) the important general areas of surgical practice. For example, an error tying a suture might be simple human error in execution, in which case the problem and remedy are apparent and not worth the entire department's time. However, a suturing error that resulted in intestinal leakage could also be a catalyst for a discussion of the biology of wound healing, suture selection and spacing, and which knot to use as a function of patient age and nature and location of the wound. In that situation, the case could be selected. Four cases are covered each week during the 1-hour meeting, so about 200 cases are presented each year. Dr. Allen may choose more cases in areas of greater frequency or concern, such as postoperative infection. He also looks for the potential for evidence-based learning relevant to the case.

Presentations are always deidentified so that patient confidentiality is preserved. Also, because it is part of a quality control effort, presentations are protected from legal discovery. Dr. Allen has complete control over personnel attending the D&C conferences and may deny attendance to anybody he feels would focus on blame rather than learning. In this way, the legal risk deterrent to revelation is mitigated.

A senior surgeon in the department is selected to moderate each D&C conference. For example, Dr. Lemaster has been the moderator on many occasions. The presentations are submitted to the moderator several days before the meeting. The moderator looks these over and anticipates how to manage the discussion so each case lives up to its learning potential, yet ends on time so the other cases can be discussed. All attendees receive a short summary of the cases to be presented.

The conference is held from 7:00 to 8:00 a.m. every Thursday morning. Around 6:55 a.m., the department personnel filter into the auditorium. There are no formally assigned seating areas, but the auditorium is divided into three sections by aisles, and as a matter of habit medical students sit in the right-hand section, residents in the middle, and attending physicians on the left. The medical students are not yet surgical residents, and most are still deciding if that career path is suitable for them. They generally remain silent during the conference, because they have little to offer given their current level of training and experience.

The moderator announces the first case, and the resident associated with the procedure begins his or her presentation. All presentations have the same general format:

- An introduction, including the patient, symptoms, vital signs, test results, and other data pertinent to surgical cases

- The death or complication

- An analysis of the situation, including questions for the audience regarding important aspects of the treatment course relevant to the case

- A presentation of scientific data culled from the literature related to this and similar cases

- The recommendations for process improvements, which may be specific ("if you ever see problem A, we recommend you do B") or more general systemic suggestions ("we need a better handoff process to the PACU, ICU, or step-down")

When the presentation reaches a point where questions are posed for the audience, the moderator selects a resident in the audience to respond. Any resident may be asked to respond, but the process is semirandom because the moderator (having seen the presentations and knowing what the questions are) can direct easier questions to more junior residents and more difficult problems to senior residents. Because they may be called upon, without warning, to answer questions in front of the entire department, residents are strongly inclined to carefully read the short summary of the cases prior to coming to conference and to anticipate and study the possible issues that may arise during the case.

Most residents answer the questions with impressive completeness, a testament to these incentives and their dedication to preparation. Sometimes, however, the answer is not complete. In these cases, the moderator will not directly berate the resident but instead will signal incompleteness in a more benign way. He may say, "You're close..." or "You got some of it right...," but these euphemisms are clearly interpreted by everyone in the audience as signaling an incomplete answer.

After the presentation is complete, the moderator asks if there are any questions from the audience. There is typically little critical discussion if the presenter has been complete in his or her presentation of the case, the scientific literature, and recommendations. Discussion might ensue, however, in several situations:

- The presenter appeared to miss something important in the case, such as a diagnosis that was consistent with the symptoms being presented and was potentially fatal, yet was not mentioned as a possibility in the presentation. These comments are not made in an accusatory manner. Rather, a member of the audience might ask, "Did you consider…"

- A death has occurred after heroic measures to save the patient. The discussion may be about the ethics of heroic care for patients that are, in all likelihood, destined to die. Or, if the patient was transferred in on a medivac aircraft but really had no chance of survival, the discussion might be around the ethics of allocating such expensive resources to a lost cause.

- Members of the audience have some personal experience beyond the surgical literature with the type of case being presented and can add something useful to the recommendations being made. An important caveat, however, is that evidence-based recommendations trump individual experience.

- There was a "system error," meaning the context within which people work (extending outside the Department of Surgery) had a large role in the death or complication. These cases typically end with a recommendation for better system communication or coordination.

The form of these discussions reinforces the social dynamics at play. Attending physicians will protect their residents. If the presenting resident begins to founder under questioning, his attending physician will speak up and handle the discussion. Although attending physicians may be quite harsh with residents within the privacy of their team, they will defend them in front of the department. This is important in maintaining the resident's allegiance, and hence the attending physician's respect and leadership role within the team.

Attending physicians respect other attending physicians, because everyone makes mistakes.

Humiliating a peer is neither useful nor productive, even among these highly competitive people. For example, if an important possibility has been missed, the benign question, "Did you consider…" invites an answer that can be made in an open and nondefensive manner. Recognizing the possibility of a mistake in judgment, the attending physician on the case will speak up to answer the question, taking the risk away from the presenting resident. Whatever the attending physician on the case says, the questioner will seldom press the issue. It will be apparent to the entire audience, without a public display, what has transpired.

The moderator's responsibility is to allow the discussion to proceed but not degenerate into either blame assignment or interpersonal competition. Comments should be sharp but not personal. Ideally, any critique or rebuttal should be data-based, not just opinion.

The Western Hospital D&C conferences succeed in encouraging the revelation and discussion of private information for the benefit of the entire Department of Surgery. They accomplish this by accommodating the intricate web of motivations and incentives among the departmental personnel. Learning ends, however, at the departmental boundary. Western still has no well-functioning mechanism for data collection, discussion, and learning across departments or across hospitals. Although there are formal reporting systems in place, the combination of private information and contrary incentives render these less useful.

After the conference was complete, a visitor mentioned to Dr. Allen the stressful nature of random questions to the residents and how impressively complete most of the residents' answers were. These future surgeons evidently had extensive knowledge of human anatomy and chemistry. "They better be good," Dr. Allen observed. "If they're called into the Emergency Department to consult on a complex case, they won't have time to go into some back room and read up. They need to know what to do."

The visitor also mentioned none of the medical students in attendance spoke up. All the talking was done by the residents and attending physicians. "The medical students don't know enough yet," explained Dr. Allen. "They're still deciding on their career path. Most of them are concluding this is not for them. But there are about 10% sitting there watching the nature of the discussion, watching residents fielding random questions and rising to the occasion, and thinking, 'That's for me!' Those are the students we want."

The Western Hospital D&C Conference is an ingenious balance of incentives that solves the significant problem of organizational learning from private information with all its disincentives to report. It does so with a delicate balance among the aspirations and values of the surgeons and residents. Along the way, it has become an integral part of resident training and even an experiential screen for medical students considering a career in surgery.

4.5 Conclusions

The practice of surgery is supremely challenging due to the inherently dangerous aspects of invading a human body. It has generated its own supporting architecture and subculture characterized by care and sophistication. The management of surgical departments is important to hospitals because a high percentage of total revenues can commonly be traceable to surgical procedures and patients' pre- and postoperative stays. The key management challenges faced by surgical hospitals and departments include the appropriate marshalling and allocation of resources and improvements in clinical practice, examples of which we covered in this chapter.

Problems of resource acquisition and use can often be addressed using our generic principles-driven "responsiveness" table. There, known principles of physics and management are used to generate a broad landscape of options for consideration.

The critical issue of patient safety and improving clinical outcomes could potentially proceed based on published "best practices" culled from medical journals, but in surgical hospitals there is great potential for learning from the experiences of the surgeons and staff. This, however, is complicated by an aversion to admit errors or near misses, due to the possibility of adverse professional or legal consequences. Some carefully orchestrated organizational remedies exist for this challenge, as shown by example here.

There are, of course, many challenges we could not cover in limited space. These include crafting a strategy that defines a portfolio of procedures in which the department will excel and marketing the department to referring physicians to secure market share for select procedures, among others. The strategic challenge would share common market-assessment themes with the Seaberg hospital case in Chapter 3. Marketing the department externally would build on the material in this chapter, where the key stakeholders are referring physicians who need to see a positive personal benefit-cost ratio to change their referring behaviors. With only modest adaptation, the tactics used here to understand and convince key stakeholders that change is good can apply.

4.6 Stakeholders' Perspectives

January 2011

The flow improvement efforts initiated by Tony Tenore and Nate Greene had gained momentum in the ED and some key nursing units. Each project in their program focused on patient-centric physical or information flows and on key stages of those flows that were clearly potential bottlenecks. Each measurable improvement created new evangelists. From the ED to the nursing units, the perception was growing that real change was afoot.

Greene continued to use Sally Oldham's journey as the catalyst to focus on critical flows throughout the hospital. In January, his attention turned to the question of why Sally was unable to get into an OR.

His team found that on the evening of March 24, 2010, both the ICU and PACU were full. Noting that this should not have delayed a time-sensitive emergent case, Greene pursued an easy fix by revising the authority of the after-hours OR schedulers. But, in an attempt to address the problem at a more fundamental level, the team sought to deal with the fact that a full 6% of all procedures at University Hospital experienced a "bed hold," meaning that patients could not move out of, or into, an OR because there was no postoperative bed.

A key underlying cause for the bed hold situation was that, even when a patient in the ICU or PACU had been cleared for transfer to a regular inpatient unit, there was frequently no inpatient bed to move them to. So, Greene's team pursued their root cause analysis one level deeper by asking why there were no inpatient beds. His staff pulled together some data on patient census and trajectories and found that many extra bed days were used up by patients who were medically ready to go home but had not been officially cleared for discharge (their paperwork was missing some signatures) or the nonmedical aspects (transportation for example) of the discharge process were not complete.

The parallel team working on the nursing units had focused on the discharge process, which would undoubtedly improve this bottleneck. 5B now had a "discharge lounge" for patients who were cleared for discharge and were only waiting for a ride or some paperwork. This, along with other improvements in the ownership and organization of the discharge process, promised to help alleviate ICU and PACU congestion.

A PACU team was looking at the relationship between the pattern of arrival of patients to the PACU and the surgical schedule, because the latter drove the former.

There were also clear physical congestion problems in the ORs. The data gathered by an OR team demonstrated that the crowded surgical schedule along with emergency intrusions caused excessive disruptions and delays to both elective and required surgeries, resulting in more "near miss" events than anybody wanted. Surprisingly, however, they also found that, overall, the surgical suite was only 80% utilized on average, and the many conflicting agendas in the surgical scheduling system combined to make poor use of the OR resources. The implication was that it should be possible to improve flows through the OR without having to invest in more rooms and capital equipment. From his experience in the ED and nursing units, Greene now understood that these problems were not inevitable but were entirely predictable and manageable using established management principles.

Another striking feature of Sally's story that Greene sought to analyze was the delay getting her into the OR for exploratory surgery, even after evidence began to mount that she might have a small bowel obstruction. From Hospital Operations, he learned about the natural human tendency for people to stick with an initial diagnosis (such as stomach flu), almost as if it was the default hypothesis that could not be dislodged except by strong evidence. Worse, there could be a natural tendency to filter information to confirm that hypothesis, especially if accepting an alternative was inconvenient. Nobody consciously did this, but lack of conscious intent did not help the patient.

With the information he and others had at the time, the odds were that Sally had stomach flu. That would be uncomfortable but was not likely to be fatal in a person of Sally's general good health. However, it was also clear that the small bowel obstruction was a possibility early in Sally's information flows, yet, due to the poor CT scan, the surgical shift change, and other phenomena, an urgency to validate or refute this diagnosis was lacking. Greene concluded that, although there was no case for negligence, the combination of clinicians falling prey to these natural perceptual biases along with the physical flow bottlenecks that delayed action when it was warranted combined to produce the worst of all possible outcomes.

The process improvement Greene sought to enact was educating clinicians to these possible biases. Already doctors and nurses were required to periodically take "medical continuing education" courses, and Greene secured the help of a renowned medical decision making expert to give an accessible presentation on how to be wary of biases we all bring to the interpretation of evidence.

By now, many in the hospital knew that Greene's teams were following a patient's path through the system and focusing on its critical physical and information flows. The intensely human perspective this introduced into the improvement process tapped into peoples' best sense of purpose and increased their willingness to embrace new initiatives in their own areas.

"I can see where my part is in the whole!" was a common reaction. Although the number of projects was actually lower than in years past, the efforts were strategically focused for maximal, and measurable, effect.

Before the end of January, Greene and his teams had leveraged principles of flexible resources to justify the transformation of several beds in nursing units to be capable of holding intensive care patients if required, so no flows into or out of the OR would be held up for lack of a PACU or ICU bed. Trained staff from the ICU and PACU could "float" if necessary to these locations. This initiative, although taking place well away from the OR complex, succeeded in reducing the number of bed holds to practically zero.

But this use of flex beds was a short-term fix; the longer term problem was to free up hospital beds more quickly. This would help more than the bed-hold problem; it would also increase the hospital's overall patient throughput. Greene championed the installation of observation beds in the ED for patients who were awaiting some test outcomes before the decision to admit, or not. These patients currently occupied in-patient beds, so this move alone would free up more beds and allowed patients to flow from the PACU and ICU down to regular beds as needed.

Earlier efforts by the nursing team on 5B had already demonstrated the value of their discharge lounge, with delayed discharges declining by 34%! It was time to extend these trial efforts to other units.

Finally, one of the key surgical services was working on designing a scheduling system with some dedicated block time for surgeons, as well as some "shared" time that would serve to buffer the variability in demand for OR time from one surgeon to another, exploiting "risk pooling economies," as described in the *Hospital Operations* book.

After a sloppy, sweaty session of basketball at the end of January, Greene commented optimistically on some of his initiatives and the results they were showing.

"It sounds like you're making progress, Nate."

Even as he listened to the compliment, Greene knew that there was a "but" coming, and it did.

"But, it sounds to me like you're successfully fighting some fires. The difference between you and me is that we never caught fire in the first place. So you're killing yourself to beat a little bit of quality into your system, while it's naturally built into ours."

"There is some truth to that," conceded Greene reasonably. "You have a very low variability system that allows you to operate with less buffer time and capacity than we can."

Greene wagged his index finger as he launched his own "but."

"But you don't handle emergencies, and you can pick and choose your patients. The variability we're coping with is coming from serving people who need care!"

"Huh?" Arnold said. "Variability? Buffering? Are you reading textbooks in your spare time?"

"Indeed, I am." Greene slung his duffel over his shoulder. "Maybe you should try it."

"Nah," Arnold scoffed. "I'd rather do than read. My job is to serve our niche really well, and I can do that already. If enough other specialty hospitals open to serve different niches, then the entire system will be better for everyone."

"Not for the general hospitals," Greene objected. "If you little guys pick off all the profitable surgery cases and leave us with the gen med and charity cases, we'll go out of business."

"That may be," Arnold admitted. "But the reason for that is our reimbursement and insurance system is screwed up."

"Well, at least we agree on that!"

4.7 References

Atkinson, J.W. "Motivational Determinants of Risk-Taking Behavior." In J.W. Atkinson and N.T. Feather (eds). *A Theory of Achievement and Motivation*, Wiley, N.Y. 1966, 11–30.

Bosk, C. *Forgive and Remember: Managing Medical Failure.* University of Chicago Press, Chicago 1979.

Fischer, M., K. Mazor, J. Baril, E. Alper, D. DeMarco, and M. Pugnaire. "Learning from Mistakes." *Journal of General Internal Medicine* 21, 2006, 419–423.

IOM (Institute of Medicine). *To Err Is Human.* Kohn, L., J. Corrigan, M. Donaldson (editors). National Academy Press, Washington, D.C. 2000.

Jackson, R. "The Business of Surgery: Managing the OR as a Profit Center Requires More Than Just IT. It Requires a Profit-Making Mindset, Too." Operating Room Info Systems. *Health Management Technology*, 2002.

JCAHO. Joint Commission on Accreditation of Healthcare Organizations organization website http://www.jointcommission.org/. February 2010.

Kuhn, J. "Operating Room Management." In Malangoni, M. (ed). *Critical Issues in Operating Room Management.* Lippincott-Raven, NY, 1997.

Lawrence, P. *Essentials of Surgical Specialties* (with R. Bell and M Dayton, editors). Williams and Wilkins, Baltimore, 1993.

Levitt, B., and J. March. "Organizational Learning." *Annual Review of Sociology* 14, 1988, 319–340.

Loudon, I. *Western Medicine (An Illustrated History).* Oxford University Press, Oxford 1997.

Lovejoy, W., and Y. Li. "Hospital Operating Room Capacity Expansion." *Management Science* 48, 2002, 1369–1387.

March, J., L. Sproull, and M. Tamuz. "Learning from Samples of One for Fewer." *Organization Science* 2(1), 1991, 1–13.

Maslow, A. "A Theory of Human Motivation." *Psychological Review*, 1943, 370–396.

Miner, J. *Theories of Organizational Behavior.* The Dryden Press, Hinsdale, Illinois, 1980.

Peters, J.. and T. Blasco. "Enhancing Hospital Performance Through Perioperative Services. *Physician Executive*, Nov–Dec 2004.

Rosenthal, M., P. Cornett, K. Sutcliff, and E. Lewton. "Beyond the Medical Record." *Journal of General Internal Medicine* 20, 2005, 404–409.

Sagan, S.D. "Toward a Political Theory of Organizational Reliability." *Journal of Contingencies and Crisis Management* 2(4), 1994, 228–240.

Schenkel, S., R. Khare, M. Rosenthal, K. Sutcliff, and E. Lewton. "Resident Perceptions of Medical Errors in the Emergency Department." Academic Emergercy Medicine 10(12), Dec 2003, 1318–1324.

Sullivan, J.T., K. Sykora, J. Schneiderman, C. Naranjo, and E. Sellers. "Assessment of Alcohol Withdrawal: Revised Clinical Institute Withdrawal Assessment for Alcohol Scale (CIWA-Ar)." *British Journal of Addiction* 84, 1989, 1353–1357.

Tamuz, M. "Learning Disabilities for Regulators: The Perils of Organizational Learning in the Air Transportation Industry." *Administration and Society* 33(3), 2001, 276–302.

Tamuz, M., and M. Harrison. "Improving Patient Safety in Hospitals: Contributions of High-Reliability Theory and Normal Accident Theory." *Health Services Research* 41(4), 2006, 1654–1676.

Tamuz, M., and E. Thomas. "Classifying and Interpreting Threats to Patient Safety in Hospitals: Insights from Aviation." *Journal of Organizational Behavior* 27, 2006, 919–940.

USP, The United States Pharmacopeia (USP) website http://www.usp.org/aboutUSP/, 2010a.

Venzmer, G. *Five Thousand Years of Medicine*. Taplinger Publishing, NY, 1972.

Vissers, J., and R. Beech (eds). *Health Operations Management*. Routledge, Taylor and Francis Group, London 2005. This book has chapters on various aspects of patient flow logistics through health systems, with an applied Operations Research emphasis using math programming and simulation techniques.

Walker, K. *The Story of Medicine*. Oxford University Press, NY, 1955.

5

DIAGNOSTIC SERVICES

Coauthored with Jeffrey Myers, MD

5.1 Stakeholders' Perspectives

Monday March 22, 2010, 4:40 p.m.

Four vials of blood accompanied by a requisition form for Mrs. Sally Oldham were delivered to the specimen receiving window of the University Hospital clinical chemistry lab by a phlebotomist. A few minutes later, Francine Watts, an accessioner, picked up Sally's sample, along with several others, and returned to her workstation. Noting that Sally's form was marked "stat," she added it to the sizeable priority pile already on her table and resumed her work of sorting submissions. The lab was backed up because it was a busy afternoon in the hospital, they had received several large deliveries of specimens from outside the hospital, and several requisitions had been incomplete, forcing the accesssioners to either get the information or send the samples back to the requesting clinicians.

Within a few minutes, Francine checked Sally's requisition and placed her tubes on the incoming rack in batches destined for various tests. Her tubes waited from 5 to 15 minutes before being moved by a medical assistant to the appropriate analysis station. There, they were loaded into analyzers. Finally, when the last test in Sally's panel was completed and autoverified, her results were posted to the information system at 5:45 p.m..

The 65-minute turnaround time (TAT) for Sally's tests was longer than the hospital target of 45 minutes. Because Dr. Greene was approaching the end of his shift and wanted to get Sally settled, he checked the system twice for the results before finally accessing them at 5:47. They showed an elevated white blood count of 14,500 (normal 4,000–10,000), blood urea nitrogen of 32 (normal <20), and creatinine of 1.4 (normal 1.0).

Although the process for Sally's test was somewhat slow, it was otherwise normal. But Jeannette Wu, a 38-year-old mother of two and nurse practitioner, had a much more flawed experience with her lab results. She arrived at the ED two hours before Sally, also with acute abdominal pain, but with a very different back story.

A week ago, Jeannette had undergone routine laparoscopic *cholecystectomy* (gall bladder removal) surgery on an outpatient basis. There had been some minor complications, which caused her procedure to take longer than expected, and she had been told to expect some pain and discomfort. But she was sent home with oxycodone/paracetamol (Percocet) for pain and an expectation of a normal recovery.

A day later, however, Jeannette was experiencing severe pain and returned to the hospital. Her surgeon examined her and, suspecting a retained stone in the bile duct, ordered an ultrasound. When the ultrasound confirmed his suspicion, he scheduled her for a second surgery that day. This proceeded normally and, after a day in the hospital, Jeannette was again sent home, this time with hydromorphone to control her pain.

Two days later, Jeannette was in even more pain and went to the ED. Among other tests, the ED physician ordered a standard liver function test panel, which included Albumin (Alb), Alinine transaminase (ALT), Aspartate transaminase (AST), and other levels. The ED physician noted that Jeannette's levels were getting better, and Jeannette, who asked to see them, agreed. He concluded that Jeannette's pain was normal surgical pain aggravated by a urinary tract infection (UTI). He sent her home with a prescription for ciprofloxin, an antibiotic, in addition to a stronger dosage of her pain medication.

Jeannette was skeptical about the UTI diagnosis and did not fill the prescription for the antibiotics. She did take the pain meds, but her pain continued to intensify. She grew increasingly pale, weak, and sweaty. After two days, she returned to the ED and saw the same doctor. Noting again that her blood work was improving, he scolded her for not taking the antibiotics, took her off the pain medication, and signed her discharge orders. Jeannette knew full well that he suspected her of drug seeking. But convinced that something more serious than a UTI was wrong with her, she pleaded with a staff nurse to get a surgeon involved. With a moderate stretch of her authority, the staff nurse managed to get a young surgical resident to come and evaluate Jeannette.

The surgical resident looked at the blood work history and immediately noted that the newest test was on the right, not the left, implying that the doctor had repeatedly read the trends in the wrong direction. In reality, the numbers showed that Jeannette's condition was not improving but instead was dangerously deteriorating. In particular, the indicators of liver function were alarming. AST level had increased to more than 2,000 (normal is 5–40), ALT was above 1,500 (normal is 7–56) and albumin had fallen below 1 (normal 3.5–5). Strongly suspecting a liver problem, the resident notified the ED physician who pulled the discharge orders, ordered a CT scan, and restarted the pain meds.

The CT scan indicated portal vein and arterial thrombosis (blood clots) in the liver. When he talked to her about her condition and course of treatment, the attending surgeon confirmed Jeannette's suspicion that taking antibiotics could have been very dangerous given the weakened state of her liver. Jeannette wound up spending nearly two months in the hospital receiving surgical and medical treatment. But, although she lost a significant portion of her liver, she ultimately made a full recovery.

In addition to the intense pain, the part of Jeannette's experience that she would never forget was the fine line between benefit and harm from diagnostic test results. All her blood samples had been properly collected, delivered, and analyzed. But in the last step of communicating the results to the requesting physician, a breakdown had occurred. Several people, including Jeannette herself, had looked at the blood work history, and every one of them had read the results backward. Convinced that her levels were improving, when precisely the reverse was the case, the ED physician locked in on the normal pain/UTI infection hypothesis. The result was several days of pain and discomfort to Jeannette, although thankfully no degradation in her ultimate outcome. If, however, she had taken the prescribed antibiotics, the consequences of the misinterpreted results could have been much more dire.

Monday March 22, 2010, 9:20 p.m.

"Hello. Come on in." A Radiology Department tech, whose badge identified her as Keisha Clark, motioned the transport tech to roll Sally's bed into the empty CT room. Sally wondered about the absence of patients, because she had been waiting a long time to get into the "busy" CT, but she was too sick to ask about it.

Keisha helped the tech move Sally on to the scanning bed and nodded as he departed.

"Are you cold?" Keisha asked. "I can get you a blanket."

Sally shook her head.

"All right." Keisha smiled. "You let me know if you need anything. Now, before we start, I need to ask you a couple of questions. First, can you please tell me your full name?"

"Sally Barbara Oldham," Sally replied softly.

"And your date of birth is three, fifteen, sixty five?"

"Three, fifteen, fifty five," corrected Sally.

"Well, bless your heart!" Keisha exclaimed, glancing back down at Sally's wristband. "You sure look good."

"I don't feel so good." Sally could still taste the contrast agent she had thrown up an hour ago.

Keisha explained that the CT scan would only take a few minutes, but they needed to set up some things first.

"I'm going to give you a contrast agent that will make you feel a little warm," Keisha warned. "It may also make you feel like you need to pee. But you won't, and the feeling will go away soon."

Sally watched resignedly as Keisha injected iodinated contrast into her IV. At first she felt nothing. But within moments a warm sensation arose in her throat and quickly washed over her entire body in a sickening flush. A strong metallic taste formed in her mouth and triggered a spike in her nausea. She turned her head to vomit but had so little in her stomach that she mostly dry heaved. Keisha came out of her booth with a towel to wipe Sally's mouth. When the nausea had subsided a bit, she helped position Sally's arms over her head and went back into the booth.

Sally did her best to remain still as the table slid her in and out of a smooth white ring with flashing lights, first quickly and then slowly. Keisha asked her a few times to take a deep breath and hold it. But Sally could not keep from choking, and moving, when she inhaled. Keisha repeated some portions of the exam in hopes of a sharper image, but she stopped when she felt the images were as good as she would be able to get. In all, Sally's exam took just over 30 minutes.

Keisha made the last keystrokes to post Sally's scan to the system, called the ED for a transport tech, and came out of the booth to talk to Sally.

"You did real well." She patted Sally's arm encouragingly. "Are you still hot?"

Sally nodded.

"Do you feel any itching or difficulty breathing?"

Sally shook her head.

"Good. They'll keep an eye on you just to make sure you don't have any reaction. I hope you feel better soon."

Sally was rolled back to the ED feeling sicker than when she left. But Keisha was right that the contrast dye symptoms passed quickly.

Meanwhile, Dr. John Amiri, a Radiology resident on late-shift duty in the reading room, pulled up Sally's images on his screen just after 10 p.m. He observed that her stomach was distended and filled with fluid and noted distended small bowel loops. These, he knew, could be consistent with a bowel obstruction or with simple gastroenteritis. So he continued looking for a point of demarcation above which the intestine was markedly more distended. But the lack of oral contrast agent made the GI tract less visible than it would have been otherwise, and some of the images had a significant amount of motion blurring. Although he could not find definitive evidence, he considered a blockage to be a possibility, along with severe gasteroenteritis. He put this in the "wet" (preliminary) read he posted for the ED at 10:25 p.m.

Tuesday March 23, 2010, 9:20 a.m.

Dr. Claudia Perez, the faculty member in charge of the Abdominal Imaging residency program, pulled up Sally's scan on her reading room screen. She had arrived that morning to a large backlog of images requiring final reads. She went first to the two images for abdominal trauma patients, and then she looked at images roughly in the order in which the exams were done. As Dr. Amiri had noted in his report, the image quality was poor. But by carefully working through the axial images, she was able to determine that the intestine did indeed narrow significantly.

She could not tell how quickly the narrowing occurred because the region of interest was obscured by a motion blur. Nevertheless, she increased Dr. Amiri's assessment of a "possible" obstruction to a "likely" obstruction. Because the image was not definitive, she recommended that "clinical correlation" was still needed.

When she finished posting her report at 9:50 a.m., Dr. Perez noted in the system that Sally had been moved to Internal Medicine and was under the care of Dr. Bennett, whom she knew slightly from past encounters. Concerned about a potentially dangerous condition, Dr. Perez picked up the phone and dialed Dr. Bennett's number. She got his pager and left her number. Within minutes, her phone rang.

"Perez."

"Hi, Claudia. Ron Bennett."

"Hey Ron," Perez returned. "I called you about Mrs. Oldham's abdominal scan. I just posted my report, and I think there's a decent chance of a lower bowel obstruction. The details on location are in the report."

"Thanks, Claudia." Bennett sounded in a hurry. "I was worried about the same thing myself. In fact, I've got someone from Surgery coming up to look at her. So your report is just in time. See you."

"Bye." Perez hung up and moved on to the next image.

Wednesday March 24, 2010, 2:15 p.m.

Dr. Perez leaned over the shoulder of a first-year resident and peered at the screen as he stepped through a sequence of images.

"Nope," she said. "Too smooth and too small. That's a benign nodule. He looks clean. Go ahead and write it up."

Dr. Perez and the resident were looking at the lung scan of Arturo Guzman, a former smoker and 43-year-old father of three. Generally healthy, he had been motivated to go in for an overdue physical exam when a cough lingered after a mild cold. His primary care physician had recommended a CT scan as a precaution against lung cancer.

Lung cancer! The words hit Arturo like a fist. He had quit smoking over 15 years ago precisely out of a fear of cancer. Now, in the thick of child rearing, it was one of his greatest worries.

Arturo had received his CT scan early that morning after a two-week wait on the schedule. It had gone smoothly, and the technician had told him that he would be contacted by his doctor with the results. But, although the results were posted before 3 p.m. the day of his test, his primary care physician was overloaded with patients on Wednesday and out of the office on Thursday and Friday. As a result, the physician did not access the results until the following Monday, and it was not until the following Wednesday that his nurse made contact with Arturo to let him know that his results were normal. But, although the final outcome was good, Arturo had endured a week of unnecessary stress before getting the good news.

5.2 Introduction to the Diagnostic Units

Diagnostic units are part of the *ancillary services* in a hospital, which are support services provided to patients other than room, board, and medical and nursing services. These include, among others, Pharmacy, Physical Therapy, Speech Therapy, Health and Wellness Education and, of particular interest to us in this chapter, Clinical Laboratories (Pathology Departments), Imaging Services (X-ray, ultrasound, CT, MRI), and Nonimaging Tests (EKG, EEG).

Diagnostic units are central to patient diagnosis and treatment. Estimates are that laboratory tests are involved in more than 70% of medical decisions (ACLA 2010). Medical imaging is not far behind and is growing as a diagnostic tool; for instance, the fraction of all ED patients who received a CT scan increased from 3.2% in 1996 to 13.9% in 2007 (Kocher et al. 2011). As such, these ancillary services play a major role in the cost and quality of hospital health care.

In their role of supporting diagnosis and treatment of patients, diagnostic units function as cost centers. But they can also act as revenue centers that charge patients directly for services. Consequently, some hospitals have followed a strategy of expanding their ancillary services (for example, by creating freestanding imaging centers) for outpatients as a means of generating additional revenue. However, other hospitals, faced with heavy capital costs and staffing challenges, have moved toward outsourcing some ancillary services (for example, contracting with a commercial laboratory to do nonroutine tests).

Whether they are employed by the hospital directly or work for outside organizations, physicians in the diagnostic units can be thought of as "doctors' doctors." When a patient is sick, he goes to a doctor. When a doctor needs help diagnosing a patient, she consults a radiologist or pathologist. Consequently, most work in the diagnostic units is initiated through referrals or support requests. However, self-referrals for tests (for example, mammograms) do occur and are becoming more common as imaging equipment becomes more prevalent (for example, scanners in shopping malls). As a result, diagnostic units do sometimes interface directly with patients, rather than indirectly through support of other units.

5.2.1 History

In ancient cultures that believed in supernatural explanations of illness, diagnosis (at least as we think of it today) was not part of the treatment process, which involved selecting appropriate prayers or rituals. The roots of modern diagnostics lie with the Greeks, and Hippocrates (460–377 BCE) in particular, who were the first to accept wholly physical causes of disease. However, although ancient physicians sought logical explanations for sickness and classified diseases according to symptoms, they lacked the science and technology to identify causes or cures for these symptoms. Although some medicinal (herbs, quinine, and so on) and physical (bone splinting, surgery to remove foreign objects, and the like) treatments developed by trial and error were helpful, other common practices (for example, bloodletting) did more harm than good.[1]

Furthermore, even though the Hippocratic school espoused systematic *observation* of patients, it did not make use of detailed *examination* of patients. Instruments, experiments, and measurements were not yet part of the physician's arsenal because it was believed that the roots of disease were holistic in nature, caused by an imbalance of the bodily humors. Resistance to detailed analysis of organs or physical samples persisted for centuries. Indeed, on the cusp of the Enlightenment, Thomas Sydenham (1624–1689), the "Father of English Medicine," was still reinforcing the Hippocratic view, rejecting the use of microscopes on the basis that examination of minute processes of the inner body was contrary to God's will (Rosenfeld 1999a).

From the Enlightenment onward, a stream of scientific discoveries (see Tables 5.1 and 5.2) laid the foundations for analytic medical diagnosis. But two key developments, which launched the medical diagnostics field in earnest, occurred at the end of the nineteenth century:

- **Germ theory of disease**—Demonstrated by Louis Pasteur and Robert Koch in the 1870s

- **X-rays**—Discovered by Wilhelm Röntgen in 1895.

Germ theory laid the foundation for pathology laboratories, whereas X-rays marked the beginning of imaging units. These two streams of diagnostic technology map into the basic split between *in vivo diagnostics*, which are tests that obtain information directly from the body (that is, images, as well as nonvisual readings, such as an EKG), and *in vitro diagnostics*, which are tests that gain information from bodily specimens (that is, lab tests).

Next we survey the key developments in these two fields and their role in spurring the evolution of modern hospital diagnostic units.

5.2.1.1 CLINICAL LABORATORIES

The word *pathology* literally means "the study of suffering," but it is more broadly defined as "the scientific study of the nature of disease and its causes, processes, development, and consequences."

Throughout history, medicine has looked to an array of theories to explain disease. Humorism, which explained all disease in terms of imbalances among the four bodily humors (black bile, yellow bile, phlegm, and blood), was the first widespread physical theory to compete with supernatural explanations. It influenced practice from the time of Hippocrates all the way into the nineteenth century. But because this model was not very convincing for explaining epidemics (why should everyone's humors suddenly go out of balance at the same time?), medical people sought external explanations for diseases, such as smallpox, measles, plague and cholera, that seemed to spread from one person to another. For some, this meant a return to religious explanations of disease. For others, it meant looking for environmental explanations.

The most widely accepted environmental model of infection from the middle ages into the nineteenth century was miasma theory, which held that "bad air" was responsible for disease. Because bad air was thought to be caused by poor sanitation and organic decay, miasma theory was used to advocate for sanitation and hygiene approaches to public health by innovative practitioners such as Florence Nightingale (1820–1910), the founder of modern nursing. Indeed, because Nightingale was also a skilled statistician (she is sometimes accorded the title of "founder of biostatistics"), she was able to document the impact of her hygienic practices on mortality rates of hospital patients, which she regarded as support of miasma theory.

Although miasma theory was consistent with the occurrence of epidemics, it was still not a very satisfying explanation of person-to-person transmission of disease. Consequently, starting in the Renaissance, some physicians and scientists began to speak of a germ theory of disease. For example, Venetian physician Girolamo Fracastoro (1478–1553) proposed that epidemic diseases are caused by "seminaria contagiosa," or "disease seeds," that are transmitted from one person to another. Dutch scientist Antonie van Leeuwenhoek (1632–1723), regarded as the father of microbiology, developed an improved microscope and used it to observe single-celled microorganisms for the first time. Italian entomologist Agostino Bassi (1773–1856) combined Fracastoro's theory with Leeuwenhoek's discovery by proposing that some diseases are caused by living microorganisms. To back up his theory, he demonstrated that a silkworm disease, muscarine, is caused by a fungus by infecting healthy silkworms with fungus from dead silkworms.

Although germ theory remained unproven, it led to some advances in therapy in the eighteenth and nineteenth centuries. In particular, English physician Edward Jenner (1749–1823) noted that milkmaids rarely contracted smallpox. Hypothesizing that this was because their contraction of the milder disease of cowpox had somehow made them immune, he inoculated a small boy with material from the cowpox blisters of a milkmaid. He then exposed the boy to smallpox and found that he was indeed immune. Through additional research (and tireless promotion), Jenner eventually convinced the medical community of the effectiveness of the cowpox vaccine. In 1840, the English Parliament banned *variolation* (the dangerous practice of using controlled injection of smallpox to stimulate immunity) and began providing the cowpox vaccination to the public free of charge. As a result, the practice of vaccination began well before the mainstream medical community understood and accepted germ theory.

A second important advance was the discovery by University of Glasgow surgeon Joseph Lister (1827–1912), published in 1867, that using carbolic acid to clean hands, instruments, and wounds could prevent infections (Osborne 1986). Prior to this innovation, compound fractures were tantamount to death sentences, due to the extremely high risk of sepsis. Because of this risk, most surgeons elected to amputate limbs with fractures associated with a break in the skin, even though this also posed a substantial danger of death from infection. Initial acceptance of Lister's claims was slow, but the dramatic reductions in surgical infections achieved by virtually everyone who adopted his antiseptic methods gradually won over the medical community. In little more than a decade, Lister's methods were nearly universal.

Although these advances in treatment were of vast importance to medical practice, the development with the most wide-ranging impact on medicine and public health was the convincing demonstration of germ theory by French chemist Louis Pasteur (1822–1895) and German physician Robert Koch (1843–1910). In the early 1860s, Pasteur demonstrated that microorganisms caused spoilage of beverages, such as wine and milk, and that heat killed these organisms. Subsequently, by means of his famous "Swan-necked bottle experiment," he showed that the organisms travelled through the air. Pasteur followed up these discoveries by developing sterilization (pasteurization) methods and developing the first attenuated virus vaccine (for rabies in 1885). He was honored with the Grand Croix of the Legion of Honor, France's most prestigious award, and attained a stature of secular sainthood during his lifetime. With Pasteur, medicine became irrevocably linked to laboratory science.

Koch provided additional scientific rigor for germ theory by developing a systematic process for documenting a cause-and-effect relationship between a pathogen and a disease. This involved: (1) observing that a microorganism is always present in diseased host, (2) isolating the microorganism and cultivating it in a pure culture, (3) injecting the cultivated microorganism into a healthy host and observing that the disease occurs, and (4) isolating the microorganism from the infected host and comparing with the microorganism from the original culture. Koch used his process to document the bacterial causes of anthrax, tuberculosis, and other diseases. He was awarded the Nobel Prize in Medicine in 1905 and is widely accorded the honorific title "Father of Bacteriology."

The work of Pasteur and Koch to validate, develop, and apply germ theory gave scientific support to the hygiene and sterilization practices of Nightingale and Lister. It also launched the age of vaccines (between 1885 and 1925 vaccines were developed for rabies, plague, cholera, typhoid, diphtheria, tuberculosis, and other infectious diseases) and paved the way for the development of antibiotics. (The first sulfa drugs were discovered in 1935.) Taken together, these practices for preventing bacteria-related illness were responsible for most of the nearly twofold increase in life expectancy during the twentieth century. No other scientific discovery has had such an enormous impact on medicine.

Widespread acceptance of germ theory at the end of the nineteenth century led to the establishment of laboratories in hospitals. However, prior to World War I, such clinical laboratories were small and ill-equipped, generally tucked away somewhere in the basement. Even in the newly built (in 1889), state-of-the-art Johns Hopkins hospital, the lab was only a twelve-foot-by-twelve-foot room equipped at a cost of $50 (Lindberg et al. 1984). It was thought that, although lab tests for some infectious diseases were clearly useful, most of the emerging tests of blood and urine had little diagnostic value.

This changed in the years leading up to World War I with two major developments: (a) Otto Folin (1867–1934) developed a colorimetric test of creatinine in urine in 1904 (Duboscq had invented his colorimeter in 1854, but it did not find much use in medical chemistry until the work of Folin showed its value and touched off a burst of development of colorimetric methods in clinical testing of blood and urine), and (b) Donald Van Slyke (1883–1971) developed a gas apparatus in 1914 for measuring sodium bicarbonate in a milliliter of blood, paving the way for other blood gas tests.

Military physicians learned the value of these new pathology services during the war and demanded such services from civilian hospitals upon their return. Between the 1920s and the 1950s, lab tests and assays became a routine part of the diagnostic process in hospitals. By 1926, the American College of Surgeons' accreditation standards required all hospitals to have a clinical laboratory under the direction of a physician.

Through the 1950s, most lab tests were done manually. For instance, the Malassez hemocytometer requires the technician to visually count (blood or other) cells through a microscope. As the volume of routine tests grew, innovators sought means to increase the capacity and efficiency of hospital laboratories. Looking to manufacturing and agriculture, where automation has been used to increase productivity since the industrial revolution, laboratory researchers began to develop means for automating the repetitive processes involved in labeling, preparing, analyzing, and summarizing tests on fluid and tissue samples.

One of the earliest automated testing devices was the Coulter counter, which uses an electrical charge to determine the size and number of particles in a solution. The underlying theory was developed in 1947 by American electrical engineer Wallace Coulter (1913–1998), who received a patent for the device in 1953. It replaced the tedious manual counting of cells in a hemocytometer in complete blood counts. Also, because the new device could test multiple samples and count many more cells, this automation improved accuracy as well as speed.

At nearly the same time the Coulter counter was being introduced to automate cell counts, the Technicon Corporation introduced the AutoAnalyzer to automate chemical testing of samples (Whitby 1964). By using bubbles to segment a continuous flow of a fluid (for example, serum), combining the segments with reagents, and measuring the color changes, an autoanalyzer could rapidly test a series of samples under the supervision of a single technician. Multichannel autoanalyzers, which could perform multiple tests on the same sample in parallel, soon followed. In 1959, American inventor Hans Baruch (1925–) began marketing a competing Robot Chemist, which used robotics to combine discrete samples with reagents. Unlike the continuous flow analyzers, which inject samples into a continuous stream of reagents, discrete analyzers like the Robot Chemist kept the reagents and samples entirely separate. Although the Robot Chemist was not a commercial success, discrete analyzers gradually become the dominant approach to automation of routine biochemistry tests in clinical laboratories, largely because they make more efficient use of samples and reagents.

In the latter half of the twentieth century, as automation technology continued to increase the speed and efficiency of routine blood and urine tests, scientific breakthroughs increased the scope and sensitivity of tests. Electron microscopes, invented in the 1930s, began to find diagnostic use in the clinical laboratory in the 1960s, beginning with differential diagnosis of smallpox (Long et al. 1970).

But the major medical revolution, whose impact at the end of the twentieth century is comparable to those of germ theory and X-rays at the end of the nineteenth century, occurred in genetics. Although gene theory dates back to the pea plant experiments of Gregor Mendel (1822–1884) in the mid-seventeenth century, the modern era of genetics began with the discovery of the double helix structure of DNA by James Watson (1928–) and Francis Crick (1916–2004). In 1977, Frederick Sanger (1918–) and Walter Gilbert (1932–) independently devised methods for determining the order of bases in a strand of DNA. This led to high-speed sequencing machines, which were used in the Human Genome Project to map (almost) the full human genome between 1990 and 2003 (U.S. Department of Energy 2009).

Although the popular press has focused on applications in forensics and genetic engineering, the genetics revolution has also had important implications for clinical laboratories. Four applications of genetic testing are

---

- **Post-symptomatic diagnosis**—Use of a genetic test to confirm that symptoms are due to a genetically linked disease (for example, confirming that a patient's mental impairment is due to Fragile X syndrome).

- **Presymptomatic diagnosis**—Use of a genetic test to identify a victim of a genetic condition with delayed symptoms (for example, Huntington's disease) (McPherson 2006).

- **Pharmacogenetics**—Use of a genetic test to ascertain the effectiveness of a particular course of therapy (for example, a genomic test of whether a breast cancer is estrogen receptor positive is used to determine whether or not a hormone suppression treatment is likely to be effective).

- **Risk prediction**—Use of a genetic test to evaluate risks of diseases that have been identified to have statistical correlations with genetic conditions (for example, elevated risk of breast or ovarian cancer).

The medical, social, and ethical implications of genetic testing go far beyond this brief history of the clinical laboratory. But, from the perspective of lab operations, the implication is that the volume of tests will continue to grow, and lab technology will continue to increase in sophistication. Moreover, as the laboratory becomes an even more central element of the hospital than it already is, operational efficiency and effectiveness of the lab will become ever more critical to hospital success.

Table 5.1   Milestones in Clinical Laboratory Science and Practice

Date	Development or Discovery
c. 400 BCE	Greek physician Hippocrates categorizes diseases and advocates careful observation and documentation in their study.
c. 300 BCE	Greek physician Herophilos performs first systematic dissections of human cadavers.
c. 1130	Arabian physician Avenzoar discovers that scabies is caused by a parasite, causing him to reject the bodily humors theory of disease.
1546	Venetian physician Girolamo Fracastoro proposes that epidemic diseases are caused by spores or "disease seeds."
1628	English physician William Harvey publishes his discovery that blood circulates due to pumping by the heart, marking the beginning of an era of mechanical explanations of bodily functions and disease.
1676	Dutch merchant and scientist Antonie van Leeuwenhoek observes single-celled organisms using his improved version of the microscope.

Date	Development or Discovery
1761	Italian anatomist Giovanni Battista Morgagni publishes his opus *De Sedibus*, which introduced the organ as the seat of disease, laying the foundation for the field of anatomical pathology.
1796	English physician Edward Jenner demonstrates that exposure to cowpox makes humans immune to smallpox.
1827	English physician Richard Bright establishes connection between albumin in urine and kidney disease, launching scientific urinalysis as a practical diagnostic tool.
1835	Lombardi entomologist Agostino Bassi concludes on the basis of experiments that the silkworm disease muscardine is caused by living microorganisms. He speculates that some human diseases (measles, syphilis, plague) have similar causes.
1839	German physiologist Theodor Schwann proposes that cells are the basic unit of life, initiating the field of histology.
1843	French pathologist Gabriel Andral publishes *Essai d'Hématologie Pathologique* describing various connections between pathology and blood chemistry.
1845	French physician Alfred Francois Donné, English physician John Hughes Bennett, and German physician Rudolpf Virchow independently use microscopy to identify leukemia as a blood disorder, helping to establish the use of cellular pathology in diagnosing disease.
1847	Ignaz Semmelweiss at Vienna General Hospital reduces infection rates with chlorinated water.
1866	Austrian priest Gregor Mendel publishes paper on inheritance of traits in pea plants, establishing the foundation for the field of genetics.
1867	University of Glasgow surgeon Joseph Lister demonstrates that sterilizing wounds and instruments in carbolic acid reduces postoperative infections.
1870	Optician Jules Duboscq develops the Duboscq colorimeter, which eventually becomes standard laboratory equipment for measuring concentrations of solutions.
1873	French scientist Louis-Charles Malassez invents the hemocytometer for counting blood cells, which is later used to count other types of cells.
1878	French scientist Louis Pasteur presents the germ theory of disease to the French Academy of Medicine.
1878	While still a medical student, German physician Paul Ehrlich develops methods for selectively staining different kinds of cells, making it possible to diagnose many hematologic disorders.
1879	German bacteriologist Robert Koch proposes postulates for demonstrating a causal relationship between a microbe and a disease.

Table 5.1   Milestones in Clinical Laboratory Science and Practice

Date	Development or Discovery
1887	While working as an assistant in Robert Koch's laboratory, German bacteriologist Richard Julius Petri invents the Petri dish for growing bacteria on a solid surface under sterile conditions.
1889	Johns Hopkins Hospital opens as the first hospital built with a (very small) clinical laboratory.
1896	French physician Georges-Fernand Widal develops a serological test for typhoid fever.
1901	Austrian physician and biologist Karl Landsteiner identifies blood groups A, B, and C (changed to O). One year later, the AB category was added.
1904	Swedish born American biochemist Otto Folin develops colorimetric method for measuring creatinine in urine.
1906	German bacteriologist August von Wassermann develops test for syphilis.
1907	Austrian pediatrician Clemens von Pirquet introduces skin test for TB.
1914	American chemist Donald Van Slyke invents the Van Slyke volumetric gas apparatus to measure concentration of sodium bicarbonate in a milliliter of blood; it soon becomes standard equipment in clinical laboratories.
1919	English chemist Francis William Aston invents the mass spectrometer.
1931	Electron microscope constructed by German scientists Max Knoll and Ernst Ruska.
1936	Cook County Hospital in Chicago establishes the first blood bank in the United States.
1939	Austrian physician and biologist Karl Landsteiner identifies Rh factor in blood.
1950	American physicist Rosslyn Yalow and physician Solomon Berson develop radioimmunoassay, which can detect tiny concentrations of a substance in blood.
1953	American biologist James Watson and English physicist Francis Crick propose double helix model of DNA.
1953	American engineer Wallace Coulter patents a device for counting microscopic particles (for example, blood cells) in fluids, launching automated hematology.
1954	Austrian chemist Alan Walsh develops the atomic absorption spectrometer for determining concentrations of metals in liquid (for example, lead in blood).
1957	Technicon introduces the first autoanalyzer, invented by American biochemist Leonard Skeggs, which automates chemical analysis of blood and urine samples.
1959	Robot Chemist, the first discrete analyzer, is developed by American inventory Hans Baruch.

Date	Development or Discovery
1968	First random access analyzer introduced by DuPont.
1971	El Camino Hospital in California partners with Lockheed to install first computer-aided medical information system, which is a precursor to computerized physician order entry (CPOE) systems.
1977	English biochemist Frederick Sanger and American microbiologist Walter Gilbert (independently) develop method for sequencing DNA molecules.
1981	German physicist Gerd Binnig and Swiss physicist Heinrich Rohrer develop the scanning tunneling microscope.
1983	American biochemist Kary Mullis develops polymerase chain reaction (PCR) technique for amplifying DNA sequences, which allows genetic testing from small samples.
1983	Genetic marker found for Huntington's disease using recombinant DNA techniques.
1985	Genetic marker for cystic fibrosis discovered.
1992	U.S. Department of Health and Human Services issues regulations that require laboratories to have quality assurance and quality control programs in place to receive certification.
2003	Human Genome Project announces a nearly complete map of the human genome.

5.2.1.2 IMAGING UNITS

For thousands of years, medicine was practiced with no way to diagnose internal medical problems other than cutting open the patient. Because this generally did more harm than good, doctors undoubtedly dreamed of a way to see into the human body without harming it. But virtually no one could foresee this as a practical reality. Indeed, when President James Garfield was shot in the summer of 1881, it was sound, not light, that the medical team turned to in a desperate attempt to find the bullet (Kevles 1998). While the President clung to life for an anxious 80 days, Alexander Graham Bell devised a crude metal detector using induction technology developed for the telephone. Sadly, the device did not locate the bullet (probably because of static caused by the metal bed), and the President died. Only decades later would Bell's vision of "hearing" solid objects be realized in sonar and ultrasound technology.

But long before the sonic approach became a practical option for exploring the interior of the human body, the dream of a visual method became a reality via a serendipitous discovery. On November 8, 1895, German physicist Wilhelm Conrad Röntgen (1845–1923) was experimenting with an induction coil in a partially evacuated tube. Even though the tube was covered with cardboard to prevent light from escaping,

Röntgen noticed that passing a charge through the tube caused a phosphorescent (barium platinocyanide) screen across the room to shimmer. He speculated that this was the result of a new type of radiation, which he temporarily labeled "X-rays" (because "x" represents an unknown in mathematics).

Having observed that the rays penetrated cardboard, Röntgen began a series of experiments to see what stopped them. Almost immediately, he tried his own hand and observed that not only did the rays pass through his hand, they showed a contrast between his dense bones and less dense flesh. Less than two weeks after his initial discovery, he replaced the phosphorescent screen with a photographic plate and, after 30 minutes of exposure, produced the first internal image of the human body, a radiograph of his wife's hand (Assmus 1995).

Almost never has technology advanced from basic discovery to practical application so quickly. Within a month of Röntgen's announcement of his discovery on December 28, 1895, physicians were using X-rays to locate bullets in human flesh and fractures in bones. Within a year, the Glasgow Royal Infirmary had established a Radiology Department. Within 10 years, almost all hospitals had X-ray equipment, and many had X-ray Departments. A popular craze also ensued, in which X-rays were featured in magic acts, coin-operated novelty machines, and shoe-fitting equipment. These frivolous uses of X-rays, along with cavalier use of radioactive substances as patent medicines, soon fizzled as the health risks of radiation became known. In the military, X-rays were used for medical purposes in the field in the Boer War (1899–1902) on an experimental basis and achieved widespread use in World War I (1914–1918).

Tragically, when President William McKinley was shot twice by an anarchist at the Pan-American Exhibition in Buffalo on September 5, 1901, the new imaging technology did not lead to a different outcome from that in the Garfield assassination 20 years earlier. Even though an X-ray machine was on display near the scene of the shooting, the physicians who treated McKinley were evidently unfamiliar or uncomfortable with it and did not try to use it. Unable to find one of the bullets surgically, they closed up the president with the bullet still inside. Shortly afterward, as the president lay recuperating in a private home (not a hospital), Thomas Edison rushed an X-ray machine to him. But again the doctors declined to use it (Kevles 1998). One week after the shooting, McKinley died of infection, sparking endless debate about whether an X-ray might have saved him.[2]

But despite this early and visible lack of use, X-ray technology and its imaging successors evolved steadily into a fixture of the medical system during the twentieth century. The progress of diagnostic imaging since the discovery of X-rays can be divided into two phases. Prior to World War II, developments focused on improving conventional radiography, in which X-rays are used to produce a photographic image on a single piece of film. Since World War II, developments have concentrated on other, more precise but less harmful, mechanisms for generating images and computer integration of data to produce detailed 3D images.

An important advance in X-ray technology was the development in 1913 of an improved X-ray tube that made use of a tungsten filament in a vacuum tube by American William Coolidge (1873–1975) of General Electric. Because it produced a stable, controllable beam, X-ray machines using the Coolidge tube instead of the Crookes tube used by Röntgen were easier to operate, longer lived, and capable of producing sharper images. Coolidge tubes are still used to generate X-rays in modern imaging equipment.

A second early advance in X-ray diagnostics was the use of contrast agents. This technology got its start in 1897, when Walter Cannon (1871–1945), a medical student at Harvard University, demonstrated that bismuth salts are opaque to X-rays and used them to study the digestive tract. This innovation led to use of other radiocontrast agents (such as barium and iodine) to facilitate imaging of soft tissue organs.

For the most part, medical imaging prior to World War II was done by passing X-rays through the body to produce a photographic image on a single piece of film. The resulting 2D projections through the body were fine for viewing hard structures, such as bones and teeth, but were less effective for viewing soft organs. To create sectional images of these 3D structures, Italian radiologist Alessandro Vallebona developed the tomography method of moving the X-ray source and film in opposite directions during exposure to pick out structures in the focal plane. But the mechanics of motion are complex, and the quality of the images is limited in manual tomography. So the real impact of this approach awaited the advent of the computer, which made it possible to synthesize multiple cross-sectional X-ray views into a 3D image of an internal structure. Computerized Axial Tomography (CAT or CT) was invented independently in 1972 by British engineer Godfrey Hounsfield (1919–2004) and South African physicist Allan Cormack (1924–1988). CT scans have proven useful in evaluating the brain, neck, spine, chest, abdomen, pelvis, and sinuses, where 3D images make it possible to diagnose conditions that cannot be detected by 2D images.

A major drawback to X-ray technology, whether used in conventional radiology or CT, is that radiation can cause irreparable damage to cells and tissues. Early X-ray equipment required massive doses of X-rays and long exposure times to produce images. For instance, a head X-ray could take 11 minutes and require 50 times the dosage used in a modern X-ray that requires milliseconds. Because controlling and recording X-rays were crudely done, early radiographs could only distinguish hard objects (bones, teeth) from soft objects (tissue). But advances in control of X-ray levels, recording sensitivity, and contrast agents made it increasingly possible to distinguish more subtle density differences, and thereby create images of more internal structures (Hessenbruch 2002). Table 5.2 summarizes major advances and the steady progression of body parts that have become amenable to imaging.

Although dosages have been greatly reduced over the years, to levels well below that of background radiation from the sun, there may still be risks (for example, to unborn fetuses). So technologies that avoid X-rays altogether offer a potential safety benefit, as well as the possibility of greater resolution under certain conditions. The two non-X-ray technologies currently used for imaging are Magnetic Resonance Imaging (MRI) and ultrasound.

MRI has its roots in a scientific discovery from the 1930s. Felix Bloch (1905–1983), working at Stanford University, and Edward Purcell (1912–1997), from Harvard University, found that when certain nuclei are placed in a magnetic field, they absorb energy in the radio frequency range of the electromagnetic spectrum, and they re-emit this energy when the nuclei transfer to their original state. For decades, this nuclear magnetic resonance (NMR) technology was used to characterize the chemical structure of substances but saw only limited attempts at biological or medical use.

Magnetic resonance became an imaging technology in 1973 when Paul Lauterbur (1912–1997), a physicist at Stonybrook University, developed a technique for using gradients in the magnetic field to produce a two-dimensional image. Later in the 1970s, Peter Mansfield (1933–), a physicist from Nottingham University, worked out a mathematical method for efficiently producing an image from these gradient signals. The first practical MRI scanners appeared in the 1980s, and use of the technology expanded rapidly after that. There are currently more than 20,000 MRI scanners in use around the world (Institute of Physics 2009).

Another non-X-ray imaging technology that became common in the latter half of the twentieth century is ultrasound. This technology had its roots in sonar technology, which measures echoes of high-frequency sound waves. Sonar was introduced in World War I and refined as a practical tool for detecting objects underwater during World War II. In the 1940s and 1950s, researchers adapted ultrasonic methods for medical imaging purposes. Significantly, Scottish gynecologist Ian Donald (1910–1987) developed a method for creating images of dense masses (such as cysts) within less dense tissue. In 1957, Donald developed the first practical ultrasound scanner and used it to monitor unborn fetuses, an application that has since become standard obstetric practice.

The history of medical diagnostic technology, in the clinical laboratory and the imaging unit, reads like a veritable who's who of Nobel Prize winners. Indeed, the first physics prize, awarded in 1901, went to Wilhelm Röntgen for his work on X-rays. Since that time, many of the innovators in medical diagnostics have been recognized with prizes in physics, chemistry, and medicine.

Not surprisingly, the intensity of competition to develop new medical technologies has led to a number of controversies concerning precedence and credit. Indeed, that first physics prize that went to Röntgen was hotly contested by Hungarian physicist Phillipp Lenard, who had developed the basic apparatus and experimental setup used by Röntgen (Eisenberg 1993). Even though Lenard received the Nobel himself for his work on cathode rays, he continued to criticize Röntgen. But he undermined his credibility when, as chief of physics under Hitler, he also criticized the physics of Albert Einstein, which inadvertently hindered Nazi efforts to develop an atomic weapon.

More than a century later, when Paul Lauterbur and Peter Mansfield were recognized with the 2003 Nobel Prize in Medicine for development of MRI, American physician/inventor Raymond Damadian was similarly incensed. Damadian published a paper in 1971 describing how nuclear magnetic resonance can be used to distinguish between normal and cancerous tissue, received the first MRI patent for his scanning device in 1974, and produced the first MRI scan of the human body in 1977. Yet he was overlooked by the Nobel Committee, to his very public (full-page ads in prominent newspapers) chagrin (Judson 2003).

The many Nobel Prizes, as well as the controversies, are indicators of just how important advances in diagnostic technology have been. In addition to being at the center of scientific progress, these developments have revolutionized medicine. Indeed, just as advances in infection control in the nineteenth century shifted the focus of medicine from the home bedside to the hospital room, advances in diagnostic technologies promoted a further shift from the hospital room to the laboratory.

At the turn of the twentieth century, diagnostic units were experimental afterthoughts in cramped basement quarters that had at best a modest impact on patient care. By the beginning of the twenty-first century, the diagnostic units had become the brain of the hospital, in which the leading edge of science was applied to the care of virtually every patient. This shift has steadily increased the volume and complexity of the work done in the imaging units. It has also increased the reliance of the other units of the hospital on the ancillary services provided by the laboratory and imaging units. Consequently, operational efficiency of these units is not only important to their effectiveness, but vital to the hospital as a whole.

Table 5.2   Milestones in Medical Diagnostic Imaging

Date	Development or Discovery
1761	Austrian physician Leopold Auenbrugger develops diagnostic percussion (chest tapping) methods for evaluating internal organs.
1816	French physician Rene' Laennec invents stethoscope.
1847	English mathematician and engineer Charles Babbage invents ophthalmoscope, which enables viewing of the interior of the eye. German physician Hermann von Helmholtz independently reinvents the ophthalmoscope in 1851.
1891	Austrian physician Samuel Siegfried Karl Ritter von Basch invents the sphygmomanometer for measuring blood pressure.
1895	German physicist Wilhelm Conrad Röntgen discovers X-rays and uses them to produce the first X-ray picture of the body (his wife's hand).

Date	Development or Discovery
1897	American physiologist Walter Cannon uses heavy metal salts to create X-rays of the digestive tract, launching the use of contrast agents in imaging.
1898	Polish physicist Marie Curie and her French physicist husband Pierre isolate the first radioactive isotopes.
1901	Dutch physician/physicist Willem Einthoven invents electrocardiograph (EKG).
1913	American physicist William Coolidge invents the hot cathode X-ray tube, which produces predictable amounts of radiation and sharper images.
1927	Portuguese physician Egas Moniz develops technique of angiography, which creates images of blood vessels by injecting a contrast agent into them.
1929	German physician Werner Forssmann performs first cardiac catheterization—on himself!
1934	Irène and Frédéric Joliot-Curie discover how to produce artificial radioisotopes, providing a source of material for nuclear medicine applications.
1955	X-ray Image Intensifier-Television units allow dynamic X-ray imaging of beating heart and its blood vessels.
1957	South African-born physician Basil Hirschowitz pioneers fiber endoscopy at the University of Michigan.
1957	Scottish physician Ian Donald develops ultrasound imaging. It finds use in obstetric examinations within a year.
1958	American cardiologist Mason Sones develops method for selective imaging of the heart via the diagnostic coronary angiogram that uses a catheter to introduce a contrast agent into the coronary artery.
1967	Center for Genomics Research in France introduces first dedicated mammography machine, but mammography does not become commonplace until the early 1970s when screen/film machines are introduced.
1972	British engineer Godfrey Hounsfield builds the first computed tomography (CT) scanning machine.
1973	Chemist Paul Lauterbur at SUNY, Stony Brook, produces the first Nuclear Magnetic Resonance (NMR) image.
1979	German computer scientist Heinz Lamke publishes a paper on applied image processing and computer graphic methods that describes a modern picture archiving and communication system (PACS).
1980	British scientist Paul Lauterbur develops Magnetic Resonance Imaging (MRI), used to create image of the brain.
1982	First large-scale installation of a PACS at University of Kansas.

Date	Development or Discovery
1985	Scientists at the University of California develop Clinical Positron Emission Tomography (PET) scanning.
1987	French dentist Francis Mouyen develops digital X-ray system using CCD-based technology for dentistry.
1989	Spiral CT allows fast-volume scanning of an entire organ during a single, short patient breath hold of 20 to 30 seconds.
1990	Full-body MRI scanners are introduced into hospitals.
1992	First entirely filmless large-scale Radiology Department is opened in the Danube Hospital in Vienna.
1993	Echo Planar MR Imaging (EPI) enables functional imaging of the brain and early detection of acute stroke.
1993	Open MRI Systems developed to allow MR scanning of claustrophobic or obese patients who cannot tolerate conventional MR imaging in a close bore system.

5.2.2 Physical Assets

The hospital of the early twenty-first century is very different from the hospital of the early twentieth century in terms of physical equipment. We noted earlier that the most modern hospital of its day, the Johns Hopkins Hospital, completed in 1889, had only a tiny lab with a few dollars of equipment in it. At the time, having a lab at all was distinctive. Indeed, for the first two decades of the twentieth century, the diagnostics equipment of a hospital generally consisted of little more than some microscopes and an X-ray machine.

But accelerating technological innovation in the twentieth century, illustrated in Tables 5.1 and 5.2, rapidly changed this. As an ever-expanding array of diagnostic equipment became available, hospital laboratories grew and multiplied. Whereas hospitals once had at most a single lab, larger hospitals now have multiple labs (for example, a dedicated lab in the ED in addition to the general hospital lab) and distributed diagnostic equipment (for example, a CT scanner in the ED or imaging units that support image directed surgery in the operating room, or OR). The trend toward more sophisticated, more automated, and more ubiquitous diagnostic technology in the hospital is likely to continue for the foreseeable future.

Here we provide an inventory of the configuration and equipment of a typical clinical laboratory and a typical Radiology Department in a large hospital. We recognize that these are likely to evolve rapidly with the advance of technology and the ever-deepening role of diagnostic testing in the health care process.

5.2.2.1 CLINICAL LABORATORY DEPARTMENT

The primary function of a clinical laboratory (Pathology Department) of a hospital is to support clinicians in the diagnosis, treatment, and prevention of disease by conducting bacteriologic, biochemical, histologic, serologic, and cytologic tests. The clinical laboratory is also usually responsible for the blood bank and the morgue.

The laboratory services of the clinical laboratory can be divided into two main categories, which generally correspond to divisions within the department:

- **Clinical Pathology**—This field is concerned with the diagnosis of disease via laboratory testing of bodily fluids (such as blood and urine) and tissues. Clinical Pathology is divided into subspecialties that reflect the disciplines on which the tests are based: these include Chemical Pathology (also called Clinical Chemistry), Hematopathology, Clinical Microbiology, Cytogenetics, and Molecular Genetics Pathology.

- **Anatomical Pathology**—This field is concerned with the diagnosis of disease through examination of tissue samples and whole bodies (autopsy) using gross (visual), microscopic, chemical, immunologic, and molecular analysis. Anatomical Pathology is divided into subspecialties that reflect the source or type of tissue sample being examined: the main ones are Surgical Pathology, Cytopathology, and Forensic Pathology.

Hospital laboratories have a wide and varying range of equipment in them, making a comprehensive or standard list impossible. But common items found in most laboratories include the following.

Manual laboratory equipment:

- Autoclaves
- Centrifuges
- Cold storage equipment
- Cutting tools
- Fluid handling tools
- Incubators
- Microscopes (light and electron)
- Mixing equipment
- Slides
- Weighing equipment

Automated laboratory equipment:

- **Routine biochemistry analyzers**—Automatically conduct a range of chemical tests, such as measuring blood glucose level.

- **Immuno-based analyzers**—Use reaction of antibodies to measure low concentrations of a substance in a biological liquid as done, for example, in detecting HIV in blood.

- **Cell counters**—Count cell populations in blood samples (for example, red and white blood cell counts).

- **Coagulometers**—Measure the ability of blood to clot.

- **Tissue processors**—Fixate and section tissues into thin films for slides.

- **Autostainers**—Apply dye to tissue to bring out various cellular components.

- **Automated immunohistochemistry platforms**—Automate major portions of the sample preparation, analysis, and interpretation process.

5.2.2.2 IMAGING DEPARTMENT

The Imaging (Radiology) Department supports clinicians in the diagnosis and treatment of disease by providing images of bodily structures, ranging from cellular-level tissue to entire body scans. A wide, and steadily expanding, array of technologies is used to generate these images. Basic categories of equipment include

- **Conventional X-ray equipment**—All hospitals have various types of X-ray machines. Some are portable (even handheld), whereas others are stationary units. Some are dedicated to particular parts of the body (for example, mammography or vascular X-ray units). In addition to being located within the Imaging Department, X-ray equipment is often found elsewhere (for example, in the ED) in the hospital.

- **CT scanner**—Although based on traditional X-ray technology, CT uses computer algorithms to combine radiographic data into cross-sectional images of organs. Specialized CT scanners for generating high-resolution images or specific body parts (for example, coronary angiography) are common in larger hospitals.

- **MRI scanner**—Among the most expensive imaging devices, magnetic resonance imaging uses a magnetic field and radio waves to generate an image of soft or hard tissue. Various types of MRI scanners exist, including traditional (tunnel) scanners, short-bore scanners, open scanners, and stand-up scanners. The trade-off is one of accuracy (closed tunnels yield more precise results) versus comfort (less enclosure makes the test easier to tolerate).

- **Ultrasound equipment**—Scanners use high-frequency sonic waves to generate images. This can include conventional 2D scanners, which generate a flat cross-sectional image, 3D scanners that translate the sound wave into a three-dimensional image, 4D scanners that generate 3D images moving over time, and Doppler ultrasound scanners that evaluate blood velocity as it flows through the body.

- **Nuclear medicine equipment**—Includes PET, single photon emission computed tomography (SPECT), and other technologies that use radiocontrast agents to image flows (for example, blood) and organs.

Depending on its size, the Imaging (Radiology) Department may be divided into divisions corresponding to clinical focus (for example, abdominal, breast, cardiothoracic, musculoskeletal, neuro, vascular), patient focus (for example, pediatric), or technology (CT, MRI, ultrasound). The location and configuration of the imaging equipment will follow the divisional structure of the department.

5.2.3 Human Assets

5.2.3.1 PATHOLOGY DEPARTMENT

Hospitals generally divide laboratories into Clinical and Anatomical Pathology, either by creating two departments or by having two divisions within a single department. Laboratory operations are often further separated by specialty (for example, chemistry, hematology, microbiology) or patient type (for example, outpatients, inpatients, ED patients). Others centralize laboratory operations for the entire hospital or multihospital medical system. Staffing and organizational structure will vary accordingly. However, common personnel within most clinical labs include

- **Director**—The Pathology Department is headed by a director or chair who is a licensed physician specializing in pathology (that is, a pathologist) and is certified by the American Board of Pathology.

- **Scientists**—Large hospital laboratories typically employ MD or PhD trained pathologists, clinical biologists, microbiologists, and biochemists who head/staff specific labs within the Pathology Department.

- **Residents**—Most teaching hospitals offer residencies in pathology; some offer residencies in clinical microbiology. Residents in these programs are medical school graduates who participate in clinical case management (that is, oversight of testing and interpretation of patient samples) as well as research studies.

- **Pathology assistants**—Pathology assistants work under the supervision of anatomical pathologists and do all the work leading up to, but not including, diagnosis. They often require a master's degree.

- **Medical technologists and technicians**—The bulk of the sample preparation, testing, and result summarization in clinical labs is carried out by medical technologists (who generally have a four-year BS degree) and medical technicians (who generally have a two-year AS degree). The analogs for Anatomical Pathology labs are *histotechnologists* (who prepare tissue samples) and *cytotechnologists* (who study cells), both of whom generally require a four-year degree. Some states require licensing of these laboratory personnel, whereas many hospitals also require them to be certified by a professional society.

- **Phlebotomists**—Although requests for tests involving tissues typically arrive with specimens (for example, from a biopsy), requests for tests involving bodily fluids often require the lab to collect the needed specimens. Clinical laboratories employ phlebotomists who specialize in the collection of blood and other bodily fluids, both from outpatients who come to the lab and from inpatients who are visited in their rooms. Phlebotomists typically complete a training course at a community college or trade school and are certified by one of several professional organizations.

- **Transcriptionists**—Most labs employ medical transcriptionists to translate dictated reports by pathologists into written reports for the requesting clinicians.

- **Administrative staff**—Depending on the size of the department, the director will be supported by managers of various administrative units, such as Finance, Information Systems, and so on. These are generally headed by nonmedical staff and employ clerical personnel.

5.2.3.2 Imaging Department

The size and complexity of Imaging Departments vary greatly between hospitals. A teaching/research hospital with the most advanced medical technology will often have a multidivisional, multilocation Radiology or Imaging Department, with a staff structure to match. A small community hospital may offer only basic X-ray and other imaging services through a single organizational unit. Nevertheless, common personnel in an Imaging Department include

- **Director**—The Imaging or Radiology Department is headed by a director or chair, who is a licensed physician specializing in radiology and is certified by the American Board of Radiology (or the American Board of Osteopathic Radiology).

- **Radiologists**—Images are evaluated by radiologists (board-certified physicians who have completed a residency in Radiology). Many radiologists have different anatomical specialties (for example, breast imaging, cardiovascular radiology, abdominal radiology, gastrointestinal radiology, musculoskeletal radiology, neuroradiology, head and neck radiology) or functional specialties (for example, nuclear medicine, emergency radiology, pediatric radiology).

- **Radiologist assistants**—High-level radiologic technologists who work under the supervision of a radiologist to perform examinations, make judgments about image quality, and take part in patient management and evaluation are called radiologist assistants. A relatively new profession, radiologist assistants must generally have a bachelor's degree and are increasingly expected to have a master's degree. They must also complete a clinical internship and be certified by the American Registry of Radiologic Technologists.

- **Radiologic technologists**—The primary operators of radiologic equipment are radiologic technologists. These technologists generally have a two-year degree and certification from the American Registry of Radiologic Technologists. Individual certification for radiologic specialties (CT, MRI, ultrasound, mammography, bone densitometry) is usually required to operate equipment beyond basic X-ray machines.

- **Radiological nurses**—Larger Radiology Departments may employ radiological nurses who assist with patient examinations, help patients during testing and recuperation, and record findings. Like all nurses, radiological nurses must graduate from an accredited nursing school and pass a licensing exam.

- **Administrative staff**—Beyond the clinical staff, Radiology Departments employ a range of administrative managers and staff members. These people perform a range of functions including billing, engineering services, computing services, purchasing, finance, quality assurance, and other important activities.

5.2.4 Flows

5.2.4.1 CLINICAL LABORATORY DEPARTMENT

Labs are high-volume production environments. Hospitals typically draw blood from inpatients on a daily basis. Add to this other inpatient tests, outpatient tests, and samples from the OR, and the clinical lab is a busy place. Furthermore, because the lab conducts a range of tests, there are many routings that samples can follow. But at a high level, a flow through a typical clinical lab can be depicted as shown in Exhibit 5.1 and consists of the following steps:

1. **Request**—A physician orders a test via a paper form or (increasingly) a computer entry. The order may be for a single test or for a schedule of tests (for example, daily blood work for an inpatient). This creates an entry in the laboratory database that specifies the patient, test, and other particulars (for example, urgency level and where to send results).

2. **Collection**—For blood and other bodily fluid samples, laboratory phlebotomists often collect the specimens from patients, in hospital rooms, or at other collection points in the hospital (which may not be contiguous with the laboratory itself). In other settings (for example, biopsies from the OR), collection is conducted by people outside the lab. In either case, the collection tubes are placed in plastic bags, along with the order form that requested the test, and are sent to the lab. This often occurs in batches, such as when a phlebotomist collects blood samples from an entire section before sending them to the lab.

3. **Labeling**—In most hospitals, labels that contain the patient name, a laboratory number, and a bar code label are printed in advance and are attached to the specimen tubes by the phlebotomists at the patient's bedside. This coding connects the specimens to their request records in the database, which are used to specify which tests are to be done and later to record results.

4. **Transportation to Lab**—Labeled samples are physically sent to the lab, which may be on- or offsite, depending on the hospital and the desired test. Because phlebotomists typically collect samples from many patients in succession (either during rounds to patient rooms or at walk-in collection sites), samples are frequently sent to the lab in batches. In some hospitals, central collection points are placed strategically among the nursing units, and runners periodically bring samples from the collection points to the lab.

5. **Preparation**—Depending on the test, the raw specimen may require preparation. For example, blood that is destined for a variety of tests is typically centrifuged into serum and clot. Tissue samples sent for rapid diagnosis require visual inspection ("grossing"), freezing, slicing, and staining for analysis in a microscope.

6. **Analysis**—Once prepared, the specimens undergo one or more tests. Many of these tests are carried out by automatic analyzers that process the specimen and return results. For example, automated cell counters count red blood cells, white blood cells, and platelets in a sample of blood. A coagulometer performs tests of the ability of blood to clot. Some testers perform only a single test, whereas others can perform multiple functions. Some systems use robotic handlers, which minimize the amount of human intervention needed during testing and reduce the chance of contamination. Many automated analyzers process samples in batches to increase their capacity.

7. **Interpretation**—No matter how highly automated the testing equipment is, a medical professional must verify the results. In routine settings (for example, standard blood assays), this may consist only of overseeing a monitoring software program. In more complex settings (for example, assessing a tumor biopsy), it may involve detailed examination by a highly trained pathologist.

8. **Reporting**—The results of the test interpretation, whether this consists of a set of simple numeric values placed in context of population norms or a detailed pathology report, is communicated to the requesting physician. Traditionally, this was done by means of a paper report. But in most clinical laboratories, it is now done electronically by attaching the report to the database record created by the initial request.

9. **Archiving**—In addition to recording the result of the test in an information system, a portion of the physical sample may be retained for possible retest or for future research. Many universities and other institutions are building up vast tissue banks of frozen specimens for research purposes.

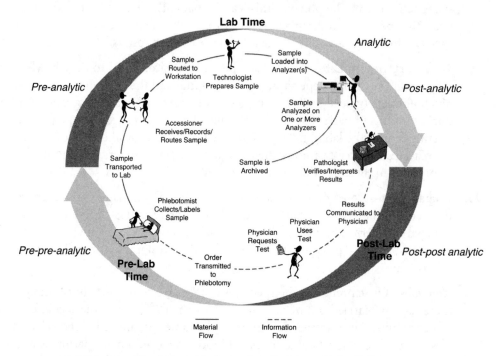

Exhibit 5.1   Physical and information flow in a clinical laboratory.

We can aggregate these steps into five stages: *pre-preanalytic* (steps before the sample reaches the lab), *preanalytic* (steps inside the lab before testing begins), *analytic* (actual testing steps), *postanalytic* (steps after testing inside the lab) and *post-postanalytic* (steps outside the lab after testing). This breakdown is commonly used in the literature on clinical laboratory management to distinguish points of major handoffs. A less detailed breakdown of the flow shown in Exhibit 5.1 is to divide total turnaround time (TAT) for a test into *prelaboratory time* (from order of test by physician to receipt of sample by laboratory), *laboratory time* (from receipt of sample to generation of results), and *postlaboratory time* (from generation of results to receipt of report by requesting physician).

This breakdown highlights geographic and functional differences in the processes that generate test results.

Of course, depending on the laboratory, there may be more steps inside the steps shown in Exhibit 5.1. For example, sample preparation may involve *aliquoting* (division into parts) and relabeling samples. Analysis on an automated analyzer may involve reagent preparation, system calibration, programming, and other tasks. We will subsume these lower-level tasks into the five steps of Exhibit 5.1. But, when performing a process flow analysis of a diagnostic unit, it is important to call out these details, because they may present opportunities for improvements.

The flow of work into most labs is uneven. Some of this fluctuation is unpredictable, but some follows a regular pattern. For instance, an early morning peak results from phlebotomists collecting samples during a morning run to allow blood count and chemistry tests to be completed in time for attending physicians' morning rounds. An afternoon peak may be caused by specimen deliveries from private physicians' offices after they close. Many hospitals have bursts of bed availabilities at shift changes (for incentive reasons described in Chapter 3), which in turn create bursts of patient admissions and attending lab orders.

To provide timely turnaround in the face of an ongoing and fluctuating workload, many hospital laboratories operate 24 hours a day, 7 days a week.

5.2.4.2 IMAGING DEPARTMENT

Flows in Imaging Departments are logically similar to those in clinical laboratories. In both settings, information is obtained from patients, analyzed, and converted into a report that is sent to the requesting physician. However, the flows differ in one important regard: patient contact. For laboratory tests, all that is needed from a patient is a specimen, which can be collected remotely in a hospital room, clinic, physician's office, or even by the patient himself at home. With a few exceptions (for example, portable X-ray and ultrasound units), patients must generally come to a central location to be scanned to produce images. Because of this, most imaging exams are scheduled, whereas most laboratory tests are not.

The basic flows associated with a stationary scanning unit can be depicted schematically as shown in Exhibit 5.2. The main steps are

1. **Scheduling**—Although occasionally a patient requests an imaging exam directly, physicians request most images. These can be for inpatients, outpatients or patients in the ED. For inpatients and ED patients, who are already in the hospital, the request goes directly to the imaging unit, where a scheduler either selects an exam time or puts the patients on a list to be seen when the scanning unit becomes available. For outpatients, who must return to the hospital for their exams, the scheduling process involves negotiation with the patient to find

an acceptable time. Because there are many types of patients and constraints involved, scheduling is a complex process. But, because time spent waiting on the schedule is the largest source of delay in getting an image for most patients, it is a particularly important one.

2. **Scanning**—The actual imaging process can be labeled scanning, whether the image is produced via X-rays, magnetic resonance, or other technologies. In addition to production of the image, this step involves any setup (for example, preparing/positioning the patient and adjusting the equipment) or wrap-up (for example, assisting the patient out of the scanner) procedures that are part of the examination.

3. **Reading**—After images are produced, they are sent, as physical films or digital images, to radiologists to be analyzed. Most often, these radiologists are located within the hospital in a reading room. But increasing prevalence of digital imaging is making it possible to send images electronically to offsite, and even overseas, radiologists; this practice is known as *teleradiology*. Whether the radiologists are local or offsite, the flow of images to them must consider their specialties (for example, breast, cardiovascular, abdominal, gastrointestinal, musculoskeletal, neuroradiology, head and neck, and so on). Although almost any radiologist can interpret some images, others require a specialist in a specific area.

   The radiologists study the images and produce reports, usually by dictating them into a recording device. These reports describe what is on the image and interpret the clinical implications.

4. **Transcription**—To produce a written report for the requesting physician, transcription takes place on the oral reports that the radiologists generate. Traditionally, this was done by medical stenographers or transcriptionists, who listened to the recordings and typed the reports. Increasingly, however, technologies are becoming available that partially automate the transcription process and allow the radiologist to generate the written report without assistance from a transcriptionist. The most common technology is speech recognition, which produces text from oral speech. However, because speech recognition software is not perfect, radiologists must monitor and correct what is generated. A less common technology is structured reporting, which enables radiologists to generate portions of the report by selecting from standard choices and modifying the details to fit the case. Like speech recognition systems, structured reporting systems eliminate the separate transcription step. But both of these technologies can slow down the radiologist, who may spend more time watching the text being generated than the image being analyzed.

5. **Signoff**—Once a report has been transcribed (or generated by a semiautomated system), the responsible radiologist must check and approve it before it is sent to the requesting physician.

These basic steps may vary by patient, imaging technology, or hospital. For instance, some images may demand a second opinion, which adds additional tasks to the reading step. Some imaging technologies may require a separate patient preparation stage. For example, endoscopy patients are usually sedated prior to the exam. Hospitals also differ according to their archival and transmission protocols. For example, a hospital with a PACS (picture archiving and communication system) will store and access images via a database, whereas a hospital using films will have a physical storage room.

But, such variations aside, Exhibit 5.2 and the preceding descriptions indicate that imaging processes are multistage flows, often with heavily utilized resources (for example, expensive scanners) and the possibility of waiting at each stage. Because of this, we will see next that waiting time metrics are key measures of performance for most imaging processes.

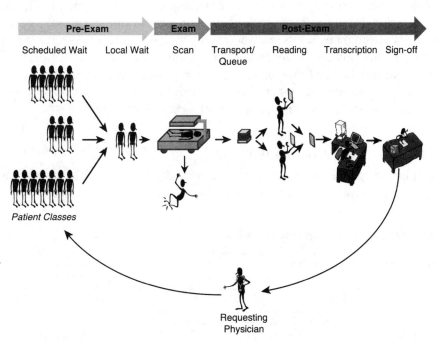

Exhibit 5.2   Flow schematic for an imaging scanner.

5.3 Managing a Diagnostic Unit

5.3.1 Performance Metrics

Like other units of the hospital, the diagnostic units can be evaluated in terms of clinical, operational, financial, and organizational performance metrics. In general, laboratory and imaging services are evaluated in terms of time, quality, and cost. Of these, time is most frequently stressed, for a variety of reasons. First, patient and physician satisfaction are negatively impacted by delays in getting lab or image results. Second, patient outcomes generally benefit from faster intervention (see, for example, Montalescot 2004, Vacek 2002), and the speed of treatment often depends on turnaround time from the lab or the Radiology Department. Third, delays can have indirect impacts on care quality and efficiency; for example, inpatient length of stay has been found to correlate with ED length of stay (Richardson 2002, Liew et al. 2003).

Although clinical laboratories and Radiology Departments are similar with regard to performance measurement, with both emphasizing turnaround time (TAT), there are some differences. Laboratories are high-volume processes involving samples often being sent to the lab from many locations, whereas imaging units are lower-volume processes in which patients must visit the facility in person. As a result, laboratories tend to respond to an unscheduled flow of sample arrivals, whereas imaging units frequently use scheduling to manage patient arrivals. With this in mind, we discuss and summarize performance metrics for labs and imaging units separately below.

5.3.1.1 CLINICAL LABORATORY DEPARTMENT

Although labs vary in terms of the metrics they track, all hospital laboratories measure quality, time, and cost. Table 5.3 gives typical metrics in these three categories.

Table 5.3   Sample Performance Metrics for the Pathology Department

Clinical Metrics	Operational Metrics	Financial Metrics	Organizational Metrics
Quality-Collection	*Time*	*Costs*	*Staff Satisfaction*
Error rate— Percentage of tests that contain one or more defects	Mean TAT—Average time from when test is ordered (or received) to when report is received	Labor expenses	Responses to satisfaction surveys

Clinical Metrics	Operational Metrics	Financial Metrics	Organizational Metrics
Specimen rejection rate—fraction of specimens deemed inadequate for testing	Turnaround time outlier percentage (TAT OP)—Percentage of responses that take longer than a specified time	Material and services expenses	Staff turnover rates
Blood culture contamination rate—Fraction of positive blood cultures identified as contaminated	Pre-analytic TAT—Time from order placement to start of analysis	Capital expenditures	
Specimen information error rate—Fraction of specimens sent to lab with inaccurate or inadequate information	Analysis TAT—Time from start to finish of test	Fully allocated cost per test	
Lost specimen rate	Post Analytic TAT—Time completion of test to time results are reported		
	Percentage of inpatients for whom tests are available for morning rounds		
Quality-Analysis			
Proficiency testing performance—Percentage of correct proficiency test results			
Diagnostic discordance rate			
Quality-Reporting			
Percentage of laboratory reports revised/amended			
Percentage of tests with all critical values reported			

Table 5.3 Sample Performance Metrics for the Pathology Department

Clinical Metrics	Operational Metrics	Financial Metrics	Organizational Metrics
Client Satisfaction	*Volume*	*Revenues*	*Learning*
Average overall patient satisfaction score	Total test volume—total number of a particular test per year	Billable test revenue from inpatients	Rate of change in established metrics (for example, error rates, TAT)
Average requesting clinician satisfaction score	Billable tests or relative value units (RVUs) per full time equivalent (FTE)	Total gross revenue from outpatients	Number of new initiatives (for example, ideas in suggestion boxes)
	Percentage of utilization of key resources		

Measures of clinical quality include objective measures of errors, in collection, analysis, and reporting, as well as subjective measures of client satisfaction, where clients include both patients and clinicians who are served by the lab. The latter must generally be collected via survey forms.[3]

Operational measures include TAT, plus metrics of laboratory volume. TAT can be measured as either total TAT (time from order to receipt of test) or response TAT (time from receipt of order to completion of test). It can also be broken down into times of various stages—preanalytic, analytic, and postanalytic—of the laboratory process. Although most Pathology Departments track average TAT, the high volume of tests can cause a slow response to get buried in the average. That's why some departments also track extreme values, measured by the percentage of tests that take longer than a specified time. For instance, Holland et al. (2005) defines outliers as more than 30 minutes for CBC counts, 40 minutes for chemistry measurements, and 60 minutes for troponin I measurements. Finally, lab volume is measured in total number of tests conducted, broken down by test type or normalized by the number of people in the lab.

Financial metrics measure costs (labor, operating, capital) and revenues. In a given hospital, the clinical laboratory may be viewed as a cost center (that is, for servicing inpatients), a revenue center (that is, generating revenue in the form of billable tests for inpatients and outpatients), or both. For instance, a small hospital may treat the entire lab as a single cost center, whereas a larger hospital may treat sections (for example, Hematology and Cytology) as separate revenue centers. The way a hospital views the lab affects the performance metrics that make up its financial reports. But, at a high level, all such reports track costs and revenues. To compare costs and revenues, accounting procedures are often used to allocate indirect labor, capital, and other indirect expenses to compute a cost per test.

Organizational metrics address the health of an organization, in terms of staff satisfaction, and its ability to learn. Staff satisfaction is often measured directly via surveys that ask questions such as, "How likely are you to recommend Hospital X as a place to work?" An important indirect measure of staff satisfaction is turnover rate. A clinical lab that has a higher-than-average turnover rate is likely suffering from staff dissatisfaction problems. Metrics of organizational learning are difficult to specify precisely. The most direct evidence of an organization's ability to learn is progress in other performance metrics. For example, a lab that exhibits a steadily decline in error rates is clearly learning in some dimension. Other less direct measures, such as the number of improvement suggestions that come from staff members, monitor organizational characteristics that facilitate learning.

5.3.1.2 IMAGING DEPARTMENT

Clinical metrics for an Imaging Department attempt to measure the quality of the images and the accuracy of the reports delivered to the requesting physician, as well as the experience of the patient. As indicated in Table 5.4, some quality metrics are objective; for instance, we can measure the number of diagnoses by independent experts that differ (are discordant) from the original diagnoses in a sample of images. But most Radiology Departments rely on subjective metrics of satisfaction (for example, compiled from surveys of requesting physicians) as proxies of overall quality and responsiveness. Similarly, surveys are used to assess patient satisfaction with the overall process.

The bulk of the performance metrics tracked by Radiology Departments are operational, particularly related to time. The most important time is the turnaround time (TAT), which measures the time from when a physician requests an image to the time she receives it. Of course, this metric needs to be reported separately for different technologies (for example, an MRI scan generally takes longer than a standard X-ray) and for different types of patients (for example, a potential stroke victim may need a CT scan right away, whereas a patient with ongoing joint pain can wait days or weeks for an X-ray).

Table 5.4   Sample Performance Metrics for the Radiology Department

Clinical Metrics	Operational Metrics	Financial Metrics	Organizational Metrics
Quality	*Time*	*Costs*	*Staff Satisfaction*
Number of discordant diagnoses in rereview of films by independent experts	TAT—Average time from when image is requested to when report is received	Staffing levels	Responses to staff surveys

Table 5.4 Sample Performance Metrics for the Radiology Department

Clinical Metrics	Operational Metrics	Financial Metrics	Organizational Metrics
False-positive and false-negative rates	Turnaround time percentiles—For example, fraction of reports completed within 24 hours	Fixed unit expenses	Staff turnover rates
Percentage of examinations with unnecessary recommendations	Reading time—Time from completion of exam to completion of dictation	Cost per relative value unit (RVU)	
Total number of incident reports (preventative reports and adverse outcomes)	Transcription time—Time from completion of dictation to completion of transcription	Hours worked per RVU	
	Signature time—Time from completion of written report to radiologist sign-out	Supply cost per RVU	
	Scheduled wait time—Time from physician order to scheduled exam appointment		
	Actual wait time—Time from physician order to actual exam		
	Local wait time—time from patient arrival at facility to beginning of exam		
Patient Satisfaction	*Volume*	*Revenues*	*Learning*
Average overall patient satisfaction score	Examination volume—Total number of exams per year	Percent of billings reimbursed	Rate of change in established metrics (for example, TAT)
Average referring physician satisfaction score	Billable exams or RVUs per full time equivalent (FTE)	Collections per FTE	Number of new initiatives (for example, improvement suggestions from staff)
			Number of courses or training sessions requested and delivered

5.3.2 Management Decisions

Management decisions in a diagnostic unit (laboratory or imaging) can be divided into long, intermediate, and short term. Long-term decisions deal primarily with capacity. Intermediate decisions involve mostly scheduling of people and supplies. Short-term decisions focus on flow of patients and tests.

- **Long-term capacity decisions**—These decisions include physical space design (for example, layout and construction of rooms), equipment purchase (for example, automated analyzers or scanners), and personnel hiring (for example, physicians, technicians and other staff). The advance of technology means that these decisions must be constantly revisited, to ensure that unit capacity is adequate to the needs of the hospital and that facilities are configured to take advantage of available technology. For instance, a layout that was suitable to a highly manual laboratory may become inefficient when automation is introduced. Hence, new equipment purchases often involve physical reconfiguration, as well as staffing changes. Exhibit 5.3 illustrates a generic layout of a hospital laboratory showing areas where flexibility is most valuable for adapting to changing needs. Beyond decisions to alter the lab within the hospital, capacity decisions can include relocation of laboratory testing offsite and developing reference laboratory capabilities that may allow the hospital laboratory to transition from a cost center to a revenue center.

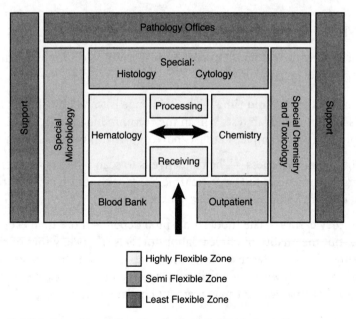

Exhibit 5.3   Sample layout of a hospital Pathology Department
(from Battisto and Allison, 2002, p. 40).

- **Intermediate-term scheduling decisions**—These decisions create plans for using capacity to meet demand. This involves creation of various types of schedules. Personnel schedules determine staffing plans. Patient schedules establish plans for examination times, either in the form of appointment times for patients at collection or imaging sites, or for hematologist rounds for visiting patients. Maintenance schedules determine the planned availability of equipment. Purchasing schedules set replenishment plans for consumables (such as reagents and film).

- **Short-term flow decisions**—These decisions determine any real-time actions taken to promote the speed and quality of flow of patients, samples, and information through the diagnostic units. These can involve batching, sequencing and expediting of transport, analysis, and reading steps. They can involve shifting labor from one task to another (such as a transcriptionist switching between sample accessioning and report transcription). They can involve responding to real-time signals (such as control charts) of quality or flow problems. Because there are many ways to promote flow and quality, laboratories are increasingly turning to organized systems, such as Lean and Six Sigma, for ideas. But the leverage of short-term decisions is largely determined by the long- and intermediate-term decisions that have created the system in which they are made. So it is vital to coordinate decisions across the three levels to improve performance.

5.4 Key Management Issues in the Diagnostic Units

Following the pattern of earlier chapters, we now zero in on three common management challenges in diagnostic units:

- **Laboratory turnaround time**—The challenge is to reliably deliver accurate results for requested lab tests within the recommended limit for the particular type of test. (For example, stat tests have tighter limits than do routine tests.)

- **Imaging responsiveness**—The challenge is to scan patients and deliver reports within recommended test-specific time limits without excessive patient waits at the facility or capital costs for scanner capacity.

- **Laboratory errors**—The modern hospital depends more than ever on lab results, but the quality of clinical laboratories is still below that of many manufacturing processes. Because errors in the lab can contribute to errors in diagnosis and treatment, with potentially disastrous consequences, delivering accurate test results is a paramount management challenge for all hospital laboratories.

Because the first two issues are related to waiting time, we will invoke the management principles related to queueing and generic Table A.1 from Appendix A for both. These concepts are broadly applicable in hospitals due to the prevalence of waiting times. However, differences in the service process in a lab (unscheduled, high volume, multi-stage process) and in an image scanning facility (scheduled, lower volume, single-stage process) necessitate invoking other principles to identify effective improvement policies.

As we did in earlier chapters, for each issue we will first identify a relevant set of management principles and then use these to enumerate a comprehensive set of generic improvement levers. By tracing the logical implications of each of these until we get to specific actions, we will generate a range of sample improvement policies for each management challenge.

5.4.1 Laboratory Turnaround Time

5.4.1.1 PROBLEM

The modern hospital relies heavily on laboratory tests to support the diagnosis and treatment of patients. Most inpatients receive lab tests on a daily, or at least frequent, basis. Outpatients seen at clinics and physician offices affiliated with the hospital also rely on the hospital lab for tests. As a result, hospital laboratories are busy places. For example, the Department of Pathology and Laboratory Medicine at Henry Ford Hospital performs more than 11 million clinical tests per year, making it one of the largest hospital-based laboratories in the United States.

Because treatment decisions hinge on tests, the speed of care can depend on the speed of the testing process. For instance, patients in the ED may wait in examination rooms for test results. Inpatients may have their releases delayed if attending physicians do not have lab results at the time of their rounds. Outpatients may have their treatment delayed if their primary care physician has to wait for results. Consequently, speed is a critical, and commonly measured, indicator of laboratory performance.

But speed can be measured in a variety of ways. The measure most closely connected to the care of an individual patient is *total TAT*, which is defined as the time from a test request to the delivery of results. However, because TAT varies from test to test, we must define statistical metrics to characterize it. The most familiar such metric would be average total TAT. But the high volume of most hospital laboratories causes the average to be insensitive to a few excessively long tests. So percentile metrics (for example, the percentage of tests with TATs less than X hours) are often used instead of the average.

Because total TAT includes time before the specimen reaches the lab and time after the results have been generated, many labs track an internal TAT, defined from the time the sample is registered in the lab to the time results are reported. For example, in a review of the literature on hospital laboratory performance, Hawkins (2007) notes that TAT is widely used as a key indicator and suggests *completion time* (defined from sample registration to result reporting) of common laboratory tests within 60 minutes for common laboratory tests as an initial goal for acceptable TAT. But, because the wait experienced by patients and physicians includes time before and after completion time, we focus on total TAT instead.

Although total TAT matters for all lab tests, it matters more for some than others. "Urgent" or "stat" (from the Latin *statim*, meaning immediately) tests are generally ordered when fast response is needed to manage medical emergencies. TAT for these tests is clearly more critical than TAT for routine tests (for example, a blood test ordered as part of an annual checkup). Indeed, a survey of 162 hospitals found that nurses regarded urgent test TAT as both the most important aspect of laboratory service and the one with which they were least satisfied (Jones et al. 2006). Hence, for purposes of analysis, we will focus on total TAT, with particular emphasis on urgent tests.

5.4.1.2 PRINCIPLES

Exhibit 5.1 gives a schematic illustration of the information and material flows in a clinical laboratory. From a logical standpoint, it makes little difference whether the physical flow involves blood being analyzed in a chemistry lab or tissue being analyzed in a histology lab. The high-level issues are the same. Of course, the details of the technologies and procedures differ among tests, so the specific low-level policies for improving performance will also differ. But, given that total TAT is a key performance metric for all clinical lab tests, Exhibit 5.1 suggests that reducing delay at each of the steps involved in the flow is the way to improve performance. We can identify ways to do this by appealing to the management principles that pertain to waiting and delay. We summarize these briefly now; for a more complete discussion, see Appendix A.

Principle (Variability)—Variability causes congestion.

For example, uneven arrival of samples to the lab can cause pileups and delay at accessioning. If arrival fluctuations are passed on to the workstations, they cause queueing delay there as well. Delay caused by variability gets worse when resources are busy, as noted in the following principle.

Principle (Utilization)—Utilization magnifies congestion in a highly nonlinear fashion.

For instance, the higher the utilization of the phlebotomists, the longer it takes to collect samples from inpatients. Collection delays can lead to delays in getting test results, which can lead to delays in treatment or discharge. The congestion caused by variability and amplified by utilization leads to performance degradation due to the following principle.

Principle (Variability Buffering)—All variability is buffered by some combination of inventory, capacity, time, quality, and system degradation.

Queueing delay at any step in the process is a time buffer. Because we are concerned with total TAT, time buffers are a problem in labs. But quality buffers (for example, a phlebotomist incorrectly labels a sample because he is hurrying to catch up) and system degradation (for example, an accessioner becomes discouraged about coping with periodic overloads of stat tests, causing his productivity and accuracy to decline) can be as bad or worse. To improve performance, we can seek policies that replace the preceding buffers with capacity (for example, adding phlebotomists) buffers. But, because lab tests are a service, they cannot be produced in advance. So, the following corollary to the Variability principle applies.

Corollary (Variability Buffering in Service Systems)—In a pure service system, inventory is not available as a buffer, so holding quality and human resource costs constant, there is a trade-off between variability, excess capacity, and waiting time.

The implication is that two key levers for reducing time delays that inflate total TAT are capacity enhancement and variability reduction. A third lever is buffer flexibility, as described in the following principle.

Principle (Buffer Flexibility)—Flexibility in variability buffers reduces the amount of buffering required for a given amount of variability.

For example, cross-training technicians to enable them to float between workstations as needed can reduce waiting within the lab. Alternatively, cross-training can enable the lab to achieve acceptable TATs with lower staffing levels by making better utilization of existing personnel.

To identify nonobvious ways to increase capacity and reduce variability, we invoke the following principles to make individual tasks more efficient and predictable.

Principle (Task Simplification)—Reducing task complexity reduces the mean and variance of the task times and the likelihood of errors.

Principle (Task Standardization)—Using clearly specified best practice procedures for repetitive tasks reduces the mean and variance of task times and the likelihood of errors.

For example, pneumatic tubes have long been used in hospitals to simplify the task of delivering samples to the laboratory. In more recent years, automated testing and handling of samples have simplified tasks internal to the lab. Checklists or electronic forms are examples of standardization of the test-ordering task. Because lab testing is a highly repetitive process, many other opportunities exist for simplification and standardization of tasks.

The high volume of samples processed by a clinical lab provides incentive for batching. For instance, to reduce walking time, phlebotomists may collect large batches of samples before delivering them to the lab. Making a delivery to the lab constitutes a setup time (because it is done once per batch). Increasing the batch size reduces the total setup time, but it makes the arrival of samples to the lab more uneven (more variable). This trade-off is described in the following principle.

Principle (Batching)—When tasks involve setup time, performing them in batches makes better use of capacity but also introduces waiting time for tasks that must wait behind the batch.

Policies that reduce setup times (for example, pneumatic tubes speed transmission of samples to the lab) make if feasible to use smaller batch size, which smooth flow and reduce downstream delay.

Because stat tests demand faster TAT than other tests, another tool for improving performance is sequencing. The following principle describes the underlying logic.

Principle (Critical Ratio Sequencing)—In a multiclass system with dynamic arrivals, prioritizing entities according to the ratio c/t, where c is the delay cost per unit time and t is the expected process time, minimizes total cumulative delay over the long term.

For most lab tests, the actual process time is similar regardless of the patient priority. (For example, a stat blood chemistry test takes the same amount of time as a regular blood chemistry test.) So the Critical Ratio Sequencing principle simply implies, not surprisingly, that stat tests should get priority over regular tests. At points in the system where queues exist (for example, at accessioning), it is fairly simple to move stat tests to the head of the line. Inserting a stat test on an analyzer that is already running may be more difficult. Although some analyzers use continuous loading, which makes it easy to get an urgent test started, others are essentially batch units, which must complete their current cycle before becoming available. Because test times are generally short, it does not make sense to interrupt tests in an attempt to speed stat tests.

Even if it does not involve 'breaking setup," prioritizing stat tests involves some amount of disruption. Operators must note the high-priority tests and take steps to ensure that they pass routine tests. If queues are long, this will make a difference. But, if other categories of improvements can reduce overall TAT to a low enough level, prioritizing (short) queues will have little effect. Consequently, some hospitals, such as Oklahoma University Medical Center, have eliminated prioritization of stat tests altogether (Blick

2005). Evidently, at OUMC, physicians in the ED still mark tests "stat," but the lab ignores this and processes specimens in first-in-first-out order.

One last source of potential source of inefficiency in all multistage processes is handoffs, so the following principle is relevant.

Principle (Handoffs)—Unless the individuals contribute new knowledge, information is degraded as it is passed from one individual to another.

Within the process that makes up total TAT for laboratory services, there are several important handoffs. The requesting physician must pass the request to the lab (which may involve another handoff from the physician to a nurse or an assistant who enters the request), the request must be passed to the phlebotomist, who in turn must transmit the sample to the lab, the accessioner must pass the sample to the appropriate workstation, the technologist may need to pass results to a pathologist, and finally these results must be given to the requesting physician. Each of these transfers is an opportunity for delay or error. Hence, streamlined flows that limit the number of handoffs and high efficiency in the transfers that remain are key components of a responsive laboratory testing process.

5.4.1.3 PRACTICES

To use the preceding principles in a structured fashion to identify practices for reducing laboratory TAT, particularly for urgent requests, we appeal to Table A.1 of Appendix A. This table identifies five generic options for improving responsiveness in a service system: reduce workload, increase capacity, improve synchronization, reduce variability, and improve sequencing.[4] To translate these generic options into specific improvement policies for the lab, we look again at the flow in Exhibit 5.1. This highlights the separation of total TAT into three components: prelab, lab, and postlab time. Although many labs focus only on lab time, a physician or patient cannot tell whether a delayed test result is due to slow laboratory procedures or holdups in getting the order/sample to or from the lab. So we include both time inside and outside the lab in defining total TAT.

In Table 5.5, we break total TAT into prelab (from the requesting physician to the lab and from the lab back to the requesting physician), lab (from the requesting receipt of sample in the lab to completion of the requested tests), and postlab (from completion of the test to receipt by the physician) time. Then we apply the preceding principles to enumerate ways to reduce each of these. By pursuing each improvement path in increasingly specific fashion, we generate a range of improvement alternatives.

Table 5.5   Generic Operations Improvement Policies: Laboratory Turnaround Time

Level 1 Objectives	Level 2 Objectives	Level 3 Objectives	Example Policies
Reduce prelab time	Reduce collection workload	Reduce test requests	Replace recurring orders with individual test requests to reduce unnecessary blood draws
		Simplify collection process	Standardize procedures to propagate best practices among phlebotomists; Assign phlebotomists to zones that reduce walk time; Preload forms with known patient information
	Increase collection capacity	Add personnel	Hire more phlebotomists; Hire runners to deliver samples to lab
		Increase personnel productivity	Measure and post productivity statistics; Incent productivity (for example, via shift rewards); Improve design of phlebotomy carts
		Automate portions of collection process	Pneumatic tube delivery of samples to lab; Use mobile technology to generate labels and barcodes and enter sample into database at patient bedside
	Improve synchronization between collection capacity and workload	Adjust demand	Start collection earlier in the morning
		Adjust capacity	Use nonphlebotomists as supplemental collection capacity for morning spike

Level 1 Objectives	Level 2 Objectives	Level 3 Objectives	Example Policies
		Improve batching	Facilitate smaller collection batches without sacrificing capacity by using runners or pneumatic tubes to deliver specimens
	Reduce collection variability	Level predictable demand spikes	Stagger rounds; Start specimen collection earlier
		Reduce variability in collection process	Standardize methods and improve training to reduce collection errors; Standardize order forms to reduce communication errors
	Improve collection sequencing	Sequence collection to support rounding	Prioritize collection of specimens from patients who are candidates for release
		Sequence collection to support patient priorities	Assign phlebotomist(s) to collect samples for stat tests before collecting them for routine tests
	Increase collection flexibility	Increase time flexibility	Adapt collection schedule to favor priority specimens over routine specimens
		Increase capacity flexibility	Cross-train other personnel to do blood draws during peaks
Reduce lab time	Reduce laboratory process workload	Reduce number of tests	Structure order forms to encourage targeted test requests
		Reduce work per test	Streamline delivery to minimize sorting and distribution; Reduce information errors by simplifying forms or improving technology

Table 5.5 Generic Operations Improvement Policies: Laboratory Turnaround Time

Level 1 Objectives	Level 2 Objectives	Level 3 Objectives	Example Policies
	Increase laboratory process capacity	Add labor capacity	Add technologists; Add support staff
		Add physical capacity	Add analyzers; Replace analyzers with newer, faster models
		Increase laboratory productivity	Develop standard procedures based on best practices; Improve ergonomics of lab stations; Streamline lab layout
		Automation	Automate specimen processing, material handling, testing
	Improve synchronization of laboratory capacity with workload	Adjust demand	Align specimen collection schedule with laboratory staffing schedule
		Adjust capacity	Cross-train technicians to float between stations; Analyzers that can process a broader range of test types
		Improve batching	Facilitate smaller batches through automated reagent preparation and continuous flow processing
	Reduce laboratory variability	Reduce variability laboratory workload	Stagger rounds; Reduce batching in phlebotomy; Pool demand from multiple units or locations

Level 1 Objectives	Level 2 Objectives	Level 3 Objectives	Example Policies
		Reduce variability in test times	Improve quality control to reduce rework; Reduce time to set up a test (for example, reagent prep); Protecting technicians from interruptions
		Process standardization	Document standard procedures; Standardize station configuration
		Error prevention	Train technologists and lab supervisors in root cause analysis and other quality improvement methodologies; Reward rapid deployment of countermeasures
		Synchronization	Adjust technician schedules to match predictable demand patterns
	Improve sequencing within the lab	Provide information relevant to sequencing decisions	Introduce priority category for morning tests to ensure they are ready for physician rounds
		Dynamically prioritize cases	Update priority status of tests based on due dates; Draw tests into system based on critical ratio rule
Reduce postlab time	Reduce delivery demand	Reduce number of tests	Structure order forms to encourage targeted test requests
		Reduce delivery work per test	Perform simple tests locally (for example, in an ED lab)

Table 5.5   Generic Operations Improvement Policies: Laboratory Turnaround Time

Level 1 Objectives	Level 2 Objectives	Level 3 Objectives	Example Policies
	Increase delivery capacity	Increase physical capacity	Add runners to deliver test results; Schedule delivery runs more efficiently
		Automate process	Deliver test results to physicians via electronic system
	Improve synchronization of delivery capacity with workload	Adjust demand	Move discharge schedule later in day to delay demand for some results
		Adjust capacity	Cross-train staff to act as runners to deliver tests during peak times; Float pathologists between stations for report writing/result checking
		Improve batching	Use electronic delivery to eliminate walking time and facilitate delivery batches of one
	Reduce delivery variability	Process standardization	Store results in a laboratory information system (LIS)
		Error prevention	Simplify test order forms; Pull patient and physician data from existing database
	Improve delivery sequencing	Provide information relevant to sequencing decisions	Identify stat test results; Identify test results relevant to discharge decisions
		Prioritize deliveries	Use wireless system to deliver results of stat tests to physicians not at computers; Deliver stat results first; Synchronize discharge patient results to rounding schedules

Each time segment (prelab, lab, postlab) has five generic paths for reducing TAT: reduce demand, increase capacity, improve synchronization between capacity and demand, reduce variability, and improve sequencing. We highlight a few of these paths to provide a sense of how these generic responsiveness improvement options can be converted into concrete TAT improvement policies for the lab.

Reducing Prelab TAT

Reduce Workload

In the prelab portion of the process, reducing workload is an attractive option, because additional samples contribute not only to the collection workload, but to the laboratory and results delivery workload. At first blush, it may seem unreasonable to reduce collection workload, because the lab cannot deny necessary services in the pursuit of faster TATs. But there may be ways to reduce workload without compromising care.

For instance, Beland et al. (2003) performed an audit of a neurological ICU and found instances of blood being drawn without orders, duplicate blood draws, and blood work continuing beyond medical need. If unnecessary tests are being done in the ICU, where patients are particularly sensitive to blood loss, they are almost certainly being done elsewhere. Indeed, May et al. (2006) reported a 12% reduction in inpatient lab tests after reconfiguring the electronic order system to limit recurring test requests and force physicians to order each test individually. Georgiou et al. (2007) reviewed 19 studies of computerized physician order entry (CPOE) systems and found several studies indicating that adoption of such systems leads to a decrease in the volume of ordered tests and (presumably consequently) a reduction in TAT. Any way it is achieved, avoiding unnecessary tests would help reduce laboratory workload and thereby improve responsiveness.

Increase Capacity

Another attractive option, which is almost always relevant to increasing responsiveness of manual operations, is to increase capacity, which can be done by adding people, making people more productive, and supplementing (or even replacing) people with automation. Adding phlebotomists is straightforward but expensive, so a cleverer option is to substitute less expensive labor where feasible. For instance, assigning low skill staff to serve as "runners" to carry samples from rooms to the lab could free up phlebotomists from this duty and thereby enable them to collect more samples per hour.

To increase the productivity of the phlebotomists themselves, we could pursue training and incentive policies. For example, Hooper et al. (1989) reported that rewarding the most productive phlebotomists and technologists by giving them first choice of available shifts led to significant improvements in productivity. Evidently, because staff members have strong preference for some shifts (for example, days during the weeks over nights and weekends), using productivity rather than seniority to allocate shifts provided a strong incentive to work hard. Alternatively, we could increase phlebotomist productivity by improving the support systems around them. For example, redesigning phlebotomy carts can ensure that phlebotomists have everything they need, so they do not need to go looking for supplies. A well-designed cart can also eliminate tasks associated with blood drawing (for example, automatically printing labels for samples so they do not need to be handwritten) and thereby enable phlebotomists to collect more specimens per hour. Making sure that all carts are standardized (for example, with standard inventory arranged in standard fashion) will also eliminate wasted time by phlebotomists. Going even further, we could increase collection capacity by automating steps in the process. For instance, a labeling machine that creates bar-coded specimen labels can eliminate the manual step of writing out labels. Of course, to save time at collection, the automated labeling process must take less time than the manual process (for example, by pulling patient information from a database, rather than requiring the technician to enter it); otherwise, such automation might speed flow within the lab at the expense of slowing it through the collection process.

Increase Synchronization

Instead of increasing total capacity or reducing total demand, we can reduce TAT by better synchronizing fluctuations in capacity with fluctuations in demand. Morning rounds generate demand for many tests due around the same time. To meet this spike in demand, the lab either needs to overstaff phlebotomy or find a way to spread out the spike. Starting collection earlier in the morning and making temporary use of nonphlebotomists are ways to increase collection capacity to match the spike in demand created by tests needed in morning rounds.

Another way to better align capacity with demand is by optimizing batching. For instance, if a phlebotomist collects 25 specimens before delivering them to the lab, the first specimen collected waits for the next 24 before being delivered. Although the first specimen was ready for delivery at the beginning of the batch, the delivery capacity was not delivered until the end of the batch. The larger the batch size between deliveries, the longer the added delay. So, ideally, we would like to deliver samples in batch sizes of one. Unfortunately, because walk times (setups) rob the system of capacity, batch sizes that are too small also cause the capacity to fall behind demand. As a result, the batch size that best matches capacity to demand may be larger than one.

But we can reduce the optimal batch size, and thereby better match capacity to demand, by reducing walk times, perhaps by automating delivery. Fernandes et al. (2006)

reported that adoption of a pneumatic tube system reduced TAT (from order to report) for mean hemoglobin from 43 to 33 minutes and for mean potassium from 72 to 64 minutes. Part of this reduction was due to an increase in collection capacity (not waiting for a phlebotomist to walk over samples), and part of it was due to a reduction in batching (not waiting for the phlebotomist to collect enough samples to warrant a trip to the lab).

Theoretically, another way to reduce the time to get samples from patients to the lab, and thereby facilitate smaller batch sizes, is to locate the lab closer to the patients. The most common way to do this is to locate a stat lab in the ED. Although this certainly shortens transportation, it may or may not reduce total TAT. For example, Lewandrowski et al. (2004) reported that a satellite laboratory in the ED reduced TAT for some tests by an average of 51.5 minutes. At the same time, Steindel and Howanitz (1993) reported that urgent laboratories had the slowest 10% of samples, presumably due to inadequate staffing and equipment for peak times. Consequently, some hospitals (for example, Henry Ford Hospital) have opted not to use satellite urgent laboratories, concentrating instead on rapid transit to a central lab and responsiveness within it.

An extreme form of local testing is point of care testing (POTC), in which tests are done at patient bedsides. Portable testing units exist for performing basic blood and urine tests; these will undoubtedly be extended to more test types and become increasingly accurate with time. Some studies have indicated positive impacts on TAT. For example, Singer et al. (2005) reported that troponin I point-of-care testing by treating nurses achieved a mean TAT of 14.8 minutes, as compared to 83 minutes in the central lab. This facilitated a reduction of ED length of stay for chest pain patients from 7.1 hours to 5.2 hours. However, not all hospitals have achieved such dramatic gains through POTC. For example, Winkelman et al. (1994) found that POTC of glucose only reduced total TAT by 1–2 minutes, compared to a central lab that used pneumatic tube delivery of samples to the lab and electronic broadcast of results. However, they reported that POTC is roughly twice as expensive as testing in a lab.

Reduce Variability

Closely related to improved synchronization is the important, but often overlooked, option of variability reduction. Staggering physician rounds so that tests are due on a more level schedule is an option for reducing demand variability. Smoothing admissions across the day would smooth the admissions-related demand for diagnostic services. Reducing collection variability can be accomplished by reducing time spent on error correction (for example, a mislabeled specimen that requires recollection) and searching for information or materials (for example, an ambiguous order that requires tracking down the ordering physician to ascertain the correct specimen to collect). Policies that minimize these will both augment capacity (by eliminating wasted time) and reduce variability (by making collection more regular). Both of these benefits will serve to reduce delays in specimen collection.

Improve Sequencing

One final option for improving collection responsiveness is to improve sequencing so that the samples collected first are those that most need it. Although this will not reduce average TAT, it can improve other responsiveness metrics, such as the fraction of tests completed by their due dates. In the lab, two factors influence patient priority: medical urgency and inpatient release schedule.

Medical urgency is always considered by hospital laboratories. The "stat" designation indicates that a test is critical to a treatment decision and therefore is to be given top priority. However, although "stat" tests are given priority within the laboratory, they are not always prioritized in the specimen collection process. For the sake of efficiency, phlebotomists tend to visit patient room in sequence. However, if some patients need test results more urgently, it may make sense to either abandon the most efficient paths, in order to put high-priority patients first, or designate one phlebotomist as the "stat" collector and assign him to the job of getting high-priority specimens.

In addition to medical urgency, the inpatient release schedule should also be considered when sequencing patients for specimen collection. If a test is not available during morning rounds for a patient who will be staying in the hospital for at least another night, the attending physician may be able to get the results by phone or computer later in the day. Although this is not optimal, it still allows the physician to monitor the status of the inpatient. However, if a test is not available during morning rounds for a patient who is a candidate for release, the delay could result in another night in the hospital. Because this could result in "bed block" that could affect patient flow out of the ED or OR, the cost of such a delay is potentially much higher than that for a patient not scheduled to be released. Hence, it may make sense to have phlebotomists collect specimens from potential release candidates first, or to assign some phlebotomists to attend to these patients, to minimize the likelihood of a test being unavailable during rounds.

Reducing Laboratory TAT

To reduce lab time, we can use pretty much the same generic options listed earlier as approaches for reducing collection time. But the detailed actions will differ because the process steps are different. That is, because both the prelab and lab phases can be viewed as multistage queueing systems, the same principles apply, but, because the domains are different, the policies for implementing these principles also differ.

Reduce Workload

Although elimination of unnecessary tests is a generic option, which reduces workloads in all segments of the testing process, steps that reduce the work per test are specific options for reducing laboratory workload. A system (pneumatic or manual) that delivers specimens directly to the proper section of the lab reduces workload by eliminating a sorting and distribution step. Steps that improve information accuracy (name of patient, required tests, and so on), such as simplifying forms or drawing patient information automatically from a database, can reduce effort spent tracking down the information needed to process a sample. Many other options exist for eliminating unnecessary steps in handling and processing specimens in the lab.

Increase Capacity
Laboratory capacity can be augmented directly by adding people (for example, technologists or support staff), equipment (for example, more analyzers or faster ones), or time (for example, expanding off-hour shifts to increase utilization of equipment). But subtler ways to add capacity are to increase productivity of existing people and equipment or to automate manual tasks to make them faster. Increasing productivity can be accomplished in myriad ways, ranging from standardized procedures that propagate best practices across the lab to improved ergonomics that prevent fatigue and errors.

Automation is an increasingly common option for productivity enhancement. Automated analyzers are ubiquitous for some tests and are becoming available for an increasingly wide range of tests. Automated specimen-handling systems are not yet universal but are already common. Total laboratory automation (TLA) systems, which combine automated specimen processing, handling, processing, and reporting, are not the norm, but various vendors are refining them. There is ample evidence of the impact of automation on TAT. For example, Berry (2006) reported that automation resulted in a 30% increase in availability of urinalysis reports within 30 minutes and a 44% increase in full blood count (FBC) reports within 30 minutes.

Improve Synchronization
Two options for better synchronizing lab capacity to demand are increased flexibility and improved batching. Flexibility can be enhanced through cross-training technicians so they can move to the point in the lab where queues are longest. However, to facilitate this, it is important to standardize stations and procedures, so that people can easily shift positions without errors or delays. In addition to personnel flexibility, labs can exploit equipment flexibility to increase responsiveness. For example, an analyzer that can perform a broader range of tests eliminates the need for a technician to switch from one apparatus to another to accommodate a shifting mix of tests.

As in the prelab portion of the process, reducing setup times allows for smaller batches, so that processing of specimens can better match their arrival. For example, if a test requires mixing of a batch of reagents, automated reagent preparation could eliminate the need to run the test on multiple samples. Alternatively, if a test requires incubation in an oven that processes samples in parallel, replacing it with a conveyor-type oven would eliminate the need to incubate samples in batches. If the setup reduction goes far enough, the optimal batch size will fall to one. Indeed, Persoon et al. (2006) reported on an overhaul that streamlined the number of steps in the preanalytic process (from accessioning to analysis) and handled samples in batches of one to achieve a reduction in median preanalytic processing time from 29 to 19 minutes.

Reduce Variability

Variability in test process times can be reduced by standardizing procedures, eliminating errors, reducing setup times, and protecting technicians from interruptions or anything else that can lead to an unusually long time to process an individual test.

Improve Sequencing

When TAT is long, sequencing can be an important responsiveness option. Indeed, most laboratories have "stat" and "routine" priority categories, which are used to jump stat tests to the front of queues within the lab. However, some labs have been able to reduce TAT via other means to the point where they have been able to abandon (or ignore) this distinction (Blick 2005). In addition to the stat distinction, another criterion for prioritization is whether or not the results are needed for morning rounds. By giving a special priority status to tests needed by rounding physicians, particularly those for patients who are candidates for release, a laboratory can help improve the flow of patients through the hospital. If this is achieved at the expense of slightly longer TATs for other routine tests, the results of which may not be needed for hours, the net effect will be an improvement.

Reducing Postlab TAT

The options for reducing TAT in the postlab portion of the process are analogous to those for the previous stages.

Reduce Workload

We can reduce workload on the distribution end of the process by avoiding unnecessary tests and by reducing the work per test required in the delivery stage. A specific option for the latter is performing tests locally to eliminate or reduce the work involved in delivering tests to physicians. Portable point-of-care testing devices can generate results for several basic blood tests right in the patient room, so no delivery is required. Having a separate laboratory within the ED shortens the distance (and presumably the delay) in delivering results to physicians. However, if results are delivered electronically, distance is not an issue. This is probably the reason that Winkelman et al. (1994) found that point of care testing of glucose had a minimal effect on TAT, compared to a central lab using pneumatic tube delivery of samples to the lab and electronic broadcast of results.

Increase Capacity

If physical reports are being delivered to physicians, then adding runners would help deliver high-priority tests more quickly. However, because the days of paper are clearly numbered, a more effective way to increase capacity is to automate delivery by having results broadcast electronically. The easiest way to do this is via an laboratory information system (LIS) that records results from the laboratory and can be accessed by physicians from computer terminals anywhere in the hospital (or beyond). If reaching physicians on the move who do not have access to a terminal is important, wireless access to the information system can be provided through handheld devices.

Improve Synchronization

A standard way to match capacity to demand is to use flexibility in capacity, inventory, or time. Because tests are a service (and hence cannot be inventoried in advance) and because time is what we are trying to shorten, the flexibility we can use here is in capacity (that is, labor). If we have manual delivery of tests, then having people who can switch from other activities to run test results during peak periods could reduce delay. Further upstream, having pathologists consciously float to stations with heavy loads to check results or write reports can similarly reduce delays due to fluctuating workloads.

Reduce Variability

As with the other stages, reducing variability in either delivery workload or delivery time can cause congestion and delays. In paper-based systems, a major source of variability is the location of the patient or physician (for example, searching for a physician on the move or trying to deliver test results to a patient who has changed rooms). Using a laboratory information system accessible from anywhere vastly reduces such variability.

But an even more corrosive form of variability, which going paperless does not eliminate, is error correction. If a test has incorrect patient or physician data on it, it may be difficult or impossible to deliver to the correct place. Such errors can be caused by overly complex systems. For instance, we have seen systems that require entry of the requesting physician via an ID number and lead to all kinds of errors from mistyped digits or forgotten numbers. Modifying the system so that physician names are selected from a list would make such errors much less likely. Any form of error prevention that avoids having to make unusual efforts to get results to the right place, or even redo the test, reduces variability and delay.

Improve Sequencing

Finally, as noted for the earlier segments of TAT, sequencing tests to favor high priority (stat tests or tests for patients who are candidates for discharge) can reduce delays for patients for whom it matters most.

5.4.1.4 Case: Reducing TAT in Anatomic Pathology at University of Michigan Hospital

In 2006, a new management team took over the Anatomic Pathology Department at the University of Michigan Hospital System (UMHS). Although responsiveness had not traditionally been a high priority, the new team declared TAT to be a key metric. They began their drive to improve responsiveness by generating previously uncollected statistics on TAT. Exhibit 5.4 shows the results for the general surgical pathology service, which, along with various specialties (breast, dermatology, gastrointestinal, genitourinary, renal, and gynecology) provides tissue testing services to the UMHS. This graph showed dramatically that TAT had increased discontinuously in 2000 (when the lab had divided services into specialties) and had been drifting steadily upward ever since. Clearly, the department lacked a culture of responsiveness.

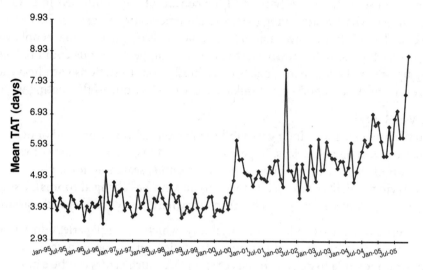

Exhibit 5.4   Turnaround time in general surgical pathology of the
UMHS Anatomic Pathology Department.

To cultivate broad involvement and jump-start the improvement process, the leadership encouraged *gemba* (direct observation) walks.[5] These revealed large batches of specimens that had been received but not accessioned, large batches of specimens that had been *accessioned* (formally received and recorded) but not *grossed* (examined by the bare eye), large batches of cassettes that had been prepared but not processed, and large batches of cases being signed out at the completion of the process. Everywhere, work was piled up in queues and being processed in lumpy, inconsistent batches. The system was the antithesis of a smooth flow-oriented process.

In 2007, a cross-functional team was formed to redesign the process to achieve smoother and faster flow. The team came up with five recommendations:

1. **Accession cases to specific faculty**—Instead of accessioning specimens to a queue, accessioners were asked to assign specimens to individual faculty. To identify the needed faculty expertise, accessioners used information about the source of the specimen (such as lung or breast), the requesting physician (for example, oncologist, dermatologist, or surgeon), and patient history (including age, prior diagnoses, and so on). To make assignments to the proper faculty member within a specialty, accessioners consulted sign-out schedules to see who would be on duty when the specimens were expected to be ready for sign-out. This simplified flows by eliminating the need for a separate assignment step (Task Simplification principle). By making a direct link from the accessioner to

the responsible faculty member, this policy reduced the potential for "stalled cases" to get overlooked (Handoffs principle). By making faculty responsible for completion of specific cases, this new assignment process became an important step in creating a culture of flow.

2. **Increase grossing of small specimens by histotechnologists**—Having histotechnologists gross small specimens (such as needle biopsies), which require less skill than larger, more complex specimens, not only reduced costs relative to examination by more expensive physician assistants (PAs) and residents, it also increased grossing capacity to allow more constant examination of specimens. This reduced delay in the grossing step by reducing both utilization and variability (Utilization and Variability principles).

3. **Partner PAs and residents to provide steady grossing coverage in all services**—For example, in a given service (for example, breast), a resident might be assigned to gross in the morning, whereas a PA is assigned to gross in the afternoon. This further reduced variability in staffing and reduced congestion and delay (Variability principle). After the initial program, these assignments were broadened to allow PAs to float between services to gross samples wherever work was piling up. This flexibility in PA capacity (Buffer Flexibility principle) better synchronized capacity with demand (Variability principle).

4. **Stagger sign-outs for more effective utilization and sign-out space**—Although the lab could not control variability in the arrival of samples, it could smooth flow within its own process to level workloads and provide a pacing mechanism. By scheduling final sign-out of various specialties to specific time windows, the lab set a target for smooth flow into the sign-out space. The resulting decrease in flow variability reduced queueing in sign-out (Variability principle) and made better use of the people and space at sign-out.

5. **Align laboratory/transcription priorities with service expectations**—With a target schedule established for sign-out, the lab instituted a system for coordinating priorities within the lab to synchronize with the sign-out schedule. To do this, they divided work in the various specialties into subsets. If the last case in a subset was scheduled to be signed out at 2 p.m., transcription for this case was expected to be completed by 1 p.m., and so on upstream through the process. The result was that the sign-out scheduled effectively "pulled" work through the system. The smooth flow reduced queueing and delay throughout the process (Variability principle).

Note that several of these policies match those suggested in Table 5.5 shown earlier, with particular emphasis on reducing variability in flow. The overall impact was to accelerate the improvement in laboratory TAT that had begun in 2006 with the renewed focus on flow. The reductions from 2005 to 2008 for each specialty are shown in Exhibit 5.5. Note that several of these had TAT reduced in half or more. In addition to dramatically improved TAT, the lab increased on-time delivery from roughly 75% in mid-2007 to 95% by early 2008. It also reduced cost by increasing the percentage of specimens grossed by histotechnologists from roughly 50% in 2007 to nearly 70% by the end of 2008 and by reducing the number of overtime hours required to meet demand. Even more impressively, these improvements were made while patient volumes grew steadily, from around 4,000 cases per month in 2007 to more than 4,500 by the end of 2008.

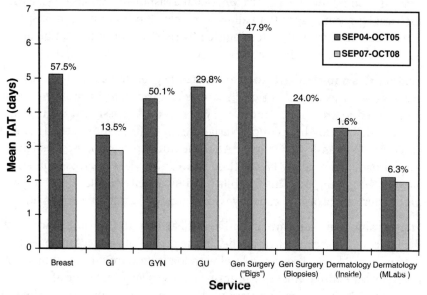

Exhibit 5.5   Percentage reductions in TAT by specialty in
UMHS Anatomic Pathology Department.

5.4.2 Imaging Responsiveness

5.4.2.1 Problem

The purpose of medical images is to aid in the diagnosis and care of patients. To be useful, the images must be available to the requesting physician in a timely fashion. But what is "timely" depends on the nature of the patient and the test. For instance, an emergency patient who needs a scan to determine the best course of immediate intervention needs results stat. An outpatient who needs a scan to help diagnose a noncritical chronic condition can wait, although not indefinitely.

So, for the purposes of framing the problem of improving imaging responsiveness, we will assume that patients can be categorized and that maximum recommended TATs can be specified for each category.

Schematically, the process that makes up the TAT for an image can be depicted in three stages—preexam, exam, and postexam—as shown in Exhibit 5.2. The preexam stage starts when a physician requests a test and the patient is placed on the schedule. It ends when the exam begins. The exam stage consists of the setup and actual examination. The postexam stage includes reading, transcription, and reporting of the results. Both pre- and postexam stages may also include transfer steps as the order/report is passed from one person/place to another.

The relative contribution of these three stages, and the steps inside them, to total TAT differ by technology. For example, because it is relatively inexpensive, the hospital may have ample capacity for conventional chest X-rays, so that getting an appointment may require almost no time. In contrast, an expensive MRI scanner may be booked weeks in advance. Consequently, preexam time may be a minor contributor to total TAT for an X-ray but may represent the majority of TAT for an MRI. In spite of differences like this, however, TAT is virtually never dominated by actual exam time. Even including setup time, most scans take from a few minutes to an hour. But TATs range from several hours to several days. Hence, it is pre- and postexam times that govern imaging responsiveness.

5.4.2.2 PRINCIPLES

This means that improving imaging responsiveness is primarily a matter of reducing delays before and after the actual exam. From Exhibit 5.2, we note that a substantial portion of these delays are queue times. Patients queue up on the schedule. They may wait in queue in the imaging facility. The images queue up for reading by the radiologists. Their dictations queue up for transcription. The reports wait in queue for final approval by the radiologists. And so on. Each step in the process presents an opportunity for waiting and batching, both of which introduce delay. The net result is that the TAT is generally much longer than the total time spent examining the patient and producing the report. Hence, the starting point for identifying opportunities to improve imaging responsiveness is understanding the queues that make up a substantial portion of total TAT.

The principles relevant to reducing imaging TAT are largely the same as those invoked earlier to reduce laboratory TAT. We list these with imaging-specific examples here.

Principle (Variability)—Variability causes congestion.

If, for instance, images were to arrive to a radiologist at a rigidly regular rate and the radiologist read them at a completely uniform rate, there would be no build-up of images waiting to be read (provided that the radiologist had sufficient capacity to keep up with the arrival rate of images). However, if the arrival rate is uneven due to variations in the types of patients, the lengths of scans, and the process of delivering images to Radiology, and the service rate is uneven because images vary in the time they take to read and because radiologists take breaks, there will be intervals during which images pile up in Radiology.

Such pile-up events will be worse if the radiologists are heavily utilized because of the following principle.

Principle (Utilization)—Utilization magnifies congestion in a highly nonlinear fashion.

Of course, because radiologists are an expensive resource, they will be scheduled in expectation of being busy. So, the combination of high variability and high utilization will naturally result in (possibly substantial) queueing delays at the reading step of the postexam stage of TAT.

The congestion caused by the combination of variability and utilization will lead to costly inefficiencies. Although the form of these inefficiencies will vary from system to system, the following principle enumerates the possible types.

Principle (Variability Buffering)—All variability will be buffered by some combination of inventory, capacity, time, quality, and system degradation.

In many of the steps in imaging TAT, the primary buffer against variability is time—namely, delay time. But, in an attempt to avoid excessive delay time, other forms of buffers may arise. For instance, radiologists may rush their analysis of images when faced with a large backlog, leading to errors (a quality buffer). Or, transcriptionists may load up on caffeine to cope with a consistently stressful workload and wear down over time (a system degradation buffer).

To the extent that procedures and policies rule out quality and system degradation responses to queueing delays, the Variability principle reduces to the following corollary in the service steps involved in the imaging process.

Corollary (Variability Buffering in Service Systems)—In a pure service system, inventory is not available as a buffer, so holding quality and human resource costs constant, there is a trade-off between variability, excess capacity, and waiting time.

Unlike a manufacturing setting, where the time to respond to a customer request can be minimized by holding on-hand inventory, imaging is a service process that is customized to each patient. Because we cannot produce images or reports in advance of patient arrivals, it is not possible to buffer variability in the imaging process with inventory. Hence, improvement is primarily a matter of managing the variability, capacity, and time trade-off.

If there were dials for controlling variability and utilization within the system, the preceding principles would be enough to guide us to design highly responsive imaging processes. We would simply dial variability down to the minimum level that is technologically and economically feasible and then set utilization low enough to keep queue times within acceptable limits for this level of variability. Unfortunately, variability comes from a host of factors that may be controllable in a variety of ways. Similarly, there are multiple ways to impact utilization. Hence, the next step in finding ways to improve imaging responsiveness is to drill down into the causes of variability and utilization at the task level.

Two fundamental principles that describe how task characteristics contribute to the high utilization and variability that causes queueing delay are

- **Principle (Task Simplification)**—Reducing task complexity reduces the mean and variance of the task times and the likelihood of errors.

- **Principle (Task Standardization)**—Using clearly specified best practice procedures for repetitive tasks reduces the mean and variance of task times and the likelihood of errors.

As indicated in Exhibit 5.2, the imaging process involves a number of tasks. (Indeed, there are more tasks than shown in that stylized diagram, which omits various handling, checking, searching, and communication steps that may be present in some imaging processes.) Simplifying or standardizing any of these can speed the flow of cases and reduce disruptions that cause variability and backups. The most important tasks to standardize and simplify are those with highly utilized resources (that is bottlenecks) and with highly variable operations. For instance, because we expect radiologists to be bottlenecks, simplifying and standardizing their work will have a substantial impact on reading time.

In the short term, improvements may be best achieved by low-technology solutions. For example, if one radiologist is particularly efficient about reading images, the department could get him to describe his simplified process and then train others in it to achieve greater standardization around it as a best practice. In the long run, technology will present more sophisticated alternatives. For instance, automated reading of digital images via pattern recognition software will eventually become an extreme form of task simplification/standardization, because it will collapse the reading process to the running of a computer program. However, although this is appealing from an operations standpoint, it is unlikely that reliable technology for full automation will be available anytime soon. So, such pattern recognition systems will probably find use as decision support systems, which give radiologists a fixed starting point for reading an image. This will still constitute a task standardization policy and hence may provide a way to increase capacity and reduce variability of the reading step.

Another form of variability that is prevalent in many diagnostic processes, including imaging, is batching, which is described in the following principle.

Principle (Batching)—When tasks involve setup time, performing them in batches makes better use of capacity but also introduces waiting time for tasks that must wait behind the batch.

For example, if a Radiology technologist must walk images down to a reading room, the walking time constitutes a setup (that is, a fixed time that must be incurred whether she is delivering one image or a dozen). To avoid wasting too much time walking, the technologist may collect a number of images before making a delivery. This results in images waiting with the technologist and a lumpy (variable) arrival process to the reading room.

Analogously, if radiologists divide their time between reading images and other activities, the time required to shift from reading to other activities and the time required to switch back constitutes a setup time. To avoid wasting time walking back to the reading room and refocusing attention on a new task, the radiologist is apt to read images in large batches, rather than reading one or two between stints on other tasks. If this results in batches of dictations being sent to transcription and batches of reports sent for approval, the uneven flow and time spent waiting in batches can substantially increase total TAT.

The preceding principles provide guidance on how to reduce average TAT by reducing queueing delays. But this average can be allocated among patients in various ways. By delaying less urgent patients in favor of more urgent ones, we can improve responsiveness where it is needed most. The following principle describes the sequencing rule that efficiently balances the waiting times of different types of patients.

Principle (Critical Ratio Sequencing)—In a multiclass system with dynamic arrivals, prioritizing entities according to the ratio c/t, where c is the delay cost per unit time and t is the expected process time, minimizes total cumulative delay over the long term.

For example, let us return to the image reading process. If all images take the same amount of time to read, this principle implies the intuitive result that radiologists should process images in order of urgency. If times differ substantially, it may become reasonable to process a quick, lower-priority image ahead of a time-consuming, higher-priority image. Of course, to apply the critical ratio rule, we need a delay cost rate for each patient type. Although it is impossible to compute these costs with precision, we can still use this rule for insight and an approximate guide. In many settings, the difference between patient urgency is considerably larger than the difference between processing times, so prioritizing only on urgency is a reasonable policy.

To the extent we can approximate the delay cost rate, it is relatively straightforward to apply the critical ratio rule in unscheduled queueing environments (for example, images arriving to reading, dictations arriving to transcription, and so on). We simply select the available job with the highest critical ratio. If specialization requires separation of the jobs (for example, radiologists have different specialties), we apply the rule within the specialties.

Because patient arrivals to the examination process are scheduled, the critical ratio rule must be implemented via decisions on how to place patients on the schedule. We can do this and get around the problem of specifying a delay cost rate by specifying a maximum allowable TAT for each type of patient. From this, we subtract a standard allotment for the examination and postexamination time to get the maximum allowable preexamination (scheduled wait) time. The goal then becomes one of putting as many patients on the schedule within their maximum scheduled wait time.

A procedure that will achieve this is as follows. First, for patients with the highest priority, place them in the earliest available slot on the schedule. Then, for patients in lower-priority categories, place them in the latest available slot on the schedule that is within their maximum scheduled wait time. This ensures that patients will meet their TAT targets while maintaining maximum flexibility for higher-priority patients who may arrive later.

Of course, so many image requests might come in that it is impossible to schedule them all within the maximum wait times. For example, suppose five days' worth of patients needing 24-hour TATs arrive all at once. Unless we have overtime available or can divert patients to other facilities (that is, have capacity buffers available), we will not be able to serve them in time.

But when multiple types of patients are involved, many scenarios lead to delays that are more amenable to correction through flexibility. The principle that applies is the following one.

Principle (Buffer Flexibility)—Flexibility in variability buffers reduces the buffering required for a given amount of variability.

One form of flexibility could be preserving the option to reschedule patients to later time slots. For instance, suppose a high-priority patient requiring 24-hour TAT arrives when today's schedule is completely full. The soonest open slot on the schedule is tomorrow and will result in a 48-hour TAT—a significant delay for this patient. To avoid this, we could reschedule one of the lower-priority patients on today's schedule into tomorrow's open slot. Because that patient was originally scheduled for his maximum TAT, he will be 24 hours late. But, because the cost of a 24-hour delay is greater for the high-priority patient than for the lower-priority patient, this switch realigns the schedule with the Critical Ratio rule. Of course, it does so at the expense of inconveniencing the lower-priority patient.

Bumping patients back in time is not the only way to use time flexibility to achieve a more efficient sequence. If we use the previous cited procedure and schedule lower-priority patients as late as possible given their maximum TATs, it is quite possible that some slots will go unfilled. This will result in lost capacity of the scanner that cannot be used to cover a future period of heavy demand. To avoid wasting capacity, we could pull patients forward into open slots, giving them earlier results and opening up capacity we might need later. This is analogous to permitting a passenger to get on an earlier flight to fill an empty seat a free up a potentially useful seat on a later flight. Unfortunately, in the short-sighted pursuit of revenue, airlines discourage this behavior by charging passengers to get on earlier flights, even when seats will go unused.

As evidence that hospitals are not making use of this type of flexibility, we offer the story of one of the authors who was scheduled for an MRI exam. Knowing how expensive this equipment is, he was not surprised to hear that it was scheduled "24/7." Because his condition was painful but not life threatening, he did not expect a prompt appointment. But he was a little surprised to get put on the schedule for 2 a.m. on a Sunday morning three weeks hence. Nevertheless, when the day came, he struggled through a late-night snowstorm to arrive at his appointment on time.

"Boy, you guys must really keep busy here," he remarked after a bit of conversation about the vicious weather.

"Not really," the woman who checked him in replied. "We haven't had anyone in here for almost six hours."

Our author could have come in at a civilized hour under less treacherous driving conditions, but no one in the facility thought to pull him forward in the schedule. Worse, it is possible that the MRI was booked for the rest of the night and unable to deliver timely service to an emergency patient. A simple phone call during the idle six hours could have made him, and that hypothetical emergency patient, much happier.

Situations like this are frustrating because of the psychology of waiting.

Principle (Waiting Time Psychology):

> Occupied time feels shorter than unoccupied time.
>
> People want to get started.
>
> Anxiety makes waits seem longer.
>
> Uncertain waits feel longer than known, finite waits.
>
> Unexplained waits feel longer than explained waits.
>
> Unfair waits feel longer than equitable waits.
>
> The more valuable the service, the longer the customer will wait.
>
> Solo waits feel longer than group waits.

Even if we cannot reduce the actual TAT for a patient image, we can make the wait on the schedule and in the examination room less onerous by providing patients with better information about their waits. For example, if patients might be bumped from the schedule to make room for emergencies, it may be a good idea to inform lower-priority patients of this possibility up front. If a patient who arrives for an examination appointment is delayed because an emergency patient has been squeezed into the schedule, it is only fair to tell the patient what has happened. Armed with a prediction of when the test will actually begin, the patient may be able to run an errand or make adjustments to his schedule for after the exam. Although this won't get the patient through the process any faster, it may well get him through it happier.

The idea of managing the psychology of waiting by providing customers information and making them feel actively involved in the process, rather than passive victims of it, is not brain surgery. But there seems to be a deep-seated cultural aversion to providing feedback about waiting times in health care systems. Disney World provides estimates of wait times throughout its theme parks, but almost no hospitals do. We are more likely to get a phone call from the pizza place explaining that our deep dish will be late than we are to get a call from a medical facility explaining that it is running behind.

Presumably this has something to do with item (vii) in the Waiting Time Psychology principle. Certainly health care is important, so we will wait for it. But competition in the health care sector is increasing. For instance, there are independent, for-profit imaging units that offer same-day scheduling, 24-hour report TAT, and open MRI technology (for patient comfort). If we don't have to endure unpleasant waits and stressful procedures, we won't. So, to keep their Radiology Departments and the revenue streams they generate, hospitals need to focus on improving both the duration and the quality of patient waiting times.

Finally, because the process of ordering exams, scanning patients, analyzing images, generating reports, and returning results involves a number of handoffs, the following principle comes into play.

Principle (Handoffs)—Unless the individuals contribute new knowledge, information is degraded as it is passed from one individual to another.

For instance, when a physician requests a CT scan, he may give a paper order to a unit secretary to convert into a computer order; this constitutes a handoff. If the appropriate information is not properly recorded in the computer order, then information degradation, which could cause efficiency and quality problems later on, occurs. We have observed an example of such degradation that occurred because the hospital computer system required entry of the requesting physician by an ID number. Even though the clerk knew the physician's name, he entered the incorrect number. As a result, the requested results were sent back to the wrong physician and a convoluted, ad hoc process ensued to get the report to the right physician. Because there are several such handoffs in the imaging process, many such information problems can disrupt the flow efficiency of the process.

5.4.2.3 PRACTICES

By combining the insights of the preceding principles, as encapsulated in Table A.1 of Appendix A, with the process breakdown shown in Exhibit 5.2, we can now use our standard procedure to enumerate a range of alternatives for improving imaging responsiveness. Not surprisingly, many of these options are analogous to those suggested for reducing laboratory TAT. But there are two important differences that lead to new streams of improvements.

First, unlike the clinical lab, most tests in an Imaging unit are scheduled. This means we can increase the utilization of the scanner by increasing the arrival rate of patients to shorten the time patients must wait on the schedule. Indeed, if there were no variability in the scanning process or in the times patients show up relative to their scheduled arrival times, we could schedule each patient to arrive just as the previous patient departs and achieve 100% utilization with no waiting. But because there is always variability, this is not possible. The Utilization principle implies that the higher utilization is at the scanner, the longer average patient wait times will be at the facility. If we assume that there is a maximum acceptable local wait time, this places a limit on the allowable utilization of the scanner. To achieve this, we must schedule *white space* (extra spacing) between patients. The more variability there is in the system, the more white space we will require to keep wait times below the maximum allowable time. Hence, we would need to reduce arrival or process variability at the scanner.

Second, because people, rather than specimens, wait for a scanner, we can invoke the Waiting Time Psychology principle to identify ways to make waiting less onerous. If this allows waits within the imaging unit to be slightly longer, scanner utilization can be pushed slightly higher, which shortens waits on the schedule.

In Table 5.6, we apply the generic improvement options from Table A.1, with additional considerations, to the objectives of reducing preexam and postexam time and successively narrow these objectives until concrete improvement policies are revealed. By working in this fashion, we generate a fairly comprehensive range of alternatives.

Table 5.6   Generic Operations Improvement Policies: Imaging Responsiveness

Level 1 Objectives	Level 2 Objectives	Level 3 Objectives	Example Policies
Reduce preexam time	Reduce scanning workload	Schedule fewer scans	Physician education on evidence-based medicine; Require physicians to personally order low-yield tests
		Divert patients to other facilities	Provide real-time estimates of wait times so physicians can direct patients elsewhere when waits are long
	Increase scanning capacity	Add physical capacity	Buy another scanner
		Speed up scanners	Replace older, slower scanners with newer, faster ones; Optimize sequences to complete scans more quickly

Level 1 Objectives	Level 2 Objectives	Level 3 Objectives	Example Policies
		Streamline setup	Automate protocol settings; Simplify and standardize setup tasks; Externalize portions of setup by prepping patient prior to scanner being available
		Increase availability	Improve preventive maintenance
	Increase scanning utilization	Reduce scan time variability	Optimize sequences to maximize image quality in a prescribed time window
		Reduce variability in setup times	Standardize setup process; Train operators in best practices
		Reduce rework/error correction	Simplify procedures; Improve operator training
		Decrease no-shows	Make reminder calls on day prior to scan
		Decrease late arrivals	Send patients instructions; Clarify signage to make facility easy to find; Ensure that escorts are available to transfer inpatients when scheduled

Table 5.6 Generic Operations Improvement Policies: Imaging Responsiveness

Level 1 Objectives	Level 2 Objectives	Level 3 Objectives	Example Policies
		Increase allowable local wait times	Make longer waits seem more acceptable by providing patients with better support and information
	Improve synchronization of scanner capacity with demand	Insert lower-priority patients into earlier slots as date approaches	Release unused times in blocks by a specified date; Allow centralized scheduler to put lower-priority patients into slots prior to their recommended response time if excess slots are available
		Reschedule lower-priority patients into earlier slots as date approaches	Call lower-priority patients and invite them to move up their appointments to make use of unfilled slots
	Reduce scanning workload variability	Level predictable demand spikes	Stagger physician rounds to stagger imaging requests; Eliminate batching of physician orders for inpatient exams
		Pull patients onto schedule	Scan inpatients opportunistically to fill holes in schedule
	Improve scanning sequencing	Reserve white space on schedule for high-priority patients	Use block scheduling to give guaranteed access to scanner; Use centralized scheduler to control access to schedule
		Slot patients by priority class	Schedule highest-priority patients into earliest available slot and schedule lowest-priority patients into latest available slot that meets recommended response times for their classes

Level 1 Objectives	Level 2 Objectives	Level 3 Objectives	Example Policies
Reduce postexam time	Reduce reading/ transcription workload	Schedule fewer scans	Physician education on evidence-based medicine
		Divert patients to other facilities	Provide real-time estimates of wait times so physicians can direct patients elsewhere when waits are long
	Increase reading/ transcription capacity	Add physical capacity	Hire radiologists/ transcriptionists
		Task simplification	Improve ergonomics (for example, lighting, chairs, software); Institute hanging protocols
		Automation	Use PACS to facilitate offsite second opinions; Install voice-automated transcription
	Improve synchronization of transcription capacity with demand	Adjust capacity	Cross-train accessioners to do transcription and use them to match transcription capacity to demand
		Reduce batching	Use PACS to transfer images and reports individually from scanner to reading to transcription; Encourage radiologists to switch frequently between reading and review/approval
	Reduce variability in reading/ transcription	Level spikes in overall reading/transcription workload	Stagger physician rounds; Pull inpatients into scanner during low demand periods

Table 5.6 Generic Operations Improvement Policies: Imaging Responsiveness

Level 1 Objectives	Level 2 Objectives	Level 3 Objectives	Example Policies
		Level mix of cases	Stagger images on schedule by radiologist specialty
		Process standardization	Establish uniform hanging protocols; Use structured reporting systems
		Error prevention	Improve technologist training and tools for monitoring image quality
		Pooling	Use teleradiology to pool radiologists across regions; Use cross-training to pool transcription and accessioning capacity
	Improve sequencing at reading/transcription	Provide information relevant to sequencing decisions	Use whiteboards to display case status (physician request time, image arrival time, urgency, and so on)
		Dynamically prioritize cases	Order cases on whiteboard accordingly to critical ratio

Reduce Preexam Time

Reduce Workload

Reducing the number of tests demanded can reduce the scheduled wait time to get those tests. If physicians are scheduling more tests than are consistent with optimal care,[6] training might ease the load. Alternatively, requiring physicians to order low-yield tests personally (rather than having a nonclinician do it) can add a barrier that results in a second thought and hence fewer orders for unnecessary tests. (See Vartanians 2010 for a discussion of a trial of this policy.) Finally, if an alternate source of capacity (such as a standalone imaging unit) is available, patients could be diverted during busy periods. Any of these approaches would serve to bring down prescan wait time. Although turning away business may actually be a plausible strategy in some cases, this path is not likely to be the one most Radiology Department managers pursue first.

Increase Capacity

We can also reduce scheduled wait times by increasing scanning capacity. Obviously, this can happen by simply buying more scanners or replacing existing ones with faster technology. But, because this is expensive, the more appealing option is to increase the effective capacity of the scanners already in place. Optimizing scanning sequences could shorten the scan time, while improving preventive maintenance could increase availability, both of which would increase effective capacity.

Note that because actual exam time is a small portion of the total TAT (from request to results), speeding up examination time has a small direct impact on TAT.

For instance, suppose a scan takes 20 minutes, and the total TAT is 4 days and is made up of 3 days of preexam time on the schedule and one day of postexam time to prepare a report. Then the direct effect on TAT of reducing exam time by 5 minutes is negligible—who cares if we take 5 minutes off a 4-day time?

But a 5-minute reduction from 20 minutes to 15 minutes means that the capacity of the scanner has increased from 3 patients per hour to 4 patients per hour—a 33% increase! If the scanner runs 24 hours a day, this means the capacity increases from 72 patients per day to 96 patients per day. The 3 days of preexam time in the original TAT represents the time to scan $72 \times 3 = 216$ patients. At 96 patients per day, this will take only $216 / 96 = 2.25$ days. Hence, the increase in capacity reduces preexam time by 0.75 days. So, the indirect capacity effect of reducing exam times on total TATs is much larger than is the direct effect. Hence, we will consider such capacity enhancement policies as options for addressing preexam time.

The really big opportunity for finding "free" capacity in the imaging process lies in the setup process. Any time the scanner is sitting idle while a patient is prepping, entering, or exiting the scanner, or the technologist is inputting protocols, adjusting other scanner settings, or any other nonscanning activity is going on, can be regarded as setup time. In lean speak, such time is "nonvalue add" or "waste." More importantly, it is lost capacity. So anything we can do to either eliminate setup steps (for example, automating, simplifying, or standardizing tasks such as entry of protocol settings) or externalize these steps (for example, prep a patient while a previous scan is still going on) will drive out this waste and increase scanning capacity.

Increase Utilization

As we noted earlier, we can also increase effective capacity of the scanner by increasing utilization. To do this without increasing wait times within the imaging facility, we must reduce variability in either scan times or arrivals. We can reduce variability in scan times by optimizing sequences or by simplifying/standardizing setup procedures to avoid repetition and adjustments that lead to an occasional long exam time. We can reduce variability in arrivals with simple measures to prevent no-shows (for example, reminder phone calls) or late arrivals (for example, better signage).[7]

Improve Synchronization

We can better match capacity to demand by bumping lower-priority patients to accommodate higher-priority patients and by pulling patients forward in the schedule to fill up open slots. Although this is straightforward to describe in theory, it takes some care to implement in practice. For instance, bumping a patient who has already arrived at the facility, and who may have ingested a nasty tasting contrast agent, will not be well received. So, an alternative approach may be to bump a patient in the near future who has not yet arrived or made invasive preparations and simply run behind schedule until that patient's slot is reached. Similarly, pulling patients forward in the schedule may not be simple, because it involves connecting with patients. Leaving messages offering earlier slots to patients would be a nightmare. Should we offer multiple patients a switch in hopes of getting one acceptance? Or should we call patients sequentially? If so, how long should we wait for a response before moving on to another patient? Or, should we just make multiple offers and allow the first person who returns the call to move up in the schedule? Coming up with something that is fair but not oppressive from an execution standpoint presents a challenge. Eventually, other forms of communication (such as email and text) will make this easier. So Radiology Departments need to remain on the lookout for technological opportunities to make adjusting their schedules more convenient.

Reduce Variability

Reducing variability of work coming into the schedule can also reduce waiting times. For instance, suppose patients needing urgent CT scans routinely arrive in bursts of several patients interspersed with periods of no arrivals. Then, no matter what scheduling procedure is used, the bursts will cause periodic work backups that prevent rapid response to the needs of some patients. If instead these high-priority patients arrived in a more uniform way, the scanner could keep up and provide faster average TATs.

So, if controllable factors lead to demand peaks (for example, physician rounding schedules send predictable bursts of patients into Radiology), there may be opportunities for workload leveling that could reduce preexam wait times for some patients. One simple way to level the workload of a scanner is to "pull" inpatients onto the schedule opportunistically. That is, instead of giving inpatients scheduled times for their exams, come and get them whenever there is a gap on the schedule. This would provide a means for making use of slots that do not get scheduled or which open up due to a patient no-show.

Improve Sequencing

In many imaging units, we need to reserve space on the schedule for high-priority patients. Some Imaging Departments do this by reserving blocks for various units. For instance, primary care physicians may get only a few slots per day for outpatients, to reserve time for ED and hospital inpatients. (This accounted for the author's three-week delay in getting on the MRI schedule.) The procedure we described earlier, in which patients are placed on the schedule at the latest point in the schedule consistent with their maximum TAT, accomplishes the same thing but is better tuned to individual patient needs than is a block scheduling system in which blocks are allocated by care units. But because patients come into the system in random order, no advance scheduling method can ensure an optimal patient sequence. So we must couple it with the flexibility measures mentioned earlier as means for improving synchronization.

Reduce Postexam Time

Reduce Workload

For a fixed scanner capacity, anything that reduces the reading/transcription workload will shorten the average time to generate reports. Hence, scheduling fewer scans or diverting patients to other facilities, which were suggested as means for reducing preexam TAT, will also serve to reduce postexam TAT. However, as we noted earlier, the trend in medicine is toward more testing, not less. So workload reduction may not be a viable option in many cases.

Increase Capacity

Other than reducing workload, the other way to reduce utilization, and hence waiting time, is by increasing capacity. The most straightforward, but expensive, way to do this is by adding people (radiologists, transcriptionists, or support personnel). But a cleverer, and less expensive, way to increase capacity is by improving the productivity (for example, cases) per hour of the radiologists and transcriptionists. Two ways to do this are task simplification and automation.

The Task Simplification principle implies that we can increase capacity of a process by reducing the number of actions and information cues required to complete tasks. Reading and transcription have many wasted steps that can be eliminated without affecting the actual work. For instance, adjusting position to compensate for an uncomfortable workstation and rereading information because of poor lighting are wasted steps that we can eliminate through better ergonomic design. Excessive clicks by radiologists and transcriptionists to access and enter information are wasted steps that can be eliminated through better IT system design. Sifting through images with unknown or mislabeled orientation and setting them up to facilitate reading are wasted steps by radiologists that can be eliminated through the use of hanging protocols.[8]

We can go even further down the task simplification path by automating some of the steps involved in the reading and transcription tasks. For instance, a PACS can automate the transfer of images between radiologists in a consultation. Voice recognition software is already automating the transcription process and, eventually, pattern recognition software will partially automate the interpretation of digital images.

Improve Synchronization

We can better match reading/transcription capacity to demand by building flexibility into the system that enables it to adjust to fluctuations in demand. For instance, we can cross-train accessioners and use them to augment transcription capacity when needed. We can also improve synchronization by reducing batching that serves to offset deliveries from demand. For instance, in a film-based X-ray unit, if films are transferred to the reading room in batches, then some images will wait unnecessarily at the scanner. Furthermore, images will arrive to the reading room in lumpy bursts, which will aggravate queueing there. So, using a runner to transfer the images more frequently will reduce TAT. Moving to digital images that can be transferred electronically one at a time will reduce delay even more. Speeding and smoothing transfer of images from the scanner to reading to transcription to the requesting physician is one of the key operational benefits of a PACS.

Reduce Variability

As in all queueing systems, once utilization has been explored for opportunities to reduce waiting, the next improvement opportunity to consider is variability reduction. This can be done by moderating arrival variability or process variability. On the arrival side, spikes in overall workload at both reading and transcription can be leveled through steps such as staggering physician rounds (to spread out imaging requests) and pulling inpatients into imaging opportunistically to fill gaps in the schedule.

Even if the total load is reasonably level, individual radiologists can still experience spikes if the mix of cases is uneven. For instance, a burst of abdominal images could back up behind the abdominal specialist while the cardiothoracic specialist is idle. So, to make more even use of the various specialties, the scanner scheduling system should be designed to level the mix of patient types. For instance, if the previously described rule for placing patients as late as possible on the schedule results in a clump of same-type patients in a time interval, it may make sense to schedule a few patients into earlier available slots to allow for a better mix. In addition, inpatients can be pulled opportunistically onto the schedule in a manner that maintains a degree in constancy of mix.

On the process side, we can reduce variability by standardizing reading and transcription tasks. We can do this by finding best practices and adopting them as standards. For instance, encouraging the use of uniform hanging protocols that have been found to be efficient can decrease variability in reading time. We can also develop tools that reduce the difference in work content of cases. For example, software that enables transcriptionists to generate common phrases, paragraphs, or even entire short reports with a few keystrokes can both increase productivity and reduce variability of transcription time.

Another form of process standardization in image reading is structured reporting, which mandates use of standard formats and terminology (Weiss and Langlotz 2008). The primary benefits cited for these computer-supported systems are reports that (a) have less chance of misinterpretation by requesting physicians, and (b) can be archived in a database for future retrieval and reuse. By making report construction a more uniform activity, structured reporting systems may also reduce variability of the image reading process. However, with current workflows and software systems, most clinicians find that standardized reporting is slower than free-form reporting. It remains to be seen whether technical improvements and familiarity will make structured reporting both more efficient and less variable than free-form reporting.

Process standardization is only one way to reduce task variability. Another is to focus on specific causes of variability. In reading and transcription, as in many processes in health care and elsewhere, an important source of variability is error correction. For example, poor image quality due to an exposure error in the exam can require reexamination of the patient, resulting in a substantial delay in reading the image. Steps that eliminate this wasteful rework step constitute task simplification strategies, which by the Task Simplification principle serves to reduce both the average and standard deviation of reading TAT. Examples of such steps could include better training of technicians and tools that enable the technologist to check image quality before the patient leaves the scanner.

Analogously, dictation errors that lead to transcription errors must be corrected by post-transcription editing. This not only delays the reports of the affected reports, but causes congestion-inducing variability at transcription, which delays other reports. Hence, error-prevention measures that address process accuracy at reading and transcription, as well as upstream from these processes, reduce postexam TAT. They also reduce the chance of patient harm that can occur if the errors are not caught and affect treatment decisions based on the imaging report.

Another generic variability reduction strategy is pooling. For instance, teleradiology allows a pool of radiologic specialists to receive images from many sites, which levels their workload and allows them to respond more consistently than an individual specialist in a hospital subject to a highly fluctuating load. Similarly, transcription services pool report requests from multiple sites to take advantage of load leveling to provide quick turnaround more efficiently (that is, with less excess capacity) than is possible in a small Transcription unit inside an individual hospital.

Finally, for variability that cannot be eliminated, synchronization strategies can mitigate the impact of the variability. The ideal is to have capacity fluctuate in a manner that exactly follows fluctuations in workload, so that no congestion occurs. Although it is never possible to match capacity to demand precisely, there are strategies for making an approximate match. For example, we can cross-train accessioners to perform transcription (and vice versa). Then, whenever transcription workload becomes high, we can increase transcription capacity by shifting some accessioners to transcription. In contrast, when accessioning workload is high, we can shift some transcriptionists to accessioning. The result is less congestion, and hence faster TATs, at both accessioning and transcription.

Improve Sequencing

As we noted in the previous discussion of preexam TAT, sequencing patients appropriately can allocate TAT efficiently among patients. That is, it can keep TATs short for the patients who need it most, at the expense of longer TATs for patients for whom speed is less critical. However, the benefits of sequencing patients into the examination process cannot be fully realized if the sequence is not maintained in the postexamination stage. For instance, a high-priority patient might have her image languish in the reading room if radiologists choose images according to fit with their interests and expertise and the image in question "falls between the cracks."

To maintain an effective sequence, two steps are necessary. First, radiologists and transcriptionists need information about the cases to enable them to sequence them. For instance, displaying the cases on a whiteboard, which shows physician request time, arrival time to reading/transcription, patient criticality, and so on, would make inappropriate delays visible to staff and management. Second, radiologists need to follow an effective sequencing policy. Earlier we noted that a critical ratio, which balances urgency and process time, can form the basis for a sequencing rule that minimizes urgency-weighted TAT. Calculating such a ratio and including it on the whiteboard display would help radiologists and transcriptionists select cases to maintain an efficient sequence. Furthermore, Halsted and Froehle (2008) found that using a system that automatically prioritizes cases reduced interruptions and time spent by radiologists on manually prioritizing cases and resulted in reduction of postexam TAT of more than 30%.

Table 5.6 gives us a logical framework for identifying ways to reduce pre- and postexam time in an imaging process. This framework is comprehensive in terms of Level 1 Objectives, reasonably thorough at Level 2 and Level 3 Objectives, but only illustrative with regard to Example Policies. Implementation of the broad concepts highlighted by the management principles is necessarily domain and technology dependent. For instance, a hospital with digital imaging units and a PACS may focus on establishing a wireless notification system to speed transfer of a completed report to a requesting physician, whereas a hospital using film and paper reports may need to focus on improving its system of runners to physically deliver results to physicians.

Furthermore, as technology improves, new policy options may emerge. For example, when pattern recognition software becomes advanced enough to give preliminary interpretations of images (for example, whether a mammogram indicates a malignancy), it may be possible to classify images according to their difficulty. Radiologists can use this information and the Critical Ratio principle to prioritize images for reading. Images classified as "easy" by the computer are more likely to be obvious, and hence quick to interpret. Because reports can be generated quickly, these cases should receive higher priority under the Critical Ratio sequencing rule. In contrast, images the computer classifies as "hard" are more likely to be subtle to interpret, and hence may require more time or even input from multiple radiologists to interpret. Under the Critical Ratio principle, these cases should receive lower priority to prevent them from holding up the faster jobs in the queue.

The preceding are illustrations of the "practices progress but principles persist" dictum. Short of eliminating the need for images due to prevention or fully automated home imaging and interpretation, neither of which seems remotely imminent, there will be a diagnostic imaging process that includes multiple steps containing nonvalue-added delays. While this is the case, the characterization of the imaging process in terms of management principles shown in Table 5.6 will provide a logical means for identifying the next step in the continual improvement process.

5.4.2.4 CASE: REDUCING MRI WAIT TIMES AT WINDSOR REGIONAL HOSPITAL

In April 2009, Windsor Regional Hospital, a large, two-campus community hospital in Ontario, Canada, had 1,424 unprocessed MRI requests and a 90th percentile of wait time for nonemergent scans of 117 days (Windsor Regional Hospital 2011). Faced with rising demand for service and the prospect of even longer delays, Director of Diagnostic Imaging Ralph Nicoletti put together a cross-disciplinary lean team to find ways to reduce wait times.

Starting with a value stream mapping process, the team identified each step in the process of providing a patient with an MRI scan and collected data on wait times and error rates at each step. A major source of variability and delay was found to be incomplete requisitions sent in by ordering physicians. These could lead to repeated phone calls to correct information, waits to administer contrast dyes or drugs, or even rebooking of patients. To address these and other inefficiencies observed in the process, the team implemented a number of changes, including the following (Health Care Ontario 2011):

- **Revising the requisition form for ordering an MRI**—Because important information was being lost in the requisition process (Handoffs principle), the team standardized forms (Standardization principle) to clarify the exact information that ordering physicians needed to communicate to the radiologist.

- **Tracking which ordering physicians repeatedly sent in incomplete requisitions and having them resubmit**—By giving physicians negative attention and extra work to correct their errors, the hospital helped align personal costs with system costs and thereby encouraged physicians to act in the interest of the overall system (Self-Interest principle) by getting it right the first time.

- **Using an electronic scheduler system**—This made it easier to track appointment times (Task Simplification principle), which in turn helped catch and correct errors (Redundancy principle) that might lead to patient no-shows and lost scanner capacity.

- **Implementing standardized protocols**—This straightforward application of the Standardization principle reduced the time radiologists spent on designing the protocols, decreased the use of contrast dye (which is costly and adds extra time), and shortened the average time per patient by decreasing the number of unnecessary scans that were sometimes included in protocols.

- **Instituting ten-hour shifts for nursing staff responsible for pediatric sedations**—This reduced sedation delays (Utilization principle), which in turn reduced MRI delays.

- **Booking similar body parts on the same day**—Grouping similar tests together reduced set-up time to change coils on the machine and thereby increased the effective capacity of the scanner (Batching principle). For example, the group created "spine Fridays."

- **Scheduling complex cases during the day and simpler cases during later hours**—Because simpler cases do not require other resources, they can be scheduled after hours without requiring extra staffing of the outside resources. Offloading some cases from the regular day hours increased the effective capacity of the MRI and hence reduced utilization and delay (Utilization principle).

- **Systematic evaluation and tracking of daily and monthly MRI reports on volumes and efficiency**—To elevate consciousness of responsiveness and provide continual feedback on the effectiveness of changes, waiting time and other statistics were prominently posted.

Because of these and other related changes, the 90th percentile of MRI wait times fell from 117 days in April 2009 to 29 days in April 2011. Over the same time period, unprocessed MRI requests had dropped from 1,424 to 156, even though patient volume had increased by 11%. In addition, radiologist protocolling time had decreased from 120 to 45 minutes per day. Finally, the use of standardized protocols resulted in a decrease in the fraction of MRI exams that used contrast agents from 21% to 15%, with an attendant time and cost savings. In recognition of its accomplishment, Windsor Regional Hospital received the Leading Practice Award at the Ontario Hospital Association (OHA) International HealthAchieve Conference in November 2011 (Musyj 2011).

5.4.3 Laboratory Errors

5.4.3.1 PROBLEM

A cursory glance at the statistics on laboratory errors might suggest that they are a small and declining problem. Indeed, errors in the analytic processes of laboratory testing are becoming less prevalent, due largely to automation and improved technology. For instance, Plebani (2010) contrasted a 1947 study of laboratory quality that reported

162,116 errors per million tests (16.2%) with a 1997 study that showed 447 errors per million tests (0.045%), and concluded that laboratory error rates have been falling over the past several decades. Leape (2009) cited recent studies indicating that the average error rate in the analytic portion of laboratory testing may be as low as 0.002%.

But analysis is only part of the laboratory testing process. In recognition of this, the International Organization for Standardization (ISO) has defined *laboratory error* more broadly as "failure of planned action to be completed as intended, or use of a wrong plan to achieve an aim, occurring at any part of the laboratory cycle, from ordering examinations to reporting results and appropriately interpreting and reacting to them" (ISO 2008). This definition encompasses all stages shown in Exhibit 5.1, from pre-pre-analytical to post-postanalytic. This is important because studies show that error rates are much higher before and after analysis than in analysis itself (see Bonini et al. 2000).

Plebani (2010) compiled the extant studies into a framework consistent with the ISO definition and concluded that laboratory errors are distributed as shown in Exhibit 5.6, where the min and max values represent the ranges observed across the various studies. This summary indicates that the direct analytic stage, which has benefited from decades of attention and automation, is responsible for only 7–13% of the total errors associated with laboratory testing. The pre-preanalytical stage, which includes the predominantly manual test ordering and specimen collection tasks, is responsible for 46–68%, whereas the post-postanalytic stage, which includes the subjective task of interpreting the results, accounts for 25–46% of laboratory errors. Clearly, most laboratory errors do not occur in the laboratory at all, but are instead the result of activities before and after the lab.

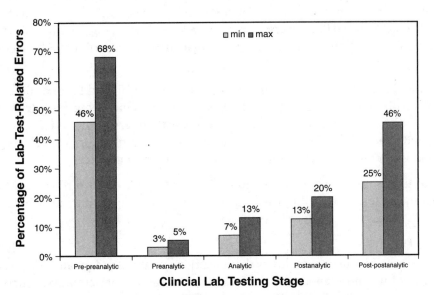

Exhibit 5.6   Distribution of errors reported in published studies of hospital laboratory errors. (Source: Plebani 2010)

When we consider the full process, the error rate in the laboratory is much higher than the 0.002% reported by Leape (2009) for the analysis stage alone. For example, in a study of the "stat" section of a hospital laboratory, Plebani and Carraro (1997) found an overall error rate of 0.47% (189 mistakes out of 40,490 analyses, of which only 13.3% came from the analytic stage).

Still, an overall error rate of less than 1% might not seem like a huge problem. But, as we noted previously, it is not uncommon for hospital laboratories to process millions of tests per year. One percent of a million is 10,000 errors per year. Although not all of these errors lead to patient harm, some do. Plebani (2010) reported that a range of research studies have concluded that 24.4% to 30% of laboratory errors had an effect on patient care (for example, performance of additional unnecessary tests), whereas 2.7% to 12% of laboratory errors led to adverse events or inappropriate care. To put these numbers into perspective, a large laboratory that processes 5 million tests per year with an error rate of 0.05%, of which 5% of errors lead to adverse events, will cause 1,250 adverse events per year.

Worse yet, such events can be tragic. For example, in 2001 at St. Agnes Hospital in Philadelphia, lab technicians used the wrong sensitivity factor in calculating the blood clotting rate for 932 patients over a seven-week period (Burling 2001). This led to many patients receiving an overdose of the blood thinning agent warfarin. Two patients died, and others suffered adverse consequences before the problem was identified and corrected.

Clearly, laboratory errors are a serious problem in the hospital. But, because hospital laboratories also support outpatient care, laboratory errors can have consequences throughout the health care system. For instance, Lundquist (2003) reported that in a study of more than 100,000 adverse clinical events observed in outpatient facilities, 34% were related to medication errors, but more than 10% were attributable to laboratory errors.

Given the importance of clinical tests to medical diagnosis in and beyond the hospital, current error rates are too high. Indeed, in most manufacturing industries, where defects seldom lead to customer harm, a process with an error rate of 0.5% would be considered unacceptable. So it is reasonable to expect a standard for hospital laboratory tests that is several orders of magnitude better than current practice.

The question is how to get there. Although we cannot give detailed directions, we can say that the path is paved with principles. We review the relevant ones next.

5.4.3.2 PRINCIPLES

From the earlier discussion, we know that the pre-preanalytic and preanalytic phases are the source of the most laboratory errors. So these stages are of paramount importance in error reduction. But for the lab to get to parts-per-million quality levels, improvements are needed in the other stages as well.

Within each stage, different types of errors are possible because the testing process involves different types of tasks. Specifically, it requires *decisions* about the course of action, *execution* of the elected course of action, *prevention* of errors that do occur from causing adverse events, and *recovery* from adverse events in a manner that mitigates patient harm as much as possible. Hence, we can classify laboratory errors (and indeed all errors related to patient safety) into the following categories:

- **Decision errors**—These are failures to elect the correct course of action. Examples are ordering an inappropriate test and using a test result incorrectly in the treatment process.
- **Execution errors**—These are failures to carry out the elected course of action properly. Such errors can occur outside the lab (for example, a sample is contaminated during collection) or inside the lab (for example, an equipment failure produces an erroneous reading).
- **Protection and recovery errors**—These are failures to catch and correct errors (of either of the preceding types) before they present an opportunity to result in patient harm. Exhibit 5.7 provides a schematic of the process by which errors present dangerous situations. It can be resolved through routine defenses or through exceptional intervention (resulting in a near miss). The layers of protection are described by the Swiss cheese model (Reason 2000), which posits that most system failures are due to breakdowns at multiple levels.

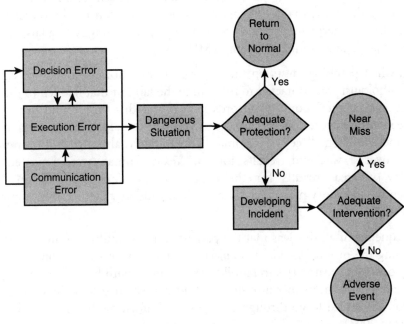

Exhibit 5.7   Errors, incidents, near misses, and adverse events.
(Adapted from van der Schaaf 1992.)

- **Communication errors**—These are failures to transfer information needed to carry out decision, execution, and protection/recovery tasks. As such, communication errors are not really a separate class of errors, but a contributing factor to the other three classes. However, because accurate and timely information is essential to error prevention, we call out communication errors explicitly to highlight their importance.

We can illustrate the preceding types of errors and the Swiss cheese model of system failure by means of a case. In 2000, a 34-year-old Texas woman went to the dentist with a nagging toothache (Burton 2003). An X-ray revealed a cyst under her gum, so she was referred to a facial plastic surgeon who took a biopsy. The lab result indicated small cell carcinoma with neuroendocrine features, an aggressive form of cancer. Because this cancer is also quite rare, the pathologist called the lab to see if any other tests had been done on the same day as the patient's, which could possibly have presented a source of contamination. She was informed that no such tests had been done. So she reported the test results as indicating metastatic small cell neuroendocrine carcinoma of primary lung origin.

The plastic surgeon referred the patient to an oncologist, who ordered additional scans. While awaiting tests, the oncologist went out of town, leaving his partners in charge of the case. When the new tests failed to confirm the original cancer diagnosis, the patient was referred to an otolaryngologist. He had the patient's slides reviewed by another pathologist, who agreed that they showed metastatic small cell carcinoma. Even though further testing did not provide independent evidence of cancer, the otolaryngologist recommended and performed surgery to remove the cyst along with a large portion of the patient's jaw and a number of teeth (TMLT 2010).

However, when pathology tests on the removed tissue showed no sign of cancer, the original pathologist was contacted to reexamine the lab test that had led to the diagnosis. She rechecked the laboratory records herself and this time found that there had indeed been another test done on a patient who had undergone a lymph node biopsy showing metastatic small cell carcinoma. Unfortunately, although both samples were processed over a weekend, results for the Texas woman were reported out on Wednesday, whereas results for the other patient were reported on Monday. Consequently, laboratory personnel did not initially identify them as overlapping in the lab (TMLT 2010).

The consequence of all this was that the patient endured multiple unnecessary surgeries, including the original *hemimandibulectomy* (removal of the jaw on one side) and several reconstructive surgeries to rebuild her mandible with bone from her leg and to replace teeth. Furthermore, because she was told that she had only three to six months to live, she was forced to go through the agony of informing her 10- and 12-year-old sons (Burton 2003).

The patient's unnecessary surgery and personal anguish (an adverse event if ever there was one) was the result of the contamination of her sample in the laboratory (an execution error). But, by itself, this error would not have led to patient harm. A number of other errors were made, along with failures of protective mechanisms to catch these errors. For example, neither the lab nor the original pathologist clearly flagged the result as suspicious and incongruent with other clinical data (prevention errors). Then, although both the original pathologist and the original oncologist testified that they favored a rebiopsy, neither of them put this in writing, and this recommendation was evidently lost in the transmission of the case to other oncologists and the otolaryngologist (a communication error). The recommendation also did not reach the patient. Finally, despite an array of tests that did not support the cancer diagnosis, the otolaryngologist decided on invasive surgery without an additional biopsy to confirm the diagnosis (a decision error).

Exhibit 5.8 summarizes this sequence of failures schematically using the Swiss cheese construct. The implication here is that processes need not be error free to protect patients. But multiple failures that are dangerously aligned can lead to patient harm. Hence, in addition to reducing the rate of errors in decision, execution, and communication, we can enhance patient safety by reducing prevention errors through implementation of more layers of protection.

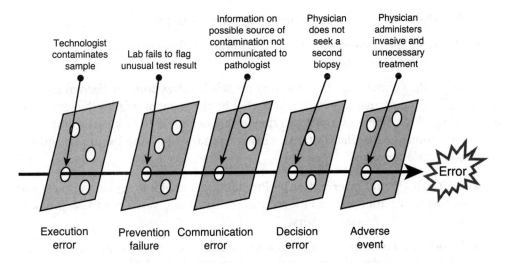

Exhibit 5.8   An example of the "Swiss cheese" system failure model of Reason (2000) applied to patient safety in clinical laboratory testing.

With this case and the previous breakdown in mind, we can identify the management principles that are applicable to reducing laboratory errors and the patient harm they can cause.

Principles that deal with the quality of decisions and conditions that affect them are relevant to decision errors. These include

- **Principle (Value of Information)**—The value of information lies in its ability to avoid a suboptimal decision. Hence, information that cannot change a decision has no value.

- **Principle (Test Quality)**—All else equal, tests with higher specificity and higher sensitivity are better in supporting rapid and accurate diagnoses.

- **Principle (Incidence Rate)**—The lower the incidence rate of a condition, the more likely a test is to yield a false positive result.

- **Principle (First Impressions)**—First impressions are critical inputs to medical decision making, because they are psychologically self-reinforcing and because even an objective statistician will not alter strongly held beliefs without significant contrary evidence.

- **Principle (Workload)**—Work efficiency and accuracy exhibits an inverted-U shaped relationship with workload.

- **Principle (Interruptions)**—Interruptions degrade decision making in complex tasks.

- **Principle (Fatigue)**—Fatigue impairs decision making.

- **Principle (Foolproofing)**—Using constraints to force correct actions reduces the likelihood of errors.

Execution of the various steps in the testing process involves both intellectual and physical tasks. The intellectual aspects are impacted by the same principles that affect decision making. But to these we must add the principles related to task performance (that is, Simplification and Standardization). This gives us the following list of principles relevant to execution errors:

- **Principle (Visual Information)**—Providing essential information visually and in tight association with a task reduces the mean and variance of task times, as well as the likelihood of errors.

- **Principle (Handoffs)**—Unless new knowledge is contributed by the individuals, information is degraded as it is passed from one individual to another.

- **Principle (Task Simplification)**—Reducing task complexity reduces the mean and the variance of the task times and the likelihood of errors.

- **Principle (Task Standardization)**—Using clearly specified best practice procedures for repetitive tasks reduces the mean and variance of task times and the likelihood of errors.

- **Principle (Workload)**—Work efficiency and accuracy exhibit an inverted-U shaped relationship with workload.

- **Principle (Interruptions)**—Interruptions degrade decision making in complex tasks.

- **Principle (Fatigue)**—Fatigue impairs decision making.

- **Principle (Foolproofing)**—Using constraints to force correct actions reduces the likelihood of errors.

Finally, no matter how much we improve decision making and execution, some errors will occur. But these need not necessarily harm patients, or at least they need not harm them as much. Principles that can be invoked to protect patients from harm or mitigate the harm they incur include

- **Principle (Redundancy)**—Independent layers of protection increase the reliability of a system.

- **Principle (Foolproofing)**—Using constraints to force correct actions reduces the likelihood of errors.

5.4.3.3 PRACTICES

To generate specific policies with which to reduce errors related to hospital laboratories and the patient harm associated with them, we invoke the generic options from Table A.2 of Appendix A, which are based on the preceding principles, and apply them to each step in the overall testing process. The major steps in this process (from Exhibit 5.1) and the distribution of errors associated with them (from Exhibit 5.6) are

1. **Pre-preanalytic stage (46–68% of errors)**

   Ordering—Physician decides what tests are needed for a patient and places an order

   Collection—Phlebotomists are notified of the test order and collect the necessary specimens from patients

2. **Preanalytic stage (3–5% of errors)**

   Accessioning—Accessioner receives, records, and routes sample within lab

   Preparation—Technologist prepares sample for tester

3. **Analytic stage (7–13% of errors)**

   Analysis—Technologist loads samples into analyzer and oversees test

4. **Postanalytic stage (13–20% of errors)**

   Validation—Technologist or pathologist validates results and may include interpretative comments with the report

   Reporting—Results are communicated to the physician who ordered the test

5. **Post-postanalytic stage (25–46% of errors)**

   Interpretation—Ordering physician interprets the test results and uses them to help determine course of patient treatment

Because the preanalytic stage is responsible for only a small fraction of errors, we will collapse accessioning and preparation into a single task (even though these are often done by different people), to keep our analysis from becoming too long. Similarly, we will collapse validation and communication into a single task, because they are closely related (that is, the same pathologist who validates and interprets the results is also involved in communicating them to the physician via his report). This leaves us with six distinct tasks: ordering, collection, accessioning/preparation, analysis, validation/reporting, and interpretation.

Within each of these tasks, we generically consider decision errors, execution errors, and protection/recovery failures. However, not all types of errors are uniformly applicable to all tasks. From the nature of the tasks, and from the empirical evidence (see Plebani 2010 for a survey), it is clear that decision errors are of particular concern in the ordering and interpretation tasks. In contrast, execution errors are the primary issue in the collection, accessioning/preparation, and testing tasks. But protection failures can occur at any stage of the process and must be considered as potential improvement options throughout the system.

The most obvious observation we can make about Table 5.7 is that it is long. Like most hospital systems, the laboratory testing process involves many steps. And, like most hospital performance metrics, error rate can be influenced along a number of dimensions, represented by a variety of management principles. When we consider the combination of steps and dimensions, we get a large number of generic improvement options (Level 4 Objectives in Table 5.7). When we consider the various options for implementing these objectives, we get an even larger number of candidate improvement policies. In Table 5.7, we list only one or two specific policies for each generic improvement option; in practice, there could be many more.

Table 5.7   Generic Operations Improvement Policies: Laboratory Errors

Level 1 Objectives	Level 2 Objectives	Level 3 Objectives	Level 4 Objectives	Example Policies
Pre-preanalytic			Improve information availability	Electronic records that provide access to prior test results
		Improve information	Improve information quality	Integrated clinical information and order entry system to provide comprehensive basis for selecting tests to order
			Improve recognition of relevant information	Test algorithms that provide guidance on appropriate ordering and use of tests
		Improve task assignments	Clarify staff authority for decision making	Rules regarding who is authorized to order which tests
Reduce ordering errors by requesting physicians	Improve decisions by physicians about which tests to order		Have formal referral protocols	Guidelines for consultation on which tests to order
		Improve training	Enhance domain knowledge	Continuing ed courses Medical abstract services
			Enhance decision process knowledge	Training on common biases and decision errors
			Test skills	Periodic quizzes on which tests to order given symptoms
			Enrich experience	Simulation-based training
		Improve incentives	Use direct method	Reduced reimbursement for tests deemed unnecessary
			Use indirect method	Requirement of physicians to personally order low-yield tests

Table 5.7 Generic Operations Improvement Policies: Laboratory Errors

Level 1 Objectives	Level 2 Objectives	Level 3 Objectives	Level 4 Objectives	Example Policies
		Simplify/ standardize decision process	Reduce/clarify choices	Order sets that include recommended tests for specified patient conditions
			Standard protocols	CPOE system that provides guidelines for test ordering
		Improve focus	Optimize workloads	Monitoring of physician patient loads in ED and wards; Flex schedules to respond to overloads
			Avoid fatigue	Shift length restrictions; Casino scheduling
			Minimize distractions/ interruptions	Whiteboards/visual displays or written protocols that reduce the number of physician queries for information
		Increase redundancy	Active checks	Seeking advice on which tests to order for difficult cases
			Passive checks	CPOE system with automated order sets of tests consistent with specified symptoms

Level 1 Objectives	Level 2 Objectives	Level 3 Objectives	Level 4 Objectives	Example Policies
	Improve execution of the test ordering process by physicians and any other people involved in placing orders	Improve information		Paper or electronic order forms that include intuitive ordering instructions
		Improve training		Training of physicians/nurses on proper procedure for ordering tests
		Improve incentives	Use direct method	Charging units for tests with incorrect information that must be corrected by laboratory
			Use indirect method	Refusal to process test orders with incomplete information, so that reorders and delays result
		Simplify/ standardize tasks		Standard forms or CPOE procedures for ordering tests
				Automation of some information entry (for example, physician info)
		Enhance focus		Same policies as for enhancing decision focus by physicians; Analogous policies for nurses/ technicians who execute test orders
	Improve protection and recovery from errors that occur in test ordering	Improve information		Tracking down ill-specified and unidentified samples to uncover causes and prevention opportunities; Rewarding "good catches"

Table 5.7 Generic Operations Improvement Policies: Laboratory Errors

Level 1 Objectives	Level 2 Objectives	Level 3 Objectives	Level 4 Objectives	Example Policies
		Increase redundancy	Have active checks	Consistency checks in lab (for example, flagging fasting tests where patients have not been confirmed as having fasted)
			Have passive checks	Electronic system that will not process order unless all critical fields have been filled in
		Mitigate patient harm	Increase speed of response	Accelerated retest of flawed test orders
			Increase effectiveness of response	Test protection by deliberately submitting orders with incomplete/incorrect information
Reduce collection errors by phlebotomists	Improve decisions by phlebotomists about when, where, and how to collect specimens	Improve information	Improve information availability	Generate summary from patient record relevant to collection (for example, mastectomy patient requiring venipuncture in specific arm)
			Improve information quality	Provide phlebotomists with test-specific patient requirements (for example, 24-hr fast for glucose; 6-hr fast for lipids)
			Improve information recognition	Color-coded wristband indicating risk factors (for example, mastectomy patient)
		Improve task assignments	Make authority clear	Rules for who decides if a second sample is needed (for example, may require doctor/nurse approval for pediatric patients)
			Have protocols for delegation	Guidelines for calling nurse/doctor (for example, patient has allergic reaction)

Level 1 Objectives	Level 2 Objectives	Level 3 Objectives	Level 4 Objectives	Example Policies
		Improve training		Continuing education for phlebotomists, which includes decision scenarios for unusual patients and new tests
		Improve incentives		Premium pay for certification
		Simplify/ standardize decisions	Reduce/clarify choices	Indication of collection details on test order
			Have standard protocols	Recommended collection procedures based on best practices
		Improve focus	Avoid fatigue, interruptions, distractions	Collection for morning rounds started early enough to avoid stress on phlebotomists
		Increase redundancy	Have active checks	Supervisor making spot checks on phlebotomists
			Have passive checks	Specimen label will not print until phlebotomist has certified check of patient information
	Improve execution of the specimen collection process	Improve information	Improve information availability	Specimen collection protocols for various patient/test type combinations
			Improve information quality	Protocols on patient fasting, specimen handling, and so on updated in light of new tests
			Improve information recognition	Numbers on containers indicating collection order

Table 5.7   Generic Operations Improvement Policies: Laboratory Errors

Level 1 Objectives	Level 2 Objectives	Level 3 Objectives	Level 4 Objectives	Example Policies
		Improve assignment	Clarify authority	Certification requirements to collect blood from infants or elderly patients
			Provide protocols for delegation	Guidelines for calling a senior phlebotomist (for example, can't find a vein)
		Improve training	Provide information	Periodic courses for phlebotomists (and others who collect samples)
			Test skills	Observation of phlebotomists in action, with feedback provided
			Enrich experience	Role-playing training in new methods
		Improve incentives		Tracking of specimen acceptance rate and rewarding of high performers with scheduling preferences, bonuses, and so on
		Simplify/ standardize tasks	Remove steps	Phlebotomy cart organized to eliminate searching
			Automate steps	Bar-coded specimen labels with onsite printer
			Transfer best practices	Documented procedures of best performers and recommended practice from literature to incorporate in training and protocols
			Have uniform protocols	Written checklists for specimen collection process; Standardized transport carts designed to prevent breakage or sample mix-ups

Level 1 Objectives	Level 2 Objectives	Level 3 Objectives	Level 4 Objectives	Example Policies
		Enhance focus	Optimize workloads	Match of phlebotomist schedules to arrival patterns; Use of floaters for collection during peak times
			Avoid fatigue, interruptions, distractions	Overtime scheduled sparingly; Senior phlebotomists paged or texted, rather than called, for consultation
		Increase redundancy	Have active checks	Patient ID information entered in two ways for consistency check
			Have passive checks	Containers that signal underfill
Improve protection and recovery from errors that occur in specimen collection		Improve information	Improve incentives	Quality awards implemented for "good catch" (near miss) identification
			Improve reporting	Electronic records record error corrections assured
			Improve monitoring	Use of "delta analysis" to flag unlikely shifts in patient readings
			Use cause and effect analysis	Time stamp steps, so errors can be tracked to their source
		Increase redundancy	Have active checks	Patient ID compared on sample and order in the lab

Table 5.7   Generic Operations Improvement Policies: Laboratory Errors

Level 1 Objectives	Level 2 Objectives	Level 3 Objectives	Level 4 Objectives	Example Policies
				Sample quality (clotting, temperature, ruptured RBCs, and so on) checked in the lab, and substandard specimens rejected; Retest samples flagged by delta analysis (or other suspicious conditions)
			Have passive checks	Automatic generation of specimen labels from barcode on patient wristband; Collection containers with outer housing to prevent contamination of specimens
		Mitigate patient harm	Increase speed of response	Control chart of test averages to detect a systematic error; Database capable of pulling up tests by result and time in lab (for example, to identify a possible source of contamination)
			Increase effectiveness of response	Contingency plans for identifying and responding to most common treatment errors; Simulation-based exercises to build problem solving confidence and expertise

Level 1 Objectives	Level 2 Objectives	Level 3 Objectives	Level 4 Objectives	Example Policies
Preanalytic Reduce errors in sample receipt/ preparation	Improve decisions by accessioners and technicians regarding whether and how to accept/prep samples for testing	Improve information	Improve information availability	Indicators of patient info (for example, fasting) with which lab can screen potentially erroneous results
			Improve information quality	Barcodes that eliminate transcription errors (for example, in patient ID)
			Improve information recognition	Color-coded test labels that indicate routing/preparation requirements
		Improve assignment	Clarify authority	Conditions under which accessioner can reject sample
			Have protocols for delegation	Guidelines for accessioner to consult technician/pathologist about ambiguous or suspicious test request or sample
		Improve training	Provide information	Periodic training sessions, which cover protocols for decision scenarios (for example, ambiguous sample)
			Test skills	Fictional test request occasionally sent to test lab response
			Enrich experience	Simulation of decision scenarios as part of training sessions

Table 5.7 Generic Operations Improvement Policies: Laboratory Errors

Level 1 Objectives	Level 2 Objectives	Level 3 Objectives	Level 4 Objectives	Example Policies
		Improve incentives		"Good catches" by accessioners tracked and displayed
		Simplify/ standardize decisions		Automated routing via bar coding
		Enhance focus		Specimen drop-off protocols that do not interrupt accessioner in the process of routing/preparing samples
		Increase redundancy		Protocols for checking patient information (for example, fasting) against test requirements
	Improve execution of the process of accessioning and preparation of samples	Improve information	Improve information availability	Order sets in CPOE that provide complete details on tests requested; Specimen labels that are durable under laboratory conditions
			Improve information quality	Bar codes that increase accuracy of patient ID and test request info by reducing transcription errors
			Improve information recognition	Color-coded labels that indicate tests to be performed on sample; No handwritten labels or small fonts used

Level 1 Objectives	Level 2 Objectives	Level 3 Objectives	Level 4 Objectives	Example Policies
		Improve assignment	Clarify authority	Division of prep work between accessioner and technician
			Have protocols for delegation	Guidelines for when a grossing technician can reroute a sample to another technician (for example, specimen was routed to incorrect cell in lab)
		Improve training		Periodic sessions to update accessioners and prep/grossing technicians on new techniques and to review basic skills
		Improve incentives		Bonus for ASCP certification; Error rates tracked and displayed
		Simplify/ standardize tasks	Remove steps	Durable bar codes used to eliminate need for transcribing labels on specimens
			Automate steps	Automated sample handling/prep stations
			Transfer best practices	Best-performing accessioners/technicians provide instruction to others
			Have uniform protocols	Written guidelines on receipt/preparation procedures
		Improve focus		Techs rotated between tasks to avoid fatigue; Batch-processing of samples avoided to prevent mix-up errors

Table 5.7 Generic Operations Improvement Policies: Laboratory Errors

Level 1 Objectives	Level 2 Objectives	Level 3 Objectives	Level 4 Objectives	Example Policies
		Increase redundancy		Prep/grossing technician reads aloud patient info and compares with requisition form to catch upstream labeling errors
		Improve information		Root cause analysis of adverse events to identify errors most likely to lead to patient harm
	Improve protection and recovery from errors that occur in accessioning or preparation	Increase redundancy		Technologists reads aloud patient ID and tests info as a check on inconsistencies; System set up for attending physicians to report errors/concerns back to lab
		Mitigate patient harm		Develop protocol for tracking down and following up on unidentified samples
Analytic			Improve information availability	Durable labels/bar codes to prevent loss during processing; Guidelines on common decisions (for example, when to reject a sample or flag a potential error)
Reduce errors in analysis of sample	Improve decisions by technologists concerning whether and how to analyze samples	Improve information	Improve information quality	Monitoring of literature for innovations in laboratory procedures; Near misses (good catches) tracked as a source of information about where technologist decision processes can be refined

Level 1 Objectives	Level 2 Objectives	Level 3 Objectives	Level 4 Objectives	Example Policies
			Improve information recognition	Flowchart posters on basic procedures; Color-coded indicators of testing requirements
		Improve assignment	Clarify authority	Designating of lead technicians for prep stations based on expertise, but technicians rotated to maintain flexibility and alertness
			Have protocols for delegation	Guidelines for deferring questions to lead technologists or pathologists
		Improve training		Requiring/encouraging professional certification of technicians/technologists; Subsidizing classes for technicians to train as technologists
		Improve incentives		Reviews/raises based in part on quality performance metrics
		Simplify/ standardize decisions	Reduce/clarify choices	Specialized cells for classes of tests
			Have standard protocols	Automated testers that standardize procedures
		Improve focus		Multiple steps completed on one sample (a la Subway sandwich preparation) before moving to the next to avoid interruptions/ handoffs that could cause errors

Table 5.7   Generic Operations Improvement Policies: Laboratory Errors

Level 1 Objectives	Level 2 Objectives	Level 3 Objectives	Level 4 Objectives	Example Policies
		Increase redundancy		Tracking of test results on a statistical process control chart to identify an out-of-control event or trend
	Improve execution of the analysis process	Improve information	Improve information availability	Innovations in lab procedures culled from literature
			Improve information quality	Errors tracked and posted, so technologists know where risks are greatest
			Improve information recognition	Large print, color-coded labels indicating test requirements
		Improve assignment	Clarify authority	Designating lead technologists for cells to enhance skills, but rotate technologists to build flexibility
			Have protocols for delegation	Guidelines for deferring a test to a lead technologist
		Improve training		Refresher courses on basics (for example, pipetting technique); Updates on new analytic techniques/equipment; Training in statistical quality control methods
		Improve incentives		Rewards, such as scheduling preferences, for accuracy and "good catches"

Level 1 Objectives	Level 2 Objectives	Level 3 Objectives	Level 4 Objectives	Example Policies
		Simplify/ standardize tasks	Reduce/clarify choices	Preparation stations automated
			Have standard protocols	Standard procedures posted for reagent preparation, slide preparation, and so on
		Improve focus		Multiple steps completed on one sample before moving to the next one
		Increase redundancy		Electronic cross-checking of patient IDs on orders, blocks, and slides; Specimen checks to reveal possible collection errors (for example, infusion contamination or lack of temperature control)
	Improve protection and recovery from analytic errors	Improve information		Root cause analysis to trace adverse events to analysis errors
		Increase redundancy		Automatic alert triggers when values suggest possible testing error
		Mitigate patient harm		Rapid physician notification of suspected errors; Feedback to lab and follow-up in lab on all errors discovered after reporting
Postanalytic Reduce validation/ reporting errors by technologist/ pathologist	Improve decisions by the technologist or pathologist who interprets the results of tests and prepares/certifies reports for the requesting physicians	Improve information		All the preceding steps for reducing the likelihood of an erroneous test

Table 5.7 Generic Operations Improvement Policies: Laboratory Errors

Level 1 Objectives	Level 2 Objectives	Level 3 Objectives	Level 4 Objectives	Example Policies
		Improve assignment		Pathologist checks suspicious results for standard tests (normally reported by technologist)
		Improve training		Ongoing pathologist training in discipline; Training in decision biases/heuristics for pathologists
		Improve incentives		"Good catches" by pathologists posted and tracked to encourage reporting of errors
		Simplify/ standardize decisions		Image-guided decision support systems to assist interpreting pathology slides
		Enhance focus		Scheduling of consulting hours for pathologists to reduce interruptions
		Increase redundancy		Second opinions on ambiguous tests Retest of highly unlikely results
	Improve execution of the process of converting test results into reports	Improve information	Improve information availability	LIS that displays patient and test information for pathologist to interpret
			Improve information quality	All the preceding steps to avoid errors that compromise the quality of reported results; Use of standard report templates to improve completeness and clarity
			Improve information recognition	Reports to highlight key information for physicians

Level 1 Objectives	Level 2 Objectives	Level 3 Objectives	Level 4 Objectives	Example Policies
		Improve assignment	Clarify authority	Tests grouped by pathologist specialty
			Have protocols for delegation	Guidelines for seeking a second opinion
		Improve training		Physician training in decision biases/ heuristics
		Improve incentives		Random physician surveys on satisfaction with reports and posting of pathologist ratings based on these
		Simplify/ standardize tasks		Report templates that automatically create structure and insert basic data
		Improve focus	Optimize workloads	Inpatient tests spread out to avoid spikes that could cause pathologists to rush
			Avoid fatigue, interruptions, distractions	Consulting hours scheduled for pathologists to reduce interruptions
		Increase redundancy		Queries of pathologists facilitated by physicians, which could uncover errors Report review by second pathologist (for example, senior physician supervising resident)
	Improve protection and recovery from errors in the reporting process	Improve information		Pathologist consultation with physician
		Increase redundancy		Retesting of unlikely or suspicious outcomes, especially when decisions are serious (for example, involve surgery or dangerous medication)

Table 5.7   Generic Operations Improvement Policies: Laboratory Errors

Level 1 Objectives	Level 2 Objectives	Level 3 Objectives	Level 4 Objectives	Example Policies
		Mitigate patient harm		Protocols for responding to adverse events that include consideration of the possibility of an erroneous test
Post-postanalytic	Improve decisions by the physician concerning the use of diagnostic reports	Improve information	Improve information availability	Steps in Table 5.5 to reduce lab TAT and make information available for diagnostic use in timely fashion; Review of near misses and adverse events for evidence of misinterpretation of reports; and use to improve reports
			Improve information quality	Pathologists include interpretative comments with results
Reduce interpretation errors by physician			Improve information recognition	Most useful values in results are highlighted, rather than buried in an overload of data
		Improve assignment	Clarify authority	Pathologist interprets results (for example, blood smear), rather than leaving this to physician
			Have protocols for delegation	Physician consultation with more senior or more specialized colleague
		Improve training		Periodic physician updates of new tests and reporting formats
		Improve incentives		Not applicable—physicians' fundamental motivation to provide quality care does not need to be supplemented by specific incentives to interpret reports accurately

Level 1 Objectives	Level 2 Objectives	Level 3 Objectives	Level 4 Objectives	Example Policies
		Simplify/ standardize decisions		Image-guided interpretative flowchart included with test results
		Improve focus		Limited patients/physicians in ward and ED to prevent rushed interpretation
		Increase redundancy		Consultation between physician and pathologist if interpretation is unclear or consequences are grave
	Improve execution of the report interpretation process			Not applicable—interpreting report results is primarily a decision process without significant opportunity for execution errors
	Improve protection and recovery from report interpretation errors	Improve information		Laboratory generates explicit warnings of readings that could indicate medication errors (for example, warfarin and digoxin)
		Increase redundancy		Use of multiple, independent tests when outcome is unlikely given prior information or implied treatment decision is risk or irrevocable; Patients with direct access to results, including access to pathologists, to allow them to serve as an additional layer of protection
		Mitigate patient harm	Increase speed of response	Wireless communication between lab and physician or lab and outpatient to eliminate notification delays; Protocols for responding to adverse events that include consideration of the possibility of an erroneous test

Table 5.7 Generic Operations Improvement Policies: Laboratory Errors

Level 1 Objectives	Level 2 Objectives	Level 3 Objectives	Level 4 Objectives	Example Policies
			Increase effectiveness of response	Training (including simulation exercises) of care teams on procedures for handling unexpected patient reactions (such as to medication errors, lack of treatment); for example, emergency physicians could give tutorials to hospitalists on procedures for handling uncertain and chaotic situations

The first conclusion from the analysis of Table 5.7 is that reducing laboratory errors is not a simple one-dimensional problem. There is no single "silver bullet" for enhancing patient safety in the clinical lab. Rather, it is necessary to fight against laboratory errors on multiple fronts as an ongoing process of continual improvement.

The next implication of Table 5.7, which follows from its size and breadth, is that a campaign to reduce laboratory errors must prioritize initiatives. It is neither possible nor desirable to pursue all the candidate improvement policies at once. One reason is that resources are always limited. Another is that some improvement policies may be substitutes for one another. (For example, instituting a system that generates specimen labels automatically from a database would obviate the need for a training system that increases the accuracy with which phlebotomists manually fill out labels.) So, to be successful, a laboratory error reduction effort should focus initially on a limited set of coordinated initiatives that will have the greatest impact. As progress is made along some dimensions, others can be introduced as new initiatives.

Based on the distribution of errors, it would seem that most labs would see maximum results by focusing on improvements in the ordering, collection, and interpretation tasks, all of which take place outside the lab. However, although it is certainly the case that these tasks deserve serious attention, we should be careful about ignoring the preanalytic, analytic, and postanalytic steps within the lab. Despite the improvements over the past several decades, the error rates in these steps are still too high to enable hospital labs to get to parts-per-million quality levels, which would match the performance of the best industrial processes. Furthermore, in addition to considering the likelihood of an error, we must consider the likelihood that an error causes patient harm.

For instance, an ordering error in which the physician fails to identify himself could lead to extra effort to communicate the results to the right place, or it might require a second request, but it is unlikely to result in improper patient treatment. In contrast, using an incorrect sensitivity factor in lab calculations would lead to an erroneous test result that could be difficult to catch before it leads to harmful treatment errors. So it is essential to do ongoing root cause analysis of both errors and near misses to identify which errors present the greatest risks to patient safety. Errors within the laboratory may be comparatively rare and yet still contribute to adverse outcomes.

Finally, an observation we can make from Table 5.7 is that information is ubiquitous in the laboratory testing process. Ordering a test, identifying a patient, presenting instructions for a task, communicating results—virtually every step of the testing process depends on information, much of which needs to be transferred accurately from one person/place to another. Because of this, many of the steps are amenable to electronic information management, in the form of laboratory information systems, bar coding systems, CPOE systems, and the connections between these and other hospital information systems. To keep up with constant technological change in medical IT, interested readers can obtain surveys, product reviews, and summaries of research on evidence-based medicine from the CMIO magazine and website (CMIO 2010).

5.4.3.4 CASE: REDUCING SURGICAL PATHOLOGY MISIDENTIFICATION ERRORS IN THE HENRY FORD HEALTH CARE SYSTEM

The Department of Pathology and Laboratory Medicine oversees clinical laboratory testing for all hospitals and clinic delivery sites of the Henry Ford Health System. With an annual volume of more than 12 million clinical laboratory tests, it is one of the largest hospital-based clinical laboratories in the nation. In the Anatomic Pathology Department, the lab system handles more than 80,000 surgical pathology cases, 2,500 frozen sections, 85,000 cytology specimens, and 200 postmortem examinations a year.

In 2006, the lab introduced a Toyota-style system of continual improvement it dubbed the Henry Ford Production System.[9] One of the first targets for attention was the Surgical Pathology lab, for which management sought improvements in both efficiency and quality. Relying on the management adage, "You can't manage what you can't measure," the team started with a data-gathering exercise.

Prior to the introduction of the Henry Ford Production System, the Surgical Pathology lab used a bar-coding system that had been installed in 2002. However, because the hospital did not have a CPOE system, paper requisitions arrived at Accessioning and had to be manually keyed into the laboratory information system (LIS). This same information had to be keyed into the printer that produced labels for the cassettes because it had no interface with the LIS. The simple barcodes on these labels could be read at subsequent steps to generate case number, patient name, and medical record number.

After Accessioning, cases progressed to Grossing, where data was entered by keyboard for simple cases or dictated for complex cases. Cases then went to Histology, where specimens were fixed, embedded, and cut, while slides were labeled by hand with a pencil to indicate accession number, block number, level of slide, and technician's initials. Slides were then stained and reassembled in order of sections on a table, relabeled with LIS printed labels, and sent to the pathologist along with a printed working draft of the case up to that point.

In July 2006, the entire laboratory staff, consisting of 21 pathologists and 38 technical staff members, participated in a 3-week error documentation exercise. Using highly visible whiteboards, staff members recorded—in an anonymous and blameless environment—all defects (defined as any flaw, imperfection, or deficiency that requires work to be stopped, delayed, or returned to the sender). Nearly one out of three cases was found to have at least one of the defects listed in Table 5.8.

Table 5.8   Defects found in the Henry Ford Hospital Surgical Pathology Lab (D'Angelo and Zarbo 2007)

Process Step	Defect Type
Specimen receiving	Not on manifest/batch
	No specimen in container
	Misplaced specimen
	Specimen and tag information discrepant
	No physician or service documented
	Wrong physician code
	No International Classification of
	Diseases, Ninth Revision code
Specimen accession	Wrong part type
	Wrong description
	Wrong physician or staff name
	Block discrepancy
	No or wrong gross description present
Specimen gross examination	Unfixed block or too large
	Wrong measurement
	Wrong number of pieces
	Poorly sampled or labeled
	Clarification needed
	Slides with wrong case number

	Wrong level
	Wrong stain label
	Poor stain quality
	Section too thick
	Section not deep enough
	Orientation incorrect
	Bar code not readable
Stains, including special and immunostains	Wrong stain ordered
	Wrong label
	Wrong pathologist name
	Poor quality
Recuts	Not deep enough
	Embedded incorrectly
	Not received, misplaced, or lost
Amended reports	Additional specimen received
	Misidentification
	Report errors

Of course, because the staff identified all these defects, they were corrected, albeit at a significant cost of time and money. But these detected defects raised the possibility of undetected defects that might affect patient safety. Of particular risk to patients are errors of misidentification. So, although the lab team took many corrective steps to address the issues in Table 5.8, we will focus here on those aimed at reducing patient misidentification errors. The 2,694 cases accessioned during the 3-week study involved 4,413 individual specimen parts, 8,776 blocks, and 14,270 slides. Among these there were 45 misidentification defects resulting from 45 cases, of which 10 were found in the accessioning process, 5 in blocks, and 30 in slide identification.

Root cause analysis of the defects revealed that the preponderance of them were the result of slide labeling at two places: (1) during manual slide labeling in Histology where slides were annotated with a pencil, and (2) after staining, where new labels were affixed to the slides. With this in mind, the team implemented the following changes to the process:

- **Interfaced cassette labeling**—An interface between the LIS and a new cassette labeler was developed to eliminate the need for dual entry of data. This exploited both the Task Simplification and the Handoffs principles to reduce both time and error rate at the Accessioning stage.

- **Produced all labels for entire case at once**—Rather than producing labels for each cassette in a case one at a time, the lab redesigned the label printing process to generate all the labels for an entire case at the time the first cassette was pinged. This was an application of the Batching principle, which increased efficiency by reducing the number of print cycles. But, because it also eliminated steps, it was another application of the Task Simplification principle, which reduced opportunities for errors.

- **Encoded work process standardization**—Because the new cassette printer used laser etching to engrave a 2D bar code, it was possible to include more data on each slide. The lab encoded standardized process instructions in the LIS, which could be accessed at each station by scanning the barcode. For instance, in Histology, the system would generate a clear set of instructions on the number of levels to be cut on each cassette and the stains to be performed. Because it associated key information with a task in a simple and accessible way, this was an application of the Intuitive Information principle, which could be expected to further improve speed and accuracy.

- **Chemical-resistant barcode slide labeling**—By replacing paper slide labels with chemically resistant labels, the lab eliminated the need to label slides with a pencil prior to staining and the need to relabel the slides after staining. With the new labels, the slides could be labeled once when the cassette was cut. This was a significant application of the Task Simplification principle aimed directly at the portion of the process most prone to errors.

- **Pencil labeling as a backup**—Despite no longer needing to do so, the histotechnologists chose to retain pencil labeling of slides as a manual quality control check against loss of the chemically resistant label or miscassetting upstream at Grossing. This application of the Redundancy principle was progressively abandoned as the new system proved reliable.

- **Development of standard slide-divider tool**—The histotechnologists designed a slide-divider tool to hold the blank slides with chemically resistant labels in a properly separated and oriented manner. The goal was to simplify labeling and handling (Task Simplification principle) and standardize processing (Task Standardization principle) to improve speed and accuracy. Indeed, because it constrained orientation decisions by the position of the slides, this tool was also an application of the Foolproofing principle.

- **Verification of patient information**—As an additional check on the accuracy of the slide identification, the lab implemented a step in which an optical character recognition of a scan of the paper requisition was compared to the information associated with the barcode on a case. If a mismatch was discovered, the case would be reaccessioned using the correct information. This application of the Redundancy principle put one more layer of patient protection into the system.

In 2007, one year after the start of the improvement project, the lab performed another defect identification exercise. The 2007 results are compared to the 2006 results in Table 5.9. This shows a dramatic reduction in the overall misidentification rate by approximately 62% (from 1.67% to 0.63%) and a vast reduction in slide misidentification of 95% (from 0.21% to 0.01%). Moreover, the elimination of repetitive manual labeling of each slide by pencil was estimated to save 96.7 work days per year (Zarbo et al. 2009). By diligently exploiting principles of flow and protection, the lab team demonstrated that efficiency can go hand in hand with patient safety.

Table 5.9   Results of Process Improvements in Henry Ford Hospital Surgical Pathology Laboratory (Zarbo et al. 2009)

Analytic Category	2006			2007		
	Volume	Number of Defects	Defect Rate (%)	Volume	Number of Defects	Defect Rate (%)
Surgical cases	2,694	45	1.67%	2,877	18	0.63%
Specimen parts	4,413	10	0.23%	4,725	11	0.23%
Tissue cassettes	8,776	5	0.06%	9,167	5	0.05%
Slides	14,270	30	0.21%	17,927	2	0.01%

5.5 Conclusions

Laboratories and imaging units are a core function of the modern hospital. With more than 70% of medical decisions hinging on diagnostic tests, the speed and accuracy of the testing process is fundamental to the quality of hospital care. Furthermore, although laboratory and imaging costs are still a relatively small fraction of total hospital cost,[10] they are growing. For this reason, a McKinsey study cited the trend toward more tests and more expensive tests as a driver of rising health care costs (Farrell et al. 2008). The implication is that performance of the hospital along the key dimensions of responsiveness, safety, and cost is intimately tied to performance of the diagnostic units.

Reliance on diagnostics will only increase as technology advances and treatment practice moves toward evidenced-based medicine. This means that improvements in the ED, OR, and bed floors will become increasingly dependent on progress in the diagnostic units. So, although it is certainly possible to improve patient care via policies entirely within individual units (for example, better matching capacity to demand in the ED, improving scheduling in the OR, enhanced infection control on the bed floors), elevating overall hospital performance ultimately requires improvement policies that cut across units.

Because the diagnostics units serve as an informational hub for the hospital, they are a natural place to begin addressing the key interfaces between hospital units. For example, prioritizing images and tests is one means for striking a balance between competing needs of the ED and OR. Synchronizing tests to rounding schedules is one way to facilitate patient discharge and thereby open up beds for patients coming from the ED and OR. Linking hospital information systems to digital test and image results is a key step toward an integrated hospital information system. These and other links between diagnostics and the rest of the hospital represent opportunities to develop the integrated operations needed to offer better, faster, and cheaper patient care.

5.6 Stakeholders' Perspectives

Wednesday September 8, 2010, 10:05 a.m.

"I'm sorry I'm late." Nate Greene had never been to the Pathology Department conference room and had wandered for several minutes before asking directions.

"That's okay," reassured Dr. Clinton Manchester with a bemused smile that made Greene suspect he wasn't all that late. "We're still waiting for a couple of people."

Manchester, head of Clinical Pathology and the only person in the room that Greene knew, introduced a lab assistant, a medical technician, a phlebotomist, and a grad assistant. While they were getting acquainted, a Pathology resident, another med tech from Clinical Pathology, and a med tech from Anatomical Pathology joined them and were introduced.

"Hello everybody." Dr. Manchester called the meeting to order. "Welcome to the Clinical Lab flow team. I want to particularly thank Nate and Anna for joining us."

Anna Pierce, the med tech from Anatomical Pathology, had been asked to join the team to contribute ideas, but mostly to gain experience that would help in a similar improvement effort planned for the Anatomical Pathology lab in November.

"As you all know," Manchester continued, "the clinical labs are getting a major renovation in January. We've been talking about layout changes and automation upgrades for the past several months. But if we're going to get the full benefit of the physical changes, we also need to improve our management policies. If we do, I think we can reduce average TAT by at least half and meet our target times on stat tests at least 90% of the time. And we can do it while increasing accuracy and reducing cost."

Manchester looked around at his team for signs of enthusiasm but was met with uncomfortable stares. Finally, Adrian Dundee, a senior med tech, broke the silence.

"I don't know," he said skeptically. "Those are pretty ambitious goals. While I'm sure we can do our jobs better, I don't see how we can do anything about the big spikes in our workload. When those happen, it's impossible to turn tests around quickly."

"Clint," Greene jumped in before Manchester could reply. "Can I comment on that?"

Manchester nodded, and Greene continued.

"We have exactly the same situation in the ED," he explained. "We get spikes in patient arrivals, some of which are predictable and some of which aren't. But we've already managed to reduce our patient length of stay by almost 35% without increasing our costs, and I'm confident we'll get it even lower when some of our current efforts start to pay off."

"That's great," replied Dundee unenthusiastically. "But that's the ED. Our work in the labs is completely different. So we can't do the same things you did."

"But that's just it," Greene countered excitedly. "What we did in the ED was use generic strategies that can be adapted to any setting. In fact, because your flows in the lab are a lot more structured than ours in the ED, I think the strategies will work even better here."

"Can you give us an example of some of the management strategies you used in the ED that might make sense for us?" asked Dr. Manchester.

"Sure." Greene stood up, walked over to a flip chart, and picked up a marker. This was a softball, because Greene knew that the more routinized parts of the diagnostic flows were natural candidates for classical lean strategies. But it was an excellent opportunity to make the point that there were fundamental principles underlying it all.

"First," he said, writing the word *Responsiveness* on the chart, "what you have is a responsiveness problem. What matters most in the lab is that you get timely and accurate test results to providers, right?"

Heads nodded, but Greene could almost hear the calls of "well, duh!" so he hurried on.

"The first lever for improving responsiveness is capacity." He wrote *capacity* on the chart, "Anything you do that increases your effective capacity enables you to respond to spikes in demand. These don't need to be hiring more people or adding more analyzers. There are lots of ways you can get more capacity by eliminating waste."

He wrote *waste* under *capacity*.

"For example, do you have to walk around to move specimens from one place to another?

Heads nodded.

"Do you have to search for materials or supplies sometimes?"

More heads nodded.

"Do you have to call requesting physicians to get missing information?"

All heads nodded emphatically.

"Those things, and a thousand others, are waste. Every one you can eliminate will give you more capacity to work off a spike in work when it occurs."

"But," Greene continued, writing the word *flexibility* on the chart, "eliminating waste isn't the only thing you can do to give you more effective capacity. You can also increase your flexibility. For instance, do you move from one part of the lab to another to help with a glut of work?"

One of the technicians nodded weakly while the others glanced around uncertainly.

"Could you do it more often?"

"We could if we knew where help was needed," said the technician who had nodded. "But we usually can't see where the backups are."

"Well then," Greene replied, "maybe that's something we can work on in the revised layout."

"Also," Greene went on, writing *variability* and *batching* on the chart, "you shouldn't give up on leveling your workloads, at least to some extent. For instance, you get an early-morning spike on account of rounds, right?"

Everyone nodded.

"Well," Greene continued looking at the phlebotomist, "could that be leveled out a bit by staggering specimen collection?"

"It depends on how early they'll let us start," said the phlebotomist.

"And on how early we staff the lab," added one of the technicians.

"Well?" Greene shrugged his shoulders and looked around the room to indicate that these were questions worth answering.

"Finally," Greene resumed, "some of your workload spikes may be of your own doing. For instance, do you move work in batches within the lab?"

Several "yeses" accompanied the head nodding.

"Those batches create mini-spikes that hinder the flow of your work. If you could get to where you work on specimens one at a time, as they arrive to the lab, you could turn them around much more quickly. And if you turned around your tests more quickly, you'd help us reduce our patient length of stay in the ED."

Dr. Manchester smiled as he watched his team nod and look at each other. Whether they understood Greene's "generic strategies" or not, it was clear that his oration had stimulated some hope in them. Now it was time to capitalize on that hope.

Over the next several weeks, the two clinical lab med techs and the grad assistant compiled TAT statistics by month and test. The statistics showed TAT gradually drifting upward over the past three years, during which test volume had increased by nearly 40%. Their best estimate of current median TAT (from phlebotomy to result posting) for blood chemistry was 56 minutes for stat tests and 2–4 hours for routine tests. But times varied among tests. For instance, median stat TAT was 44 minutes for hemoglobin tests but 57 minutes for potassium tests. Manchester didn't just propose incremental improvements to these current values. He both dropped the target TAT for stat blood tests from 45 minutes to 30 minutes and set a goal of meeting this target 90% of the time, setting out a frighteningly ambitious aspiration for the team.

While the statistics collection was going on, the two med techs and the grad assistant constructed process flow diagrams for the various clinical labs. On these, they noted that specimens often waited in queues before and after accessioning. Because the lab was organized in islands, technicians had to walk back and forth between locations to perform tests, so they tended to collect batches to reduce the number of trips. They also noted that techs were frequently interrupted to collect supplies from storage locations that were distant and sometimes poorly organized.

In the run-up to the physical remodeling of the lab, the team worked on details of the layout. For instance, they located the high-volume chemistry testing area next to accessioning to encourage movement of specimens directly from receiving to testing without batching. They planned for material supply locations to be located close to testing locations. They arranged instruments into U-shaped cells to allow a single tech to monitor the status of several automated testers at once. To further enable techs to monitor several processes, the new equipment was equipped with audible alarms that signaled when tests were complete.

In January, the construction crew removed some walls, which had previously blocked both flow and visibility, and set up connections for the new equipment. The flow team worked up formal 5S organization schemes for the supply locations. They also created whiteboard displays to give technicians real-time feedback on workloads and performance metrics.

The new equipment was installed and calibrated at the end of January, providing both an increase in capacity and an elimination of steps by combining previously separate testing steps. The new equipment and layout also allowed a single tech to follow tests through more stages of the process than before, thereby eliminating handoffs.

Once the new equipment was in, the team shifted its focus to designing work standards to propagate best practices throughout the lab. In the first few weeks with the new equipment, these standards changed frequently as techs and lab assistants found better ways to do things. There was also a conscious effort to shift simpler tasks (for example, restocking supplies) from the techs to the lower-paid assistants and to do some tasks, such as instrument calibration, during nonpeak hours.

With the aid of the open layout and the whiteboard displays, techs were able to spot work backups throughout the lab. To allow them to shift where capacity was needed, techs and assistants were cross-trained to staff several stations.

Finally, as the lab stabilized, the team extended its focus to the collection process. Shifts were staggered for both phlebotomists and technicians to allow collection and testing to start earlier in the morning and thereby smooth out the morning spike in work. The team also made a compelling case to hire another phlebotomist. The objective was to give phlebotomists enough time to make more trips to the tube stations and thereby deliver specimens to the laboratory in smaller batches.

The combination of new equipment and new processes had a dramatic effect. By the end of March 2011, median TAT for blood chemistry had fallen to 26 minutes for stat tests, with 76% under the new 30-minute target. Even more remarkably, median TAT for routine tests decreased to 35 minutes, with 41% completed within 30 minutes. Results available for morning rounds increased from 62% to 91%. Of particular delight to management, monthly lab costs fell by 14% from the previous year, despite a 9% increase in volume. The two primary sources of savings were attrition in the number of techs and a reduction in the amount of overtime pay, both made possible by the increase in capacity from the physical and operational changes.

When he saw that routine tests had become nearly as fast as stat tests, Manchester was tempted to drop the stat designation altogether. But the team convinced him to retain prioritization at accessioning so that stat tests would be less affected by spikes in arrivals, which were bound to occur. However, beyond accessioning, the team ceased using priorities and began processing everything on a first-come-first-serve basis, which further simplified flows. With additional improvements that occurred as technicians came up the learning curve and the smoothed specimen collection process was implemented, the lab more than achieved Manchester's goals. Similar improvements were achieved using similar interventions in Hematology, Urine Chemistry, and other units within Clinical Pathology.

In parallel with his participation with the Clinical Lab flow team, Dr. Greene also sat in on an analogous effort in Radiology, which focused on reducing imaging TAT, first in CT and then in MRI. The team that mapped the current state of the CT scanning process noted that the major points of delay were queueing to get on to the CT schedule and waiting for a radiologist to read the image. Two significant sources of lost capacity that contributed to the queueing in front of the process were: (1) next patient not ready when scanner becomes available, and (2) inefficiencies in the setup and scanning procedures. Contributing factors to delays in image reading included: (1) radiologists were often diverted from reading scans by the need to protocol cases (that is, identify the scan and oral preparation needed for patients' diagnoses), (2) batching of images, which caused some early scans to wait until late in the day to be read, and (3) inconsistent priorities for reading inpatient images.

One subset of the CT flow team focused on the flow of patients into the scanner. For outpatients, the team enhanced maps, instructions, and signage to assist people in preparing for and arriving to the CT scanner in time for their appointment. Team members also modified reminder calls to include reminders about fasting and oral and IV prep instructions.

For inpatients, this team set up an online schedule display that showed patient progress in real time. This, along with some meetings with the transport techs, helped ensure that patients arrived before the scanner was ready for them. It also helped the CT techs pull patients into earlier slots when cancellations occurred. To avoid delays due to fasting violations, the team developed protocols for improving communication of inpatients' "nothing by mouth" status to the food service and medical units. To better spread workload over the day, the team instituted a campaign (with posters and candy bars) for residents and physicians to write early orders. To translate orders into same-day results, the team dedicated two scanners to inpatients in the early part of the day.

For all patients, the team designed an "On Deck Room," where patients could receive oral prep and from where the CT tech could pull patients as soon as scanner slot becomes available.

A second subset of the CT flow team focused on the setup and scanning process itself. One particularly experienced and efficient tech wrote up standard sequences and procedures for various types of scans and conducted instructional sessions for the other techs. The team offloaded some tasks (for example, room preparation and patient positioning) to CT assistants to free up techs for their core tasks. Finally, members focused intensely on the room turnover process, reducing the time between scans from 15 minutes to 6 minutes through a combination of simplification and urgency.

A third subset of the CT flow team focused on the reading and report generation process. To address delays caused by radiologists being pulled away from reading to do protocolling, the team recommended hiring a nurse practitioner to protocol all but the most difficult cases. This helped team members sell the idea of having radiologists read images promptly one-at-a-time instead of in batches. Finally, at the team's urging, the hospital equipped several radiologists with high-resolution monitors at home so they could read images remotely while covering on-call shifts during off hours.

By April 2011, the fraction of routine CT reports that were delivered in the same day as the scan rose from 16% to 47%, giving the group hope that same-day results could become the norm. For ED scans, the group set targets for TAT of 60 minutes for scans without contrast and 120 minutes for scans with contrast. Prior to the improvement project, only 15% of scans without contrast and 7% of scans with contrast met these targets. In April, 56% of scans without contrast and 38% of scans with contrast met the targets. Moreover, the average TAT for CT scans without contrast fell from 92 minutes to 59 minutes, and the average TAT for CT scans with contrast fell from 163 minutes to 135 minutes.

Thursday April 14, 2011, 8:32 p.m.

"Nice shot!" Dr. Arnold held out his hand to congratulate Dr. Greene, who had just swished a rare shot from the top of the key to win the final game of the evening by a close 5–4 score.

"Thanks." Greene slapped his hand and trotted to the corner of the gym, where he collapsed on an exercise mat next to his duffle. He pulled out a towel and mopped his brow. They had played 2-on-2 without subs all evening, and he was winded but satisfied with the workout.

"You were on fire tonight," Arnold complemented Greene. "Good week at the office?"

"Good year at the office!" Greene's adrenaline was pumping from the game, but he was also on a high from the recent results with the hospital flow improvement teams. "We're really starting to push the envelope on some of our metrics. For instance, we're turning more than half of our CT scans without contrast in less than an hour."

"We do our simple CT scans in under 45 minutes," Arnold retorted smugly.

"Yeah, but how many do you do?"

"A dozen a day, sometimes more."

"A dozen a day!" Greene snorted. "We do more than 250,000 a year!" Greene pulled his sweats from his duffle muttering, "A dozen a day."

When Arnold did not press his point, Greene went on while struggling to pull his sweats over his shoes.

"We're also doing really well in turning around Clinical lab tests in 30 minutes and Surgical Pathology tests in less than a day." He stood to pull up his sweats. "I suppose you're faster on those, too?'

"Actually," conceded Arnold, "we send most of our lab work to you. And I have to admit that we are getting better turnaround."

Greene grinned. "Mighty big of you to say so."

"Yeah, well." Arnold was stuffing a basketball into his own duffel. "I thought you got into all this management stuff to improve patient safety. But all I hear from you is speed and flow and turnaround time…"

"I did." Greene slung his gear over his shoulder. "But responsiveness is a big part of patient protection. And nothing we've done has promoted speed at the expense of safety."

"Do you have statistics to back that up?"

"Some," Greene responded, "from some of our earlier efforts in the ED and nursing units. But a lot of the changes are too new to tell yet. And measuring safety is a lot harder than measuring TAT. But I'm convinced in my soul that all of our attention on flow processes has made us more conscious of safety than we've ever been."

"You're convinced in your soul!" Arnold scoffed. "I'm convinced in my soul that a focused specialty hospital is safer than a general hospital every day of the week. And we have the stats to show it. We track patient outcomes, adverse events, return visits, satisfaction, and everything else you'd ever want to know. And, as I keep telling you, we're good."

"And as I keep telling you," Greene shot back, "you're only good for a few people. A dozen scans a day! See you next week."

5.7 References

ACLA. 2010. "The Value of Clinical Laboratory Services." American Clinical Laboratory Association. http://www.clinical-labs.org/issues/value/index.shtml [accessed August 5, 2010].

Assmus, A. 1995. "Early History of X Rays." *Beam Line*. Stanford University. Available: http://www.slac.stanford.edu/pubs/beamline/25/2/25-2-assmus.pdf [accessed November 9, 2009].

Battisto, D., and D. Allison. 2002. "Nature and Rate of Change in Clinical Laboratories." The Coalition for Health Environments Research (CHER), San Francisco.

Beland, D., C. D'Angelo, and D. Vinci. 2003. "Reducing Unnecessary Blood Work in the Neurosurgical ICU." *Journal of Neuroscience Nursing* 35(3), 149–152.

Blick, K.E. 2005. "No More STAT Testing: Improve Critical Results Management and Lab Efficiency Through Automation and Data Management." *Medical Laboratory Observer* 37(8), 22–26.

Bonini, P., M. Plebani, F. Ceriotti, and F. Rubboli. 2002. "Errors in Laboratory Medicine." *Clinical Chemistry* 48(5), 691–698.

Burling, S. 2001. "Lab Error Blamed in Pair of Deaths." *Philadelphia Inquirer*, August 16, 2001.

Burton, S. 2003. "The Biggest Mistake of Their Lives." *New York Times Magazine*. March 16, 2003. http://www.nytimes.com/2003/03/16/magazine/the-biggest-mistake-of-their-lives.html [accessed June 17, 2010].

CMIO. 2010. "Information, Evidence & Effectiveness in Medicine." http://www.cmio.net [accessed August 10, 2010].

D'Angelo, R., R.J. Zarbo, and R.J. 2007. "Measures of Process Defects and Waste in Surgical Pathology as a Basis for Quality Improvement Initiatives." *American Journal of Clinical Pathology* 128, 423–429.

Eisenberg, R.L. 1992. "Cathode Rays and Controversy." *American Journal of Radiology* 160, 62.

Fernandes, C.M., A. Worster, K. Eva, S. Hill, and C. McCallum. 2006. "Pneumatic Tube Delivery System for Blood Samples Reduces Turnaround Times Without Affecting Sample Quality." *Journal of Emergency Nursing* 32, 139–43.

Farrell, D., E. Jensen, B. Kocher, N. Lovegrove, F. Melhem, L. Mendonca, and B. Parish. 2008. "Accounting for the Cost of US Health Care: A New Look at Why Americans Spend More." McKinsey Global Institute http://www.mckinsey.com/mgi/publications/us_healthcare/ [accessed August 9, 2010].

Filler, A.G. 2009. "The History, Development and Impact of Computed Imaging in Neurological Diagnosis and Neurosurgery: CT, MRI, and DTI." *Nature Precedings* hdl:10101/npre.2009.3267.4: Posted 30 Jun 2009. http://precedings.nature.com/documents/3267/version/4 [accessed December 1, 2009].

Ford, H. 1926. *Henry Ford: Today and Tomorrow*. Doubleday, Page & Co., New York.

Foster, W.D. 1958. "The Early History of Clinical Pathology in Great Britain." *Medical History* 3(3), 173–187.

Georgiou, A., M. Williamson, J. Westbrook, and S. Ray. 2007. "The Impact of Computerised Physician Order Entry Systems on Pathology Services: A Systematic Review." *International Journal of Medical Informatics* 76(7), 514–529.

Halsted, M, and C. Frohle. 2008. "Design, Implementation, and Assessment of a Radiology Workflow Management System." *American Journal of Radiology* 191, 321–327.

Hawkins, R.C. 2007. "Laboratory Turnaround Time." *Clinical Biochemistry Review* 28(4), 179–194.

Health Quality Ontario. 2011. "Examples of Success—MRI Wait Times." *Health Quality Ontario*. http://www.ohqc.ca/pdfs/2011_success_story_4_en.pdf [accessed March 1, 2011].

Hessenbruch, A. 2002. "A Brief History of X-rays." *Endeavour* 26(4), 137–141.

Holland, L.L., L.L. Smith, and K.E. Blick. 2005. "Reducing Laboratory Turnaround Time Outliers Can Reduce Emergency Department Patient Length of Stay." *American Journal of Clinical Pathology* 124, 672–674.

Hooper, A.D., W. Simons, and M. Stevenson. 1989. "Using Schedule Rewards to Boost Productivity." *Medical Laboratory Observer* 21(1), 43+.

Institute of Physics. 2009. "MRI: Magnetic Resonance Imagery." http://www.iop.org/activity/policy/Publications/Case%20Studies/file_35555.pdf [accessed March 17, 2010].

Jones, B.A., M.K. Walsh, and S.G. Ruby. 2006. Hospital Nursing Satisfaction with Clinical Laboratory Services: A College of American Pathologists Q-Probes Study of 162 Institutions." *Archives of Pathology and Laboratory Medicine* 130, 1756–1761.

Judson, H.F. 2003. "No Nobel Prize for Whining." *New York Times*, October 20, 2003. http://www.nytimes.com/2003/10/20/opinion/no-nobel-prize-for-whining.html?pagewanted=1 [accessed March 17, 2010].

Kennedy, M.T. 2004. *A Brief History of Disease, Science & Medicine*. Asklepiad Press, Mission Viejo, CA.

Kevles, B.H. 1998. *Naked to the Bone: Medical Imaging in the Twentieth Century*. Rutgers University Press, New York.

Kocher, K.E., W.J. Meurer, R. Fazel, et al. 2011. "National Trends in Use of Computed Tomography in the Emergency Department." *Annals of Emergency Medicine* 58(5), 452–462.

Lewandrowski K. 2004. "How the Clinical Laboratory and the Emergency Department Can Work Together to Move Patients Through Quickly." *Clinical Leadership and Management Review* 18, 155–159.

Liew, D., D. Liew, and M.P. Kennedy. 2003. "Emergency Department Length of Stay Independently Predicts Excess Inpatient Length of Stay." *Medical Journal of Australia* 179, 524–526.

Lindberg, D.S., M.S. Britt, and F.W. Fisher. 1984. *Williams' Introduction to the Profession of Medical Technology*. 4th ed. Philadelphia, PA: Lea & Febiger.

Long, G.W., J. Noble Jr., F.A. Murphy, K.L. Herrman, and B. Loric. 1970. Experience with electron microscopy in the differential diagnosis of smallpox. *Applied Microbiology* 20(3), 497–504.

May, T.A., M. Clancy, J. Critchfield, et al. 2006. "Reducing Unnecessary Laboratory Testing in a Teaching Hospital." *American Journal of Clinical Pathology* 126(2), 200–206.

McPherson, E. 2006. "Genetic Diagnosis and Testing in Clinical Practice." *Clinical Medicine & Research* 4(2), 123–129.

Miyakis, S., G. Karamanof, M. Liontos, and T. Mountokalakis. 2006. "Factors Contributing to Inappropriate Ordering of Tests in an Academic Medical Department and the Effect of an Educational Feedback Strategy." *Postgraduate Medical Journal* 82, 823–829.

Montalescot G., M. Borentain, L. Payot, et al. 2004. Early vs Late Administration of Glycoprotein Iib/Iiia Inhibitors in Primary Percutaneous Coronary Intervention of Acute ST-Segment Elevation Myocardial Infarction: A Meta-Analysis." *Journal of the American Medical Association* 292, 362–366.

Mustapha, M., S. Reicks, J. Rieken, et al. 2009. "Innovations in the Clinical Laboratory: TAT Reduction Through Workflow Improvement in Renal Function Lab." Mayo Medical Laboratories. http://www.mayomedicallaboratories.com/mediax/outreach/resources/whitepapers/tatreduction.pdf [accessed November 25, 2009].

Musyj, D. 2011. "How LEAN, Teamwork Solves Efficiency, Safety Issues." *Hospital Impact.* http://www.hospitalimpact.org/index.php/2011/11/16/title_32 [accessed March 1, 2011].

Osborn, G.G. 1986. "Joseph Lister and the Origins of Antisepsis." *Journal of Medical Humanities and Bioethics.* 7(2), 91–105.

Patrick, J., and M.L. Puterman. 2007. "Improving Resource Utilization for Diagnostic Services Through Flexible Inpatient Scheduling: A Method for Improving Resource Utilization." *Journal of the Operational Research Society* 58, 235–245.

Patrick, J., M.L. Puterman, and M. Queyranne. 2008. "Dynamic Multipriority Patient Scheduling for a Diagnostic Resource." *Operations Research* 56(6), 1507–1525.

Persoon, T.J., S. Zaleski, and J. Frerichs. 2006. "Improving Preanalytic Processes Using the Principles of Lean Production (Toyota Production System)." *American Journal of Clinical Pathology* 125, 16–25.

Phend, C. 2010. "Unnecessary Imaging Drops with Ordering System Rule Change." *Medpage Today* http://www.medpagetoday.com/Radiology/DiagnosticRadiology/20283 [accessed July 12, 2010].

Plebani, M. 2010. "The Detection and Prevention of Errors in Laboratory Medicine." *Annals of Clinical Biochemistry* 47, 101–110.

Reason, J. 2000. "Human Error: Models and Management." *British Medical Journal* 320, 768–770.

Richardson, D.B. 2002. The Access-Block Effect: Relationship Between Delay to Reaching an Inpatient Bed and Inpatient Length of Stay." *Medical Journal of Australia* 177(9), 492–495.

Rosenfeld, L. 1999a. *Four Centuries of Clinical Chemistry*. Gordon and Breach Science Publishers.

Rosenfeld, L. 1999b. Otto Folin and Donald D. Van Slyke. "Pioneers of Clinical Chemistry." *Bulletin for the History of Chemistry* 24, 40–47.

Simoni, R.D., R.L. Hill, and M. Vaughan. 2002. "The Measurement of Blood Gases and the Manometric Techniques Developed by Donald Dexter Van Slyke." *Journal of Biological Chemistry* 277, 33–34.

Singer, A.J., J. Ardise, J. Gulla, and J. Cangro. 2005. "Point-of-Care Testing Reduces Length of Stay in Emergency Department Chest Pain Patients." *Annals of Emergency Medicine* 45(6), 587–591.

Steindel S., and P. Howanitz. 1993. "Emergency Department Turnaround Time: Data Analysis and Critique." *Quality Assurance Q-Probes* 93-04. Northfield, Il: College of American Pathologists.

Terry, M. 2007. *Lab Industry Strategic Outlook: Market Trends and Analysis 2007*. Washington G-2 Reports.

TMLT. 2010. Texas Medical Liability Trust. *Closed Claim Studies*. "Pathology: Pathology Contamination." http://www.tmlt.org/newscenter/closedclaims/pathology.html?x=3 [accessed June 17, 2010].

U.S. Department of Energy. 2009. "Human Genome Project Information." http://www.ornl.gov/sci/techresources/Human_Genome/home.shtml [accessed March 15, 2010].

Vacek, J.L. 2002. "Classic Q Wave Myocardial Infarction: Aggressive, Early Intervention Has Dramatic Results." *Postgraduate Medicine* 112, 71–77.

van der Schaaf, T.W. 1992. *Near Miss Reporting in the Chemical Process Industry*. Eindhoven: Technische Universiteit Eindhoven, Proefschrift.

Vartanians, V.M., C.L. Sistrom, J.B. Weilburg, D.I. Rosenthal, and J.H. Thrall. 2010. "Increasing the Appropriateness of Outpatient Imaging: Effects of a Barrier to Ordering Low-Yield Examinations." *Radiology*: 255(3), 842–849.

Weiss, D.L, and C.P. Langlotz. 2008. "Structured Reporting: Patient Care Enhancement or Productivity Nightmare?" *Radiology* 249(3), 739–747.

Whitby, L.G. 1964. "Automation in Clinical Chemistry, With Special Reference to the AutoAnalyzer. *British Medical Journal* 2, 895–899.

Windsor Regional Hospital. 2011. "Polarizing MRI Wait Times." http://www.wrh.on.ca/webbuild/site/wrh-internet-upload/file_collection/ Polarizing_MRI_WaitTimes.pdf [accessed March 1, 2012].

Winkelman, J.W., D.R. Wybenga, and M.J. Tanasijevic. 1994. "The Fiscal Consequences of Central Vs Distributed Testing of Glucose." *Clinical Chemistry* 40(8), 1628–1630.

Zarbo, R.J., J.M. Tuthill, R. D'Angelo, R, Varney, B. Mahar, C. Neuman, and A. Ormsby. 2009. "Reduction of Surgical Pathology In-Process Misidentification Defects by Bar Code–Specified Work Process Standardization." *American Journal of Clinical Pathology* 131, 468–477.

---

[1]   Indeed, William Osler (1849–1919), the "Father of Modern medicine" who was known for his careful analysis of the efficacy of treatment procedures, was sometimes called a "therapeutic nihilist" because his insistence on demonstrating the efficacy of a therapy before adopting it led him to reject many common medicines and therapies of his time.

[2]   In a case of cruel irony, another Edison invention did get used in the McKinley case. The Edison Company employed his motion picture camera to film a reproduction of the electrocution of Leon Czolgosz, McKinley's assassin.

[3]   Note that clinician satisfaction is considered a quality metric, because clinicians are clients (customers) of the labs, whereas staff satisfaction is considered to be an organizational metric, because technicians/pathologists are staff members who facilitate functioning of the lab. Obviously both are important, but they impact performance in different ways and are subject to different interventions.

[4]   Table A.1 also identifies "enhance patient perceptions" as an option for mitigating the psychological impact of service delays. But because the objective here is to reduce laboratory TAT, we limit our focus to physical improvements only.

[5]   *Gemba* is a Japanese term for "the real place," so gemba walks encourage direct observation of the system under question, rather than indirect study through data alone.

[6]   The ultimate irony of the previous story of the author's trip through a midnight snowstorm to an MRI exam is that the exam itself was almost certainly unnecessary.

[7]   In a 2008 week-long study of an offsite Radiology unit at the University of Michigan Hospital, a student team observed 11% of patients scheduled for CT scans did not show up for their appointment. An even higher percentage of patients were late for their appointments. The unpredictability of patient arrivals was the main cause of schedule disruption and underutilization of the scanning equipment.

[8]   A *hanging protocol* refers to the sequence of actions involved in arranging images for viewing. The term comes from the era of film images, which were hung on light boxes, but now usually refers to computerized display of digital images in a format that facilitates reading.

[9]   This name has deep roots. In 1926, long before Toyota had begun its revolutionary lean journey, Henry Ford wrote in his autobiography, "Our finished inventory is all in transit. So is most of our raw material." He went on to claim that Ford could take newly mined ore from the Upper Peninsula of Michigan and convert it into a finished car in just four days (Ford 1926). As the epitome of a lean, flow-oriented system, it is no wonder that Taiichi Ohno, the architect of the Toyota Production System, cited Ford as a major inspiration of his approach.

[10] Kane and Siegrist (2002) estimated in 2000 that the laboratory accounted for 9.4% of total direct inpatient cost, whereas Radiology accounted for 4%.

6

HOSPITAL OF THE FUTURE

6.1 Stakeholders' Perspectives

Monday February 25, 2012

Dr. Arnold's son Bobby was one of those rare people gifted with both a love of sports and natural athletic ability. He excelled in almost everything he attempted, and his athletic development was slowed only once, and then only briefly, by an inguinal hernia at the age of 13. Dr. Arnold wondered if the constant lifting and straining in practice was responsible, but Bobby's pediatrician had been equivocal about that. Regardless, the outpatient repair procedure had been straightforward.

Over time, Bobby gravitated toward water sports, and in his senior year of high school, he was the first student to be voted co-captain of both the swimming and the water polo teams. Of course, being a captain meant that his parents were "captain's parents" who were responsible for fund-raising, timing and scoring at meets, providing food for hungry teens, arranging travel to away meets, and many other support activities. Because his father worked long hours, first at University Hospital and later at the Orthopedic Surgery Center, most of this work fell to his mom, Peggy. She did not mind, really, and forged lasting relationships with the other swim and polo parents.

Now 20 and a college sophomore, Bobby was majoring in history and was a central player on his Division 1 water polo team. As he had done the year before, during winter break he went back to his high school to help his former coach mentor younger athletes. This year a particularly virulent flu had depleted the ranks of the swimmers who showed up at the pool at 5:30 a.m. each morning. So when he began experiencing increasing abdominal pain, Bobby assumed that he had picked up the bug. But other swimmers who were hurting continued to show up and soldier through the morning workouts. Not wanting to risk his star status to criticisms of being "soft," Bobby also continued swimming.

When he was home, Bobby did not see much of his father, outside of weekends, because they both went to bed early to be ready for their morning commitments. On Sunday, they had gone cross-country skiing on a local golf course. Afterward, Bobby's intestinal pains became more acute.

"I'm fighting a virus," he told his parents. "I think I'll go to bed early to try to chase it." He vomited once during the night but laid back down, hoping that quiet rest would settle his stomach.

In the morning, Bobby was still feeling ill. He managed to drive to the pool but realized quickly it was a mistake. No amount of determination could overcome the lightheadedness and nausea he felt. He excused himself from the pool deck and vomited in the bathroom. Then he apologized to the coach and drove back home. His mom was out and his dad was working, so he left a note on the kitchen table and went to bed.

Later in the afternoon, his mom came in to check on him.

"I really don't feel well, Mom," Bobby groaned. "I'm going to skip dinner tonight and just try to sleep."

His mother agreed. Bobby was still sleeping when his father came home.

When the alarm went off the next morning at 4:30 a.m., Bobby could not get up. He called one of the other swimmers and told him he was sick and would not be at the pool that morning.

"Please tell coach I'm sorry."

He resolved later to call the coach and explain that he might not be able to be with the students for a few days, and fell back to sleep.

Bobby did not go in the next day, as his pain worsened.

Wednesday February 27, 2012, 7:00 p.m.

A minimal diet of soup and toast, along with constant rest, had not reduced Bobby's level of abdominal pain. Around noon, Bobby's mother had tried to call her husband, but she was told he would be in surgery for most of the day. An hour later she had called Bobby's primary care physician, only to find that she was on vacation and that all open slots with her practice partners had already been taken by other flu victims. She decided to wait for her husband to come home.

At 7:00 p.m., Dr. Arnold had still not returned, so Peggy called his office. She was told that there had been a complication in the operating room (OR) and it was not clear when Dr. Arnold would be coming out. Concerned that Bobby's pain was not subsiding, she finally decided to take him to the University Hospital Emergency Department (ED).

The triage nurse greeted them as soon as they walked in the door.

"Hi, how can we help you today?"

"Bad case of flu," Bobby said as nonchalantly as he could manage. When asked about his level of pain, he shrugged and replied, "Moderate." The nurse classified Bobby as an ESI-3 and placed him into the "simple" track in the ED, as she had been doing all week with flu patients. After only about 5 minutes in the waiting room, Bobby was taken into a small room where a physician assistant (PA) interviewed him, took vital signs, and drew some blood.

Twenty minutes later, the lab test results came back showing elevated blood urea nitrogen (BUN) and creatinine (Cr) levels. This, along with Bobby's distended abdomen, caused the PA to flag Bobby as potentially unsuited for the simple track. He called the attending physician in charge of the simple track, who agreed that it could be more than a case of flu. He ordered a CT scan and diverted Bobby off the simple track.

The switch in tracks was invisible to Bobby and Peggy, because he did not immediately move anywhere physically. But he was reassigned from the PA to a senior ED resident, Dr. James Gunn, who was working under the supervision of attending Dr. Nathanial Greene.

Within minutes, Bobby was given oral contrast, along with an antiemetic to help him keep it down, as called for by best practices for cases like his. Forty minutes later, he was wheeled to Radiology where he waited for ten minutes in a prep room outside the CT room. Once inside, the scan was conducted swiftly and efficiently.

Because it was past 8:30 p.m., a senior radiologist was not onsite. Instead, the image was transmitted electronically to an on-call radiologist working from home for a check on image quality while Bobby waited. The response came back quickly that the image was fine, but Bobby was not. The radiologist immediately followed with a call to Dr. Gunn indicating that a small bowel obstruction was likely and that immediate clinical confirmation was indicated. Minutes later, he posted his report documenting this conclusion in writing.

Dr. Gunn immediately contacted General Surgery for a consultation. Shortly after 9 p.m., GS resident Dr. Leslie Mason examined Bobby and the radiology report. She confirmed that emergency surgery was warranted and started the process.

Although the elective surgery schedule had closed, as had most of the ORs, the hospital had developed a system to enable them to rapidly open a room for emergent cases. Under this system, Department of Surgery techs routinely prepared the "ED-OR" which was kept at ready after hours for just such emergencies. On-call surgeons were never more than 30 minutes from the hospital, and on-call duties were spread across several surgical services so that level of responsiveness did not come at great personal cost to any one surgeon. As a result, by 10:15 p.m., Bobby's surgical team had been assembled, the room had been prepped, and the surgical nursing and PA staff were in place.

Dr. Arnold arrived just in time to squeeze his son's hand as he was being rolled into surgery. He and Peggy then waited in the surgical waiting room like any other nervous family member of a surgery patient. Ninety minutes later, the surgeon, Dr. Ann Arbor, came out and informed the relieved couple that everything went perfectly.

"However," she said, "it's a good thing we operated when we did. The blockage was total and any delay could have been very serious. We'll keep him here for a day for observation, but I'm sure he's going to be just fine."

Dr. Arnold was relieved, thankful, anxious, and thoughtful all at once. He knew, more than anybody else in his family, how serious this could have been. When he and Peggy were finally permitted to see Bobby in the Post Anesthesia Care unit (PACU), Arnold kissed his son on the forehead in emotional relief and gratitude.

Later, when he and Peggy were leaving the PACU to accompany Bobby up to his room, he asked a nurse if she knew who had been involved in treating his son. She informed him that, in addition to the surgeons Drs. Mason and Arbor, the ED doctors were the resident Dr. Gunn and his attending Dr. Greene.

Thursday February 28, 2012, 7:00 p.m.

When Dr. Arnold arrived at the gym, Dr. Greene was the only one there, warming up by trotting up and down the court making easy layups. When Arnold walked out to him, Greene stopped at center court and held the ball.

"Do you remember the young man last night with a small bowel obstruction and volvulus?" Arnold asked. "Your resident Gunn treated him."

"Yeah..."

"That was my son..."

They looked at one another wordlessly for a long moment. Finally, Arnold broke the silence.

"Thank you," he said softly.

After a thoughtful pause, Dr. Greene responded.

"You're welcome, friend."

And he launched a high arcing shot that touched nothing but net.

6.2 Product and Process Integration

Bobby's experience might sound like optimistic fiction. The perception of today's hospitals as expensive, crowded, inefficient, and dangerous makes it difficult to imagine a smooth, almost pleasant, experience in a hospital. But all the practices that facilitated Bobby's efficient trip through the hospital are already in use in some hospitals. On the experience frontier, a number of hospitals have even consulted with the Disney Institute

Healthcare Service Program, and many have adopted the service focus of a top-end hotel or (dare we say it) theme park. Even transformative technological innovations with the potential to further enhance performance are not far-fetched. For example, in the past decade, ultrasound technology has benefited from both miniaturization and resolution enhancement to the point where bedside scanning can produce high-quality images of many different organs. So the components of a radically improved hospital experience are already here or coming.

But the overall vision of cost-effective, patient-centric care is not yet reality. Hospitals remain vastly complex systems of poorly connected silos of specialization that frustrate patients and clinicians alike. Efforts to borrow successful practices from other industries, such as Lean and Six Sigma, have been limited to *point kaizens* (small, isolated improvements that are easy to implement quickly) rather than systemic transformations. The gap between the actual and the possible remains wide.

In this regard, the health care industry has defied the natural pattern of industrial evolution, in which economic pressures drive industry structure from a jumble of loosely coordinated activities to a tightly linked set of coordinated processes. Although economic pressures have not been absent in health care, they have been muted in their effect due to some distinctive aspects of the decision making and reimbursement environment. Nevertheless, we forecast that these pressures must eventually be responded to. In this final chapter, we use an operations management lens to project the ways in which that response is likely to manifest itself. Although we predict that hospitals will change significantly over the next few decades, we are confident that the management principles we have introduced, described, and applied in this book will remain in force more than ever. This is because these principles are not the product of any one health system or structure, but rather tenets of physics and human nature that will stand the test of time.

Of course, it is easier to talk about the future than it is to create it. Words about breaking down silos and end-to-end patient flow are simple to write but difficult to carry out. A few more words in this final chapter will not make the way ahead any less demanding. But, by stepping back and highlighting the major goals, trends, and challenges facing hospitals, we can at least shed some light on the path ahead and the steps needed to reach the hospital of the future we know is possible.

6.2.1 Process Hierarchy

A major issue faced by almost all enterprises is matching process with product.[1] Different products demand different delivery processes to provide the right mix of cost, quality, variety, and speed. For example, a five-star restaurant uses a general-purpose kitchen staffed by skilled cooks to produce expensive gourmet food, whereas fast food restaurants use standardized, semi-automated production lines staffed by low-skill workers to produce inexpensive fast food. Federal Express uses a hub and spoke delivery system to deliver traceable overnight packages at a premium price, whereas the U.S. Postal Service uses a regional post office system to deliver packages at a discount, but with slower speed and less traceability. A pharmaceutical company uses a highly flexible research laboratory to produce small batches of new drug candidates, but it uses a rigidly focused production line to produce large quantities of commercial drugs.

Although there are innumerable ways to configure the product delivery processes, they can be grouped into three broad categories:

- **Job shops**—These are highly flexible organizations capable of producing a range of products and adapting to production of new products. Examples include prototyping facilities, consulting firms, and hospital EDs. Job shops require highly skilled personnel, general-purpose equipment, and flexible work methods. Because products are not standardized, job shops typically charge for inputs (for example, time and materials or consulting hours) rather than for outputs.

  - **Flow shops**—These are highly efficient organizations focused on producing a narrow range of products. Examples include automotive assembly lines, insurance underwriting groups, and some clinical laboratory procedures. Flow shops require more narrowly trained personnel than do job shops because equipment is specialized and work methods are structured. Because products are well defined and predictable, flow shops generally charge for outputs (such as fixed prices for products backed up by warranties).

- **Self-service**—These are systems in which customers produce all or part of their product value with the assistance of technology or social networks. Examples of technology-enabled self-service include self-checkout lanes, ATMs, and self-administration of insulin via injection pens. Examples of social network facilitated self-service include online auction sites (for example, eBay) and patient support networks (for example, dLife.com for diabetics, and y-me.org for breast cancer survivors). Businesses based on self-service charge for either the facilitating technology (for example, insulin pens) or the facilitating network services (for example, eBay).

Organizations are often dominated by one type of delivery system. For instance, consulting firms are mainly configured as job shops, mass production factories are set up predominantly as flow shops, and online download providers (for example, iTunes) are presented primarily as self-service systems. But organizations can use a mixture of delivery systems to deliver different products to different customers. For example, a consulting firm uses a job shop system to deliver customized consulting services and a flow shop system to deliver standardized training or audit services. A factory uses a flow shop process to assemble standardized products, but it uses a self-service online portal to deliver even more standardized order entry services. Hospitals are predominantly job shops because they are designed to provide a range of medical services in a flexible manner. But they also contain flow shops (for example, some clinical lab processes) and possibly even self-service systems (for example, online bill payment).

Industries often go through a natural progression from job shop to flow shop to self-service driven by a combination of technology and economics. Technology facilitates this progression by standardizing and automating the delivery of a class of products. For example, automobiles were initially produced in job shops staffed by highly skilled artisans using simple tools and flexible methods. But the advent of the moving assembly line and more sophisticated assembly tools simplified automobile production to the point where it could be carried out in flow shops. Similarly, the advent of barcode scanning technology made the grocery checkout process so simple that it could be shifted from flow lines staffed by moderately skilled cashiers to self-service lines operated by the customers themselves.

But, although technology facilitates simplification of the delivery process, it is economics that motivates it. In general, the progression from job shop to flow shop to self-service promotes an increase in cost efficiency, albeit at the expense of a decrease in flexibility. For instance, a patient could receive insulin shots at an integrated hospital, at a storefront clinic, or at home via self-administered injection. The cost of the shots would be highest in the hospital, less in the clinic, and even less at home. But the hospital can provide almost any medical service, the clinic can provide a limited range of services, and an insulin pen can do only one thing. Hence, an important management challenge that faces any organization is finding an array of delivery processes that provide the desired range of products at an efficient cost. This is not a challenge that has been well met by today's hospitals.

When processes become misaligned with products, the consequences can be disastrous. Imagine how quickly a five-star restaurant would go broke if it tried to offer fast-food-quality burgers produced by expensive chefs in expensive kitchens. Faced with a $100 fast food meal, customers would desert the restaurant in droves.

But these kind of mismatches can and do happen. A recent one occurred in the publishing industry. Although we usually think of the products in this industry as books and periodicals, the real product is the reading experience. Starting with a finished manuscript, the traditional paper-based process delivers this service by means of a book printing and binding process (often carried out in highly flexible job shops) followed by a retailing process (which mixes job shop functions, such as customer support, and flow shop functions, such as checkout).

This traditional business model was attacked by two waves of innovation. First, online retailing (primarily by Amazon) replaced the job/flow shop mix of retail outlets with flow/self-service activities involved in e-tailing and mail delivery. This model also took advantage of pooled inventories to reduce costs and improve product availability. So it was inevitable that, as web technology made the online ordering process easier and more secure, Amazon gained significant market share. Second, electronic books, which can be delivered completely through self-service downloads, were introduced as substitutes for paper books. This model also eliminated paper and printing costs. So as e-reader technology advanced to the point of providing a satisfactory e-book reading experience, digital delivery began to grow rapidly.

Unfortunately, Borders, which had achieved nationwide success as a pioneer of the book superstore concept, failed to establish an effective online presence. After a seven-year effort at tying its web presence to Amazon, Borders.com reemerged as an independent entity but was woefully behind the competition. Meanwhile, it was also late to the e-book revolution. Forced to rely on declining revenues from the brick-and-mortar portion of its business, Borders slipped into unprofitability and liquidated in 2011. Health care organizations whose processes are not well aligned with their products risk the same fate.

The Borders case illustrates an example of a product/process mismatch that occurred because a firm lagged behind in the evolution to more efficient delivery processes. But a reverse type of mismatch can also happen if procedures are prematurely standardized before the organization is sufficiently down the learning curve toward stable best practices. For example, in the 1970s, Material Requirements Planning (MRP) systems were touted as the information-age key to unlocking business productivity. These systems standardized lead times, batch sizes, and other key manufacturing decisions into information systems that told managers when and how much of each required input to order, to meet forecasted demand. Unfortunately, in many firms, none of those inputs, and especially not demand, was constant over the planning lead times. So, rather than resulting in smooth, optimal flow, MRP systems resulted in chaotic behavior that was euphemistically dubbed *nervousness*. In the end, workers had to circumvent the "official" system with all kinds of interventions, such as "expediting," to get things done. Prematurely standardizing practice before it has reached stability can be as inefficient as not standardizing practice once it has reached stability.

6.2.2 Product Variety

Because medical conditions, and our knowledge of how to diagnose and treat them, vary greatly, so does the range of medical products. Christensen, Grossman and Hwang (2009) have elegantly grouped the types of medical services into the categories of intuitive, empirical, and precision medicine, which are defined as follows:

- **Intuitive medicine**—This describes treatment of conditions for which diagnoses must be made on the basis of imprecise symptoms and for which outcomes from available treatment options are highly uncertain. Most maladies are initially treated via intuitive medicine. For example, the condition labeled as consumption (phthisis in Greek) was known in ancient times. But, lacking diagnostic technology, physicians could only identify the disease by general symptoms such as fever and coughing up blood. Because several diseases, including tuberculosis, pneumonia, pulmonary edema, and others, can produce these symptoms, no precise diagnosis was possible. Worse, no consistently effective treatment was available. Physicians variously attributed consumption to heredity, demons, vampires, bad air, sugar, and a host of other causes. Consequently, they experimented with all manner of treatments, including opium, bloodletting, specialized diets, the "royal touch" of a monarch, extra-pleural *thoracoplasty* (injecting air into the pleural cavity to collapse the lung), spending time in caves, spending time at high altitudes, isolation in sanatoriums, and many others. This type of trial-and-error treatment is characteristic of intuitive medicine.

■ **Empirical medicine**—This describes treatment of conditions where diagnosis and treatment have a statistical basis. Specifically, using the terminology of the management principles found in Appendix A, empirical medicine becomes possible when we have enough data to separate effective from ineffective treatments. For example, in the 1820s, French physician Pierre Charles Alexandre Louis applied the statistical correlation methods of Pierre-Simon Laplace to understand tendencies in the progression of tuberculosis and the efficacy of various treatments. Although none of the treatment options available at the time were broadly effective, the statistical work of Louis and those who followed gave physicians a logical basis for choosing between alternatives. In general, statements like, "This drug is 85% effective in patients with your symptoms" are characteristic of empirical medicine.[2]

■ **Precision medicine**—This describes the medical ideal in which the state of knowledge about a disease enables high-diagnostic accuracy and predictable treatment effectiveness. For example, in 1882 Robert Koch identified the bacterium that causes tuberculosis (TB) and made a precise diagnosis possible. Instead of relying on general symptoms that could be produced by a variety of conditions, physicians could cultivate a sputum sample to find out definitively whether the patient was infected. Koch's discovery also led first to a preventive vaccine in 1906 and finally to an effective antibiotic therapy in 1944. With these innovations, diagnosis and treatment of TB were transformed from matters of art and professional judgment into a simple deterministic procedure—administer a TB test and, when positive, prescribe antibiotics.[3] Such rule-based diagnostic and treatment procedures are characteristic of precision medicine and are the ultimate goal of medical research.

Prior to the late nineteenth century, most treatment fell into the category of intuitive medicine. Since then, a steady stream of research results has revealed the underlying causes of many medical conditions and has led to predictably effective treatments.

Consequently, most treatment today falls into the empirical medicine category, with some approaching the ideal of precision medicine.

6.2.3 Product/Process Matrix

A fundamental premise of operations management is that there should be a match between products and the processes used to produce them. A common framework for describing this match is the well-known product/process matrix introduced by Hayes and Wheelwright (1979). A version of this, adapted to health care and making use of the preceding categories, is given in Exhibit 6.1. The basic concept captured by this exhibit is that, although many different delivery processes can be used to produce a product, there are natural fits between product and process types. This fit is indicated by the diagonal of the product/process matrix. Combinations above the diagonal are generally inefficient, whereas combinations below it are generally ineffective.

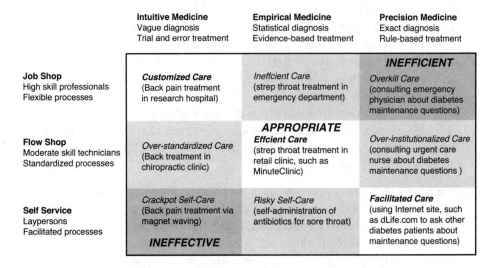

Exhibit 6.1   Health care product/process matrix.

To see this, consider the first column in the matrix in Exhibit 6.1, which addresses the condition of chronic back pain. The symptoms are clear enough—pain! But there are many potential causes, including bulging/herniated disks, spinal degeneration, osteoporosis, and skeletal irregularities, as well as maladies whose causes are still unknown, such as fibromyalgia and spondylitis. As a result, it is often difficult to diagnose the specific cause of chronic back pain. None of the myriad treatment options, including exercise, massage therapy, physical devices, acupuncture, surgery, laser surgery, and many more, are uniformly effective. So treatment of chronic back pain is still largely in the intuitive medicine stage. Given this, back pain patients are best off in a job shop–type integrated health care system that can provide a range of treatments and experiment with these to find the best therapy for each patient. A flow shop–type system that focuses on a narrow range of therapies (for example, a chiropractic clinic) may be effective for a few patients but useless for many others. Self-treatment via home remedies has an outside chance of providing relief but is far more likely to benefit the retailers of the remedies than the chronic back pain sufferers. The bottom line:

> *Conditions that have not advanced beyond the state of intuitive medicine are best suited to job shop delivery systems.*

The second column in Exhibit 6.1 considers strep throat. The symptoms—sore throat, fever, headache, nausea—are easy enough to observe. But these can be caused by viruses as well as the strep bacterium. Fortunately, physicians can use a rapid strep test or a throat culture to determine whether the patient has strep throat. If he does, a well-defined regimen of antibiotics has a high likelihood of being effective. Because both diagnostic tests and treatment options are good but less than perfect, strep throat falls into the category of empirical medicine. But the high reliability of the tests and the robust effectiveness of the treatment put it closer to precision medicine than intuitive medicine. As such, strep throat treatment is amenable to a flow shop delivery system.

MinuteClinic is a commercial example of a flow shop for treating strep throat and similar maladies. Launched in 2000 in the Minneapolis/St. Paul area as the first system of retail health clinics, MinuteClinic initially made use of small offices located in shopping malls, grocery stores, and other retailing centers. In 2006, MinuteClinic was acquired by CVS Corporation, and locations were consolidated into CVS drugstores. Staffed by a single midlevel practitioner (nurse practitioner or PA), these clinics rely on standard diagnosis and treatment protocols enforced by a computer program to provide highly efficient diagnosis and treatment of a small set of conditions (for example, strep, ear infections, pinkeye, mono, flu, pregnancy tests, and so on). Patients with conditions outside this specified set are referred to a hospital or private physician. Patients who are treated are done so within predictable 15-minute time windows so that they can walk up without appointments and either be served immediately or given a firm time to return. This allows them to shop or run errands instead of waiting idly. MinuteClinic reports high levels of patient satisfaction with the overall experience, and online comments on customer review sites support this.

Clearly, treatment of strep patients in the job shop environment of an ED can be done in a clinically acceptable manner. But it will be much slower and more expensive than at MinuteClinic. Conversely, although self-treatment of sore throat symptoms might someday be possible with appropriate technology, today it runs the risk of inappropriate diagnosis and treatment (for example, ineffective use of antibiotics for viral infections). Hence, the insight here is:

> *Conditions that fall into the realm of empirical medicine are often most effectively treated in flow shop systems.*

The third column in Exhibit 6.1 considers diabetes maintenance. A chronic disease with no cure currently available, diabetes must be treated through a combination of medication and lifestyle changes. On the medication side, the responses to hyperglycemia (that is, insulin injection) and hypoglycemia (that is, consumption of fast-acting carbohydrates) are standard and reliably effective, so treatment falls into the category of precision medicine. Armed with the right technology (for example, blood sugar monitors and insulin-injection devices), diabetes patients can diagnose and treat themselves effectively. On the lifestyle side, although doctors and nurses can provide general guidance, they are a poor source of information on some specific, but important, questions. For example, finding recipes for diabetes-friendly dishes, helping a diabetic child cope at school, and developing an exercise routine, are issues about which reliable information exists but is more easily obtained from diabetic peers than from medical providers. Hence, a web-enabled "crowd sourcing" solution, like that offered by dLife.com, is an appropriate delivery model for diabetes lifestyle information delivery. In general:

> *Conditions that can be addressed through precision medicine are amenable to technology or network-enabled self-service systems.*

Finally, notice that product-process combinations below the diagonal are potentially dangerous, because they apply overstandardized procedures that may not fit the condition. Combinations above the diagonal may be medically acceptable, but they are inefficient because the delivery systems are overdesigned for the products. One does not need a fully equipped, technologically advanced, integrated hospital to treat strep throat. Unfortunately, this type of overmatching of process to product is rampant in the health care industry.

As we observed earlier, competition drives most industries toward more efficient production processes. Efficiency improvements can take the form of *incremental enhancements*, which increase effectiveness within a delivery model, and *transformative shifts*, which alter the basic delivery model. These are illustrated in Exhibit 6.2. Non-health care examples of incremental enhancements include Boston Consulting, which improved the job shop delivery of consulting services by shifting the focus from execution to strategy; Toyota, which improved the flow shop production of vehicles by systematically eliminating waste and variability; and Skype, which improved the efficiency of self-service communication by using low-cost data networks to transmit voice. Examples of transformative shifts include Ford, which transformed auto assembly from an artisan job shop environment to a repetitive flow shop through use of a moving assembly line, and eBay, which transformed third-party retailing into a self-service network of Internet-enabled auctions.

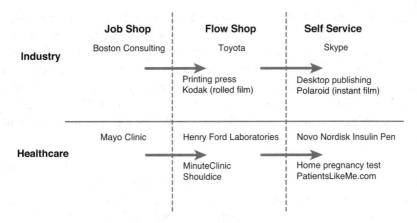

Exhibit 6.2   Incremental Innovations within Delivery Models and Disruptive Innovations that Shift Delivery Models (adapted from Christensen et al 2009).

Analogous examples exist in health care. For instance, Exhibit 6.2 lists Mayo Clinic as an industry leading example of an integrated hospital (job shop), Henry Ford Laboratories as an innovative user of lean methods in a clinical laboratory (flow shop), and the Novo Nordisk insulin pen as a significant innovation in insulin delivery (self-service). MinuteClinic, as we mentioned earlier, is an example of an organization that introduced a flow shop system to offer medical services that were previously available only through job shop systems.

Another famous example of a transformative shift from job shop to flow shop in health care is that of Shouldice Hospital (Heskett 2003).[4] Opened in 1945 in Toronto by Dr. Earl Shouldice, this hospital treats only patients requiring surgical hernia repair using a highly standardized procedure developed by Dr. Shouldice. The processes for admitting and preparing patients on the day prior to surgery, and caring for them during the two or three days of postsurgery recovery, are also highly standardized. Moreover, some tasks, such as shaving the surgical area, are carried out by the patients themselves in self-service mode. The result is an assembly-line-like process through which patients flow smoothly and efficiently. Christensen, Grossman and Hwang (2009) report that the cost of a hernia repair at Shouldice is 30% less than that at a typical U.S. hospital, even though Shouldice includes a 3–4 day stay in a pleasant facility, whereas a typical hospital performs the procedure on an outpatient basis. Because it makes use of standard repetitive processes, it is not surprising that Shouldice achieves a significant cost advantage over the unstandardized job shop processes of a typical hospital. But it may be surprising that Shouldice also engenders higher levels of patient satisfaction due to the amenities and collegial environment the hospital is able to wrap around its efficient flow process. Indeed, patients feel so connected to their experience that for many years Shouldice held well-attended reunions for former patients.

Although MinuteClinic and Shouldice are excellent examples of transformative shifts in health care delivery processes, such examples in health care are far rarer than are examples in other industries. The health care industry has continued to provide many services through hospitals, clinics, and physician offices configured as highly flexible job shops. Although technological advancements have improved the quality of care greatly, the basic delivery systems have remained relatively unchanged. Despite some localized shifts to more efficient delivery modes (for example, Fast Tracks in EDs), most health care is still provided through costly and inefficient job shops.

A major reason for this is that the market forces that drive innovation toward greater efficiency (from job shop to flow shop to self-service) are largely absent in health care. Fee-for-service (or time and materials) payment schemes pay for inputs rather than outputs, so they can actually reward inefficiency. Any industry buffered from market forces is likely to lag in efficiency innovations. Like health care, national defense has benefited from payments for inputs (via cost-plus contracts) and has similarly been criticized for being inefficient in its use of resources. In health care, distorted economic signals have retarded the natural progression toward more efficient delivery modes. In terms of Exhibit 6.1, many medical conditions continue to be treated with processes in the upper-left portion of the product/process matrix. That is, even though technology has advanced to the point at which certain conditions are amenable to empirical medicine, hospitals continue treating them with job shop processes because there has been insufficient economic pressure to force a shift to the efficiencies of flow shop delivery. Consequently, we have a much less efficient health care system than we should have at this stage of the development of medical technology.

Although we could wring our collective hands about the reasons for this past market failure in health care, the more important questions are those about the future. Are there trends that will finally force health care to make radical improvements in efficiency? If so, how will these impact hospitals and their future roles? What can hospital managers do to adapt their institutions to the health care landscape of the future?

To consider these, we first need to describe that landscape, and then we need to interpret it in light of the industrial dynamics model depicted in Exhibits 6.1 and 6.2, as well as the principles-based management framework presented in this book.

6.3 Looking to the Future

Wayne Gretzky, widely acknowledged as the greatest hockey player of all time, described the key to his success with the quote, "I skate to where the puck is going to be, not where it has been." Unfortunately, unlike "The Great One," hospitals are skating to where the puck has been. Configured as job shops, they are adapted to intuitive medicine in an age in which empirical medicine is becoming the norm. Adapted to complex and arbitrary reimbursement policies, hospitals have evolved physical and human capacities that are ill-suited to the true economic realities of the present and are even less suited to the future.

But how can hospitals know where the puck is going to be? Health care is influenced by so many disparate parties (including patients, employers, insurers, providers, and politicians) that it is impossible to make detailed predictions about the future. However, at the macro level, we can confidently project that two major trends from the present will continue. Viewing these through an operations management lens suggests that current hospital configurations will not remain viable, but that two very distinct roles for hospitals will be well suited to future needs. This perspective also suggests that decisions made by hospital personnel will critically influence the health care landscape of the future. That is, hospital managers can not only skate to where the puck is going, they can influence where it will go.

6.3.1 Key Trends

Two well-established trends that are certain to continue are

- **Improving technology**—As medical science advances, diagnostic accuracy and treatment efficacy will continue to improve. Consequently, more and more conditions will progress up the scale of empirical medicine toward precision medicine.

- **Increasing cost pressure**—With health care costs already consuming 17.6% of GDP and continuing to rise, it hardly takes a crystal ball to predict ongoing and increasing pressure to reduce health care costs. This will come in varying degrees from patients, employers, insurance companies, the government, and providers.

Taken together, these trends scream for restructuring of the health care delivery process. Technological advances are increasing the number of conditions amenable to the repetitive processes of flow shop systems, or even self-care, whereas cost pressure is increasing the incentive to make use of these more efficient systems.

How this restructuring plays out depends on how the cost pressure is applied. In most industries, cost pressure comes from market competition. But because health care occupies a special status somewhere between a fundamental right and a luxury good, the federal government supports it through entitlement programs and favored tax status. As a result, most treatment services are paid for by public or private insurers, rather than by patients themselves. Because they do not bear the costs directly, patients do not usually shop around for the best deal and hence do not provide incentive for providers to increase efficiency. Whatever cost pressure providers do experience comes through the reimbursement policies of insurers.

The traditional reimbursement scheme, which Medicare and private insurers still use, is *fee-for-service*, in which providers are paid for office visits, tests, procedures, and other activities based on a set fee schedule. As one would expect in a system that tries to set prices in a sector as complex as health care, all rates are subject to negotiation, in which providers lobby payers for adjustments.[5] Because it rewards services rendered rather than services avoided, fee-for-service is fundamentally inflationary. It provides economic incentive to overprovide treatment and underinvest in more efficient delivery (including prevention measures).

Seeking to rein in costs, Medicare and private insurers are moving toward *bundling*, in which fees are paid for combinations of services, rather than for each service. For example, a bundled payment for a hip replacement would cover presurgical preparation, anesthesiology, surgery, the hospital stay, OR fees, the hip implant, radiological examinations, laboratory tests, rehabilitation, and everything else associated with treating the patient. Because the provider receives the same fee regardless of the number of services provided, this type of *fee-for-episode* reimbursement provides incentive to streamline, integrate, and otherwise improve efficiency. An even more aggressive form of bundling is to reimburse a provider with a fixed fee for delivering all the health care services needed by an individual during a year. Like fee-for-service, this type of *fee-for-membership* or *capitation* payment incents efficiency. Because it pays providers even if no treatment is provided, it also incents prevention.

Designing a bundled payment scheme involves many decisions about what to bundle, how to set fees, how to divide payments among providers, and other details. Countless different payment systems are possible. What mix of these emerges will depend on the actions of patients, providers, employers, and politicians. So predicting the exact nature of medical reimbursement is futile. Fortunately, hospital managers do not need to predict the details of the future to prepare for it. Knowing that the health care puck is sliding toward technologically standardized treatment and bundled payment cost pressure is enough for hospital managers to figure out where to skate.

6.3.2 Alternate Futures

Bundled payments that reward efficient providers naturally encourage flow shop delivery systems. For example, Shouldice Hospital is configured as a focused flow shop that can treat hernia patients for significantly less than the cost of an integrated (job shop) hospital. If cost pressures drive down the (bundled) reimbursement rate for hernia patients, there will come a point at which a Shouldice-type system can treat them profitably but integrated hospitals cannot.

If they do not mount a defense, integrated hospitals will see more and more business picked off by third-party providers that target patients requiring empirical/precision medicine with high-efficiency flow shops. Under this scenario, focused hospitals like

Shouldice, retail clinics like MinuteClinic, and even physician's offices will increasingly treat patients who currently go to hospitals. Cost is clearly one reason for this. If reimbursement rates for some patient types fall to the point at which hospitals cannot compete with these alternate providers, they will naturally decrease their capacities to treat these patients and thereby lose market share.

But another reason third-party flow shops will steal business from hospitals is speed. Even if reimbursement rates remain high enough to compensate hospitals for their inefficient job shop delivery, alternate providers using flow shop models will be able to provide faster, more responsive service. For instance, someone with a sore throat might well choose MinuteClinic over the local ED, even if their copay is identical, because MinuteClinic has a substantially shorter wait time. If flow shop providers are able to establish themselves for a class of patients on the basis of speed, insurers will have incentive to decrease reimbursement rates to levels in line with the costs of these more efficient systems. Thus, the competitiveness of hospitals could ultimately be undermined by both the speed and cost advantages of their flow shop rivals.

If this scenario plays out over a significant portion of the health care sector, we can expect hospitals to face increasing financial stress as they lose business that helps cover fixed costs and cross-subsidizes unprofitable activities. Many traditional hospitals will close, leaving a smaller and smaller set of institutions dedicated to the activities that have not yet been targeted by outside institutions. We refer to this as the *disintegration future.*

For hospital administrators, the disintegration future represents a serious threat. But it has undeniable appeal to patients and tax payers. After all, who doesn't want faster, cheaper health care? But the disintegration future is neither assured nor necessarily rosy. In addition to plain old momentum, which puts third-party providers at a disadvantage, two major obstacles could undermine the evolution of the disintegration future. These are (1) the lack of effective gatekeepers and (2) the risk of overstandardization.

Gatekeepers are needed in health care because medical services are not like typical consumer products in which selection can be left to the customer. We require the help of trained professionals to determine which health care services we need. If this function is left up to primary care physicians, who are affiliated with hospitals, patients are unlikely to be directed to third-party providers. If insurers try to play this role themselves and are perceived as denying care in pursuit of cost efficiency, they are likely to face a backlash from both patients and medical professionals like that prompted by health maintenance organizations (HMOs) in the 1990s. Unless insurers can establish gatekeepers that are both medically credible and cost conscious, the emergence of efficient third-party providers may be painfully slow.

Even if appropriate gatekeepers can be found, flow shop delivery should be applied only to conditions in which medical science has made standardization appropriate. But judging which conditions are amenable to standardization is not easy. In a conventional competitive environment, the market would determine this. For instance, if a software consultant could standardize the procedure for installing an enterprise system to the point where it could predict both the cost and the outcome, it could conquer the market by quoting fixed fees with guaranteed results. But until technology justifies such a shift, consultants will continue charging for their time in fee-for-service fashion.

In health care, where reimbursement rates are set more by mandate than by market, decisions about what services to bundle and what rates to set may not be at all aligned with the state of technology. Indeed, in the pursuit of cost efficiency, insurers are likely to ignore the previously cited dictum—rationalize the repeatable, but only the repeatable—and apply bundled reimbursement to patients requiring intuitive medicine. Because the services, and hence the costs, for such patients are inherently unpredictable, the resulting fees will produce economic distortions that overincent some types of treatment and underincent others. So, as is the case today, we will wind up with too much capacity for some types of medicine (which increases costs) and too little for others (which increases patient wait times).

But an even greater danger at the hospital level of an overzealous push toward bundled reimbursement could be overreliance on rigid protocols for medical conditions that are not ready for them. Faced with standardized reimbursement and mounting cost pressure, providers may feel forced to standardize treatment of patients requiring intuitive medicine. Doing so would make them guilty of a blunder described by another famous dictum:

> A foolish consistency is the hobgoblin of small minds.
>
> —Ralph Waldo Emerson

Legitimate resistance from the medical community to inappropriate protocols could easily carry over to the standardization process as a whole and impede progress toward an efficient decentralized delivery system.

If the disintegration future does not materialize because of obstacles like those already mentioned or because hospitals do mount a credible defense against third-party attackers, what would the alternate future look like? We can say with confidence that it will not look like the current health care system. The relentless progression of technology and cost pressure *will* ultimately force a shift to more flow shop and self-service health care. The only question is whether this transformation will be carried out by outside parties or within existing hospital systems.

There is no fundamental reason that an integrated hospital system could not include efficient flow shops for delivering empirical medicine or even facilitated networks for supporting self-care. Indeed, an integrated system offers two important advantages over a disintegrated system:

- An integrated system can serve as an unbiased gatekeeper, because it directs patients within its own system, rather than to competitors. For instance, a physician in an independent unit within a disintegrated system has incentive not to direct patients to a third-party low-cost clinic, because it would take money out of his own pocket. In contrast, a salaried physician in an integrated system both serves his employer and retains his salary by appropriately directing patients to a low-cost clinic within the system.[6]

- The issue of dividing bundled fees is less problematic than in a decentralized system because fees are divided within the same system rather than between independent systems. This latter advantage makes integrated systems particularly well suited to fee-for-membership or capitation style reimbursement. Indeed, integrated providers, such as Kaiser Permanente, have made successful use of fee-for-membership compensation for a long time.

The implication is that advancing technology and increasing cost pressure could also lead to an *integration future*, in which providers consolidate into comprehensive care networks. To be successful, these networks have to go beyond the considerable amount of consolidation in the hospital industry that has occurred in recent years, which was largely driven by the need to pool resources for large capital purchases and the desire to build negotiating power with insurers. Existing consolidated systems consist largely of collections of integrated hospitals and offsite facilities, which still operate predominantly in job shop mode. In the future, motivated by rising cost pressure and facilitated by increasingly standardized technology, integrated provider networks need to make radical improvements in delivery efficiency of empirical/precision medicine to remain competitive. If they do, hospital-centric networks in the integration future could offer a credible alternative to the third-party attackers of the disintegration future.

6.4 Management Challenges

Joseph Schumpeter used the term *creative destruction* to describe the process by which existing products, firms, and industries are made obsolete through innovation. From buggy whips to Betamax, history books are filled with examples of successes that became obsolete and rapidly vanished. Whether modern hospitals evolve into key players in the health care landscape of the future or wind up in Schumpeter's dustbin will depend in great part on their own actions.

6.4.1 Shaping the Future

As we noted earlier, the mechanism by which third-party providers can steal market share from hospitals is by delivering faster or cheaper health care services. This can be done by focusing on a specific segment of patients amenable to empirical/precision medicine and serving them with a simpler delivery model. MinuteClinic did this by setting up a flow shop system to treat a small set of minor conditions. Dlife.com did this by establishing a self-service network specifically for diabetics. We can expect many more such efforts.

Of course, high-efficiency competitors can only steal patients from hospitals if they generate a significant advantage over the status quo. So the most direct defense against such attacks is for hospitals to improve their own efficiency. The flow principles described in this book provide a framework for doing this. Innovations that take advantage of simplification, standardization, variability reduction, critical ratio sequencing, and other concepts that underlie the responsiveness improvement framework shown in Table A.1 in Appendix A can eliminate considerable waste in existing systems. This can make possible faster treatment in the ED, quicker access to elective surgery, and shorter stays in the hospital, as well as reduced costs and improved patient safety. In parallel, hospitals can continually improve patient safety by exploiting the concepts of redundancy, foolproofing, decision making, and execution, as outlined in Table A.2. Traversing the learning curve toward standardized best practices and promulgating them across the enterprise can be facilitated with the organizational learning tools implicit in Table A.3. The more progress hospitals make on the responsiveness, safety, and learning fronts, the more difficult it will be for competitors to poach patients.

But effective use of management principles in the current hospital structure will not be enough to head off all third-party attacks. The most efficient job shop cannot compete with a well-designed flow shop, and an exceptional flow shop cannot outperform an appropriate self-service system. So, if hospitals are going to defend their central role in the health care system, they cannot rely on incremental innovation alone. They must also use transformative innovation. Specifically, they must replace job shop delivery with flow shop and self-service delivery for patients where this makes sense.

In manufacturing, firms often use specialized facilities configured as high-efficiency flow shops where demand volume justifies the necessary scale. For example, a chemical company might set up a plant to produce nothing but polystyrene. Because this specialty plant would have less variability and complexity than a general-purpose chemical plant, it would be capable of producing polystyrene more efficiently (and hence at a lower cost) than would a general-purpose plant.

In health care, laser eye surgery clinics, Shouldice Hospital, and MinuteClinic are all examples of such specialty facilities. Although these examples are third-party entities that run independently of a central hospital, there is no reason that a hospital system could not set up its own network of specialty facilities. For example, a hospital could open high-efficiency clinics in high-traffic areas that are geographically separated from the hospital. By referring patients who fall outside the appropriateness guidelines for care to the central hospital for further diagnosis and treatment, the integrated hospital system can, in theory at least, offer a better combination of cost, convenience, and safety than can third-party specialty facilities.

When demand volume is insufficient to justify an entirely separate specialty facility, manufacturing firms often incorporate high-efficiency production systems into existing facilities by using a *factory-within-a-factory* approach. For instance, a highly flexible job shop designed to produce a variety of products can be adapted to produce a limited family of products efficiently by setting up a separate flow line for those products. Such lines are often called *cells* because equipment is located in close proximity to promote flow. The result is that the plant can produce the narrow set of products assigned to the cell rapidly and efficiently, while it continues using the job shop in the rest of the factory to produce the range of other products flexibly but less efficiently.

In a hospital, the analogous strategy would be a *hospital-within-a-hospital* approach. For example, a hospital could set up an urgent care clinic within its footprint using high-efficiency flow methods like those used by MinuteClinic. Or it could set up a separate surgical unit for hernia procedures using a production-line approach like that of Shouldice. In principle, any delivery system that could be introduced by a third party could be introduced within or beyond a conventional hospital.

Why then haven't hospitals done this? Why haven't most hospitals set up clinics staffed by nurse practitioners, surgical production lines, or online support networks? Part of the answer may be a lack of scale. A community hospital simply doesn't have enough hernia patients to support a surgical unit dedicated to hernias alone. This suggests that general hospitals may be vulnerable to destination hospitals that can amass the necessary scale to justify specialization. Indeed, they almost certainly will be if they continue to rely on their traditional job shop practices. But creative versions of the high-efficiency hospital-within-a-hospital and offsite clinic concepts might still give the general hospital a fighting chance. For instance, suppose a few ORs were deticated to hernias on Fridays, procedures were carried out in production-line style, and patients were allowed to recover as a cohort, as is done at Shouldice. With some effort to craft an efficient and convenient patient experience, the general hospital might close the gap sufficiently to make a trip to a destination hernia hospital comparatively unattractive.

Another way to address the scale problem is by sharing specialized resources. There are many examples of this already. For example, a small hospital lab that cannot justify the specialized equipment for exotic tests will simply outsource those tests to a larger hospital lab or national reference lab. But both need and technology suggest that more sharing is likely to occur in the future.

The need for resource sharing will come about as specialty facilities arise within and without hospitals. Because, by definition, such facilities have a narrow range of capabilities, they will need to make use of capabilities from elsewhere to deal with the inevitable patients who require them. For example, a MinuteClinic-type facility run by an MLP (mid-level practitioner) will be highly efficient for the majority of patients. But to provide for patients whose needs require prompt higher-level judgment, the clinic could share an attending physician with a number of other such clinics. With simple phone (or video) consultations, a single physician could provide diagnostic support for a range of geographically distributed facilities.

Advancing technology will broaden the range of services that can be shared in this manner. For example, by matching high-resolution monitors with data networks (connected by technologies ranging from phone lines to computer clouds), various entities are already offering versions of *teleradiology* (to share scans) and *telepathology* (to share test images, such as pictures of slides). Even *telesurgery*, which adds robotic control of surgical instruments (such as a laparoscopic device) to image transfer to allow a surgeon to conduct procedures remotely, is beginning to emerge.

The possibilities presented by these capabilities are tantalizing. At the low end, narrowly focused, highly efficient clinics will be able to make occasional use of sophisticated resources without having to incur the high fixed cost of installation and the significant overhead costs. At the high end, advanced research hospitals will be able to offer their leading-edge services to a much broader market and thereby generate demand to justify their investments in them. Because they would be able to send services to patients, rather than having patients come to them, these hospitals would become destination hospitals without the destination.

But describing a network of providers that use high-efficiency flow shop facilities and specialized resource sharing to deliver health care is much easier than actually doing it. The problems we have raised in the context of a single hospital (for example, scheduling surgical procedures, prioritizing diagnostic tests, ensuring patient safety in the face of handoffs, promoting organizational learning) will still exist and indeed will become even more complex in a network of shared resources. So the management principles of this book will be more necessary than ever.

In addition to these management challenges, a significant obstacle to a restructuring of hospitals away from their traditional job shop forms is institutional inertia. Doctors, nurses, and administrators have trained and worked extensively in hospitals. As a group, they are dedicated to their professions and believe in their institutions. So it is not surprising that the collective reaction of physicians to MinuteClinic was one of suspicion and concern. Most could not imagine a clinic without onsite physician supervision being safe. They also found the concept of retail health care worrisome because it does not link to primary care physicians who can ensure continuity of care.

Although such concerns may be legitimate, they do not imply that the concept of retail health care is not viable. A third-party attacker like MinuteClinic has clear economic incentive to find creative ways to overcome these concerns. For example, a retail health care provider might address the issue of continuity of care by partnering with firms, such as ZebraHealth and The Living Record, that offer personal health record (PHR) support, so that patients can document their care regardless of where it is received. But familiarity and inertia tend to cause many within the established medical profession to defend the status quo, rather than seriously consider radical alternatives. So attacks like MinuteClinic often come from outside the mainstream rather than from within.

Nevertheless, as more outside attacks come, the medical mainstream will be faced with a choice of either embracing the path of transformative change, very possibly through their own version of retail health care, or watching their institutions be whittled down to much smaller roles than they play today. If hospital professionals choose the former and evolve efficient flow shop delivery systems as (on- or offsite) cells within their diagnostic job shops, they will make it much easier to partner (merge?) with insurers to form integrated accountable care organizations (ACOs). In this integrated future, hospitals will be the foundation of the health care delivery system. If ACOs fail to emerge, due to institutional inertia, turf battles, or whatever, the likely outcome is the disintegrated future, in which a few hospitals will serve in specialized roles, but the rest will wither away. We examine these future roles next.

6.4.2 Roles in the Future

In the current health care system, hospitals play a major role as the go-to place for medical treatment. Most tests and treatments that cannot be done at home or in the physician office are carried out in hospitals and their satellites (for example, offsite labs and radiology facilities). Hospitals are also the hub of the powerful medical research engine that is steadily converting conditions from the exploratory realm of intuitive medicine to the rule-based protocols of precision medicine. Hence, it is no surprise that hospital care accounts for nearly a third of total health care spending in the United States.

But, as we noted earlier, it is not at all clear that hospitals will remain the provider of choice for many types of health care. Handheld scanners, minimally invasive surgical techniques, medications for conditions currently treated with surgery, and many other technological advances will make it possible to treat a range of patients via simpler systems than those in use today. Indeed, the simplest form of care of all is prevention, in which networks of nonpatients take advantage of technology and education to maintain their health and thus avoid entering the Subacute and Acute Care segments at all. Even though it is naïve to expect prevention to entirely replace care, the trends in place imply a progression from job shop to flow shop to self-service, which in turn implies a relentless reduction of the average skill level (and hence the cost) to provide medical services.

The net result will be a progressive deskilling of the health care industry (in those processes that migrate into empirical medicine) like that which has occurred regularly in other industries. For example, auto assembly once required highly skilled mechanics; it now requires narrowly trained line workers. Tax preparation once required skilled accountants; we can now do it ourselves using software. Coronary blockages once required highly skilled cardiac surgeons to conduct bypass surgery; they can now be resolved by less broadly skilled cardiologists or vascular surgeons using angioplasty and stent technology, or even primary care physicians using medication.

We classify the levels of health care, from simplest to most complex, and their connection to delivery system and provider skill in Exhibit 6.3. These are:

- **Prevention**—Don't get sick at all. This aspirational zenith of all health care is, ironically, no care at all. Like dentistry, where fluoridation and improved cleaning and maintenance greatly reduced the need for restoration care, improved prevention in medicine will obviate some care (and some caregivers).[7] Of course, although prevention eliminates the need for a provider of medical treatment, there may still be the need for a provider of preventive services (for example, a dietary consultant, personal trainer, or meditation instructor), but these will almost certainly be less highly skilled and less expensive than medical providers.

- **Self-care**—If you do get sick, resolve the issue without professional help. This can be done by using pure self-service (for example, as when diabetics self-administer insulin shots) or with the help of support networks (such as Dlife.com for diabetics). Self-treatment is obviously less expensive than professional treatment, because one does not need to pay a provider. It is often more convenient as well, because care can be administered at home. So we can expect health care to follow banking (ATMs), retail (self-checkout), and gas stations (self-serve pumps) in the migration from service to self-service.

- **Minimal care**—If you can't cure yourself, get care from the lowest-level personnel/facility that can provide quality care. Lower-level providers are cheaper and usually more accessible than higher-level providers. So, for example, seeing a therapist before a nurse before a doctor before a specialist or receiving care in a nonmedical site before a clinic before a community hospital before a research hospital will reduce both costs and access delays. We have used MinuteClinic as a well-documented example of minimal care, but there are many lesser known competitors in the retail health care space, including MediMin in Arizona, RediClinic in Texas, and Soltanic in Florida.

- **Specialized care**—If you can't be cured with minimal care, get treatment from an advanced facility that is well suited to your needs. For example, a cardiac patient may be best off being treated at a specialty heart hospital, whereas a patient with unclear symptoms may be best diagnosed in a research hospital. Because highly specialized hospitals may need to become destination sites to generate sufficient scale, we would expect relatively few such hospitals compared to what we have today. Specialized testing facilities (for example, standalone MRI units) are also possible, but as imaging technology becomes simpler, there would seem to be less incentive to create destination testing facilities. But specialty hospitals, which integrate testing, diagnosis, treatment, and education of a specific type of patient, have already emerged (for example, for cardiac, cancer, and patients) and are likely to become more common in the future.

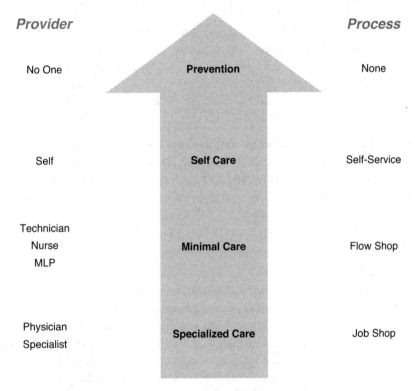

Exhibit 6.3   Efficiency hierarchy of health care.

Unfortunately, current general hospitals are not particularly good at delivering any of these levels of care. Prevention and self-care barely exist in current hospital practice. Minimal care is inefficiently provided because hospitals are insufficiently focused. And specialized care, which should be the strength of hospitals, is less effective than it could be because hospitals are inadequately coordinated.

The fundamental problem is that current hospitals are a jumbled combination of flow and job shops, which make them not particularly good at delivering either intuitive medicine or empirical/precision medicine. Caregivers in hospitals are expected to simultaneously focus on flow for patients with predictable needs and flexibility for patients with unpredictable needs. But the structure and discipline required to deliver efficient flow are fundamentally incompatible with the agility and resourcefulness required to deliver flexible response.

To see that a hospital is not an effective flow shop, compare the flow of tonsillectomy patients in a surgical unit with the flow of automobiles on an assembly line. The assembly line is dedicated to one model (or at most a few similar models) of automobile and uses a highly repetitive process made up of standardized tasks to produce vehicles at an efficient and predictable rate. In contrast, a surgical unit shares resources (ORs, anesthesiologists, scrub teams, ICU beds, and so on) among many other types of patients, which presents a complex scheduling problem and an inefficient need to set up resources. Consequently, tonsillectomies are slower and less efficient than automobile assemblies. An example of a surgical unit that operates (literally) like an assembly line is a cataract surgery facility, which takes advantage of an exclusive focus on a single procedure to achieve highly repetitive, highly efficient, and highly predictable performance.

To see that a hospital is not an effective job shop, compare the treatment of a patient with uncertain symptoms in a hospital with the processing of a custom design job and uncertain requirements in a prototyping facility. Unencumbered by the need to produce high-volume production parts, the prototyping facility is set up as a highly flexible organization that can adapt to almost any work request. To meet the request by a client to mock up a completely new part, the prototyping facility puts together a team of engineers and technicians with the requisite skills, and they work collaboratively with the client to design and produce the part.

In contrast, when a patient is sent to the hospital with an undiagnosed malady, he is passed from specialist to specialist, with some tests in between. Although someone will ultimately take responsibility for the patient and try to coordinate his journey through the system, it is rare for physicians to act as a true team and treat the patient as a collaborative problem-solving challenge. Physicians are too busy trying to serve a steady stream of other patients with needs of varying complexity to be preempted to join a responsive problem-solving team. This is similar to asking machinists to service both routine production and prototyping tasks. It simply cannot be done well. Routine production requires consistent staffing of repetitive high-volume activities, whereas prototyping demands adaptive shifting and grouping of staff to meet unpredictable requirements. But this untenable position is exactly what many hospital providers face every day.

Although there is probably no hospital in the world today that can match the job shop performance of a top-notch prototyping facility or consulting firm, some hospitals are better job shops than others. Mayo Clinic, for instance, is well known for its collaborative culture (Berry 2004), in which doctors consult flexibly and often on issues of diagnosis and care. But even Mayo has patients posting online comments questioning the amount of collaboration that occurs in actual practice, which serves to point up how difficult it is to form adaptive teams in the inconsistent and overloaded environment of a modern hospital.

What does all this mean for the future role of hospitals? To begin with, the history of industrial dynamics suggests that health care cannot continue to offer standardized services through inefficient job shops. They also cannot continue to blur their delivery systems so that they are effective neither as flow shops nor as job shops. Instead, there seem to be two viable roles for hospitals in the future:

- **Integration hub hospitals**—These hospitals will serve as the gatekeepers and coordinators of an array of efficient flow shops set up to handle well-defined categories of patients in need of empirical/precision medicine. Built on the hospital-within-a-hospital model, these hospitals will contain flow shop "cells" for testing and treating patients with predictable needs. These cells will be similar to today's Fast Track Departments in EDs but will serve a much broader set of patients requiring diagnostics, surgery, and nonsurgical procedures. Integration hub hospitals could serve as the core of an integrated network in the integration future or could coordinate specific contract services in the disintegration future. In both cases, they could also serve as a repository of specialized services that could be distributed electronically via various telemedicine channels.

- **Custom care hospitals**—These facilities will offer highly individualized care for specific classes of patients requiring intuitive medicine. To succeed, these will need to be organized as highly flexible and responsive job shops. In addition to revolutionary models of team diagnosis and treatment, these facilities will need to offer an outstanding patient experience in order to be competitive as destination sites. Custom care hospitals could be wholly owned parts of an integrated network in the integration future or focused providers in the disintegration future. Because they will presumably require specialized capabilities suited to their focus (for example, a cancer clinic would require world-class pathology and oncology diagnosticians), they could also offer some of these as telemedicine services.

To highlight the differences between the hospitals of today and these two types of hospitals of the future, we offer patient flow schematics in Exhibits 6.4, 6.5, and 6.6. Exhibit 6.4 shows that, in the general hospital of today, a patient may enter the hospital through various entry points (for example, ED, OR, Inpatient unit, Outpatient unit). Once in the hospital, patients may be routed from one unit to another and from one caregiver to another. Because units treat a variety of patient types, they operate as job shops and cannot offer flow shop efficiency to patients with predictable needs. But, because caregivers are busy with their own caseloads, it is difficult and slow for them to collaborate with caregivers from other units. So the overall hospital also functions poorly as a job shop for patients with complex needs.

Hospital

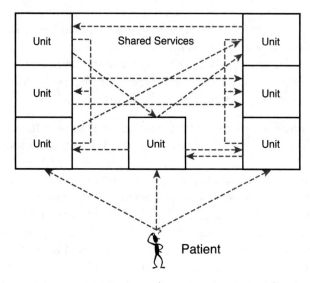

Exhibit 6.4   Patient flow in a typical general hospital.

Exhibit 6.5 provides a schematic of patient flow in an integration hub hospital. Patients are guided into the hospital by a gatekeeper, who directs them to the appropriate treatment option. If patients are in need of empirical/precision medicine, they are sent to a supported self-care network, an external clinic offering minimal care, or an internal unit set up as a flow shop. Hence, an essential element of an integration hub hospital is a well-designed set of self-care and flow shop units that are capable of providing full service to narrowly targeted classes of patients. For patients requiring empirical medicine, the gatekeeping function must recognize this and route them to an internal or external job shop. Note that the gatekeeper function need not be set up as a centralized referral system but could include rule-based protocols that permit multiple decision makers to refer patients into the hospital system. Any way it is structured, this gatekeeping function must be well managed in order for a coordination hub hospital to function effectively.

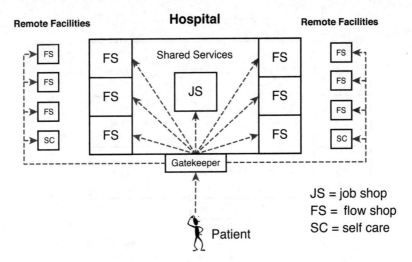

Exhibit 6.5   Patient flow in an integration hub hospital.

Exhibit 6.6 illustrates patient flow in a custom care hospital. Instead of a gatekeeper, who guides patients to units, a custom care hospital uses a team formation process, which assigns caregivers to an individualized care team for each patient. This team formation process is not an exogenous judgment made prior to starting care, but rather a collaborative effort among caregivers to flexibly evolve the right combination of expertise. Once in the hospital, patients are diagnosed and treated in team fashion by a set of caregivers, whose makeup may evolve according to the needs of the patient. Consequently, the essence of a custom care hospital is a culture of adaptability.

Hospital

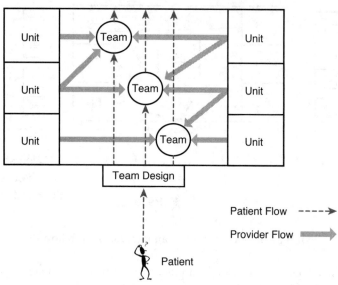

Exhibit 6.6   Patient flow in a custom care hospital.

The coordination hub and custom care hospitals are very different and therefore present very different management challenges. However, as we will describe next, both of them require sound application of management principles—just not the same principles.

Integration hubs present the challenge of delivering efficient service to a range of patients. In this regard, they are similar to manufacturing facilities, which must make a variety of products with production line efficiency. In manufacturing, this is done through cellular manufacturing, in which products are grouped into families and assigned to high-efficiency cells. The trick is to ensure that products in a family are similar enough to allow a cell to switch between them with little loss of efficiency. An integration hub hospital faces the analogous challenge of determining which patients to group together for assignment to cells (units) that can handle them efficiently.

Current hospitals already face a simple version of this problem in the ED when they set up Fast Tracks to handle low-acuity patients. For these to work well, it is essential that Fast Track patients can be treated with clear protocols and little variation in basic flow. If this is not the case, say because patients requiring advanced tests or significant physician consultation are sent to the Fast Track, the desired flow will be disrupted and the Fast Track will no longer be fast.

Creating an effective cell depends critically on the Standardization, Simplification, and Variability principles. The cell design process begins with identification of a set of patient types that can be treated via a standard work flow. For example, MinuteClinic limited its target population to patients with only a few conditions so it was possible to conduct the diagnosis/test, prescribe medication, and counsel the patient within a 15-minute time window. For some patient types, this required simplification of steps (for example, test protocols) to enable them to fit into the standard work flow. For all patients, controls were implemented to regulate variability (for example, procedures for avoiding excessive social conversation that could cause appointments to run long). The designers of the MinuteClinic process explicitly patterned their system after production cells at Toyota and made use of similar tools, such as process flow mapping and statistical control charts, to those used in manufacturing. In the language of this book, MinuteClinic adapted many of the generic options of Table A.1 in Appendix A to achieve responsiveness. They also used policies from Table A.2 to ensure patient safety.

In addition to creating efficient cells, the other critical piece of an integration hub hospital is the gatekeeping function. In a factory, it is a simple matter to route casings to the casing cell and circuit boards to the circuit board cell. But in a hospital, it may be difficult to know whether to send patients with flu-like symptoms to a minimal care MinuteClinic-type facility staffed by a mid-level practitioner, an urgent-care-type clinic staffed by primary care physicians, or an ED unit staffed by emergency physicians with access to specialists. Undoubtedly, there will be incorrect assignments, resulting in inefficiencies and rerouting of patients. Because the process must involve patient observation and interview and may often involve testing, Bayes' Rule and the decision-making principles related to it—namely, the Incidence Rate, First Impressions, Value of Information, and Test Quality principles—are essential to effective gatekeeping. Adapting these to more sophisticated environments than that of MinuteClinic will represent a major challenge in the evolution of integration hub hospitals.

Armed with good information and an appropriate decision-making process, the gatekeeping function of an integration hub hospital will strive to send a patient to the most efficient cell that can meet his needs. In terms of Exhibit 6.3, gatekeepers should send patients to minimal care cells, or even facilitated self-care systems, rather than to specialized care facilities wherever possible. The fact that gatekeepers would be medically credible in an integrated hub hospital gives them an advantage over a disintegrated network, in which the insurer often plays the role of gatekeeper. If hospitals do this well, they can potentially head off the disintegration future, in which much of their business will be co-opted by third parties. Indeed, a well-run integrated delivery network hub would make a good candidate for merger with an insurer to produce an ACO.

Although simplification and standardization are the foundation of the flow shops that make up a coordination hub hospital, they are much less relevant to a custom care hospital because the work is largely nonrepetitive. The Variability principle is still relevant, because it implies that a capacity cushion is needed to cope with the unavoidable workload variability in a job shop environment. Also central to a custom care hospital are the

Information and Organizational Learning principles, which are the foundation of the needed culture of flexibility.

A flexible team environment must first overcome individual behaviors that work against it. These are characterized in the Knowledge Sharing, Self-Interest, Hoarding, and Inertia principles. Those with decision-making power must support the team culture and other necessary changes. This requires application of the Key Stakeholders, Veto Power, Pareto Efficiency, and Motivation for Change principles. Finally, continually evolving a culture that can adapt to the ever-changing demands placed on a custom care hospital requires adaptation of the generic process of organizational learning depicted in Table A.3 in Appendix A.

A strong custom care hospital can thrive in the disintegration future because there will always be patient conditions that require intuitive medicine. Even if insurers co-opt the gatekeeper role, they need providers who can provide job shop services to patients with complex diagnostic or care needs. However, as third parties pick off the increasing number of patients with treatment needs amenable to self-care and standardized care, the overall need for job shop style hospitals will decrease. Successful custom care hospitals will increasingly become destination sites, whereas hospitals that maintain a muddled mix of job shop and flows shop structures will wither and disappear.

Assuming that specialization leads to a need for scale and hence stimulates a competition among hospitals to become destination sites, the patient experience will become a key competitive dimension. Once patients get over the hurdle of getting on a plane to receive diagnosis or treatment, they become fair game for hospitals around the world. So, successful destination hospitals will be those that provide high-quality care in terms of both clinical outcomes and patient experience. This implies that perception concepts, such as those embodied in the Waiting Time Psychology and Negative Experiences principles, will become even more relevant than they are today. Given this, it is no wonder that Disney is moving into the health care consulting space.

In summary, hospital roles are likely to change substantially in the not-too-distant future. But, although the processes will look very different from those in use today, the underlying principles will remain the same. The generic issues of responsiveness, safety, and organizational learning, as interpreted through management principles in Tables A.1, A.2, and A.3 in Appendix A, will remain relevant as long as medicine is practiced. The challenge will be to find new ways to operationalize these more effectively in the hospitals of the future.

6.5 Final Message

The health care debate is generally carried out in high-level terms, with reference to politics and payment structures. We've indulged in a tiny bit of that in this chapter. But, although it's fine to think about health care very broadly as a critical part of the economy, we must never forget that each day health care is delivered in millions of transactions between providers and patients. So the cost, convenience, and quality of health care ultimately come down to managing those transactions. It comes down to operations management.

This means that no matter how the politics of health care play out, successful hospitals in the future will be those that manage their operations well. Hospitals that stay on their current path and resist all but the most incremental changes to their systems are likely to see their market shares erode, their units contract and, ultimately, their viability vanish. But hospitals that embrace a clear strategy as either integration hubs of efficient flow shops providing empirical/precision medicine or custom care job shops providing high-quality, responsive, intuitive medicine can thrive, and can reshape the very landscape of the health care industry.

6.6 References

Berry, L. 2004. "The Collaborative Organization: Leadership Lessons from Mayo Clinic." *Organizational Dynamics* 33(3), 228–242.

Christensen, C.M, J.H. Grossman, and J. Hwang. 2009. *The Innovator's Prescription: A Disruptive Solution for Health Care.* McGraw-Hill, New York.

Hayes. R.H., and S.C. Wheelwright. 1979. "Link Manufacturing Process and Product Life Cycles." *Harvard Business Review.* 57(1), 133–140.

Heskett, J. 2003. "Shouldice Hospital Limited." Harvard Business Case 9-683-068, Harvard Business School, Boston, MA.

1   Note that we are using the term "product" broadly to include both physical and service products.

2   When the effectiveness numbers get high enough, such statistics can be used as the basis for rules of the type "when patient exhibits symptom set X, apply treatment option Y." Such rules are referred to as *evidence-based medicine*.

3   In the 1980s, previously effective antibiotics began to fail, as patients who discontinued their therapy regimens inadvertently cultivated antibiotic-resistant strains of bacteria. This created a new condition, labeled extensively drug-resistant tuberculosis (XDR-TB), which is more difficult to diagnose and treat than conventional TB. As a result, a condition that was well down the path toward precision medicine reverted to the status of intuitive medicine as the search for effective therapies began anew.

4   Shouldice Hospital Limited is one of the best-selling cases offered by the Harvard Business School, which is why every year thousands of business students, most of whom have nothing to do with health care, read this case as an example of the power of operational focus.

5   Christensen, Grossman and Hwang (2009) liken the amalgam of arcane algorithms and backroom negotiations involved in setting reimbursement rates to the price-setting mechanism of a communist central planning system.

6   Of course, there will always be some reluctance to refer patients elsewhere as units within an integrated system jockey for negotiating position in the budget planning process. For instance, a unit that serves more patients this year will be able to argue for a larger budget next year. But a performance evaluation process that recognizes and rewards units and individuals for actions that both serve patients and reduce overall system costs can help discourage such parochial behavior.

7   Whether improved prevention will cause medicine to follow dentistry into greater emphasis on elective services, such as cosmetic treatments, remains an open question. Proliferation of hair replacement, wrinkle removal, weight loss, and other forms of cosmetic medicine, suggest this is a possibility, albeit one we decline to analyze.

MANAGEMENT PRINCIPLES

A.1 Introduction

Managing complex organizations, such as businesses, government agencies, and hospitals, is a challenging endeavor that requires deep domain knowledge, sound judgment, creativity, leadership, and a host of other skills. Fortunately, experience and research have revealed certain basic insights about the performance of complex organizations. In this appendix, we give a summary of key management concepts that are relevant to improving the operations of a hospital.

We do this by encapsulating major ideas as principles. A *principle* is a "comprehensive and fundamental law, doctrine, or assumption" (Webster's Dictionary). Consequently, only ideas about which we are confident can be so classified. To qualify as a principle, an insight must be both highly *general* (applicable to many settings) and *stable* (relevant now and in the future). This means that there is much about management that cannot yet be captured in principles, leaving us to rely on other faculties, such as judgment and creativity. But it also means that overlooking the things that can be captured in principles can lead to fundamental errors. Hence, understanding management principles is extremely valuable as a starting point for managing hospital operations.

In this appendix, we begin by summarizing principles that are particularly relevant to hospital management. We then state the main categories of performance metrics for a hospital and identify the specific principles that have a direct bearing on each metric. By doing this, we direct the reader interested in making improvements along a particular dimension to the management insights that might be helpful. Finally, we identify three generic management issues—improving responsiveness, enhancing patient safety, and promoting organizational learning—that are ubiquitous concerns across the hospital. For each of these, we use the relevant principles to identify generic improvement paths in the form of tables. In the chapters on individual hospital units, we flesh out these tables in the context of specific environments and use these to enumerate candidate policies for addressing key management concerns.

A.2 Management Principles

Because management is a multidisciplinary activity, consisting of both theory and practice, there are many dimensions of management principles (for example, related to accounting, marketing, finance, economics, strategy). No single book could summarize all knowledge on such a wide range of subjects. So we will only attempt to summarize the three main categories of principles that relate strongly to the operations focus of this book. These are

- **Flows**—The operations of any complex organization center on entities that move through the system as a consequence of the organization's function. These could be jobs in a factory, customers in a call center, containers in a transportation system, financial transactions in a bank, and so on. In a hospital, the main flows involve patients, because the primary function is patient care, but other flows (for example, involving money, materials, and orders) are also relevant. The speed and efficiency of flows within an organization are almost always important drivers of its performance. Certainly in a hospital, the speed with which patients are treated and the effectiveness of the care they receive are core concerns.

- **Information**—All organizations rely on implicit and explicit data and knowledge to support operations. Product specifications, task descriptions, customer orders, local knowledge of the competitive market, and numerous other categories of information are essential to planning and execution decisions. In a hospital, many forms of information (test results, task instructions, patient data, and so on) are critical to performance. Consequently, collection, transmission, and use of information are vital to hospital operations.

- **Human behavior**—Operations, as well as every other function of an organization, are defined and implemented by the people involved in them. Managers, staff members, customers, and consultants influence operating performance via their decisions, actions, preferences, biases, and other behaviors. In a hospital, physicians, nurses, technicians, support staff, administrators, and patients play key roles in both executing day-to-day operations and carrying out improvement programs.

Next we summarize principles in these three categories. We cluster the relevant principles in each category into narrower subcategories for purposes of discussion and to make them easier to connect to specific hospital problems.

A.2.1 Flow Principles

A *flow* is a sequence of steps through which entities move to provide a good or service. An example of a flow in a factory is an assembly line, which is made up of a sequence of machines through which parts move to produce a finished product. In a hospital, the sequence of treatment, test, and administrative steps a patient goes through in the Emergency Department (ED) constitutes a flow. The series of steps to complete a laboratory test, from specimen collection to results reporting, is another example of a flow.

Key concerns about a hospital flow are *volume* (how many patients, tests, or other entities can be processed in a given period of time), *time* (how long it takes to process a patient, test, or other entity), and *quality* (how accurately or effectively the patient, test, or other entity is processed). The following clusters of principles are relevant to the volume, time, and quality of a flow.

A.2.1.1 CAPACITY PRINCIPLES

In a flow, the starting point for all questions of volume, and many questions of time, is the concept of capacity. At the level of a single resource (physician, phlebotomist, CT scanner, operating room (OR), and so on), capacity is defined as:

Definition (Resource Capacity)—The capacity of a resource is the throughput it can achieve provided that it is never starved for work.

For example, suppose each patient in the ED requires ten minutes for the triage nurse to classify according to his Emergency Severity Index (ESI). This includes the time for the nurse to walk over to the patient, to record the result in the hospital information system, and to carry out any other activities directly associated with triaging an individual patient. Consequently, the triage nurse can classify six patients per hour (that is, 1/10 patients/minute $\times$ 60 minutes/hour = 6 patients/hour), which is her capacity.

Now, suppose that between 8 a.m. and 10 p.m., patients arrive to the ED at a rate of 5 per hour. The triage nurse can handle 6 patients per hour, so she should be able to keep up with this workload. Indeed, if we divide the arrival rate by her capacity, we get (5 patients/hour) / (6 patients/hour) = 83%, which represents the fraction of time she will be busy triaging patients. Because this is less than 100%, she does not have a capacity overload. However, if patients were to arrive at a rate of 12 per hour, the triage nurse's capacity is not sufficient to keep pace, and her ratio would become (12 patients per hour)/(6 patients per hour) = 200%, which is either impossible, or it means she is somehow able to work twice as fast as the rate we specified as her capacity. Despite motivational speeches urging athletes or employees to "give 120%," the most a person can work is 100%. So capacity overloads cannot persist over the long term.

The triage nurse is a human resource. But we can use the same approach to evaluate the capacity of a physical resource, such as the examination rooms in the ED. However, note that although the triage nurse handles patients *serially*, examination rooms handle patients in *parallel*. To compute the capacity of a parallel resource, we must multiply the capacity of an individual unit by the number of units in the resource. For instance, suppose patients spend an average of a half hour in an examination room. This means that the capacity of a single examination room is two patients per hour. If the ED has 8 examination rooms, then the total capacity is $2 \times 8 = 16$ patients per hour. If the arrival rate to the ED between 8 a.m. and 10 p.m. is 5 patients per hour, the examination rooms will have enough capacity to keep up and will be busy on average 5/16 = 31% of the time.

The preceding calculation gives us a formal definition of a capacity overload of an individual resource—namely, that the arrival rate exceeds the capacity. But, like most hospital flows, the patient flow through the ED involves many resources and does not have a single capacity. To define the capacity of a complex system like an ED, we must determine which resource limits system capacity. We do this by first defining the following.

Definition (Utilization)—Utilization of a resource is the long-term fraction of time it is busy, which is given by the average arrival rate of work (for example, patients per hour) at the station divided by the resource capacity over the long term.

Note that this is the same calculation that we did earlier to determine the fraction of time a resource is busy. And indeed, that is what utilization means. However, when we refer to utilization, we are always talking about *long-term averages*. Hence, the utilization of a resource is the fraction of time it will be busy over the long term. The resource in a system with the highest utilization has the least capability to catch up from a capacity overload. Because of this, we define the following.

Definition (Bottleneck)—The bottleneck of a system is the resource with the highest utilization.

We define the bottleneck to be the resource with the highest utilization, because if we progressively increase the arrival rate proportionally at each resource, the one with the highest utilization at the outset is the first one to exceed 100%. When this happens, the system reaches its maximum output rate, so any further increase in arrival rate only leads to a backlog. As such, the bottleneck constrains the maximum rate of the system and hence defines its capacity. We state this as the System Capacity principle.

Principle (System Capacity)—The capacity of a system is defined by its bottleneck, which is the resource in the system with the highest utilization. If the capacity of a system is less than the demand placed on it, the demand cannot be met.

Let us apply these definitions to perform a capacity analysis of a simple ED in which each arriving patient requires 10 minutes from the triage nurse, 5 minutes from the registration nurse, 30 minutes from the emergency nurse, and 15 minutes from the emergency physician. Patients also require 90 minutes in an examination room. The ED consists of 12 examination rooms and is staffed by 1 triage nurse, 1 registration nurse, 3 emergency nurses, and 1 emergency physician. Suppose that the daily arrival rate to the ED between 8 a.m. and 10 p.m. averages 5 patients per hour.

The table that follows summarizes the capacity calculations for this simplified ED. Note that although the examination rooms have the longest processing times, they are not the resource with the least capacity because there are 12 of them. Likewise, the emergency nurses, who are the human resources that spend the most time with patients, are not the resource with the least capacity because there are 3 of them. The resource with the smallest capacity is the emergency physician. Because we are assuming that all patients use all resources in this simplified ED, the arrival rate is the same to each resource. Hence, the resource with the smallest capacity is the resource with the highest utilization, which means that the physician is the bottleneck.[1] Thus, the capacity of the ED is the capacity of the emergency physician, which is 4 patients per hour.

Resource	Number	Treatment Time (Min)	Unit Rate (Patients per Hour)	Capacity (Patients per Hour)
Exam rooms	12	90	60 / 90 = 1.33	12(1.33) = 8
Triage nurse	1	10	60 / 10 = 6	6
Registration nurse	1	5	60 / 5 = 12	12
Emergency nurse	3	30	60 / 30 = 2	3(2) = 6
Emergency physician	1	15	60 / 15 = 4	4

Because arrivals average five patients per hour, this system will experience a capacity overload during the 8 a.m. to 10 p.m. time window.[2] Clearly, this situation is not sustainable indefinitely, because patients cannot continue backing up without bound.

But patients do not arrive at a steady rate indefinitely. Historical data shows that some hours of the day typically experience more arrivals than others. In general, more patients arrive during daytime hours than at night.

In Exhibit A.1, we show what would happen in the ED if staffing were to remain constant over the course of the day, but patients were to arrive at a rate of 5 per hour from 8 a.m. to 10 p.m. and a rate of 2 per hour for the rest of the night. Note that during the day when arrivals exceed capacity, patients build up in the system. Indeed, by 10 p.m., there will be 14 patients in the ED, presumably filling all 12 examination rooms plus 2 seats in the waiting room. When arrival rates fall off overnight, the ED begins catching up because now capacity exceeds demand. But it takes until 5 a.m. for the backlog to clear. Then the cycle starts again the next day. Because such behavior is common in EDs, it is no wonder that staff develop a "siege mentality" as they face a new crush of work each day.

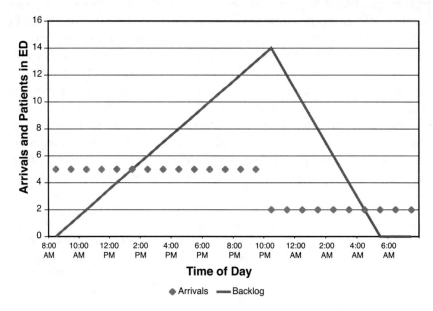

Exhibit A.1   Patient buildup in a simplified ED.

As illustrated in the preceding example, overloaded resources lead to backups. Such situations occur because there are powerful economic incentives to load expensive resources heavily. For example, underutilization of an OR means fewer procedures can be performed, and less revenue can be generated. Underutilization of an MRI machine could make it impossible to keep up with demand, leading to expensive purchase of an additional unit. Consequently, managers often seek ways to increase resource utilization. However, even if this does not lead to a capacity overload (that is, utilization greater than 100%), this can be dangerous, due to the following principle:

Principle (Utilization)—Utilization magnifies queueing in a highly nonlinear fashion.

The intuition behind this principle is that the busier the system the less excess capacity it has for catching up from backups that result from fluctuations in the rate of demand or processing. For example, imagine an OR that is fully scheduled 24 hours a day, 7 days a week. In such a setting, if a patient is late for a procedure or a procedure runs long, the start times of every procedure from then on will be delayed. There is simply no slack in the schedule to catch up. If we pig headedly continue to schedule the OR without any catch-up time, each disruptive event will push the start times further and further back. The *backlog* (queue) of procedures, and the delay time for a given procedure, will head toward infinity in the long run.

Of course, the preceding scenario never happens in a hospital or any other operating system. Eventually, when things get bad enough, someone takes action. The scheduler backs off on the schedule and builds in some white space to allow recovery from disruptions. Hospital management authorizes additional capacity, such as another OR. Or surgeons find a way to adjust capacity to keep up with demand, perhaps by speeding up procedures when the system falls behind schedule. All these interventions serve to ensure that the OR runs at less than 100% of capacity. The further below 100% the system operates (for example, the more white space that is built into the schedule), the more quickly the system can recover from disruptions, and the shorter the average delay time is.

This behavior, which is captured in the Utilization principle, is illustrated graphically in Exhibit A.2. The main insight is that the waiting time for a resource grows rapidly as it approaches 100% utilization. This principle is at work all over the hospital. Busy EDs have long patient average length of stay (LOS). Busy labs have long turnaround times (TATs). Busy ORs have frequent backups and even procedure cancellations. The Utilization principle, along with the closely related Variability principles (whose role will be explained below) are among the most broadly useful management insights in a hospital.

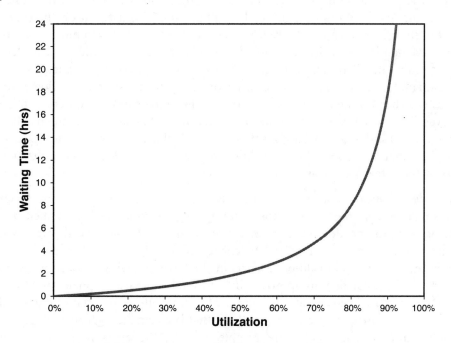

Exhibit A.2   Impact of utilization on waiting time.

Although the Utilization principle implies that carelessly increasing resource utilization can lead to undesirable consequences, there are ways to make more effective utilization of resources. One approach is batching, which leads to the trade-off described in the following principle.

Principle (Batching)—When tasks involve setup time, performing them in batches makes better utilization of capacity but also introduces waiting time for tasks that occur after the batch.

An illustration of batching is the process of specimen collection by hospital phlebotomists. Typically, phlebotomists visit several patients to draw blood before delivering the specimens to the laboratory—in a batch. If, instead, they were to hand-deliver each specimen to the lab, they would use up much of their time walking to and from the lab and have less capacity to collect specimens. In this context, the lab deliveries constitute setup times, so delivering specimens in batches instead of individually saves total delivery time and increases the effective capacity of the phlebotomists. Factories do the same thing by stamping out a batch of one type of parts before setting up the machine to stamp out a different type of parts. Both practices use batching to limit the number of setups per day.

However, as the Batching principle notes, batching also increases waiting time. For instance, the first blood sample drawn by a phlebotomist must wait on the collection cart until the entire batch is delivered. As a result, it arrives at the lab much later than it would have had it been delivered immediately after collection. Avoiding such delays is the reason that the literature on Lean espouses "batch sizes of one." If each entity (job, part, patient, lab sample, and so on) moves on to the next resource in a flow immediately after it has finished with the previous resource, batching delays are eliminated. However, if such moves involve significant setup times (to change over the machine, to walk to the lab, and so on), batch sizes of one use valuable capacity. This can lead to high utilizations that cause delay like that illustrated in Exhibit A.2, or even utilizations in excess of 100% that are infeasible in the long term.

The "trade-off buster" related to batching is setup time reduction. If setup times are made small enough, the extra setups resulting from making batches smaller, or even reducing them to one, doesn't cause excessive waiting. Knowing this, Toyota has spent decades reducing the time required to change dies in large punch presses; this has enabled them to stamp out different parts in small batches without wasting too much time on setups. An analogous approach in a hospital is the use of pneumatic tube systems, which replace lengthy walks to the lab with drop-offs at tube stations. This allows phlebotomists to make deliveries more often (that is, in smaller batches) without using up too much time. The result is that samples arrive at the lab more quickly, but phlebotomists can still collect high volumes of specimens.

To this point, the definitions and principles presented in this section characterize the physical capacity of a system. But they do not fully describe the economics of the decisions faced when matching capacity to demand. Because demand is almost never known with precision, the challenge is to install capacity that is appropriate for a probabilistic forecast of demand. Hospitals face this question when choosing the number of hospital beds, or ORs, or ED bays to build in a facility designed to serve a forecasted patient load.

It must be answered when a nurse manager decides how many nurses to schedule to show up for work four weeks from now. It must be answered when a purchaser decides how many stents to stock in inventory, knowing the distribution of daily stent usage. In short, it must be answered every time a capacity decision (beds, rooms, nurses, stents) must be made to address random demand.

A plausible but naïve strategy for this situation is to plan for the middle of the demand distribution (the median). For example, if the forecasted demand for nurses on a unit four weeks from now is Normally distributed with a mean and median of 7 (the *mean* is the median for symmetric distributions like the Normal) and a standard deviation of 2, we might decide to schedule 7 nurses to work that day. Because we are just as likely to need more than 7 nurses as we are to need less than 7 nurses, this would seem to balance the upside and downside risk.

What this naïve logic ignores is the important consideration that the situations of over-capacity and undercapacity may have significantly different consequences. Sizing capacity to the median demand level does not balance the upside and downside economic risks when these two are asymmetric in their consequences.

For example, suppose it costs less to send home a nurse when capacity exceeds demand (a capacity overage) than it does to bring in a nurse when capacity is insufficient to meet demand (a capacity underage). The policy of staffing to median demand results in equal frequency of capacity overages and capacity underages. But, because overages are less costly than are underages, a better policy is to staff above median demand, so that there are more overages and fewer underages.

The problem posed by this common situation is referred to in the operations management field as the *newsvendor problem* because, on any given day, a newsvendor must determine capacity to meet demand by choosing the number of newspapers to buy to have in stock at the start of the day. Because demand is uncertain, on any given day the newsvendor may have too many newspapers (an overage) or too few newspapers (an underage). Overages are costly because they represent newspapers that were unnecessarily purchased. Underages are costly because they represent lost sales.

We can formally state the logic for balancing overage and underage costs where demand is uncertain (see Nahmias 2000 or Hopp and Spearman 2007 for derivations) in the following principle.

Principle (Newsvendor)—In a single demand period with uncertain demand, the capacity level that optimally balances the cost of too much capacity with too little capacity is given by Q^*, where

$$F(Q^*) = c_u / (c_o + c_u)$$

and

$F(\cdot)$ = cumulative distribution function of demand (that is, $F(x)$ = probability that demand is less than or equal to x)

c_o = cost of overage = cost per unit overstocked relative to demand

c_u = cost of underage = cost per unit understocked relative to demand

Note that, because $F(Q^*)$ represents the probability that demand is less than or equal to Q^*, the Newsvendor principle states that we should size capacity to the point where the probability of meeting demand is equal to $c_u / (c_o + c_u)$. This is the point where overage and underage costs are balanced to achieve the lowest expected total cost. Setting Q^* higher than this point results in overage costs being too high; setting Q^* lower than this results in underage costs being too high.

A practical difficulty of using the formula in the Newsvendor principle is that we must find the Q^* (possibly by trial and error in a spreadsheet) that makes the probability of meeting demand equal to $c_u / (c_o + c_u)$. However, when demand is Normally distributed, the newsvendor formula can be simplified into a closed-form expression for Q^*, as described in the following corollary.

Corollary (Newsvendor with Normal Demand)—In a single demand period with Normally distributed demand, the capacity level that optimally balances the cost of too much capacity with too little capacity is given by Q^*, where

$$Q^* = \mu + z\sigma$$

where

μ = mean (expected) demand

σ = standard deviation of demand

z = the $[c_u / (c_o + c_u)]^{th}$ percentile of the standard Normal distribution (that is, $\Phi(z) = c_u / (c_o + c_u)$, where Φ is the Standard Normal distribution)

To illustrate the application of this principle, suppose the demand for nurses on a future shift is Normally distributed with a mean of 7 nurses and a standard deviation of 2 nurses. Further suppose that if we have too many nurses scheduled, the extra nurses are sent home but are paid $5 per hour. Hence, the overage cost (the extra amount the hospital pays above what it would have paid if it had scheduled 1 fewer nurse) is c_o = $40 for an 8-hour shift. If, instead, we have too few nurses, nurses are called in and are paid an hourly bonus of $10 per hour above their normal rate. Hence, the underage cost (the extra amount the hospital pays above what it would have paid if it had scheduled 1 more nurse) is c_u = $80 for an 8-hour shift.

This implies that our "critical ratio" is $c_u / (c_o + c_u) = 80/120 = 2/3$. Hence, we should choose Q* to be the number that puts 67% of the probability in the lower tail of the demand distribution. Because demand is Normal, we can compute the z value by looking up $\Phi(z)$ in a Standard Normal table and finding the z that makes $\Phi(z)$ equal to 0.67. Alternatively, we can use the internal functions in Excel and find that z = NORMSINV(0.67) = 0.44. Hence, the nursing capacity we need to meet demand 67% of the time is

$$Q^* = \mu + z\sigma = 7 + (0.44)2 = 7.88 \approx 8 \text{ nurses}$$

Note that because the cost of having too few nurses is higher than the cost of having too many, the optimal capacity (staffing level) is greater than the mean demand of 7 nurses.

A.2.1.2 VARIABILITY PRINCIPLES

The dynamics in Exhibit A.1 partially explain how and why flows experience queueing, but they do not tell the whole story. If we really did know the arrival rates of patients hour by hour, as we assumed in that example, the natural response would be to staff the ED accordingly. In our tiny sample ED, this might take some imagination, because we need 1.25 emergency physicians on duty from 8 a.m. to 10 p.m. and half a physician during the other hours. Such fractional capacity might be provided by sharing a physician with another part of the hospital, using a physician assistant or resident, or by training nurses to take on physician duties. But in larger hospitals, with higher staff levels, matching staffing to a known demand is straightforward; it simply involves scheduling enough people of each job class to cover hourly demand.

Unfortunately, real life is not so simple. Even if we were to staff the ED to perfectly match expected demand, there would still be queueing. The reason is the influence of variability, which we summarize succinctly as follows.

Principle (Variability)—Unsynchronized variability causes queueing.

Here, variability refers to everything that prevents work from arriving and being completed in a regular, clocklike fashion. An example of variability is the deviation of the actual number from the expected number of patient arrivals to the ED in a particular hour. Just because historical data shows that an average of five patients arrive between 1 and 2 p.m. doesn't mean that exactly this many will arrive on any given day.

The Variability principle states that unsynchronized variability causes queueing.[3] The term *unsynchronized* refers to mismatches between demand and capacity. For instance, if patient arrivals to the ED moved up and down, so that the arrival rate was high from 8 to 9 a.m., low from 9 a.m. to 10 a.m., moderate from 10 a.m. to 11 a.m., high from 11 a.m. to 1 p.m., low from 1 p.m. to 4 p.m., and so on, but staffing levels fluctuated in the same manner (for example, due to some staff members switching back and forth between the ED and another hospital unit), the queue of patients would not build up.

But if arrivals fluctuate substantially, while staffing levels remain nearly constant (that is, demand and capacity are unsynchronized), the system will experience backups. This observation is important to practice, because it implies that one way to mitigate the consequences of variability is to take measures to synchronize variability in demand and capacity (that is, by either adjusting capacity to match fluctuations in demand or adjusting arrivals to match fluctuations in capacity).

In addition to fluctuating patient arrivals, other issues can cause unsynchronized variability. For instance, even if five patients did arrive during the specified hour, the amount of work they require could vary greatly. Five serious cardiac patients will take much more time than five minor trauma patients. Even if we account for the type of illness or injury, the treatment time may vary greatly. (For example, some cardiac patients require more care than others.) The net result is that no amount of historical data or forecasting can enable us to predict the workload that the ED will receive during any interval of time. Beyond variability in workload, there could be variability in the time to get a test result, variability in the number of staff who show up for work (due to absenteeism), variability in the time it takes to clean a room on a bed floor, and many, many others.

Variability causes queueing because idle periods do not offset busy periods. For instance, suppose that the ED is empty at 8 a.m. and on average five patients arrive between 8 a.m. and 9 a.m. But suppose that no one arrives until 8:45 a.m. and then five patients come in between 8:45 a.m. and 9:00 a.m. The fact that the staff has been idle for 45 minutes does nothing to help them deal with this surge of work because they cannot start caring for patients until they actually arrive. Consequently, patients will wait longer for treatment than they would have if they had arrived uniformly over the hour.

The more variability there is in the system, the more violently it lurches between busy and idle periods. If busy periods occur more suddenly, they cause more backups. For instance, a clinical lab that can process 100 basic blood chemistry tests per hour (with no variation in processing time) and receives a steady 90 samples per hour to test will easily keep up with demand. The same lab faced with an average demand rate of 90 samples per hour, but with arrivals that fluctuate wildly, from zero in some hours to 500 in other hours, will experience substantial backups and lengthy delay.

As we noted earlier in the Utilization principle, the higher the utilization of a system, the slower it is able to catch up when a work backlog forms. For instance, the utilization of the previously mentioned lab is given by the arrival rate divided by capacity (90 samples per hour ÷ 100 samples per hour), which is 90%. This means that the lab is working 90% of the time, leaving it only 10% to catch up when a pileup occurs. The same lab facing demand of only 70 samples per hour will have utilization of 70%, and hence will have 30% extra time in which to catch up. Accordingly, the average amount of work backlog in the lab with 70% utilization will be lower than that in the lab with 90% utilization.

What this means is that variability causes backup events, and utilization amplifies their impact. So variability and utilization combine to cause queueing. We illustrate this in Exhibit A.3. For a given system, increasing either variability or utilization will increase queueing and hence waiting time.

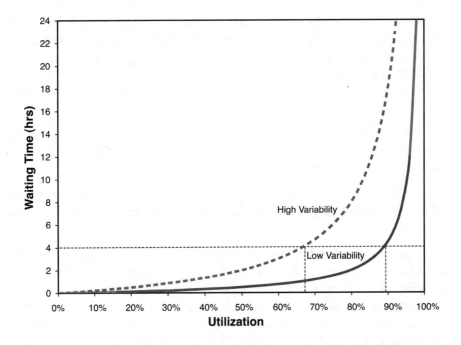

Exhibit A.3   Impact of utilization and variability on waiting time.

This interaction between variability and utilization means that variability reduction can serve as a substitute for increasing capacity. For example, suppose that Exhibit A.3 refers to an ED where the High Variability case represents current practice. If the hospital establishes a policy that average waiting time in the ED cannot exceed four hours, the current ED cannot operate at more than 67% utilization. (That is, it must go on diversion to limit patient arrivals, increase the number of staff to increase capacity, or both.)

Now suppose the ED were to adopt a variability reduction program. This might include measures to encourage the EMS system to distribute patients to EDs in the community more evenly, measures to prevent delays in getting patient test results, and other policies to smooth out arrivals into the ED and times for treating patients within the ED. If the Low Variability curve represented the improved ED, then, as shown in Exhibit A.3, a four-hour limit on average waiting time would translate into 89% utilization. Because less variability means fewer backup events from which to catch up, we can operate the system closer to its capacity level without causing serious disruption. Because this would allow the ED to function with fewer staff or to handle more patients with the same staff, the variability reduction policies are a form of virtual capacity.

The observation that variability reduction can serve as a substitute for capacity increase is actually part of a more general principle.

Principle (Variability Buffering)—All unsynchronized variability will be buffered by some combination of inventory, capacity, time, quality, and system degradation.

The basic idea here is that the tendency toward queueing referred to in the Variability principle can manifest itself in a variety of ways. To illustrate this, suppose the hospital cafeteria has a taco bar, which is staffed by a single cook, Ingmar. Customer arrivals to the taco bar fluctuate unpredictably. (That is, there is demand variability.) As a result, whenever there is a burst of customers, a line forms, and people have to wait for their tacos. This constitutes a time buffer.

Suppose Ingmar feels that waiting times are too long. One option for reducing wait times is to prepare tacos in advance and have them held for customers on a warming table. This is an inventory buffer.

If the warming table makes the tacos soggy and unappetizing, Ingmar could lobby for an assistant who would help respond more quickly during busy periods.[4] This is a capacity buffer.

Finally, Ingmar could respond to busy times by working faster. If he can do this without stress, then his normal rate had slack in it, which would constitute a capacity buffer. But if speeding up causes him to cut corners in his taco making, it amounts to a quality buffer. Alternatively, if speeding up causes Ingmar to become stressed, then fatigued, then sick and absent, it is an example of a system degradation buffer, since the short-term gain from rushing leads to a long-term loss from absenteeism.

The point is that variability is costly, in the near term, the long term, or both. Most systems use multiple forms of buffers against variability. Ingmar might use some combination of all forms of buffering. That is, he could hold tacos on the warming table during the lunch hour rush, hire a part-time assistant, work faster during busy periods (causing both quality problems and degradation's due to stress), and still have customer waits when the place gets too busy.

Similar variability buffering choices exist all over a hospital. For instance, an OR can reduce the time patients spend waiting to get into surgery by increasing capacity (for example, by adding ORs or extending hours). This would constitute substituting a capacity buffer for a time buffer. An ED could institute full capacity protocols, under which some activities are streamlined during busy periods to speed up the treatment process. This would represent substituting a quality buffer for a time buffer (and possibly a system degradation buffer if straining to deal with peak workloads leads to future problems such as a demoralized, and less productive, workforce). A lab could collect blood samples earlier in the day so that it is able to complete tests in time for morning rounds without adding staff. This would be an example of substituting a time buffer for a capacity buffer.

Most of what the hospital provides is in the form of services. Unlike tacos, services cannot be made up in advance, so inventory is not possible. In hospital settings, the following reduced form of the Variability Buffering principle is often relevant.

Corollary (Variability Buffering in Service Systems)—In a pure service system, inventory is not available as a buffer, so holding quality and system degradation costs constant, there is a trade-off between variability, excess capacity, and waiting time.

For example, a hospital laboratory can reduce turnaround times by adding capacity (for example, more technologists, equipment, and so on) or by reducing variability (for example, staggering specimen collection to smooth out the arrival of samples to the lab).

Although we cannot get around the fact that we must buffer variability, we can sometimes make buffering more efficient by exploiting the following principle.

Principle (Buffer Flexibility)—Flexibility in variability buffers reduces the amount of buffering required for a given amount of variability.

To illustrate this, let us return to the hospital cafeteria taco bar. If Ingmar sells tacos with both hot and mild sauce, he needs to stock both types on his warming table if he wants to be ready for a spike in demand for either type. Alternatively, he can stock plain tacos and only apply the sauce after the customers place their orders. Even better, he can sell plain tacos and let customers apply their own sauce. Under either of these "delayed differentiation" schemes, a plain taco can satisfy demand for either a hot or a mild taco. So Ingmar needs to carry fewer total tacos on the warming table to provide a given level of responsiveness. Plain tacos are an example of flexible inventory.

In a hospital, where inventory is not central, flexibility is most helpful in time and capacity buffers. For example, if patients can be called in early to fill empty time slots (for example, due to cancellations) on an MRI schedule, the average waiting time can be reduced. This is an example of a flexible time buffer.

An example of a flexible capacity buffer is cross-trained personnel. For instance, suppose that Radiology technicians are certified to conduct multiple types of scans (for example, X-rays, CT scans, ultrasound, and MRI). If patients are waiting for CT scans but not ultrasounds, the ultrasound tech can shift over to CT to help work down the backlog. We need fewer total technicians to achieve the same level of responsiveness if the technicians are cross-trained (flexible) than if they are not.

The Variability Buffering principle gives us one relationship between capacity, inventory, and time. Another is the following.

Principle (Little's Law)—Over the long term, the rate (R), in-process inventory (I), and waiting time (T) of a system are related according to:

$$I = R \times T$$

The easiest way to appreciate the intuition of Little's Law is to think of a conveyor. For example, consider the conveyor that transports used trays of dishes back into the hospital cafeteria kitchen. Suppose that trays are placed on the conveyor at a rate of 1 every 5 seconds. Because what goes on must go off, they are also removed at the other end (inside the kitchen) at a rate of one every 5 seconds. Hence, the rate of the conveyor is R = 1/5 tray per second, or 12 trays per minute.

Further suppose that the trip down the conveyor takes 30 seconds, so that T = 30 seconds. During the 30 seconds a particular tray spends on the conveyor, 6 trays (30 seconds ÷ 5 seconds per tray) are loaded onto the conveyor. So as that tray is exiting, there are 6 trays on the conveyor. Indeed, when any tray is exiting, there are 6 trays on the conveyor, so the in-process inventory is I = 6 trays.

Note that these numbers obey Little's Law:

6 trays (I) = 1/5 trays/second (R) × 30 seconds (T)

Little's Law is invoked whenever people refer to inventory in units of time. For instance, a hematology lab that uses an average of 3 cases of blood collection vials per day and maintains an average supply of 60 cases on hand can be described as carrying a 20-day supply of inventory. In Little's Law terms, the rate at which vials enter (and exit) the lab is R = 3 cases per day, the average inventory level is I = 60 cases and the average time vials spend in inventory awaiting use is T = 20 days. Again, Little's Law is satisfied:

60 cases (I) = 3 cases per day (R) × 20 days (T)

Note that Little's Law does not require the inventory, rate, or time to be constant. As long as I, R, and T represent long-term averages, Little's Law holds.

In the hospital, one valuable application of Little's Law is when the inventory term represents people. For example, if a hospital averages R = 40 admissions per day and the LOS is T = 2.5 days, the average number of patients in the hospital will be I = R × T = 40 patients per day × 2.5 days = 100 patients. If the hospital were to implement policies that reduced the LOS to 2 days, the average number of inpatients would fall to I = R × T = 40 patients per day × 2 days = 80 patients.

Numerically, Little's Law can be used to compute the third term given knowledge of any two of I, R, and T. In terms of intuition, Little's Law describes the impact of changes in any of the three parameters on the others.

Little's Law supplements the Variability Buffering principle by describing how the impact of changes can ripple through performance metrics. For instance, we know from the Variability Buffering principle that reducing variability can reduce waiting time, as shown in Exhibit A.3. So if we reduce variability in an ED to the point where average patient waiting time (T) is reduced in half, but the patient arrival rate (R) remains constant, then Little's Law implies that the number of patients waiting in the ED (I) will also be reduced in half. Alternatively, if variability reduces average waiting time (T) in half, but the average number of patients waiting (I) remains constant, the average rate of patients going through the ED (R) must double.

Because reducing variability has so many operational benefits, we often seek to reduce it. One generic way to reduce variability is pooling, which is characterized in the following principle.

Principle (Pooling)—Combining sources of variability so that they can share a common buffer reduces the total amount of buffering required to achieve a given level of performance.

A common example of pooling is a regional warehouse that stocks products that can be sold in a number of retail outlets. If, in one month, retail outlet A has high sales, and retail outlet B has low sales, the warehouse will send more stock to retail outlet A. If, in the next month, the situation is reversed, the warehouse will send more stock to retail outlet B. The warehouse serves to "pool" customer demand by servicing it from a common source. Because high demand in one retail outlet is averaged out by low demand in another outlet, the warehouse will require less safety stock to provide reasonable product availability than would be required if each retail outlet carried its own safety stock.

Pooling can be used in various ways to mitigate the effects of variability in a hospital. For instance, some health care systems use a single laboratory to service multiple hospitals. By combining (pooling) demand for testing services, the centralized lab can provide comparable turnaround times with less total capacity than would be possible with individual labs in each hospital. Similarly, transcription services are often centralized (pooled) across radiology services, rather than distributed among various specialties. This avoids the inefficiency of having one transcriptionist idle while another is overwhelmed with work. As a result, the centralized system can achieve faster turnaround times with the same total capacity as the decentralized system.

We note, however, that sometimes hospitals deliberately avoid pooling to attain other efficiencies. For instance, hospitals often have remote imaging units. Although these will be less efficient in using capacity than would be a single centralized unit, they can be geographically distributed, saving patients travel time and inconvenience. So the efficiency benefits of pooling must be compared to the localization benefits of unpooling before concluding that pooling is right for a given situation.

A.2.1.3 Task Efficiency Principles

As we noted earlier, a flow is a sequence of steps through which entities (patients, physical samples, patient records, and so on) move. The steps themselves can be further broken down into tasks, which we define as follows.

Definition (Task)—A task is an identifiable and cohesive piece of a job or project, which is carried out by an individual or team.

Of course, we have some discretion in defining tasks. For example, we might choose to regard all activities involved in triaging a patient in the ED as a single task. Or we could further break down these activities by regarding initial patient examination as one task, evaluation using a decision support system as a second task, and generating a triage tag as a third task. There is no theoretical importance to the precise divisions of work into tasks. But there is practical value to finer breakdowns of steps under scrutiny for improvement opportunities. Process flow mapping and value stream mapping are formal methods for breaking down a flow into tasks to highlight inefficiencies (Rother and Shook, 2003).

Because flows are made up of tasks, improving tasks is an important way to address the capacity, variability, and accuracy of a flow. The key characteristic of tasks that affects all aspects of flow performance is complexity, which we define as follows.

Definition (Task Complexity)—The complexity of a task is increasing in the number of actions, precedence constraints, and information cues needed to specify it.

Exhibit A.4 illustrates the structure of a task implied by the preceding definition. A task involves multiple actions, each of which requires processing of information (each piece of which is called a *cue*) and each of which may require other actions to be completed before it can start. For instance, the task of drawing blood involves (D) swabbing the arm with alcohol, (E) applying a tourniquet, (F) inserting a needle, and other actions. The alcohol and tourniquet must be applied before the needle can be inserted, so activities (D) and (E) are predecessors of task (F). For task (F), the information cues that must be processed include instructions about how much blood is required, conditions of the patient's veins, verbal comments of the patients, and many others. Broken down in this way, even a relatively straightforward task like blood collection has a substantial degree of complexity to it. Surgical procedures and other activities in the hospital are vastly more complex.

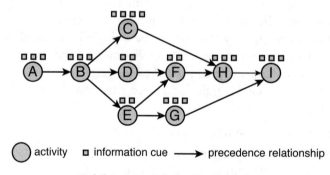

Exhibit A.4   Schematic of a task.

The implication of the preceding definition of task complexity is that there are multiple ways to reduce complexity. First, we can reduce the number of activities. For example, a well-organized phlebotomy cart might eliminate activities involved in finding and organizing the equipment needed to draw blood. Second, we can streamline the number of information cues that must be processed. For instance, someday phlebotomists may be equipped with scanners that automatically determine whether a patient has been fasting and flag a patient who has not complied with testing requirements. This would eliminate the need for phlebotomists to query the patient about their food consumption and compare the answers to testing requirements.

Third, we could reduce precedence constraints to allow more flexibility in the sequence of activities. For example, a conventional collection process has phlebotomists put raw specimens in containers and deliver them to the lab, where they are prepared and tested. Hence, delivery must precede preparation, which must precede testing. But newer collection containers contain reagents, which start the preparation process prior to delivery (that is, by removing the precedence constraint). This can stabilize the specimen, and thereby allow the phlebotomist more flexibility in delivery without damaging the sample, which in turn enables him to make more efficient collection/delivery rounds. Point of care testing (POCT) pushes this even further, but allowing some tests (for example, glucose levels) to be done at bedside, effectively removing the constraint that delivery be done before testing. This could facilitate quicker access to results.

Knowing that we can reduce task complexity in these three ways, we now observe the benefits of such reductions.

Principle (Task Simplification)—Reducing task complexity reduces the mean and variance of the task times and the likelihood of errors.

Notice that this principle implies that complexity reduction can improve three major operational performance metrics: volume, time, and quality. By reducing the mean time to complete tasks, simplification (complexity reduction) increases the capacity of a resource, and hence the volume of work it can handle. By reducing the variance of task times, simplification reduces queueing and waiting (by the Variability and Variability Buffering principles). And by reducing the likelihood of errors, simplification improves quality. As such, this principle is broadly applicable to improvement efforts in the hospital.

Indeed, simplification is at the root of most lean practices, in health care and in other industries. For example, a common lean practice is 5S (which stands for Sort, Stabilize, Shine, Standardize, Sustain, or some variant of similar S-words). The basic idea behind 5S is to organize a system so that it has a logical order and stays in that order. A typical application of 5S is an equipment room, where pieces of equipment are given clearly marked positions and whiteboards on the wall are used to record where the equipment has gone when it is removed from its position. The result is that the task of equipment collection is simplified due to activity elimination (walking around) and information cue elimination (calling people in search of the information that is now on the whiteboard). By making equipment collection faster and more reliable, we reduce the chances of delaying a procedure that requires the equipment.

A similar example of task simplification that is widespread in hospitals is visual display of information. For example, many EDs, nurse stations, diagnostic units, and ORs make use of physical or electronic whiteboards to display key information about the unit. An ED whiteboard typically identifies which patients are in which exam rooms and give some basic information about patient status. The purpose is to simplify tasks by reducing the information cues that must be processed (for example, by providing quick access to the information an ED physician needs to decide which patient to see next).

We note that because task completion involves processing information cues, there is a cognitive element to task execution. Task efficiency also depends on behavioral issues, such as motivation. We consider principles related to cognitive efficiency and other behavioral issues in the section on behavioral principles in section A.2.3.

A related practice that goes hand in hand with task simplification is task standardization.

Principle (Task Standardization)—Using clearly specified best-practice procedures for repetitive tasks reduces the mean and variance of task times and the likelihood of errors.

In essence, simplification seeks to make tasks more efficient; standardization seeks to make them more uniform. Standardization is a cornerstone of the Toyota Production System. The basic idea is to define the "best" way to perform each task by (a) breaking down the task into well-defined steps, (b) determining the best procedure and time required for each step, and (c) defining the proper sequence for the steps. Ideally, these specifications should be developed jointly by the people responsible for the tasks, although the primary input will probably come from the most skilled or knowledgeable individuals in this set.

Once standard procedures have been specified, everyone is expected to follow them— but not blindly. Workers are encouraged to suggest improvements in a spirit of continual improvement. At Toyota, written standards exist for tasks ranging from installation of a door to greeting visitors to processing an invoice. The goal is to make sure everyone is using current best practices, as well as thinking about ways to improve those practices in the future.

A famous medical example of standardization is the process used by Shouldice Hospital in Ontario, Canada, in which all surgeons use exactly the same procedure for performing hernia repair operations (Heskett 2003). Such consistency facilitates training and quality control. The result is that Shouldice achieves very good performance on both operational and clinical performance metrics.

To make effective use of standardization, hospitals must develop methods for *finding* and *sharing* best practices. For example, in large hospitals, IVs are inserted in patients hundreds of times per day by many different individuals. When it goes well, this is a fairly simple and relatively painless procedure. But when it goes badly, getting an IV can be an extremely painful experience that results in blood everywhere and a large, tender bruise on the patient's hand or arm. For patients with cancer or other conditions that require them to get IVs frequently, bad IV experiences make a bad experience even worse.

However, almost no hospitals record the percentage of times that IVs are inserted successfully on the first try. Consequently, although almost any chemotherapy patient knows that skill levels among those charged with IV insertion vary widely, hospital managers have no way of identifying their most skilled people. Until they start tracking IV outcomes, managers will not be able to find best IV insertion practices or facilitate sharing of them, and patients will go on being bloodied and bruised.

Standardization can apply to infusions as well as the IVs used to introduce them. For example, Parshuam et al. (2008) performed an experiment in which physicians, nurses, pharmacists, and pharmacy technicians, all of whom prepared infusions as part of their professional duties, prepared specified morphine infusions. They observed that 34.7% of the infusions had errors leading to incorrect concentrations, and that errors were more serious in infusions made from 10 mg/mL stock than in infusions made from 2 mg/mL stock. This suggests that the standardization strategy of stocking only the diluted 2 mg/ML solution could prevent potentially dangerous errors.

Wood et al. (2008) reported that adopting a standard procedure for obtaining and recording key clinical information during outpatient visits to the Mayo Clinic resulted in significantly improved accuracy and completeness in the medication list for patients. In addition to increasing medication accuracy and compliance with safety standards, this standardized process shifted much of the burden for dictating clinical notes from the physicians to clinical assistants.

In addition to a range of repetitive tasks, medicine involves many knowledge-intensive, creative tasks. For instance, triaging a patient, deciding what tests or specialist opinions are needed, carrying out a cutting-edge organ transplant, and many other medical tasks require judgment on the part of the caregiver. In such cases, it may be impossible to prespecify best practices, and hence standardization could degrade performance. So, when selecting tasks for standardization, we should keep in mind the following maxim:

> *Rationalize the repeatable, but only the repeatable.*

In other words, if each instance of a task is (or could be) essentially the same, finding a single best procedure is a sensible strategy. But if each instance is fundamentally unique, requiring judgment or creativity on the part of the people involved, standardization will only serve to stifle the needed creativity.

Note, however, that even creative tasks can make use of standardization for some steps. For example, an artist might use a standard setup for her paints, even though the actual painting process may vary greatly from one picture to the next. In the ED, the triage process may follow a standard framework; indeed, there are computerized systems designed to implement such a framework. But when circumstances warrant (for example, the patient exhibits a sudden change in status), the triage nurse can and should modify the procedure (for example, stop the evaluation and call for help). Using standardized procedures for routine aspects of the job can improve efficiency and treatment speed, while empowering providers to act on their judgment when needed can make the system more accurate and flexible with regard to patient needs.

Completing a project, such as diagnosing a patient, carrying out a surgical procedure, or installing a piece of equipment, typically involves multiple repetitive or creative tasks, which may be executed in series (for example, the phlebotomist can only deliver a sample to the laboratory after collection has been completed) or in parallel (for example, a pre-op nurse may administer intravenous fluids and collect patient information simultaneously). We can describe the precedence relationships between tasks in a project by means of a network, analogous to the one shown in Exhibit A.4, which breaks down a task into a network of activities. In a project network, an important property is described by the following principle.

Principle (Critical Path)—In a process with parallel activities, the throughput time for the process is determined by its critical path, which is the longest of the parallel paths in the process.

For example, Exhibit A.5 shows the network for a highly stylized surgical procedure. Note that there are three paths through this network, A-B-E-F-G, A-C-E-F-G, and A-D-E-F-G. The longest one is the first of these, which requires 15 + 20 + 40 + 10 + 5 = 90 minutes to complete. Hence, A-B-E-F-G is the critical path. Because the procedure can only be completed when all paths are complete, the duration of the project will be 90 minutes.

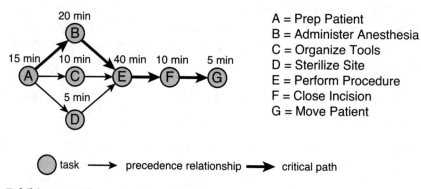

Exhibit A.5   Schematic of a project/process network showing the critical path.

If we want to shorten the project time, we can only do so by shortening tasks along the critical path. Shortening a noncritical task (for example, D = Sterilize Site) will not reduce the project time, because these tasks already have slack built into them. That is, noncritical tasks can be extended without causing the path(s) they lie on to exceed the critical path. So if Task D takes 5 minutes longer than planned, it won't affect the completion time of the surgery.

The key insight from the Critical Path principle is that reducing the duration of a one-time project (for example, installation of a new OR scheduling system) or process (for example, surgical procedure for a given patient) requires speeding up or eliminating tasks along the critical path.

A.2.1.4 SEQUENCING PRINCIPLES

So far, the principles in this section have described how we can improve the performance of a flow by increasing capacity (which reduces utilization) or reducing variability (which reduces queueing). We can accomplish both of these by improving flows at the task level via simplification or standardization.

But sometimes it is possible to improve performance at the patient level without improving the average performance of a flow. That is, even though the average throughput and the average flow time (LOS or TAT) are unchanged, we can provide better service to patients who need it more, at the expense of poorer service to those who need it less. We do this by prioritizing resources to favor some entities (patients, tests, medical units, or whatever) over others. This procedure is generically known as *sequencing*.

Sequencing involves a balancing act because, in addition to urgency considerations, there is the issue of the number of resources required. For example, consider patients in the ED, who are classified in triage according to their urgency and number of resources required. As we noted in Chapter 2, many hospitals use an Emergency Severity Index (ESI) system to classify patients. ESI-1 is reserved for patients who cannot wait due to risk of death. ESI-2 is for patients who are not at risk of death but cannot wait due to a risk of other negative outcomes (for example, loss of function). ESI-3, 4, and 5 all designate patients who will not be medically harmed by waiting. The difference is that ESI-3 patients require multiple resources (for example, tests) as part of their evaluation/treatment, ESI-4 patients require a single resource, and ESI-5 patients do not require any resources. Hence, in general, medical urgency and the amount of time/resources are decreasing in the ESI level of patients.

In some situations, medical urgency dominates. For instance, no ED would keep an ESI-1 patient waiting while it treated patients in less urgent categories. The mission to save lives takes precedence over other performance metrics, so ESI-1 patients get priority. But medical urgency is not always sufficiently different to distinguish patients. For example, ESI-3, 4, and 5 patients can all wait without medical consequences. If there were truly no difference in their urgency levels, there is incentive to treat fast patients before slow patients. That is, we should favor ESI-5 patients before ESI-4 patients before ESI-3 patients so we can finish them more quickly and reduce ED LOS.

The principle that balances urgency and time is the following.

Principle (Critical Ratio Sequencing)—In a multiclass system with dynamic arrivals, prioritizing entities according to the ratio c/t, where c is the delay cost per unit time and t is the expected process time, minimizes total cumulative delay cost over the long term.

This principle gives us a way to think about sequencing patients who differ with regard to both urgency and time. For example, suppose that ESI-3, 4, and 5 patients differ according to discomfort level. That is, on average, suppose that ESI-3 patients suffer more than ESI-4 patients who suffer more than ESI-5 patients. No one will die or suffer serious consequences from waiting, but the patients who suffer more are more likely to write complaining letters about their waits. Putting ESI-3 patients before ESI-4 and ESI-5 patients will favor the individuals most likely to complain but will also put the slowest patients first, causing everyone else to wait.

For purposes of illustration, suppose the ED director wants to minimize the rate of complaint letters by sequencing ESI-3, 4, and 5 patients. Suppose further that she knows from past history that ESI-3 patients write complaints at a rate of 0.05 letters per hour of wait time. ESI-4 patients write complaints at a rate of 0.04 letters per hour of wait time. And ESI-5 patients write complaints at a rate of 0.02 letters per hour of wait time. Finally, suppose that the expected treatment times for ESI-3, 4, and 5 patients are 60 minutes, 40 minutes, and 15 minutes.

We can compute the c/t ratios as follows:

ESI	c	t	c/t
3	0.05	60	0.00083
4	0.04	40	0.001
5	0.01	15	0.00067

This calculation suggests that the ED should process patients in order of ESI-4 before ESI-3 before ESI-5. The logic behind this is that ESI-4 patients complain almost as frequently as ESI-3 patients, but they take substantially less time to treat. So taking ESI-4 patients first introduces less delay for the other patients waiting behind them than would taking ESI-3 patients first. ESI-5 patients complain at such a low rate that taking them last does not lead to too many complaints, even though they wait behind all other classes of patients.

Strictly speaking, the critical ratio results for this example imply that an ESI-4 patient who has just arrived should get priority over an ESI-3 patient, regardless of how long that patient has been waiting. The reason for this is that the Critical Ratio principle is premised on an assumption of constant cost rates. In this example, this means that an ESI-5 patient has an additional 1% chance of writing a complaint for every extra hour he spends waiting in the ED. But in practice, the likelihood of an unhappy (and letter writing) patient may grow more quickly once the wait time goes above a level perceived as reasonable (for example, two hours). If this is the case, it makes sense to violate the critical ratio priority order to take patients who have been waiting too long, regardless of their ESI level.

As long as we can establish holding cost rates (that is, c values), the critical ratio rule can be used to set sequencing priorities for all kinds of things at a hospital. Possibilities include patients being scheduled for elective surgery, patients being scheduled for scans or other tests, specimens in a clinical laboratory, images being read by radiologists, and many others.

However, there are many instances in which we cannot or do not distinguish entities according to urgency. For example, walk-in patients getting routine blood work at a lab are usually regarded as having equal priority. In terms of the Critical Ratio principle, this means that everyone can be given a delay cost of c = 1, so that the critical ratio becomes 1/t. This means that entities should be prioritized in inverse order of their process time, as stated in the following.

Corollary (SPT Sequencing)—Processing entities in order of shortest processing time (SPT) minimizes average wait time.

This SPT rule is a classic result of scheduling theory. But it is also part of our daily intuition. For example, most of us have witnessed (or been part of) the following scenario. Individual A walks up to the cash register at the grocery store with one item and sighs as she gets in line behind Individual B who has two fully loaded carts and is holding a couple of items without price tags or bar codes. Individual B hears the sigh, turns around, and takes note of the situation.

"Here," she says, "why don't you go ahead of me?"

Individual A happily accepts and is rung up in one minute. The cashier then takes ten minutes to ring up Individual B.

Note that, under this scenario, Individual A takes 1 minute to get through the line, while Individual B takes 11 minutes, for an average of (1 + 11) / 2 = 6 minutes. If Individual B had not let Individual A go first, Individual B would have gone through the line in 10 minutes and Individual B would have taken 11 minutes, for an average of (10 + 11) / 2 = 10.5 minutes. As we all know intuitively, putting long process times at the front of the line keeps everyone waiting. So, putting short process times in front reduces average wait time.

Returning to the ED patient sequencing example, suppose that the consequences of waiting (for example, likelihood of medical problems, pain, and amount of complaining) are equivalent for ESI-3, 4, and 5 patients. Then the SPT Sequencing rule applies. Because, in general, ESI-5 patients require less treatment time than ESI-4 patients, who in turn require less time than ESI-3 patients, this rule suggests that patients be sequenced with ESI-5 patients before ESI-4 patients before ESI-3 patients. Of course, as we have noted, the ED might want to modify this rule to intervene on behalf of someone who has been waiting for a long time. But the ED would not want to sequence patients in reverse of this order, because that would constitute a longest process time (LPT) rule, which would maximize expected wait time.

A.2.1.5 PROTECTION PRINCIPLES

Recall that three key operational performance metrics are volume, time, and quality. The bulk of the preceding principles pertain to volume and time, although some (for example, the Simplification and Standardization principles) also deal with quality. We conclude our summary of flow principles with two fundamental principles that apply specifically to quality.

The first principle encapsulates the intuition of the Swiss cheese model of system failure (Reason 2000). This model views system failures as the consequence of breakdowns in multiple layers of protection. For example, an automobile accident might occur because one car had a tire blowout and worn struts that hindered emergency handling, another (oncoming) car had a driver distracted by a text message and was therefore slow to take evasive action, and the road was covered by loose gravel that compromised braking and maneuverability of both cars. In this scenario, better maintenance of the first car, more attentiveness on the part of the second driver, and improved condition of the road are all layers of protection (cheese), any one of which could have prevented the accident.

We can summarize the essential insight of the Swiss cheese model in the following principle.

Principle (Redundancy)—Independent layers of protection increase the reliability of a system.

Notice that this principle calls for *independent* layers of protection, not just more layers, to increase reliability. For instance, suppose a restaurant purchases a backup electric freezer, in which to keep its frozen foods in case of failure of the primary electric freezer. Although this would represent an added layer of protection, it would not do any good if the only reason for failure of the primary freezer is a power outage. In such a case, failure of the two freezers would be completely *dependent* events. In contrast, a gasoline-powered backup freezer could still fail but would do so independently of the electric freezer.

Hospitals are full of redundant layers of protection aimed at increasing patient safety. Attending physicians check the decisions of residents. Doctors check the work of nurses. Nurses check the work of doctors. Phlebotomists ask patients to state their name as an identity check. Laboratories make use of multiple patient identifiers to permit cross-checking of patient names. Surgeons mark surgical sites to help prevent wrong site surgery. Radiologists ask for second opinions on ambiguous images. And patients are asked to repeat the same information over and over to different clinicians. Because patient safety is such a high priority, there are many examples of redundancy in hospital processes.

But redundancy can be expensive. For example, we are aware of a hospital in which scheduling of patient tests was difficult and error prone. Consequently, physicians routinely checked the schedules to make sure their urgent patients were actually scheduled for when they thought they were. Obviously, spending time checking schedules and correcting errors was a poor use of a highly trained physician. But because the physicians perceived the consequences of errors to be serious and the opportunities for resolving the root problem to be remote, they did it anyway.

The reason redundancy can be expensive is that it often involves adding steps. Checking the work of others, repeating tasks, collecting the same information multiple times, and many other forms of redundancy require additional time, and hence expense. This expense may be justified in many situations. However, because cost is a vital concern in health care, hospital professionals must be open to cheaper alternatives for protecting patients from harm.

One way to do this is by removing opportunities for errors. The generic term for this is *foolproofing*, which we describe in the following.

Principle (Foolproofing)—Using constraints to force correct actions reduces the likelihood of errors.

Examples of foolproofing abound in mechanical devices. For instance, in a car, you cannot take out your key until you shift into park (preventing you from leaving it in a gear that might allow the car to roll away), you can only fit an unleaded fuel nozzle into the gas tank (preventing you from using leaded fuel or diesel by mistake), anti-lock brakes do not allow the wheels to lock up (preventing an uncontrolled skid), and many other safety devices prevent dangerous behavior. Note that none of these protective mechanisms require additional checks or remedies; they simply make undesired behaviors impossible.

In the hospital, foolproofing strategies can be highly effective and cost efficient. For example, single-dose packaging of medications eliminates the potential for bedside dosage errors. Using unique connectors for different gases makes it impossible to accidentally hook up a tube (patient) to the wrong gas. Auto analyzers that accept samples with rubber stoppers in place prevent contact between lab technicians and blood that could contaminate the sample or infect the technician. Oral syringes that will not fit into IV tubing prevent accidental intravenous administration of oral medication. Needleless syringes prevent the transmission of disease and infection via accidental needle sticks. The Bloodloc device prevents units of blood from being administered unless their code matches that of the patient, thereby avoiding transfusion errors due to misidentification of patient or sample. A door lock system prevents a centrifuge from being run without being latched and locked (which could damage samples). Many other examples of foolproofing in hospitals exist, and many more are possible.

Foolproofing is a powerful tool for preventing mistakes in settings where the correct action is precisely known and can be forced via a physical device. In settings where actions are more complex (for example, requiring judgment) and cannot be specified precisely in advance, mechanical foolproofing devices are not possible. A less rigid, but still effective, method for error prevention is to present key information in an intuitive (often visual) format.

Principle (Intuitive Information)—Providing essential information visually or orally in tight association with a task reduces the mean and variance of task times, as well as the likelihood of errors.

This principle is at the heart of the old saying, "A picture is worth a thousand words." Human brains can process information quickly and accurately when presented in intuitive visual form. Automobiles exploit this via warning lights (for deficient oil pressure, malfunctioning alternator, unlatched doors, low tire pressure, and so on), analog speedometers with pronounced markings for highway speed limits, tachometers with red lines indicating excessive engine speed, and many other visual signals. Humans also take in information efficiently when it is presented acoustically. Seat belt warning buzzers, chimes that indicate the lights have been left on, and beeping backup sensors are just a few automotive examples of intuitive acoustic information. Intuitive information can make use of senses beyond seeing and hearing. For instance, an odorant is added to natural gas (which has almost no smell of its own), allowing people to use their sense of smell to detect its presence and avoid dangerous explosions.

The Intuitive Information principle is closely related to the Task Simplification principle we introduced earlier. Recall that we defined *task simplification* to mean a reduction in the number of activities, information cues, or precedence constraints. Often the intuitive presentation of information amounts to a reduction in the number of information cues that must be processed during a task. For example, a patient with a medication allergy could have this fact noted in his file. But checking this written information requires scanning through the file (that is, processing many information cues). In contrast, a color-coded wristband that indicates a medication allergy communicates this same essential piece of information at a glance. Putting the necessary information in visual format and in plain view of the nurse who administers medications reduces the chance that the information will be overlooked or misinterpreted. This is an example of the Task Simplification principle applied to the information aspect of medication administration.

However, the Intuitive Information principle is not entirely a consequence of the Task Simplification principle, because there may be cases in which providing the essential information may have impacts beyond the task itself. For example, putting a warning buzzer on a specimen refrigerator that indicates when the temperature has gone outside the acceptable range could simplify the task of monitoring sample storage (for example, by allowing fewer visits to check the temperature). So for the person charged with this task, the buzzer is a form of task simplification. But if someone other than the person charged with sample monitoring hears the buzzer and takes action (for example, calls a repair person, moves samples to another refrigerator, and so on), this is more than task simplification. In this case, the intuitive information serves as a type of redundancy protection by allowing additional people to serve as guardians of the refrigerator. Because intuitive information can facilitate an added layer of protection by involving previously uninvolved people, we call out this principle separately from the Task Simplification principle.

In the hospital, the Intuitive Information principle takes up where the Foolproofing principle leaves off. Any error-prone step that is not amenable to a constraint-based approach for making errors impossible can potentially apply an intuitive information approach to make errors less likely. For example, color-coding medications to indicate their type and dosage makes medication errors less likely than if look-alike packaging is used for different medications. A bag that changes color in the presence of carbon dioxide can be used to visually detect esophageal intubation. Sensors can detect when patients have gotten out of bed or have fallen. Computerized physician order entry (CPOE) systems can be programmed to provide warnings to physicians (for example, possible effects of a particular medication on elderly patients, drug interactions, or possibly suspicious changes in dosage) as a means of catching errors.[5] Grout (2007) offers many other examples of foolproofing and intuitive information in the context of a hospital.

The Intuitive Information principle is the core concept underlying the practice of visual management systems (VMS). (See Grief 1991 for an overview.) The mantra of VMS is "make it obvious." We see examples of visual management all the time in daily life in the form of walk signals at crosswalks, colored cones, and barriers marking construction zones. Manufacturing firms have widely adopted visual management methods, such as whiteboard displays of production output, lights indicating stoppages or quality problems and statistical process control charts of all kinds of performance metrics. Hospitals have implemented analogous methods, such as whiteboards summarizing patient status, call lights indicating patient needs, and statistical process control charts for metrics such as laboratory turnaround time or ED patient left-without-being-seen (LWBS) rates.

Finally, we note that the Intuitive Information principle implies efficiency benefits as well as safety benefits from properly placed intuitive information. For example, a well-organized tool rack that visually signals where each tool goes will save time in putting away equipment. The same rack with whiteboards to indicate where a removed tool has been taken will save time in tracking down needed equipment. This sort of "a place for everything and everything in its place" policy is the essence of 5S policies (Rona 2009). Conceptually, these exploit the simplification benefits of visual information to reduce the mean and variance of the time to complete tasks.

A.2.2 Information Principles

Although many of the preceding flow principles involve information, their focus is on physical flows—patients, specimens, supplies, and so on. But in the functioning of a hospital, the flow of information is every bit as important as the flow of people and material. Patient records, doctors' orders, test results, and many other types of information are essential to patient care. Consequently, the following principles related to the transfer, use, and value of information are strongly relevant to management of hospital operations.

A.2.2.1 INFORMATION TRANSFER

Before information can be used to make decisions and carry out tasks, it must reach those who need it. Consequently, the transfer of information from one person or place to another is vital in hospitals. Unfortunately, information errors are common and are involved in many incidents that harm patients. For example, a patient misidentification error could lead to surgery on the wrong patient. An ambiguous prescription could lead to a medication error. Miscommunication between nurses during a shift change could lead to dangerous inattention to patient needs.

We encapsulate the tendency to lose information integrity in the following principle.

Principle (Handoffs)—Unless new knowledge is contributed by the individuals, information is degraded as it is passed from one individual to another.

The classic illustration of this principle is the children's "telephone" game, in which a message is whispered from one child to the next and winds up thoroughly distorted from its original form. In health care, passing a patient from one doctor to another, or one nurse to another (across shifts, say), are opportunities for information degradation.

However, we must balance this degradation problem with the benefit of "two heads are better than one." If new knowledge is contributed, involving more people can be good. For example, although handing off a patient from an emergency physician to a specialist could be an opportunity for error (for example, if the emergency physician fails to communicate an essential piece of information about the patient's status), it is far more likely to lead to a better diagnosis and plan for treatment as a result of the specialist's added expertise.

But, there are many handoffs in which little additional information or knowledge is added by the exchange. For instance, a handoff of a patient from one nurse to another at a shift change is a situation in which degradation of information may lead to a degradation of quality. Indeed, Steitenberger et al. (2006) suggest caution in using intermediaries (for example, admission nurse or bed management specialist) who may add complexity and steps to the process, without contributing knowledge to it. By the Handoff principle, such intermediaries may be a source of errors.

The Handoff principle deals with accidental impediments to information transfer. But there are also structural impediments, as we note in the following.

Principle (Knowledge Sharing)—Knowledge is power, so people need a good reason to share it.

For instance, a hematologist who is particularly skilled in drawing blood and does it faster and more accurately than anyone else might be reluctant to train other hematologists in his methods if it means that he will lose stature (for example, employee of the month recognition, scheduling preferences, and so on). In general, revealing private knowledge to others yields power to others, so there must be other perceived benefits to the individual to induce sharing of such knowledge. This means that work standardization initiatives, which seek to transfer best practices across the organization, need to provide incentives to the best performers who are expected to share their "tips and tricks." These could be tangible (for example, bonuses or privileges for people who get chosen to act as trainers) or intangible (for example, the stature inferred by being recognized as a best performer). But neglecting to acknowledge the personal benefits from guarding personal knowledge can seriously impede the organizational learning process. We will delve into other such issues in the section on behavioral principles and the discussion on organizational learning therein.

A.2.2.2 INFORMATION USE (DECISION MAKING)

Transferring information is only a means to an end. The ultimate reason for collecting information is to use it to make better decisions. The prototypical hospital decision is the diagnostic one of how to treat a patient. But thousands of other decisions are made in hospitals every day. A charge nurse in the ED must decide which patient to bring next from the waiting room to an examination room. A hospitalist in a patient ward must decide whether to call a specialist for a patient who is exhibiting new symptoms. An imaging technician must decide whether an image is satisfactory or a rescan is necessary. And so on.

The underlying structure of all these decisions is similar. There is a set of alternatives, which may be clear or unclear, from which one must be chosen. Before digging into the details, the decision maker will have a sense of the likelihoods that each alternative is the right one. She can then collect information, through direct observation, formal testing and investigation, or both. This information may alter her sense of the likelihoods of each alternative being the right one. At some point, the decision maker decides that her sense of the likelihoods is sufficiently clear and selects one or more of the alternatives.

To be more concrete, let us consider the specific decision problem presented by the diagnosis and treatment of patients in a clinic, ED, or physician's office. Patients enter in an "undifferentiated" state, meaning that physicians do not yet know what is wrong with them. Physicians use a process of "differential diagnosis" to gather information and recommend actions (therapies, or more testing) from that information. The information gathering process begins as soon as the physician encounters the patient, through observation and interview. The physician observes the patient's demographic (age, gender, weight) and, based on this information, the described symptoms, and known frequencies of occurrence of different diseases in the population, forms some ideas about what might be causing the reported symptoms. The physician can choose from a range of additional information-gathering options, such as additional clinical signs, a physical examination, blood tests, radiological exams, and so on. These options will differ according to their cost, invasiveness, test quality, and value of information.

The information garnered from these activities and tests is used to refine the physician's beliefs about what might be wrong with the patient. Sometimes there is a clear line between information gathering activities and the prescription of a course of therapy. That is, the physician may continue gathering information via tests and examinations until, in his estimation, the evidence is sufficiently convincing of a specific diagnosis to warrant stopping information gathering and starting therapy. Sometimes these activities are intertwined. For example, giving an antibiotic may cure the patient, but if it does not, the physician will know that the disease is not due to those pathogens that should have succumbed. In that case, information accrues as a result of therapy. In still other cases, some actions are proactive. For example, an overweight individual undergoing emergency abdominal surgery who is likely to be immobilized for a while after surgery is a high-risk candidate for postoperative *thrombosis* (development of a clot in a vein or artery). Hence, in such a case, information gathering includes assessing the patient's risk level for thrombosis, which could lead to recommendation of preventive measures (for example, compression stockings for the legs, or use of an anticoagulant such as Heparin). In all these cases, the general process is information gathering and then taking action based on that information. The "actions" can include gathering more information, treating for specific diseases, or both.

Unfortunately, no matter how much effort is devoted to information gathering, some uncertainty almost always remains. Few tests, no matter how costly and advanced, are absolutely definitive in their results. The reason is a lack of sensitivity or specificity, which are defined as follows.

Definition (Test Sensitivity)—The sensitivity of a test is the true positive rate, which is the probability of yielding a positive result when the condition being tested is present.

Definition (Test Specificity)—The specificity of a test is the true negative rate, which is the probability of yielding a negative result when the condition being tested is not present.

Note that we need both sensitivity and specificity to be high in order for a test to be accurate. For example, a test that always yields a positive result has sensitivity of 100% and specificity of 0% and is entirely useless because it does not distinguish between positive and negative conditions. Analogously, a test that always yields a negative result has specificity of 100% and sensitivity of 0% and is equally useless. A test that has sensitivity and specificity both equal to 100% will correctly identify all positive and negative conditions. But, sadly, almost all real-world tests have sensitivity and specificity below 100%.

As a result, it may not be possible, or even desirable (given the required investment in time, money, and physical discomfort) to discover the patient's disease state exactly. If the physician is 99% sure that the patient is suffering from a specific disease, further testing is probably not necessary or desirable. Living in this world of uncertainty is philosophically challenging when human lives are at stake. However, it is an inevitable reality given imperfect testing. Because of this, physicians adjust their activities with human consequences in mind. A disease that is unlikely but fatal will justify a more aggressive information gathering strategy than one that is likely and benign.

There is a statistical language to describe this process of investigation and prescription, centered on an information updating law known as *Bayes' Rule*. Although most physicians do not make formal use of statistical methods, their intuitive processes generally conform to them. However, sometimes intuition can be flawed. So it is helpful to understand the statistical underpinnings of decision making and the insights that follow from these. But it is also useful to understand how behavioral biases can distort decision making. We address the statistical aspects of decision making here in our discussion of information principles and take up the behavioral aspects in section A.2.3.

We present Bayes' Rule in the context of differential diagnosis, but note that it applies to any sequential process of information collection and decision making. A Bayes' Rule model of differential diagnosis views the patient as being in one of a list of possible disease states. To capture the uncertainty about which state the patient is in, the model designates probabilities that each state is the true one. Before information is gathered, these probabilities are called the *prior probabilities* (or just *priors*). After information is gathered, and the probabilities are updated, they are called the *posterior probabilities* (or just *posteriors*). Note that the basic step of priors-information-posteriors may be repeated several times; in each case the posteriors from the last stage of the process become the priors for the next stage.

For example, suppose an overweight, 65-year-old male smoker walks into a clinic with *angina* (chest pain). There are several possible explanations for the pain, including musculo-skeletal (rib fracture, muscle strain) and lung-related (pneumonia, pneumothorax) conditions. However, it is coronary heart disease with which the physician is most concerned, because a delay in treatment could prove fatal. After conducting a physical exam and an interview, the physician makes an estimate of the prior probability of coronary disease.[6]

If this prior is sufficiently high, the physician might elect to begin treatment right away. If not, she could choose to pursue additional tests. For example, the physician might have the angina patient undergo an exercise electrocardiogram (possibly combined with a radionuclide scan), an echocardiogram, or potentially a more invasive option. Her recommendation would be based on both the sensitivity and specificity of the available tests, as well as the cost (financial and physical) and risks involved.

Bayes' Rule is the statistical tool for computing posterior probabilities that a condition is present from prior probabilities and test sensitivity/specificity. We can state it as follows:

Definition (Bayes' Rule): The posterior probability that a condition is present given a positive test is

$$\text{Posterior}^+ = \frac{\text{Sensitivity} \times \text{Prior}}{\text{Sensitivity} \times \text{Prior} + (1 - \text{Specificity}) \times (1 - \text{Prior})}$$

and the posterior probability that the condition is present given a negative test is

$$\text{Posterior}^- = \frac{(1 - \text{Sensitivity}) \times \text{Prior}}{(1 - \text{Sensitivity}) \times \text{Prior} + \text{Specificity} \times (1 - \text{Prior})}$$

For example, suppose the physician orders an exercise electrocardiogram for the angina patient. Then the Prior is the physician's estimate of the probability that the patient has coronary heart disease before the test is done. The Posterior$^+$ is the estimate of the probability of coronary heart disease if the test results are positive, and Posterior$^-$ is the estimate of the probability of coronary heart disease if the test results are negative.[7] The Sensitivity and Specificity are descriptors of the accuracy of the test, which must be estimated from historical data.

Exhibit A.6 shows the posterior probabilities of coronary disease given a positive test result as a function of the prior probability, and Exhibit A.7 shows the posterior probabilities given a negative test. The three lines in each graph show the results for three different levels of test quality (specificity and sensitivity of the test, which are assumed to be equal in this example, but they do not have to be). From these graphs, and the Bayes' Rule formula from which it is derived, we can observe the following:

- **Prior probabilities are persistent**—In Exhibits A.6 and A.7 this is illustrated by the fact that the posterior probability is increasing in the prior probability. In the context of our example, this means that if the patient has a high likelihood of coronary heart disease before the test, then a positive test may boost this likelihood to a very high (that is, conclusive) level. Even if the test is negative, if the prior probability is extremely high, the posterior may still remain high (that is, we suspect the test result is a false negative). But if the patient has a low likelihood of coronary heart disease before the test, then a positive result may leave us with still low (that is, inconclusive) likelihood of disease.

- **Increasing accuracy increases the influence of a test**—In Exhibit A.6, this is illustrated by the fact that, for a given prior probability, higher sensitivity/specificity leads to a higher posterior probability. In Exhibit A.7, higher sensitivity/specificity leads to a lower posterior probability. In the context of our example, a test with higher sensitivity and specificity will result in greater confidence in either confirming the diagnosis of coronary heart disease if the test is positive, or rejecting it if the test is negative.

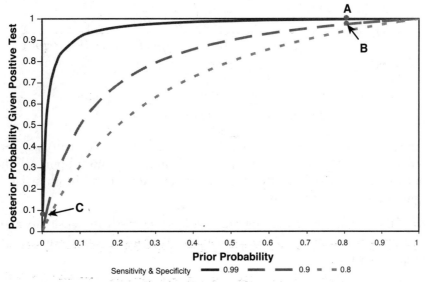

Exhibit A.6   Impact of prior and sensitivity/specificity on posterior given a positive test.

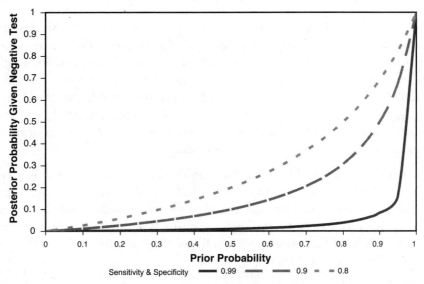

Exhibit A.7   Impact of prior and sensitivity/specificity on posterior given a negative test.

To illustrate these observations quantitatively, suppose that, based on her training, experience, and observations, the physician estimates there is an 80% chance that the angina patient has coronary heart disease. Further suppose that the exercise electrocardiogram test has sensitivity of 99% (that is, a 1% false negative rate) and specificity of 99% (that is, a 1% false positive rate).

Then we can compute the posterior probability of coronary heart disease given a positive test result by using Bayes' Rule as follows:

$$Posterior = \frac{Sensitivity \times Prior}{Sensitivity \times Prior + (1 - Specificity) \times (1 - Prior)}$$

$$= \frac{0.99 \times 0.8}{0.99 \times 0.8 + (1 - 0.99) \times (1 - 0.8)} = 0.997$$

Hence, the positive test increases the likelihood that the patient has coronary heart disease from 80% to 99.7%. (We show this graphically in Exhibit A.6 as point A.) This level of certainty may well be sufficiently conclusive in the judgment of the physician to warrant beginning a course of treatment.

However, if the exercise electrocardiogram were less accurate, with sensitivity and specificity only equal to 90%, the posterior probability of coronary heart disease given a positive test decreases to:

$$Posterior = \frac{0.90 \times 0.8}{0.90 \times 0.8 + (1 - 0.90) \times (1 - 0.8)} = 0.973$$

which is illustrated graphically as point B in Exhibit A.6. Although this is still pretty high, the physician may decide that it leaves enough doubt to warrant following up with another test, such as an echocardiogram. If that were done, the posterior probability from the first test (97.3%) would become the prior probability for the new test. If the second test is positive, this probability will be boosted to an even higher level (the size of the boost will depend on the sensitivity/specificity of the second test). If the second test is negative, it will result in a posterior probability below 97.3%, and potentially cast doubt on coronary heart disease as the correct diagnosis.

To appreciate the influence of the prior probability on the posterior probability, suppose the clinic considers giving random exercise electrocardiograms to young, apparently healthy people. Suppose further that the likelihood that such people have coronary heart disease is 1 in 1,000. Hence, the prior probability is only 0.001. Even if the sensitivity and specificity of the test were 99%, a Bayes' Rule calculation shows that the posterior probability after a positive test is only:

$$Posterior = \frac{0.99 \times 0.001}{0.99 \times 0.001 + (1 - 0.99) \times (1 - 0.001)} = 0.09$$

which is illustrated in Exhibit A.6 as point C. Hence, for these random patients, a positive test is hardly convincing evidence of heart disease. Even worse, because there is only a 9% likelihood that a person with a positive test has the disease, there is a 91% chance that he does not. Consequently, a random testing program will produce far more false positives than true positives. The result will be anguish and additional testing to sort out who actually has the disease. So, unless the benefit of each true positive result is extremely high, the financial cost of the testing and the psychological costs of the false positives will make random testing unattractive.

Exhibit A.6 and the preceding exercises show that prior probabilities (that is, first impressions) matter greatly. For the obese patient with angina, first impressions led to a fairly high prior for coronary heart disease. With this high prior, a positive test led to a convincingly high posterior. But for random young people, first impressions are that coronary heart disease is unlikely. So, although a positive test results in a posterior probability that is much higher than the prior probability, the resulting posterior is still much too low to conclude that the disease is present.

When the posterior probability is low despite a positive test, this implies a high likelihood of a false positive. In the example of random exercise electrocardiograms on young, apparently healthy people, only 9% of positive tests are true positives, and 91% are false positives. We summarize this important result in the following principle.

Principle (Incidence Rate)—The lower the incidence rate of a condition, the more likely a test is to yield a false positive result.

Sox et al. (1988) offer the following maxim in keeping with this principle.

If a test result surprises you, repeat the test before taking action.

For example, if we get a (surprising) positive test result for coronary heart disease in a young, otherwise healthy, patient, the Incidence Rate principle implies that it is statistically unlikely that the result is accurate. So following up with an independent second test to make sure is a wise course of action.

In addition to their statistical persistence, there is a psychological reason why prior beliefs are so important. People sometimes have a tendency to ignore or interpret away evidence contrary to their beliefs, so first impressions can be self-reinforcing. Crosskerry (2009) gives an overview of research on cognitive biases and identifies a list of specific behaviors that can influence medical decision making. These include *anchoring*, which is the tendency to lock onto salient features of the patient's initial presentation early in the diagnostic process and then fail to adjust these; *confirmation bias,* which is the tendency to look for confirming evidence to support a hypothesis and to not look for disconfirming evidence; and *ascertainment bias,* which results from stereotyping or gender bias (Croskerry 2009). In addition, a *sunk cost* bias can occur when considerable time and energy (and ego) have been invested in a particular diagnosis, leading a physician to be reluctant to give it up. All these contribute to a tendency to weight initial impressions even more heavily than statistical reasons justify.

Combining the statistical role of priors with psychological inertia gives us the following.

Principle (First Impressions)—First impressions are critical inputs to medical decision making, because they are psychologically self-reinforcing and because even an objective statistician will not alter strongly held beliefs without significant contrary evidence.

Taken together, the Incidence Rate and First Impressions principles imply that prior probabilities have great influence over posterior probabilities, and hence our decisions. We already noted that taking into account this influence can help guide us in what not to do (that is, not to make decisions based on unexpected results without further confirmation). But it can also help guide us in what to do. Sox et al. (1988) encapsulate this in the following maxim:

> *If you hear hoof beats, think of horses not zebras.*

That is, all other things being equal, a physician should consider the likely explanations for a patient's symptoms first because these are the scenarios with high prior probabilities. For such scenarios, supportive test results can provide convincing evidence. For unlikely scenarios (zebras), the First Impressions principle implies that it will be much harder to provide strong statistical evidence. This means that multiple tests are likely to be needed, precisely when such tests are most likely to be negative. Hence, in the interest of spending financial, time, and discomfort budgets most wisely, physicians should start with the obvious.

We should note, however, that the preference for likely explanations is only when all other things are equal. If the zebras in the above maxim are vicious killers, and the horses are mild-mannered pets, we might want to think of zebras even if they are unlikely. In an example with more medical relevance, the most likely explanation of a patient's dizziness might be an inner ear infection. But the physician might choose to test to rule out stroke as a cause because failure to do so could result in a delay that might cause real harm to the patient. We address the influence of the consequences of a decision in the following section on information value.

A.2.2.3 INFORMATION VALUE

With the formal structure for decision making provided by Bayes' Rule, we can state some principles that describe the value of information and the factors that determine it.

As we noted at the beginning of the previous section, the ultimate purpose of information is for use in decision making. As we observed in our discussion of Bayes' Rule, the way information changes decisions is by updating prior probabilities into posterior probabilities and thereby clarifying the basis for selecting a course of action. However, we noted that not all information is equally helpful in doing this. For example, a test like an exercise electrocardiogram is likely to be useful in confirming a diagnosis of coronary heart disease and motivating treatment decisions for an angina patient with other risk factors. But this same test is unlikely to have any influence on the treatment of a random, young, and apparently healthy patient.

We can collapse this insight that information is only valuable to the extent that it helps us make better decisions in the following principle.

Principle (Value of Information)—The value of information is determined by the expected improvement in outcome with the information over that without it. This implies that information that will not change a decision has no value.

Because it states value in terms of the *expected* improvement in outcome, this principle implies that two factors determine the value of information: likelihood that the information will change the outcome, and magnitude of the change in outcome. The expected improvement is the product of these.

For example, suppose a physician feels that a tumor, which has been revealed by a CT scan, should be removed whether it is benign or malignant. Then there is no value to a biopsy, because the result would not change the decision to proceed with surgery. The likelihood of an improved outcome is zero. Similarly, if a patient shows signs of infection and is given an antibiotic, the value of a test to determine the specific bacterium depends on how it might impact treatment. If the same antibiotic would continue being administered regardless of the outcome, then, again, the test is valueless.

Sox et al. (1988) summarize this insight with the following maxim:

> If a test is unlikely to change the management of the patient, don't do the test.

The likelihood that a test will change the outcome in a decision scenario can be low for a variety of reasons. As we noted, if the treatment is the same regardless of the test result (for example, surgery will be undertaken regardless of whether a biopsy indicates a tumor is malignant, or the same antibiotic will be administered regardless of the outcome of a test to identify the bacterium), the value of information from the test is useless. We also noted that if the prior probability is very high (for example, we are virtually certain that the angina patient has coronary heart disease) or very low (for example, we are almost certain that a random healthy patient does not have coronary heart disease), the test is unlikely to change the course of treatment. Other reasons a test might have little chance of changing the outcome include the time to get test results (for example, safety may dictate that an antibiotic regimen begin before the pathogen can be cultured) and lack of an effective treatment (for example, a test that indicates a poison for which there is no antidote).

But a particularly important determinant of a test's ability to change the outcome is the accuracy of the test. As we observed in Exhibit A.6 and the numerical examples associated with it, more accurate tests lead to more conclusive posterior probabilities. Hence, we can summarize the influence of test quality on the value of information as follows.

Principle (Test Quality)—All else equal, tests with higher sensitivity and higher specificity are better in supporting rapid and accurate treatment.

From Bayes' Rule, we know that higher specificity and sensitivity lead to more definitive posterior probabilities (for example, high level of certainty in either confirming or ruling out a disease). This leads to greater confidence in selecting the best treatment alternative(s). Better accuracy also reduces the need for additional testing and therefore can speed the process of selecting a course of treatment.

But, as we noted, the likelihood that information changes the outcome is only part of what determines the value of the information. The other part is the magnitude of the change in outcome. For example, faced with a patient with a soft tissue infection, a physician could do a test to try to determine whether the bacteria strain is a common variety, which can be treated with an inexpensive antibiotic (for example, penicillin, erythromycin, streptomycin, or tetracycline) or a gram-positive (resistant) variety, which requires a newer (and more costly) antibiotic (for example, daptomycin or linezolid). Alternatively, the physician could proceed without a detailed test and just prescribe one of the newer antibiotics. If the newer and older antibiotics are equally effective against conventional strains, the only value of the test is the potential cost savings that would result if the test allowed the use of a cheaper antibiotic. However, if the newer antibiotics are ineffective against gram-negative bacteria, the value of the test is much higher, because the physician would need to know the type of bacterial strain to prescribe an effective antibiotic. Hence, the value of the test would include the expected cost of avoiding potential massive infection and death, which would be much higher than the cost of prescribing an overly expensive antibiotic.

Sox et al. (1988) capture this insight concerning the magnitude of the consequences of a wrong decision with one final truism:

> *The first priority in differential diagnosis is to think about the diseases you can't afford to miss.*

There are several ways in which the preceding concepts about information and decision making can be used. In this book, we are primarily interested in making qualitative use of the insights captured in the information principles, along with those in the flow principles and behavioral principles, to structure analysis and improvement of hospital operations. But Bayes' Rule can also be used quantitatively as the basis for clinical decision support systems that partially automate the diagnostic and testing decision process. In addition to these practice-oriented uses of Bayes' Rule, the normative framework provided by it can be used in a research context. By contrasting the decisions people should make with those they do make, we can uncover and correct decision biases in health care systems. All these uses can contribute to better understanding of the decision processes on which hospital systems rely, and thereby facilitate better performance.

A.2.3 Behavioral Principles

Hospital operations are essentially about managing flows of patients, materials, and information. But, because it is people who control those flows, hospital management is ultimately about managing people. As a result, management principles that describe essential aspects of human behavior are a fundamental part of the knowledge base underlying hospital operations management.

Of course, the study of human behavior is a vast and varied endeavor. Because it is such a complex subject, no overview could hope to be comprehensive. Therefore, rather than making any pretense at completeness, we offer key principles in four areas that are directly relevant to the impact of human behavior in hospital operations management settings. These are

- **Cognitive efficiency**—Factors that impact the ability of people to plan and execute health care treatment procedures

- **Experience**—Issues that affect the personal experience of patients in a health care system

- **Individual behavior**—Habits, tendencies, and biases that influence the actions of individuals, particularly in work settings such as hospitals

- **Group behavior**—Factors and issues that impact the performance of organizations made up of groups of people

We discuss each of these individually next and call out the essential insights as principles.

A.2.3.1 COGNITIVE EFFICIENCY PRINCIPLES

Carrying out the work of treating patients in a hospital involves the two basic activities of planning and execution. *Planning* involves establishing an agenda (plan) for what should be done, whereas *execution* is the act of carrying out the plan. Both of these involve the mental functions of accumulating information, assessing it, and making decisions. For example, in patient diagnosis (a planning activity), the information includes patient symptoms and test results, the assessment involves enumerating explanations for the symptoms and estimating their likelihood, and decisions are the choices of testing and treatment steps. In surgery (an execution activity), the information includes observations of patient conditions and instrument readings, the assessment involves continual evaluation of patient status, and decisions include what to cut, what not to cut, and when to stop.

Because they rely on mental functions, both planning and execution rely on the cognitive efficiency of the people carrying them out. A person's cognitive functions can be affected by a variety of environmental conditions, as we summarize in the principles in this section. The first factor we consider is workload.

Principle (Workload)—Work efficiency and accuracy exhibit an inverted-U shaped relationship with workload.

This is a version of the Yerkes-Dodson Law, which is named for the two psychologists who first proposed it in 1908 (Yerkes and Dodson 1908). Their conjecture, based on learning experiments with mice, was that performance increases with arousal, but only up to a point. Eventually, too much arousal (stress) is detrimental to performance. In the many years since Yerkes and Dodson proposed it, arousal theory has been widely studied. (See Neiss 1988 for a survey.) One qualification of the original conjecture that seems widely accepted is that a high level of arousal is more helpful to simple tasks than complex ones (see Exhibit A.9). Presumably, that is because the down side of the inverted-U curve is due to some kind of overload. In complex, intellectual tasks, cognitive overload can occur relatively quickly. In contrast, simple, physical tasks can benefit from quite high levels of physical stress before overload occurs.

However, as Neiss (1988) notes, arousal does not fully characterize one's psychological state, so the inverted-U relationship can be modified by other conditions (for example, anger and fear). For this reason, we state the Workload principle in narrower terms, with *workload* rather than *arousal* and *efficiency/accuracy* in place of *performance*. Although the Yerkes-Dodson Law may not hold for all tasks and all circumstances, it captures a reality about human motivation that has been observed in contexts as varied as caffeine use, driver alertness, athletic training, and video games.

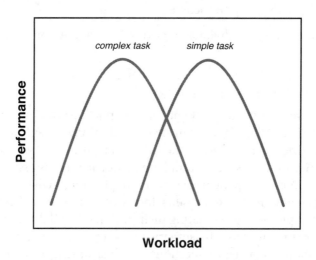

Exhibit A.8   Graphical illustration of Yerkes-Dodson Law.

In health care, the Workload principle is something of an article of faith. Physicians, whose training (for example, residency) is stressful by design, routinely say that a certain amount of stress helps to keep them sharp. But for tasks such as diagnosis, which are cognitively complex, even moderate stress may well put them on the negative slope of the inverted-U curve. Several studies have found a statistical association between high workload and patient mortality (see, for example, Diwas and Terwiesch 2009, Richardson 2006, Sprivulis et al. 2006), suggesting that the stress of a heavy workload is detrimental to patient safety.

The implied mechanism is that the pressure of work may lead to hurrying, skipping steps, and other errors that would not occur under less stressful conditions. On the other end of the scale, low workloads may also inhibit maximum efficiency and accuracy. For example, faced with a lightly loaded ED, staff may feel entitled to work at a slower-than-optimal pace, possibly as psychological compensation for the overload they know is coming. Although a slow pace may have only a moderate effect on waiting times when workloads are light, it may have a more damaging impact on quality. Without the adrenaline boost that comes from a bit of pressure, people may be less sharp, causing them to overlook information, fail to consider alternatives, or make poor choices.

The implication is that matching capacity to demand, in a manner that maintains a busy, but not hectic, workload, can promote more accurate treatment.

Another feature of a chaotic and stressful environment, like that often found in the ED and other parts of the hospital, is frequent interruption of tasks. Indeed, in a study of 5 hospitals and 22 primary care physician offices, Chisholm et al. (2001) found that emergency physicians were interrupted an average of 9.7 times per hour, compared to 3.9 times per hour for primary care physicians. Particularly when the system is busy, a provider who is trying to diagnose or treat one patient is frequently pulled away to tend to another patient or is interrupted by another staff member with questions. We summarize the impact of such interruptions in the following principle.

Principle (Interruptions)—Interruptions of complex tasks degrade the quality of decision making and the efficiency of execution.

Experimental research suggests that, although interruptions can improve performance on simple tasks, it degrades decision making in complex tasks (Speier 1999). The theory that explains this effect is one of information overload. That is, an interruption diverts some attention away from the processing of information cues in the task. In a complex task, in which the decision maker has little cognitive capacity to spare, the distraction of the interruption results in relevant cues being overlooked and hence errors (for example, forgetting to complete actions already begun prior to the interruption). In contrast, in a simple task, in which the decision maker has ample capacity to process the relevant cues, an interruption can actually be beneficial. By using up some of the excess capacity, the interruption can prompt the decision maker to avoid wasting time on irrelevant cues and thus be more efficient. Furthermore, as we noted earlier in the Workload principle, interruptions may move a decision maker away from a low utilization situation that leads to lethargy and lack of acuity. But, from a practical standpoint, because hospitals involve many complex tasks, the important implication of this theory is the negative impact interruptions have on the accuracy of decision making.

A final consequence of a stressful environment is fatigue. Although people can run on adrenaline for a while, eventually they tire. We state this intuitive observation as a principle as follows.

Principle (Fatigue)—Fatigue impairs decision making and task execution.

It is widely known that fatigue degrades mental processes. For instance, Williamson and Feyer (2000) found that being awake for 17 to 19 hours is equivalent to a blood alcohol level of 0.05% on performance in a variety of cognitive tests. Of particular concern is the fact that fatigue specifically affects high-level cognitive functions involved in innovation, flexibility of thinking, risk assessment, awareness of what is feasible, and ability to communicate effectively (Harrison and Horne 2000). Because patient diagnosis and treatment often rely on these skills, the consequences of fatigue can be serious errors. Indeed, Landrigan et al. (2004) found that interns in the Intensive Care unit (ICU) who worked 24-hour shifts made 36% more serious medical errors than interns who worked shorter shifts.

This principle provides a long-term counterbalance to the short-term effect described in the inverted u-shaped relationship of the Workload principle. High workload, pressure, and stress can lead to increased performance for a while. Eventually, however, fatigue becomes a factor and performance declines. This is precisely what Kc and Terweisch (2009) found in studies of patient transport services and cardiothoracic surgery. In both of these very different systems, workers were found to speed up in response to short-term increases in workload. But long-term increases in workload led to decreases in rate, as well as increased mortality rates.

A.2.3.2 PERCEPTION PRINCIPLES

How people perceive a service depends on both their physical experience and their emotional/psychological experience. In a hospital, a patient's physical experience is measured by objective criteria such as LOS, clinical outcome, facility cleanliness, and so on, whereas his emotional/psychological experience is often captured in satisfaction surveys. Patient perceptions, including psychological ones, influence future decisions about choice of hospital, which impacts hospital finances. They also affect word-of-mouth exchanges, which impacts hospital reputation. Hence, it is important for hospital staff to be sensitive to patient perceptions of performance, as well as to objective measures of performance.

One arena where perceptions are particularly important is waiting. Because they do so much of it in a hospital, how patients experience waiting has a strong impact on how they perceive their hospital visit. David Maister (1985) made a number of key observations about the psychology of waiting, which we summarize in the following principle.

Principle (Waiting Time Psychology):

    a. Occupied time feels shorter than unoccupied time.

    b. People want to get started.

    c. Anxiety makes waits seem longer.

    d. Uncertain waits feel longer than known, finite waits.

    e. Unexplained waits feel longer than explained waits.

    f. Unfair waits feel longer than equitable waits.

    g. The more valuable the service, the longer the customer will wait.

    h. Solo waits feel longer than group waits.

These insights have potential for application almost anywhere in the hospital where patients wait. For example, in the ED, studies have consistently shown a strong influence of perceived wait time and provision of information/explanation on patient satisfaction. (See Taylor and Benger 2004 for a survey.) Researchers have also found that people who feel more informed about wait times are less likely to leave the ED without being seen (Arendt et al. 2003).

The idea of managing the psychology of waiting by providing customers information and making them feel actively involved in the process, rather than passive victims of it, is not brain surgery. But it remains an uncommon practice in medicine. There seems to be a deep-seated cultural aversion to providing feedback about waiting times in health care systems. Disney World provides estimates of wait times throughout its theme parks, but few hospitals do. We are more likely to get a phone call from the pizza place explaining that our dinner will be late than we are to get a call from a medical facility explaining that our test or examination appointment will be delayed.

Nevertheless, some hospitals are experimenting with policies to improve the waiting experience. A few hospitals (for example, Detroit Medical Center) are publicizing current times in their EDs, via the web, and through text message. Such a practice could have an objective impact (that is, smoothing arrivals by encouraging people who can wait to come when the ED is not busy) and a subjective impact (that is, make patients feel more informed about their wait times). Some hospitals push the psychological dimension even further by deliberately quoting wait times that are longer than expected, so that patients will be pleasantly surprised (Goldstein 2008).

Another psychologically motivated ED tactic that is being adopted by some hospitals, such as Florida Hospital DeLand, is to advertise "No Wait" emergency rooms. Despite the name, these EDs do not literally offer zero waiting. Instead, they typically promise rapid triage (for example, within 5 minutes) and a limited wait to see a physician (for example, within 30 minutes). Moreover, they usually strive to shift patients from the waiting room into exam rooms and observation units. Consequently, although the total waiting time may be only slightly reduced, patients, who are better informed and more engaged in the process, perceive their waits to be less onerous.

Despite these examples, active management of the psychology of waiting is still rare in hospitals. Presumably this has something to do with item (g) in the Waiting Time Psychology principle. Because health care is important, people will wait for it. But there is competition in the health care sector. For instance, there are independent, for-profit imaging units that offer same-day scheduling, 24-hour report turnaround time, and open MRI technology (for patient comfort). If patients don't have to endure unpleasant waits and stressful procedures, they won't. Hence, hospitals risk losing time-sensitive patients, and the revenue streams they generate, if they don't improve both the duration and the quality of patient waiting times.

Patient perceptions are not just important because of their impact on individual patient visits. They also have a spillover effect, due to the following principle.

Principle (Negative Experiences)—People react more strongly and more durably to negative service experiences than to positive ones.

Marketing research on dissatisfied customers consistently finds that the majority of them do not complain directly to the provider of the negative experience (Hart, Heskett, Sasser 1990). They do, however, tell other people, as noted in the well-worn marketing maxim:

A happy customer tells a friend; an unhappy customer tells the world.

In the past, such a statement was hyperbole. But in the Internet era, it is becoming literally possible. (For example, see the book *Satisfied Customers Tell Three Friends, Angry Customers Tell 3,000* by Blackshaw (2008).)

In hospital settings, the implication is that patient complaint letters are only the tip of the iceberg. There are many more unhappy patients than there are letter writers, and all of them are spreading their negative experiences.

But the Negative Experience principle is manifest in ways beyond word-of-mouth communication. For instance, research shows that customers are more likely to be influenced by negative product reports than positive ones (Herr, Kardes and Kim 1991). Research in a range of settings (relationships, financial transactions, sexual encounters, education, health care, and others) shows a "negativity bias," in which humans give more weight to negative experiences than to positive ones (Baumeister et al. 2001). In marketing, the impact of good and bad experiences on customer loyalty, word of mouth, and other behaviors is so central that the *Journal of Consumer Satisfaction, Dissatisfaction and Complaining Behavior* is devoted exclusively to research on such issues.

In markets where patients have choices about their health care, the impact of negative patient experiences can be substantial. A patient who leaves an ED without being seen despite a long wait is likely to share his negative experience with many people, whereas a patient who is seen promptly is apt to share his positive experience with only a few. A few negative reviews from new mothers on Yelp or Angie's List could drive down volume in a hospital's obstetrics unit. Rudeness at the reception desk may not be overcome by attentiveness in the examination room. These types of psychology-driven impressions can already seriously affect a hospital's reputation. In the future, as electronic networking continues to grow, the impact is likely to be even greater.

A.2.3.3 INDIVIDUAL BEHAVIOR PRINCIPLES

Because a hospital is an organization, we are primarily interested in organizational behavior. But because all organizations are made up of people, the behavior of the organization is strongly influenced by the behavior of the individuals in it. So before we consider principles concerning organizational behavior, we first consider some basic principles about individual human behavior.

We begin with a fundamental reminder about the primacy of individual behavior in organizations.

Principle (Self-Interest)—Individuals, not organizations, are self-optimizing.

This may seem self-evident, because all it states is that people act in their own self-interest. That interest might include a sense of moral commitment or concern for others, but it is nevertheless the objectives of the individual that guides actions, not the objectives of the organization. Even individuals who join an organization strongly believing in its goals, and willing to endure personal sacrifice to promote them, can be worn down by contrary incentives. If the person's self-interest is consistently violated by attending to organizational goals, his loyalty to those goals will diminish over time. At the risk of oversimplifying the complexities of human motivation and behavior, we can avoid a lot of organizational mistakes by assuming self-interest on the part of stakeholders, and designing the community so that those interests align with organizational goals to the extent possible.

The tension between individual goals and organizational goals can play out in transparent ways. A nurse may call in sick to attend a friend's wedding. A technician may receive training to get certification that raises his pay, at a job outside the hospital. A specialist may fail to pick up the phone when on call to spend time with her children. These actions are made in the self-interest of the individual, not the interest of the organization.

Hence, one way to improve organizational performance is to design incentives that align people's self-interest with organizational goals. For instance, offering staff paid personal days, which must be requested in advance, would provide incentive for people to signal planned absences, rather than calling in sick at the last minute, and hence would facilitate better staff scheduling. Setting up clear career paths, through which staff can obtain raises and promotions within the hospital by advancing their skills, could reduce turnover and facilitate coverage of key positions. Providing home videoconferencing connections for on-call specialists, to allow them to consult from home, might make on-call duty less onerous and hence easier to arrange.

But the Self-Interest principle is about more than organizational inefficiency caused by many people going their own ways. In addition to having implications for incentives, this principle can inform operating policies.

For example, the Pooling principle we discussed earlier states that combining sources of variability smoothes out the fluctuations and thereby reduces the need for buffering. A specific application of the Pooling principle would be revisiting the policy of a hospital that has separate CT scanners for the ED, inpatient floors, and outpatient offices. Such an "antipooling" policy could result in one unit's CT being overloaded while another has slack capacity. Centralizing the CT scanners in a single department (Radiology) would pool demand from the various units and reduce waiting due to capacity overloads.

But the benefits of pooling may not be as clear when self-interest is taken into account. Because the hospital units have competing objectives, and people are rewarded for local performance, rather than overall hospital performance, the pooled CT facility may not properly sequence patients. For instance, given full access to the CT schedule, the outpatient offices, which are able to schedule their patients with longer lead times, might tie up blocks of time and prevent the inpatient and ED patients from getting CT scans in a timely fashion.

Hence, to balance the needs of the different types of patients, it may be necessary to introduce constraints on access to the schedule by reserving blocks of time for the various units. Although this might be suboptimal from a capacity utilization perspective, it would preserve the opportunity for ED patients and inpatients to get on the CT schedule more quickly. Once this has been accomplished, the hospital could turn to flexibility measures (for example, releasing unused schedule time to other units) to reduce the utilization inefficiency of the antipooling approach of block scheduling.

The general insight here is that we must recognize the objectives of the individuals in an organization to predict how they will behave. By doing this, we can design organizational policies that strike a better balance between conflicting objectives than might occur naturally.

One behavior that occurs in the context of optimizing individual objectives is hoarding, which we describe in the following principle.

Principle (Hoarding)—People hoard resources in uncertain environments as buffers against an uncertain future.

A prototypical example of resource hoarding in a hospital occurs with regard to beds. In busy teaching hospitals, with occupancy rates in excess of 90%, beds can be a scarce resource. Bed block can lead to patient boarding in the ED or Post Anesthesia Care unit (PACU) and elective surgery cancellation in the OR. But in many hospitals, beds are controlled by more than one unit. If the cardiac unit has an open bed but anticipates a patient arrival soon, it might delay action to release that bed. Multiple units doing the same thing could lead hospital records showing full utilization when in actuality several beds are available. Failing to make full use of these beds is suboptimal for the hospital as a whole but serves the objectives of the individual units.

Hoarding occurs all the time in inventory management settings. Product managers get scolded at for carrying excess inventory but fired for failing to meet customer needs. So they play all kinds of games with record keeping (for example, placing orders immediately after the monthly stock measurement) to keep inventory as high as possible to avoid stockouts. On nursing units, nurses sometimes hoard infusion pumps because they want to be sure one is available when they need it. This behavior is a direct result of being uncertain that, if they order a pump from material services, it will arrive in a timely fashion. They may also place phantom orders to be sure they have the inventory they need. Understanding these incentives and changing the supply or reward system is an essential part of implementing Lean, in industry and in hospitals.

Finally, we state one final principle concerning individual behavior, which plays a large role in all efforts at organizational change.

Principle (Inertia)—People resist change because they know the system they are familiar with, but do not know firsthand the strengths and weaknesses of alternative proposals. Unless there are compelling reasons to believe that significant advantages will accrue, the certain status quo will be preferred to an uncertain future.

Just as a chemical reaction requires an activation energy to get started, organizational change requires some impetus to get over its members' natural, and rational, resistance. For change to occur in an organization, the motivation to change must outweigh the resistance to change for each key stakeholder. This principle has consequences in two situations. The first is in generating a motivation for change in the first place. The second is when some subgroup (perhaps a study group investigating an issue and making recommendations) wants to roll out a change to the rest of the organization.

For example, consider the problem that some patients do not leave their hospital room even after they have been cleared for discharge, pending transportation. Transportation can take hours to arrive, delaying the admission of another patient who may be boarding in the ED or PACU. To address this, the administration might propose a "discharge lounge" where patients can wait, so the rooms can be turned over for new patients. But floor nurses might rationally oppose this. In addition to increasing their workload (more patients flowing through the system), they might be uncertain about: (a) what their responsibility will be for somebody cleared for discharge but still on premises, (b) where the lounge will be, (c) how much attention they need to give lounge patients, and (d) how attending to lounge patients will interfere with their work on the floor. Overcoming their resistance would require addressing these uncertainties, and possibly changing assignments, rewards, or involvement in the project to give floor nurses a positive incentive that would outweigh their inertial resistance.

A.2.3.4 GROUP BEHAVIOR PRINCIPLES

Organizational behavior is the result of individual behavior. Decisions can only be made by minds, and only people have minds; organizations do not (Litterer 1969). But, as we noted in the Self-Interest principle, individuals make decisions based on their own objectives. An organization is a collection of individuals who believe they can attain at least some of their objectives better by being part of the organization than by leaving it. In contrast to economic models that treat organizations as unitary optimizing agents within a competitive landscape, behavioral theories of organizations begin with the explicit or implicit bargains by which individuals become participants (Baumol 1964). As Cyert and March (1963) observe:

> It has been proposed that organizations be considered as coalitions of people who have agreed to join together in return for satisfaction of certain of their objectives. This agreement is arrived at by a process of bargaining and is recorded in the organizational structure, the budgets, and the policies.

The resources that feed these goal attainment desires come from the external market as reward for the social role the organization plays. A hospital is an organization with two broad sets of goals: one aimed at the needs of its customers (patients), and the other aimed at the organization's members (staff). Revenue generated from customers allows the hospital to invest in internal operations that support the collective goals of members, who otherwise would not remain with the organization. For example, a hospital OR invests revenues from patients in surgical facilities and equipment that facilitate better patient treatment and, because they are too expensive for individual surgeons, provide incentive for surgeons to remain affiliated with the hospital.

Once an organization has struck the necessary bargains to ensure member participation, the collective decisions by the members determine the behavior of the organization. However, the objectives and decisions of individuals within an organization are not weighted equally. All organizations have power structures that weight the influence of some members more than others. Therefore, the manner in which individual behavior is translated into group behavior depends critically on the following principle.

Principle (Key Stakeholders)—All organizations have key stakeholders with veto power whose approval is necessary to implement changes.

Note that for purposes of this principle, we distinguish between *stakeholders*, who are people with an interest in an organization, and *key stakeholders*, who are people with effective veto power. For example, in the OR, surgeons, administrators, and representatives of the nurses' union are typically key stakeholders. On the hospital floors, hospitalists and staff supervisors are key stakeholders. Any major initiative will need their approval to be implemented. If any key stakeholder perceives a proposed action as conflicting with his goals, he may block, delay, or alter the action.

Hospitals tend to have more key stakeholders than other types of organizations. Unlike a factory or military organization, in which a hierarchical organization ensures that control rests with a relatively small number of individuals, hospitals are flat organizations with many key stakeholders—administrators, hospitalists, surgeons, nurses, technicians—all of whom are potentially capable of preventing initiatives from going forward.

Combining the Self-Interest and Key Stakeholders principles leads to the following principle.

Principle (Veto Power)—For a proposal to be implemented, all key stakeholders must perceive themselves to be better off with the proposal than without it.

In other words, if the team trying to implement a change does not take the time to (a) identify the key stakeholders affected by the change, and (b) solicit and understand their concerns, the implementation is likely to fail. For example, suppose the hospital administration wishes to extend the hours of operation in the ORs to make better use of existing resources and increase revenue. But suppose also that surgeons, who are key stakeholders, regard late-afternoon surgeries as personally inconvenient and potentially unsafe (because of fatigue problems within the surgical staff and because of inadequate evening coverage of the surgical ICU [SICU]). Without attention to the concerns of the surgeons, the extended hours will not happen.

If a change makes at least one key stakeholder better off and makes no key stakeholder worse off, then we describe the change as *Pareto efficient*. The term comes from the Italian economist Vilfredo Pareto (1848–1923) who introduced the idea in studies of income distribution. It has since become a standard concept in economics. The following principle gives the conditions under which a Pareto-efficient outcome is possible.

Principle (Pareto Efficiency)—If benefits can be transferred from one group to another (for example, via the transfer of money or time or some other medium of exchange) and if there exists a policy that improves the overall performance of a system, there exists an allocation of the total benefits that makes all key stakeholders better off.

Note that there are two requirements for making all key stakeholders better off: (1) the change must make the overall system better off, and (2) it must be possible to transfer benefits from one group to another. The first condition is obvious—a change that makes the overall system worse off cannot possibly benefit everyone in it. But the second condition is more subtle. If we are talking about outcomes that are entirely measured in monetary terms, as Pareto did in his income distribution studies, it is clear that a change that increases the total amount of money can make everyone better off. All we have to do is find a way to share the extra money among everyone.

There are hospital scenarios in which benefits can be monetized to facilitate sharing. For example, suppose that the only problem with expanding the OR schedule to late afternoon hours is the personal inconvenience of surgeons and surgical staff members. Then one potential solution would be to ask the surgeons and staff members how large a "shift bonus" would be required to make them indifferent between an early-morning procedure and a late-afternoon procedure. The additional pay required would differ among individuals, based on their personal preferences for time and money. Once these amounts are known, the administration could establish bonus levels that are large enough so that enough people will find them attractive to staff the later hours. If the increased revenue from the expanded hours exceeds the extra pay, then everyone—administrators and clinical staff alike—will be better off.

Unfortunately, it is not always possible to monetize the impact of changes. For example, beyond a certain salary level, surgeons may no longer be motivated by money and may value their quality of life instead when considering proposals to work longer hours. If they will not accept money in exchange for time, there is no common medium of exchange between the hospital administration and the surgeon.[8]

It can be the case, however, that a monetary exchange is possible through an indirect means. For example, if the impediment to extended OR hours is surgeon concern about safety in the ICU, due to the number of staff on duty, then giving surgeons bonus pay is unlikely to resolve the problem. Surgeons, like all clinical staff, have individual objective functions that include concerns for patient well-being, so they are not prone to exchanging patient safety for personal gain. However, if the hospital invested some of the increased revenue into increased evening ICU staffing, the surgeons' concern over safety might be assuaged.

Another example of indirect compensation arises if the surgeon concern about late afternoon surgeries is start time reliability. For instance, unlike a 7 a.m. procedure, which has nothing scheduled ahead of it and is likely to start on time, a 4 p.m. procedure could be delayed if any of the preceding procedures in the same OR run long. Although it might be possible to compensate surgeons and other staff for the possibility of having to wait, another option would be to increase the white space between procedures to reduce the likelihood that a procedure that runs long will delay subsequent procedures. Which alternative is better depends on surgeon preferences (that is, their "price" for delays) and the variability of procedure times, which influence the amount of white space needed to protect downstream procedures. (See Lovejoy and Li 2002 for a discussion of assessing surgeon preferences and modeling OR start time reliability.)

Finally, even if a Pareto-efficient improvement exists, it will not come about unless the key stakeholders are motivated to change. In general, people are motivated to change something when there is sufficient dissatisfaction with the status quo, as a result of a divergence between the goals of some key stakeholders and the performance of the organization (in meeting those goals). Of course, one possible outcome is dissatisfied members choosing to leave. But, if they still believe the organization in some altered form can offer them net benefits, the members will argue for change. This can also occur if members are motivated by forecasting a future divergence, rather than by experiencing a current one. For example, if external customers abandon the organization because its performance does not meet their needs, this will rob the organization of the resources it needs to attend to internal stakeholders. If internal stakeholders see deterioration in financial performance metrics, they can be motivated to act to stave off the impending problems.

We can summarize the motivation for change within an organization as follows.

Principle (Motivation for Change)—Motivation for change comes from a perceived or projected divergence between organizational performance and the goals of its key stakeholders.

For example, the physicians in a hospital ED might perceive the patient overcrowding situation to be contrary to their goals. So they might push for increased staffing to reduce wait times and increase patient safety. But motivation alone is not sufficient to bring about change. Change, particularly if it involves adding staff or resources, is costly. So there must be some organizational slack (time and surplus resources) to invest in the change process. Organizations with no slack may understand the need for change but may not be able to do anything about it. They are doomed to the status quo, no matter how unsatisfactory that is.

Given motivation and resources, an organization carries out change by going through three basic stages: concept generation, concept selection, and implementation.

In the *concept generation* stage, many alternative routines are developed and considered, usually by some subgroup within the organization. Often this involves more data gathering and interpretation as new concepts are built up by mixing and matching desirable components of older concepts.

The principles offered earlier in this appendix and the generic improvement tables we develop from them later are intended to help hospital staff identify an ample range of possible improvement alternatives. For example, the Variability principle states that variability causes queueing. So an alternative to adding staff to reduce ED overcrowding is to reduce the variability that causes the queuing. The many ways patient arrivals might be smoothed are candidate ways to address overcrowding at a lower cost than adding staff.

In the *concept selection* stage, the best among the generated alternatives is selected. The challenge here is to define *best*. This should be defined relative to the key performance metrics of the organization. If best cannot be defined to align with those key performance metrics, those metrics are not useful and may be dysfunctional for guiding the organization. But, another consideration in selecting the best solution is its chances of successful implementation, which requires (by the Veto principle) that the goals of all key stakeholders be taken into account. Note that the goals of key stakeholders may diverge in some significant ways (but not in totality) from the goals of the organization, so when one considers the goals of the organization as a whole and the goals of its individual subgroups, best may be a compromise between the ideal and the politically feasible.

Finally, in the *implementation* stage, the results are communicated to the organization and steps are taken to institutionalize them. This can be easy if the previous stages were executed well. If a clear need for change is apparent and the best concept was selected with implementation in mind, roll-out should be relatively straightforward. However, as a standalone activity, implementation requires that (a) a convincing need for change is effectively communicated, (b) the reservations of all key stakeholders are recognized and defused, and (c) a plan for implementation is followed. Part (b) includes making a convincing case to all key stakeholders with veto power that the proposed change will offer them net benefits in excess of its costs. This is why change within a department is always easier than systemic change, because the latter must co-opt people with different parochial objectives and metrics.

A.3 Performance Metrics

The bridge between principles and practices is a set of performance metrics that we can use to rank and evaluate alternate improvement plans. But selecting metrics to represent the objectives of the hospital can be a thorny task because, as we noted earlier, hospital objectives are a complex composite of the objectives of the key stakeholders. Ideally, a hospital would use a bargaining process to evolve a global set of metrics, to which local metrics of individual units would be aligned. But the reality is that such bargaining processes rarely converge. So hospitals wind up with global metrics that may or may not influence local metrics and local metrics that may or may not be aligned with one another.

However, misalignment in metrics is usually not the result of a fundamental disagreement about the underlying issues that make up performance. No one thinks that more patient injuries or slower response times are good. Where the disagreements occur is in the weighting of the elemental metrics, especially where there is competition for resources. For example, the ED and the OR may disagree on whose patients should receive priority for lab test results. Two inpatient units may disagree over whose patient should receive priority for a bed. (For example, can the cardiac unit hold a bed in anticipation of a patient rather than release it to an obstetrics patient who is already waiting?) And any two units within the hospital are almost certain to disagree about whose capital improvement project is more worthy of funding.

We cannot resolve the problem of priority conflicts at the operational level, because these are an issue of strategy. An institution that has staked out a strategic position as a cardiac destination hospital should have different priorities from an institution that has strategically positioned itself as a local family hospital. So we will sidestep the weighting issue and instead focus on the basic metrics that serve as building blocks for measuring performance of any hospital unit.

At the detailed level, metrics vary greatly between units and institutions. For instance, a common metric in the ED is "door to balloon time" for ST segment elevation myocardial infarction (STEMI) patients. Although very important to this one class of patients in the ED, this metric is not applicable to other classes of ED patients or patients beyond the ED. However, it belongs to a generic class of metrics, namely time metrics, which are broadly applicable to many settings. Other examples of time metrics are LOS in the ED, TAT in the pathology lab, delay from diagnosis to surgery in the OR, hospital bed turnaround time, and so on.

But time isn't the only category of metrics that matters in a hospital. Quality metrics, which include accuracy of diagnosis and treatment, as well as patient safety, are also essential. We can create a reasonably comprehensive list of hospital performance metrics by starting with the extremely broad operational, clinical, financial, and organizational categories and then breaking these down into (still very broad) generic classes as follows:

Operational Metrics

> **Volume**—Number of patients treated

> **Time**—Time to begin treatment, length of treatment

Clinical Metrics

> **Quality**—Effectiveness of care

> **Patient satisfaction**—Happiness of patients with their experience

Financial Metrics

> **Cost**—Cost per patient to deliver care

> **Revenue**—Rate of money collected

Organizational Metrics

Staff satisfaction—Happiness of staff with their working environment

Learning—Number and effectiveness of new practices adopted by organization

In an improvement initiative, a unit, task force, committee, or whatever group of people is responsible, will specify a performance metric or metrics to be improved. In cases involving operations issues, these metrics will almost always fall into the preceding eight categories. For example, the OR might seek to increase the number of procedures per day (a volume metric). The ED might seek to reduce time to first treatment of patients (a time metric). An inpatient unit might seek to reduce the number of patient falls (a quality metric). An outpatient clinic might seek to improve its scores on patient evaluation surveys (a patient satisfaction metric). A clinical lab might seek to reduce the cost per test (a cost metric). A hospital might seek to increase profit (a combined revenue and cost metric) from its cardiac unit, to support other hospital functions. A nursing unit might seek to increase the level of dedication indicated by nurses on an employee satisfaction survey (a staff satisfaction metric) as part of an effort to increase the number of process improvement ideas submitted to suggestion boxes (a learning metric).

Once metrics have been established, the next step in the improvement process is to identify candidate policies for addressing them. This is where management principles come in. By breaking down the structure of each of the eight generic metrics, we can identify principles that are likely to be relevant to improvements aimed at each one. We do this for each of the generic metrics next.

A.3.1 Volume Metrics

For any resource, the fundamental relationship for volume is:

throughput = capacity × utilization

where throughput is the output rate of the process, capacity is the maximum rate that could be achieved if the resource were always busy, and utilization is the fraction of time the resource is actually busy.

As an example, consider an OR and suppose that procedures take 2 hours on average. Then, assuming a 24-hour day, the capacity of the OR is 12 procedures per day. However, due to unscheduled hours in the night, scheduled white space between procedures, cancellations, and other factors, suppose the OR is actually being used for surgery only 50% of the time. Then the throughput is capacity × utilization = $12 \times 0.5 = 6$ procedures per day.

This expression for throughput implies that actions that increase either capacity or utilization will increase throughput. So the System Capacity and Utilization principles are obviously relevant to any effort to increase volume. The Batching principle, which identifies a trade-off between resource capacity and batch size, is also directly applicable.

Principles that deal with task efficiency provide insights into how to increase capacity by reducing task times. The Task Simplification, Task Standardization, Intuitive Information, Workload, and Interruptions principles provide a variety of levers for speeding tasks.

Finally, the Variability Buffering in a Service System corollary tells us that variability and utilization interact. That is, if we want to keep delay times in a variable service process below an acceptable level, we must buffer the process with capacity (that is, by keeping utilization below some limit). For example, if we want rapid turnaround times in an ED lab, then, because lab orders are necessarily variable, we must staff the lab so that utilization is not too high. If, however, we could reduce the variability, we could operate the lab at a higher level of utilization without increasing turnaround times.

This implies that the principles related to variability—namely, the Variability, Variability Buffering, Buffer Flexibility, and Pooling principles—are all relevant to increasing volume of a process without increasing delay. For example, folding the ED lab into the clinical lab of the hospital is a form of pooling, which would reduce arrival variability and hence permit higher utilization while maintaining short turnaround times. This is the reason that some hospitals have gone to centralized labs without priority schemes; by reducing variability and operating at moderate utilization levels, they are able to provide rapid turnaround times for all tests.

A.3.2 Time Metrics

For any entity (patient, lab specimen, test result, and so on), we can divide the system time (flow time, LOS, turnaround time, or whatever this time is called in the specific application) into the following:

system time = sum of service times + sum of queue times

That is, entities are either being served or are waiting to be served.[9] This implies that there are two basic ways to reduce system time: (1) speed up the actual service steps, or (2) reduce queueing.

Speeding up service is generally a matter of *waste reduction*, which amounts to elimination of actions that do not directly contribute to servicing the entity. For example, carrying specimen to the laboratory does not directly contribute to the generation of test results. So a pneumatic tube delivery system that eliminates this step is a form of waste reduction.

Several principles, including the Task Simplification, Task Standardization, Intuitive Information, Workload, Interruptions, and Fatigue principles, deal with ways to reduce mean task times. Hence, all of these are relevant to initiatives to improve time metrics.

Although speeding up service tasks can certainly help speed entities through hospital systems, reducing queueing can usually help even more. The reason is that most entities spend more time waiting than being served. For instance, the LOS of patients in the ED might be more than four hours, when the actual hands-on treatment time adds up to less than 30 minutes. Hence, the first places to look for ways to speed up a hospital flow are the places where entities wait. For example, ED patients wait in the waiting room, in the examination rooms, at imaging facilities, for lab test results, for transport personnel, and so on.

The Utilization and Variability principles tell us that queueing is a consequence of utilization and variability. Hence, these two principles are germane to the task of increasing speed through the elimination of queueing. They also imply that principles dealing with increasing capacity (which decreases utilization) or reducing variability are relevant to speeding hospital flows. Principles that deal with increasing capacity are the Task Simplification, Task Standardization, Intuitive Information, Workload, Interruptions, and Fatigue principles. Principles that deal with reducing variability and its consequences are the Variability Buffering, Buffer Flexibility, Pooling, Task Simplification, Task Standardization, and Intuitive Information principles.

The Batching principle implies that reducing batch sizes is another way to reduce waiting times. For example, collecting patient specimens in batches means that the first specimen in the batch will wait until the last specimen in the batch before it is delivered to the lab. Runners or pneumatic tubes that permit specimens to be delivered one at a time (or at least in smaller batches) reduce this waiting time.

Finally, the Critical Ratio Sequencing principle implies that queue times of some classes of entities can be reduced at the expense of the queue times of other classes of entities. For example, reserving some space on the MRI scanner schedule for emergency cases reduces the waiting time of these cases but increases the waiting time of less urgent cases.

A.3.3 Quality Metrics

Ideally, the quality of a hospital would be measured against the perfection of patient outcome. But this isn't a realistic standard given incompleteness of medical knowledge, limitations in technology, and the complexity of the human body. So a more realistic target is implementation of the best decisions and treatment actions possible given the current state of medical knowledge and technology. Under this standard, an undesirable outcome that results despite care that is judged to be consistent with best practice is not considered an error. However, if in retrospect, trained professionals would judge the decisions or procedures administered to a patient to be inconsistent with best practice, this constitutes a breach of quality.

There are two basic ways to attain the best patient care consistent with the current state of the art:

- **Do it right the first time**—That is, make the right decisions and take the right actions at each step in the process. In industry, this is referred to as *quality at the source*. Because it is the most efficient way to achieve a quality outcome, this is the gold standard of quality control.

- **Make corrections so that the ultimate outcome is correct despite intermediate errors**—If decision or execution errors are made during the process, the outcome can still be consistent with best practice provided the errors are caught before the end of the process. For instance, if a physician makes an incorrect diagnosis but corrects it upon consultation with a specialist before treating the patient, the ultimate treatment may still be as good as possible from the patient's perspective. Similarly, if a lab test is improperly done but the error is detected before any results are reported, the ultimate report may still be as good as possible from the perspective of the physician who requested the test. In industry, this is referred to as *inspecting quality into* or *reworking* the process. Because it generally requires more steps, more cost, and more time than doing it right the first time, rework is a less desirable form of quality. But it is better than letting errors escape the process and harm patients.

We measure the extent to which we "do it right the first time" via *accuracy metrics*, and the extent to which we "ultimately get it right" via *protection metrics*. An example of an accuracy metric is the percentage of laboratory orders that are entered correctly. There are literally thousands of first-pass quality metrics with which to characterize the extent to which tasks are done correctly without repetition. An example of a protection metric is a count of *near miss* (or *no harm* or *good catch*) incidents in the OR, which represent errors that did not lead to patient harm. Identifying and studying such incidents can help improve accuracy to avoid future errors and build stronger protection mechanisms for keeping patients safe from errors that do occur.

Like all knowledge-based work systems, hospital processes involve decisions and tasks. So accuracy is a matter of both making the correct decisions and executing tasks in accordance with best practices. Principles that deal directly with the accuracy of decision making include the Test Quality, First Impressions, and Incidence Rate principles. Principles that deal with environmental conditions that can degrade decision making accuracy are the Workload, Interruptions, and Fatigue principles. Finally, the Intuitive Information principle is related to decision-making accuracy because correct decisions require correct processing of information.

Because the accuracy of task execution is directly influenced by the complexity of the task, the Task Simplification and Task Standardization principles are also central to efforts to improve accuracy of hospital processes. Less directly, queueing can lead to a degradation of execution accuracy by promoting hurrying. The Variability Buffering principle, which points out that all variability will be buffered somehow, includes two types of variability that affect accuracy. These are *quality variability*, which refers to the short-term phenomenon that quality (execution accuracy) declines as task times are compressed, and *system degradation variability*, which refers to the long-term phenomenon that performance (execution accuracy again) is degraded when people are stressed by repeatedly coping with overloads. This implies that all the principles dealing with utilization and variability (Utilization, Batching, Variability, Buffer Flexibility, Pooling, Task Simplification, and Task Standardization) are also relevant.

Note that task simplification and task standardization are mentioned twice in the preceding paragraph. This is not a mistake. Simplifying the tasks in a process (by reducing complexity) reduces opportunities for error, whereas standardizing the tasks in the process (by using best practice procedures) makes errors less likely. So applying simplification and standardization directly to a process is one way to improve execution accuracy. At the same time, simplification and standardization of upstream processes will reduce variability of the flow into the process in question. This will reduce queueing backups and hence the need to hurry and the errors this causes.

For example, simplifying/standardizing the procedure for conducting an MRI will reduce errors in the MRI process. But simplifying/standardizing the upstream processes of scheduling, receiving, and prepping patients will smooth the flow of patients into the MRI. This will reduce the need for the technician to hurry to catch up and hence will reduce errors due to haste.

Sadly, no amount of effort devoted to accuracy can ensure that every decision and every action in a complex process is carried out correctly. There are simply too many ways to go wrong to prevent them all. Mistakes *will* happen.

But mistakes need not lead to bad outcomes. For example, an extended power outage might cause a refrigerator full of spoiled food in one house but not another, because the second house has a backup generator, a form of protection. A laboratory test might be carried out incorrectly (contaminated, preparation error, wrong reagent, incorrect tester settings, and so on) but lead to a result that is caught in an out-of-range value check (a form of protection) that is detected and used to stop the report from going forward. Redoing the test might slow the turnaround time but will avoid a potentially disastrous diagnostic error.

The two principles that pertain directly to protection are the Foolproofing and Redundancy principles. Somewhat less directly, the Intuitive Information principle applies to protection, because information is essential to spotting errors and circumventing their consequences. The previous example of an out-of-range value check is made possible by displaying information in an obvious manner (for example, warning message on report, alarm on tester, and so on).

A.3.4 Patient Satisfaction Metrics

Patient satisfaction is an inherently subjective measure. Only an individual patient can say whether he is happy with his hospital experience. Because people are different, one person might perceive a hospital visit positively, even though another perceives an identical (in terms of all measurable metrics) visit negatively. Hence, satisfaction metrics are always based on patient responses to surveys, given onsite or as follow-up questionnaires/interviews. Many hospitals use home-grown survey tools, but there are efforts to create standardized instruments so that satisfaction metrics can be compared across institutions (see, for example, HCAHPS 2010).

When tracking patient satisfaction, hospitals usually look at the average response score to a single summary question. (For example, "Rate on a scale of 1 (bad)—4 (excellent) your overall satisfaction with your recent hospital stay.") But more specific questions ("Rate the frequency with which nurses treated you with courtesy and respect during your stay: 1 (never)—4 (always)") can be useful in evaluating units or processes within the hospital. Furthermore, in addition to the mean response to a question, it is sometimes useful to note percentages (for example, the percent of patients who rated their experience as "bad"). The reason is that a score of 3.5 has a very different meaning if it results from an even split of "4 (excellent)" and "3 (good)" responses or from 83% "4 (excellent)" responses and 17% "1 (bad)" responses. If the latter were the case, we should dig deeper into the reasons that so many patients were miserable during their stays.

Obviously, the most direct way to make patients happy is to provide them with responsive, high-quality care. So all the previous avenues for treating more patients (volume), treating them more quickly (time), and treating them well (quality) are avenues for increasing patient satisfaction. Hence, all the previously mentioned principles are relevant to satisfaction improvement initiatives.

But good, fast service is not always enough to result in high satisfaction. The reason, again, is that experience is subjective. If hospitals are going to measure themselves in terms of subjective patient experience, they must also actively manage those experiences. Although there are many results from the field of psychology that may apply to how patients experience hospitals, the insights that are most relevant to hospital operations are those captured in the Waiting Time Psychology principle. The main implication of this principle is that shortening waiting times is not the only way to make patients less happy about waiting. We can also improve the experience of waiting.

A.3.5 Cost Metrics

No hospital, whether for-profit or not-for-profit, can survive if it consistently operates at an overall loss. So management of finances is a crucial component of hospital management. We can use many metrics to track financial performance, including profitability, liquidity, debt-to-asset ratio, net patient revenue per full time equivalent (FTE), and many others. But, because this is a book on hospital operations, not hospital accounting, we will focus on unit cost as an essential financial metric that is closely linked to operating performance.

Unit cost (the cost to deliver a specific service) is important to solvency because reimbursement rates are often set by the government (Medicare, Medicaid) or insurance companies. If unit cost exceeds the reimbursement rate for a procedure, the hospital will run an operating loss on that procedure. In the American system, reimbursement rates vary widely for the same procedure. Furthermore, market rates for different services differ greatly with regard to their costs, making some procedures highly profitable and others highly unprofitable. As a result, all hospitals make profits on some patients and take losses on others. The goal, therefore, is not to achieve unit costs that make all patients profitable, but to hold costs down so that the hospital does not run an operating loss in the aggregate.

We can express the unit cost for a specific procedure as follows:

$$\text{unit cost} = \text{variable unit cost} + \frac{\text{fixed cost}}{\text{volume}}$$

where variable unit cost consists of all costs directly related to provision of the service (for example, labor and materials), fixed (or overhead) cost is made up of all costs that are not directly associated with specific services (for example, administrative/supervisory labor, depreciation of physical plant and equipment, and so on), and volume represents the number of services provided in the period over which fixed cost is measured (usually a year). In a highly specialized hospital that provides only one type of service (for example, Shouldice Hospital, which only performs hernia repairs) calculation of unit cost is straightforward, because all fixed costs are allocated to the same service type. But in typical hospitals that provide many different services, the accounting problem of allocating fixed costs to services is a thorny one. As a result, hospitals seldom know the true costs of their services, a fact that greatly complicates the health care debate.

But for purposes of identifying principles that are related to cost control, the preceding equation, without details of fixed cost allocation, is sufficient. It tells us that reducing unit cost requires reducing variable unit cost, reducing fixed cost (without losing volume), increasing volume (without increasing fixed cost), or some combination of these.

The most direct way to reduce variable cost is by increasing task efficiency and quality to reduce labor and correction costs. The Task Simplification and Task Standardization principles address both efficiency and accuracy, so they are directly relevant to cost control. Other principles that deal with reducing (costly) errors, including the Foolproofing, Redundancy, Intuitive Information, Value of Information, Test Quality, Handoffs, First Impressions, Workload, Interruptions, and Fatigue principles, are also relevant.

To address the fixed cost component of unit cost, we note that

$$\frac{\text{fixed cost}}{\text{volume}} = \frac{\text{fixed cost}}{\text{capacity}} \times \frac{\text{capacity}}{\text{volume}} = \frac{\text{fixed cost}}{\text{capacity}} \times \frac{1}{\text{utilization}}$$

where the last step follows from the definition of utilization as

$$\text{utilization} = \frac{\text{volume}}{\text{capacity}}$$

The implication is that the fixed cost contribution to unit cost can be reduced in the obvious way by reducing total fixed cost (for example, by streamlining administrative costs, instituting energy conservation measures, negotiating better terms on equipment purchases, and countless other ways). But it can also be reduced by increasing capacity or utilization. Hence, the Utilization and Batching principles are directly relevant.

Less direct, but just as important, is the fact that the Variability and Utilization principles imply that variability and utilization combine to cause queueing. If the hospital places a limit on queueing delay (for example, the ED sets an upper bound on LOS or a lab establishes a maximum turnaround time), then for a given level of variability, utilization must be kept below some limit. However, if variability were reduced, utilization could be increased without increasing queueing delay. Hence, principles that deal directly with reducing variability, including the Variability Buffering, Buffer Flexibility, Pooling, Task Simplification, and Task Standardization principles, can serve as tools for reducing the fixed cost component of unit cost. Because errors induce variability by leading to unpredictable correction times, principles that deal with error mitigation, including the Foolproofing, Redundancy, Intuitive Information, Test Quality, Handoffs, First Impressions, Incidence Rate, Workload, Interruptions, and Fatigue principles, are also relevant.

A.3.6 Revenue Metrics

In addition to cost control, the other lever for avoiding solvency is revenue enhancement. Although total hospital revenue may include charitable donations, government support, research grants, and other streams not directly generated by patient care, the portion of revenue associated with hospital operations is operating revenue, which is given by

$$\text{operating revenue} = \text{patient volume} \times \text{revenue per patient}$$

Here, operating revenue is measured in dollars per year, patient volume is measured in patients per year, and revenue per patients is measured in dollars.

The implication is that we can enhance operating revenue by increasing either volume or the revenue per patient. Revenue per patient is influenced by collection (that is, making sure that the hospital is reimbursed as fully as possible for services provided). Because the American health care system is so complex, collection is often a nightmare that occupies substantial amounts of staff time and has even spawned a cottage industry of third parties that earn tidy livings by taking over the billing and collection process for hospitals. Revenue per patient is also influenced by hospital strategy, which influences patient mix. For example, the fraction of fully insured patients, or the fraction of patients who require high reimbursement services like cardiac care, will significantly influence the average revenue per patient. Important as they are, these issues are outside our operations scope, so we will not go beyond mentioning them.

However, the option of increasing volume is very much inside our scope. The Variability and Utilization principles imply that volume can be increased without increasing queueing delay by either increasing capacity or by reducing variability. The Batching, Task Simplification, and Task Standardization principles deal directly with ways to increase capacity. The Variability Buffering, Buffer Flexibility, Pooling, Task Simplification, and Task Standardization principles deal with ways to reduce variability. And the Foolproofing, Redundancy, Intuitive Information, Test Quality, Handoffs, First Impressions, Workload, Interruptions, and Fatigue principles deal with ways to reduce errors, which also reduce variability.

A.3.7 Staff Satisfaction Metrics

Members of the hospital staff must ultimately carry out all hospital performance improvements. A workforce that is unhappy, bitter, and disengaged is unlikely to execute or innovate well. In contrast, vibrant, happy employees who feel a strong sense of loyalty to the organization and commitment to a higher purpose can be an immense source of creativity, flexibility, and quality.

Within the performance improvement process, flexible staff who see what needs to be done and do it serve as capacity buffers via the Variability Buffering and Buffer Flexibility principles. They also serve as quality filters via the Foolproofing and Redundancy principles. But, even more importantly, as engaged problem solvers, satisfied staff members are key contributors of ideas on how to improve operations via the Task Simplification, Task Standardization, Pooling, and many other principles. In short, virtually every idea in this book is easier to translate into practice if a satisfied workforce is in place to make it happen.

A.3.8 Learning Metrics

Changing technology, patient expectations, public policy constraints, and competitive landscapes demand that hospitals continually improve performance over time. This requires ongoing learning, not just by individual staff members, but by the organization as a whole. Learning by an organization involves learning by the individuals in it, but it also involves sharing knowledge among individuals and translating it into improved practices.

Measuring learning is difficult enough at the individual level, as evidenced by the persistent debates over standardized testing in schools. At the organizational level, it is even more difficult. Complex organizations like hospitals do many different things, so they must "learn" in many dimensions. The most direct way to measure learning with respect to a specific performance objective, therefore, is to measure improvement in the metric(s) for that objective. For instance, a steadily declining turnaround time is by definition a measure of a clinical lab's learning to be responsive.

But direct performance measures of organizational learning do not shed much light on how to improve learning. So scholars and practitioners alike look to indirect measures of an organization's ability to learn, such as the number of ideas submitted to a suggestion box, the number of new initiatives adopted, and the number of interpersonal connections maintained beyond one's home unit. These and many other metrics can indicate a culture that supports learning across the organization.

Measured in these terms, it is clear that organizational learning centers on generating, sharing, and using information. Hence, the information principles are core to organizational learning. For instance, the Handoffs and Knowledge Sharing principles are essential to information sharing, whereas the First Impressions principle describes a fundamental tendency toward inertia in the use of information. But organizational learning is about more than information. Because people must work together to facilitate organizational learning, the group behavior principles of Key Stakeholders, Veto Power, Pareto Efficiency, and Motivation for Change characterize human realities that must be recognized in forging a collaborative environment that supports learning. Because organizational learning is vital to all ongoing process improvement efforts, we probe it more deeply next as a generic management challenge.

A.4 Improvement Policies

The previous section generates lists of principles that apply to each of the eight main classes of performance metrics that characterize operating performance of a hospital. But it was probably obvious that the same principles were repeated in different contexts. For instance, reducing variability can be a means to increase volume or speed, which in turn can reduce cost or increase revenue. Conversely, the things we can do to improve quality also reduce variability, which means that they apply to these performance metrics as well. Because there is so much overlap, simply knowing which principles to invoke is not enough. We must also know how to use them.

In this section, we carry the application of principles to performance improvement a step further by systematically invoking the relevant principles to generate generic improvement strategies for three ubiquitous hospital issues: responsiveness, patient safety, and organizational learning. These three issues cut across all areas of the hospital. For example, responsiveness is relevant to the ED in efforts to reduce patient LOS, to the labs and imaging units in efforts to reduce TAT, in the hospital floors in efforts to speed bed turnover, and in the OR in efforts to ensure that procedures are completed in time to maintain the schedule. Patient safety is such a universal concern throughout the hospital that it hardly needs motivation. And organizational learning, the process by which the hospital upgrades its institutional capabilities, is essential to all efforts to improve over time.

For each of these objectives, we appeal to the principles identified earlier to identify generic improvement strategies. Using common-sense logic, we further break down each strategy into more specific paths of action. The result is a table that provides a checklist of improvement options.

In the chapters on specific hospital units, we start with these generic tables and add environmental details to translate the general improvement options into candidate policies for addressing particular problems within the units. For example, we address problems like mitigating ED overcrowding, reducing laboratory turnaround time, lowering the likelihood of hospital bed unavailability, and reducing errors in the OR. At the generic level, these are challenges of responsiveness, safety, or learning. But, because the contexts differ between units, the details of the improvement policies will also differ.

Our intent is that the detailed tables in the chapters will provide insights into hospital problems of current importance, whereas the generic tables in this appendix will provide a structured framework for dealing with other problems of responsiveness, safety, and learning, now and in the future.

A.4.1 Responsiveness

Responsiveness is fundamentally about the speed with which a particular service can be provided. We can invoke the previous principles in a systematic manner to address the problem of increasing speed by addressing the problem in four levels. First, we consider *capacity* by identifying the factors that can avoid a system overload. The only two means for doing this are to reduce workload or increase capacity. Next, we consider *variability* as a cause of queueing congestion that occurs even without a capacity overload. The two ways to reduce variability-induced queuing are to increase synchronization (between demand and capacity) or to reduce variability. Then we consider *sequencing* as a means for improving overall responsiveness by speeding service to some cases at the expense of others. Finally, we consider the *psychology* of waiting to identify ways of increasing patient perceptions of their care in spite of having to wait.

We discuss each of these in turn here and then summarize the overall structure in Table A.1.

Reduce Workload—Reducing workload lowers utilization, which, by the Utilization principle, reduces congestion. There are two ways to reduce workload:

- **Reduce case rate**—The fewer cases (patients, tests, images, or whatever constitutes the unit of work in a system), the less work the system will have to do and hence the better it will be able to keep up.

- **Reduce work per case**—Even if the number of cases does not decrease, if the work per case goes down, the system will have less work and hence will be more responsive.[10]

Increase Capacity—Increasing capacity also reduces utilization and congestion. Note that increasing the capacity of a flow requires increasing the capacity of the bottleneck resource. As we note in the options that follow, this can be done by directly adding capacity to that resource or by reducing blocking/starving of this resource by other resources, which decreases the effective capacity of the bottleneck.

- **Add physical/human resources**—The simplest way to add capacity is to add more physical resources (ED examination rooms, CT scanners, auto analyzers in the lab, hospital beds, ORs, and so on). Of course, this is also the most expensive way to add capacity, so we generally look for alternatives first.

- **Eliminate steps**—Time spent on unnecessary steps constitutes waste or nonvalue added activity. Eliminating this provides more capacity for the (value-added) activities that need to be done. In industry, this type of waste elimination has been promoted under various names, such as *Lean* and *Business Process Engineering*. Certainly, the idea of efficiently completing tasks by avoiding unnecessary steps is as old as the concept of human work and has been a pillar of the industrial revolution. For example, the efficiency brought to Adam Smith's imaginary pin factory by the division of labor was the direct result of dividing work into small, repetitive tasks that could be performed without unnecessary motions (for example, switching from one task to another). The Scientific Management movement of the early twentieth century carried time and motion efficiency to new heights. Anyone who has read the book *Cheaper by the Dozen*, which describes how Scientific Management pioneer Frank Gilbreth applied his work studies to his own household (for example, to tasks ranging from daily showering to tonsillectomies on the kitchen table), knows the almost religious fervor with which efficiency can be pursued.

In hospitals, opportunities for eliminating unnecessary tasks abound. For example, most studies of nursing work have found that nurses spend more time on indirect activities (for example, collecting materials and supplies, confirming doctor's orders, walking, and so on) than on direct patient care. Finding ways to eliminate these nonvalue added steps is an important way to increase capacity, which is often much less expensive than adding more people or equipment.

- **Reduce process times**—Once unnecessary tasks have been eliminated, further increases in capacity can be achieved by making the remaining tasks faster. The default way to do this is to simply work harder. Hospital staff members often work faster during heavy demand periods. But this is not a sustainable strategy. Consistently working beyond a healthy, vigorous pace leads to frustration and errors. This is what the Variability Buffering principle means by *system degradation*. For example, the negative consequences of handling too many patients are apparent in statistics showing that medical outcomes degrade when the ED is overloaded (see, for example, Cowan and Trzeciak 2005).

Standard ways of speeding tasks without working harder and degrading the system include using technology, standardizing procedures, and simplifying tasks. For example, a technology option for speeding the task of triaging patients in the ED is an e-triage system, which structures the sequence of questions and examinations needed to classify patients according to their treatment needs. Because it imposes a set procedure, an e-triage system is also a means of standardizing the process. An example of a task simplification policy might be using a 5S system to organize ORs, to position materials and equipment in a manner that supports rapid cleaning and preparation of the ORs for surgery.

Task elimination and simplification are ongoing processes that require diligence and perseverance. For example, Toyota spent 25 years reducing setup times on punch presses (largely by eliminating unnecessary activities) from several hours to several minutes. An organizational tool for driving this type of continual improvement is the *kaizen event*, in which teams focus on a narrow objective (for example, simplify the check-in process) and are authorized to make changes in layout, procedures, work assignments, or whatever else is necessary. Typically, a kaizen is done quickly, say over a weekend, to maintain a sense of urgency and pace.

- **Balance workloads**—Eliminating steps and speeding process times create capacity from within by either eliminating or speeding tasks to free up resources. Another way to create capacity from within is by balancing workloads, which increases capacity at bottlenecks by borrowing it from nonbottlenecks. That is, it shifts work from high-utilization resources to low-utilization resources. This can be done in both the long term through reassignment of tasks and the short term through dynamic sharing of tasks. An example of a long-term task reassignment would be training an orderly to do a task that a nurse normally does. An example of short-term work sharing would be having a lab technician whose area is currently experiencing a light workload shift over to help out in another area where workload is currently heavy.

A generic difficulty with work sharing programs is one of fairness. If the program makes you believe that by slacking off you will be able to shift some of your work to someone else, it creates a moral hazard to working hard. The result can be that good, hardworking employees wind up carrying their less devoted colleagues and feel resentful for having to do so. In the long run, this can lead to everyone becoming less productive.

There are two approaches for overcoming this problem: (1) rewarding individual performance and (2) rewarding team performance. An example of rewarding individual performance would be instituting a tracking mechanism for a staff member who moves from his station to help out at another station to log this activity. By rewarding such activity via bonuses or consideration in performance evaluations, the hospital can provide incentive for the hard workers to continue to work hard. Of course, it is easier to describe a reward system than it is to make one work. If workloads are unbalanced (as they always will be in practice), the person with the lighter average workload will have more opportunity to take on outside work and gain reward than will the person with the heavier average workload.

The second approach to rewarding team performance gets around the tendency to pit individuals against one another by rewarding the team as a whole. Whether the rewards are in the form of a financial bonus, public recognition (for example, team of the month), preferential treatment on the work schedule, or whatever, they are given out to the team as a whole. For example, if everyone on the staff of the hematopathology lab gets a bonus if they bring turnaround times below a targeted level, technicians will have incentive to switch from clinical flow cytometry to the coagulation laboratory if needed to keep up with workload fluctuations.

In general, teamwork approaches work best in systems with relatively few people (Kameda et al. 1992). When teams get large, the problem of "free ridership" creeps in because an individual may feel that his effort has little impact on the performance of the overall team. So, if a hospital wants to promote work sharing across a large team (for example, nurses on a floor), it may be necessary to reward highly productive people individually.

■ **Increase task parallelism**—Yet another way to create capacity from within is by doing more than one thing at once by multitasking. This can be made possible through technology; for instance, a pneumatic tube delivery system makes it possible for a phlebotomist to send a specimen to the lab even while he continues collecting samples. It can also be facilitated by job design. For example, nurses multitask routinely when they interview patients while they are taking blood pressure or setting up supplies.

■ **Reduce blocking/starving**—All the preceding options are means for directly increasing the capacity of a flow. But recall that we noted earlier that

$$\text{throughput} = \text{capacity} \times \text{utilization}$$

Hence, the other way to increase the amount of work that can be processed by a flow is to increase utilization. To do this, we must reduce either blocking or starving of the bottleneck resource. An example of blocking is when a patient continues to occupy an ED exam room because he is waiting for a hospital bed to open up. Hence, reducing the frequency of this bed block phenomenon will act very much like increasing exam room capacity. An example of starving is when a heavily scheduled MRI scanner is idle because of a glitch in the patient prep process.

Note that blocking can be caused by downstream variability, whereas starving can be caused by upstream variability. Hence, variability reduction (for example, leveling hospital bed occupancy or making MRI patient prep more reliable) can serve as a source of effective capacity by allowing better use of the bottleneck. But, by the Variability principle, variability reduction can also improve responsiveness by reducing queueing. So we will bring up variability reduction again later.

Improve Synchronization—According to the Variability principle, unsynchronized variability causes congestion, so measures to better synchronize fluctuations in demand and capacity will reduce congestion. There are only two ways to synchronize demand and capacity: either adjust capacity to meet demand, or adjust demand to meet capacity.

■ **Adjust demand rate**—The standard way to adjust demand rate is by making appointments. This is routine for procedures like scans and elective surgery that require expensive capacity. As long as people show up for their scheduled appointments, demand will closely match scheduled capacity. Of course, if people miss appointments or are late for them, the match will be degraded, leading to queueing and underutilization of capacity. So policies that help maintain schedule adherence (for example, reminder phone calls) are also part of a synchronization strategy. Finally, even when scheduling is not possible (for example, when cases are emergencies, as in the ED), it may still be possible to partially synchronize demand with capacity. For instance, posting response times in the ED might encourage nonemergency patients to time their visits with lulls in demand.

- **Adjust capacity**—In environments where work cannot be scheduled, it may be possible to schedule capacity instead. The most easily scheduled capacity is human labor. To the extent that demand is predictable in advance, the staff schedule can match people to demand. For example, phlebotomists and lab technicians can be scheduled to cover the spike in demand for blood tests associated with morning rounds. However, when demand is unpredictable, a staff schedule will only be able to adapt to expected demand patterns. For example, the ED has discernible patterns in average daily demand (see Exhibit 2.5). But on any given day, demand may depart substantially from the average. To synchronize capacity to unpredictable demand, a system can use responsive capacity (for example, calling in ED staff members to cope with a spike in demand).

- **Improve batching**—As noted in the Batching principle, increasing batch size increases capacity when setups are involved. For example, the time for a phlebotomist to deliver samples to the lab can be viewed as a setup because it does not depend on the number of samples being delivered. Hence, if the phlebotomist delivers samples to the lab in batches, he will spend less time walking to the lab than he would if he were to deliver each one individually. The extra capacity gained by delivering samples less frequently can be used to avoid delivery delays due to backups caused by spikes in collection workload.

  However, the Batching principle also implies that increasing batch size too much will increase delay because the first items in a batch (for example, the first sample collected) must wait for the rest of the batch. If batch sizes get large enough, the waiting time penalty will overwhelm the capacity benefit. So maximizing responsiveness requires setting batch sizes to strike a balance between additional capacity and additional waiting time. However, if we can also reduce setup times (for example, reducing delivery times of specimens by establishing multiple drop-off points with transport done by pneumatic tube or human runners), we can gain capacity and reduce waiting times by using smaller batches. So setup time reduction is an option for better matching capacity to demand wherever entities are processed in batches.

Reduce Variability—Reducing variability, in either arrivals or process times, reduces queueing congestion according to the Variability principle. Arrival and process variability have a roughly equivalent impact on queueing, so which one is a more attractive target depends on which is larger or more controllable. However, the Utilization principle implies that the impact of variability is highest at bottlenecks (high utilization resources), so targeting either variability into bottlenecks or process variability at bottlenecks will be more effective than similar improvements at nonbottlenecks.

- **Reduce arrival variability**—Smoothing arrivals of entities to a process reduces queueing by making it less likely that they arrive in bunches. This can be done in many ways depending on the specifics of the system. For example, the arrival of patients to a CT scanner could be smoothed through scheduling (for example, making outpatient appointments). Arrivals could be smoothed by removing sources of variability in the arrival process itself (for example, providing reminder calls so patients don't forget their appointments and providing clear signage so patients are not delayed by getting lost). And arrivals could be smoothed by removing variability in upstream processes (for example, physician rounds could be staggered so that inpatient test requests are spread out over the day). We have already noted that the impact of arrival variability can be mitigated if it is correlated with capacity; for instance, pulling inpatients into the scanner when there are gaps in the outpatient schedule aligns demand with capacity and thereby reduces queueing.

- **Reduce process variability**—Making process (task) times more regular also reduces queueing by making it less likely that an unusually long time for one entity causes a backup of the entities behind it. There are many ways that variability can be introduced into the time to process an entity. For example, in a clinical lab, the time to process a test may vary from one specimen to the next because of setups (for example, reagent preparation), failures (for example, autoanalyzer breakdown), rework (for example, a test must be redone due to an error), operator variation (for example, one tech is more efficient than another, or the same tech is distracted by personal matters on a given day), environmental factors (for example, a bug flies in a tech's eye), and many, many other causes. Identifying variability and driving it out is an important way to improve responsiveness and is a core practice in lean production.

Improve Sequencing—The Critical Ratio Sequencing principle implies that average waiting times of entities can be reduced even if demand, capacity, and variability are not changed. By sequencing entities such that those with short processing times do not wait behind those with long processing requirements, we can reduce the overall average time in a system. Doing this involves two key steps:

- **Generate information**—To sequence entities effectively, we must have information about them in advance of processing. The Critical Ratio Sequencing principle implies that the two key pieces of information are priority and processing time. Priority information is quite common in hospitals. For example, in the ED, priority is estimated in triage, with ESI-1 patients classified as more urgent than ESI-2 patients, who are more urgent than ESI-3 patients. But it is not generated everywhere it might be useful. For example, lab tests for patients who are scheduled to be released are not usually prioritized over tests for other patients. This could result in discharge delays, which in turn could result in bed unavailability that leads to cancellation of a surgical procedure. So there may be additional opportunities to prioritize work in the hospital.

Hospitals generate processing time information even less frequently than they generate priority information. One partial attempt to do so is in triage categories in the ED. Patients classified as ESI-5 require no resources (for example, tests), whereas ESI-4 patients require only one resource and ESI-3 patients require multiple resources. Patients in these categories are not time critical (as are ESI-1 and ESI-2 patients), so they do not differ in priority. Because ESI-5 patients require less time in exam rooms and with ED personnel, SPT (shortest processing time) logic suggests that they should be prioritized over ESI-4 patients, who should be prioritized over ESI-3 patients. Indeed, EDs that use Fast Tracks, which shunt ESI-4 and ESI-5 patients around the rest of the ED, do exactly this. However, large variations in patient treatment times occur within ESI categories, and virtually no EDs attempt to predict these in advance and use them to sequence patients more effectively.

- **Optimize sequence**—Once we have information about priorities and times, we can use it to sequence entities. Depending on the environment, sequencing can influence different things.

To begin with, the Critical Ratio Sequencing principle implies that sequencing entities according to the ratio of priority to process time will strike an efficient balance between urgency and speed. That is, we should process short, urgent entities before long, nonurgent ones. If all entities have the same priority, this rule reduces to sequencing in order of shortest process time, which serves to minimize the average waiting time of entities. If all entities become available at the same time, implementing this rule is relatively straightforward. For example, if a nurse is given a set of patients, each of which must be visited sometime during a shift, then visiting patients with short care times first and long care times last minimizes the average time patients wait for care. If we can attach a cost for waiting (for example, patients who have painful conditions are deemed ten times as "expensive" to keep waiting than patients without painful conditions), then the nurse should visit patients in order of their cost/time ratio. In this case, in which the waiting cost of patients with pain is very high compared to that of patients without pain, this would boil down to first visiting all patients with pain (in inverse order of their expected treatment time), and then visiting all patients without pain (again in inverse order of their expected treatment time).

Sequencing gets more complicated when entities arrive over time (for example, patients arrive at the ED, specimens arrive at the lab, images arrive at the Radiology reading room, and so on). In this situation, taking entities in order of largest critical ratio or shortest process time may violate considerations of equity. For example, taking a patient who just arrived to the ED ahead of a patient who has been waiting for hours because the former requires less treatment time may be efficient, but it may not be fair. So, although critical ratio logic is useful in improving overall responsiveness, it must be tempered by other considerations. For instance, the ED might institute a rule that gives priority to patients who have waited longer than a specified time, regardless of their processing time.

Sequencing can get even more complicated when the impact of a sequence extends beyond the process that is being sequenced. For example, if the sequence in which images are read in Radiology affects the flow of patients through the ED, OR, and inpatient units, then the "cost" coefficient in the critical ratio should reflect this. Of course, saying that we need to define coefficients to reflect the relative urgency of images ordered by different units in the hospital is easier than actually defining them. Understandably, the ED, OR, and inpatient units all think their images should receive top priority. Only by establishing priorities at a hospital-wide level can we hope to facilitate sequencing decisions that involve choices between units.

Another way the impact of sequencing can extend beyond the immediate process is when supporting resources are required. Consider, for example, the problem of sequencing procedures in the OR. If all procedures were equally urgent and all patients came in at the same time (for example, everyone needing surgery on a given week made a request for a time slot on Friday of the previous week), the Critical Ratio Sequencing principle would suggest scheduling the short procedures early in the week and the long procedures late in the week to minimize the average patient wait. If some procedures are more urgent than others, the sequence could be set according to the critical ratio (waiting cost coefficient divided by expected procedure time). If patients arrive over time (as, of course, they do), we might deviate from a strict critical ratio to prevent excessive waiting by lower-priority patients. But, because surgical procedures require resources beyond ORs, we must also consider the impact of the sequence on these. For instance, surgeons and scrub teams may desire contiguous schedules (that is, to avoid having one procedure in the morning and one in the evening, with nothing in between). Procedures may require equipment, such as heart-lung machines, which are in limited supply. So the OR sequence needs to be set so as not to exceed the supply of such equipment. These and other considerations make sequencing and scheduling a difficult and technical management problem. Nevertheless, the Critical Ratio Sequencing principle provides an intuitive starting point from which we can build to meet the needs of specific sequencing challenges.

Enhance Patient Perceptions—There will always be waits in the hospital, despite our best efforts to improve responsiveness. So, one final option for managing wait times is to address the psychology of waiting. Of course, this option only applies to people; specimens in a lab or images in a reading room do not perceive their waits in psychological terms. According to the Waiting Time Psychology principle, a number of factors make waits feel longer or more aggravating, so addressing these can improve patient experiences (and evaluation scores on surveys):

- **Make waits more enjoyable**—A comfortable environment, reading materials, refreshments, a television, a quiet space away from the television, and so on, are examples of options for making waits less onerous.

- **Get patients started**—Because patients are in the hospital to receive care rather than to wait, the most direct way to improve their experience is to get them going on the care process as quickly as possible. For instance, an ED that triages patients quickly and has a physician consult with them early on is apt to be perceived more positively by patients than one that lets patients wait a long time before any clinical contact, even if the total LOS is the same. This is behind the strategies of EDs that make guarantees that patients will see a physician within a reasonably short time (for example, 30 minutes).

- **Reduce patient anxiety**—Hospital visits are often stressful experiences for patients. Anxiety about one's condition or the experience one is about to undergo can cause tension and strain. So anything that the hospital can do to alleviate anxiety can improve the quality of the waiting experience. These things can be large (for example, administering antianxiety medication to patients with significant problems) or small (for example, helping patients keep track of personal articles as they go through the system). The key is to be sensitive to individual patients' needs and address anxiety proactively.

- **Provide information about or explanations of waiting times**—One of the major sources of anxiety in a hospital is the lack of information. Patients often do not know what is about to happen to them or why they are waiting. As a result, they can become restless and resentful. By providing information about how long waits are likely to last, the hospital can reduce some of these negative feelings. Sadly, although Disney World and call centers routinely provide wait time estimates, hospitals seldom do.

  Although information about waits is helpful, explanations can be even more so. For example, telling a patient waiting for a scan that there will be a 30-minute delay is better than simply letting him wait. But telling him that the delay is the result of having to fit in an emergency patient makes the delay more understandable. If the personal communication with the patient can be extended to helping the patient understand his experience and allay concerns, it will go beyond simple information into the realm of emotional support.

- **Make waits more equitable**—Waiting is bad enough, but feeling that one has waited unfairly is worse. The gold standard for fairness is treating patients in first-come-first-serve (FCFS) order. Of course, medical urgency must sometimes take precedence over fairness. But if waits are explained, they can still be perceived as equitable. For example, an ED patient with a minor injury who sees a heart attack patient go ahead of him, but not other patients with minor injuries, is unlikely to feel cheated. But fairness can get complicated. For example, should an MRI operator take the 3:00 patient who is 20 minutes late or the 3:30 patient who is 10 minutes early? Although there may not be clear answers, hospital managers can at least ask whether they would find their own policies fair if they were patients themselves.

- **Make waits proportional to value**—People who would be unwilling to wait ten minutes for a hamburger will wait years for an organ transplant. Obviously, willingness to wait increases with the value of what is being waited for. So long waits for minor services are likely to be particularly irritating. For instance, an outpatient who is sent to the lab for routine blood work and experiences an hour-long wait is likely to be upset and may even leave without being seen. However, although hospitals devote considerable effort to responsiveness for critical services (for example, treatment of urgent patients in the ED or scheduling of emergency procedures in the OR), they are less diligent about noncritical services. But, because waits for these services may annoy patients and undermine their loyalty to the hospital, efforts to bring down wait times for minor services may pay long-term dividends.

- **Facilitate group waiting**—In general, solitary waits are more difficult than group waits because other people can provide entertainment, reduce anxiety, and help us maintain perspective. So, for example, policies that enable family members to stay with a patient as much as possible during their visit can make patients feel better about their waits.

We compile the preceding paths for addressing responsiveness in Table A.1. The basic structure is to start with the primary objective to increase responsiveness and follow this to two levels of more specific objectives that support it. We will use this as the starting point for all tables in the hospital unit chapters that address issues of responsiveness. There we invoke the environmental details of the individual application to pursue these generic objectives to more specific objectives and finally to candidate improvement policies.

Table A.1 Generic Options for Improving Responsiveness

Level 0 Objective	Level 1 Objectives	Level 2 Objectives
Improve responsiveness	Reduce workload	Reduce case rate
		Reduce work per case
	Increase capacity	Add physical/human resources
		Eliminate steps
		Reduce process times
		Balance workloads (for example, work sharing)
		Increase task parallelism
		Reduce blocking/starving
	Improve synchronization	Adjust demand
		Adjust capacity
		Improve batching
	Reduce variability	Reduce arrival variability
		Reduce treatment variability
	Improve sequencing	Generate information
		"Optimize" sequence
	Enhance patient perceptions	Keep patients occupied
		Get patients started
		Reduce patient anxiety
		Provide explanations of waiting times
		Make waits more equitable
		Make waits proportional to value
		Facilitate group waiting

A.4.2 Patient Safety

Ensuring patient safety is a matter of avoiding negative patient outcomes that are avoidable given current best practices. We can invoke management principles systematically by considering the types of failures that can lead to patient harm. First, patients can be harmed by a delay in treatment, which can be avoided through responsiveness. Second, patients can be harmed by errors in decisions, which lead to inadequate treatment plans. Third, patients can be harmed by errors in execution of the treatment plans. Finally, if errors are made somewhere in the treatment process, patient harm can still be avoided through protection mechanisms or reduced through mitigation mechanisms.

We enumerate the ways to improve patient safety along each of these dimensions next and then summarize the overall framework in Table A.2.

Improve Responsiveness—We already enumerated the ways to improve responsiveness. All of those approaches apply to the problem of reducing harm due to treatment delay except for the option of improving patient perceptions of waiting. A patient's clinical outcome only depends on how swiftly he is treated, not on how satisfied he is with the waiting experience. We list the remaining options without discussion, because they were already described in the previous section.

- Reduce workload

- Increase capacity

- Improve synchronization

- Reduce variability

- Improve sequencing

Improve Decisions—Treatment of patients begins with testing decisions that determine what information to gather, diagnostic decisions about the causes of symptoms, and treatment decisions that specify a planned course of therapy. The decision process can be simple (for example, a single X-ray confirms a diagnosis of a broken bone, which leads to a decision to set the limb in a cast) or complex (for example, ambiguous symptoms require multiple tests to rule out several causes before leading to sufficient confidence in a diagnosis to justify a specific course of treatment). Furthermore, decisions may iterate with execution when lack of efficacy in a course of treatment leads to a change in diagnosis. As the complexity of the decision process increases, so do the opportunities for error. The major ways to reduce the likelihood of decision errors are

- **Improve information**—All decisions are based on information. In hospital settings, the relevant information includes direct observations, test results, descriptions of hospital procedures, and general medical knowledge. Gaps or errors in any of these can lead to an inappropriate patient treatment plan. An example of an information improvement policy in the ED might be use of an e-triage system, which systematically walks the triage nurse through the steps of the triage process, helping to avoid oversights.

- **Improve assignment**—Who makes a decision can have a big impact on the quality of that decision. Hence, procedures that ensure decisions are assigned to the people most capable of making them correctly can play an important role in improving patient safety. For example, guidelines in the inpatient unit about what decisions a resident should defer to an attending physician and what decisions the attending physician should defer to a specialist could improve the accuracy of diagnosis and treatment.

- **Improve training**—Because knowledge is fundamental to decision making, training that increases the knowledge of decision makers is an obvious way to improve accuracy. A not-so-obvious type of training, however, might be instruction on decision heuristics and biases that are common in medical decision making. For example, the Persistence of Initial Impressions principle is partly based on the observation that physicians tend to overweight their initial diagnosis and stay with it too long. Learning about this tendency and the reasons for it can help physicians become more flexible in their early diagnoses and ultimately make better decisions.

- **Improve incentives**—All behaviors, including decision-making processes, are influenced by incentives. Some incentives that promote good decisions (for example, raises and promotions for physicians who are recognized as skilled diagnosticians) are obvious. But others are more subtle in their effects. For example, if physicians feel pressure to avoid malpractice suits, they may practice defensive medicine by ordering excessive testing. But, by Bayes' Rule, tests of unlikely outcomes can be much more likely to lead to false positives than true positives. So excessive testing could actually lead to more test errors and hence more treatment errors, which is exactly opposite of the intended outcome. Because incentives that influence decision processes are complex, it may be difficult to uncover misalignments directly. But they may become apparent indirectly through root cause analysis of errors and near misses. The key is to include consideration of peoples' underlying incentives when analyzing their decisions.

- **Simplify/standardize the decision process**—Because decisions are tasks, the Task Simplification and Task Standardization principles apply and provide avenues for reducing decision errors. For example, a CPOE can simplify the decision of which tests to order by offering standard order sets for various patient conditions. Because this makes the choices uniform across physicians, it is an example of a standardization policy, as well as a simplification policy.

- **Improve focus**—Even if we have the right information, person, training, incentives, and decision process, errors can still occur due to suboptimal conditions when the decision is made. The principles related to cognitive efficiency (Workload, Interruptions, and Fatigue) imply that avoiding work overloads, interruptions, and fatigue can increase the accuracy of decision making. For example, physicians in inpatient wards who are constantly interrupted while tending to patients by the lack of information, equipment, and supplies are apt to make errors of omission (for example, failing to consider a treatment option) or commission (for example, exercising flawed judgment in an effort to hurry). So, reducing the chaos that leads to these interruptions by better organizing information and materials will support more accurate decision making.

- **Increase redundancy**—Making decisions involves considering alternatives, rejecting those deemed undesirable, and settling on the best choice. So, during the decision process, we frequently entertain "wrong" options before selecting the "right" one. Hence, one final way of improving the likelihood of a good decision is to invoke the Redundancy principle and build in protective layers that reduce the chance of a "wrong" option being selected. For instance, a CPOE system that includes automatic checks that highlight potential drug interactions can prevent a physician from choosing an inappropriate combination of medications that he would have selected without the system warning.

Improve Execution—Once decisions regarding treatment have been made, they must be carried out. Even if the treatment plan is entirely appropriate, a patient can be harmed by execution failures. A nurse can misread a prescription and administer the wrong medication or dosage. A surgeon can slip and damage an untargeted organ. An orderly can drop a patient and cause an injury. Hospitals abound with opportunities for execution errors. General categories of policies for improving execution are

- **Improve execution information**—To execute a treatment task properly, the person executing it must know how to execute it. Hence, missing or erroneous information about the patient (for example, wrong patient identity), treatment plan (for example, ambiguous physician instructions), or procedure (for example, how to administer the prescribed medication) could lead to harmful errors. Policies that ensure such information is available (for example, bar-coded wrist bands that provide information about patient condition) and understandable (for example, color-coded wrist bands that flag patients with drug allergies) are key to patient safety.

- **Improve assignment**—Given the right information, people must use it correctly to execute a treatment task. But, just as people differ in decision-making skill, people differ in execution skill. Hence, assigning people to tasks in a manner that makes maximal use of high-skill individuals can reduce execution errors. For instance, some infusion technicians are more skilled than others at inserting an IV. So assigning the most skillful technicians to the patients with the most delicate veins will reduce the frequency of nerve injuries.

- **Improve training**—Once an individual has been assigned to execute a task, the likelihood of an error depends on that individual's skill and knowledge. Training, which increases skills and knowledge, is therefore a vital part of ensuring patient safety. However, the number of training opportunities will always dwarf time and budget constraints. So the key is to track performance and use root cause analysis of adverse events and near misses to spot execution flaws and direct training efforts to the areas where they will do the most good.

- **Improve incentives**—As noted earlier, all behavior is influenced by incentives, which can be tangible (for example, money) or intangible (for example, reputation). So providing incentives for improved accuracy is certainly an option for addressing patient safety. For example, a clinical lab could offer scheduling priority to technicians with the lowest error rates. However, care must be taken that incentives do not distort information collection. For example, if the technicians are the people responsible for measuring errors, they will have incentive to avoid reporting mistakes that were caught before reports were sent out of the lab. This will reduce the opportunity to detect systemic problems in laboratory processes. Hence, the lab either needs to have an independent way of measuring performance (for example, periodic audits) or should give technicians credit for spotting internal errors (good catches) as part of the incentive system.

- **Simplify/standardize the execution process**—The Task Simplification principle implies that simplifying a task, by reducing the number of actions, reduces the opportunities for errors. The Task Standardization principle implies that standardizing tasks, by applying uniform best practices, reduces reliance on inferior, ad hoc methods and reduces the likelihood of errors. There are countless ways these principles can be applied to improve execution of treatment processes. An example of a simplification policy would be predosed medication, which eliminates the step of measuring out the dosage and hence the opportunity for a dosing error. An example of a standardization policy, which is also a training policy, would be to have the most skilled infusion technicians document their methods and teach them to the other technicians, so that everyone uses the same best practice.

- **Improve focus**—Just as they can lead to decision errors, work overloads, interruptions, and fatigue can lead to execution errors. For example, a laboratory might adopt a policy in which technicians complete multiple preparation steps on a single sample before switching to another sample to avoid interrupting their train of thought and making errors as a result.

- **Increase redundancy**—If an execution error is initiated, due to a breakdown in any of the dimensions listed earlier, it is still possible to prevent the error from being completed by adding redundant layers of protection within the task. For example, issuing IM (intramuscular) drugs in single-dose syringes that do not fit into an IV (intravenous) tube would stop a nurse from committing a potentially dangerous drug administration error.

Improve Protection and Mitigation—If an error is committed and goes beyond the confines of the task, it still may be possible to prevent, or at least reduce, the harmful impact on a patient. The basic avenues for intervening between errors and patients are

- **Improve information**—Information is vital to protection/mitigation in two ways. First, we cannot install passive protection mechanism unless we know how and where errors occur. Second, we cannot take active remediation unless we detect errors that may harm or have harmed patients. Hence, both long-term information about the nature and progression of errors, and short-term information about the occurrence of errors, are relevant to protection/mitigation. An example of long-term information would be the results from follow-up studies of medication errors, which could reveal the sequence of errors and oversights that can lead to the wrong medication/dosage being administered to patients. An example of short-term information is the out-of-range warnings that highlight unusual test results as potential errors.

- **Increase redundancy**—Just as we can install layers of protection within a task to prevent an error from occurring, we can install layers of protection between tasks to prevent an error from occurring. For example, if the pharmacy misreads a physician order and issues the wrong medication, it constitutes an error. But if an alert nurse questions the appropriateness of the medication and stops it from being administered, there is no harm to the patient. The nurse acts as a form of redundant protection.

- **Mitigate harm**—If errors occur and impact patients, there may still be opportunities to reduce patient injury. For example, if an incorrect medication has been administered and an almost-as-alert nurse notices the problem and immediately initiates corrective care (for example, antidote), the harm to the patient may be less than it would have been otherwise. The nurse acts as a form of mitigation.

We compile the preceding paths for addressing patient safety in Table A.2. This starts with the primary objective to increase responsiveness and pursues this to two levels of more specific objectives that support it. We will use this as the starting point for all tables in the hospital unit chapters that address issues of patient safety. In specific applications, we will use environmental details to expand these generic objectives into more specific objectives and finally to candidate improvement policies.

Table A.2 Generic Options for Improving Patient Safety

Level 0 Objective	Level 1 Objectives	Level 2 Objectives
Increase patient safety	Improve responsiveness	Reduce workload
		Increase capacity
		Improve synchronization
		Reduce variability
		Improve sequencing
	Improve decisions	Improve information
		Improve assignment
		Improve training
		Improve incentives
		Simplify/standardize decision process
		Improve focus
		Increase redundancy
	Improve execution	Improve information
		Improve assignment
		Improve training
		Improve incentives
		Simplify/standardize execution process
		Improve focus
		Increase redundancy
	Improve protection and mitigation	Improve information
		Increase redundancy
		Mitigate harm

A.4.3 Organizational Learning

Responsiveness and safety are direct goals because they are key parts of a hospital's value proposition to patients and hence its mission. In research hospitals, learning is also a direct goal, which is an explicit part of the mission (and the value the hospital provides to its research sponsors). But organizational learning is indirectly essential to all hospitals, research and the community alike. Without the ability to learn and evolve new processes, hospitals cannot continue to deliver on their commitments to patients, and hence cannot remain competitive, over the long term. Hence, organizational learning is fundamental to improvement, and indeed survival, of hospitals.

Human understanding of how individuals, let alone organizations, learn is not sufficiently complete to permit reduction of the learning process to precise steps and mechanisms. So, we cannot hope for the same levels of precision and completeness in generating improvement options for organizational learning we were able to provide for responsiveness and safety. Nevertheless, we can appeal to management principles to provide a structured framework for generating options for improving organizational learning within a hospital.

To do this, we note that for an organization to develop or adopt new and better processes, it must first have information about what needs improvement or could be improved. Then it must generate motivation within the organization to pursue changes. Then it must execute the process of identifying and selecting improvements to make. Finally, it must implement change.

We discuss these dimensions and enumerate supporting activities for each of them next. We summarize the overall structure for improving organizational learning in Table A.3.

Improve Information—Understanding current performance is vital for creating motivation to change and identifying opportunities for improvement. But, as we have stressed in this appendix and throughout this book, hospitals are measured along many dimensions. When we consider the many different services offered by a hospital and the many different systems used to deliver these, the number of specific performance metrics becomes enormous. As a result, performance measurement is not a "set it and forget it" activity. Hospitals must constantly be on the lookout for better ways to track their performance relative to their strategic goals. Specific steps for doing this include

- **Establish appropriate metrics**—At a superficial level, this means we should measure things that matter as directly as possible. For example, suppose an inpatient unit concerned about patient falls implements a policy that nursing assistants must always wear gait belts and tracks (via disciplinary write-ups) frequency of compliance. By itself, this compliance metric is not strategic, because it only tells us whether the assistants are wearing the belts, not whether they are using them. Furthermore, even usage rate of the gait belts is an indirect measure, because it measures an action rather than a result. To understand the situation relative to patient falls, the hospital should measure the frequency and type of falls directly.

  At a deeper level, aligning metrics with strategy also requires measurement of contributing factors. For example, collecting data that shows how the rate and severity of patient falls varies by time of day, type of patient, activity being carried out, and so on, could reveal problems and opportunities that would not be evident from simple incidence rate data. Hence, identifying what to measure is the first step in improving information to support organizational learning.

- **Improve passive data collection**—Once we know what we are trying to measure, the next step is to determine how to collect the data. The simplest way to gather data internally is via passive methods, which acquire data without human intervention. For example, computer systems can keep track of when patient tests were ordered and completed and compute response time statistics as a by-product of the ordering and reporting process. In the future, passive RFID tags may facilitate passive tracking of the flow of patients and the movements of staff members and equipment, thereby providing detailed data that currently can only be obtained through invasive and expensive time studies.

- **Improve active data collection**—Although passive data collection is desirable because it is cheap, it will never be possible to obtain all key data by passive means. Technological limitations on passive collection are one reason. But a more important reason is that data collection often requires decisions. For example, collecting data on near misses (incidents that put patients in danger but did not result in injury) requires judgment of whether an error resulted in a dangerous situation. (Does messy handwriting on a prescription constitute a dangerous situation? How messy is messy?) Decisions must be made by humans; hence, data collection that requires judgment also requires active human involvement.

  When humans are involved, so are motives. This means that incentives to report data are also a lever for improving data collection. For instance, in a hospital culture where staff members are blamed for mistakes that led to dangerous situations, people will be disinclined to report their errors. In a hospital culture that rewards people for good catches, people will be more willing to report errors and the systemic conditions that led to them. (For example, "I delivered the medication to the wrong room because the patient's name was misspelled, and I often don't look at the room number because the font is so small.")

- **Improve access to external data**—Internal data, whether collected passively or actively, constitutes only part of the description of performance. To be able to judge current processes and identify opportunities, hospital personnel must also know about performance in other institutions. This may be information about practices in similar institutions (for example, turnaround times in the clinical labs of other hospitals) or research results on new methods (for example, point of care testing technologies and their efficacy in various settings).

- **Improve the interpretation of data into information**—Data is nothing but bits in a computer until it is converted into summaries, descriptions, and insights that can be used to guide decision making. For example, the surgical reports for an OR over a six-month period are data. When classified to produce a count of adverse outcomes by procedure type and presented against national averages for comparable institutions, they generate information that can be used to evaluate performance. When the adverse events are statistically correlated with variables such as time of day, surgeon seniority, patient characteristics, and so on, they produce even more information that might reveal opportunities to improve patient outcomes.

Increase Motivation—As noted in the Motivation for Change principle, organizational incentive to change arises when key stakeholders perceive a divergence between goals and performance. That is, the people with power believe that it is both possible and desirable for performance to improve along some dimension(s). However, as we noted in the Veto principle, if some key stakeholders are not convinced that this is the case, they can (and generally will) prevent change from occurring. So, motivation for organizational change occurs only when the change is Pareto efficient (that is, makes all key stakeholders better off).

For example, if all surgeons in an OR were convinced that expanding the schedule to evening hours would improve performance along all important dimensions (for example, improving patient outcomes by reducing delays in getting surgery, increasing hospital revenues by facilitating more procedures, and so on), then an effort to change the scheduling process could go forward. But if some senior surgeons are unconvinced of the benefits (for example, they resist evening procedures for family reasons or concerns about fatigue), a change proposal may be a nonstarter.

An organization can increase motivation to change in two ways:

- **Better communication of actual organizational performance**—To see potential for change, people must first know where they are now. For example, in the above OR scheduling scenario, knowing that patient wait times to receive surgery are long and rising, and that there is a negative correlation between delay and long-term prognosis, might motivate surgeons to think more deeply about options for altering their OR scheduling policies.

- **Justify and communicate aspirational goals for the organization**—Simply knowing that current performance is bad is not enough. People in an organization must also aspire to something better. For instance, if surgeons saw expanded OR scheduling as part of an overall plan to upgrade the OR into a surgical destination site and were convinced that increased revenues would be put to this purpose, they might be willing to set aside personal inconvenience in pursuit of this higher goal.

Improve Execution of the Learning Process—Like all organizational activities, organizational learning involves processes. When processes are ad hoc and chaotic, activities are inefficient and error prone. So, an essential part of improving organizational learning is improving the underlying processes that support it. This can be done in the following ways:

- **Increase time and resources allocated to learning**—The most obvious way to make a process better is by spending more on it. Assigning people to learning activities (for example, charging staff with following up on near misses) and giving them tools (for example, database software) to support these activities is a natural way to upgrade the learning process. Although it is obvious that time and resources can improve organizational learning, it is not always obvious where deployment would be most valuable. Obviously, this depends on the specifics of the individual hospital. But a general rule is to start with strategy. By constantly thinking in terms of the performance metrics that relate most closely to the mission of the hospital, we can identify places where learning is most needed.

For example, patient LOS is of particular strategic importance in many hospital EDs because it affects patient outcomes, revenue, and overall culture. So efforts devoted to improving learning processes related to ED LOS, which could range from detailed tracking of patients to studies of the perceived incentives of ED staff members, are apt to be worthwhile activities.

- **Improve the concept generation effort**—The two major stages of the process of finding improved methods are concept generation and concept selection. So, systemically enhancing a hospital's capacity for carrying out these functions is core to improving the overall learning process. An example of improving the capacity to generate improvement concepts is use of morbidity and mortality (M&M) conferences to review cases of medical errors. A major purpose of such meetings is to identify systematic issues that compromise patient care, and hence represent opportunities for improvements.

- **Improve the concept selection effort**—Once concepts have been generated, one or some subset must be selected. Organizations without an effective selection process can waste valuable time or even fail to carry out change at all due to internal arguments over the best course of action. Part of a good selection process is competent analysis of alternatives. For example, ED staff could argue ad infinitum about whether introducing a Fast Track for low-acuity patients would substantially improve performance without altering staffing levels. But a well-validated simulation model could resolve the technical questions about performance and focus discussion on softer issues of implementation. This still leaves the issue of achieving buy-in from the key stakeholders, which we address later.

- **Standardize the learning process**—Some aspects of organizational learning are generic across applications. Regardless of whether we are trying to stimulate ongoing improvement in the ED, OR, pharmacy, or cafeteria, basic elements of the learning process apply. So units can learn about learning from one another and thereby propagate best-learning processes across the organization.

In industry, this type of standardization is generally instituted by establishing a "Firm X Production System" (for example, Toyota Production System) or "Firm X Business System" (for example, Danaher Business System). Although these systems may include philosophical mission statements and tools for everything from product design to greeting customers, they usually also include guidelines for standardized learning processes. Examples include the Toyota practice of summarizing problems in specifically formatted single A3 page reports, and the Danaher process for conducting kaizen events. By using a common process for promoting organizational learning and continual improvement, firms achieve efficiencies in training and knowledge sharing.

Improve Implementation of Change—Collecting information, motivating people, and generating/selecting concepts are important parts of organizational learning. But learning is only useful if it actually leads to change. To support a culture of continual improvement, the organizational learning process must also contain an implementation process that puts new ideas into practice.

- **Improve communication of the need for change**—Implementing change successfully often requires the participation of many people, who may or may not have been involved in the concept generation and selection process. To ensure broad cooperation within the organization, it is important that people know of the need to change. For example, if administrators decide to implement a tighter OR schedule that requires turning over ORs more quickly, they need the support of cleaning crews to make the new policy a success. So communicating the reasons for the changes to the people on the cleaning crews is important to a successful implementation.

- **Reduce resistance among key stakeholders**—Although broad support of change is important to successful implementation, support from the key stakeholders is essential. Opposition from even a single person with veto power will doom a proposal. For example, if stellar surgeons refuse to support the proposal for a tighter OR schedule because they believe it will lead to delays in start times, the proposal is likely to be a nonstarter. So the proponents of the change need to win support of these key stakeholders by demonstrating feasibility of the new system by means of a computer simulation, a pilot study, or evidence from another institution.

- **Make implementation more efficient**—Finally, anything the organization does to make implementation of change faster, less costly, or more effective will stimulate the overall organizational learning process. In addition to the direct effect of facilitating process improvements, a more efficient implementation process also serves to motivate people by demonstrating the value of learning. An organization that acts on good ideas is more likely to hear them from its people than is an organization that lets ideas languish through inaction. For example, if teams charged with following up on near misses know from experience that their findings are likely to influence hospital policy in important ways, they are more likely to take their charge seriously and really dig into the root causes of the problem.

We summarize the preceding generic options for improving organizational learning in Table A.3. We use this table, or parts of it, throughout the book when addressing issues of institutionalizing the process of improvement.

Table A.3   Generic Options for Improving Organizational Learning

Level 0 Objective	Level 1 Objectives	Level 2 Objectives
Improve organizational learning	Improve information	Establish appropriate metrics
		Improve passive data collection
		Improve active data collection
		Improve access to external data
		Improve the interpretation of data into information
	Increase motivation	Improve communication of actual organizational performance
		Justify and communicate aspirational goals for the organization
	Improve execution of the learning process	Increase time and resources allocated to learning
		Improve the concept generation effort
		Improve the concept selection effort
		Standardize the learning process
	Improve implementation of change	Improve communication of the need for change
		Reduce resistance among key stakeholders
		Make implementation more efficient

A.5 References

Baumeister, R., E. Bratslavsky, C. Finkenauer, and K. Vohs. 2001. "Bad Is Stronger Than Good." *Review of General Psychology* 5(4), 323–370.

Baumol, W. 1964. Untitled review of Cyert and March text "A Behavioral Theory of the Firm" by R. Cyert and J. March, appearing in *Journal of Marketing Research* 8(1), 74–76.

Blackshaw, P. 2008. *Satisfied Customers Tell Three Friends, Angry Customers Tell 3,000: Running a Business in Today's Consumer-Driven World*. Doubleday.

Chisholm, C.D., A.M. Dornfeld, D.R. Nelson, and W.H. Cordell. 2001. "Work Interrupted: A Comparison of Workplace Interruptions in Emergency Departments and Primary Care Offices." *Annals of Emergency Medicine* 38(2), 146–151.

Cowan, R.M., and S. Trzeciak. 2005. "Clinical Review: Emergency Department Overcrowding and the Potential Impact on the Critically Ill." *Critical Care* 9, 291–295.

Crawford, M. 1997. *New Products Management.* Irwin.

Croskerry, P. 2009. "Cognitive and Affective Dispositions to Respond." In *Patient Safety in Emergency Medicine.* P. Croskerry, K. Cosby, S. Schenkel, R. Wears (eds.), Wolters Klewer, Philadelphia.

Cyert, R., and J. March. 1963. *A Behavioral Theory of the Firm.* Prentice-Hall, Englewood Cliffs, NJ.

Goldstein. J. 2008. "Inflated Wait Time Estimates Make ER Patients Happier." *Wall Street Journal Health Blog*, October 30, 2008, http://blogs.wsj.com/health/2008/10/30/inflated-wait-time-estimates-make-er-patients-happier/ [accessed 12/14/2010].

Greif, M. 1991. *The Visual Factory: Building Participation Through Shared Information.* Productivity Press.

Grout, J. 2007. "Mistake-Proofing the Design of Health Care Processes." AHRQ Publication No. 07-0020, Agency for Healthcare Research and Quality, Rockville, MD. http://www.ahrq.gov/qual/mistakeproof/mistakeproofing.pdf [accessed 9/8/2010].

Harrison Y., and J. Horne. 2000. "The Impact of Sleep Deprivation on Decision Making: A Review." *Journal of Experimental Psychology: Applied.* 6, 236–249.

Hart, W.L., J.L. Heskett, and W.E. Sasser, Jr. 1990. "The Profitable Art of Service Recovery." *Harvard Business Review.* July–August.

HCAHPS. 2010. "CAHPS Hospital Survey." http://www.hcahpsonline.org/home.aspx [accessed 10/21/2010].

Herr, P.M., F.R. Kardes, and J. Kim. 1991. "The Effects of Word-of-Mouth and Product-Attribute Information on Persuasion: An Accessibility-Diagnosticity Perspective." *Journal of Consumer Research* 17, 454–462.

Heskett, J. 2003. "Shouldice Hospital Limited." Harvard Business Case 9-683-068, Harvard Business School, Boston, MA.

Hopp, W., M. Spearman. 2007. *Factory Physics: Foundations of Manufacturing Management*, Third Edition. Waveland Press, Chicago.

Kameda, T., M. Stasson, J. Davis, C. Parks, and S. Zimmerman. 1992. "Social Dilemmas, Subgroups, and Motivation Loss in Task-Oriented Groups: In Search of an "Optimal" Team Size in Division of Work." *Social Psychology Quarterly* 55(1), 47–56.

Kc, D.S., and C. Terwiesch. 2009. "Impact of Workload on Service Time and Patient Safety: An Econometric Analysis of Hospital Operations." *Management Science* 55(9), 1486–1498.

Landrigan C.P., J.M. Rothschild, J.W. Cronin, R. Kaushal, E. Burdick, J.T. Katz, C.M. Lilly, P.H. Stone, S.W. Lockley, D.W. Bates, and C.A. Czeisler. 2004. "Effect of Reducing Interns' Work Hours on Serious Medical Errors in Intensive Care Units." *New England Journal of Medicine.* 351, 1838–1848.

Lovejoy, W., and Y. Li. 2002. "Hospital Operating Room Capacity Expansion." *Management Science* 48, 1369–1387.

Maister, D.H. 1985. "The Psychology of Waiting Lines." [Online.] Available: http://davidmaister.com/articles/5/52/ [accessed July 22, 2008].

March, J., and H. Simon. 1958. *Organizations.* Wiley, New York.

March, J., L. Sproull, and M. Tamuz. 1991. "Learning from Samples of One for Fewer." *Organization Science* 2(1), 1–13.

Nahmias, S. 2000. *Production and Operations Analysis*, Fourth Edition. McGraw-Hill, New York.

Neiss, R. 1988. "Reconceptualizing Arousal: Psychobiological States in Motor Performance." *Psychological Bulletin* 103(3), 345–366.

Pugh, S. *Total Design.* Addison-Wesley, 1991.

Richardson, D.B. 2006. "Increase in Patient Mortality at 10 Days Associated with Emergency Department Overcrowding." *Medical Journal of Australia* 184, 213–216.

Rona, J.M. *5S for Healthcare.* CRC Press. 2009.

Rother, M, and J. Shook. 2003. *Learning to See: Value Stream Mapping to Add Value and Eliminate MUDA.* The Lean Enterprise Institute, Cambridge, MA.

Speier, C., J.S. Valacich, and I. Vessey. 1999. "The Influence of Task Interruption on Individual Decision Making: An Information Overload Perspective." *Decision Sciences* 30(2), 337–360.

Sprivulis, P.C., J-A Da Silva, I.G. Jacobs, A.R.L. Frazer, and G.A. Jelinek. 2006. "The Association Between Hospital Overcrowding and Mortality Among Patients Admitted via Western Australian Emergency Departments." *Medical Journal of Australia* 184, 208–212.

Streitenberger, K., K. Breen-Reid, and C. Harris. 2006. *Handoffs in Care—Can We Make Them Safer?* Pediatric Clinics of North America 53, 1185–1195.

Taylor, C., and J.R. Benger. 2004. "Patient Satisfaction in Emergency Medicine." *Emergency Medicine Journal.* 21, 528–532.

Ulrich, K., and S. Eppinger. *Product Design and Development.* McGraw-Hill, 2000.

Williamson, A.M., and A-M. Feyer. 2000. "Moderate Sleep Deprivation Produces Comprehensive Cognitive and Motor Performance Impairments Equivalent to Legally

Prescribed Levels of Alcohol Intoxication." *Occupational and Environmental Medicine* 57, 649–655.

Yerkes, R.M., and J.D. Dodson. 1908. "The Relation of Strength of Stimulus to Rapidity of Habit-Formation." *Journal of Comparative Neurology and Psychology* 18, 459–482.

---

1   Note that the resource with the smallest capacity is not always the bottleneck. For example, if the physician only saw half the patients who came through the ED, then his arrival rate would be only half that of the other resources. To determine which resource is busiest, we must compute utilization by dividing the arrival rate by the capacity. Because the triage nurse and emergency nurse do not have twice the capacity of the emergency physician, they would have higher utilization than a physician who sees only half the patients, and hence would be the bottlenecks under these conditions.

2   An experienced ED physician knows that (a) patients are not identical, with some requiring more treatment time than others, and (b) patients do not arrive at a steady rate, so some hours experience more arrivals than others. These are forms of *variability*, for which we will present principles in the next section. A physician also knows that staff assignments, and hence processing times, may not be rigidly defined. For instance, when the ED is busy, the registration nurse may be able to perform some tasks normally handled by emergency nurses, and emergency nurses may be able to take on some of the tasks normally done by the emergency physician. This is a form of *flexibility*, which we will also deal with in the section on variability principles.

3   Throughout this book, when we refer to *variability*, we mean "unsynchronized variability." Whenever we speak of actions to coordinate supply and demand variability, we will explicitly call these out as synchronization policies.

4   Note that adding a taco maker increases capacity, which reduces utilization. As shown in Figure A.2, this would reduce average waiting time.

5   Built-in warning systems can be viewed as a form of redundancy. But because a CPOE system puts such a warning in close context with the task, and hopefully in an intuitively obvious format, we can also view such warnings as intuitive information. Thinking in terms of both providing additional layers of protection and offering key information in intuitive formats can only help in the search for effective patient protection policies. So we adopt an inclusive attitude toward these overlapping concepts.

6   Strictly speaking, this prior probability is already a posterior probability, because the initial likelihood of coronary disease has been updated via the examination and interview. But this is the iterative nature of information collection. Each time we get new information, we update the prior probability into a posterior probability, which then becomes the prior probability for purposes of the next information update.

7   When test results are not strictly positive or negative, but instead can take a range of outcomes, Bayes' Rule still applies, but we need more numbers than "sensitivity" and "specificity" to characterize the accuracy of the test. Furthermore, there will be more than two posterior equations (that is, one for each possible test outcome). Any introductory statistics text will contain a general description of Bayes' Rule, so we do not elaborate further here.

8   The cynic (or capitalist) might argue that failure to reach agreement on compensation for longer hours simply means that the price is not high enough because "everyone has his price." Although this might be true, if the "price" is so high that the increased revenue from extended hours will not cover it, no Pareto efficient solution will exist.

9   In manufacturing, service time is called *value added* time, whereas waiting (queueing) time is called *nonvalue added* time. A key focus of Lean is to eliminate as much nonvalue added time as possible.

10 We note that reducing the work/case could be viewed as increasing system capacity rather than reducing workload, because it permits the system to handle more cases per hour. But, because the purpose of these generic tables is to serve as a checklist, redundancy that highlights opportunities is preferable to parsimony that leads to oversights. Actions on the demand side that reduce work per case (for example, having patients download and fill out forms prior to their hospital visit) might not come up when thinking of ways to increase capacity but will come up when thinking about ways to reduce workload.

B

HISTORICAL JUSTIFICATION FOR AND DEVELOPMENT OF STANDARD BED/ POPULATION RATIOS

B.1 Hill-Burton Act of 1946

The Great Depression (1929–1939) took a tremendous toll on America's infrastructure, including hospitals, many of which were outdated and in poor repair by 1940. Then, World War II diverted resources to the war effort. By 1945, the country's hospitals required major upgrades, and many regions in America had no hospitals at all.

The Hill-Burton Act, passed in 1946, was a federal grant-in-aid and matching funds program for hospital construction and public health centers. Central to the legislation were target ratios of how many beds (per 1,000 people in the geographic area) *should* exist in a region. Because of the potential for risk pooling economies in urban areas and in part to gain enough votes to pass in Congress, the formula for construction favored rural areas. The suggested ratios were 4.5 beds per 1,000 people in high-density areas, versus 5.5 in low-density areas (Correia 1975). Between 1947 and 1975, more than $4.4B in grant funds were distributed, and more than $2B in loans were made or guaranteed. By 1974, about 496,000 inpatient beds and 3,450 outpatient health centers had been built with Hill-Burton support (HRA 1980). Because many of these were in rural and semi-rural areas, they suffered from chronic low occupancy rates and have since gone bankrupt (Jonas 2003).

Although the intent of the Hill-Burton Act was to anticipate how many total beds should be in a geographic area and not which specific hospitals should get the beds, individual hospital planners can use the ratios (beds per 1,000 patients in their market) as rough-cut benchmarks for sizing. The Hill-Burton formuli have an attractive simplicity for facility designers, and such formuli (updated to reflect current realities on lengths of stay, and so on) remain a common method for estimating the number of beds required to serve a patient population.

B.2 The Emergence of Central Planning Initiatives

By 1980, serious concerns had arisen about the rising cost of health care; distribution of technology; redundancy in facilities, services, and personnel; and disparity in the health status of different subgroups in the population. Between 1970 and 1980, hospital costs increased more than 260% (HRA 1980), and capital investments beyond those justified by the market were believed to be key contributors to that escalation. The perceived market failures (that justified government intervention) included limited consumer information/understanding and decisions on consumption made primarily by providers rather than consumers or payers. Due to these failures, the normal laws of supply and demand were believed to be only weakly operative, with the result that local hospitals would engage in capacity races to compete for market share to an extent that would not be justified in well-operating markets.

The environment in which the central government paid many of the hospital bills, so that the benefits for adding beds were enjoyed locally while the costs were borne socially, created a recipe for local overbuilding and justification for the government to step in to control its own costs. In addition, there was some concern that more beds might induce more, but perhaps unnecessary, demand for beds. ("If we build it, they will come.") This was known as Roemer's Law, after American health services researcher Milton Roemer who published a paper that found a positive correlation between the number of hospital beds available and the number filled, leading to a conclusion that supply may induce demand when a third party pays for usage (Roemer 1961, Christianson 1981).

Because of these emerging perspectives, the focus of government regulations changed from encouraging construction to discouraging construction beyond the "right" number of beds as computed using standardized targets. Predictably, many detractors of health planning saw this process as overly politicized and ineffectual, and others questioned the technology, information, and decision making of the planning agencies. Some legislation related to the central planning mission included (HRA 1980):

- **1972 Amendments to Social Security Act (Public Law 92-603) Section 1122—** A state can enter into an agreement with the Secretary of Health, Education, and Welfare to have the planning agency review capital expenditures greater than $100,000. Any expenditure denied would also be denied reimbursement from Medicaid, Medicare, or Maternal and Child Health programs. Within three years, 39 states had Section 1122 agreements.

- **The National Health Planning and Development Act of 1974**—This created a 2-tier system of 205 Health System Agencies (HSAs) and 57 State Health Planning and Development Agencies (SPDAs). Service areas were about 500,000 to 3 million people, and both types of agencies were in place to provide health planning and approve what new health services and facilities would be allowed in their area. Each agency was to draft a Health System Plan (HSP) of long-range goals for the community. The plan would offer benchmarks against which all requests for funding would be reviewed. Also under the 1974 Act, every state was required to pass a *Certificate of Need* (CON) act by 1980, under which all capital expenditures over $150,000, changes in numbers of beds, and all new services were to be reviewed for approval.

  The federal requirement that all states have a CON process was repealed in 1987, and over the next ten years, 14 states discontinued their CON programs. However, 36 states currently maintain some form of CON program, and those that repealed their state CON laws retain some mechanisms intended to regulate costs and prevent needless duplication of services (NCSL 2009).

- **The American Hospital Association Statistical Survey of 2007**—This revealed a range of hospital beds per thousand in the population. The highest ratios were in the Great Plains and Appalachian states, and the lowest were in the West and on the Atlantic coast. For example, the highest ratios were 5.5 and 5.3 in North and South Dakota, and the lowest were 1.7 in Utah and Washington. The nationwide average was 2.7 beds per thousand. This can be used as a reference point for how many beds is appropriate for a population, but any such calculation should also consider the local situation, which varies widely in different parts of the country. For example, the nationwide hospital bed utilization is only about 67%, but there are very high utilizations in some larger urban and tertiary care hospitals.

B.3 National Health Planning Goals

To provide an example of what national health planning goals look like, we present some key recommendations appearing in a 1980 report by a committee of the Institute of Medicine, Health Resources Administration (HRA 1980). Although outdated now, the guidelines demonstrate how the overall average target is adjusted to local demographic conditions. The 1980 guidelines specify a target of less than 4 non-federal short-stay hospital beds per 1,000 persons in the health service area, adjusted as follows:

- **Age**—Those over 65 experience longer stays in hospital beds. If their numbers are more than 12% above the national average in the population, higher planning levels can be used.

- **Seasonal fluctuations**—Predictably high seasonal fluctuations due to vacation and recreation patterns can justify higher bed levels.

- **Rural areas**—Hospital care should be accessible within a reasonable time limit. In sparsely populated rural areas, adherence to 4 beds per thousand, coupled with economies of scale in construction (so we are not building many small dispersed hospitals) may put many people farther than 30 minutes from the nearest hospital. So, a bed ratio greater than 4 per 1,000 may be justified.

- **Urban areas**—Large numbers of beds in one part of a larger metropolitan area can be compensated for by fewer in other parts, providing the overall average is less than 4 beds per 1,000.

- **Areas with referral hospitals**—If a local hospital is a referral hospital that performs a lot of specialty procedures for patients not in the area, the HSA may exclude the beds used for referral patients from being counted in the overall regional inventory.

There may be special targets for specific services, such as obstetrical services, neonatal special care units, pediatric inpatient services, open heart surgery, cardiac catheterization, CT scanners, radiation therapy, and end stage renal disease.

The 1980 report also suggests attention to future trends. For example, it saw the emergence of health maintenance organizations (HMOs), with their attention to prevention and cost oversight, as a promising development that might reduce bed inventories. The 1980 report observed that quality care might eventually be provided with as little as 3 beds per 1,000. This was prescient, because by 2010 there were about 2.9 beds per thousand nationwide.

Closely related to the number of beds per thousand in a population is the target bed occupancy rate. Historically, an average annual occupancy rate of at least 80% for all nonfederal, short-stay hospital beds was recommended (with adjustments for seasonal fluctuations in tourist locations and rural locations, as mentioned earlier). More recent work (c.f. Green and Nguyen 2001) suggests 85% as a natural bed occupancy target. Targets have generally been increasing due to cost pressures. Jonas (2003) suggests that 90% to 95% are appropriate planning targets, which would limit capital expenditures but would likely generate high congestion costs in hospitals. In a variable environment, 95% utilization is high, preordaining congestion and delays in patient care.

B.4 References

Christianson, J., and W. McClure. "On Public Sector Options for Reducing Hospital Capacity." *Journal of Health and Human Resources Administration* 4(1), 1981, 73–91.

Correia, E. "Public Certification of Need for Health Facilities." *American Journal of Public Health* 65(3), March 1975, 260–265.

Green, L., and V. Nguyen. "Strategies for Cutting Hospital Beds: The Impact on Patient Service." *Health Services Research* 36:2, June 2001, 421–442.

HRA (Health Resources Administration). "Health Planning in the United States: Issues in Guideline Development." Report of the Institute of Medicine committee contract 282-78-0163-EJM, March 1980.

Jonas, S. *An Introduction to the U.S. Health Care System*. Springer, NY, 2003.

NCSL: National Council of State Legislatures website http://www.ncsl.org/IssuesResearch/Health/CONCertificateofNeedStateLaws/tabid/14373/Default.aspx, updated April 2009.

Roemer, M.I. "Bed Supply and Hospital Utilization: A Natural Experiment." *Hospitals.* 1961 Nov 1; 35:36–42.

INDEX

C

OR organizational learning
  case study: Western Hospital D&C
    (Death and Complication) conferences,
    326-332
  improvement policies, 316-326
  nature of problem, 313-315
  relevant management principles,
    315-316
  standardizing learning process, 583
Leeuwenhoek, Antoine van, 346, 350
legislation
  1972 amendments to Social Security Act
    (Public Law 92-603) Section 1122, 590
  Emergency Medical Treatment and Active
    Labor Act (EMTALA), 31
  Hill-Burton Act of 1946, 589-590
  The National Health Planning and
    Development Act of 1974, 591
Lemaster, John, 328
Lenard, Phillipp, 356
"level demand" strategy, 286
levels of health care, 486
LH (Lincoln Hospital) ED observation unit,
  109-111
licensed practical nurses (LPNs), 38
life expectancy, U.S. versus other OECD
  countries, 6
ligature, 250
Lincoln Hospital (LH) ED observation unit,
  109-111
Lister, Joseph, 253, 347, 351
Little's Law, 52, 108, 511-513
  OR scheduling, 272
  long-range bed and nurse capacity
    planning, 165
Long, Crawford, 252
long-range bed and nurse capacity planning
  bed inventories, 162-163
  nature of problem, 161-162
  objectives and practices, 169-173
    average hospitalization rates, 171-172
    Monte Carlo simulation, 173
    queuing theory, 172

  service-line forecasting, 172
  standard bed-to-population ratios, 171
  relevant management principles, 164-169
    Buffer Flexibility, 168
    Little's Law, 165
    Newsvendor, 168-169
    Pooling, 167
    System Capacity, 166
    Utilization, 167
    Variability, 166
  Seaberg Hospital case study, 173-178
  staffing levels, 163-164
long-range strategic planning, 47
  for diagnostic units, 375
  for nursing units, 158
  for operating rooms, 266-268
Louis, Pierre Charles Alexandre, 471
Lower, Richard, 251
LPNs (licensed practical nurses), 38

M

Magnetic Resonance Imaging (MRI)
  technology, 356, 361
Malassez hemocytometer, 348
Malassez, Louis-Charles, 351
MAMC (Mercy Academic Medical Center),
  shift-to-shift nursing report practices
  change planning, 229-231
  evaluation, 234-235
  recommendations, 232-234
mammography, 358
management principles
  Batching, 504-505
    imaging responsiveness, 399-400
    laboratory turnaround time, 380
  Bayes' Rule, 530-533
  Buffer Flexibility, 52, 511
    imaging responsiveness, 401-402
    laboratory turnaround time, 379
    long-range bed and nurse capacity
      planning, 168
    nurse scheduling, 185
  categories of, 498

U

X-Y-Z